The First World War

The First World War

Germany and Austria–Hungary

1914–1918

Holger H. Herwig
Professor of History, University of Calgary

A member of the Hodder Headline Group
LONDON • NEW YORK • SYDNEY • AUCKLAND

First published in Great Britain in 1997 by
Arnold, a member of the Hodder Headline Group,
338 Euston Road, London NW1 3BH
175 Fifth Avenue, New York, NY 10010

Distributed exclusively in the USA by
St. Martin's Press, Inc.,
175 Fifth Avenue, New York, NY 10010

British Library Cataloguing in Publication Data
A catalogue entry for this book is available from the British Library

Library of Congress Cataloging-in-Publication Data
Herwig, Holger H.
    The First World War: Germany and Austria–Hungary, 1914–1918 /
Holger H. Herwig.
        p. cm. — (Modern wars)
    Includes bibliographical references and index.
    ISBN 0–340–67753–8. — ISBN 0–340–57348–1 (pbk.)
    1. World War, 1914–1918—Germany.   2. World War, 1914–1918—
Austria.   I. Title.   II. Series.
D531.H464 1996
940.4'147—dc20   96–28152
                                                                          CIP

ISBN 0 340 67753 8 (hb)
ISBN 0 340 57348 1 (pb)

Typeset in 11½pt Times Roman by Phoenix Photosetting, Chatham, Kent
Printed and bound in Great Britain by
Mackays of Chatham PLC, Chatham, Kent

For my children,
Brooke and Lars

And finally, Prussia-Germany can no longer
fight any war but a world war; and a world war
of hitherto unknown dimensions and ferocity.
Eight to ten million soldiers will strangle each
other and in the process decimate Europe as
no swarm of locusts ever did. The ravages of
the Thirty Years' War telescoped into three or four
years and extended to the entire
Continent: famine, pestilence, and the general
barbarization of both armies and peoples . . .
ending in general bankruptcy; the collapse of
the old state and traditional statecraft . . . to
such an extent that dozens of crowns will roll
in the streets and no one will want to pick
them up.

Friedrich Engels, 1887

Contents

List of Maps

General Editor's Preface

In 1930 Basil Liddell Hart published a general account of the First World War under the title *The Real War*. Renamed *A History of the World War 1914–1918* and then – after 1945 – *A History of the First World War*, it has rarely been out of print from that day to this. Its author's trenchant criticisms, sustained in telling metaphors, provided powerful insights. Its enduring influence and its continuing quotability are testified by a number of citations in this book, Holger Herwig's history of the war.

But Professor Herwig's approach constitutes a powerful corrective for an English-language audience hitherto sustained by Liddell Hart's preoccupations. First, Liddell Hart was – despite the appearances suggested by a polyglot bibliography – concerned primarily with Britain's role in the war. For Holger Herwig the focus lies with Germany and Austria–Hungary, the powers deemed by many to be the war's prime movers. Secondly, Liddell Hart's narrative was a sustained attack on the nature of continental warfare in general and of the response of British generals to it in particular. If it was not he who set this agenda, his was none the less one of the most powerful voices in its development. The bulk of the English-language literature on the war ever since has fed off these two themes. It is a literature which has convinced itself that the war was futile in its aims and so confirmed the notion that it was wasteful in its conduct. And it has focused on the alleged incompetence of the British high command as both an illustration and an extension of these points. Since Liddell Hart's death in 1970, the British records have been opened to academic research and we now have a sequence of scholarly works to correct and modify the edifice which Liddell Hart erected. None the less, those publications have continued to march to the beat of Liddell Hart's drum: their focus has remained anglo-centric. Despite the quality and quantity of the work on the war now available to English-language readers, its centres of gravity still tend to be the western front rather than other fronts, London rather than Berlin.

A principal justification for this approach, linguistic laziness apart, has been the absence of the German army's records. The majority were destroyed by allied bombing in 1945. There are therefore gaps in our knowledge which will undoubtedly never be satisfactorily filled. But the void is not as great as some seem to imagine.

First, the massive German official history of the land war, the Reichsarchiv's *Der Weltkrieg 1914–1918*, almost all of it published too late to be used by Liddell Hart even if he had been minded to do so, constitutes an extraordinarily rich source, and it can be supplemented by a number of other books written by the Reichsarchiv's historians. However tainted their preoccupations – by the need to sustain the reputation of the Wilhelmine army, by the fact that latterly their works were written under the Nazis – these men had access to the papers in a way denied to later generations.

Secondly, the absence of potentially the most significant military archive should not blind us to the unpublished material that lies elsewhere. Most important in scale and significance are the official records of the Austro-Hungarian army in Vienna. Within Germany, the papers of the states other than Prussia, particularly those of Bavaria, have proved informative. The archives of many government agencies, especially the navy's and the foreign office's, did not suffer the fate of those of the army. In recent years collections of private papers have been accumulated in Freiburg, and to these have now been added the documents held in the former German Democratic Republic at Potsdam. The end of the Cold War has thus revealed that the destruction wrought in 1945 was not as complete as previously thought: some elements of the army's archives had survived in their original home, and others had been taken to Russia.

That it remained possible for the assiduous scholar to piece together a story radically different from that put forward by the Reichsarchiv and its associates between the wars was demonstrated as long ago as 1961. Fritz Fischer's book on Germany's aims in the First World War, particularly when bracketed with its successor, *The War of Illusions*, is one of the few which merits that much overworked epithet, seminal. By culling the archives afresh, Fischer showed that the story of Germany's role in the First World War was not as closed as either the Reichsarchiv historians wished it to be or as the aftermath of the Second World War suggested it might be. The controversy which he provoked has continued to reverberate. However, its fertility has, at least until recently, been selective in its effects. German scholars have focused on Germany's role in precipitating war and on Germany's territorial and economic ambitions in that war. In the language of school textbooks, their concerns have been causes and consequences – or rather potential consequences. The course of the war and its conduct have been peripheral to German scholarship. And yet the conduct of the war explains why the possible consequences were not visited on Europe – or at least not in 1918. For one of the reasons why the German controversy has been so hard fought is that Germany's aims in the First World War are seen as prefiguring those of the Second. For Fischer and his supporters, in unleashing war in 1914 Wilhelmine Germany provided the link which sustains a fundamental continuity in German history running from Frederick the Great through Bismarck to Hitler. Expansion, nurtured by and itself nurturing Prussian militarism and autocratic government, was on this interpretation a key factor in Germany's evolution as a state.

The significance of the long view suppressed the need for proper consideration of many shorter-term issues, including the reasons for Germany's failure to win the First World War. Thus the historian was left with a paradox. The tactical and operational effectiveness of the German army was hallowed; its practices became precepts for Liddell Hart and others. And yet Germany lost the war. The outcome suggested two possible resolutions to the paradox. One was that the German army was not as good as either it or its enemies believed. The other was that in the conduct of total war in the twentieth century military proficiency was not enough: above all, the possession of resources and the ability to manage those resources effectively were fundamental.

Holger Herwig's book is built on the full range of sources now available in the German language. Whilst not losing sight of the Entente and its strategies, he at last puts the anglo-centric preoccupations of English-language historians into a long overdue perspective. He points the reader to both of the explanations for Germany's defeat suggested above. He has much to say about the economy and about the shortages from which the Central Powers suffered. Indeed in discussing these he adduces what is in effect a third reason. Germany's principal ally, Austria–Hungary, a multinational empire confronted with the challenge of national self-determination, struggled to stay in the war from 1915 onwards. Thus much of Germany's effort was expended in sustaining not only its own war effort but also that of its neighbour. Austria–Hungary resented the dependence on Germany this implied; Germany became increasingly frustrated by Vienna's refusal to subordinate itself to Berlin as fully as the economic and military realities suggested it should. For each power the description of its ally as 'the secret enemy' was applicable.

But it is in what it has to say about Germany's military performance that *The First World War: Germany and Austria–Hungary 1914–1918* provides its most telling correctives. Its core is a narrative of land operations. For British readers accustomed to criticisms of Haig and his associates, Herwig injects a comparative perspective that suggests a more general problem than that of many somewhat parochial accounts. Ludendorff was no genius: indeed, 'intellectually', Herwig avers, he 'never rose above the level of an infantry colonel'. German and, even more, Austrian generals seemed just as remote from the preoccupations of the front-line soldier as their British counterparts. And the German offensives of March 1918, developed by the inter-war theorists into a model of breakthrough operations, are criticized not just for their lack of a strategic objective but even for their tactical failings. The problems encountered by the German infantry on 21 March make the crisis in the command of the British Fifth Army and its component corps hard to comprehend.

Herwig's account is not just the war as seen by statesmen and generals. Its readers will encounter the tribulations and sufferings of many whose names are now important solely for the fact that they have left us their impressions of the war and its effect on their lives. These are the people who matter in defining the texture of modern war, in explaining the position of the First World War in the development of what war means to us today.

The men who went to war in 1914 laboured under two misconceptions – although it is less clear whether their leaders necessarily laboured under the same misconceptions. Firstly, they thought the war was going to be short. There is nothing very remarkable in that: it is a reflection of the triumph of hope over experience. Most of those who embark on a war do so with the intention that the conflict should be short; they also tend to believe that they can win it. The second misconception was that war was perceived to be personally liberating – a young man's activity fought in the open air, free from the routines of industrialized society and the values of bourgeois Europe.

In the event, the war did of course prove to be long. One of the reasons it lasted so long was that it was fought between industrialized societies. Even on the battlefield, its pattern and tempo were determined by the output of the factories that many were at least metaphorically trying to put behind them. Heavy artillery required the most sophisticated of machine tools to enable its mass production. The principal killers of the war, the guns, set a timetable for attacks as rigid as the working day of the urbanized worker. Initiative, courage and command all seemed secondary to the machinery of modern war. Its destructive effects subordinated humanity to its tyranny. If in one sense the wars of the French Revolution were the first modern war in that they witnessed the creation of mass armies through conscription, then in another the First World War was the first modern war in that it revealed the impact of the mass production of new technologies on the battlefield.

In the process some would begin to wonder about the possibility of trading off human resources for industrial resources, of making machines do the work of men, of increasing the numbers of the former while reducing the numbers of the latter. Over the last 2 years of the First World War the ratio of firepower to manpower did change, but it did so less because of a conscious wish to expend bullets rather than lives and more because men had become the resource in shortest supply. What the war revealed was that confronted with a struggle for its survival the modern state would construct as many weapons as it could *and* create as large an army as it could. The only effective constraint on the manpower mobilized for the armed services was the competing need of war industry for labour to produce the weapons with which mass armies would fight. The ratchet in which the state was caught pulled in the whole fabric of the nation, compelling it to channel all its resources into the prosecution of war. As Holger Herwig shows, for both Germany and Austria–Hungary the self-destructive consequences proved ineluctable. In the long run only the possession of nuclear weapons, themselves potentially the supreme embodiment of machine warfare, had the ability to release states from the pervasive militarization of their activities that the war of 1914–1918 demanded.

Hew Strachan

Acknowledgements

This book has been more than a decade in the making. During that time, archives have been moved from the former Soviet Union to the former German Democratic Republic, from east to west Germany, and from one district of Vienna to another. A flood of books on the Anglo-Saxon experience in the Great War especially has appeared. And a 5-year stint as Department Head during a period of radical budget and staff cuts had its negative effect.

The positive side of the ledger is represented by three people who have been of immeasurable help. First and foremost, Professor Wilhelm Deist of Freiburg University was kind enough to take time from his Visiting Killam Professorship at The University of Calgary to go over the manuscript with his customary thoroughness and great expertise. Secondly, Professor Hew Strachan of the University of Glasgow read the manuscript critically and made numerous suggestions for improvement. And finally, my wife Lorraine read draft after draft of each chapter as it developed after summer trips to research sites in Central Europe. Her usual sharp eye for syntax and organization, and her acerbic comments kept me on track. The final product owes much to these three people. As always, the shortcomings remain my own.

Holger H. Herwig
Calgary

Names, Places, and Dates

The areas of central, eastern, and southeastern Europe especially have witnessed great changes in nomenclature over the past century. By 1919 the Austro-Hungarian, German, Ottoman, and Russian empires had collapsed and a bewildering host of petty states had been carved out of their former territory. Woodrow Wilson, Adolf Hitler, and Josef Stalin with their actions altered names and regions with reckless abandon. The breakup of Mikhail Gorbachev's Soviet Empire after 1989 further compounded the situation as new states such as the Czech Republic, the Slovak Republic, Slovenia, Bosnia–Herzegovina, Croatia, Serbia, Moldavia, and Ukraine came into being. Thus it would be sheer madness to attempt to give Croat, Czech, German, Hungarian, Polish, Romanian, Russian, Serb, Slovak, or Slovene equivalents – as it would be to translate all personal names into English. I have kept especially Austrian and German names in the original. Germans do not translate English names such as Winston Churchill or David Lloyd George; why should we tamper with their names?

With regard to Russian, I have used the modified version of the US Library of Congress system that Neil Heyman and I adopted in our *Biographical Dictionary of World War I* for transliterating Russian names. In place of 'IU' and 'IA' at the start of names, 'Yu' and 'Ya' are given; thus Yudenich and Yanushkevich. Likewise, 'ii' at the end of names has been made 'y'; thus Ruzsky and Zhilinsky. Apostrophes and diacritical marks have been omitted. And throughout the book, all dates are according to the Gregorian rather than the Julian, or Old Style, calendar.

The problem of names was most acute with regard to Austria–Hungary and Germany. For personal names of officers in the *k.u.k.* Army I relied on the official history of the war: *Österreich-Ungarns Letzter Krieg 1914–1918*. With regard to place names for the period before and during the Great War, I used the then current German language names, fully aware that these changed after 1918, and again in the 1930s, and again in the 1940s, and again in the 1980s and 1990s. Hence appointments were to and battles at Agram, Brünn, Hermannstadt, and Pressburg, not Zagreb, Brno, Sibiu, or Pozsony (Bratislava); in the case of Germany, to or at Königsberg, Strassburg, Thorn, and Danzig, not Kaliningrad, Strasbourg, Toruń, or Gdańsk. As far as possible, I have tried to avoid linguistic chauvinism, but if certain usage offends, then I ask the reader's forgiveness under the trying circumstances.

The following list of cities and places is not intended to be exhaustive, but merely to offer a rough guide to places frequently mentioned in the book:

Agram	Zagreb, Zágráb
Altenburg	Magyaróvár
Bozen	Bolzano
Breslau	Wroclaw
Brixen	Bressanone
Brody	Bródy
Brünn	Brno
Cattaro	Boka Katorska; Kotor
Czernowitz	Cernauti (Rom.); Chernovtsy (Russ.); Tschernowzy (Pol.)
Danzig	Gdańsk
Esseg	Osijek
Fiume	Rijeka
Görz	Gorizia; Gorica
Flitsch	Bovec (Slov.); Plezzo (Ital.)
Görz	Gorizia; Gorica
Györ	Raab
Gumbinnen	Gusev
Hermannstadt	Sibiu (Rom.); Nagyszeben (Hung.)
Insterburg	Chernyakhovsk
Karfreit	Caporetto (Ital.); Kobarid (Slov.)
Kaschau	Kassa
Königsberg	Kaliningrad
Kronstadt	Brassó
Laibach	Ljubljana
Langemarck	Langemark
Lemberg	Lwów (Pol.); Lvov (Russ.); Lviv (Lith.)
Louvain	Löwen
Luck	Lutsk

Marburg	Maribor
Marienburg	Malbork
Monastir	Bitola; Bitolja
Niemen	Neman
Olmütz	Olomouc
Ortelsburg	Szczytno
Osterode	Ostróda
Peterwardein	Pétervárad; Petrovaradin
Pilsen	Plžen
Pless	Psczyna
Pola	Pula
Posen	Poznań
Pressburg	Pozsony (Hun.); Bratislava (Czech.)
Rastenburg	Ketrzyn
Rowno	Równe
Salonika	Thessaloníki
Scutari	Shkodër
Sieben Gemeinden	Cette communi; Sette commune
Stallupönen	Nesterov
Stolp	Slupsk
Strassburg	Strasbourg
Tarnopol	Ternopol (Pol.); Ternopil (Russ.)
Tannenberg	Stebark
Tarnów	Tarniv
Teschen	Tešin (Czech.), Cjeszyn (Pol.)
Thorn	Toruń
Tolmein	Tolmin
Trient	Trento
Troppau	Opava
Valona	Vlora; Vlone
Vilna	Vilnius
Volhynia	Volyn
Weichsel	Vistula
Weissenburg	Gyulafehérvár
Zabern	Saverne.

Finally, all times given for Austro-Hungarian or German actions are Greenwich meridian plus one.

Introduction

The war solved no problems. Its effects, both immediate and indirect, were either negative or disastrous. Morally subversive, economically destructive, socially degrading, . . . devious in its course, futile in its result, it is the outstanding example in European history of meaningless conflict.

C. V. Wedgwood, *The Thirty Years' War*

These eloquent words, penned on the eve of the Second World War with regard to a protracted struggle more than 300 years earlier, apply equally to the so-called 'Great War' of 1914–18. For, the First World War radically altered the European state system as well as European economies and societies. The Austro-Hungarian, German, Ottoman, and Russian empires collapsed. A power vacuum was created in Central Europe, one which France could not and the United States would not fill. Britain returned its attention to the Empire. Russia engaged in a vicious civil war, from which the Bolshevik dictatorship of the Soviet Union would emerge. The world's largest creditor in 1914, Europe emerged in 1918 as the world's greatest debtor. And while European nations concentrated on slaughtering each other, the rest of the world industrialized and modernized. In short, the age of European supremacy died on the battlefields of northern France and Russian Poland.

The First World War remains pivotal to understanding the twentieth century. For the first time, a generation had to come to grips with death in massive numbers: more than 9 million soldiers and 12 million civilians. Plagues and disease accounted for another 3 million lives lost. Death, or the fear and proximity of death, became an everyday experience. Death reigned during the 'battles of material' at Verdun and the Somme in 1916. Not discriminating on the basis of wealth, education, colour, or creed, death became the great leveller. After the war, death became ritualized.

Massive monuments, cemeteries, and graves heroized death and enshrined those killed between 1914 and 1918 in a new cult of nationalism. An industry of kitsch cards, posters, and books sentimentalized the dead as 'victims' who 'gave' their lives or 'fell' on the 'altar of the fatherland'.

The war marked a generation of young men for life. Some glorified the war as an epic experience; others despised its death and destruction. On the one hand, Corporal Adolf Hitler glorified struggle (*Kampf*) as the ultimate transcendental experience of mankind; on the other hand, a noble Saxon officer, Arnold Friedrich Vieth von Golssenau, writing under the pseudonym Ludwig Renn, decried it for the common man in the anti-war novels *War* and *After War*. Yet both were part of what Erich Maria Remarque in *All Quiet on the Western Front* called the 'iron youth'.

The troglodyte world of the trenches also left its scars on modern man. The spade became as important as the rifle; entrenchment as critical as the attack. Rain and rats, water and mud became as lethal as the enemy. A novel culture developed in this subterranean world, and trench experiences added new words to common vocabularies. The grey everyday of war was symbolized by what Ernst Jünger in *Storm of Steel* called the new 'workers of war' – the storm troopers dressed in grey uniforms, wearing grey steel helmets, and trudging through the grey mud. And by the millions of almost surrealistic shell craters, poisoned water holes, bombed-out hovels, broken tree trunks, shattered and scattered rotting corpses, and omnipresent filth.

Industrialized warfare also set the 'Great War' apart from its predecessors. In numbers too great for anyone to have imagined before 1914, heavy and light artillery, howitzers, trench mortars, machine guns, flamethrowers, hand-grenades, and bayonets ripped bodies open and poisoned them with gas or contaminated them with the bacteria of the richly-manured soil of northern France. Rolling artillery barrages and hurricane bombardments tore units apart. Shell shock affected perhaps as many as one in every four combatants. The dash and daring of former wars was reduced to a deadening monotony of mutual mass murder in the industrialized, technological war of 1914–18.

There was also a certain 'masculinity' to the war. Millions of men often lying 9 yards under the surface of the earth in damp, dirty trenches, eating and drinking and defecating together over 4 years, underwent a new experience. It bred a sense of group solidarity, of having to rely on one another for the most basic aspiration – survival. It erased standard peacetime divisions such as those between urban and rural dweller, Catholic and Protestant, industrial and agrarian labourer, and educated and uneducated. Hitler was hardly alone in suggesting that the war for the first time had created an – albeit idealized – national racial community (*Volksgemein-schaft*).

Pent-up sexuality found outlets in filthy jokes and whores – and in one's comrade, willing or often not. The front-line soldiers (*Frontschweine*) developed their own vocabulary, code of ethics, and norms of behaviour. Few of these had anything in common with prewar upbringing and education. Indeed, many of the front-line combatants developed a vitriolic dislike of the home front in general and of civilian 'profiteers' (*Etappenhengst*) and draft-evaders (*Drückeberger*) in particular. This 'we-versus-them' dichotomy would plague the Weimar Republic to its very end.

The First World War also affected the home front in ways unimaginable before 1914. Hunger was the main determinant. Food shortages appeared as early as the autumn of 1914; they became critical early in 1915; and the so-called 'turnip winter' of 1916–17 perhaps most prominently expressed this plague. Food riots became as commonplace as the long waiting lines – centres of rumours, distrust, and suspicion. Horse meat replaced beef and pork. A plethora of ersatz products threatened to poison consumers with chemical derivatives. By 1916 there was little coal. Few shoes. Almost no textiles. No soap. No fat. No cheese. No butter. No eggs. Overall civilian mortality and especially tuberculosis skyrocketed; fertility and average body weight plummeted. Hoarding and blackmarketing drove a wedge between city and countryside, rich and poor. Eventually, these conditions destroyed the fabric of an orderly society and undermined its very legitimacy. Perhaps it was fitting that the first volume of Oswald Spengler's *The Decline of the West* appeared in the autumn of 1918.

The war rent asunder the traditional German 'home'. Millions of husbands and fathers were absent at the front while hundreds of thousands of women worked in industrial plants – and thus were not at home to look after their children. By 1918 there existed in Germany a 'surplus' of 2 million women, mainly widows. Many were impoverished by meagre government pensions and subsidies that failed to cover the escalating costs of increasingly unavailable food. Still others entered traditional 'male' industries and gained unknown independence. Tens of thousands of youths likewise experienced financial freedom by working in armaments plants – at the cost of education and upbringing. Their young male teachers had been drafted, and established vocational training programmes were abandoned due to the ever-increasing demand for cannon fodder.

The American statesman George F. Kennan appreciated the sea-change brought about by the 'Great War': in 1979 he termed it simply '*the* great seminal catastrophe of this century'.[1] Few have disagreed with Kennan.

But do we really need yet another tome on the First World War? Certainly the British experience on the Western Front has undergone a great deal of reinterpretation by David French, John Gooch, Peter Simkins, and T. H. E. Travers, to name but a few of the most recent scholars. Yet, I would argue that with the exception of only a few, although notable tracts, most books on the 'Great War' paid but lip service to what Winston S. Churchill called 'the forgotten war' on the Eastern Front. To balance the picture, I began research in Vienna and Freiburg in the mid-1980s on an analysis of how statesmen and soldiers in Austria–Hungary and Germany, respectively, viewed the nature of a future war and planned to deal with it in the years immediately preceding the July crisis of 1914.

After I had spent a few summers of eye-opening work in the files at the Haus-, Hof- und Staatsarchiv and the Kriegsarchiv in Vienna, Hew Strachan approached me about translating Hans Herzfeld's comprehensive treatment of Germany in the First World War.[2] I praised the work – but added that it was now nearly 30 years old, that it badly needed updating because countless documents had become available since its appearance, and that the emphases of discussion had radically shifted since its inception. Moreover, it was written in a turgid and almost untranslatable style. I had made a critical mistake and soon found myself committed to undertake not only a history of Germany in the 'Great War' but to broaden the treatment to include the Dual Monarchy. I was – and remain – convinced that one cannot write the history of the Central Powers at war between 1914 and 1918 simply from the perspective of Berlin. This book represents the sins of my argument.

After completing a first draft of the work, I learned that the Military Archive at Potsdam in the former German Democratic Republic had received 2156 captured German military files from the Soviet Union in the mid-1980s and that these were being transferred to the Federal Military Archive at Freiburg. With the financial assistance of the Research Council of The University of Calgary, I examined the most important files, classified as record group W-10. These included, but were not limited to, Wilhelm Dieckmann's analysis of the Schlieffen plan, written before the destruction of the bulk of the German Army's records by Allied Bomber Command in 1944–5; the diary fragment of Kaiser Wilhelm II's military adjutant, General Hans von Plessen; and the diary fragment of the Prussian War Minister, General Erich von Falkenhayn, for the critical weeks of July–August 1914.

This book basically follows a chronological outline. With regard to the Austro-Hungarian Empire, I have concentrated on the initial stages of mobilization and the horrendous first battles in Galicia in 1914. Thereafter, the story becomes one of attempts to preserve the independence and finally the integrity of the Habsburg Monarchy against the Russians and the Italians as well as against the German ally. In the German case, I have traced the Hohenzollern war effort through five separate bids for victory: the Schlieffen plan and the First Battle of the Marne; the 'race to the sea' in 1914; the spring 1915 offensive in Poland; Verdun 1916; unrestricted submarine warfare in 1917; and the great *Michael* offensive in France in 1918.[3] Given that the appointments late in 1916 of Field Marshal Paul von Hindenburg and General Erich Ludendorff to run the Great General Staff marked what German historians such as Fritz Fischer, Andreas Hillgruber, and Gerhard Ritter have called a 'caesura' in the war, I halted the narrative after Chapter 5 and in the next two chapters addressed the critical issues of industrial and manpower mobilization. Thereafter, the book returns to its chronological progression.

Last but not least, I must belabour the patently obvious: this book could not possibly tackle all theatres and campaigns, statesmen and soldiers, issues and developments. It is not intended to be global in its coverage. It concentrates on Austria–Hungary and Germany generally and on the land war that they conducted between 1914 and 1918 specifically. Of necessity, it sidesteps the thorny issue of the combat effectiveness of the various ethnic contingents in the Austro-Hungarian and German armies; first broached by Christoph Führ in 1968, this issue requires much more study. Moreover, the book reflects both the bias and the expertise of its author. I am too old to apologize for either. To those who sought more, I can only suggest that they take comfort from the great Saint Augustine: 'I am done. . . . From all who think I have said either too little or too much, I beg pardon'.[4]

Introduction Notes

1. George F. Kennan, *The Decline of Bismarck's European Order: Franco-Russian Relations, 1875–1890* (Princeton, Princeton University Press, 1979), p. 3. Kennan also dubbed it 'that first great holocaust'.
2. Hans Herzfeld, *Der Erste Weltkrieg* (Munich, Deutscher Taschenbuch Verlag, 1968).
3. Happily plundered from Colin S. Gray, *The Leverage of Sea Power: The Strategic Advantage of Navies in War* (New York, Free Press, 1992).
4. Saint Augustine, *City of God* (New York, Image Books, 1958), book 22, p. 545.

1

Origins: 'Now or Never'

If we must go under, we better go under decently.

Kaiser Franz Joseph, August 1914

June 1914. Europe's statesmen and soldiers were busily planning to escape the approaching seasonal heat of Berlin, London, Paris, and Vienna. Most members of the British Cabinet of Prime Minister Herbert Henry Asquith were making ready to head to Scotland for salmon fishing and other forms of relaxation, while the Secretary of State for Foreign Affairs, Sir Edward Grey, longed for the solitude of casting for stippled trout in the River Itchen near Winchester. Across the Channel, French President Raymond Poincaré and Premier René Viviani were preparing for a leisurely cruise on the battleship *France* through the North and Baltic seas to meet Tsar Nicholas II at St Petersburg.

In Vienna, Kaiser Franz Joseph fondly looked forward to another summer with Katharina Schratt at the Tyrolean resort of Bad Ischl in the Salzkammergut. Archduke Franz Ferdinand, the heir presumptive to the Habsburg throne, was anxiously awaiting the end of the month when, as Inspector-General of all Austro-Hungarian armies, he could join his wife, Sophie Chotek, Duchess of Hohenberg, for their wedding anniversary (1 July) on a tour of inspection in Bosnia–Herzegovina, two provinces that Vienna had annexed in 1908. In Salzburg, an Austro-Hungarian court martial found the draft dodger Adolf Hitler, recently returned from Munich, unfit ('too weak; incapable of bearing arms') for military service.[1]

The German Reich's principal leaders likewise yearned for summer vacations. Kaiser Wilhelm II was preparing to fish the fjords of Norway; Chancellor Theobald von Bethmann Hollweg longed for the peace and relaxation of his estate Hohenfinow on the Oder River; and Foreign Secretary Gottlieb von Jagow was headed for Lake Lucerne in

Switzerland on his honeymoon. Additionally, Grand Admiral Alfred von Tirpitz, State Secretary of the Imperial Navy Office, was off to the cool climes of St Blasien in the Black Forest; General Helmuth von Moltke, Chief of the Prussian General Staff, was set to join his Austro-Hungarian counterpart, General Franz Baron Conrad von Hötzendorf,[2] at the Bohemian spa of Karlsbad; and General Erich von Falkenhayn, the Prussian War Minister, was off to vacation at Juist in the East Frisian Islands.

A certain calm had descended on Europe after the turbulent first decade of the new century. The Continent had survived revolution in Russia in 1905, two Moroccan crises in 1905 and 1911, and two Balkan wars in 1912–13. Even the Anglo-German naval arms race, which had climaxed in the 'naval scare' of 1908–9, seemed to be winding down, with London and Berlin amicably discussing both the division of the Portuguese colonial empire and the financial future of the Berlin-to-Baghdad Railway. In fact, Sir Harold Nicolson, Permanent Under-Secretary at the Foreign Office in London, confessed that he had 'not seen such calm waters' in all his days at Whitehall, while the First Lord of the Admiralty, Winston S. Churchill, later recalled that the spring and summer of 1914 'were marked in Europe by an exceptional tranquillity'.[3] Even the volatile Wilhelm II had been assured by the Hamburg banker Max Warburg that there was no cause to draw the sabre in the near future: 'Germany becomes stronger with every year of peace. We can only gain by biding our time'.[4] Hugo Stinnes, one of Imperial Germany's most dynamic entrepreneurs, likewise opined that after '3–4 years peaceful development', Germany would be 'the undisputed economic master of Europe'.[5]

For most upper- and middle-class Europeans this was the 'golden age' of law and order, respect and decency. Child mortality was down. Nutrition had improved dramatically. Real wages had shot up almost 50 per cent between 1890 and 1913. Germany was showing the way to the future social state with health insurance, accident insurance, and old-age pensions. Wilhelm II seemed to have spoken for most heads of state in 1892 when he promised to lead his Brandenburgers 'towards glorious times'.

Paris alone was seething with political excitement. In March 1914 Henriette Caillaux, the wife of Finance Minister Joseph Caillaux, had entered the offices of Gaston Calmette, editor of *Le Figaro*, and had shot him six times with a revolver concealed in her muff. Madame Caillaux had taken this grave action to prevent Calmette from publishing her love letters to Caillaux, written while the Finance Minister was married to his first wife. Paris was abuzz with rumours that the impending trial might reveal that Caillaux had conducted secret diplomacy with the Germans during the Second Moroccan Crisis in 1911. All France awaited the trial with great interest.[6] Colonel Edward House, special adviser to US President Woodrow Wilson, travelling through Europe in the spring of 1914, caught a more serious note of approaching catastrophe. There was 'jingoism run stark mad' in London, Paris, and Berlin, House wrote Wilson, and 'there is some day to be an awful cataclysm'.[7]

July 1914. Two shots fired by a Serbian high-school boy, Gavrilo Princip, shattered the air at a street corner in the Bosnian capital of Sarajevo on 28 June, the Serbian national holiday (*vidovdan*) to remember the defeat of 1389 at Kossovo at the hands of the Turks. Minutes later, Franz Ferdinand and Sophie Chotek were dead. Josef Redlich, Austrian historian and Member of Parliament, noted in his diary both the absence of mourning in Vienna and the gravity of the moment: 'This day is the day of a world historical event. . . . The hour of destiny for the Habsburgs is at hand'.[8] Within 6 weeks of the assassination, Europe was at war. Four years later, about 9 million combatants and 12 million civilians were dead; more than $36 billion in property had been destroyed; and four empires had collapsed. For 8 decades, historians have tried to explain why the great European Armageddon came in 1914 in the wake of the regicide of Sarajevo.

Vienna: war as salvation

Few in Vienna mourned the passing of Franz Ferdinand. The Archduke was staunchly Catholic, disliked the Czechs and Poles within the Empire, distrusted Vienna's ally, Italy, and hated the co-ruling Magyars at Budapest to the point that he drew the blinds of his personal train whenever he travelled through Hungary. Franz Ferdinand yearned for the day when, as ruler of the Dual Monarchy, he could curb the powers of the Magyars and reestablish the centralized monarchy as it had existed under Felix Prince zu Schwarzenberg after 1848. For the first few days immediately after the regicide, Viennese pundits spent their time less on the fate that had befallen the Archduke and his family and more on a host of possible 'conspiracies' to commit murder on the part of German intelligence, Freemasons, the son of the late Crown Prince Rudolph, and even Count István Tisza, the Hungarian Prime Minister!

Nor did Kaiser Franz Joseph particularly mourn the loss of the heir presumptive. The Emperor had disliked Franz Ferdinand's morganatic marriage to Sophie Chotek and had cut the Duchess of Hohenberg off from all royal and court functions. After Sarajevo, Franz Joseph dispatched the body of the murdered archduke in the dead of night to the memorial chapel at Artstetten in the Danubian Nibelungengau with such alacrity and lack of decorum that he later had to explain his actions. But regicide was quite another matter; the act itself demanded punishment. A swift, surgical strike against Belgrade would have found favour with Europe's crowned heads of state. But nothing ever moved swiftly in the Habsburg realm.

The first move in what historians have dubbed the 'July crisis' of 1914 thus rested with Vienna in general and with Conrad von Hötzendorf in particular. This 'dark, small, frail, thin officer with piercing and expressive eyes set in the face of an ascetic'[9] without question was the most energetic Chief of the General Staff that the Habsburg Army ever possessed. Daily, the crew-cut Conrad stood at his writing desk and poured out a veritable flood of contingency war plans. The nearly 700 officers of the General Staff were kept busy from morning until late in the evening with Conrad's memoranda heavily underlined and annotated with thick red and blue scribblings. Even today, it is amazing to see with what prodigious energy the Chief of the General Staff laboured. A glance at Conrad's outpourings during the 7 years before 1914 provides insight into his fertile mind. In 1907 Conrad demanded war against 'Austria's congenital foes' Italy and Serbia; the next year versus Russia, Serbia, and Italy. In 1909 he counselled military action against Serbia and Montenegro; in 1910 against Italy; and in 1911 versus Italy, Serbia, and Montenegro. The year 1912 saw concentration on the struggle against Russia and Serbia. The next year was especially productive, with military studies readied for conflicts with Albania, Montenegro, Russia, Serbia, and even Russian Poland. The final 6 months of peace in 1914 saw renewed plans versus Montenegro, Romania, Russia, and Serbia.[10] Each of these years also brought contingency plans against numerous combinations of the above-named powers.

Conrad's contingency war plans did not languish at General Staff headquarters: each was dutifully dispatched to Kaiser Franz Joseph at Castle Schönbrunn or the Hofburg; and to Foreign Ministers Alois Lexa von Aehrenthal (1906–12) and his successor, Leopold Berchtold, at the Ballhausplatz. The plans were followed by Conrad's request for an audience with Franz Joseph to discuss their implementation. 'The fate of nations, peoples, and dynasties', Conrad lectured his Emperor and government, 'is decided not at diplomatic conference tables but on the battlefield'.[11] Conrad argued repeatedly that the use of armed force alone could retard the centrifugal forces of nationalism in the 'multinational empire'; war was the only means of politics. During the July crisis of 1914, Foreign Minister Berchtold summarized Conrad's stance as simply: 'War, war, war'.[12]

Conrad von Hötzendorf was haunted by two historical moments. Firstly, there was the 'lost chance' of 1908–9. The diplomatic record at Vienna is chock full of his remonstrances that the Dual Monarchy had failed to seize the historical moment associated with the annexation of Bosnia and Herzegovina to crush Serbian expansion aspirations. Over and over, Conrad deprecated what he termed 'this foul peace which drags on and on'.[13] Secondly, Conrad was convinced that only a victorious military campaign could erase the stigma of 1866. In other words, Austria's humiliating defeat at the hands of Prussia near Königgrätz could be expunged from memory only by new successes on the battlefield. In February 1909, to cite but one example, Conrad lectured the Foreign Ministry that the Monarchy still suffered from the effects of the humiliation of 1866, and instructed Count Aehrenthal that a military victory alone could restore its prestige.[14]

Whatever one may think about Conrad's mind-set, he, almost alone in Vienna, at least had a clear perception of the Dual Monarchy's future. The ancient empire was under assault by corrosive nationalist elements especially in Bohemia, Bosnia–Herzegovina, Galicia, and the South Tyrol. The only way to counter those forces, Conrad never tired of lecturing the Ballhausplatz, was through a redistribution of power by way of territorial expansion. By applying the Machiavellian formula of *divide et impera*, Conrad sought to remove Serbia as a player in the Balkans and to bring Albania and Montenegro into close and personal union with the Habsburgs. A new trialistic state based on Austria–Bohemia, Hungary, and South Slavia, tied to the imperial crown and held together by a unitary imperial army, alone could guarantee the Dual Monarchy's survival. The key to success lay in Vienna's willingness to use force to bring about this realignment. War was neither moral nor immoral; it was unavoidable and an integral part of international relations. 'Only an aggressive policy with positive goals can save this state from destruction.'[15]

Not surprisingly, given this 'war-at-any-price' mentality, Conrad viewed the Sarajevo regicide as a Serbian declaration of war against Austria–Hungary. In July 1914 he was determined not to let the last moment slip by to 'settle accounts' with the Serbs. War, if need be apocalyptic war, Conrad counselled, was the only solution to retard the perceived Habsburg decline.[16] But there was also a personal motive behind Conrad's martial stance. He informed his mistress, Virginie ('Gina'), the wife of the brewery magnate Johann von Reininghaus, that he was anxious for a 'war from which I could return crowned with success that would allow me to break through all the barriers between us . . . and claim you as my own dearest wife'. Such a war, Conrad hoped, 'would bring the satisfaction in my career and private life which fate has so far denied me'.

Above all, the issue of war must not be evaded once again through diplomatic compromise. 'It will be a hopeless struggle', Conrad confided to 'Gina', 'but nevertheless it must be because such an ancient monarchy and such an ancient army cannot perish ingloriously'.[17] The files of the critical Intelligence Division of the General Staff (*Evidenzbureau*) record the receipt of three telegrams from Sarajevo on 28 June announcing Franz Ferdinand's murder; the next entry is an innocuous request for war supplies 1 year later. Obviously, Conrad chose in June–July 1914 not to leave a paper trail behind. Or, were the files 'cleansed' after the war by zealous patriotic self-censors?

Senior Habsburg military commanders seconded Conrad's aggressive stance. War Minister Alexander von Krobatin repeatedly pressed Conrad for war with Serbia. Otto Gellinek, Vienna's military attaché at Belgrade, added fuel to the fire by informing the War Ministry at Vienna that the Sarajevo murders had been engineered by Colonel Dragutin Dimitrijević ('Apis'), head of Serbian military intelligence and Europe's foremost expert on regicide. And General Oskar Potiorek, the military commander in Bosnia–Herzegovina, badgered Viennese leaders to take military measures against Belgrade.[18]

Kaiser Franz Joseph shared Conrad von Hötzendorf's mind-set in 1914, and likewise was beset by doubts and plagued by nightmares. Haunting memories of Solferino, where he had led Austrian armies to defeat at the hands of France and Piedmont-Sardinia in 1859, and of Königgrätz, where his forces had been routed by the Prussians in 1866, for years had crippled the Emperor's ability either to reject or to act on Conrad's demands for preemptive strikes. After the military manoeuvres of 1913, for example, which had ended with yet another plea for war by Conrad, Franz Joseph had strongly admonished his Chief of the General Staff not to become another Wallenstein – a painful reference to the Austrian commander, Albrecht Count Wallenstein, murdered in 1634 after draining Habsburg fortunes and treasure during the Thirty Years' War. But in 1914, Franz Joseph was prepared to draw the sword. The bearer of more than 70 august titles, he was determined to leave the stage with honour. 'If we must go under', he confided to Conrad, 'we better go under decently'.[19]

During the critical phase of the July crisis, Franz Joseph argued that the very survival of his Monarchy was at stake. The Emperor once more placed his faith in his Army, 'in its bravery and dedicated loyalty'.[20] It is revealing that Franz Joseph refused to invite the crowned heads of Britain and Russia or the President of France to Archduke Franz Ferdinand's funeral for fear that they might exert a moderating influence on Habsburg plans with regard to Serbia. 'Precious fruits for the Monarchy were to ripen', in the words of a senior Habsburg diplomat, from Franz Ferdinand's spilled blood.[21]

The pivotal role during the July crisis belonged to Foreign Minister Berchtold. Like Franz Joseph, Berchtold had repeatedly rejected Conrad's pleas for war, but after Sarajevo he came round to the conclusion that the Austro-German alliance of 1879 was engaged in a life-and-death struggle with Russia – and by extension, France. As early as 30 June, that is, 1 week before the formal decision for war, Berchtold spoke of the need for a *'final and fundamental reckoning'* with Serbia.[22] Could Conrad have remained ignorant of this?

Indeed, Berchtold had developed a plan – more, a set of assumptions – that led him to favour military measures. The Foreign Minister felt certain that early and decisive action by Vienna and Berlin would deter possible Russian intervention; that a firm stand by Germany in support of Austria–Hungary would 'localize' the war in the Balkans; and that even if Russia threw her support behind Serbia, the Dual Monarchy's flank in Galicia would be secured by German forces deployed against the Tsar. War now, better than later, was the mood also at the Ballhausplatz.

But was the Austro-Hungarian Army prepared for a mass, industrial war in 1914? Resoundingly 'No'. Around 1800 Napoleon Bonaparte allegedly had claimed that Habsburg forces were always one army, 1 year, and one idea behind; in 1900 they were several defence budgets behind the major European powers. As late as 1903 Austro-Hungarian subjects spent as much on tobacco and more on beer and wine than on defence. In terms of per-capita expenditures on the defence budget of 1906 in Austrian Kronen, Britain spent 36, France 23.8, Germany 22, Italy 11.6, Russia 9.8, and Austria–Hungary 9.6.[23] Despite a dramatic 64 per cent rise in defence spending between 1906 and 1914, the 16 corps commands of the Dual Monarchy in 1914 fielded fewer battalions of infantry (703) than in 1866 – notwithstanding a twofold increase in population over that half century. In fact, Austria–Hungary annually trained a smaller percentage of its population (0.29 per cent) than either its ally, Germany (0.47 per cent), or its potential adversaries, Russia (0.35 per cent), Italy (0.37 per cent), and France (0.75 per cent).

Put differently, the Habsburg Monarchy each year trained only between 22 and 29 per cent of draft-eligible males; the corresponding figures were 40 per cent for Germany and 86 per cent for France. And while the peace-time Army consisted of 415 000 officers and men, the imperial bureaucracy boasted 550 000 servants. At the time of the Second Hague Conference on Disarmament in 1907, Conrad had seriously suggested that Austria–Hungary not send a delegate because it was already in a state of *de facto* disarmament! And during the Second Moroccan Crisis of 1912

Vienna could not even pay the costs of mobilizing its forces, and had to borrow heavily for this from New York money markets.

The truth is that Habsburg military forces were designed not to fight a major war but rather to maintain the delicate political balance in the Empire. In 1868, in the wake of Austria's defeat at the hands of Prussia and its need to reach a 'compromise' with the Magyars, Franz Joseph had divided his armed forces into three distinct components. The joint Austro-Hungarian Imperial and Royal (*k.u.k.*) Army recruited roughly 100 000 men throughout the Empire and trained them for 3 years. Both Vienna and Budapest also established reserve formations – the imperial *Landwehr* in Austria and the royal *Honvéd* in Hungary, each about 10 000 men strong – which were to serve for 2 years. In fact, they actually trained for about 8 weeks per year. The reserves in both Austria and Hungary only gradually received artillery after 1908. The language of command was German for the *k.u.k.* Joint Army and the *Landwehr*; Magyar for the *Honvéd*; and Croatian for the reserves of Bosnia and Herzegovina. In time, army regulations stipulated formal command, service, and regimental languages to be used by each of the 11 ethnic nationalities. Budgets for the militias were approved every year in Budapest and Vienna, and adjusted every decade by a joint Austro-Hungarian budget committee. In short, three military units were ruled by three administrative bureaucracies using three separate command languages![24]

Budapest bureaucrats distrusted Austrian military policy and denied Franz Joseph's forces the requisite funds with which to modernize and expand. Most Magyars viewed the *Honvéd* not as a manpower reserve for the joint Imperial and Royal Army, but rather as the germ cell for a future Hungarian army, commanded by Hungarian nobles, using Magyar as the language of command. And although 1.8 million men were available for service in 1914, only one in four had ever been on active duty; the rest were reservists, recruited from the eight Austrian *Landwehr* (first-line reserve) commands and 41 *Landsturm* (second-line reserve) districts, and the 31 Hungarian *Honvédség* (reserve) units. First-line reservists were between 19 and 37 years of age; second-line reservists between 37 and 42.[25]

In material terms, at the divisional level there were no heavy field guns and only 42 light artillery pieces, as compared to 72 in the German armies. Most Austro-Hungarian 10 cm and 15 cm guns had bronze barrels of 1899 vintage without either shields or buffer brakes. Fortress artillery stemmed from 1880 – and some iron pieces even from 1861. Each artillery battery entered the war with only 250 training shells – the same number as before the Austro-Prussian War of 1866 – compared with around 700 for equivalent French and German units. And in the air, Austria possessed but 48 first-line machines, against 250 in Germany.[26]

The Habsburg officer corps was composed of about three-quarters of Germans – specifically, 76 per cent of the total officer corps and 57 per cent of reserve officers as well as 68 per cent of War Ministry staff. It was probably no better and no worse than most. While the historian István Deák gives the officer corps high marks overall, the public image drawn of officers by novelists in Austria–Hungary was at best contradictory. It ranged from Joseph Roth's Lieutenant Trotta in the *Radetzky Marsch*, quietly resigned to face doom in 1914, to Jaroslav Hašek's Lieutenant Lukasch in *The Good Soldier Švejk*, cynical, corrupt, cowardly, and vile – not to mention downright stupid.[27] There is no question that the Dual Monarchy's nobility no longer saw service with the military as desirable: nobles in the General Staff had declined from 60 per cent in 1863 to a mere 11.5 per cent on the eve of the Great War, and those in general rank from 90 per cent to 25 per cent. By 1913 only 58 of 503 officers on Conrad's staff were aristocratic.[28] But the officers in their splendid uniforms and led by dazzling military bands remained an anachronism of a past bureaucratic-military feudal state in an age of a rapidly modernizing industry and society.

Widespread realization that the Monarchy could not alone tackle Serbia (and much less Russia) led Foreign Minister Berchtold to consult the German ally. On 1 July he had a lengthy discussion of the Serbian affair with Viktor Naumann, a German journalist then in Vienna, who claimed to be a semi-official spokesman for Berlin. Naumann informed Berchtold that Germany was more receptive to the notion of a 'preventive war against Russia' than it had been in 1913; that Kaiser Wilhelm II would support any Austro-Hungarian action against Serbia to uphold the 'monarchical principle'; and that the diplomats at the Wilhelmstrasse in Berlin 'considered the moment opportune' to settle Balkan affairs. Ominously, Naumann warned Berchtold that Austria–Hungary would cease to be 'a great power if it allowed the moment to slip by'. Berchtold informed Naumann that he appreciated these assurances of German support.[29] It is interesting to note that Berchtold's official diary at the Foreign Office is conspicuously devoid of entries for the period between 27 June and 5 July 1914.[30]

On 4 July Berchtold despatched Alexander Count Hoyos, his personal *chef de cabinet*, to Berlin with two confidential letters from Kaiser Franz Joseph and himself addressed to Wilhelm II to ascertain what the German position would be in the event that Vienna took actions designed 'to eliminate' Serbia 'as a political power factor in the Balkans'.[31] Hoyos, along with János Count Forgách and Alexander Baron von Musulin, belonged to the younger generation of diplomats who in 1914 formulated Vienna's anti-Serbian policy. Berchtold's personal diplomacy served three important functions: it made certain that the Germans were convinced of Vienna's determination to act against Serbia; it obviated any possible conciliatory diplomatic manoeuvres by Ambassador László Szögyény-Marich at Berlin; and it short-circuited the political influence in Vienna of the Hungarian Prime Minister, Tisza, who on 30 June had recommended a diplomatic, rather than a military, offensive against Belgrade.

Kaiser Wilhelm II, on receiving Count Hoyos' letters on 5 July, hastily recalled his Chancellor from Hohenfinow. In a series of meetings with Bethmann Hollweg – later blown up erroneously by the Allies into the 'Crown Council of Potsdam' – the two men weighed their options. They decided to back their lone loyal ally. Wilhelm II assured the Austrians that Vienna could count on 'Germany's full support' in the Balkans, even if 'serious European complications' – a diplomatic euphemism for war – resulted. Additionally, he counselled Vienna not to 'delay the action' against Belgrade and added that Germany fully expected war with Russia and had made all preparations over the past few years with this in mind. War Minister von Falkenhayn unconditionally assured the Kaiser that the Army was ready for war. Bethmann Hollweg, for his part, informed the Austrians that he viewed a military strike against Serbia as the 'best and most radical solution' to Vienna's Balkan problems and pressed Vienna to take decisive steps against Serbia.[32] His Under-Secretary of State, Arthur Zimmermann, already at this point opined that the likelihood of war stood at 90 per cent. Neither Wilhelm II nor Bethmann Hollweg shied away from the prospect of war; rather, both were willing to exploit the crisis to full advantage. To do otherwise, in their view, would be tantamount to renouncing Germany's world-power status.

Armed with this German 'blank cheque', which will be analysed shortly, Berchtold convened a Common Council of Ministers at Vienna on 7 July and apprised his Cabinet of Germany's staunch backing, 'even though our operations against Serbia should bring about the great war'.[33] The Foreign Minister, supported by War Minister von Krobatin, Chief of the General Staff Conrad von Hötzendorf, Austrian Premier Karl Count Stürgkh, and Common Finance Minister Leon von Biliński, favoured a 'radical solution' of the Serbian problem by way of immediate 'energetic' military measures against Belgrade. Premier Stürgkh described the present situation as one 'that unquestionably was moving toward a military reckoning with Serbia'. Krobatin favoured war 'now better than later', and Biliński lectured the Council that 'the Serb understands only force'. Conrad's survey of the Monarchy's military situation was not taken down as it was deemed top secret. But the questions that followed the Chief of the General Staff's presentation left no doubt that a general European conflagration and not a simple Austro-Hungarian 'surgical strike' against Serbia was in the offing.

Only Hungarian Premier Tisza demurred, voicing fears that such precipitous action would bring on 'the dreadful calamity of a European war'. In the end, Tisza agreed to Berchtold's suggestion that Serbia be sent an ultimatum demanding that it allow Habsburg officials to help round up the suspected assassins – that is, one specifically designed to be rejected by Belgrade. To keep Italy, Britain, and even Russia out of the war, Tisza demanded that Serbia not be dismembered but that Bulgaria, Greece, and Albania rather than Austria–Hungary seize some of its territory. Vienna, for its part, would be content to extract the costs of war and reparations from Belgrade. Privately, Tisza favoured 'serious action' against what he termed the 'insolence of the Serbs'. Yet as Hungarian Premier he opposed war on 7 July mainly because he desired no annexation of more Slavic subjects; as a Magyar he was already a minority in his native Hungary.[34] Surprisingly, the role of the Italian ally in any future conflagration was not discussed on 7 July. Nor was any effort made to convince the Russians to stand aside in this matter. War now, better than later.

After the meeting, Berchtold departed for Bad Ischl to 'vacation' with Franz Joseph. Concurrently, he advised Conrad and Krobatin to begin their planned summer holidays 'to preserve the appearance that nothing is being planned'.[35] But before leaving Vienna, Conrad received a rude shock. Having instituted a system of harvest leaves for recruits designed to appease the Monarchy's powerful agrarian interests, Conrad on 6–7 July discovered that critical units earmarked for mobilization were already on leave at Agram, Graz, Pressburg, Cracow, Temesvár, Innsbruck, and Budapest; they would not return to barracks until 15 July. Instant recall was out of the question as this would impede the harvest, overload the Monarchy's fragile railroad system, and alert Europe to Vienna's possible military intentions.[36] The issue would have to await future resolution.

By 14 July Tisza was ready to endorse Berchtold's plan to present Belgrade with a stringent ultimatum that would permit Viennese officials to enter Serbia at any time to search for the Sarajevo murderers. If Serbia accepted the ultimatum, Berchtold calculated, it would be publicly 'humiliated', and Russia would again, as in 1908–9 over the annexation of Bosnia–Herzegovina, lose 'prestige in the Balkans'.[37] If, on the other hand, Serbian Prime Minister Nikola Pašić rejected the ultimatum, Austria–Hungary would break diplomatic relations, mobilize its forces, and shell Belgrade. Count Hoyos was ready for all eventualities: 'It is immaterial to us whether the world war comes out of this'.[38] In what undoubtedly was the single greatest case of bureaucratic bungling during the July crisis, the Austrian investigation into the regicide headed by Friedrich Wieser failed to establish that the Serbian Army had trained the assassins, that the Russian military attaché in Belgrade (V. A. Artamonov) had financed them, and that the Serbian government had foreknowledge of the plot.[39]

The final decision for war was reached at a special Common Council convened at Berchtold's private residence on 19 July.[40] All key players were ordered to arrive in unmarked cars. Berchtold opened the meeting by assuring Tisza that Vienna would not annex new Serbian territory, but seek only minor border revisions. Conrad, while pleased that war was in sight, expressed dismay at Berchtold's pronouncement. Privately, he assured War Minister von Krobatin that after a successful campaign, such a promise was of little value. In fact, there were already intimate discussions in Viennese official circles that the war might end not only with Serbia's economic integration into the Dual Monarchy but also with the annexation of Russian Poland and perhaps parts of the Ukraine. It was decided at the Council to hand Serbia the ultimatum, carefully crafted by Musulin to assure rejection, on 23 July and to demand compliance within 48 hours. Tisza's countryman, István Count Burián, laconically noted: 'The wheel of history rolls'.[41] The Army officially began its war diary on 23 July.

Not surprisingly, on 25 July Serbia, in an ambiguous reply, rejected the Austro-Hungarian ultimatum because it feared loss of sovereignty if it allowed Habsburg officials *carte blanche* over its internal affairs. Sir Maurice de Bunsen, Britain's envoy to Vienna, informed Whitehall: 'Vienna burst into a frenzy of delight, vast crowds parading the streets and singing patriotic songs till the small hours of the morning'.[42]

Still, Count Berchtold feared that the Entente powers might at the last moment clutch peace from the jaws of war. To make certain that 'clarity' was brought about by a declaration of war, Berchtold informed Kaiser Franz Joseph on 26 July that the Army had confirmed that Serbian troops from Danubian steamers had fired on Habsburg forces near Temes Kubin (Kovin). Vienna could now depict the coming war as one of defence against Serbian aggression. In fact, the incident never took place and the military report was never found in the archives.[43]

Yet it served its purpose. At Bad Ischl, Franz Joseph, 'hollow eyed', signed the order for mobilization and accepted the likelihood of war. His only recorded comment, delivered 'in a muffled, choked voice, which barely managed to fight its way out of his throat', was '*Also doch!*'; 'so, after all'.[44] Within 24 hours the mobilization decree as well as an imperial appeal to the subjects of the Multinational Empire were posted in 11 languages. Civil rights were suspended and military replaced civilian administration in most districts. On 28 July the Kaiser, with a tear in his eye, signed the declaration of war against Serbia. Berchtold slyly informed Franz Joseph that he preferred not to include the Temes Kubin 'incident' in the official declaration of war! As an act of antiquated chivalry, Franz Joseph ordered Austrian officials not to arrest the Serbian Chief of the General Staff, Field Marshal Radomir Putnik, then passing through Austria–Hungary on return from vacationing at Bad Gleichenberg in Bohemia, but to let him proceed to Belgrade unmolested.[45]

It is fair to conclude that Austria–Hungary in July 1914 went to war to save itself. Fear dominated Viennese planners: fear of Pan-Slavic nationalism; fear of losing the military advantage to Serbia, Russia, and France; and fear of forfeiting Berlin's avowed support. Planners in Vienna decided to eliminate the Serbian problem once and for all and they fully accepted the likelihood of war with Russia. Each scenario 'gamed' at the Ballhausplatz had one cardinal feature: Austria–Hungary had to emerge from the crisis as the dominant political force in the Balkans, supplanting Russia and keeping out Germany. In July 1914 nothing short of war could achieve that purpose.

For too long, Anglo-Saxons remained mesmerized with the *fin de siècle* Vienna of Gustav Mahler, Arthur Schnitzler, Gustav Klimt, Arnold Schönberg, and Sigmund Freud, and refused to accept that the home of Sacher Torte and Kaffee mit Schlag, of Karnival and Musikverein, could have initiated the great folly of 1914. But the initiative for war lay in Vienna. Habsburg and not Hohenzollern decided to settle accounts by military rather than diplomatic means. Both the direction and the pace of the July crisis were dictated by Vienna. It was Count Berchtold, according to historian Samuel Williamson, Jr., who set the tempo, defined the moves, and closed off the options in July 1914. In fact, Berchtold throughout July was most reluctant to share information with Berlin for fear that the latter might apply the brakes and seek a last-minute diplomatic resolution to the crisis. Vienna first resolved for war, sought German assurances, and then exploited them once received.[46]

Berlin: the 'calculated risk'

Leaders in Berlin faced a hard choice in the summer of 1914. Two decades of rudderless statecraft had left the Reich in a precarious situation. France, Britain, and Russia had 'encircled' Germany with an entente cordiale in answer to Berlin's fleet building and foreign ventures in Asia, Africa, the Middle East, and Latin America. Italy apparently had second thoughts about its commitment to defend the Rhine under the terms of the Triple

Alliance of 1882. Austria–Hungary alone remained a solid ally, yet that ally was also a liability. Vienna constantly demanded full backing from Berlin for any play that it chose to make in the Balkans – the very region that Otto von Bismarck had identified as Europe's potential powder keg and deemed not to be worth the 'bones of a single Pomeranian grenadier'. Statesmen and soldiers in Berlin in 1914 thus had to decide between support for a lone reliable ally or isolation in the face of a hostile coalition.

Berlin did not go to war in 1914 in a 'bid for world power', as the historian Fritz Fischer claimed, but rather first to secure and thereafter to enhance the borders of 1871. Secondly, the decision for war was made in July 1914 and not, as some scholars have claimed, at a nebulous 'war council' on 8 December 1912. Thirdly, no one in Berlin had planned for war before 1914; no long-term economic or military plans have been uncovered to suggest otherwise. The Prussian Army's refusal to expand its peacetime force of 800 000 men by three army corps in 1912–13 for fear that this would undermine the social cohesion of its officer corps alone argues against the thesis of a long-planned war of aggression. The Army's ammunition reserves in the summer of 1914 were 20 to 50 per cent short of required levels, and industrial capacity was so low that it took 6 months rather than the anticipated 8 weeks to make up the shortfall. Nor would the High Sea Fleet be completed until the early 1920s. Fourthly, there was no ready shopping list of war aims extant in July 1914. Bethmann Hollweg's infamous war-aims programme was not drafted until the critical days of September 1914, when German and French forces clashed at the Marne River in what was expected to be the decisive battle of the war.

This having been said, the fact remains that on 5 July 1914 Berlin gave Vienna unconditional support ('blank cheque') for a war in the Balkans. The larger answer for this decision lies in the prevailing mind-set rather than in any specific military algebra. Civilian as well as military planners in Berlin, like their counterparts in Vienna, were dominated by a 'strike-now-better-than-later' mentality. They were aware that Russia's 'Big Programme' of rearmament, launched in 1913 after the disastrous Russo-Japanese War, would be completed around 1916–17. Should – indeed, could – one wait until then? Or would it not be better to strike now? No one doubted that war was in the offing. The diplomatic and political record, reflecting the flood of popular literature, contains countless dire prognostications of the inevitability of a 'final reckoning' between Slavs and Teutons. Leaders in Berlin also saw war as the only solution to 'encirclement' – even if few among them accepted that this 'encirclement' had been self-imposed. In short, war was viewed as both apocalyptic fear and apocalyptic hope.

General Helmuth von Moltke (the Younger), Chief of the Prussian General Staff, like Conrad von Hötzendorf at Vienna, was convinced that what he termed Kaiser Wilhelm II's 'peace policy' would lead Prussia to disaster as a similar policy against Napoleon I had done in 1806, and that only a preemptive war against Russia could secure Germany's future.[47] Moltke understood that such a conflict would embroil the European powers. As early as 1911, in a position paper for the General Staff, he had bluntly stated: 'All are preparing themselves for the great war, which all sooner or later expect'.[48] At the putative 'war council' in December 1912, Moltke had pressed Wilhelm II for war with Russia, 'and the sooner the better'.[49] During his last peacetime meeting with Conrad von Hötzendorf at Karlsbad on 12 May 1914, Moltke had lectured his Viennese guest that 'to wait any longer meant a diminishing of our chances'.[50]

Moreover, Moltke couched the coming war in racial terms. Returning to Berlin from Karlsbad, he assured the German government of the 'deeply rooted sentiment of allied loyalty' that existed between the Habsburg and Hohenzollern dynasties. In language taken from ancient Germanic texts, Moltke spoke of *Nibelungen* loyalty. The European war would come 'sooner or later', and it would be 'primarily a struggle between Germans and Slavs'.[51] With regard to the immediate Balkan crisis, Moltke compared Serbia to an abscess that poisoned the European body politic; cauterization with a red-hot iron alone could neutralize this deadly 'abscess'.

Normally of a dour and pessimistic nature, Moltke was more convinced than even Conrad von Hötzendorf that time was against the two Germanic powers. His mind was beset with pessimism bordering on paranoia. Two months before the Sarajevo regicide, Moltke had confided to Foreign Secretary von Jagow that prospects for the future 'weighed heavily upon him'. Russia would finish rearming in 2 or 3 years. 'Our enemies' military power would then be so great', the general cautioned the diplomat, 'that he did not know how he could deal with it'. But Moltke bluntly informed Jagow that 'there was no alternative but to fight a preventive war so as to beat the enemy while we could still emerge fairly well from the struggle'.[52] While he feared a 'horrible war', one that could set European culture back decades, Moltke as late as 29 July instructed his Supreme War Lord that Germany would 'never hit it again so well as we do now with France's and Russia's expansion of their armies incomplete'.[53] During the critical days of July 1914 Moltke badly underestimated the British and French armies and vastly overrated both the Russian Army and his own.

General Georg von Waldersee, Moltke's deputy, was like-minded. Already in May 1914 he had penned a position paper in which he bluntly lectured the General Staff that Germany had '*no* reason whatever *to avoid*' a general conflict 'but *quite the opposite*, [good] prospects *today* to conduct a great European war quickly and victoriously'. During the critical phase of the July crisis on 31 July Waldersee stressed that he would 'regard it with favour if war were to come about now' because 'conditions and prospects will never become better'.[54] In other words, once Austria–Hungary had committed to war, German military planners were ready to draw the sword.

Chancellor von Bethmann Hollweg shared this *Götterdämmerung* mentality. Social Darwinism taught by teachers and professors and printed in journals and novels had taught European leaders that history rewarded only the victors, that empires rose and fell according to Machiavellian precepts, and that might alone guaranteed survival. In April 1913 Bethmann Hollweg had lectured the Reichstag about an 'inevitable struggle' in the near future between Slavs and Teutons and concurrently had warned Vienna that Russia could not possibly stay out of any future Austro-Hungarian war with Serbia.[55] Shortly after the Potsdam audience with Wilhelm II on 5 July 1914, in which the Chancellor agreed to back any Austro-Hungarian play in the Balkans, Bethmann Hollweg informed his chief political advisor, Kurt Riezler, that Russia 'grows and grows and weighs on us like a nightmare'.[56] According to Hoyos, Bethmann Hollweg bluntly stated that 'were war unavoidable, the present moment would be more advantageous than a later one'.[57] On 7 July, knowing that Vienna had made the decision for war, the Chancellor assured the Austrians that he regarded military action against Serbia as the 'best and most radical solution' to the Dual Monarchy's Balkan problems.[58]

Bethmann Hollweg was determined that all levers of decision-making remain in his hands – that is, to control the pace and the extent of Berlin's actions. He spied in the July crisis a splendid opportunity either to break the Anglo-French-Russian alliance and thus gain a great diplomatic victory, or if need be to risk a land war against France and Russia to shore up and expand Germany's semi-hegemony on the Continent. Former Chancellor Bernhard von Bülow in December 1914 condemned Bethmann Hollweg's pro-Habsburg policy during the July crisis: 'This fifth of July was a horrible day for Germany . . . a fatal day. How could Bethmann have done this!'[59]

In fact, Bethmann Hollweg had worked out in his mind a 'calculated risk'. If war came 'from the east' and Germany entered it in order to preserve the Habsburg Monarchy, 'then we have the prospect of winning it'. But should Russia remain idle, 'then we have the prospect of having outmaneuvered the Entente in this matter'.[60] In other words, victory was possible either on the field of battle or at the conference table. It is interesting that Bethmann Hollweg by 8 July placed war first, and diplomacy second, in his innermost thoughts. Above all, time was of the essence; Vienna had to be encouraged to move swiftly against Serbia. On 11 July Bethmann Hollweg encapsulated his rationale for Wilhelmstrasse staff as follows: 'A quick fait accompli, and then friendly [stance] toward the Entente; then we can survive the shock'.[61] A week later the Chancellor expressed to Crown Prince Wilhelm his delight that Germany could take part in the looming European conflagration as Austria's second, rather than as the primary agent of expansion.

Privately, Bethmann Hollweg remained pessimistic about Germany's future. He instructed his son, Felix, not to plant new trees on the family estate on the Oder River because the Russians in all likelihood would be in Hohenfinow in a few years anyhow![62] Yet Bethmann Hollweg, widely referred to as the 'Hamlet' of German politics, was resigned to war as inevitable, and at the height of the July crisis glumly confided to his closest associates: 'A fate beyond human power hangs over Europe and our *Volk*'.[63] Having decided to risk a European war over Vienna's play in the Balkans, the Chancellor suggested that the generals leave Berlin for their planned vacations to maintain the appearance of diplomatic calm.

There remained the Kaiser. Wilhelm II basically shared the prevailing mood of the inevitability of war. In the fall of 1913 he had confided this conviction to the Austrian Foreign Minister Berchtold, and 1 month before the tragedy at Sarajevo had mused whether it might not be 'better to attack' Russia 'than to wait' until its rearmament programme was completed by 1916–17.[64] Wilhelm II had been pilloried recently by the German press as being 'timid' and as posturing like a 'valiant chicken' for his lack of resolution in foreign affairs. In July 1914 he was determined not to miss what he considered to be his 'historical hour'.[65] Hence, when Ambassador Heinrich von Tschirschky from Vienna informed him on 3 July of the decision to avenge the regicide at Sarajevo, Wilhelm hastily penned 'now or never' on the report.[66] Three days later the Kaiser instructed Ambassador Szögyény-Marich that Franz Joseph could count on 'Germany's full support' even if 'serious European complications' resulted, adding that Vienna ought not to 'delay the action' against Serbia.[67] Later that evening of 6 July Wilhelm II three times reassured himself – as well as his dinner guest, Gustav Krupp von Bohlen und Halbach – that this time he would not 'cave in'.[68]

Thus, the Austro-German position by mid-July 1914 accepted the 'calculated risk'. Franz Joseph and Wilhelm II, Berchtold and Bethmann Hollweg, Conrad von Hötzendorf and Moltke were willing to gamble on a general European war ('serious European complications') for the twin purposes of ending Belgrade's 'Greater Serbia' aspirations in the Balkans and Russia's Pan-Slavic agitation. This German determination was accurately reported by the Bavarian diplomatic legation in Berlin. Since Bavaria would have to cast the critical vote for war in the Federal Chamber under Article 11 of the German Constitution, Maximilian Count von Soden called at the Wilhelmstrasse on 9 July to gather instructions for his government. Zimmermann bluntly informed Soden that Berlin viewed the moment as 'propitious' for Austria–Hungary to undertake a 'campaign of revenge' against Serbia. Moreover, Berlin, ever confident that the Balkan crisis could be 'localized', had advised Vienna 'to proceed with all means' at its disposal. Germany would support its ally 'come what may'.[69]

On 18 July the Bavarian military plenipotentiary, Hans von Schoen, informed his government of the mood at the General Staff: 'So they are of the opinion here that Austria is face to face with an hour of fate, and for this reason they declared here without hesitation, in reply to an inquiry from Vienna, that [they] would agree to any method of procedure which [Austria–Hungary] might determine on, even at the risk of war with Russia'. Schoen allowed that Austria–Hungary's 'hour of decision' was at hand and that Berlin would support any action that Vienna chose to take, 'including war with Russia'.[70]

In light of recent scholarship, the notion, first put forth by David Lloyd George and reiterated as late as 1994 by Henry Kissinger, that 'nation after nation slid into a war whose causes they did not understand but from which they could not extricate themselves',[71] is untenable. It simply served to avoid painful self-examination on the part of the 'men of 1914'. Nations rarely, if ever, 'slide' into war. Rather, as in July 1914, statesmen and soldiers carefully assess their situations, weigh their options, calculate the risks involved, and then decide on war or peace. On 23 July diplomats in Vienna handed Belgrade the Austro-Hungarian ultimatum, demanding that Habsburg agents be allowed to enter Serbia in search of the regicides. They demanded an answer within 48 hours. Wilhelm II's military entourage, cruising the waters off Norway, was fully aware that rejection by Belgrade 'pretty well meant war' in Europe.[72]

The 'leap into the dark'

The seriousness of the July crisis hit European capitals with full force on 23–4 July. All eyes turned to St Petersburg, where the visiting French delegation discussed the Balkan crisis with Tsar Nicholas II and his government. French President Poincaré had already cautioned the Austrian Ambassador to Russia, Friedrich Count Szápáry, at a diplomatic reception on 21 July not to forget that Serbia had 'some very warm friends in the

Russian people' and that 'Russia has an ally, France'.[73] The French President was determined to preserve the Franco-Russian alliance of 1894 at all costs as it alone offered France security against Germany and hope to recover the provinces of Alsace and Lorraine 'lost' to Prussia in 1871.

But Premier Viviani's mind was not in St Petersburg Rather, it was in Paris, where the Caillaux trial threatened to make public secret contacts that Caillaux had established with the Germans during the Second Moroccan Crisis and thereby embarrass the government. Additionally, Viviani was concerned about the whereabouts of his mistress from the *Comédie française*.[74] The Premier was anxious and delighted to leave Kronstadt on 23 July, and thus learned of the Austrian ultimatum to Serbia while steaming through the Baltic Sea en route to Sweden.

In Paris the caretaker government of Finance Minister Jean-Baptiste Bienvenu-Martin took the first precautionary steps toward war when it learned of the Austrian ultimatum to Serbia on 23 July. Within 48 hours it recalled generals on summer vacation and military forces on harvest leave. French units stationed in Morocco were ordered home by 27 July. The next day Chief of the General Staff Joseph Joffre hastily – and without official government sanction – assured the Russians of France's 'full and active readiness faithfully to execute her responsibilities as an ally'.[75] Yet even at this late hour, the gravity of the Viennese action was largely obfuscated by the sensational verdict of 'not guilty' in the Caillaux trial, to which *Le Temps* gave twice the coverage that it accorded the European crisis. On 29 July Poincaré and Viviani landed on French soil.

Russian Foreign Minister S. D. Sazonov was fully cognizant of the seriousness of the Austro-German initiative against Serbia and its implications for Russia. The country had suffered two stinging defeats in recent years: in 1905 it had been humiliated both on land and at sea by the Japanese; and in 1908 threats of war from Berlin had forced Russia to back down in the face of Austria–Hungary's annexation of Bosnia–Herzegovina. On 24–5 July 1914 Baron M. F. Schilling, Director of the Foreign Chancellery, recorded that Sazonov viewed war as being 'unavoidable' when news reached St Petersburg that Serbia had rejected the Viennese ultimatum. 'This is the European war.'[76] Not surprisingly, Sazonov turned for counsel to French Ambassador Maurice Paléologue. A vain, arrogant man, Paléologue assured the Russians on 24 July of 'the complete readiness of France to fulfill her obligations as an ally in case of necessity'.[77] Serbia rejected the Austrian ultimatum on 25 July and mobilized its army. Austria followed suit and declared war on Serbia on 28 July. Austrian artillery shells fell on Belgrade later that day.

Russia now faced its hour of decision. It could accept the Austro-German decision to 'punish' Belgrade for the regicide and suffer another diplomatic defeat, or it could stand firm behind the 'little Slav brother' in the Balkans and risk a European war. Russia's military leaders, War Minister V. A. Sukhomlinov and Chief of the General Staff N. N. Yanushkevich, counselled general mobilization. Foreign Minister Sazonov, although armed with Paléologue's 'blank cheque', wanted to put off such a final and irrevocable step until Austrian forces had actually invaded Serbia. However, on 28 July he convinced Tsar Nicholas II to sign a decree mobilizing 1.1 million troops in the military districts of Kiev, Odessa, Moscow, and Kazan – that is, those confronting only Austria–Hungary. Nicholas II, irresolute as ever, idled his time away at the summer residence of Tsarskoe Selo. On 29 July he noted in his diary: 'During the day we played tennis; the weather was magnificent'. On 30 July he 'had a delightful bathe in the sea'. But on 31 July he noted: 'It has been a grey day, in keeping with my mood'.[78]

The Tsar's 'grey mood' had developed around 4 p.m. on 30 July during a meeting with Sazonov. The Foreign Minister, citing support from Generals Sukhomlinov and Yanushkevich as well as French Ambassador Paléologue, had demanded mobilization of all Russian forces. There was danger in delay, Sazonov warned Nicholas II, as Austrian troops were about to cross the Danube into Serbia. Ingeniously, Sazonov lectured his sovereign that partial mobilization was out of the question as it would violate Russia's obligations to France under the provisions of the 1894 alliance. More bizarre yet, Sazonov warned that failure to mobilize immediately would give Kaiser Wilhelm II an opportunity to extract a declaration of neutrality from the French – or even to force Paris to march with Berlin against St Petersburg! Nicholas II was not the man to resist such dire prognostications. Although he lamented 'sending thousands and thousands of men to their death', the Tsar nevertheless concurred that it would be 'very dangerous' not to undertake 'timely preparations' for what after all seemed to be 'an inevitable war'. Thus he signed the *ukazes* announcing general mobilization. Thereupon, Sazonov allegedly instructed Yanushkevich to order the General Staff to smash its telephones so that the Tsar could not cancel mobilization.[79]

A final flurry of diplomatic activity gripped Berlin and London. Sir Edward Grey at Whitehall had condemned the Austro-Hungarian ultimatum to Serbia of 23 July as 'the most formidable document that I have ever seen addressed by one State to another that was independent'.[80] In fact, Grey had watched the July crisis develop in splendid isolation, seeking the counsel neither of fellow Cabinet ministers nor of senior Foreign Office professionals. The truth is that Grey thought that he could manage the crisis by himself through personal diplomacy with Berlin. And he knew fully well that the overwhelming majority of his ministerial colleagues opposed war. Thus Grey, falling back on a proposal by Nicolson, the Permanent Under-Secretary at the Foreign Office, suggested a four-power conference to deal with the Serbian matter. He found no takers. The Cabinet finally took up the European crisis on 29 July at the tail end of a lengthy discussion over Ulster's opposition to Irish Home Rule, and in the words of John Burns simply 'decided not to decide'. And when it was suggested that Germany might start military operations by invading neutral Belgium, Grey laconically replied that this would be treated as a question 'of policy rather than legal obligations'.[81]

Vienna's ultimatum to Serbia and the resulting Russian mobilization put a halt to such mental gymnastics. By 24 July the military in Berlin had taken over management of the July crisis from the Chancellor, who now became afraid of his earlier boldness and urged restraint on Vienna. General von Falkenhayn returned from Juist on 24 July and immediately grasped the seriousness of the situation. '[Austria] simply wants the final reckoning' with Serbia. The War Minister, apparently realizing that the coming struggle would be a protracted one, ordered inquiries 'about purchasing vast quantities of wheat'. Moltke arrived in Berlin 2 days later and Wilhelm II on 27 July. An *ad hoc* council of war took place and Falkenhayn summed up its results as follows: 'It has now been decided to fight the matter through, regardless of the cost'.[82]

But Falkenhayn was a little hasty in his assessment of the imperial resolve. On 28 July Wilhelm II learned that Serbia had accepted all points of the Austro-Hungarian ultimatum save one – Vienna's demand to dispatch agents to Belgrade to hunt down the assassins. The Kaiser crowed about Vienna's 'brilliant performance' and gauged that therewith 'all reason for war' had disappeared. Falkenhayn tersely denounced what he termed the Kaiser's 'chaotic speeches' and maliciously pointed out to Wilhelm II that he 'no longer had control of the affair in his own hands'.[83]

Austria–Hungary declared war on Serbia that same day. On 29 July General von Moltke urged mobilization before France and Russia could do so in order to conduct campaigns against the two continental adversaries. After reminding Bethmann Hollweg yet again of the 'deeply rooted sentiment of allied loyalty' that existed between Berlin and Vienna, Moltke demanded that the Chancellor ascertain at once whether France and Russia 'are disposed to go to the length of war with Germany'. The time to strike was at hand. 'We shall never hit it again so well as we do now', Moltke assured his government.[84]

The July crisis now entered its most critical stage in Berlin. Mobilization was the necessary preliminary step to a declaration of war, and with it control over domestic affairs – freedom of movement, distribution of vital war materials and food reserves, censorship of the press, promulgation of military law and courts-martial, confiscation of raw materials, and even the arrest of leading socialists – would pass from civilian to military leaders. Germany, in the words of the Prussian Minister of the Interior, Friedrich Wilhelm von Loebell, upon mobilizing would take on 'the character of a military dictatorship'.[85] Falkenhayn's closest associate at the War Office, General Adolf Wild von Hohenborn, informed the Saxon government on 29 July: 'We are slowly but surely moving toward mobilization'.[86]

On the diplomatic front, Moltke, ably seconded by Falkenhayn, pressed the Wilhelmstrasse also to ascertain Britain's position on war – and to make certain that the onus for declaring war fell on St Petersburg. Bethmann Hollweg, probably buoyed by Grand Admiral von Tirpitz's assurances that the Royal Navy's mobilization of the fleet was 'bluff', now decided to play his 'trump'. Shortly before midnight on 29 July the Chancellor called British Ambassador Sir Edward Goschen to his residence and laid his cards on the table: were Britain to remain neutral in the coming war, Germany would offer London a neutrality agreement, guarantee the independence of the Netherlands, and promise not to undertake 'territorial gains at the expense of France'. Shocked by the naked candour of these 'astounding proposals', Goschen merely noted that 'they reflect discredit on the statesman who makes them'.[87]

Grey received Goschen's account of the impromptu midnight meeting with Bethmann Hollweg on 30 July. It drove him into a 'white heat of rage'. Clearly, Berlin had rejected his personal diplomacy. That afternoon, Grey informed German Ambassador Karl Prince von Lichnowsky that, in case of a general war, Britain would not remain neutral, and he instructed Goschen at Berlin to inform Bethmann Hollweg that Britain would never accept the Chancellor's shameful proposal.[88] Therewith, Bethmann Hollweg's 'calculated risk' had collapsed. The war would not be 'localized' in the Balkans. Nor would it be limited to the Continent. Later that day Bethmann Hollweg informed the Prussian State Ministry that 'the hope for England [was now] zero'. He merely expressed his desire to 'depict Russia as the guilty party'.[89]

Bethmann Hollweg panicked as the likelihood of war dawned on him. He dashed off a telegram to Vienna, resurrecting the Kaiser's suggestion that Austria be asked to 'halt in Belgrade' and merely to hold the Serbian capital as a 'pledge' while the diplomats sought to resolve the crisis.[90] But General von Moltke would have none of it. He immediately informed the Austrian military attaché at Berlin, Karl Count von Bienerth, that Austria and Germany must mobilize against Russia at once. And he sent a cable to Conrad von Hötzendorf in Vienna: 'Austria–Hungary must be preserved; mobilize also against Russia. Germany will mobilize'. Not surprisingly,

Foreign Minister Berchtold was exasperated by the two conflicting telegrams from the German capital. 'Who rules in Berlin', he asked Conrad, 'Moltke or Bethmann?'[91] The answer to that rhetorical question came late on 30 July when Bethmann Hollweg agreed to War Minister von Falkenhayn's request to institute a military state of emergency – the necessary precondition for mobilization – to go into effect at noon the following day. The dice were cast.

Moltke harboured no illusions about the coming war. Pacing nervously up and down in his office, he confided to his adjutant, Major Hans von Haeften, that Russian mobilization against Austria–Hungary meant that Germany would have to honour its alliance commitments to Vienna. German mobilization, Moltke allowed, would make a European war inevitable. France, for its part, would back Russia while Britain could not afford to stay out of such a general conflagration. The war could not be localized in the Balkans, but rather would assume from the start the nature of a 'world war'.

All that remained for Bethmann Hollweg was to put the best face possible on the July crisis. He was greatly relieved around 11 a.m. on 31 July when news began to filter through from Ambassador Friedrich Count von Pourtalès in St Petersburg that the bright red mobilization orders were being posted in the Russian capital. Bethmann Hollweg could now assure the Social Democrats (SPD) that Russian mobilization had forced Germany to go to war. Within hours of the welcome news from Pourtalès, shortly after noon on 31 July, Kaiser Wilhelm II agreed to issue the decree that a 'threatening state of war' (*Zustand der drohenden Kriegsgefahr*) existed. Moltke read a draft of the proposed declaration of mobilization and an accompanying appeal to the German people with a voice 'almost suffocated by tears'. Bethmann Hollweg thereupon expressed his 'displeasure' at this usurpation of civilian authority and entered into a heated debate with the Kaiser concerning the division of powers between civilian and military authorities.[92] A formal military delegation briefed an apparently ignorant Federal Chamber on the precise meaning of mobilization.

Relief and joy prevailed in official quarters in Berlin on 31 July. The strain and stress of the diplomatic crisis was a thing of the past. Moltke was pleased. 'There was . . . an atmosphere of happiness.' Admiral Georg Alexander von Müller, Chief of the Naval Cabinet, recorded in his diary: 'The mood is brilliant. The government has managed brilliantly to make us appear the attacked'. General Karl von Wenninger, Bavaria's military plenipotentiary to Berlin, visited the Prussian War Office and noted: 'Everywhere beaming faces, shaking of hands in the corridors; one congratulates one's self for having taken the hurdle'. An 'exceedingly excited and unruly mob' stoned the British Embassy when the *Berliner Tageblatt*

leaked word that war was imminent.[93] Even Bethmann Hollweg appreciated the enthusiastic crowds outside the Chancellery – apparently organized by his cousin, Dietrich von Bethmann Hollweg.[94] Ever the
pessimist, he worried about the German 'leap into the dark', but concluded that it was his 'most solemn duty' to undertake it.[95] Almost alone,
the industrialist Walther Rathenau soberly noted: 'This war has a false
ring to it; it is not 1813, not 1866, not 1870. . . . It did not need to happen
the way it did'.[96]

The Kaiser signed the formal order to mobilize at 5 p.m. on 1 August
1914 – in the Neues Palais at Potsdam at the desk made of wood from Lord
Nelson's flagship HMS *Victory*, a present from Queen Victoria.
Falkenhayn, who had to push his way through thousands of jubilant citi-
zens ringing the castle, recorded the drama of the moment: 'Thereupon the
Kaiser shook my hand for a long time; tears stood in both of our eyes'.[97]
After a brief moment of confusion about Britain's anticipated entry into the
war, the German 16th Division was ordered to cross into Luxembourg.
Wilhelm II ordered champagne to celebrate the momentous decision.

The 'men of 1914' never exorcised the decision to go to war from their
minds. Many used the editor of the *Berliner Tageblatt*, Theodor Wolff, as
a sort of 'confessing father' to bare their souls. In February 1915, for
example, Bethmann Hollweg confided to Wolff that it would be insufficient to state that the issue of responsibility for unleashing the war
'depressed' him; instead, 'the thought never leaves me, I live with it constantly'. That same month, Wilhelm von Stumm, head of the Political
Division within the Foreign Office and a driving spirit behind the decision
for war in July 1914, assured Wolff that Germany had not 'bluffed' in
1914. 'We were prepared to accept the fact that war with Russia would
result'. Stumm merely regretted that the military calculus had proved
defective. Later in the war, Foreign Secretary von Jagow informed Wolff
that he had spent late nights with a friendly countess as he could not sleep
because he knew that Germany 'had wanted the war' which had turned
into a catastrophe.[98] Intelligent and experienced men, they had weighed
their options carefully and decided that war lay in the best interest of the
nation. Italy's Queen Mother Margherita pithily commented that if
German diplomats had not wanted war, then they behaved like 'the
biggest donkeys that the world had ever seen'.[99]

Questionable allies: Britain and Italy

London slowly managed to grope its way to war. Grey, as late as 1 August,
was still unwilling to debate the question of war in Cabinet. In fact, he had

for years studiously evaded the conclusion that a German attack on France would involve British interests, and that Britain would have to uphold the European balance of power even at the cost of a land war. With 'an ignorance whose true name was connivance', Grey had not even informed his fellow ministers back in 1911 that he had, quite on his own, authorized 'military conversations' with the French General Staff.[100] But Germany's ultimatum to Belgium to let its armies pass through unmolested en route to Paris forced Grey's hand.

'Poor little Belgium' became the decisive moral issue behind which Grey could rally the Cabinet, and it the country. Prime Minister Asquith opined as late as 2 August that 'a good ¾ of our own [Liberal] party in the House of Commons are for absolute non-interference at any price'.[101] But could Britannia really stand by and allow Germany to control the southern Channel coast and to acquire access to the Atlantic? Slowly, the idea that a naval war would be generally acceptable began to permeate the Cabinet. A substantial, stubborn minority, however, continued to oppose intervention in France. The logical approach seemed to be to use British sea power to augment French and Russian land power; or, put more bluntly, to fight Germany 'to the last Frenchman', much as Paris hoped to fight Germany 'to the last Russian'. French Ambassador Paul Cambon wondered aloud whether the word honour had been expunged from the English dictionary.

Grey was rescued from his predicament in the Cabinet by news on 3 August that Belgium intended to reject Berlin's ultimatum for free passage of German troops – much as Bethmann Hollweg in Berlin had used the Russian mobilization of 30 July to 'save face'. The Belgian decision would spare the British Cabinet what promised to be an unpleasant debate: whether war in France was in Britain's national interest. Bethmann Hollweg's unfortunate remark that the Treaty of London of 1839 was merely a 'scrap of paper', and his Machiavellian pronouncement in the Reichstag on 4 August that 'necessity knows no law', simply played into Grey's hands. Apparently no one in Berlin remembered Otto von Bismarck's warning that a German invasion of Belgium or the Low Countries would constitute 'complete idiocy' as it would immediately bring Britain into the war.[102]

On 3 August Britain was the only country in Europe where the crowds wildly cheered the war before it had even been declared.[103] In fact, the Cabinet never did decide for war. The only decisions taken by the ministers were two to resign, two to resign and retract, and the rest to remain in office. General Sir William Birdwood, Secretary to the Government of India in the Army Department, perhaps expressed the national sentiment best when he linked the news of war in Europe to the fight over Irish

Home Rule: 'What a real piece of luck this war has been as regards Ireland – just averted a Civil War and when it is over we may all be tired of fighting'.[104]

Rome faced the critical question of war and peace with even greater indecision than London. Allied to Austria–Hungary and Germany since 1882, Italy almost annually issued firm pledges of allegiance to the Triple Alliance. In October 1911, for example, King Victor Emmanuel III had assured Crown Prince Wilhelm that Germany 'could count on [Italy's] every last man' if it came to war in Europe.[105] And as late as February 1914, General Alberto Pollio, Chief of the Italian General Staff, as well as Victor Emmanuel III yet again reassured the Germans that in the event of war, Italy would transport the Third Army to the Rhine and defend Alsace within 4 weeks of the start of mobilization.[106]

But Pollio died on 1 July after suffering a massive heart attack – initially diagnosed as gastric obstruction – during an inspection tour of Turin. Victor Emmanuel III took 26 days to appoint a successor, General Luigi Cadorna, and thus the Italian Army was without direction during the most critical phase of the July crisis. A Piedmontese aristocrat who possessed absolute faith in his own strategic gifts, Cadorna at once informed the Germans that he intended to honour Pollio's pledges of military cooperation, and thereafter sought to convince Prime Minister Antonio Salandra to enter the war quickly. The General's resolve broke on the rock of obfuscation presented by Foreign Minister Antonio Di San Giuliano.

Di San Giuliano demanded that Italy receive territorial compensation – as stipulated by the terms of the Triple Alliance – in the event of an Austro-Serbian war that would likely result in Habsburg gains in the Balkans. Specifically, the Italian Foreign Minister harboured dreams of empire in Africa and sought the South Tyrol, the Trentino, Istria and Trieste, the Dalmatian Islands, and bases in Albania (*Italia irredenta*) as 'compensation' for honouring the alliance of 1882. Beyond that, Di San Giuliano, who believed that Germany would win, feared that a victorious Berlin and Vienna would be in no mood to include Rome in dividing the spoils of war. He had good reason to harbour such fears: on 9 August Wilhelm II asked Vienna to purchase Italian neutrality by giving it the Trentino – which Austria could then reclaim after a victorious war.[107] Moreover, Di San Giuliano was undoubtedly aware of a general mood of non-interventionism in the country, and he likely spied Italy's chance to exploit the coming war by bargaining for its services. He shared none of these thoughts with Cadorna.

Rome was in a state of chaos by 31 July–1 August 1914. The Navy was ready to mobilize for war. The Army, War Minister General Dino Grandi declared, was not, owing to a shortage of uniforms. On 29 July General

Cadorna asked Victor Emmanuel III for permission to send three Italian army corps to the Rhine. Two days later, the Cabinet voted for neutrality. On 2 August the King agreed to Cadorna's request, just as the Cabinet made its neutrality decision public![108]

Both Vienna and Berlin were outraged by Italy's behaviour. Conrad took malicious pleasure in reminding his government that he had warned Foreign Minister Count Aehrenthal as early as 1907 that the 'Balkan question' could only be solved after Austria–Hungary first 'settled accounts' with Italy.[109] On 3 August 1914, the day after Victor Emmanuel III informed Franz Joseph of Italy's neutrality, Conrad bitterly lectured Foreign Minister Berchtold: 'Our future lies in the Balkans; our barrier is Italy; we must finally settle accounts with Italy'.[110] Above all, Conrad warned his government not to bow to Italian greed. If Vienna yielded the Trentino today, Italy would simply demand the South Tyrol tomorrow; and Romania would want Transylvania.

Wilhelm II fumed about the incompetence of his diplomats and noted that Germany's allies were falling away 'like rotten apples' even before the first shot of the war had been fired. On 5 August Moltke dropped all positive references to Italy and endorsed Conrad's views: 'Italy's felony will be revenged in history. May God now grant you victory so that later you can settle accounts with these scoundrels'.[111] Privately, Moltke spoke of Italy's 'ignominious breach' of its 'word of honour'.[112]

Part of Italy's dilemma was the abysmal state of its armed forces. On paper, Cadorna commanded 875 000 soldiers organized into 31 divisions. In reality, he was short of 13 500 officers and 200 000 sets of uniforms. The reserves and militia, which comprised half of the total force, were poorly trained and equipped. Ten of Italy's 36 regiments of field-artillery did not exist. Nor did Cadorna relish the prospect of manning the 275-mile Italo-Austrian border from Switzerland to the Adriatic Sea with only 380 000 regulars. The Russian defeat at Tannenberg in August combined with the German setback at the Marne in September allowed Italy to remain on the sidelines. The historian John Gooch is on the mark in summing up Italy's predicament in 1914 as follows: 'Her civilian leaders were not ready to listen to public arguments from the military; her military did not speak with a single voice; and her soldiers were materially unready to fight'.[113]

Undaunted by the Italian 'felony', Wilhelm II in Berlin rallied his forces for war. At 1:10 p.m. on 3 August he instructed his orderlies to lay out the uniform for his visit to the Reichstag the next day: field grey tunic with high-top boots, brown gloves, helmet without plumes. By 3:10 p.m., obviously feeling the need for something more splendid, he decreed that all colonels and generals residing in Berlin were to accompany him to the Reichstag wearing appropriate medal ribbons and sashes. German troops crossed into Belgium on the morning of 4 August. At noon the Kaiser attended a special service at St Hedwigs Church. An hour later he informed parliament that he was about to fulfil his 'alliance obligations' to Austria–Hungary, and that he 'no longer knew political parties'. 'I only know Germans.'[114] By 11 p.m. that night a state of war existed between Germany and Britain. Wilhelm II returned his uniforms of Admiral of the Fleet and Field Marshal to King George V with the sarcastic comment that Britain's declaration of war on 4 August was 'the thanks for Waterloo'.[115] At 11 a.m. on 9 August Wilhelm II bade a personal farewell to the Potsdam Guards regiments bound for France, held a review and parade, and then returned to Berlin for a late breakfast.

The 'mood of 1914'

A chain reaction of mobilization orders and declarations of war (44 in number eventually) thundered across Europe early in August 1914. Reservists were called up from the Pyrenees to the Urals and complex train schedules for mobilization implemented. A world 'grown old and cold and weary', in the words of the English poet Rupert Brooke, suddenly found a new lease on life. Poincaré in France, Churchill in Britain, and Ottokar Count Czernin in Austria–Hungary invoked the image of a cleansing 'thunderstorm' to convey the prevailing mood of relief and rejuvenation.[116]

Much of Europe was thrilled by the news of war. The 'foul peace' (Conrad von Hötzendorf) that Bismarck had imposed on the Continent with his intricate alliance system was finally over. There would be honours, medals, promotions, profits, and new borders. No longer would the generation of 1914 have to listen at local beer halls or wine taverns to worn-out tales of the glorious deeds of their grandfathers in the wars of 1866 and 1870–1. Instead, they would create their own legends and myths. Bands played. Women wept. Rifles were studded with flowers. It was 'on to Paris' and '*à Berlin*'. 'God save the tsar' and '*Gott mit uns*' expressed the fact that Europe's youth was being asked to fight and die for Holy Russia, Britannia, *la patrie*, and the *Vaterland*. It is estimated that in Germany more than 1.5 million patriotic 'war poems' were penned in 1914 alone.

Hundreds of thousands of young men volunteered for service. But contemporary estimates of between 1.3 and 2 million *Kriegsfreiwillige* in Germany are grossly exaggerated; in fact, volunteers during 1914–15 were formed into 22 divisions, or about 308 000 soldiers. The reasons behind this spirit of voluntarism remain unquantifiable and impressionistic. Late in 1914 the Institute for Applied Psychology near Potsdam sent its staff out into the streets to query volunteers concerning their motivation. Many young men replied that the war offered a chance of adventure and action, an escape from the dreariness of everyday life. Others stated that they joined out of love of country or home (*Heimat*); a few saw war as an opportunity to 'prove' their manliness; and some simply accepted it as being 'inevitable'. Still others volunteered out of patriotism; a few from pure enthusiasm. Many argued that they were merely fulfilling their 'duty'. A good number of young men just wanted to be 'part of it', that is, not to miss out on the expected great victory. Some confessed hatred of Britain or of Russia; none felt personal animosity towards the men fighting for these countries.[117] Historians suggest that some of the volunteers welcomed war as an act of national integration, as a chance to overcome the pluralistic, modern world of self-interest and self-indulgence, and to create a new harmonious national community, or *Volksgemeinschaft*.[118] Whatever the precise nature of the voluntarism, the Army quickly closed down the Institute's polling activities.

Although some scholars dealing with Darmstadt, Freiburg, Hamburg, Saarbrücken, and Wesel have suggested that the euphoria was not as universal as has hitherto been assumed and that tens (if not hundreds) of thousands of workers took part in peace demonstrations in late July, the euphoria nevertheless was widespread, especially among students and the upper middle class. And it was shared by Europe's political and intellectual elite. In Paris President Poincaré cheerfully assured his Cabinet on 2 August that 'Russian troops will be in Berlin by All Saints' Day'.

In Vienna, Freud for the first time in three decades felt thrilled to be an Austrian; 'all my libido goes to Austria–Hungary'. Schönberg, on hearing of war, returned to Vienna to join the *Deutschmeister* regiment – and to compose victory marches for it. The radical socialist Otto Bauer volunteered for service. His colleague, Karl Renner, declared that victory by the Entente would favour 'monopoly capitalism', while victory by Berlin and Vienna would benefit socialism! The Austrian pacifist writer Stefan Zweig twice offered his literary skills to the Habsburg state – only to be rejected, whereafter his war enthusiasm waned. This notwithstanding, 30 years later Zweig still acknowledged the euphoria of August 1914:

> The trains filled with freshly arrived recruits. Flags waved, music boomed.
> I found the entire city of Vienna in a state of intoxication. . . . Processions
> formed in the streets, suddenly flags were unfurled everywhere, bands and
> music, the young recruits marched in triumph and their faces were radiant
> because one cheered them – them, the little common people, who other-
> wise no one notices or celebrates. And to be truthful, I must admit that I
> found something great, magnetic, irresistible, and even seductive in this

first popular awakening. . . . Thousands and hundreds of thousands of people felt something as never before that they should better have felt in
peacetime: that they belonged together.[119]

Many Austrians rushed to the colours with a feeling of wanting to be part
of a grand thing, just to be there. Still, the suspicion remains that much of
the 'euphoria' may have been 'cognitive dissonance' – the joyous,
released relief at the end of weeks of anxiety and uncertainty.

In Germany, War Minister von Falkenhayn cynically confided to the
Bavarian military plenipotentiary: 'It is critical that we use the prevailing
euphoria before it goes up in smoke'.[120] The novelist Thomas Mann
allowed that he was 'tired, sick and tired' of peace and depicted the coming war as 'a purification, a liberation, an enormous hope'. His colleague,
Hermann Hesse, considered 'the moral values of the war on the whole
rather highly', and stated that it was salutary for Germans 'to be torn out
of a dull capitalistic peace'.[121] The philosopher Max Scheler argued that
the war would unify the nation, mobilize its dormant power, and bring out
the 'noble beast' in Germany's young men. The economist Johann Plenge
contrasted the German 'ideas of 1914' – duty, order, justice – with the
French 'ideas of 1789' – liberty, fraternity, egality.

On the political front, the Liberal Theodor Heuss stressed that the war
would be a test of 'moral strength' and 'moral right', while his colleague
Conrad Haussmann deemed the war to be one of 'the will to assert one-
self'. Elections were suspended for the duration of the war and seats
opened by illness or death were to be filled by the party of the deceased.
Beyond the political mainstream, Magnus Hirschfeld, leader of the
German homosexual movement, saw the war as defence of Teutonic 'honesty and sincerity' and the omnipresent uniforms, badges, and guns as sex-
ual stimulants.[122] In Munich, Hitler, the erstwhile draft dodger, volunteered
for the Bavarian Army: 'The war liberated me from the painful feelings of
my youth. . . . I fell down on my knees and thanked heaven with an over-
flowing heart for granting me the good fortune to be alive at that time'.[123]

Gertrud Bäumer, head of the Federation of German Women's
Associations (BDF), rallied her nearly 600 000 members behind the war
effort. Bäumer asked women to put their demands for the vote and for
greater access to education and state employment in abeyance for the
duration of the war. 'We are *Volk*', she reminded her followers.
Individualism needed to be subsumed into the national cause. 'The great
alternative: to win or to die, a greater fatherland or death; this suddenly
raises the nation above all other treasures of life.'[124] The BDF's members
rallied behind a National Women's Service and ran soup kitchens, improvised hospital wards, tended to the rising number of orphans, and knitted
woollen clothing for the troops at the fronts.

Army reservists perhaps had a more realistic conception of the coming war. On 1 August Wilhelm Schulin, a cobbler, was called to the colours of the 119th Grenadier Regiment of the 29th Infantry Division near Öhringen, Württemberg. Private Schulin heard 'trains running day and night', loaded 'only with military personnel' and exuding a 'muffled sound'. The news of war that Saturday evoked 'incredible tension' among the people Schulin met. The mood quickly turned into 'something horribly heavy, dark, a pressing burden'. Many wept openly; others muttered astonishment at the news. The next day, Sunday, it was church service with communion, and communion again that evening. 'One *Volk* after the other declared war; our thoughts became ever greater and more grave.'[125]

There was no doubt that the war would be offensive. In Germany, Alfred von Schlieffen had preached that 'attack is the best defence' to a generation of General Staff officers; his successor, Moltke, likewise endorsed 'the principle that the offensive is the best defence'. In France, Joseph Joffre announced that the French Army 'no longer knows any other law than the offensive'. Ferdinand Foch trumpeted that the nation knew but one formula for success, 'the decisive power of offensive action undertaken with the resolute determination to march on the enemy, reach and destroy him'. Across the Channel, General W. G. Knox noted that the defensive was alien to the British character, and that his countrymen made 'little or no study of it'. And Russia's Minister of War, Sukhomlinov, crowed that his army also had adopted the doctrine of 'dealing rapid and decisive blows' to its enemies.[126]

This 'cult of the offensive' helped Europe's military convince the public to accept war in 1914 with assurances that the conflict would be brief. Somewhere in northern France or Galicia there would be a single, decisive battle, another Cannae or Sedan. Then all would return home to 'business as usual', as Churchill put it. This 'short-war illusion' dominated European capitals. In Vienna the War Ministry advised workers called to the colours not to apply for unemployment compensation because they would be back at their factories before the bureaucracy could process the applications. In St Petersburg the War Ministry rejected requests for new typewriters from front-line staffs, arguing that the old ones would do for this short campaign.

But was the 'short-war illusion' realistic? Or was it really designed to conceal the true nature of the coming struggle from the nation? Perhaps it would be more appropriate to use the term 'short-war *delusion*'. On 28 July 1914 General von Moltke in a confidential memorandum confessed that he harboured no 'short-war illusions'. He spoke of a 'world war', a 'horrible war', one 'which will annihilate the culture of almost all of Europe for decades to come'.[127] But was that not the price of great-power status? Could the head of the world's most prestigious General Staff openly concede that war was no longer a feasible option in 1914? Nor were such musings restricted to the General Staff. The Grand Duchy of Baden's envoy to Berlin on 3 August ominously informed his government at Karlsruhe: 'A war of everybody against everybody will break out, the likes of which the world has not yet experienced'.[128] General von Falkenhayn took leave of his old regiment, the 4th Foot Guards, with the words, 'This war will last at least one-and-a-half years'.[129] On 4 August he boldly informed Bethmann Hollweg: 'Even if we go under as a result of this, it still was beautiful'.[130] The sparkling optimism of Europe's 'golden age' died with the declarations of war.

There is no question that European statesmen sent millions of young men lemming-like to their destruction in autumn 1914 out of fear that this cannon fodder might come too late to participate in the one great 'cleansing thunderstorm' that would resolve the 'Serbian crisis'. Classical scholars all, they forgot the warnings contained in Thucydides' 'Melian Dialogue', wherein Melos had cautioned Athens: 'Do not be led astray by a false sense of honour – a thing which often brings men to ruin when they are faced with an obvious danger that somehow affects their pride'.[131]

Chapter I Notes

1. Werner Maser, *Adolf Hitler. Legende, Mythos, Wirklichkeit* (Munich, Bechtle, 1974), p. 12.
2. Conrad had the highest rank in the Habsburg armies, *Feldmarschalleutnant*. This was followed by *Feldzeugmeister* for commanders of the artillery, infantry, and engineers, or General of Cavalry, and (after 1908) General of Infantry. I have used the more familiar English rank of 'General' throughout. The family's name originally was simply Conrad, but the General's grandfather adopted the maiden name of his wife (von Hötzendorf) when he was raised into the nobility. Conrad was given the title 'baron' in 1910.
3. Cited in Zara Steiner, *Britain and the Origins of the First World War* (New York, St Martin's Press, 1977), p. 215.
4. Cited in Fritz Fischer, *Krieg der Illusionen. Die deutsche Politik von 1911 bis 1914* (Düsseldorf, Droste Verlag, 1969), p. 658. Conversation of 21 June 1914.
5. Cited in Wolfgang J. Mommsen, *Grossmachtstellung und Weltpolitik. Die Aussenpolitik des Deutschen Reiches 1870 bis 1914* (Frankfurt and Berlin, Ullstein, 1993), p. 293.
6. See Christopher Andrew, 'France and the German Menace', in Ernest R. May, ed., *Knowing One's Enemies: Intelligence Assessment Before the Two World Wars* (Princeton, Princeton University Press, 1984), p. 144.
7. Arthur S. Link, ed., *The Papers of Woodrow Wilson* (69 vols, Princeton, Princeton University Press, 1979) 30, pp.108–9. Note of 29 May 1914.
8. Fritz Fellner, ed., *Schicksalsjahre Österreichs 1908–1919. Das politische Tagebuch Josef Redlichs* (2 vols, Graz and Cologne, Hermann Böhlaus Nachf., 1953–4) 1, p. 235. Diary entry of 28 June 1914.
9. Winston S. Churchill, *The World Crisis* (London, Thorton Butterworth, 1931), p. 30.
10. These plans were culled from Österreichisches Staatsarchiv-Kriegsarchiv, Vienna (hereafter ÖStA-KA), Conrad Archiv, B Flügeladjutant, vol. 1.

11. Gerhard Ritter, *Staatskunst und Kriegshandwerk. Das Problem des 'Militarismus' in Deutschland* (4 vols, Munich, R. Oldenbourg, 1965) 2, pp. 282–6.
12. Cited in Hugo Hantsch, *Leopold Graf Berchtold. Grandseigneur und Staatsmann* (2 vols, Graz, Verlag Styria, 1963) 2, pp. 558–9.
13. Cited in Gina Gräfin Conrad von Hötzendorf, *Mein Leben mit Conrad von Hötzendorf. Sein geistiges Vermächtnis* (Leipzig, Grethlein & Co., 1935), pp. 30–1. Letter of 26 December 1908.
14. Conrad's talk with Aehrenthal, 18 February 1909. ÖStA-KA, Conrad Archiv, B Flügeladjutant, vol. 1.
15. Conrad von Hötzendorf, *Aus meiner Dienstzeit 1908–1918* (5 vols, Vienna, Leipzig, and Munich, Rikola Verlag, 1921) 1, p. 537.
16. Notes on Conad's audience with Franz Joseph, 5 July 1914. ÖStA-KA, Operations Büro, General Stab 91.
17. Cited in Gina Conrad von Hötzendorf, *Mein Leben mit Conrad*, p. 114. Letter of 28 June 1914.
18. Samuel R. Williamson, Jr., *Austria–Hungary and the Origins of the First World War* (New York, St Martin's Press, 1991), pp. 192–3.
19. Cited in Gina Conrad von Hötzendorf, *Mein Leben mit Conrad*, p. 118. Dated 18 August 1914.
20. Cited in Gunther E. Rothenberg, *The Army of Francis Joseph* (West Lafayette, Ind., Purdue University Press, 1976), pp. 176–7.
21. Baron Leopold Andrian, cited in Manfried Rauchensteiner, *Der Tod des Doppeladlers. Österreich-Ungarn und der Erste Weltkrieg* (Graz, Vienna, and Cologne, Verlag Styria, 1994), p. 68.
22. Tschirschky to Bethmann Hollweg, 30 June 1914, cited in Imanuel Geiss, ed., *Juli 1914: Die europäische Krise und der Ausbruch des Ersten Weltkriegs* (Munich, Deutscher Taschenbuch Verlag, 1965), pp. 39–40. Italics in the original.
23. Eugenie Maria Müller, 'Der Konflikt Conrad Ährenthal', unpubl. diss., Vienna University 1978, pp. 299–300.
24. Rudolf Kiszling, 'Heer und Kriegsmarine in den Letzten Jahrzehnten vor Ausbruch des Ersten Weltkrieges', *Österreich in Geschichte und Literatur*, 6 (1963), p. 252. The Dual Monarchy's land forces broke down along ethnic lines as follows: Germans 26.7 per cent, Magyars 22.3 per cent, Czechs 13.5 per cent, Poles 8.5 per cent, Ruthenians 8.1 per cent, Croats and Serbs 6.7 per cent, Romanians 6.4 per cent, Slovenes 2.6 per cent, and Italians 1.4 per cent.
25. Rudolf Hecht, 'Fragen zur Heeresergänzung der gesamten Bewaffneten Macht Österreich-Ungarns während des Ersten Weltkrieges', unpubl. diss., Vienna University 1969, pp. 8–9.
26. See Rothenberg, *The Army of Francis Joseph*, pp. 172–4; Rudolf Kiszling, 'Die Entwicklung der österreichisch-ungarischen Wehrmacht seit der Annexionskrise 1908', *Berliner Monatshefte, 12* (1934), p. 747; and Wilhelm Czermak, *In deinem Lager war Österreich. Die österreichisch-ungarische Armee, wie man sie nicht kennt* (Breslau, W. G. Korn, 1938), pp. 37–9.
27. István Deák, *Beyond Nationalism: A Social and Political History of the Habsburg Officer Corps 1848–1918* (Oxford, Oxford University Press, 1990), p. 190.
28. Johann Christoph Allmayer-Beck, 'Die Träger der Staatlichen Macht', in Otto Schulmeister, *Spectrum Austriae* (Vienna, 1957), pp. 272–4.
29. Haus-, Hof- und Staatsarchiv, Vienna (hereafter HHStA), Politisches Archiv (PA) VII Gesandschaft Berlin 196, Separat Akten. Ballhausplatz notes on the conversation of 1 July 1914.
30. HHStA, PA I Cabinet des Ministers. Protokoll 1913–1915, vol. 592.
31. Franz Joseph to Wilhelm II, 5 July 1915, cited in HHStA, PA VII Gesandschaft Berlin

196. See also Luigi Albertini, *The Origins of the War of 1914* (3 vols, London, Oxford University Press, 1953) 2, p. 134.

32. Cited in Fritz Fischer, *Griff nach der Weltmacht. Die Kriegszielpolitik des kaiserlichen Deutschland 1914/18* (Düsseldorf, Droste Verlag, 1964), pp. 63–4.

33. The following is from *Protokolle des Gemeinsamen Ministerrates der Österreichisch-Ungarischen Monarchie (1914–1918),* ed. Miklós Komjáthy (Budapest, Akadémiai Kiadó, 1966), pp. 141–50.

34. See Williamson, *Austria–Hungary and the Origins of the First World War*, pp. 202–4.

35. Geiss, ed., *Juli 1914*, pp. 56–65; Albertini, *Origins of the War of 1914*, 2, pp. 165–9.

36. Williamson, *Austria–Hungary and the Origins of the First World War*, p. 200.

37. Albertini, *Origins of the War of 1914*, 2, pp. 286–9.

38. Fellner, ed., *Schicksalsjahre Österreichs*, p. 237. Entry of 15 July 1914.

39. Williamson, *Austria–Hungary and the Origins of the First World War*, pp. 188–9.

40. See *Protokolle des Gemeinsamen Ministerrates*, pp. 151–4.

41. Cited in Williamson, *Austria–Hungary and the Origins of the First World War*, p. 204.

42. Bunsen to Grey, 8 August 1914. HHStA, PA VIII England. Berichte 1913, Weisungen Varia 1914.

43. See Rauchensteiner, *Der Tod des Doppeladlers*, pp. 92–4. Even after the Second World War, Rudolf Kiszling, Austria's eminent military historian, continued to write articles about the Temes Kubin 'action'.

44. Albert von Margutti, *Kaiser Franz Joseph. Persönliche Erinnerungen* (Vienna and Leipzig, Manz'sche Verlags- und Universitätsbuchhandlung, 1924), p. 414. See also James Joll, *1914: The Unspoken Assumptions* (London, Weidenfeld & Nicolson, 1968), who wondered whether the Kaiser spoke the words with pain, regret, relief, or surprise.

45. See Margutti, *Kaiser Franz Joseph*, pp. 420–1.

46. Williamson, *Austria–Hungary and the Origins of the First World War*, has cogently revised the claims of the Hamburg historian, Fritz Fischer, that Vienna was taken on the 'leash' by Berlin in 1914.

47. For background on this, see Holger H. Herwig, 'Strategic uncertainties of a nation-state: Prussia–Germany, 1871–1918', in W. Murray, M. Knox, and A. Bernstein, eds, *The Making of Strategy: Rulers, Strategy, and War* (Cambridge, Cambridge University Press, 1994), pp. 242–77.

48. See the General Staff's memorandum of 2 December 1911 in Auswärtiges Amt, Politisches Archiv, Bonn (hereafter AA-PA), Deutschland Nr. 121 geh., vol. 1.

49. Cited in Fischer, *Griff nach der Weltmacht*, p. 233.

50. Cited in Conrad von Hötzendorf, *Aus meiner Dienstzeit*, 4, p. 670.

51. Moltke to Conrad, 27 August 1913, ÖStA-KA, Conrad Archiv, B Flügeladjutant, vol. 4. See also Eliza von Moltke, ed., *Generaloberst Helmuth von Moltke. Erinnerungen. Briefe. Dokumente 1877–1916. Ein Bild vom Kriegsausbruch, erster Kriegsführung und Persönlichkeit des ersten militärischen Führers des Krieges* (Stuttgart, Der Kommende Tag Verlag, 1922), p. 6.

52. AA-PA, Nachlass Jagow, vol. 8, pp. 69 ff. Discussion in the spring of 1914; scholars differ whether the talk took place on 19 May or 3 June.

53. Cited in Imanuel Geiss, ed., *Julikrise und Kriegsausbruch 1914: Eine Dokumentensammlung* (2 vols, Hanover, Verlag für Literatur und Zeitgeschehen, 1964), 2, p. 299.

54. Geiss, ed., *Julikrise and Kriegsausbruch 1914* 1 (1963), p. 75. Comment of 3 July 1914. Waldersee repeated this comment almost verbatim on 31 July to the Bavarian envoy to Berlin (Lerchenfeld). The General's statement of May 1914 is cited in Wolfgang Michalka, *Der Erste Weltkrieg. Wirkung, Wahrnehmung, Analyse* (Munich and Zurich, Piper, 1994), p. 208.

55. *Verhandlungen des Reichstages. XII. Legislaturperiode, I. Session*, vol. 189, pp. 4512–13. Session of 7 April 1913; August Bach, ed., *Deutsche Gesandschaftsberichte zum*

Kriegsausbruch 1914. Berichte und Telegramme der badischen, sächsischen und württembergischen Gesandschaften in Berlin aus dem Juli und August 1914 (Berlin, Quaderverlag, 1937), p. 12.

56. Cited in Kurt Riezler, *Tagebücher, Aufsätze, Dokumente,* ed. Karl Dietrich Erdmann (Göttingen, Vandenhoeck & Ruprecht, 1972), p. 183. Entry for 7 July 1914.
57. Cited in Mommsen, *Grossmachtstellung und Weltpolitik,* p. 306.
58. See Geiss, ed., *Juli 1914,* p. 52.
59. Theodor Wolff, *Tagebücher 1914–1919,* ed. Bernd Sösemann (2 vols, Boppard, H. Boldt, 1984) 1, pp. 139–40. Entry for 15 December 1914.
60. Riezler, *Tagebücher,* pp. 183 ff.
61. Riezler, *Tagebücher,* entry for 11 July 1914. Under-Secretary Zimmermann seconded this position.
62. Eberhard von Vietsch, *Bethmann Hollweg. Staatsmann zwischen Macht und Ethos* (Boppard, H. Boldt, 1969), p. 143.
63. Riezler, *Tagebücher,* p. 192. Bethmann Hollweg's comment of 27 July 1914.
64. See Fischer, *Krieg der Illusionen,* p. 684.
65. See Holger H. Herwig, 'Imperial Germany', in May, ed., *Knowing One's Enemies,* pp. 81, 94.
66. Geiss, ed., *Julikrise,* 1, p. 59.
67. Geiss, ed., *Juli 1914,* p. 52.
68. Cited in Fischer, *Krieg der Illusionen,* p. 692.
69. Soden to Count Hertling, 9 July 1914. Bayerisches Hauptstaatsarchiv, Munich (hereafter BHStA), MA 3077, Militär-Bevollmächtigter Berlin.
70. Cited in Geiss, ed., *Julikrise,* 1, p. 213.
71. Kissinger in the *New York Times* 11 March 1976; cited in Marc Trachtenberg, *History and Strategy* (Princeton, Princeton University Press, 1991), p. 99. Kissinger repeats this line of argument in *Diplomacy* (New York, Simon & Schuster, 1994), Chapter 8.
72. Bundesarchiv-Militärarchiv, Freiburg (hereafter BA-MA), MSg 1/3251 Frhr. v. Lyncker, Kriegsbriefe 1914. Dated 25 July 1914.
73. Raymond Poincaré, *Comment fut déclarée la guerre de 1914* (Paris, Flammarion, 1939), pp. 34–5.
74. See John F. V. Keiger, *France and the Origins of the First World War* (New York, St Martin's Press, 1983), pp. 147 ff.
75. Cited in Graydon A. Tunstall, Jr., *Planning for War Against Russia and Serbia: Austro-Hungarian and German Military Strategies, 1871–1914* (New York, Columbia University Press, 1993), p. 150.
76. See D. C. B. Lieven, *Russia and the Origins of the First World War* (New York, St Martin's Press, 1983), p. 140.
77. Albertini, *Origins of the War of 1914* 2, pp. 536–9.
78. Cited in Albertini, *Origins of the War of 1914* 2, *p. 569.*
79. Albertini, *Origins of the War of 1914* 2, p. 572.
80. Cited in Steiner, *Britain and the Origins of the First World War,* pp. 221–2.
81. Steiner, *Britain and the Origins of the First World War,* pp. 222–4.
82. BA-MA, W-10/50635 Tagebuch v. Falkenhayn, dated 27 July 1914. Holger Afflerbach, *Falkenhayn. Politisches Denken und Handeln im Kaiserreich* (Munich, R. Oldenbourg, 1994), first discovered this diary and I have followed his analysis.
83. BA-MA, W-10/50635 Tagebuch v. Falkenhayn, dated 28 July 1914.
84. Geiss, ed., *Julikrise und Kriegsausbruch 1914* 2, p. 299; Albertini, *Origins of the War of 1914* 2, p. 489.
85. Cited in Afflerbach, *Falkenhayn,* p. 156.
86. Cited in Afflerbach, *Falkenhayn,* p. 157.
87. Cited in Geiss, ed., *Juli 1914,* pp. 302–4.

88. Geiss, ed., *Juli 1914*, pp. 320–2; Steiner, *Britain and the Origins of the First World War*, p. 227.
89. Geiss, ed., *Julikrise und Kriegsausbruch* 2, p. 373.
90. See Volker Berghahn, *Germany and the Approach of War in 1914* (New York, St Martin's Press, 1973), p. 201.
91. Cited in Conrad von Hötzendorf, *Aus meiner Dienstzeit* 4 (1923), pp. 152 ff.
92. BA-MA, W-10/50635 Tagebuch v. Falkenhayn, dated 31 July 1917.
93. Goschen to Grey, 8 August 1914. HHStA, PA VIII England.
94. Fellner, ed., *Schicksalsjahre Österreichs* 2, p. 44.
95. J. C. G. Röhl, 'Admiral von Müller and the Approach of War, 1911–1914', *The Historical Journal*, 12 (1969), p. 670; Riezler, *Tagebücher*, p. 185; Bayerisches Hauptstaatsarchiv, Kriegsarchiv, Munich (hereafter BHStA-KA), MKr 1765, Mobilmachung 1914. Report of 31 July 1914.
96. Cited in Mommsen, *Grossmachtstellung und Weltpolitik*, p. 321.
97. BA-MA, W-10/50635 Tagebuch v. Falkenhayn, dated 1 August 1914.
98. Wolff, *Tagebücher* 1, pp. 156, 166; and 2, p. 665.
99. Cited in Bernhard von Bülow, *Denkwürdigkeiten* (4 vols, Berlin, Ullstein, 1931) 3, p. 225.
100. Elie Halévy, *A History of the English People in the Nineteenth Century* 1: *The Rule of Democracy, 1905–1914* (New York, Barnes & Noble, 1961), p. 438.
101. Cited in Cameron Hazlehurst, *Politicians at War, July 1914–May 1915. A Prologue to the Triumph of Lloyd George* (London, Cape, 1971), p. 33.
102. Cited in Bülow, *Denkwürdigkeiten* 4, p. 556.
103. Steiner, *Britain and the Origins of the War of 1914*, pp. 233–40; Geiss, ed., *Juli 1914*, p. 347.
104. Cited in John Gooch, *The Plans of War: The General Staff and British Military Strategy c. 1900–1916* (London, Routledge & Kegan Paul, 1974), p. 300.
105. Bienerth to Conrad, 12 October 1911. ÖStA-KA, Conrad Archiv, B Flügeladjutant, vol. 2.
106. Gooch, *Army, State and Society in Italy*, pp. 152–5.
107. Szögyény to Berchtold, 9 August 1914. HHStA, PA VII Gesandschaft Berlin 196.
108. Gooch, *Army, State and Society in Italy*, pp. 156–9.
109. See Conrad to Aehrenthal, 18 December 1907. ÖStA-KA, Conrad Archiv, B Flügeladjutant, vol. 1.
110. Cited in Conrad von Hötzendorf, *Aus meiner Dienstzeit* 4, pp. 169–70.
111. Conrad von Hötzendorf, *Aus meiner Dienstzeit 4*, pp. 193–4. Moltke to Conrad, 5 August 1914.
112. Moltke, ed., *Generaloberst von Moltke*, p. 9. November 1914.
113. Gooch, *Army, State and Society in Italy*, p. 156.
114. BA-MA, PH1 Militärkabinett, Mobilmaching 1914, vol. 4. See also Szögyéni to Berchtold, 5 August 1914, HHStA, PA III Preussen Berichte 171. Few in Berlin noticed that the Conservatives were left 'ice cold' by the speech.
115. Walter Görlitz, ed., *The Kaiser and His Court: The Diaries, Note Books and Letters of Admiral Georg Alexander von Müller Chief of the Naval Cabinet, 1914–1918* (New York, Harcourt, Brace & World, 1959), p. 17. Entry for 8 August 1914.
116. See Frederic Morton, *Thunder at Twilight: Vienna 1913/14* (New York, Macmillan, 1989), pp. 322–3.
117. Paul Plaut, 'Psychographie des Krieges', *Beihefte zur Zeitschrift für angewandte Psychologie* 20 (Leipzig, Johann Ambrosius Barth, 1920), pp. 10–14.
118. See the contribution by Thomas Rohkrämer in Michalka, ed., *Der Erste Weltkrieg*, pp. 760–1.
119. Cited in Michalka, ed., *Der Erste Weltkrieg*, pp. 8–9.

120. BHStA-KA, HS 2546 Tagebuch Wenninger. Dated 16 August 1918.
121. Morton, *Thunder at Twilight*, pp. 328–33.
122. Modris Eksteins, *Rites of Spring: The Great War and the Birth of the Modern Age* (Boston, Houghton Mifflin, 1989), pp. 91–3.
123. Adolf Hitler, *Mein Kampf* (Munich, F. Eher Nachf., 1939), p. 165.
124. Gertrud Bäumer, *Weit hinter den Schützengräben. Aufsätze aus dem Weltkrieg* (Jena, Eugen Diederichs, 1916), pp. 29, 31.
125. BA-MA, MSg 2/4537 Tagebuch Schulin. Entries for 1 and 2 August 1914.
126. Cited in Stephen Van Evera, 'The Cult of the Offensive and the Origins of the First World War', *International Security* 9 (1984), pp. 59–61.
127. Moltke, *Generaloberst Helmuth von Moltke*, pp. 3–7.
128. Graf Berckheim to Baron von Dusch, 3 August 1914. Cited in Bach, ed., *Deutsche Gesandschaftsberichte zum Kriegsausbruch 1914*, p. 141.
129. Cited in Afflerbach, *Falkenhayn*, p. 171.
130. Cited in Riezler, *Tagebücher*, p. 228. Dated 22 November 1914.
131. Thucydides, *History of the Peloponnesian War* (New York, Penguin, 1954), p. 406.

2

The Plans of War

War is the realm of uncertainty. . . .

Carl von Clausewitz

The military strategies of Austria–Hungary and Germany, both before 1914 and during the opening phases of the First World War, are intimately tied to the two respective Chiefs of the General Staff. While Conrad von Hötzendorf has enjoyed a splendid press, both within and outside Austria, the Younger Moltke has been vilified for his alleged failure to execute Schlieffen's bold gamble of a two-front war. Austria's eminent military historian, Edmund Glaise von Horstenau, unabashedly claimed that Conrad 'belonged to the best in a very thin row of great captains produced by the world war', a commander 'hundredfold worthy to be included in the annals of the Greater German Army'.[1] August von Urbánski concurred, stating that Conrad 'is to be counted among the greatest captains of all time'. General Alois Klepsch-Kloth von Roden, Vienna's plenipotentiary to the *OHL* and no admirer of Conrad, as late as the 1950s still asserted that Conrad 'undoubtedly was the greatest strategist of the First World War, far above all others'.[2] Non-military writers also lavished praise on Conrad. The publicist Karl Friedrich Nowak called him one of the true 'heroes' of history, and the historian Oskar Regele assured Austrians that Conrad was their 'greatest commander since Prince Eugene of Savoy'.[3] Anglo-Saxon scholars readily adopted this high praise: the English military historian Cyril Falls, for example, declared that Conrad simply was 'the best strategist at the outset, probably of the war' of 1914–18.[4]

Moltke, the nephew of the victor of Sedan (1870), in contrast, has been made to bear the blame for the failure of the German offensive in France in 1914. Contemporaries such as Generals Wilhelm Groener, Hermann von Kuhl, and Wolfgang Foerster, to name but a few, distorted the historical record by suggesting that Schlieffen had opposed Moltke's appointment in 1906. Additionally, they argued that Moltke was inexperienced in staff matters, without knowledge of military history, and preoccupied with the occult and theosophy.[5] In short, as Groener later put it, the 'great symphony' of the Schlieffen plan could only be played once; in 1914 the 'conductor' bungled it.

Both General Staff chiefs were complex and peculiar personalities. Conrad preferred to read the works and hear the music of serious, pensive, introverted artists, statesmen, and writers. He favoured men who saw little value in human existence – Prussia's King Frederick the Great, Vienna's poet Franz Grillparzer, Germany's legendary composer Ludwig van Beethoven, and its renowned misogynist Arthur Schopenhauer. Some of Conrad's staff officers found it strange that he had never 'studied the German masters or, apparently, modern military history'.[6] Later in life, Conrad developed a great fascination with the work of Charles Darwin. In fact, Conrad's intellectual development ran from Schopenhauer's *The World as Will and Mental Representation*, from which he derived his own 'will to live' and 'will to perform', to Darwin's concept of the struggle for survival, which Conrad viewed as 'the driving force' in all endeavours. Life to Conrad was a never-ending ebb and flow of peace and war. Friedrich Nietzsche's 'will to power' became in him 'the will to survive in the struggle for existence'. Conrad also shared the prevailing anti-Semitism of his age. He called Karl Friedrich Nowak a 'filthy Jew' – conveniently overlooking that Nowak placed Conrad's bulky five volumes of memoirs with Rikola Publishers, and that Nowak later paid Conrad's widow royalties for translations from the Italian that 'Gina' never produced fit for print.[7]

Above all, Conrad regarded war as a necessary condition, a 'given' in the constant struggle for survival among the Great Powers. War was neither moral nor amoral; it was simply a way of life. In a classic reversal of Clausewitz's dictum that war was but the extension of politics by other means, Conrad firmly believed that during a time of national emergency, responsibility for the fate of the nation rested with its Chief of the General Staff. 'The essence of politics lies in the use of the means called "war".'[8] At times, Conrad even contemplated fighting Germany in order to maintain Habsburg predominance in the Balkans.[9] Buddhism and Christianity were 'too soft' for Conrad, who liked Islam's notion of holy war and Shinto's emphasis on heroic ancestors and hero worship.[10]

Moltke was anything but the stereotypical Prussian Army officer. A highly cultivated man, he developed serious interests in art history, oriental studies, and theology. He was equally at home organizing annual military manoeuvres, visiting medieval monasteries, or demonstrating stereoscopic photography. In 1906 Moltke had accepted the Kaiser's call to succeed Schlieffen as Chief of the General Staff with grave reservations about his own abilities, and only on condition that Wilhelm II stop meddling in annual manoeuvres by way of deciding these through heroic but archaic cavalry charges.[11] While some contemporary observers, including Klepsch-Kloth von Roden, denounced Moltke as an officer of at best 'average ability', 'flat and shallow', a 'pleasant socializer endowed with special musical talents',[12] Schlieffen as late as January 1905 praised Moltke's 'practical bent of mind' in his successor's last fitness report – which strangely disappeared from army files until after the First World War.[13]

But Moltke, like Conrad, had a dark, fatalistic side. His wife, Eliza, imbued him with a strong veneration for spiritualism and the occult, and held séances to establish contacts with historical figures in the hereafter. Not surprisingly, Moltke developed a passionate interest in understanding life after death – which led him to Rudolf Steiner and theosophy. A missionary philosophy, theosophy claimed to be a dynamic system based on intuitive knowledge and an understanding of the underlying ebb and flow of the invisible forces of world history. Through Eliza and Steiner, Moltke came to the Book of Revelation, which predicted the second coming of Christ amid chaos and terror of epic proportions.[14] The near total destruction of the General's papers after the First World War – the result of tremendous pressure exerted by Prussian Conservatives on Eliza to publish only an expurgated version of her husband's memoirs – precludes formal connection between Moltke's mind-set and the push for war in July 1914.

Almost allies: Conrad and Moltke to 1914

Conrad as well as Moltke fully appreciated that any war would be fought on two fronts: in Conrad's case, against Russia in the northeast and Serbia in the south; in Moltke's case, against France in the west and Russia in the east. While Conrad readily accepted that Russia was the major adversary, Moltke acknowledged that France was the most dangerous opponent in the short run. There was consensus within the Germanic alliance that Austria–Hungary would bear the brunt of the struggle against Russia while Germany would seek a quick and decisive victory over France. Moltke lectured Conrad in February 1913 that 'Austria's fate will not be definitively decided along the Bug but rather along the Seine'.[15]

Moltke therewith reiterated verbatim the German position first enunciated by Schlieffen in the winter of 1905–6. The epitome of the Prussian professional soldier, Schlieffen had come to his position as Chief of the General Staff in 1891 convinced that a two-front war with France and Russia was unavoidable – given that Kaiser Wilhelm II the previous year had refused to renew Otto von Bismarck's Reinsurance Treaty with Russia. Whereas the legendary Elder Moltke by 1890 realized that the next conflict in Europe would likely be a 'Seven or Thirty Years' War' and that German security could be achieved not by military action alone but rather through diplomatic means, Schlieffen refused to address Germany's diplomatic weakness and instead sought to secure the future through a General Staff *tour de force*. Arguing that Russia would be slow to mobilize due to its underdeveloped transportation system, and haunted by the Napoleonic nightmare of spectacular but meaningless victories in the east – victories that would only suck German forces ever deeper into the Russian vastness while French armies charged through Lorraine and across the Rhine into central Germany – Schlieffen opted for a western orientation in his military strategy.

By 1892, already, Schlieffen had posited that France was Germany's most lethal opponent, that the Reich could ill afford a protracted war, that only a gigantic battle of envelopment and annihilation (*Kesselschlacht*) such as Cannae (216 BC), Leuthen (1757), or Sedan (1870) could break the iron ring of the hostile coalition that 'encircled' Germany, and that offensive operations in the west alone promised success.[16] Consequently, Schlieffen proposed to send seven-eighths of his available forces, organized into six armies, against France in an all-out attack lasting 40 days from the start of mobilization.

The keys to victory lay in rapid mobilization and numerical superiority at the decisive point. The 'hammer', or right wing, of the German Army would have to march through the Netherlands, Belgium, and northern France before descending into the Seine basin west of Paris in order to drive the French, Belgian, Dutch, and (possibly) British armies against the 'anvil' of German forces stationed in Lorraine. This invading force needed to be seven times as strong as the German left wing anchored in Lorraine. Originally, Schlieffen proposed to allocate 85 per cent of his forces to the right wing in the north and only 15 per cent to the left wing in the south. As soon as the French were engaged in Alsace-Lorraine, Schlieffen wanted to shuttle two army corps north to reinforce the right wing, which would then contain 91 per cent of all German troops in the west. In the east, a single army was to conduct a holding action against the Russians, divided into two groups by the Masurian Lakes; Schlieffen hoped that this army would be able to attack each Russian force singly.

Railroads were critical. The inadequate Russian rail system convinced Schlieffen that the Tsar's forces would not be able to cross Germany's eastern borders before the 40th mobilization day. Conversely, superb Belgian and Dutch railroads would allow a rapid German thrust first west and then south, where they would link up with the French rail network. The lightning pace of the German assault would catch British and French armies by surprise and annihilate them in one Armageddon. German planners argued that a delay of just 72 hours in railroad deployment could spell disaster. Finally, Schlieffen feared that a protracted war could awaken the 'red ghost' and plunge Germany into domestic turmoil.

The Schlieffen plan was a high-risk operation born of hubris and bordering on recklessness. One throw of the dice would determine the nation's future. Mesmerized by visions of a gigantic *Kesselschlacht*, Schlieffen, in the words of the historian Gordon Craig, 'disregarded not only the demographic, technological, and industrial factors which affected the war effort of Great Powers in the modern age, but also the political and psychological forces which are apt to make peoples fight even against hopeless odds'.[17] Above all, Schlieffen imbued German military planners with tunnel vision: all attention was focused on the final operational goal, the battle of annihilation in the west. Cast overboard were flexibility, the chance for partial envelopments, and exploitation of local breakthroughs. The word strategy rarely, if ever, appeared in Schlieffen's writings – hardly surprising for a man who devised a grandiose operational plan designed to win the opening campaign of an uncertain war.

In retirement in 1908 Schlieffen boldly predicted a new style of warfare. In place of the personal command of a warrior-king (*le roi connétable*) such as Frederick the Great or even Wilhelm I, Schlieffen postulated a distant, highly-centralized command and control system. The theatre commander would be far removed from the din of battle, sited in 'a house with roomy bureaus, where wire and wireless telegraphy, telephones and signal apparatus, as well as hordes of trucks and motorcycles' were at his instant beck and call. The 'modern Napoleon' would conduct battle seated in a 'comfortable chair at a broad table containing a map of the entire battlefield; from there, he will telephone crisp orders and there he will receive reports from army and corps commanders'. Dirigibles would reconnoitre enemy positions; cavalry would seek, probe, and charge the enemy rear; and infantry would deliver the 'final victory'. Each army corps of 25 000 rifles and 144 heavy guns would be able to attack, hold territory seized, sustain losses of up to 50 per cent of strength, and still be sufficiently powerful to launch a final assault. Several million men could be moved about a campaign area of 40 000 square miles like pieces on a chessboard.[18] There was little or no room in this rigid scheme for imponderables such as friction, interaction, or the 'genius of war'. Well should Schlieffen have read Clausewitz: 'War is the realm of uncertainty; three quarters of the factors on which action in war is based are wrapped in a fog of greater or lesser uncertainty'.[19]

To be sure, Schlieffen's thaumaturgic strategy engendered criticism. Chancellor Leo von Caprivi, an army general, as early as 1892 warned that 'war just against France' would be 'tenacious and protracted'.[20] Senior officers such as Field Marshal Colmar von der Goltz harboured doubts about the short-war scenario and feared instead that any war in Europe would become a long and difficult enterprise. General Ernst Köpke, Schlieffen's Quartermaster-General within the General Staff, as early as August 1895 had warned that France's superiority in troops and its network of fortresses along the eastern border with Germany precluded a repeat of Sedan (1870). 'We cannot expect quick, decisive victories. Army and nation will slowly have to get used to these unpleasant perspectives if we wish to avoid a worrisome pessimism already at the outset of [the next] war, one that could lead to grave danger regarding its outcome.' Even 'the most offensive spirit', Köpke warned Schlieffen, could achieve little more than 'a tedious and bloody crawling forward step-by-step' in what would essentially become 'siege-style' warfare.[21] In May 1910 the Third Department (Intelligence) of the General Staff reiterated Köpke's concerns and added that the French could always withdraw into the interior of the country and thus deny Schlieffen his rapid victory.

Schlieffen apparently accepted Köpke's arguments – without in the least revising and much less abandoning his strategy of annihilation for fear that such a course would undermine the General Staff's prestige and influence on national policy. To admit that armed violence no longer served German interests would have called into question the General Staff's very existence. Schlieffen thus clung to his plan – an act both of despair and of self-justification.

On another level, General Karl von Einem warned Schlieffen that never in history had a great captain commanded 23 army corps, an undertaking that lay in the 'realm of fantasy'.[22] The Prussian War Minister well remembered that the Elder Moltke had mobilized only 280 000 soldiers against Austria in 1866; Schlieffen was now contemplating directing nearly 3 million men in war. Military planners in Berlin were also apprehensive about the human cost of battle: in each minute of combat a modern brigade of 3000 men with artillery expended a volume of fire equal to the volley and salvo firing delivered by the Duke of Wellington's entire army of 60 000 men at the Battle of Waterloo in 1815.[23] Army corps, especially, had become deadly forces: each of Schlieffen's corps with 144 artillery tubes and 25 000 magazine rifles possessed an aggregate fire-power 10 times that of Wellington's muzzle-loader armies. This new 'storm of steel' had caused 68 per cent casualties at Mars Le Tour in 1870, and 90 per cent in the Japanese Nambu brigade during the Russo-Japanese War.[24] Would modern, industrialized societies accept such horrendous losses over time?

Schlieffen's critics within the Prussian military establishment also pointed out that the decisive right wing of the 'wheel' that was to sweep the English Channel with its right sleeve required 13 army corps alone – at a time when Schlieffen could commit but five corps to it. Others argued that Schlieffen blithely ignored anticipated British forces on the Continent, overestimated the combat readiness of German reserves, overlooked Clausewitz's notion of the 'diminishing force of attack', and contemplated a siege of Paris requiring seven or eight army corps – forces that existed neither in reality nor yet even on paper. Grandiose visions of German units marching through the French capital with bands playing the *Paris Entrance March* substituted for Bismarckian *Realpolitik*.[25] Critics may also have wondered whether corps commanders (average age above 55) and army commanders (average age between 60 and 70) would stand up to the strains of marching more than 400 miles in just 40 days – not to mention conducting major engagements with superior forces. General Hans von Seeckt, one of Germany's most able commanders during the Great War and creator of the *Reichswehr* in the 1920s, in retrospect lamented Schlieffen's obsession with the battle of annihilation. 'Cannae: no slogan became so destructive for us as this one.'[26]

Apart from never having read Polybius' account of the Second Punic War,[27] Schlieffen ignored that Rome, while losing the Battle of Cannae, had won the war by the skilful deployment of its sea power. And one can only question whether in an age of universal male conscription, France would have capitulated once German forces stormed Paris. Would France not have resorted to guerrilla warfare as it had in 1871, thereby forcing the Germans to occupy the entire country and in the process denying them the ability to shuttle forces east to meet the approaching Russian 'steam-roller'?

Most critically, German military planners continued to question Schlieffen's obsession with a victorious 'short war'. The Younger Moltke in 1905 expressed to his wife his innermost fears that the future war would be 'a peoples' war', a 'long and tedious struggle', whereafter even a victorious Germany would be 'utterly exhausted'.[28] The Imperial Navy Office the following year expected a European war to last 18 months, while the Imperial Statistical Office prognosticated a war of 2 or even 3 years. The Prussian War Office in 1911 and again in 1912 depicted a 'nine-months-long war' as the norm. Moltke in 1912 and 1914 reiterated his belief that a future war would be 'a protracted struggle on two fronts'. And his Chief of Operations, Colonel Gerhard Tappen, when asked by the Ministry of the Interior how long it would have to feed Berlin in a future war, replied that 'the next war will last at most 2 years'.[29]

The Schlieffen plan was also born in isolation. Both the War Ministry, which had to provide the requisite forces, and the Chancellery, which had to make the necessary diplomatic and political preparations for the German advance through neutral Belgium and the Netherlands, were kept ignorant of the plan's exact details until December 1912. Nor was the German Navy, which might be called on to interdict British cross-Channel troop transports, brought into the planning process.[30] Not even the Reich's sole steadfast ally, Austria–Hungary, was consulted. Quite apart from his general dislike for and distrust of alliances, Schlieffen specifically had grave misgivings about the efficacy of Habsburg forces. The General so distrusted Vienna's top military leadership that after 1896–7 he limited contacts to annual festive greetings. At no time was he willing even to discuss the matter of a unified military command in what, after all, could only be a coalition war.[31]

The Younger Moltke was hardly the man to question the basic tenets of Schlieffen's plan. To be sure, convinced that the next war could possibly be a prolonged 'world war', Moltke abandoned the politically indefensible march through the Dutch Maastricht Appendix to maintain the Netherlands as a 'windpipe' to world trade. He strengthened the German left flank in the south to protect the vital industries of the Saar, expanded the Prussian Army by 137 000 men, and instituted logistical exercises in annual manoeuvres. By enlarging the German left wing in Alsace-Lorraine, Moltke reduced the ratio of forces between the right and left wings from Schlieffen's original seven-to-one to its final calculus of three-to-one.

But further Moltke would not go. He never challenged Schlieffen's proposition that Germany could defeat France in 4 weeks, and thereafter shuttle the bulk of its forces east to halt the Russian advance into East Prussia and Silesia. Nor did he question Schlieffen's France-first strategy. Neither the swampy bogs nor the fortified crossings at the Niemen and Narew rivers offered much prospect for swift, decisive military action. And the Russian rail network in Poland was only single-track and of different gauge from German rolling stock. And when the Franco-Russian alliance held firm during the December 1912 diplomatic crisis, Moltke in 1913 cancelled contingency planning for the east.

On the other hand, Moltke improved relations with Vienna. After 1906 he regularly exchanged letters and intelligence and arranged personal meetings with Conrad. Yet neither Moltke nor Conrad was willing to bare his innermost thoughts and plans to the other. Each pursued his own strategy independently. Conrad sought to commit Moltke to deploy specific numbers of troops in the east, to offer precise dates for full-force intervention against the Russians, and to define individual military operations. But Conrad never openly informed the Germans of his determination to tackle Serbia concurrently with Russia. He even struck a stamp, 'Not to be Relayed to the German General Staff', for sensitive information! Conversely, while Moltke tried to commit Conrad to assume the brunt of the war against Russia as German forces stormed into France, the German refused tenaciously to make firm promises as to his deployment strength, to set timetables for bringing his armies from the west to the east, and to coordinate specific operations.[32] For 6 years both heads of their respective General Staffs danced a polite polonaise around the vital issue of joint military planning. Yet the historian Dennis Showalter surely hit the nail on the head when he commented that only a military innocent – which Conrad was not – could have expected eight Prussian reserve divisions composed of 'greenhorns and grandfathers' to have mounted a major offensive against superior Russian forces in the Polish salient.[33] In the end, Conrad was a victim of his own pre- and misconceptions.

Romanticized assurances of standing 'shoulder-to-shoulder' and pledges of legendary Germanic loyalty (*Nibelungentreue*) substituted for realistic planning. Each general *assumed* that the other would launch a major offensive against Russia at the outset of war. Each *intended* to strike out against his principal enemy the moment that war broke out. Additionally, both men were blinded by ethnic and racial animosities. While Conrad constantly railed against 'dog Serbia' and the 'snake Italy', Moltke frequently reminded Conrad that any future war would be 'a struggle between Slavs and Teutons' for the preservation of 'Germanic culture'.[34] Yet even there the two soldiers were at odds. Moltke dismissed Conrad's charges of Italian 'perfidy', and insisted that Rome would honour its pledge to deploy three army corps on the Rhine by the 22nd mobilization day. Conrad rejected Moltke's hypothesis of a 'racial war' and testily reminded his German counterpart that Slavs made up 47 per cent of the Habsburg Empire.[35]

At their last prewar meeting at Karlsbad on 12 May 1914 the two soldiers once more politely sidestepped the critical issue of common strategy and command. Both were convinced that war was imminent and unavoidable. 'To wait any longer', Moltke lectured Conrad, 'means a diminishing of our chances'. Both agreed that the war would have to be short, especially given Russia's numerical superiority. And both identified their principal opponent. Conrad promised to hurl the major part of his forces against Russia in Galicia; Moltke reiterated his intent to concentrate against France. The issue of joint command was not raised.[36]

Thus it is hardly surprising that Austria–Hungary and Germany went to war in 1914 without a coordinated military strategy. No one in the German military had bothered to undertake careful and critical assessment of the military strength and preparedness of the Viennese ally, much less of its industrial and manpower reserves. No one in German political circles had demanded that once the dice were cast for war, Austria–Hungary as the 'junior' partner coordinate and, if need be, subjugate, its policies and strategies to those of the 'senior' partner in Berlin. German soldiers and statesmen alike merely *assumed* that all was well with the Habsburg ally.

On 30 July 1914 Lieutenant-Colonel Karl von Kageneck, the Reich's military attaché in Vienna, anxiously pleaded with Moltke's deputy, General Georg von Waldersee, 'to play absolutely with open cards in order not to repeat the [negative] experiences of all coalition wars'.[37] Nothing was done. By 4 August Kageneck grew more anxious. 'It is high time that the two general staffs consult now with absolute frankness with respect to mobilization, jump-off time, areas of assembly and precise troop strength', he cabled Moltke. 'Everyone has been relying upon the belief that the two chiefs of staff had worked out these most intimate agreements between themselves'.[38] Instead, Conrad had sent the bulk of his forces south to smash Serbia, while Moltke had unleashed his armies against Belgium and northern France, en route to Paris.

Conrad von Hötzendorf: war at any price

The Imperial and Royal Habsburg Army marched off to war on two fronts in 1914. In the south, the punitive expedition launched against Serbia on 12 August ended in defeat and the loss of about 100 000 soldiers. In the north, Conrad von Hötzendorf's offensive against Russia, mounted in Galicia on 22 August, brought defeat at Lemberg and the surrender of the great fortress at Przemyśl, along with a further loss of 500 000 irreplaceable front-line troops. In some respects, it would not be too far off the mark to state that the twin disasters in Serbia and Galicia deprived Austria–Hungary of any chance to score a military victory against its adversaries. Conrad quickly pinned responsibility for defeat on railroad technicians, Viennese diplomats, and the German ally.[39] The truth is more complex and it lies with Conrad.

Like Germany, Austria–Hungary in 1914 acknowledged the need to conduct a two-front war. Like most contemporary commanders, Conrad believed that infantry remained the queen of battle and that élan could overcome superior numbers as well as defensive fire. Like Moltke, Conrad knew that he would not have the luxury of superior numbers: quite the contrary, his 48 infantry divisions would be pitted against 11 Serbian and 55 Russian divisions. Thus, like Germany, Austria–Hungary could not possibly conduct offensives on both fronts but had to concentrate against the power it hoped to be able to defeat most easily, before turning to meet the more slowly materializing threat. Conrad, in reaching his final operational deployment, proceeded on the basis of several assumptions. Firstly, the war would be short, lasting at most 6 weeks. Secondly, it would take Russia at least 30 days to mobilize the bulk of its forces. Thirdly, Habsburg armies could be operational against Serbia in 15 days. And fourthly, Austro-Hungarian units would have to secure Germany's eastern front while Moltke sought victory in France.

Conrad resolved his two-front predicament by way of a flexible response. He divided his field army into three separate parts. The largest of his forces, *A-Staffel*, consisting of nine army corps with 27 infantry divisions, nine cavalry divisions, and 21 hastily formed and poorly equipped supplementary (or third-line) reserve infantry brigades (*Marschbrigaden*), would deploy in southern Poland against Russia. *Minimalgruppe Balkan*, comprising three army corps of nine infantry divisions and seven supplementary reserve brigades, would operate against Serbia. Critical to Conrad's plans was the strategic reserve, *B-Staffel*, made up of four army corps of 11 infantry divisions, one cavalry division, and six supplementary reserve brigades. It would be a swing force: against Serbia in case of an Austro-Serbian war, and against Russia in case of a general European war.[40]

This sensible equation failed to take into account one critical constant: Conrad's visceral hatred of Serbia and his determination to destroy it.[41] In 1912–13, for example, the Operations Bureau of the General Staff had stated confidently that in case war broke out with Serbia, followed by Russian mobilization against the Dual Monarchy, Austrian forces would first 'settle accounts' with Serbia before turning north against the major threat. Conrad's cheery prognostication was that *A-Staffel* could be operational against Russia by the 15th mobilization day, and that the strategic reserve (*B-Staffel*) could deploy in Galicia by about the 25th mobilization day – thus leaving it plenty of time to march through Belgrade.[42] Once united in Galicia, Conrad's forces, consisting of four armies of 2 million men and 1 million horses, would strike out from Lemberg deep into

Volhynia. At no time during the July crisis did Conrad share these plans with the politicians who led Austria–Hungary into war.[43]

Conrad's calculations were based on wishful thinking. As the historian Gunther Rothenberg has put it, 'On paper Conrad's plans always had an almost Napoleonic sweep, though he often lacked the resolution to carry them out and also forgot that he did not have the instruments to execute them'.[44] Quite apart from the fact that in 1914 his forces would be about a dozen infantry divisions inferior to those of his adversaries, Conrad ignored that Russian mobilization schedules had been cut down dramatically by the extension of the Russian rail network in Poland. In fact, Moltke warned Conrad in February 1914 that Russia would complete mobilization of two-thirds of its forces 18 days after a declaration of war.[45] Austria–Hungary's mobilization pace of 153 trains per day would be dwarfed by Russia's rate of 360 trains per day – with the result that Russia would have sent 6760 and Austria–Hungary only 3978 trains to the front by the 30th mobilization day.[46] One wonders whether Conrad ever understood that Serbia's fate would ultimately be decided on the Vistula, not the Danube.

The outbreak of war between Austria–Hungary and Serbia on 28 July 1914 revealed Conrad's shortcomings as a strategic planner. The Dual Monarchy declared war knowing that its forces could not be fully mobilized before 12 August; Conrad never explained that 'oversight'. In fact, Conrad immediately instructed both *Minimalgruppe Balkan* and *B-Staffel* to mobilize against Serbia, but the eight army corps of *A-Staffel* were not mobilized for fear that such action might provoke Russia. Additionally, since Austrian military regulations stipulated that the first day of mobilization was a 'free' or 'alarm' day, designed for troops to settle their private affairs, many anxious volunteers were turned away at barracks gates on 29 July and told to report the following day 'according to schedule'.[47] On 30 July Conrad ordered *Minimalgruppe Balkan* and *B-Staffel* to operate against Serbia. As late as noon of 31 July Conrad still insisted that Russia's position remained unclear and that operations proceed against Serbia.

All available evidence indicates that Conrad knew well before 31 July that Russia would mobilize. The German military attaché in Vienna, Kageneck, informed Conrad as early as 25 July that Russia would support Serbia in any future conflict, 'otherwise Russia will cease to be a great power'.[48] Conrad's military attaché at St Petersburg, Franz Prince zu Hohenlohe, stated on 26 July that Russia would mobilize against the Dual Monarchy. Foreign Minister Berchtold seconded that opinion three days later. Conrad admitted as much during an audience with Franz Joseph on 29 July.[49] The next day, Conrad received confirmation from St Petersburg that Russia was mobilizing its four military districts bordering on the Dual Monarchy. On 31 July Conrad's man in St Petersburg again instructed Vienna that Russia had mobilized these four military districts. Conrad finally had to face reality on the evening of 31 July. General Viktor Dankl, designated commander of the First Army, appreciated that the war would extend to most of Europe: 'Thank God, it is the great war!'[50]

Germany proclaimed general mobilization around noon on 31 July. Kaiser Wilhelm II, Chancellor von Bethmann Hollweg, Foreign Secretary von Jagow, and General von Moltke, unaware that Conrad had dispatched half of his army against Serbia, immediately informed Vienna that the time had come for Austria to concentrate the greater part of its forces against Russia.[51] Panic-stricken, Conrad now demanded that his railway staff halt the 12 divisions bound for the Serbian frontier and reroute *B-Staffel* at once to Galicia.[52] Additionally, Conrad wished to put *B-Staffel* units not yet en route to the Danube on hold in their barracks.

Colonel Johann Straub, head of the War Ministry's Railroad Bureau, became irate. He lectured Conrad that such precipitous action would destroy the tactical cohesion of these units and bring 'chaos' to the mobilization schedule. Moreover, Straub argued, the Dual Monarchy's railway network and staff of 1059 officers and 46 350 men, the largest single military contingent in the *k.u.k.* Army, could not possibly sustain the strain of such radical rerouting. After all, prewar planning had given priority to trains bound for the Balkans over those headed for Galicia. The Austro-Hungarian Railroad Bureau had made no plans for such an eventuality. In the end, the General Staff agreed to follow the suggestion of Major Emil Ratzenhofer, Conrad's own railway expert on Russia, that the troops of *B-Staffel* continue on to Serbia, disembark, and then reembark for Galicia by about 18 August.[53] Ratzenhofer refused suggestions that *B-Staffel* troops not yet on board trains for Serbia be detained in their home barracks until the situation had cleared, arguing that the sight of flower-bedecked and beflagged troops returning unbloodied to barracks would cause 'moral, political, and disciplinary damage'.[54] In August 1914 Conrad experienced the Elder Moltke's admonition that a mistake made during the original concentration of forces could not be rectified during the entire course of a campaign.

The hastily redirected mobilization against Russia unravelled much slower than anticipated. Instead of the 11 000 trains that Ratzenhofer claimed could be used for this purpose, a mere 1942 were activated. The truth is that the Austro-Hungarian General Staff still operated with timetables dating from the Franco-Prussian War and had failed to take advantage of existing modern railroad technology such as more powerful locomotives, automatic interlocking brakes, and signal apparatus. Further, in order to oversee every aspect of mobilization, Conrad's planners had decreed that all trains were to roll at approximately the same speed – that is, the speed of the slowest, about 10 miles per hour (compared with average German speeds of 20 miles). As a result, Austrian trains, whether narrow-gauge Alpine spurs or double-track commuter lines, lumbered on at the speed of bicycles. Overly cautious engineers in the Carpathian passes insisted on absurd braking requirements and pulled troop trains apart to meet local regulations.[55] Sidings and platforms for detraining soldiers limited troop trains to 50 cars. No one thought to exploit recent technological advances on the vital double-track line between Budapest and Przemyśl. And although each army unit carried along its own field kitchen, railway officials ordered that all trains stop each day for 6 hours for victualling and water resupply. The net result was that rail traffic during the critical northern mobilization moved at half the speed realized in peacetime manoeuvres. The short haul from Pressburg to Sambor, for example, took 16 hours – a time in which a healthy pedestrian could have made the journey![56] On 11 August Kageneck in classic understatement reported to Moltke that the Austrian public was 'somewhat nervous' about the snail's pace of mobilization.[57]

In the end, *B-Staffel* spent much of the opening phase of the war in railroad cars. Conrad's vaunted strategic reserve, in Churchill's words, left General Potiorek in Serbia 'before it could win him a victory. It returned to Conrad in time to participate in his defeat'[58] in Galicia. The truth is that Conrad, without informing Moltke, on 13 July had abandoned plans to launch an offensive from Lemberg into Volhynia. Instead, he unloaded the four armies of *A-Staffel* and later *B-Staffel* well behind the Russian front in a half-moon configuration in front of the San and Dniester rivers. Three armies were to assume defensive positions; First Army and Fourth Army alone were instructed to advance against the enemy.

Conrad's railway staff worked feverishly throughout late July and early August to revise no fewer than 84 boxes of detailed instructions to accommodate their commander's latest deviation.[59] Austro-Hungarian troops paid the price in physical exhaustion as they marched to the front on foot. It is estimated that the four Habsburg armies in Galicia undertook daily forced marches of almost 20 miles between 19 and 26 August just to reach the Russian border. A weary army confronted the Russians at Lemberg early in September 1914.

Moltke: the march to the Marne

German mobilization was highly complex and consisted of seven distinct phases. Stage one ('state of security') alerted the Army to new and threatening intelligence. Stage two ('political tension') put commanders on ready alert. Stage three ('imminent threat of war') was the first to be made public: leaves were cancelled, reserve staffs were ordered to duty, 11 of the 25 army corps called up their first-line reserves, and the state of siege law, designed to suppress possible civilian (read, socialist) unrest, was enacted. Stage four ('war mobilization') ordered all active, first- and second-line reserve (*Landwehr* and *Landsturm*) units to report to their military commands and directed 21 brigades to move to the borders. Eighth Corps at Saarbrücken was to seize the Alzette River basin in southern Luxembourg; six infantry brigades were to advance against Liège in eastern Belgium; and civilians near the Russian frontier in East Prussia were to be evacuated to 'safe' areas.

Stage five was the actual Military Travel Plan, which began on 4 August and ran through to 20 August 1914. In the west, seven armies took up ready positions along the line Aachen-Metz, Saarburg-Millhausen; in the east, Eighth Army assumed a ready position between Hohensalza and Insterburg; and Silesia was defended by one *Landwehr* corps. Stage five was perhaps the most critical phase of mobilization because it depended on the equal and constant speed and intervals of troop trains moving roughly 3 million men and 600 000 horses (which required 10 times the food of men) on the same stretches of track. Stage six was simply dubbed 'concentration'. Soldiers were to be off-loaded from trains and assembled in formation at border crossings. Stage seven ('attack march') was designed to bring troops into contact with the enemy. The General Staff demanded that each war-mobilized corps of 41 000 men, 14 000 horses, and 2400 wagons, occupying 30 miles of road, be formed at the border in 24 hours.[60]

The Great General Staff was the brain centre of this gigantic mobilization. It had grown from a minuscule agency of 15 officers which the Elder Moltke had taken into battle in 1870 to a bureaucratic labyrinth of 650 officers in 1914. Schlieffen had stamped his personal motto, 'Say little, do much. Be more than you appear', on the General Staff.[61] The work ethic of this Hutterian Pietist, whose day began at 6 a.m. in the map room and ended at 11 p.m. at his desk, followed by reading military history to his daughters at home, became the expected norm. His tone – sarcastic, heavy with scorn and ridicule – likewise was emulated by what Bismarck had termed the 'demigods' of the General Staff.

Six major sections handled the General Staff's workload: Central Section, composed of deputy chiefs, adjutants, and secretaries, controlled the flow of paperwork and monitored work completion; First and Third Sections dealt with intelligence, analysing foreign armies east, west, and south of Germany; Second Section was responsible for mobilization and thus railroad schedules; Fourth Section directed staff rides and supervised the War Academy in Berlin; and Fifth Section handled military history. Rapid victories against Denmark in 1864, Austria in 1866, and France in 1871 had given the General Staff the aura (and arrogance) of invincibility. In fact, it was said that Europe had created five perfect institutions: the Roman curia, the British Parliament, the Russian ballet, the French opera, and the Prussian General Staff.

In August 1914 time was of the essence. The Schlieffen plan was predicated on Germany being the first to mobilize, to cross enemy borders, and to drive in behind Paris and annihilate the Anglo-Belgian-French armies in the field within 40 days of stage five (mobilization). Nor were the Germans alone in their anxiety over speed: General Joffre, Moltke's French counterpart, stated on 31 July 1914 that every delay of 24 hours in mobilizing the reserves would force France to yield 12 to 15 miles of border lands.[62] Time meant space (and blood) in modern war planning.

The complexity of German mobilization largely accounts for Moltke's mental crisis of 1 August. Wilhelm II, momentarily convinced that the British would apply the brakes to the French and that the war could thus be limited to Russia, demanded that Moltke recast the Schlieffen plan – now in stage four – and 'simply deploy the whole army in the east'! Aghast at the Kaiser's ignorance of German mobilization plans and deeply shaken, Moltke with 'trembling lips' interjected: 'The deployment of a host of millions of men cannot be improvised'. To which Wilhelm II acidly replied: 'Your uncle [the Elder Moltke] would have given me a different answer'.[63] Therewith, in Moltke's mind, the Emperor had broken his pledge of 8 years' standing not to interfere in General Staff matters. Irate, Moltke wondered aloud whether Russia might also rein in short of war, thereby erasing all prospects of war! War Minister von Falkenhayn found Moltke to be 'totally broken' in spirit because the Kaiser apparently still 'hoped for peace'.[64] Later that 1 August, Moltke spilled 'tears of despair' over the Kaiser's orders to halt the German 16th Division at the Luxembourg frontier, an expression of 'disappointment' and 'hurt' from which he never recovered.[65] Nor did Schlieffen's 1908 vision of the 'modern Napoleon' eventuate. Six years later, 27 days after mobilization, Moltke sat in an empty girls' schoolhouse in Luxembourg, his desk lit only by a few dim oil lamps, contemplating the unknown advance of his armies through northern France.[66]

The Central Section of the General Staff in Berlin became a 24-hour electronic communications centre. Telephones and telegraphs as well as a pneumatic tube connected it to Berlin's major post offices, from where 200 000 telegraph employees and 100 000 telephone operators manning 32 847 telephones communicated the state of 'imminent war' to the 106 infantry brigades scattered throughout the Reich. The General Staff's Railroad Section, augmented by 23 railroad directorates beyond Berlin, commanded 30 000 locomotives as well as 65 000 passenger and 800 000 freight cars to assemble 25 active German army corps.

Initially, military planners gauged an army corps to be a formation equal to the number of soldiers that could come into action from a single road in a single day – about 30 000 men – but the increasing size of artillery units and ammunition trains had raised that figure to 40 000 by 1914. Corps commanders were given six aircraft for reconnaissance and one battalion of sixteen 15 cm howitzers, the best medium-range guns in the world. Below the corps level, German higher formations were organized by twos: two divisions to a corps; two brigades to a division; and two regiments to a brigade. The two infantry brigades of each corps were supported by a regiment of cavalry – four squadrons each of 170 'sabres'. In a short war, cavalry was a one-shot shock weapon that was to expend itself at the decisive moment in a campaign.

The heart of the German Army was the mixed combat arms division. Its four regiments each of slightly more than 3000 soldiers boasted three battalions made up each of four companies of 250 men. On the eve of the Great War, each division had added a 13th company composed of six water-cooled Maxim automatic machine guns. The MG 08 had a range of 12 000 feet and fired 400 to 500 shots per minute. Moreover, German divisions were given an artillery brigade of two regiments, each with two 18-gun battalions, or 72 tubes. Three of the four battalions per division after 1905 manned 54 flat-trajectory 77 mm guns (FK 96 nA); these pieces had recoil buffer brakes and an optimum range of 25 000 feet. They were considered to be inferior to the French 75 mm guns in range, accuracy, and rate of fire. The high cost of upgrading artillery had prevented the German Army from adopting a new design before 1914. But the fourth artillery battalion of every division enjoyed eighteen 105 mm field howitzers, a weapon without equal in Europe. Krupp also produced superb 21 cm howitzers, but its experiments with mammoth 42 cm howitzers stagnated as the gun required 36 hours to assemble and could be moved only on rails. And whereas in the Franco-Prussian War artillery's primary role had been to batter hostile artillery, after 1907 the German Army ordered it first and foremost to support infantry.

Infantry remained the 'queen of battle'. The German Field Regulations of May 1906 were simple and direct on this point:

Infantry is the primary weapon. In tandem with artillery, its fire will batter the enemy. It alone breaks his last resistance. It carries the brunt of combat and makes the greatest sacrifices. Consequently, it garners the greatest glory. Infantry must nurture its intrinsic drive to attack aggressively. Its actions must be dominated by one thought: Forward against the enemy, cost what it may![67]

But debates within the Prussian Army revealed concern that infantry's role was more and more reduced to 'offering targets for the artillery'. While few generals deemed this a 'worthy' goal, they nevertheless agreed that 'it would come down to this' in the next war.[68]

German soldiers carried the Rifle 98, a 7.9 mm Mauser design with a range of just over 6000 feet. It was a sturdy and reliable weapon, one that would serve German infantry for the next half century. Colourful tunics had been relegated to the parade square by 1910 in favour of field grey, a colour that blended well with smoke, mud, and autumn foliage. Soldiers wore calf-length boots as well as the famous (but useless) leather spiked helmet (*Pickelhaube*), and carried a square knapsack weighing up to 70 lbs, bayonet, entrenching tool, haversack, mess kit, and six ammunition pouches. The haversack contained tinned meat and preserved vegetables, biscuits, coffee, and salt as emergency rations; field bakeries on wheels made bread while mobile field kitchens provided hot meals.[69] All things considered, a German Army corps was akin to a small village on the move.

The German mobilization and advance in August 1914 was also complicated by the compression of terrain: the entire west front early in August 1914 was a rough triangle 400 miles by 230 miles by 260 miles at its greatest extension, about 55 000 square miles. While General Alexander von Kluck's First Army of 320 000 men had to pass through a 6-mile-wide strip between the Dutch border and Liège, General Karl von Bülow's Second Army of 260 000 men had to march through and immediately south of Liège. Nearly 600 000 German troops along with their horses and gear had to squeeze through a narrow funnel 12 miles wide and to cross the Meuse (Maas) River. Their further advance north on to the Belgian plain necessitated the capture of Belgium's principal fortress, Liège, by six German infantry brigades – and thus entailed violation of Belgian neutrality at the outset of war.[70]

Aachen, the ancient capital of Charlemagne, was the major German choke point. No fewer than six army corps had to pass through the city on their way to Liège. Each army corps stretched about 20 miles; each division nine miles. The munitions train for an army corps required 12 miles of road; the baggage train another 4 miles. Army corps were required to carry food for 4 days; cavalry and infantry units additionally received 'iron rations' for 3 days. Each infantry company of 250 men was assigned one food supply wagon and one field kitchen pulled by horses.

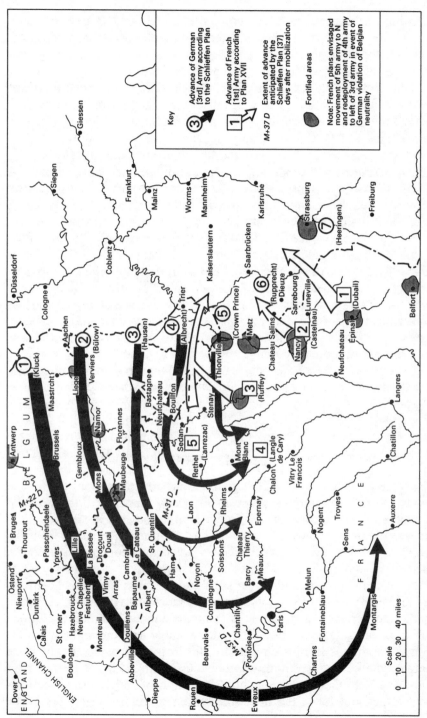

Map 1. The French and German plans of war, 1914

To funnel this massive force, which took up about 200 miles of roads, through the streets of Aachen, General Staff planners had worked out elaborate logistics plans. First and Second Armies left their heavy gear and supplies in Düsseldorf, to be sent after them once they had passed Aachen. Food for the 600 000 soldiers was sent ahead, to be distributed by reserve units stationed in Aachen. Martial law was declared to keep civilians off the streets and military police manned every major intersection. Still, it took 5 days (13 to 17 August) for Kluck's and Bülow's men to march through the city. They crossed the Meuse on 18 August.[71]

Last but not least, the Germans were painfully aware of their numerical inferiority on both fronts. Moltke, in his last prewar calculations, estimated that his 70 divisions earmarked for the west would be met by 92 Belgian, British, and French; in the east, 48 Austro-Hungarian and nine German divisions would face 112 (!) Russian and Serbian. In raw totals, Moltke calculated that Berlin and Vienna had available 3 547 000 soldiers against 5 379 000 Allied. The General Staff took only 'white' troops into account and left aside the 477 000 'non-white' soldiers available to the Entente.[72] A war of attrition remained a distinct possibility but also a nightmare, given that Germany and Austria–Hungary combined had a population of only 118 million against an Allied aggregate of 258 (not counting 420 million 'coloureds').[73] One simply hoped that the Schlieffen plan would bring a rapid victory early in the war in France and thereby accord the Reich an advantageous position from which to plan its next step.

Plan 19: the Russian 'steamrolller'

Strategic planners in St Petersburg, like their counterparts in Berlin and Vienna, faced the daunting prospect of a two-front war. War Minister Sukhomlinov and Quartermaster-General Y. N. Danilov as early as 1910 had devised Mobilization Schedule 19, an 'active defence' in the west that featured the concentration of 53 infantry divisions against Germany, with a secondary deployment of 19 infantry divisions against Austria–Hungary. In the face of immense political pressure from Paris to hasten mobilization and secure in the promise of an 'immediate and decisive' French offensive against the Germans 'with all forces', Danilov, the real architect of Russian prewar planning, agreed not only to mount a major offensive between the 15th and 30th mobilization day, but to shift its thrust from the lower to the middle Narew – that is, still more against Germany.[74]

In May 1912 General Y. G. Zhilinsky, Danilov's successor, undertook what turned out to be the final fine-tuning of Russia's war plan. The revised Mobilization Schedule 19 offered two variants: 'A' against Austria–Hungary and 'G' against Germany. Under variant 'A', Russia agreed 'to go over to the offensive' against Habsburg armies (with lesser forces detailed against Hohenzollern forces) 'with the objective of taking the war into their territory'. Forty-five infantry divisions organized into four armies would constitute the southwest front against Austria–Hungary, and 29 infantry divisions gathered in two armies the northwest front against Germany; a reserve of two armies would guard the approaches to St Petersburg and Bendery. The two armies massed against Germany were to destroy 'German forces remaining in East Prussia' and then to use this province as an 'assembly area for further operations', that is, an assault on Berlin.

Variant 'G' had 43 Russian infantry divisions organized into three armies 'go over to the attack' against the nine German divisions defending East Prussia, while 31 divisions in two armies would head southwest to 'paralyze' the Habsburg enemy 'on the remaining fronts'.[75] Since Russian planners expected Germany to be involved in a two-front war with France and Russia, Zhilinsky argued that variant 'A' was the most likely scenario. Just over 1.3 million peacetime troops would be mobilized in case of war.

Indeed, Russian mobilization, beginning on 30 July 1914, unfolded according to Schedule 19 (A). Southwest front under General N. Y. Ivanov consisted of 16 army corps ranged in a 250-mile semicircle against Austria–Hungary. One army group of the seven corps of Fourth and Fifth armies struck south out of the Polish salient against the great Austrian fortress Przemyśl. A second army group of the nine corps of Third and Eighth armies advanced west from the Ukraine across the Dniester River. Ivanov's forces were to destroy Austro-Hungarian armies in Galicia, to storm the Carpathian passes, and thereafter to deploy on to the Hungarian plain.

General Zhilinsky's northwest front consisted of nine army corps deployed against East Prussia over a broken line 150 miles in length. The four corps of General P. K. Rennenkampf's First Army concentrated west of the middle flow of the Niemen River above the Masurian Lakes, while the five corps of General A. V. Samsonov's Second Army marshalled along the line Grodno-Lomza-Belostok below the Masurian Lakes. Russian planners saw three options: an advance against Königsberg, the Hohenzollerns' coronation site; an assault against Allenstein; or a drive across the Vistula, past Thorn, toward Berlin. While the French encouraged the Russians to choose the latter option, Zhilinsky in 1914 decided to destroy the German forces in East Prussia by mounting twin drives with 800 000 men by the 15th day of mobilization against both

Königsberg and Allenstein. Thereafter, he planned to advance across the Vistula into Silesia, and eventually against Berlin.

Given the overwhelming German concentration against France, it is not surprising that East Prussia was thinly guarded against the Russian invasion. General Maximilian von Prittwitz's Eighth Army consisted of but nine divisions, including two reserve and one cavalry. He hoped that superior German leadership, spirit, training, and tactics would enable him to keep the Russians at bay until the crucial decision had fallen in France – roughly by the 40th mobilization day. Geography was Prittwitz's great ally: the Masurian Lakes would force Zhilinsky to divide his invading armies, and thus accord the German the advantage of manoeuvre. For, in the words of French General Joffre, East Prussia was 'an ambush' waiting to happen.[76]

The keys to Russian success were time and mass. Assured by Paris that France would mount an offensive with more than 800 000 men by the 15th mobilization day, Zhilinsky was to launch his own attack into East Prussia concurrently. The prevailing 'short-war illusion' allowed no time for a leisurely massing of reserves. Above all, Zhilinsky would have to pass his armies north and south of the Masurian Lakes in quick order so that they could join up again deep in East Prussia. Given that under Schedule 19 (A) Russia would concentrate only 60 per cent of its forces against Austria–Hungary, Danilov's assurance that victory could be attained with merely a 20 per cent superiority was a first casualty of the war.

The Russian Army in 1914 was prepared to fight a short war of annihilation (*sokrushenie*). Each artillery piece had a thousand shells, and the entire Army possessed 2.5 billion rounds for small arms – up to normal prewar levels. Field Regulation PU-1912 deemed the offensive to be dominant, left a great deal of initiative to field commanders, and asserted the triumph of morale and will on the modern battlefield. Infantry, the queen of battle, was taught that both the rifle (Mosin-Nagant) and the machine gun but especially the 30-inch bayonet were decisive. Cavalry was trained to screen infantry's advance, to attack enemy cavalry, and eventually to dismount to 'get at close quarters with the bayonet'. Cossacks were issued sabres for close combat, and since 1912 all cavalry units again carried lances as shock weapons. Artillery was to fire in short, rapid bursts and field guns to fire over the heads of advancing infantry. Artillery's major goals were to engage hostile artillery and machine guns, seal off enemy routes of approach, breach obstacles by fire, and batter down counterattacks.[77]

Organizationally, the Russian Army mirrored its German counterpart. Army corps consisted of two infantry divisions each of two brigades and four regiments; each regiment of four battalions and a company of eight heavy Maxim machine guns. Russian divisions each had a brigade of 48 Putilov field guns arranged in six companies of eight tubes each. But whereas German corps boasted 48 light and 16 heavy howitzers, Russian corps were undergunned with only 12 122 mm howitzers. Thirty divisions of cavalry were arranged in four regiments each of 4500 riders; and regiments were subdivided into six squadrons of about 1000 'sabres'.

On 2 August 1914 Grand Duke Nikolai Nikolaevich, Tsar Nicholas II's uncle, was given overall command of Russian armies deployed along a 1000-mile front. Known as a reformer and enjoying a reputation for personal honesty, the Grand Duke, who had expected no more than command of the Sixth Army guarding St Petersburg, found himself at a post which he had not anticipated and in charge of carrying out a plan with which he was barely familiar. He reached Supreme Headquarters (*Stavka*) at Baranovichi on 14 August. General N. N. Yanushkevich served as his chief of staff and the ubiquitous Danilov once more as Quartermaster-General. Since the war was to be short, the War Ministry denied *Stavka* modern communications equipment. General Samsonov's Second Army, for example, possessed only 25 telephones, several Morse-coding machines, and one slow Hughes teleprinter. Nor did it have encoders at its disposal.

The one thing that Russian forces – or, at least, their commanding officers – possessed was confidence. They had been prepared for a short war of annihilation and they were ready to fight it. The alliance with France provided further assurance of victory. General Sukhomlinov's army reforms after 1906 and especially his 'Big Programme' of 1912 had generated an aura of euphoria at headquarters. The Army was willing to accept great risks for a great victory. And the betrayal to Russia of Conrad's war plans by Colonel Alfred Redl, chief of staff of the VIII Corps at Prague, apparently gave Russian commanders the decisive edge in military intelligence.[78] It is even likely that a second mole in the Austro-Hungarian General Staff continued the treason after Redl's exposure in 1913.

Plan XVII: *à Berlin*

France, unlike Austria–Hungary, Germany, and Russia, was not troubled by the prospect of having to fight a two-front war. Instead, it could concentrate against a single opponent, Germany. If the Schlieffen plan was born of a desperate strategic logic, the French war plan was the product of a desperate national psychology. France had not accepted the historical verdict delivered by the twin defeats of Emperor Napoleon III's armies in 1870 and of Adolphe Thiers' republican forces in 1871. The 'lost' provinces of Alsace and Lorraine – the proverbial 'gap in the Vosges' – remained the focal point of a pathological hatred of Germany. No government in Paris dared accept their loss. *Revanche* was the one national policy that united the disparate political elements of the French polity.

Thus it is hardly surprising that various French governments defended the Army passionately during the notorious Dreyfus Affair[79] and lavished enormous funds on it. In a word, France led the European drive to militarization. Its defence expenditures comprised 36 per cent of the national budget, compared with only 20 per cent in Germany. France conscripted 5620 men for each million inhabitants, compared with 4120 per million in Germany. Yet, in raw totals, France, with a population of 25 million fewer inhabitants, could never match German mobilization, and certainly could not accept a prolonged war against a numerically superior adversary. The only solution, French planners argued, lay in overcoming superior German numbers with valour and morale. The lesson of the lost war of 1870–1, successive generations of officers at the *École de guerre* were instructed, was that the defensive had been discredited in favour of a new 'mystique of the offensive'.

Joffre, appointed Commander-in-Chief of the French Army (*commandant en chef des armées françaises*) in 1911, was the most persistent advocate of the offensive. He reminded his soldiers of the French military tradition of the *arme blanche* and the *Furia Francese*, stressed the superiority of the Gallic genius over the slow-witted Hun, admonished French planners to reconstruct the *élan vitale* of the revolutionary armies of 1789, and argued that spirit and guts (*cran*) could overcome firepower. General Adolphe Messimy, who as War Minister had appointed Joffre to command French forces in 1911, perhaps put it best: 'Neither numbers nor miraculous machines will determine victory. This will go to soldiers with valour and quality – and by this I mean superior physical and moral endurance, offensive spirit'.[80] General Foch, while head of the French Military Academy St Cyr, lectured a generation of French officers: 'victory = will'.[81]

Planners in Paris were not ignorant of the Schlieffen plan. In 1903–4 French intelligence agents had obtained the basic contours of what soon would become the German blueprint for war in the so-called 'Vengeur' documents. While some scholars have suggested that these were tainted or bogus German 'plants', their accuracy concerning the planned German march through Belgium was confirmed that same year by an unimpeachable source. In January (and again in December) 1904, Kaiser Wilhelm II demanded that King Leopold II of Belgium pledge Germany safe passage through his country in case of war. Failure to do so, Wilhelm warned Leopold, would mean that Germany would 'immediately invade Belgium'.[82] And French agents in Berlin could hardly have missed the open speculation in political salons by socialites such as Hildegard Baroness Spitzemberg, among many, concerning the Schlieffen plan.

For nearly 2 years Joffre and the *Troisième Bureau* (Operations) of the French Army struggled with the problem of blunting a German offensive, which they expected through the Ardennes. War Plan XVII, which Joffre presented to the War Board in April 1913 and which became official policy in May 1914, was the incarnation of the *offensive à outrance*. Joffre estimated that France, on the basis of the 3-year service law of 1913, could pit 710 000 soldiers against an expected 880 000 German troops. He was certain that Germany would mount a two-pronged offensive consisting of an advance westward out of Alsace-Lorraine and a drive across Belgium toward Mézières, avoiding the Meuse River but crashing through the Ardennes forest. Joffre ignored warnings by senior commanders such as Joseph Galliéni, Charles Lanrezac, and Pierre Ruffey that the Germans would mount a large-scale crossing of the Meuse in hopes of enveloping the French left wing. The General Staff argued instead that the Germans would limit their offensive to the land south of the Meuse because an invasion north of the river would force them to divide their forces into two groups to bypass the Belgian fortresses. Joffre ordered his forces simply to charge through Lorraine into central Germany. He again dismissed a German drive through Belgium because it would encounter the combined resistance of Belgian and English forces, and thus most likely lead to stalemate on the battlefield.

In the firm belief that the war need be short and that the offensive alone guaranteed victory, Joffre divided his available forces into five armies. In May 1914 he decreed that three armies would be deployed along the borders of Alsace-Lorraine between Verdun and Epinal; that the Fifth Army would man the Franco-Belgian frontier from Montmédy to Sedan to Mézières; and that the Fourth Army, a strategic reserve ('army of manoeuvre'), would be held at St Dizier, ready either to join the French attack on Thionville or to assist the Fifth Army if the Germans came through the Ardennes.[83] For political reasons Joffre avoided assigning specific areas of concentration, much less of attack, to Belgian and British troops. As a result, Joffre left exposed the 110-mile left flank from Mézières to the English Channel.

In terms of strategy, Joffre gave his senior commanders no ultimate objective – apart from the advance through Lorraine into central Germany. He vaguely alluded to a 4-week offensive, relatively aimless, featuring major thrusts eastward but devoid of an overall concept. His primary political-strategical objective appears to have been an offensive designed to tie down German forces in the west while the 800 000 Russian troops promised by the 15th day of mobilization 'occupied Berlin'. The dazzling combination of a French breakthrough in Lorraine and a Russian advance on Berlin, Joffre argued, would create confusion leading to retreat and eventually to surrender by Imperial Germany.[84] The Battle of Tannenberg between 27 and 30 August 1914, however, would force Joffre to rely on his own forces.

Joffre's miscalculations concerning German intentions stemmed in part from abysmal military intelligence. As late as May 1914 *Deuxième Bureau* (Intelligence) still insisted that the main German assault would come against Nancy, Verdun, and St Dié, that any German operation in Belgium would stay well south of the Sambre and Meuse, and that the Germans would not deploy reserve formations equally with regular units.[85] In short, the Second Bureau prophesied the war that it wished to see, in the process fortifying Joffre's own preconceptions.

Britain's role in any future continental war remained the great unknown in French planning. While expecting Britain's entry into the war owing to 'the interest of English commerce', Joffre nevertheless refused to count on active British deployment on the Continent for lack of a written agreement to this effect. 'We will thus act prudently in not depending upon English forces in our operational projects.'[86] Joffre regarded British intervention at best as an insurance policy, especially should the war, against all expectations, not be short. In 1909, when asked by British General Sir Henry Wilson as to the 'smallest British military force' that he deemed 'of any practical assistance' to France, Joffre maliciously replied: 'One single private soldier, and we would take good care that he was killed'.[87]

Nor was Joffre's relationship with the Belgians any easier. Wary of French intentions at least since Napoleon III to seize Belgian territory and yet apprehensive that Germany planned to invade Belgium in any future war, statesmen and soldiers in Brussels had tried to walk a fine line between benevolent and armed neutrality. For years Belgium had maintained a relatively small field army of 100 000 soldiers, augmented by 80 000 fortress troops, and had rejected all French entreaties, however gentle, to enter into an alliance with Paris and London. But in 1912–13, in the wake of reliable information about the Schlieffen plan, Belgium underwrote a massive expansion of its armed forces by 1917 to 150 000 field soldiers, 130 000 fortress troops, and 60 000 reservists.[88] Yet, for political reasons, Joffre was reluctant to assign neutral Belgium a definitive role in Plan XVII.

It would not be too far off the mark to suggest that Plan XVII was primarily a political document. In a short war it left the decisive battles to the

Russians; in a prolonged war it relied on British 'insurance' against the Germans. As the historian L. L. Farrar has put it: 'Designed for military victory, it prevented political defeat'.[89] For Plan XVII, combined with German diplomatic blundering, assured France of superior numbers in 1914: 92 Anglo-Belgian-French divisions of 2.38 million soldiers against 73 German divisions of 1.8 million.[90]

Britain: continental commitment?

23 August 1911 was a fateful day in British strategic planning. At an unprecedented all-day, secret meeting of the Committee of Imperial Defence, Sir Henry Wilson, Director of Military Operations at the War Office since August 1910, expressed to Prime Minister Asquith his alarm over news that in case of war on the Continent the Royal Navy was considering nothing more than a small series of feints against Bremerhaven, Cuxhaven, the Kiel Canal, and Wilhelmshaven. Wilson, who had established intimate ties with General Foch of the French *École supérieure de guerre* while commandant of the Staff College at Camberley between 1907 and 1910, had argued long and loud that in the event of war a British Expeditionary Force (BEF) be deployed on the left wing of the French Army in the area of Le Cateau-Hirson-Maubeuge. But the Royal Navy's plans in 1911 seemed to obviate the need for sending '*l'Armée W*' to France. To buttress his case for continental commitment, Wilson, who expected the main German advance to come through the 90-mile gap between Verdun and Maubeuge, presented the Committee with three suppositions: that London mobilize on the same day as Paris; that it send all six regular divisions to France at the outbreak of war; and that it commit to maintaining a force of this size in France for the duration of the war.[91] Above all, General Wilson argued eloquently that the insertion of a mere six divisions on the left flank of the French Army could be decisive.

Reginald McKenna, the First Lord of the Admiralty, fired back that the Admiralty could supply neither the men nor the ships to transport the BEF to France. The First Sea Lord, Sir Arthur Wilson, sought to defuse General Wilson's plans with the technical argument that the Royal Navy could not simultaneously mobilize the fleet and transport the BEF to France. When this ploy was defeated under close questioning by the Home Secretary, Churchill, and the Chancellor of the Exchequer, David Lloyd George, Admiral Wilson offered his studied opinion that the Germans would not possess the ability to swing north of the Meuse into France between Lille and Maubeuge for another 10 years! Instead, the First Sea Lord reiterated the Admiralty's European strategy: a close blockade of German ports followed by small landings at the mouth of the Jade and Weser rivers, and eventually by more substantial operations against Helgoland Island and Wilhelmshaven in the North Sea, and Danzig and Swinemünde in the Baltic Sea. Wilson argued that at least two regular divisions needed to remain in Britain to guard against a German invasion.

Admiral Wilson's performance was a disaster. His call for a close blockade of Germany contradicted his own published views to the contrary, and he failed to provide any details to support either the blockade or the success of landings as far away as Danzig. Nor could he answer Churchill's query as to how German ships could transport an invading army to Britain if the Royal Navy maintained a close blockade of German ports! The Cabinet concluded that the First Sea Lord possessed no war plans worthy of the name. 'Continental intervention', in the words of the historian Samuel Williamson, Jr., 'had become the accepted dogma'.[92] Churchill replaced McKenna at the Admiralty within 2 months of the 23 August 1911 meeting; one of his first actions was to fire Admiral Wilson.

Neither the Committee of Imperial Defence nor the Cabinet was prepared to debate the details of continental commitment. Hence, when the War Council met on 5 August 1914, the day after Britain's declaration of war against Germany, there existed no plans concerning military strategy, the likely size of the BEF, or its probable destination and deployment. General Sir John French, the designated commander of the BEF, sought quick agreement on Antwerp as the landing site, but Secretary of State for Foreign Affairs Grey, passionately, if inaccurately, argued against this move as it would violate Dutch (!) neutrality. Horatio Herbert, Lord Kitchener, literally snatched off a Channel boat and appointed Secretary of State for War 48 hours earlier, suggested Amiens. After what General Wilson termed 'desultory strategy (some thinking Liège was in Holland) and idiocy',[93] the Cabinet accepted the octogenarian Field Marshal Frederick Lord Roberts' advice to let the French decide where to deploy the BEF. The continental school, having won on the basic question of commitment, easily convinced the Cabinet to dispatch a cavalry division and two infantry corps of the BEF to France.[94] The 6th Division remained at home, ostensibly to guard against a German invasion but also to guard against internal disorder.

Firm in the belief that the war would be but a short cleansing thunderstorm, the BEF crossed the Channel en route to glory and victory. It was a splendid little army, in the words of the military historian B. H. Liddell Hart, a 'rapier among scythes'.[95] But it was better prepared for an action in the veldt or east of Suez with its lances, khaki uniforms, and carbines. It did not take howitzers, hand-grenades, or wireless equipment to the

Continent. At Le Cateau it would suddenly and unexpectedly find itself in the path of two German armies heading to Paris.

Chapter 2 Notes

1. Edmund Glaise von Horstenau, 'Feldmarschall Conrad von Hötzendorf', *Soldatische Wirklichkeit* (n.p., n.d.), pp. 58, 60.
2. Peter Broucek, 'Chef des Generalstabes und Oberster Kriegsherr. Aus den Erinnerungen des Feldmarschalleutnants Alois Klepsch-Kloth von Roden, K.u.K. Delegierten im Deutschen Grossen Hauptquartier, 1915/19', *Mitteilungen des Österreichischen Staatsarchivs* 27 (1974), p. 394.
3. Kurt Peball, 'Briefe an eine Freundin. Zu den Briefen des Feldmarschalls Conrad von Hötzendorf an Frau Walburga von Sonnleithner während der Jahre 1905–1908', *Mitteilungen des Österreichischen Staatsarchivs* 25 (1972), pp. 492–3.
4. Cyril Falls, *The Great War* (New York, Putnam, 1959), p. 36.
5. See Jehuda L. Wallach, *The Dogma of the Battle of Annihilation: The Theories of Clausewitz and Schlieffen and Their Impact on the German Conduct of Two World Wars* (Westport, Conn., and London, Greenwood Press, 1986), p. 88. The charge of occultism was firmly rejected by the General's son, Adam von Moltke, after the war. BA-MA, Nachlass Moltke, N 78, vol. 37, pp. 4–5.
6. ÖStA-KA, Nachlass Schneller, B/509, vol. 2. Entry for 1 July 1915.
7. Peter Broucek, ed., *Ein General im Zwielicht. Die Erinnerungen Edmund Glaises von Hostenau* (2 vols, Vienna, Cologne, and Graz, Böhlau, 1980) 1, p. 354.
8. Conrad's marginal notes on a memorandum from Foreign Minister Aehrenthal, 15 August 1909. ÖStA-KA, Conrad Archiv, B Flügeladjutant, vol. 1.
9. Conrad to Berchtold, 28 July 1913. ÖStA-KA, Operations Büro, General Stab 91.
10. See Alfred von Wittich, 'Zur Weltanschauung Conrads von Hötzendorf', *Militärwissenschaftliche Mitteilungen LXXV* (1944), pp. 4–15; August Urbánski von Ostrymiecz, *Conrad von Hötzendorf. Soldat und Mensch* (Graz, Leipzig, and Vienna, Ulrich Mosers Verlag, 1938), pp. 355–9; and Ferdinand Käs, 'Versuch einer zusammengefassten Darstellung der Tätigkeit des österreichisch-ungarischen Generalstabes in der Zeit von 1906 bis 1914 unter besonderer Berücksichtigung der Aufmarschplanungen und Mobilmachungen', unpubl. diss., Vienna University 1962, pp. 250–1.
11. See, for example, the Kaiser's glowing evaluation of Moltke as future staff chief on 20 December 1903 in BA-MA, Nachlass Schlieffen, N 43, vol. 124. Wilhelm II had equated a change in the General Staff's top post to 'an event of world importance'.
12 ÖStA-KA, Operations Büro, General Stab, F 59. Reports of 16 November 1906 and 12 January 1904.
13. BA-MA, Nachlass Moltke, N 78, vol. 37. Comments by Moltke's son, Adam.
14. Arden Bucholz, *Moltke, Schlieffen, and Prussian War Planning* (New York and Oxford, Berg Publishers, 1991), pp. 217–19.
15. Moltke to Conrad, 10 February 1913. ÖStA-KA, Conrad Archiv, B Flügeladjutant, vol. 3.
16. See Gerhard Ritter, *The Schlieffen Plan. Critique of a Myth* (New York, Frederick A. Praeger, 1958); also L. C. F. Turner, 'The Significance of the Schlieffen Plan', *The Australian Journal of Politics and History* 13 (1967), pp. 47–66.
17. Gordon A. Craig, *The Politics of the Prussian Army 1640–1945* (Oxford, Oxford University Press, 1955), p. 281.
18. BA-MA, Nachlass Schlieffen, N 43, vol. 101. 'Der Krieg in der Gegenwart'. Schlieffen later published his views in the *Deutsche Revue* (January 1909), pp. 13–24.
19. Carl von Clausewitz, *On War,* eds Michael Howard and Peter Paret (Princeton, Princeton University Press, 1984), p. 101.

20. Reichsarchiv, *Der Weltkrieg 1914 bis 1918, Kriegsrüstung und Kriegswirtschaft* (2 vols, Berlin, E. S. Mittler & Sohn, 1930) 1, p. 327.

21. BA-MA, W-10/50220. Unpublished manuscript by Wilhelm Dieckmann, 'Der Schlieffenplan', pp. 53–7. I am indebted to Stig Förster for alerting me to this document.

22. Cited in Ludwig Rüdt von Collenberg, 'Graf Schlieffen und die Kriegsformation der deutschen Armee', *Wissen und Wehr* 10 (1927), pp. 624 ff.

23. John Keegan, *The Mask of Command* (New York, Viking, 1987), p. 248.

24. BA-MA, Nachlass Schlieffen, N 43, vol. 101. 'Der Krieg in der Gegenwart'.

25. Wallach, *Dogma of the Battle of Annihilation*, p. 58; and Gerhard Ritter, *Staatskunst und Kriegshandwerk. Das Problem des 'Militarismus' in Deutschland* (4 vols, Munich, R. Oldenbourg, 1965) 2, pp. 256–8. As late as 1912 Wilhelm II concluded from the annual manoeuvres that the main thing was to come to close grips with the enemy 'and then, drums beating and flags unfurled, on into the annals of history'. BA-MA, Nachlass Moltke, N 78, vol. 23, p. 15.

26. Hans von Seeckt, *Gedanken eines Soldaten* (Berlin, Verlag für Kulturpolitik, 1927), p. 17.

27. Wolfgang von Groote, 'Historische Vorbilder des Feldzugs 1914 im Westen', *Militärgeschichtliche Mitteilungen* 47 (1990), p. 41.

28. Eliza von Moltke, ed., *Generaloberst Helmuth von Moltke. Erinnerungen, Briefe, Dokumente 1877–1916. Bild vom Kriegsausbruch, erster Kriegsführung und Persönlichkeit des ersten militärischen Führers des Krieges* (Stuttgart, Der Kommende Tag, 1922), p. 308. Letter of 29 January 1905.

29. Reichsarchiv, *Kriegsrüstung und Kriegswirtschaft* 1, pp. 327–31.

30. See Holger H. Herwig, 'From Tirpitz Plan to Schlieffen Plan: Some Observations on German Military Planning', *Journal of Strategic Studies* 9 (1986), pp. 53–63.

31. Franz Conrad von Hötzendorf, *Aus meiner Dienstzeit 1906–1918* (5 vols, Vienna, Leipzig, and Munich, Rikola Verlag, 1923) 4, p. 259. See also Lothar Höbelt, 'Schlieffen, Beck, Potiorek und das Ende der gemeinsamen deutsch-österreichischen-ungarischen Aufmarschpläne im Osten', *Militärgeschichtliche Mitteilungen* 36 (1984), pp. 7–30.

32. This and the following discussion of Conrad's relations with Moltke is taken from ÖStA-KA, Conrad Archiv, B Flügeladjutant, vol. 3, which contains their letters and accounts of their meetings, mainly at Karlsbad, between 1909 and 1914. See also Gerhard Ritter, 'Die Zusammenarbeit der Generalstabe Deutschlands und Österreich-Ungarns vor dem ersten Weltkrieg', in *Zur Geschichte und Problematik der Demokratie: Festgabe für Hans Herzfeld* (Berlin, Duncker & Humblot, 1958), p. 538; and Holger H. Herwig, 'Disjointed Allies: Coalition Warfare in Berlin and Vienna, 1914', *The Journal of Military History* 54 (1990), pp. 265–80.

33. Dennis E. Showalter, 'The Eastern Front and German Military Planning, 1871–1914 – Some Observations', *East European Quarterly* 15 (1981), p. 174.

34. Moltke to Conrad, 10 February 1913. AA-PA, Deutschland 128 Nr. 128 Nr. 1, secr., vol. 32.

35. Conrad to Moltke, 15 February 1913. ÖStA-KA, Conrad Archiv, B Flügeladjutant, vol. 3.

36. Conrad, *Aus meiner Dienstzeit* 3 (1922), p. 670.

37. BA-MA, MSg 1/1914 Tagebuch Kageneck.

38. Cited in Gordon A. Craig, 'The World War I Alliance of the Central Powers in Retrospect: The Military Cohesion of the Alliance', *Journal of Modern History* 37 (1965), p. 338.

39. Max von Pitreich, *1914: Die militärischen Probleme unseres Kriegsbeginnes. Ideen, Gründe und Zusammenhänge* (Vienna, Selbstverlag, 1934), p. 226. See also Dieter Degreif, 'Operative Planungen des k. u. k. Generalstabes für einen Krieg in der Zeit vor 1914 (1880–1914)', unpubl. diss., Mainz University 1983.

40. Conrad von Hötzendorf, *Aus meiner Dienstzeit* 1 (1921), pp. 361 ff.; and Bundesministerium für Landesverteidigung, *Österreich-Ungarns Letzter Krieg 1914–1918. 1: Das Kriegsjahr 1914* (Vienna, Verlag der Militärwissenschaftlichen Mitteilungen, 1931), p. 17.

41. Conrad reiterated his determination to destroy Serbia to Foreign Minister Berchtold at the height of the July crisis on 22 June 1914. ÖStA-KA, Operations Büro, General Stab, Fasz. 44.
42. ÖStA-KA, Operations Büro, General Stab, Fasz. 26, 'R-Alarm, Kriegsfall R 1912/13'. General Karl Christophori's memorandum on railway mobilization.
43. Josef Stürgkh, *Im Deutschen Grossen Hauptquartier* (Leipzig, Paul List Verlag, 1921), p. 100. Comment by the Hungarian Prime Minister, István Tisza, late in 1914.
44. Gunther E. Rothenberg, *The Army of Francis Joseph* (West Lafayette, Ind., Purdue University Press, 1976), p. 178.
45. Conrad-Moltke letters of February 1914. ÖStA-KA, Operations Büro, General Stab, Fasz. 89a.
46. Norman Stone, 'Die Mobilmachung der österreichisch-ungarischen Armee 1914', *Militärgeschichtliche Mitteilungen* 16 (1974), pp. 75–6.
47. Stone, 'Mobilmachung', p. 78.
48. BA-MA, MSg 1/1914 Tagebuch Kageneck.
49. ÖStA-KA, Armeeoberkommando, Operationsbüro, vol. 1, Op. Nr. 35.
50. ÖStA-KA, Nachlass Dankl, B/3, vol. 5/1, entry of 31 July 1914. Two days later, Dankl penned: 'The world war is at hand!'
51. ÖStA-KA, Verbindungsoffiziere, Oberost, Fasz. 6180. Reports of Captain Moritz Fleischmann von Theissruck and Colonel Karl von Bienerth from Berlin. See also Conrad von Hötzendorf, *Aus meiner Dienstzeit* 4, p. 275.
52. *Österreich-Ungarns Letzter Krieg 1914–1918* 1, pp. 22–3.
53. Ratzenhofer's critical role in the mobilization process – and his later denials of it – have been analysed by Graydon A. Tunstall, Jr., *Planning for War Against Russia and Serbia: Austro-Hungarian and German Military Strategies, 1871–1914* (New York, Columbia University Press, 1993), pp. 159–210.
54. Stone 'Mobilmachung', pp. 79, 82.
55. Stone, 'Mobilmachung', p. 83; Tunstall, *Planning for War*, p. 186.
56. ÖStA-KA, Neue Feldakten (NFA), 3. Operierendes Armeekommando, vol. 42. Tagebuch 1, pp. 6–8.
57. BA-MA, MSg 1/1914 Tagebuch Kageneck.
58. Winston S. Churchill, *The Unknown War: The Eastern Front* (New York, Charles Scribner's Sons, 1931), p. 132.
59. Stone, 'Mobilmachung', p. 91.
60. German mobilization has been brilliantly analysed by Bucholz, *Moltke, Schlieffen and Prussian War Planning*, pp. 300–2.
61. Hugo Rochs, *Schlieffen: Ein Lebens- und Charakterbild für das deutsche Volk* (Berlin, Voss, 1921), p. 90. The motto apparently came from Johann Wolfgang von Goethe, who had taken it from Tycho de Brahe.
62. Stephen Kern, *The Culture of Time and Space, 1880–1918* (Cambridge, Mass., Harvard University Press, 1983), pp. 270–3.
63. Moltke to Plessen, 2 May 1915. BA-MA, Nachlass Moltke, N 78, vol. 6, pp. 12–15.
64. BA-MA, W-10/50635 Tagebuch v. Falkenhayn, dated 1 August 1914.
65. BA-MA, Nachlass Moltke, N 78, vol. 37, p. 18.
66. Moltke, ed., *Generaloberst von Moltke*, p. 382. 29 August 1914.
67. Cited in Militärgeschichtliches Forschungsamt, *Handbuch zur deutschen Militärgeschichte 1648–1939* (5 vols, Munich, Bernard & Graefe, 1979) 3, p. 159.
68. See the comments of General von Bock in Bernd F. Schulte, *Die deutsche Armee 1900–1914. Zwischen Beharren und Verändern* (Düsseldorf, Droste Verlag, 1977), p. 217.
69. *Handbuch zur deutschen Militärgeschichte*, 3, pp. 160, 166, 172, 174, 177-8. See also Dennis E. Showalter, *Tannenberg: Clash of Empires* (Hamden, Conn., Archon Books, 1992), pp. 117–21, 148–9.

70. BA-MA, PH 5 II/119 General Staff, First Army Retrospect; see also Ritter, *Schlieffen Plan*, p. 166.
71. BA-MA, PH 5 II/119 General Staff, First Army Retrospect.
72. Reichsarchiv, *Der Weltkrieg 1914 bis 1918*, 1: *Die Grenzschlachten im Westen* (Berlin, E. S. Mittler & Sohn, 1925), pp. 22–3.
73. Reichsarchiv, *Der Weltkrieg 1914 bis 1918*, 1, p. 37.
74. Bruce W. Menning, *Bayonets before Bullets: The Imperial Russian Army, 1861–1914* (Bloomington, Ind., Indiana University Press, 1992), p. 242.
75. Menning, *Bayonets before Bullets*, pp. 242–3. See also William C. Fuller, Jr., *Strategy and Power in Russia 1600–1914* (New York, Free Press, 1992).
76. Norman Stone, *The Eastern Front 1914–1917* (New York, Charles Scribner's Sons, 1975), pp. 54–5.
77. Menning, *Bayonets before Bullets*, pp. 255–65.
78. Conrad von Hötzendorf, upon discovering Redl's treason, quickly altered Habsburg mobilization plans; he informed Foreign Minister Berchtold on 31 May 1913 that the Dual Monarchy's military situation had been secured. ÖStA-KA, Conrad Archiv, B Flügeladjutant, vol. 3. An internal review by the Army's judicial branch – sealed in the archives until recently – suggests instead that the Redl affair had caused considerable damage.
79. In the fall of 1894 Captain Alfred Dreyfus, an Alsatian Jew serving with the Infantry of Paris, was arrested, charged with, and wrongly convicted of treason. For 12 years, the France of '1789' battled with the Army and the church over the case, which reached new lows in hatred and anti-Semitism.
80. Cited in Douglas Porch, *The March to the Marne: The French Army 1871–1914* (Cambridge, Cambridge University Press, 1981), p. 227.
81. Wolfgang Michalka, ed., *Der Erste Weltkrieg. Wirkung, Wahrnehmung, Analyse* (Munich and Zurich, Piper, 1994), p. 258.
82. Memorandum by Hans Adolf von Bülow, First Secretary at the Brussels legation, 30 December 1914. Norman Rich and M. H. Fisher, eds, *The Holstein Papers* (4 vols, Cambridge, Cambridge University Press, 1963) 4, pp. 358–9.
83. S. R. Williamson, 'Joffre Reshapes French Strategy', in Paul M. Kennedy, ed., *The War Plans of the Great Powers, 1880–1914* (London, George Allen & Unwin, 1979), p. 148.
84. See L. L. Farrar, Jr., 'The Short-War Illusion: The Syndrome of German Strategy, August–December, 1914', *Militärgeschichtliche Mitteilungen* 12 (1972), p. 45; and von Groote, 'Historische Vorbilder des Feldzugs 1914 im Westen', p. 47.
85. Williamson, 'Joffre Reshapes French Strategy', p. 145; Porch, *March to the Marne*, p. 231.
86. Cited in Williamson, 'Joffre Reshapes French Strategy', p. 146.
87. Cited in C. E. Callwell, *Field Marshal Sir Henry Wilson: His Life and Diaries* (2 vols, London, Cassell & Co., 1927) 1, pp. 78–9.
88. BA-MA, PH 2/99 Kriegsministerium. Denkschrift über Belgien.
89. Farrar, 'The Short-War Illusion', p. 45.
90. *Der Weltkrieg 1914 bis 1918* 1, p. 22.
91. John Gooch, *The Plans of War: The General Staff and British Military Strategy c. 1900–1916* (New York, Wiley, 1974), pp. 290–1.
92. Samuel R. Williamson, Jr., *The Politics of Grand Strategy: Britain and France Prepare for War, 1904-1914* (Cambridge, Mass., Harvard University Press, 1969), p. 307.
93. Cited in Callwell, *Sir Henry Wilson* 1, p. 158.
94. See Williamson, *The Politics of Grand Strategy*, pp. 364–6.
95. Basil Liddell Hart, *The Real War 1914–1918* (Boston, Little, Brown, 1930), p. 42.

3

The Great Gamble, 1914

If war was once a chivalrous duel, it is now a dastardly slaughter.

General Arthur von Bolfras, September 1914

Europe was on the move by early August 1914. The Military Telegraph Section of the German General Staff mobilized 3 822 450 men and 119 754 officers as well as 600 000 horses. This gigantic force transported to the front in 312 hours by 11 000 trains. More than 2150 54-car trains crossed the Rhine River over the Hohenzollern Bridge at Cologne in 10-minute intervals between 2 and 18 August.[1] The west army, consisting of 1.6 million men organized into 23 active and 11 reserve corps (or 950 infantry battalions and 498 cavalry squadrons), thundered across the various Rhine bridges at a rate of 560 trains per day, travelling at the then unheard-of speed of almost 20 miles per hour. In the east General von Prittwitz used the sparse railroad network of East Prussia to gather his Eighth Army, comprised of nine active and reserve infantry divisions, or 158 battalions, by 22 August to await the approach of advance Russian forces. The English-born Evelyn Princess Blücher, no admirer of Prussia, was deeply impressed by the 'overpowering' mobilization. The Germans, she noted in her diary, 'take to war as a duck takes to water'.[2]

The Prussian General Staff was transformed into the Great General Staff at the onset of hostilities and its powers were extended over the royal armies of Bavaria, Saxony, and Württemberg. Hugo Baron von Freytag-Loringhoven was dispatched to Austrian headquarters as the Kaiser's special military plenipotentiary. At home, the General Staff formally exercised command and control through a newly-created Supreme Army Command (*Oberste Heeresleitung*, or *OHL*). Under the Prussian Law of Siege of 4 June 1851, the 24 Deputy Commanding Generals of the German Army Corps Regions as well as governors of military fortresses organized recruitment, labour distribution, and food supply; controlled the dissemination of news and information; and ensured domestic order. How many of the 16 million letters, cards, packages, and newspapers sent to the front every day – 28.7 billion pieces including 50 000 varieties of 'war postcards' by 1918 – they actually read and censored remains an open question.

'This war is great and wonderful'

Prewar fears concerning the 'unpatriotic' Social Democrats proved unfounded. Wilhelm II stood alone in his desire to arrest their leaders; the government on 24 July rejected such action. On 3 August Berlin cleverly produced a so-called *White Book* to show that the 'ring of Entente politics' had in recent years 'encircled us ever more tightly'. Few knew that half of its 30 documents were blatant forgeries. That same day the SPD's party caucus, which had assured the government of its support already at the end of July, voted 78 to 14 in favour of granting war credits. Still, just to be on the safe side, the party sent its treasury to Switzerland. On 4 August the SPD closed ranks and unanimously voted for war credits of 5 billion Marks. Its military expert, Gustav Noske, admitted that he feared being 'trampled to death' at the Brandenburg Gate in case of a negative vote. The Baden Social Democrat Ludwig Frank, a Jew, volunteered for service at the front and on 3 September at Lunéville became the first deputy to die in the war. SPD trade unions informed the government that they would not strike during the war.

Most SPD leaders supported the war in the hope that their 4 million voters could thereby escape the isolation of the past and be integrated into the national state. The Prussian police appreciated the SPD's positive stance. Traugott von Jagow, Police President of Greater Berlin, informed his government that workers even in the predominantly working-class and 'least patriotic' districts in the north and east of the capital displayed countless black-white-red flags. 'Social Democracy is no longer capable of action', Jagow cheerily reported, 'since almost half of its functionaries have been called to the colours and those left behind display little interest'.[3] The only sour note on 4 August came from the middle class, where many withdrew their savings from banks, bought up and hoarded food, and refused to accept paper money.

But few in Germany worried about money in 1914, secure in the knowledge that the Julius Tower of the Spandau Citadel in Berlin literally bulged with gold. In truth, the old fortress housed 1200 iron-banded wooden crates holding about 205 million Goldmarks – the last of the French reparations payments after 1871.[4] No one cared to calculate that this would run a modern, industrial war of millions of men for about 2 days.

Wilhelm II headed for the 'front' on 16 August. The war started with a scare: an 18-year-old Berlin youth accosted His Majesty at the Potsdam railroad station, shouting 'Doesn't anyone have a revolver?'[5] The Kaiser assumed supreme command over all land forces under Article 63 of the Constitution. Like his grandfather Wilhelm I in 1866 and 1870, he remained for the duration of the war at army headquarters, established on 17 August in Castle Koblenz at the confluence of the Mosel and Rhine rivers, far removed from the din and confusion of battle.

At Koblenz Wilhelm II played at war, content to let others conduct the campaigns that would decide the fate of his dynasty. Dining on the silver field service of Frederick the Great, he regaled his dinner guests with gruesome tales of battle – 'Piles of corpses 6 ft. high . . . a sergeant killed 27 Frenchmen with 45 bullets' – and demanded that his troops 'take no prisoners'.[6] But Wilhelm II, who became Supreme War Lord with the onset of hostilities, from the start remained a peripheral figure. The following story, recorded by Admiral Georg Alexander von Müller, Chief of the Naval Cabinet, perhaps best epitomizes the Kaiser's position. During one of his frequent walks in the local parks with Admiral von Müller and General Moriz von Lyncker, Chief of the Military Cabinet, Wilhelm II rested on a bench. His two military paladins, not wishing to disturb the Emperor and aware that the short bench might not hold three middle-aged flag officers, pulled up another bench. 'Am I already such a figure of contempt', Wilhelm II churlishly inquired, 'that no one wants to sit next to me?'[7] The Kaiser gave up hunting to show that he too was prepared to make sacrifices. The pressure of the war took its toll even before the first major engagements were fought: on 20 August General Walter von Esebeck, the Prussian Royal Master of Horse, shot himself in a fit of depression at Koblenz.

In Austria–Hungary, Conrad von Hötzendorf became the virtual ruler of the Austrian half of the Dual Monarchy. Parliament (Reichsrat) was suspended but not closed – this would have necessitated new national elections – and in the process deputies lost their parliamentary immunity and came under military law. Command and control over large parts of Cisleithania and its war industries were bestowed on a Supreme Army Command (*Armee-Oberkommando*, or *AOK*), which activated the Empire's 16 military districts and 112 reserve districts, and raised the number of troops from a peacetime strength of 415 000 to 3 350 000 (of whom 1 270 000 were rear-echelon support forces).

Two Imperial Emergency Decrees on 25 and 31 July 1914, based on an ancient law of May 1869, suspended basic civil rights such as freedom of speech, assembly, and the press, and granted sweeping powers to a new War Supervisory Office (*Kriegsüberwachungsamt*) within the War Ministry to substitute military for civil law. On 24 August Conrad introduced special courts-martial – and thus suspended the right of appeal – in the military districts of Cracow, Przemyśl, Lemberg, and Dalmatia; and on 14 November Conrad abolished the erstwhile stipulation that trials were to be delayed as much as 48 hours to allow corps commanders time to arrive at court, thus permitting instant, on the spot courts-martial presided over by subaltern officers. The *AOK* insisted that in all cases of desertion the courts were to consider only the death sentence, that the new regulations were also to apply to civilians, and that there existed no need to inform the government in Vienna of such proceedings.[8] These emergency measures remained in effect in Austria until July 1917; Hungary, always suspicious of Conrad, refused to enact them. In time the Supreme Command's control over occupied territories as well as over imperial jurisprudence became so pervasive that Arthur von Bolfras, Franz Joseph's septuagenarian head of the Royal and Imperial Military Chancery, bitterly complained: 'We are being ruled by the *AOK*'.[9]

Since Kaiser Franz Joseph was too old and frail and Archduke Karl too young and inexperienced to lead the armies, Archduke Friedrich was appointed Commander-in-Chief in the east on 31 July 1914. Franz Joseph undertook this step mainly out of dynastic considerations, but also with an eye toward history: Friedrich was the nephew of Archduke Albrecht, victor of the Battle of Custozza in 1866, and the grandson of Archduke Karl, victor of the Battle of Aspern in 1809. But Friedrich possessed few of the requisite attributes for command, apart from being a member of the imperial and royal family and immensely wealthy. The Archduke was reticent to the point of being timid, shied away from personal initiative, and frequently consulted his wife, Isabella, concerning which uniform to wear.[10] He left the day-to-day operation of the war to Conrad and his Chief of Operations, Colonel Josef Metzger. Conrad appointed General Josef Stürgkh, brother of the Austrian prime minister, as his representative to German headquarters. In Hungary Premier Tisza stubbornly kept the Magyar representative government in session as a check on Austrian wartime measures. This shrewd decision also gave his demands and remonstrances official character and weight.

Austrian infantry divisions were made up of two brigades, each of 7300 men; a brigade consisted of two regiments each of three battalions, each of 1100 men. War fever ran so high in 1914 that recruitment depots quickly ran short of uniforms, rifles, and ammunition. Young men rallied to the colours out of patriotism, for love of adventure, to search for a purpose in life, to fulfil their ideal of masculinity, and to find personal regeneration. A large number of foreigners – Russian Jews, Greeks, Germans, Swiss, Italians, Spaniards, and Montenegrins – volunteered for the Imperial and Royal Army.[11] Vienna University boasted 148 volunteers. Desertions were few: the Ministry of the Interior reported only nine cases in the Crown lands of Bohemia, 124 in the South Tyrol, 133 in the coastal areas of the Adriatic Sea (where the ethnic Italian elements dominated), and 600 to 700 in Croatia and Slovenia.[12]

Conrad initially considered establishing his headquarters at Peterwardein on the Danube, from where he wished to conduct the war against Serbia, but then opted for Przemyśl in Galicia and later for Teschen in Austrian Silesia. There, in the words of the historian Gunther Rothenberg, Conrad and his staff 'were totally out of contact with the troops, living in luxury with uniformed lackeys, candlelit dinners, and frequent female company'.[13]

But Conrad was not alone in enjoying the perquisites of command. When Anglo-French leaders met to discuss joint strategies, they chose their sites well. In December 1915, for example, Allied generals convened at Chantilly, the Renaissance palace of the Montmorencys and the Condés. The château's English garden, replete with a Temple of Venus and Island of Love, shielded the generals' minds from the mud and blood of Flanders. Crystal, parquet floors, and jewel collections served as a resplendent backdrop for sumptuous meals prepared by Paris's finest chefs, washed down with the best vintage that Beaune, Pommard, and Reims had to offer. And when the Allies finally agreed to establish a joint military headquarters, they opted for Versailles, the epitome of decadent splendour and conspicuous consumption, home of the 'sun king' Louis XIV.

But few complained. After all, the fate of empires and peoples rested in the hands of the military. Especially in France, the war gave the generals their first real chance in decades to vent their feelings against 'the Whore', the Republic. The state of siege decreed on 2 August granted the military sweeping powers to appoint judges and subprefects, to control the press and the telephone system, and to circumvent parliamentary deputies and administrative prefects under the cover of 'military secrecy'. President Poincaré, for example, was not told the outcome of the first battles in Lorraine and at Charleroi, was denied knowledge of the staggering early losses, and was refused permission to tour the front near Alsace. Premier Viviani learned from a flower seller that the French High Command was going to leave Chantilly in the face of the German advance into France. General Hubert Lyautey voiced the feelings of many of his peers when he crowed that the country was 'getting better because the politicians have shut up'.[14] Perhaps civilians tolerated this usurpation of power secure in the knowledge that the war would be over by Christmas, whereafter the generals would again recede from view.

The war, many soldiers and statesmen hoped, would plaster over past military–civilian rifts and create at least an aura of domestic harmony and unity. Russia declared a 'civil truce' in domestic politics. Austria–Hungary suspended ethnic quarrels for the duration of the struggle. In Britain, Andrew Bonar Law's Unionists concluded a pact of common unity of purpose and solidarity with Prime Minister Asquith's ruling Liberals. France triumphantly declared a *union sacrée* to exist, while Germany countered by proclaiming a domestic peace (*Burgfriede*).

Nor were these official pronouncements entirely devoid of truth. Middle-class men of all persuasions and beliefs, long tired of peace, rallied to the defence of their nations. The avowed antimilitarist Gustave Hervé proclaimed France, 'the fatherland of revolution', to be 'in danger'. His countryman, Henri Bergson, creator of the notion of the French *élan vitale*, agreed with the paper *La Croix* that the 'History of France is the Story of God'. Alphonse Aulard and Albert Mathiez, socialist historians, saw 1914 as a rebirth of the 'spirit of 1789' and demanded anew that France's borders be extended to the Rhine. Across the river, the economist Werner Sombart in February 1915 crowed that this war was between 'the merchants', the British, and 'the heroes', the Germans. His colleague Emil Lederer believed that war would transform Germany from a *Gesellschaft* into a *Gemeinschaft*. The sociologist Max Weber trumpeted the mood of the moment: '*Regardless* of the outcome – this war is great and wonderful'.[15] Under the sobriquet 'ideas of 1914', German academicians developed a vague definition of a specific German culture centred on the authoritarian, bureaucratic, social welfare state, one that stood in opposition to the egalitarian, nationalist, French state of 1789. European socialists such as Gustav Noske in Germany, G. V. Plekhanov in Russia, Albert Thomas in France, and Arthur Henderson in Britain rallied to the war cause, each depicting the struggle purely as one of defence of the homeland.

In Britain, the patriotic spirit of 1914 changed the nomenclature of the aristocracy. The House of Hanover-Saxe-Coburg became the House of Windsor; the Tecks of Württemberg became the marquesses of Cambridge; and the Battenbergs became the Mountbattens. German shops in London were looted, German residents shipped off to the Isle of Man. 'German' shepherd dogs became 'Alsatians', and dachshunds were actually stoned on British streets. The public clamoured for a ban on performing the works of 'Huns' such as Brahms, Händel, Mendelssohn, Strauss, and Wagner. In time, Europe created a new 'royalty' of the sword: Hindenburg, 'the saviour of the fatherland'; Joffre, the 'imperturbable' one; and Kitchener, the 'organizer of victory'.[16] The stage was set for the all-decisive Armageddon in northern France or Galicia.

Tannenberg: reality and myth

East Prussia was a maze of irregular hills covered with wild brush and trees. The low terrain alternated between barren stretches of sandy soil and swampy regions of bogs, lakes, and forests. There were few decent roads and even fewer good railway lines. In its centre lay the 50-mile barrier of the Masurian Lakes, stretching from Angerburg to Johannesburg along the Russian border. General von Prittwitz had been ordered to defend this historic Prussian land with the Eighth Army – and with the admonition not to risk destruction in the open field or besiegement in the fortress of Königsberg, as had befallen French Marshal Achille François Bazaine at Metz in 1870. Prittwitz was given great latitude in developing his operations plans. He opted to send the bulk of his forces – six divisions of infantry and one of cavalry – against the northern Russian First Army commanded by General Rennenkampf; and he detached only two divisions to defend against the southern Second Army under General Samsonov. On 14 August Moltke ordered Prittwitz not to languish on the defensive, but to be 'offensive, offensive, offensive'.[17] If worse came to worst, Prittwitz was to withdraw behind the Vistula River and await reinforcements from the west. General Hermann von François, a difficult but energetic subordinate, pressed Prittwitz to conduct a series of limited sorties into Russian territory designed to disrupt and slow down the Russian 'steamroller'.

Prittwitz waited. On 14 August he received the first reports of Russian cavalry scouting ahead of General Zhilinsky's main forces. The countryside immediately was swept by a wave of reports of Cossack hordes burning houses, plundering farms, and raping women. Prittwitz ordered nine divisions to attack the Russian First Army. Three days later, at Stallupönen, the German 1st Division reported that it was being attacked along its entire front. Clausewitz's 'fog of war' quickly set in. Dust obscured accurate observation. Ammunition ran low. The chain of command broke as units rushed to the sound of the guns. Battalions plugged gaps in the line in helter-skelter fashion. Stretcher-bearers carried back the first grisly victims of high explosive and shrapnel shells. Field kitchens and ammunition carts bogged down in the sand. Panic ensued among the civilian population, who gathered whatever possessions they could carry and drove their prized livestock west, choking the few good roads. Many of the 800 000 refugees were direct descendants of the

20 000 Salzburg Protestants who 180 years earlier had found a safe religious haven in East Prussia.

Dazed, Prittwitz ordered François' I Corps, which had actually inflicted 3000 casualties on the Russian First Army's centre, to fall back on Gumbinnen. Obviously, the eastern campaign was not progressing according to Schlieffen's notes. Russian mobilization had taken place much quicker than the Germans had expected, and the Russian Second Army was advancing much more rapidly and further west than predicted. On 20 August General August von Mackensen's XVII Corps delivered a frontal attack at Gumbinnen and was badly mauled: 8000 men, one-third of the Corps, were lost and a shocked Mackensen sounded a general retreat. Prittwitz concurred and later that day broke off the action and ordered the Eighth Army to fall back 140 miles to the Vistula River. The Eighth Army had suffered 14 607 casualties in and around Gumbinnen.[18] Prittwitz's chief of staff, Waldersee, endorsed his superior's decision to retreat behind the Vistula to save the Eighth Army from defeat and possible annihilation. Moltke called Prittwitz on the night of 21 August and, receiving no reassurances concerning the situation in East Prussia, sacked the Eighth Army's commander – the first time in modern German military history that an army commander had been relieved of command in this manner.[19]

Moltke, high-strung at the best of times, must have been in a state of great anxiety on 21 August. That very day Conrad had cabled a request for an immediate German offensive in the east to relieve Russian pressure on his forces in Galicia. In the west, the French Fourth and Fifth armies were mounting a concerted offensive deep into the Ardennes. Moltke confessed to his staff that the strains of conducting two major wars in the east and the west were taking their toll. Reality contradicted Schlieffen's orderly notes: 'Ordre – contre-ordre – désordre'.[20] Moltke hardly needed Prittwitz's bleak news from East Prussia. Within 24 hours, he ordered General Erich Ludendorff, who had received the coveted *Pour le mérite* for storming the Belgian fortress of Liège on 7–8 August, to Koblenz and instructed the Kaiser to appoint Ludendorff chief of staff of the Eighth Army.

On 23 August Ludendorff's special train, en route to Marienburg, halted long enough at Hanover to pick up General Paul von Hindenburg, the new commander of the Eighth Army. Both men quickly reached agreement that German units were to remain east of the Vistula River. Unbeknownst to them, Lieutenant-Colonel Max Hoffmann, Prittwitz's first staff officer, had already given orders for German forces to halt their retreat before Rennenkampf's First Army and to concentrate against Samsonov's Second Army.[21] On 24 August Hindenburg and Ludendorff approved Hoffmann's dispositions.

The most renowned military partnership in German history thus was forged on a train bound for East Prussia. Hindenburg, born at Posen in 1847 the son of an army officer whose family had once possessed estates in East Prussia, had entered the cadet corps at age 12. Hindenburg saw action at Königgrätz in 1866 and in the war against France in 1870–1. Thereafter, he rose through the ranks, alternating studies at the War Academy and General Staff with field service at Oldenburg, Koblenz, and Karlsruhe, before commanding the IV Army Corps at Magdeburg from 1903 to 1911. Twice Hindenburg had been considered for high command – as Chief of the General Staff and as Prussian War Minister – and twice he had been disappointed.[22] In January 1911 Hindenburg retired to Hanover, seeing little prospect for war in the near future. Tall and thick-set, with brush-cut hair, beetling brows, and massive muttonchops, Hindenburg seemed the incarnation of imperturbable calm; a man of solid, simple strength, sure and steady.

Ludendorff was a study in contrast. Born in 1865 at Krusczewina in eastern Posen to a family of middle-class merchants, Ludendorff had entered the Prussian Army in 1883, and 12 years later had joined the General Staff as a captain. After a series of field commands, Ludendorff rejoined the General Staff; in 1912 as head of its Mobilization and Deployment Section under Moltke's tutelage he worked out plans for a 300 000-man increase in the Prussian Army. When the War Ministry refused to condone such drastic expansion, Ludendorff was shunted off to infantry commands at Düsseldorf and Strassburg. His stocky figure with its close-shaven head and monocle in time became a national symbol. A man of enormous energy and powers of concentration, Ludendorff was a narrow technical specialist with a limited horizon. He possessed the mental arrogance of the self-made man.[23]

The triumvirate of Hindenburg, Ludendorff, and Hoffmann, aware that they were outnumbered 485 000 to 173 000 in East Prussia, quickly agreed that their only chance lay in a bold gamble. Given that the phlegmatic Rennenkampf had not exploited his victory at Gumbinnen but that Samsonov in the south had pushed as far west as Ortelsburg, the German leaders decided to concentrate all available forces against Samsonov below the Masurian Lakes and to leave only a cavalry division between Rennenkampf and the Vistula. There was no talk of a new Cannae, only of a chance to hit the Russian Second Army in the flanks. Yet Ludendorff was sufficiently confident of his position to inform Moltke on the night of 26 August that he did not need the three corps and a division of cavalry that Moltke was sending to East Prussia. In quick order, the German XX Corps took up position north of Neidenburg; the I Corps detrained south of Deutsch Eylau; the 3rd Reserve Division deployed from Allenstein on the right of XX Corps; and reserve forces from the Vistula garrison moved east to join the concentration south of Allenstein.

Samsonov's forces by the morning of 26 August were advancing north-west along a 60-mile front on the line Allenstein–Hohenstein. For 7 days his troops had marched over hot, dusty roads without sighting the enemy. The roads were execrable and much of Second Army's transport was left behind. Reconnaissance by horse was poor and by air non-existent. Military intelligence was uncertain at the best of times and that day almost unavailable. Lacking professional coding staff, the Russians used 'clear' wireless traffic. As far as Samsonov knew, the German units flying before Rennenkampf were on their way back to the Vistula fortresses. General Zhilinsky, buoyed by news of Rennenkampf's victory at Gumbinnen and Prittwitz's subsequent retreat, pushed Samsonov hard to attack the Germans. 'Let General Samsonov show a little more courage, and everything will be all right.'[24] Samsonov dutifully drove his weary troops forward.

At dawn on 27 August François' I Corps unleashed a hurricane artillery bombardment against Samsonov's left wing (I Corps) on either side of Usdau. General L. K. Artamonov's forces broke and ran, thereby exposing their own centre. François immediately recognized the main chance and pressed his advantage by a forced march to Neidenburg in the hope of thereby cutting off any Russian retreat. The Russian right wing, near Rothfliess, had faced its trial by fire on 26 August, when the German XVII Corps and I Reserve Corps, after a forced march from Rennenkampf's front due south, attacked and completely surprised the Russian VI Corps. The latter lost 5300 officers and men as well as its confidence. General A. A. Blagoveshchensky lost his nerve and for eight hours failed to inform the Second Army of his defeat; in the meantime the VI Corps retreated almost 20 miles without being pursued. Samsonov's centre (XIII and XV Corps and half of XXIII Corps) was now threatened with a double envelopment from the north and the south.

Ludendorff decided on the morning of 27 August that his own centre had retired enough and ordered General Friedrich von Scholtz's reinforced XX Corps to attack. Scholtz's men advanced through a heavy early-morning fog. Hindenburg moved his headquarters closer to the front at Frögenau in anticipation of victory. He was not disappointed. On 28 August Samsonov mounted an attack against the Germans with his centre but it quickly ground to a halt. Thereafter, German forces charged both Russian flanks. The Russian XV Corps broke after fierce fighting and by the evening of 28 August the Russians decided that their only hope lay in retreat. Instead, a rout ensued. The soldiers of the XIII and XV Corps, exhausted and demoralized, wandered aimlessly through the dense forest

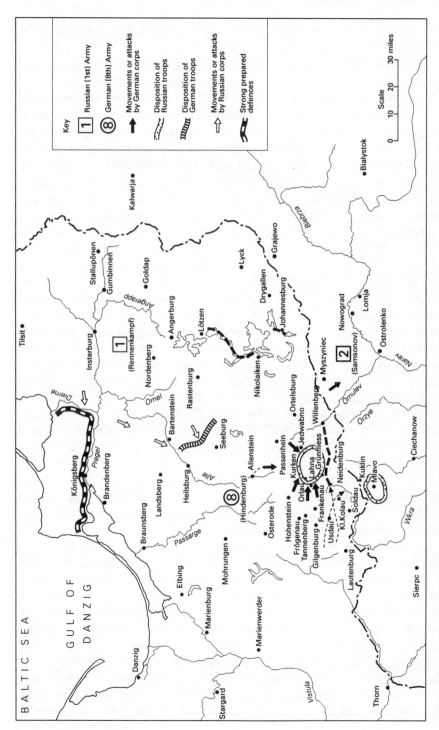

Map 2. The Battle of Tannenberg, 1914

at Grünfliess. Attempts to break out south of Muschaken and north at Kaltenborn were repulsed. Only 2000 Russian soldiers escaped the German ring. The greater part of the XII and XV Corps surrendered on 30 and 31 August.

Samsonov learned of the fate of his left and right wings at Neidenburg on 27 August. Barely had he digested that news, than the first streams of stragglers from the Russian centre appeared at headquarters. A veteran cavalry officer who preferred to lead 'from the saddle', Samsonov left Neidenburg on the morning of 28 August to take personal command of VI Corps. He never found it. In the confusion of the Russian rout, Samsonov and his staff became lost in deep forests. The commander of the Second Army was last seen heading off into the darkness alone; his staff heard a single shot but found no body. Samsonov had committed suicide at Pivnitz, near Willenberg, where the Germans later found his body.

The German official history lists 92 000 Russian prisoners taken (more than the tally of French after Sedan in 1870), 50 000 dead and wounded, and 500 guns captured or destroyed. It put its own losses at between 10 000 and 15 000 men.[25] Dead Russians bloated in the hot August sun. Roads were littered with destroyed or abandoned wagons, carts, and guns. Thousands of Russian stragglers had to be combed out of the forests. Sixty trainloads of captured material left Puchallowen for Germany and herds of Cossack mounts were gathered at Neidenburg. The Eighth Army ignored the Kaiser's startling suggestion 'that 90 000 Russian prisoners of war' be driven on to a barren peninsula at Courland along the Baltic shore and 'starved to death'.[26] Two Russian army corps had been annihilated and two others badly mauled. The Second Army ceased to be a fighting force.

At 5:30 p.m. on 28 August Ludendorff began to draft his report of the battle, giving the village of Frögenau as its site. Hoffmann suggested that Ludendorff instead use another nearby village, Tannenberg, where a Polish-Lithuanian force had defeated the Teutonic Knights on 15 July 1410, thereby ending Germanic eastward expansion. Ludendorff readily concurred. Wilhelm II, on hearing of the victory on 29 August, opted for the name Allenstein, but later also fell into line with Hoffmann's suggestion.

There remained Rennenkampf. Hindenburg and Ludendorff shifted headquarters north to Osterode and on 31 August ordered the exhausted soldiers of Eighth Army to march northeast against the Russian First Army. Reinforced by two army corps from the west, Eighth Army by 5 September deployed along the line Ortelsburg–Bischofsburg–Heilsburg. Two days later, its advance screen found Rennenkampf. Hindenburg and Ludendorff moved close to the front at Rössel, anticipating another encirclement operation. On 9 September François' I Corps was ordered to undertake a flanking movement in the direction of Goldap, designed to drive in the Russian left and thereby to threaten the enemy rear. Concurrently, Mackensen's corps was to mount a frontal attack from the south around Lötzen.

By 10 September another Tannenberg seemed in the offing as 5000 Russian prisoners and 60 guns were taken. But Rennenkampf had no desire to share Samsonov's fate. Instead, he held the Germans at bay with a series of desperate counterattacks on 11 September – and then ordered a general retreat. 'Withdrawing as far as twenty-five miles a day, the Russians literally ran faster than the Germans could chase them.'[27] On 13 September Rennenkampf was back over the Russian border. The First Army had lost as many as 100 000 men (70 000 dead and wounded and 30 000 prisoners) as well as 150 guns.[28] General Zhilinsky was relieved of command of the northwest front late in September.

The reality of Tannenberg quickly became the myth of Tannenberg. Hindenburg, awarded the *Pour le mérite*, became the war's first hero. His picture adorned newspapers and walls throughout Germany. Barber shops copied his muttonchops. War loans were enhanced by allowing subscribers to drive nails into his wooden statue in Berlin. The Imperial Navy christened a battle-cruiser and Silesia renamed the industrial city of Zabrze in honour of the victor of Tannenberg. The German official history of the war asserts that Tannenberg was the 'greatest battle of encirclement in world history' after Leipzig (1813), Metz and Sedan (1870). Even Cannae paled in comparison.[29] The architects Johannes and Walter Krüger erected a gigantic stone monument at Tannenberg in memory of the 'saviour of the fatherland'. Eight large towers were linked by a heavy wall; there was room for 10 000 'worshippers' inside the 'sacred' circle. In 1945 German engineers destroyed the monument.

Conrad's war

The battles of Tannenberg and the Masurian Lakes, while freeing East Prussia of Russian forces and soothing the nervous national psyche, were peripheral to the outcome of the war. In the west Moltke's armies continued their relentless revolving-door drive to the Channel and eventually around Paris and on to Lorraine; in the east the brunt of fighting the numerically superior Russians remained with Conrad von Hötzendorf. Before taking command of Habsburg forces in Galicia, Conrad on 7 August had appointed General Potiorek supreme commander, Balkan forces, with instructions to secure the Dual Monarchy's southern flank.

Like Conrad, Potiorek was ranked a 'genius' by senior Austro-Hungarian military leaders.

It was a poor choice. Potiorek had never commanded a division, was still bitter at having been passed over in 1906 for the post of Chief of the General Staff in favour of Conrad, and had been badly shaken by the Sarajevo murders of 28 June.[30] Yet Potiorek was highly ambitious and had intimate ties to Court. On 12 August he used those connections to claim four divisions of Conrad's strategic reserve, the erstwhile *B-Staffel* now reconstituted as the Second Army, to 'demonstrate' along the Save and Danube rivers. That same day Potiorek launched a two-pronged offensive against Serbia across the Save and Drina rivers with the 19 divisions of General Liborius von Frank's Fifth Army and his own Sixth Army. Instead of standing on the defensive against Serbia while the main decision was sought against Russia, Potiorek used the reinforced *Minimalgruppe B* to restore his tarnished reputation. On 21 August he further exploited his ties to Court to gain a command position virtually independent of the *AOK* at Przemyśl.[31]

Potiorek's armies numbered 460 000 soldiers with about 500 mobile guns, but many of his units were inexperienced *Landsturm* brigades. The wily Serbian commander, Field Marshal (*Vojvoda*) Radomir Putnik, had arrived at Serbian headquarters at Kragujevac on 5 August. He had available 400 000 soldiers, including 185 000 well trained, war experienced, and highly motivated veterans of the recent Balkan Wars armed with new Mauser rifles as well as 328 modern Schneider-Creusot M 1897 field guns. Montenegro, allied with Serbia, fielded about 40 000 men on the southern border of Bosnia–Herzegovina. Thus Potiorek had to guard not only the Danube against an expected assault by Putnik, but also Bosnia–Herzegovina's 400-mile frontier with Serbia and Montenegro. Overly confident of victory against the hated Serbs, Potiorek on 12 August drove the Fifth Army across the lower Drina and Save rivers in the direction of Valjevo. Two days later, his Sixth Army crossed the upper Drina. The two armies were about 60 miles apart. The terrain was difficult, the weather wet.

Putnik, like most generals of the day enamoured with the cult of the offensive, decided not to wait. Armed with vital intelligence that the Habsburg Second Army was about to be withdrawn to Galicia, the *Vojvoda* counterattacked at Jadar on 16 August and decisively defeated Potiorek. The Austrian 21st *Landwehr* Division bolted, leaving its equipment on the battlefield; another division was badly mauled. The Austrians withdrew across the Drina. Conrad took advantage of Potiorek's momentary embarrassment to order most of the Second Army north to Galicia. The first signs of panic appeared in civilian quarters. István Count Burián of the Hungarian Cabinet noted in his diary on 21 August: 'What horrible moral effect in the Balkan states, in Italy and Romania. . . . When will our victories arrive at last?'[32] All Habsburg forces were withdrawn from Serbian soil by the end of August. Putnik, emboldened by his success at Jadar, sent a small Serbian contingent to threaten Sarajevo early in September, forcing Potiorek to dispatch much of Sixth Army to defend the Bosnian capital.

Potiorek appealed to Vienna once more to grant him another chance at Serbia, and on 8 September launched a night attack across the Drina. It fared no better than the first. The Serbs were well entrenched and counterattacked Potiorek's bridgeheads, inflicting heavy casualties. Rain slowed the advance to a crawl. Troops drowned in the mud. Ammunition ran out. Both armies were exhausted after 10 days of vicious fighting. Habsburg forces withdrew behind the Save River to Hungary. It was an inauspicious start to the war. Potiorek had lost 600 officers and 23 000 men. Tens of thousands suffered from malaria and typhoid fever.[33] Conrad quickly disassociated himself from his former rival, leaving Potiorek to shoulder the burden of defeat. Privately, Conrad admitted that he had undertaken operations in the south for 'political reasons', that is, 'the need to slap Serbia'.[34]

Worse was to come in the north. While the Germans counted on an all-out offensive by 40 Austro-Hungarian divisions against the Russians in the direction of Volhynia at the outbreak of war, Conrad on 13 July had changed his marshalling area to behind the San–Dniester line. He now planned a more leisurely spoiling sweep with the left wing of his now only 34 divisions north and northeastward between the Vistula and the Bug rivers in the direction of Lublin and Cholm, but did not to inform Moltke of the change in plans. When Moltke finally notified Conrad on 3 August that German forces would stand on the defensive in East Prussia and not join a projected Austro-German envelopment of Russian armies in the Polish salient, the grandiose dream of a gigantic pincer movement to trap the advancing Russian armies around Siedlce died. Conrad coolly informed Moltke that he would proceed alone against Lublin and Cholm by 20 August. He declined to wait for the arrival of the Second Army from the Danube. Undoubtedly, Conrad wished to show that his Army was capable of fighting a major campaign alone.

It was a costly and imprudent decision. The critical left wing of the Habsburg Army in Galicia could muster only 17 divisions, barely equal to the Russian concentration before it, instead of the 30 divisions that Conrad had called for in his last peacetime plans.[35] Furthermore, Russian infantry divisions had a greater number of battalions than their Austro-Hungarian counterparts and thus were 60 to 70 per cent superior in numbers. Russian divisions also enjoyed 90 per cent superiority in light and 230 per cent in heavy artillery. Each Russian division had eight more machine guns. Undaunted, Conrad proposed to crush Russian forces as they assembled in central Poland with his mobile left wing and thereafter to wheel his assault forces eastward in the direction of Kiev.[36] Accordingly, throughout the first 2 weeks of August, Conrad's forces disembarked from trains behind the San–Dniester line, reformed, and marched to the front. Many units had to cover more than 100 miles on foot in 6 or 7 days. Tired and exhausted, hungry and thirsty, they trudged up to the front.

They also advanced blindly. On 17 August Conrad had sent his cavalry out on a broad sweep from the Dniester to the Vistula – an area 250 miles wide and 90 miles deep. It achieved little. Few units penetrated the Russian screen and their mounted charges were decimated by fire from dismounted Russian cavalry. Still, the deployment continued. While the Third Army and Army Group Kummer anchored the right wing of the Austro-Hungarian front, the First and Fourth armies – 17 divisions in all – marched north and northeastward against the unknown. The further they advanced, the greater their front became, and the more they diluted their strength.

In the meantime Conrad indulged in grandiose political speculation. Intelligence reports suggested that an Austro-German 'liberation manifesto' addressed to the Poles under Russian rule had been well received, and Conrad proposed to follow it up with a similar document promising to remove the Ukraine from 'Moscow's yoke'. On 17 August Conrad requested that Germany instigate a 'Moslem uprising' against the British in Egypt and India. The German military attaché at *AOK*, Kageneck, laconically noted: 'Easier said than done'.[37] And before a shot had been fired in Galicia, Berlin and Vienna quarrelled over who would possess Russian Poland in the future.

Conrad, who attached little value to fortresses and who had cut Przemyśl off from funding in 1911, now regretted his past actions. More than 27 000 construction troops were rushed to Przemyśl to expand its belt-line defences, construct new barracks for the troops, and establish a system of trenches and obstacles against Russian attacks. In short order, seven new lines of defence consisting of 24 strong points with 200 batteries as well as 30 miles of trenches and 650 miles of barbed wire were built. Next, Conrad decreed that the artillery required a clear and expansive field of fire and levelled 21 villages and 2470 acres of woodlands. In the process, Przemyśl grew to a small city of 80 000 men.

Austro-Hungarian and Russian armies soon collided in a series of heavy engagements along a 200-mile front southwest of the Pripet

Marshes. The Russians had divided their forces, consisting of 2.7 million soldiers in 96 infantry and 37 cavalry divisions, into two groups of two armies each: in the north the Fourth and Fifth armies advanced via Lublin to Cholm and Kovel; and in the south the Third and Eighth armies assembled at Dubno and Proskurov-Dunajevsky. *Stavka* hoped thereby to achieve a double envelopment of both Austro-Hungarian flanks.[38] At Poronin near Zakopane Habsburg forces captured a Russian national, V. I. Lenin, but on the advice of the Austrian socialist Viktor Adler allowed Lenin to proceed to Zurich.

Between 23 and 24 August General Dankl's First Army defeated five divisions of the Russian Fourth Army at Kraśnik after encircling its right flank. Infantry Regiment 76 (Öderburg) suffered 40 to 50 per cent losses as a result of three suicidal frontal charges. General Moritz Auffenberg's Fourth Army repelled the Russian Fifth Army at Komarów between 26 and 31 August. An ecstatic Wilhelm II awarded Conrad the Iron Cross I and II Class. 'If only I knew for what', Conrad cynically queried the German delegation at Przemyśl.[39]

Despite heavy casualties, Conrad, who still suspected the main Russian forces to the north in the Lublin-Cholm region, pressed Auffenberg and Dankl to continue their advance. In doing so, Conrad was influenced by reports that several Siberian army corps were detraining in the Ukraine, and by impatient German queries concerning the starting date for major operations in Galicia – at a time when East Prussia was threatened by two Russian armies. Alarmingly, Bolfras at the Military Chancery questioned Conrad about reports that Austrian infantry was recklessly launching suicidal frontal attacks against the Russians. On the basis of battlefront reports, Conrad had to agree that the troops were so eager to engage the Russians that they often failed to wait for the artillery to soften up enemy positions. In fact, Habsburg artillery deployed in open position and fired without cover against its Russian counterpart. On 1 September Conrad lamented to Freytag-Loringhoven, the German representative at *AOK*, what he termed the 'ill-timed bravado' of his troops. 'It stems from 1866.'[40] Bolfras and Freytag-Loringhoven wondered about the quality of Austrian prewar military training.

Troubled by his lack of military intelligence as to the whereabouts of the main Russian forces, Conrad unleashed a barrage of telegrams to Moltke – on 23, 28, 30 August and 1 September – demanding that at least 12 German divisions immediately launch an offensive in the direction of Siedlce. The Habsburg commander undoubtedly regretted his earlier failures to extract definite commitments from Moltke for a coordinated pincer movement against the Russians. Self-pity was not beyond him. 'Unfortunately, we Austrians are people of chivalrous selflessness.'[41]

Conrad did not have long to wait to discover the whereabouts of the main Russian forces. On 1 September Cossacks penetrated Auffenberg's screen and concurrently crept behind General Rudolf von Brudermann's Third Army. At Lemberg they discovered a 60-mile gap between the Habsburg First and Fourth armies because Conrad had shifted forces from his centre to his right wing in the hope of striking the Russians in the flank. Instead, the Russian Ninth and Fifth armies immediately advanced into this gap; at Ravaruska they drove a wedge between Dankl and Auffenberg. Conrad's First Army was threatened with encirclement; his Fourth Army faced annihilation from the rear. Further to the south, on the Austrian right, Brudermann's Third Army caved in before the onslaught of the 18 to 20 divisions of the Russian Third and Eighth armies. Austrian troops suffered horrendous losses, were quickly cut off from their supply train, and began a confused and demoralizing retreat. On 2–3 September Russian General Ivanov entered an undefended Lemberg. Conrad cashiered Brudermann's staff chief, General Rudolf Pfeffer, as well as numerous corps, division, and brigade commanders.

Chaos ensued. As the Austro-Hungarian Third Army struggled to reestablish its position at Lemberg, the 23rd Division, which guarded its northern flank, heard several shots fired and in utter panic raced for its barracks. It finally regrouped at its exercise square – only to discover that the divisional commander and his two brigadiers had deserted the unit and taken up quarters in a local hotel, where they could not be dislodged from their beds.[42] Many units showed more bravery than sense. At Hujcze, the 2nd Regiment Tyrolean *Kaiserjäger* mounted a bayonet charge against an entire Russian infantry division; it lost nearly 2000 men, including its colonel.[43] The 3rd Infantry Division of the XIV Corps was reduced from 10 000 to 4000 men. Fourth Army had fought for 18 of its 21 days in the field and lost 50 per cent of its officers and 25 per cent of its rank and file; combat strength had fallen from 50 000 to just 10 000 men.[44] Furthermore, the Austro-Hungarian transportation system had collapsed: 100 locomotives and 15 000 cars were lost in Galicia in the first 10 days of September; 22 000 wounded per day had to be evacuated; and thousands of refugees filled existing roads.[45] Conrad confided to his dinner circle the 'dreadful thought' that a lost war could cost him the comfort of his beloved 'Gina'.[46]

Still, Conrad refused to confront the situation. Instead, he brazenly planned a double envelopment of Russian forces in and around Lemberg and ordered Auffenberg and Brudermann to stand fast while Dankl continued his 'spoiling sweep' to the north and northeast. Conrad could hardly have been cheered by injunctions from Moltke to abandon frontal attacks in favour of flanking movements, and to be as aggressive in

Galicia as the Germans were in France. 'The devil must have a hand in this', Moltke grumbled, 'if the fine Austrian Army cannot do the same'.[47] But 2 days of murderous fighting finally forced Conrad to face reality: on 11 September he broke off the battle and ordered a withdrawal behind the San River. Brudermann, who saw himself as the hapless 'victim of circumstances', was relieved of command ('for health reasons') at the height of the battle and replaced with the energetic Croat, General Svetozar von Boroević. Disingenuously, Conrad informed the Germans that very day that he was still waiting for the Russians to charge ahead full speed so that he could 'defeat them through a counterattack'.[48] In truth, Conrad, along with Archduke Friedrich, the nominal theatre commander, and Archduke Karl, the heir to the Habsburg throne, had rushed to the front near Grodek to rally the demoralized troops.

It was not to be. General Ivanov pressed his advantage and drove Habsburg forces behind the Dunajec River, investing Przemyśl in the process. Conrad had abandoned 150 miles of territory in the Bukovina and East Galicia. General Eduard von Böhm-Ermolli's Second Army had arrived in Galicia from the Balkan theatre just in time to be caught up in the Third Army's chaotic retreat. The 22nd Division lost 6300 men, almost half its peacetime strength. The hapless Auffenberg fired two of his corps commanders, Generals Karl Count Huyn and Blasius Schemua, and then was himself stripped of command of the Fourth Army and replaced by Archduke Joseph Ferdinand. The First Army was saved from certain annihilation at Tarnów by General Remus von Woyrsch's Silesian *Landwehr* Corps, which lost 8000 men covering Dankl's retreat. In desperation, Conrad appealed for help to Józef Piłsudski's Polish Legion (*Strzelcy*) of about 3000 volunteers as well as to a nascent Ukrainian Legion (*Sichovi striltsi*) in western Galicia. Polish legionnaires in eastern Galicia spent most of their time plundering and had to be abandoned as a fighting force.[49]

Conrad was bitter that the Poles refused to see the Austrians as liberators. General Michael Tisijar von Lentulis, inspector of police in Galicia, handed Conrad a bleak appraisal of the situation in Poland. Russophiles, primarily Ruthenians (Ukrainians), assisted Tsarist forces in eastern Galicia by reporting Conrad's dispositions, strengths, signals, and supplies. Especially the educated elements – priests, professors, teachers, and lawyers – showed the Russians shortcuts through forests and marshes and helped them site machine guns in church steeples. Women sheltered wounded Russian soldiers and gave civilian garb to spies. Polish Jews bribed officials and exploited farmers – all in the name of the Viennese government. All too few Poles, Tisijar von Lentulis reported, understood that they would be best served 'under the wings of the [Habsburg] double eagle'.[50]

General Hermann Kövess informed Conrad on 7 September that his XII Corps was shattered; another offensive would 'lead to the dissolution of our forces'. Kövess' report from his sector during the Battle of Lemberg sheds light on the proverbial 'fog of war' that beset Habsburg forces in Galicia. While falling back on Bóbrka, Kövess' staff was scattered by hostile shrapnel fire and the commander thrown from his mount and trampled by a squadron of hussars. Suffering serious head contusions, Kövess nevertheless managed to swing into the saddle of a bypassing hussar's mount and to rejoin his main forces. He quickly discovered that his army group and its supply formations had scattered in all directions. 'Cowardly train personnel' at Bóbrka had prematurely abandoned the railroad station, leaving a train of severely wounded soldiers behind. With the help of three generals, Kövess gathered three divisions of the XII Corps, about 20 000 men, and resumed an orderly retreat. On 2 September he returned to Lemberg – only to witness railroad personnel pouring petrol on abundant supplies and burning them by order of the Third Army. Three days later the Austrians abandoned Lemberg in chaotic fashion, leaving behind 8000 rifles and other stores. All high-ranking officers had quietly slipped out of Lemberg.[51] Conrad fully appreciated the magnitude of his defeat, and informed his headquarters over the breakfast table that Archduke Franz Ferdinand, were he still alive, 'would have had me shot'.[52] Kövess reported to his wife that numerous Habsburg generals had suffered mental breakdowns.

Boroević concurred. He lectured his generals that the Third Army failed to pass muster. 'All too often it lacks discipline and order, it lacks obedience; apathy and lack of self-confidence have entered its ranks'. Officers had failed to 'steel' themselves in peacetime for the rigours of war. In his forty-third year of service, Boroević noted that he had spent 25 of the last 28 days with the troops in Galicia, sleeping on straw in open fields and drinking only tea. He could not say the same of his officers. He found all too many drunk at their posts; others failed to respond with proper salutes when addressed; numerous others dressed as they liked without regard to codes; and all too many read their own glowing press clippings. 'When a military formation fails, this means: the commander has failed.'[53]

Austria–Hungary had suffered 100 000 dead and 220 000 wounded, and surrendered 100 000 prisoners of war as well as 216 artillery pieces.[54] In 17 days Conrad had lost one-third of his combat effectives, including many of his regular junior officers and most of his experienced non-commissioned officers. An outbreak of cholera further decimated his already broken armies. But Conrad refused to institute courts-martial for failed corps commanders and instead spoke of the string of 'unlucky' generals

(Brudermann, Gieslingen, Hortstein, Huyn, Schemua, Wurm, Zedtwitz, Zweienstamm) that he had been forced to dismiss. Yet these were Conrad's hand-picked corps commanders and hence their inadequacy to command must rest with him. Conrad's private diary sheds light on the qualities he judged highest in army commanders before 1914. Concerning General Kövess, Conrad noted: 'A moderately talented, personally extremely vain, dutiful, loyal, reliable general; a brave, pliable man, whom I personally brought to the very spot where I needed men with such traits and compromising characters; luck also was on his side'.[55]

The 100 000-man garrison at Przemyśl was left invested by six enemy infantry divisions. Austrian Galicia was in Russian hands. Ahead of General Ivanov lay the Carpathian passes leading down to the Hungarian plain and Budapest. Fortunately for Conrad, the Russians were equally exhausted after 2 weeks of bloody combat. In Vienna, War Minister von Krobatin at last began to make plans for a winter campaign. The dream of a short, victorious war was over. Austria–Hungary was now engaged in a mortal struggle for its survival. On a personal level, Conrad's third-eldest son, Herbert, died at Ravaruska on 8 September.

The first reaction in Vienna was one of panic. A bridgehead was hastily built on the northern bank of the Danube and *k.u.k.* bureaucrats toyed with the idea of moving the state archives into the catacombs below St Stephen's cathedral. Thereafter the mood turned to one of sadness at the horrendous loss of human life and at the unlucky hand that fate had dealt Conrad. Franz Joseph, well acquainted with defeat on the battlefield, stoically refused to assess guilt: 'Today's unlucky commander may well be victorious tomorrow'.[56] At the Military Chancery, Bolfras, a veteran of the campaigns of 1859 and 1866, noted the need for ever greater amounts of 'cannon fodder'. 'Mars seems to have become very voracious.' Above all, Bolfras detected a change in the nature of war. 'If war was once a chivalrous duel, it is now a dastardly slaughter.'[57] Count Hoyos, the Foreign Ministry's *chef de cabinet* who had undertaken the special mission to Berlin on 5 July, reminded the Germans of Austria–Hungary's bloody sacrifice – and *AOK* of the need to avoid 'recriminations' concerning responsibility for the debacle in Galicia.[58]

Conrad refused to heed Hoyos' sage advice, however, and instead blamed his defeat squarely on Moltke's failure to honour alleged prewar commitments to a major German drive into Poland at the outset of hostilities.[59] In a fit of deep despair, he counselled the Ballhausplatz to seek a separate peace with Russia. 'Why', Conrad queried Foreign Minister Berchtold, 'should Austria–Hungary bleed needlessly?'[60] In a moment of extreme agitation at the height of the Battle of Lemberg, Conrad had informed Bolfras that the military disaster in Galicia was due to Wilhelm

II's desire 'to protect the stud-farms of Trakhenen and the stag hunts of Rominten' in East Prussia.[61] Privately, Conrad wallowed in self-pity. 'All reproaches over all that has not gone right in this gigantic struggle will be unloaded on to me. I will probably have to disappear from the scene like an outlaw. I have no home, no woman who will stand by my side in my final years. I have one of my sons seriously ill and the son that I idolized in a mound of corpses at Ravaruska.'[62]

Conrad compared his situation in autumn 1914 to that of Prussia's Frederick the Great in 1759. He was determined not to share the fate of another hapless Austrian commander, General Karl Mack von Leiberich, who in 1805 had surrendered to Napoleon at Ulm. Conrad's headquarters bitterly noted that 9 September was the 40th day of German mobilization – that is, the very moment that the German armies, having defeated the French, were to have been shuttled east to deal with the Russians. As a final blow to Austrian prestige, Wilhelm II on 16 September refused to place Hindenburg's newly constituted Ninth Army under Habsburg command.

Conrad's biting comments that the Germans had left him 'in the lurch' did not go unanswered. General Ludendorff went out of his way to make disparaging remarks about the Austro-Hungarian Army in general and its inept leadership in particular. When Conrad sent several officers to confer with the Ninth Army about coordinating future offensives, Ludendorff refused to receive them.[63] The German military delegation to Conrad's headquarters, now at Neu Sandec, reported that Habsburg forces had expended themselves in senseless frontal assaults and that they were incapable of renewing the attack. Freytag-Loringhoven informed Moltke that Conrad had expected too much of his forces, that the troops had lacked self-confidence, and that the great hopes placed in Polish and Ukrainian liberation movements had been misplaced. Kageneck reported that Conrad had 'lost all confidence in his army'. The two German officers concurred that only 'a quick, definitive decision' in France could save Austria–Hungary.[64]

The Battle of the Marne

Between 3 and 20 August the German Second Army's special task force of 30 000 soldiers commanded by General Otto von Emmich crossed the border between the Ardennes and the Maastricht Appendix. Before them lay a formidable barrier: the Belgian fortress of Liège, one of the strongest in Europe, guarded by a belt of 12 concrete and steel forts. A night attack on 5–6 August penetrated the outer layer of forts and on 8 August

Ludendorff took command of the 14th Brigade and after an all-night street battle entered the inner city. Thereafter, four batteries of special Austrian 30.5 cm howitzers – Krupp's massive 42 cm 'gamma-gun' had not been completed in series production in time – systematically reduced the city's cupolaed defences. Liège formally surrendered on 16 August, 2 days behind Schlieffen's blueprint.

General von Kluck's First Army and General von Bülow's Second Army quickly passed through the Liège corridor, crossed the Meuse River, and headed toward Mons, Péronne, Compiègne, and Paris.[65] Belgian forces were rapidly dispersed. Brussels was occupied on 20 August and King Albert invested at Antwerp. But the Belgians demolished their communications infrastructure as they retreated. By mid-September all 26 000 railroad personnel of the German Army were engaged in trying to repair damaged Belgian lines, water towers, bridges, and tunnels. The BEF, having landed at Boulogne on 14 August, took up positions near Mons.

Allied and German forces – 92 and 70 infantry divisions, respectively – clashed between 14 and 25 August in four simultaneous actions in what are termed the Battles of the Frontiers. On the German left flank in Lorraine, French General Paul Pau's Army of Alsace, General Auguste Dubail's First Army, and General Noël de Castelnau's Second Army hurled 420 battalions of infantry against German positions between Metz and Strassburg for a full week beginning 8 August. Ten days later, the German Sixth Army of Crown Prince Rupprecht of Bavaria and the Seventh Army of General Josias von Heeringen – a total of only 328 battalions – mounted violent counterattacks and threw French forces back to the Grand Couronné at Nancy.

To the north the advancing French Third and Fourth armies with 377 battalions of infantry launched the bloody Battle of the Ardennes on 20 August, when they collided with the 236 battalions of the German Fourth Army, commanded by Duke Albrecht of Württemberg, and the German Fifth Army, headed by Crown Prince Wilhelm. The Ardennes had been designated by Schlieffen as the pivot for the giant German 'wheel' around Paris, and the French were badly mauled in 4 days of severe fighting and had to fall back behind the Meuse River, with their right flank anchored at Verdun.

Still further to the north 358 infantry battalions of the German First, Second, and Third armies swept west and southwest from Liège. Joffre, acting in accordance with Plan XVII, thereupon ordered General Lanrezac's Fifth Army and the BEF (257 battalions) to parry this unexpected advance in the Sambre-Meuse area. The Germans attacked Lanrezac at Namur, defeated him, and stormed the Belgian fortress of

Namur in the Battle of the Sambre (22–3 August).[66] Schlieffen's master plan dictated that the Germans advance relentlessly at the rate of 20 to 25 miles per day.

The BEF came into action at the Battle of Mons. First concentrated on Lanrezac's left at Le Cateau, Joffre ordered Field Marshal French's 110 000 soldiers along with his own Fifth Army to advance against Namur. There on 23 August the BEF ran into the full force of Kluck's German First Army. French's position became precarious when Lanrezac withdrew from Namur – without informing him – and thereby exposed the BEF's flank. Bitter recriminations between the two Allied commanders ensued. For 13 days the BEF undertook a rearward odyssey of 200 miles. It is fair to say that French panicked and withdrew from Mons, certain that disaster was inevitable. Only the hasty personal intervention of Lord Kitchener brought the 'Great Retreat' to a halt by 1 September.

The Battles of the Frontiers spelled complete failure for Plan XVII. French armies had suffered about 300 000 casualties and were far from central Germany. Nor had the Russians reached Berlin. The ranks of France's generals were thinned in a manner not seen since the Revolution of 1789: Joffre sacked 140 generals, including two of five army commanders, nine corps commanders, and 38 of 82 divisional generals. But Joffre now had a clear idea of the direction of the German advance, and in adversity rallied his armies to meet the real threat. In what has been described as a 'Schlieffen plan in reverse', Joffre's General Instruction Nr. 2 ordered First and Second armies to stand at all costs at Verdun and Nancy as the pivot of his new plan. The French Third, Fourth, and Fifth armies as well as the BEF were to continue their southwesterly withdrawals. Joffre created two new armies (*masse capable à reprendre l'offensive*) from reserves and the shattered units of his right wing: General Michel J. Maunoury's Sixth Army was assembled around Paris, west of the German right, to attack east; and General Foch's Ninth Army was held in close support behind and between the Fourth and Fifth armies for a possible counterattack.

For the Germans, the Schlieffen plan seemed to be on track. While inferior forces held the left flank and the centre of the front, the critical outer right wing unfolded according to plan: 120 German battalions with 748 guns drove 52 British battalions of infantry and 336 guns before them.[67] But cracks were developing in the Schlieffen plan. Moltke, far behind the fighting at Koblenz, remained out of touch with the 54 German divisions deployed between Aachen and Metz and the 16 sited in Lorraine.[68] Faulty information and poor communications kept him in the dark concerning the landing of British forces until 20 August, and also led him to overestimate his victories in Lorraine, the Ardennes, Namur, and Mons. Seduced by the vision of a classic double envelopment of French forces, Moltke ordered Crown Prince Rupprecht and General von Heeringen to press their attacks against the fortified heights around Nancy and diverted reinforcements intended for Sixth and Seventh armies to Lorraine. Moltke's spur-of-the-moment decision to send the 16 divisions of the German Sixth and Seventh armies not north via Metz to join Bülow and Kluck but east toward Épinal, constituted one of his gravest errors during the Marne campaign.

At the same time, Moltke asked Kluck and Bülow to continue their scythe-like sweep from the Ardennes and the Sambre in behind Paris. By 25 August Moltke was sufficiently confident of victory to detach two army corps to help hold the east against the Russians. He later conceded that this was his greatest mistake of the campaign.[69] Finally, Moltke was forced to leave units behind to pen the Belgian Army up at Antwerp and to invest the French fortress of Maubeuge. On 25 August nervous German troops set fire to the centre of Louvain, destroying 1000 houses, the Cathedral of St Pierre, and the University's library. Throughout Belgium between 5000 and 6000 citizens were summarily executed as suspected spies or saboteurs.[70] Allied charges of 'Huns' and 'barbarity' were not long in coming.

Moltke's dispositions meant that the critical right wing of the Schlieffen plan was now reduced from 16 to 11 corps. By 22 August the German right wing consisted of 358 battalions and 2164 guns; it was opposed by 269 Anglo-Belgian-French battalions and 828 guns. Overall, the Germans had massed 71 infantry and nine cavalry divisions on the Western Front -- against 73 Allied infantry and 11.5 cavalry divisions.[71]

The German march to Paris continued. Kluck's First Army defeated General Horace Smith-Dorrien's II Corps at Le Cateau on 26–7 August, inflicting nearly 8000 casualties on the BEF. French's chief of staff, Sir Archibald Murray, fainted at an inn in St Quentin on hearing of the defeat. French proposed to pull the BEF out of the Allied line altogether and to withdraw to the far side of Paris. He was saved from further embarrassment by Joffre, who ordered his own Fifth Army, already engaged in heavy fighting with Bülow's Second Army, to wheel 90 degrees to the west to prevent Kluck from pursuing the BEF.

The last day of August proved critical. Lanrezac's I Corps, commanded by General Louis Franchet d'Esperey, had scored the first French tactical victory of the war by halting the German Second Army the day before. Bülow appealed to Kluck for help. Unable to establish contact with Moltke (who was moving German headquarters from Koblenz to Luxembourg) and thinking that the exposed flank of the French Fifth Army lay before him, Kluck on 2 September jettisoned the last remnants of the Schlieffen plan by ordering the First Army to march southeast and to roll up the French Fifth Army.[72] Kluck instructed his forces not to encircle Paris – as envisioned by Schlieffen – but to pass the capital to the east, where they would run into Joffre's new concentration around Paris. Kluck's open violation of orders ran against Schlieffen's cardinal tenet of enveloping the French left. On 2 September Kluck's First Army stood with its left flank on the Marne at Château-Thierry and its right on the Oise near Chantilly. Bülow's Second Army crossed the Aisne and Vesle rivers that same day. The French government hastily abandoned Paris for the safety of Bordeaux.

Moltke belatedly approved Kluck's decision not to sweep around Paris from the west, but admonished him to guard the right flank of Bülow's Second Army, which had now become the spearhead of the modified German wheel.[73] Moltke was unaware that Kluck had driven his men so hard the past 3 days that for the First Army to have guarded Bülow's flank would have required a marching halt of 2 days. Kluck feared that such a delay would allow the French either to escape or to rally. He was not about to jeopardize his place in history by letting the French Fifth Army escape. On 3 September Kluck crossed the Marne at Chézy, Château-Thierry, and Meaux just east of Paris. Bülow's Second Army was too far behind to protect Kluck's right flank.

It was a bloodied and exhausted German Army that reached the Marne on 3 September. It was also short of time and supplies. In 6 days – that is, by the 40th day of mobilization – it would have to defeat the Anglo-Belgian-French armies in order to head east to blunt the Russian onslaught. What the historian Martin van Creveld has called Schlieffen's 'ostrich-like refusal' to address logistics haunted the grand design in the west throughout August and September.[74] The men on the extreme right wing of the German advance discovered that they could not maintain the torrid pace of marching 300 miles to the west of Paris in 40 days. Artillery, whose ammunition tables were 40 years old, expended its allotted 1000 rounds per barrel within the first 40 days of fighting. Each army corps consumed about 130 tons of food and fodder per day, requiring 1168 railroad wagons for resupply. The 84 000 horses of Kluck's First Army alone ate up 2 million pounds of fodder per day – an amount requiring more than 900 wagons. Motor transport was out of the question: 60 per cent of the 4000 German trucks broke down before the armies reached the Marne; in any event, it would have taken 18 000 trucks to move just the German right wing. Existing railroads were taxed beyond their limits. During the critical first week of September 1914, most German railheads were 80 to 100 miles behind the front.[75] Improvised narrow-gauge railroads and horse-drawn wagons hauled what supplies they could from the railheads to the front. But 54 German divisions could hardly 'live off the land' in an area as compressed and densely populated as Belgium and northern France.

Joffre learned of Kluck's turn east of Paris on 3 September from French aviators and from documents taken off a dead German officer. The French High Command quickly appreciated that Kluck's right wing was now open to a flank attack from Paris. On 4 September Joffre ordered his Sixth Army to strike eastward from Château-Thierry and moved the BEF up to Montmirail, with the French Fifth Army in support. The Third Army was to drive westward from Verdun, while the Fourth Army would hold its position between the Marne and Ornain rivers. A double envelopment of the German right wing was in sight.

The Battle of the Marne began on 5 September.[76] The previous night, General Galliéni, the military governor of Paris and temporary commander of the Sixth Army, had recognized Kluck's exposed flank and besieged Joffre by telephone to strike hard at the German First Army. Joffre's orders were sufficiently vague to allow Galliéni to advance to the Ourcq River against Kluck's exposed flank. Six hundred Parisian taxicabs rushed 3000 fresh reserves to the battle. The Battle of the Ourcq raged for 2 days. Kluck, mistaking Galliéni's attack as a simple spoiling action, charged hard southward after the retreating French Fifth Army and the BEF. The German IX Corps, for example, marched nearly 40 miles on 7 September and another 40 the next day.[77] Joffre, clearly recognizing that Galliéni's brilliant insight had been correct, now took personal command of the Sixth Army. While Kluck's First Army turned west against French forces advancing from Paris, Bülow's Second Army turned south to meet another developing threat; as a result, the gap widened between the joint of the two German armies. Kluck realized his predicament by the morning of 6 September and stood fast north of the Marne. His hard charge had further widened the already existing chasm between the German First and Second armies. The BEF crossed the Marne and stumbled into the gap. Heavy fighting also ensued at Petit Morin, St-Gond, Vitry-le-François, and Nancy.

Moltke, finally ensconced in a girls' school at Luxembourg, became worried by conflicting reports from the front. There was no longer talk at German Headquarters of hurling the French armies against the Swiss border. Instead, Kluck passionately pleaded for the Second Army's III and IX Corps to reinforce him, while Bülow countered that he needed both corps to protect his right wing. The time had come for Moltke to coordinate the actions of his two army commanders. But Moltke issued no orders from 5 to 9 September; he received no reports from Bülow or Kluck from 7 to 9 September.[78]

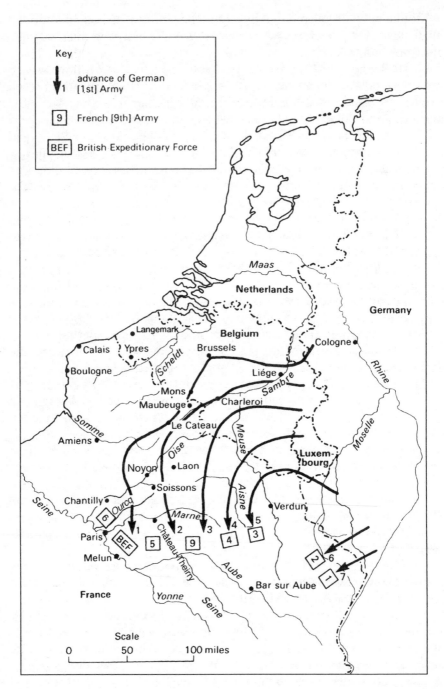

Map 3. *The German march to the Marne, 1914*

Moltke now discovered that his communications system was woefully inadequate. The Telegraph Bureau before the war had experimented with electronic communications only within armies, not between them. Thus, the first telephone line was established between Kluck and Bülow only at 2:30 p.m. on 9 September – thirty minutes after First Army had commenced its retreat! Nor had Moltke deployed automobiles, motorcycles, and airplanes. Bülow's headquarters at Montmort lay a mere half-hour by air from Kluck's base at Mareuil, but the possibility of using aerial communication was not raised even once by Moltke.[79] Instead, Moltke during the critical days between 5 and 9 September left the direction of the campaign in the hands of his two commanders. All the while, extremely severe fighting took place at the Ourcq River. Wilhelm II, perhaps sensing Moltke's lack of firmness, sought to strengthen his staff chief's resolve on 7 September: 'Attack, for as long as possible – under no circumstances a step back'.[80]

Moltke finally became aware that the moment of decision had come. Without accurate information on the condition and situation of the First and Second armies east of Paris, he convened a staff conference at Luxembourg on the morning of 8 September. It was decided to dispatch a highly gifted staff officer, Lieutenant-Colonel Richard Hentsch of the Saxon Army, with only verbal instructions to reconnoitre the situation east of Paris, to close the suspected gap between First and Second armies, and, failing that, to order Kluck's First Army to withdraw to the line Soissons–Fismes (if Kluck and Bülow concurred). Moltke apparently accorded Hentsch full powers to undertake dispositions for First and Second armies. Since Hentsch died at Bucharest in February 1918, he never published his instructions. And in July 1915 the General Staff somehow 'lost' a report that Hentsch submitted to it concerning his actions at the Marne in September 1914.[81]

Hentsch left Luxembourg at 11 a.m. on 8 September. He arrived at Bülow's headquarters in Montmort at 7:45 p.m. that evening after visits to the Fifth, Fourth, and Third armies. Almost immediately, reports came in that the French Fifth Army, now commanded by Franchet d'Esperey, had turned the German Second Army's right flank near Montmirail in a desperate night attack. Hentsch was deeply shaken by discussions with Bülow's staff officers, some of whom suggested that several units of the Second Army had been reduced to 'dregs' (*Schlacke*) by constant marching and fighting. Bülow conceded that he knew nothing of the whereabouts of Kluck's First Army. Hentsch firmly believed that the dangerous situation along the Ourcq could be salvaged only by ordering the First Army to break off the battle and to deploy on Bülow's threatened right wing. Nevertheless, while estimating Bülow's situation to be 'serious but not hopeless', Hentsch let it be known that Moltke had empowered him to order a general retreat, should that become advisable. At the height of the Battle of the Marne, the French left wing (Ninth, Fifth, and Sixth armies as well as the BEF) outnumbered the German right wing (First Army, Second Army, and half of the Third Army) by 200 infantry battalions and 190 artillery batteries.[82]

Hentsch departed for Kluck's headquarters in Mareuil at 7 a.m. on 9 September, arriving shortly after noon. En route, he encountered numerous baggage and medical units streaming back from the Ourcq in confusion and near panic. It was hardly a confidence-inspiring experience. Moreover, Hentsch discovered that five columns of the BEF had crossed the Marne (I Corps at Nogent l'Artaud and Charly and II Corps at Nanteuil and Saacy) and entered the gap between the German First and Second armies. The Second Army's situation seemed critical. But Kluck reassured Moltke's deputy that the British advance was of no consequence, given Sir John French's slow and deliberate nature. Finally, Kluck reminded Hentsch that the First Army had driven the British before it ever since Mons and Le Cateau.

Probably fearing that the First Army faced being caught in a French pincer and convinced that Bülow's Second Army was seriously jeopardized by the BEF's advance, Hentsch ordered the First Army to withdraw to Soissons. He similarly instructed Bülow to retreat from the Marne. Hentsch most likely was guided by the following consideration in arriving at this critical decision: a strategic withdrawal, allowing overall reorganization and reinforcement by way of the newly formed Seventh Army in Belgium, would permit the *OHL* to regain both direction and initiative in a renewed assault on Paris. On 10 September Hentsch briefed Moltke at Luxembourg on the situation, stressing that Kluck's First Army had already ordered a partial withdrawal the day before.

Both Moltke and Wilhelm II were relieved to learn that a greater disaster along the Marne had been averted. While Schlieffen's admirers railed for years about Hentsch's 'irresponsible' decision to withdraw behind the Marne at the very moment of alleged victory, there is little question that the retreat was necessary. The entire German campaign was at the point of collapse and failure to withdraw and reorganize would have allowed the Allies to isolate and destroy individual German armies; at worst, to envelop the overextended German armies from the rear. In May 1917 a formal inquiry headed by Ludendorff ruled that Hentsch had been 'justified' in reaching his decision and had not exceeded Moltke's instructions.[83]

For 5 days, beginning on 9 September, the Germans pulled back behind the Marne and Aisne rivers to the line Noyon–Verdun. British General

Wilson crowed that the Germans would be driven back to Elsenborn, Belgium, near their own border in 4 weeks, 'unless we made some serious blunder'. But the Allies were too exhausted to press the attack against the Germans, dug in on the heights above the Aisne River. On 11 September Moltke visited his armies and confirmed the original orders to retreat. Observers with the General Staff in Luxembourg concurred that Moltke seemed a 'broken man' and several noted physical deterioration as well. Utterly 'decimated', he called his wife Eliza to General-Headquarters on the eve of 12 September for 'psychological' counselling.[84]

Two days later, Moltke was quietly replaced by the Prussian War Minister, Falkenhayn. The latter had just turned 53 years of age – younger than all army commanders and commanding generals of active and reserve corps. The official announcement was delayed until 6 November for fear of its negative impact on the home front and to deny Allied claims that Moltke had lost the Battle of the Marne. Moltke remained at headquarters for nearly 2 months, enduring what he termed his 'martyrdom' to spare nation and Kaiser the embarrassment of publicly admitting defeat. Thirty-three German generals, including two army commanders, were sacked. Wilhelm II was 'very depressed' over the Marne, viewing the lost battle as '*the* great turning point' in his life.[85]

French General Galliéni, bitter at having been relieved by Joffre of command of the Sixth Army at its moment of repelling Kluck, later asserted: 'There has not been a Battle of the Marne'.[86] Instead, Moltke had simply broken off a series of German campaigns from Strassburg to the Petit Morin. Yet casualties had been horrendous, about 250 000 men on each side. Responsibility for having 'won' or 'lost' the Marne was quickly assessed on both sides. Claims of sole credit for the victory by Galliéni and Joffre were repeated by their respective armies of biographers and hagiographers after the war. On the German side, Hentsch was roundly condemned for ordering Bülow and Kluck to retreat, and Moltke for his lack of nerve in the heat of battle.

The Marne was an operational defeat of the first magnitude for the Germans. The Schlieffen plan was the only recipe for victory; once it had failed, there existed no fallback plan. The German campaign of 1914 was predicated on a swift and decisive victory in the west by the 40th day of mobilization; when it did not materialize, the great gamble had failed. Moltke, as its commander, must bear the responsibility for losing the campaign. Battle had not shown him to possess what Schlieffen had termed 'that certain fire of a determined will to victory, a wild drive to advance, and an unerring desire to annihilate the adversary'.[87] Whether Moltke lost his nerve remains unanswerable, given the 'cleansing' of his memoirs by patriotic self-censors during the 1920s and the destruction of the records of the General Staff by Allied Bomber Command during World War II. In May 1915 Moltke briefly broke his self-imposed silence and admitted to General Hans von Plessen, head of the Kaiser's military headquarters, 'that I became nervous during the critical days of September'. He also acknowledged that he had grown 'pessimistic' concerning the military situation east of Paris.[88] Further, he would not go.

It is at least plausible to argue that the great 'wheel' around Paris was beyond the capability of armies marching on foot with supplies drawn by horse. A giant envelopment of Paris from the north and west in all likelihood would have exposed exhausted German forces to flanking attacks by the French armies concentrated around the capital by 4 September. Nor is it at all certain that the French would have surrendered at once had Kluck defeated the French Fifth Army east of Paris. The year 1871 suggests at least another possibility.

Major Hans Tieschowitz von Tieschowa, Moltke's adjutant in the fall of 1914, left a lucid yet not unsympathetic picture of a commander plagued by doubts about the overall operation, his own abilities, and the gravity of the war. 'He was not a great captain, for he did not possess the necessary iron will or the proud belief in himself and his abilities.' On receiving orders relieving him of command on 6 November, Moltke 'collapsed completely'.[89] The Germans did not inform Conrad von Hötzendorf of the change.

In the final analysis, the Battle of the Marne revealed the shortcomings of the Prussian General Staff system. Moltke, who in the last peacetime manoeuvres had conceded that battles entailing a 200-mile front had been conducted only on paper, chose simply to issue general directives and to leave the actual campaigns with his army commanders. Neither Bülow nor Kluck was up to the task. Each went his own way. Both failed to coordinate operations east of Paris. Neither Bülow nor Kluck sought guidance from Moltke. And that a mere lieutenant-colonel from staff headquarters could redirect the operations of the two most senior commanders in the German Army (both in the rank of colonel-general), speaks volumes for the critical over-dominance of the 'demigods' of the General Staff.

Joffre rather than Moltke proved to be Schlieffen's 'modern Alexander', directing with imperturbable calm the movements and redirection of millions of men in the heat of battle. The buzzword of the 'miracle of the Marne'[90] for too long obscured the fact that Joffre and his staff brought about instead *'un miracle mérite'*.

The last hurrah

Habsburg soldiers and statesmen were told little about the debacle at the Marne. Conrad slowly put the pieces of the puzzle together from scraps of information that he received from the German officers attached to *AOK*. What readily became clear was that there would be no massive transfer of German forces from France to Poland. But the new Chief of the German General Staff, Falkenhayn, with whom Conrad never developed a close working relationship, was not blind to the Russian danger to both Austria–Hungary and Silesia. Grand Duke Nikolai Nikolaevich was planning an invasion of Silesia, a German industrial and mining centre, with the Russian Fifth, Fourth, and Ninth armies. Therefore, Falkenhayn in mid-September transferred four corps in 750 trains from the old Eighth Army in East Prussia to Conrad's northern flank near Cracow. This new Ninth Army was commanded by Hindenburg and Ludendorff, once again ably assisted by Hoffmann. The triumvirate quickly agreed on a spoiling attack to preempt the Russian operation against Silesia.

Conrad, anxious not to surrender the initiative to the Germans and still lusting for a double envelopment of Russian forces in the Polish salient, 'scraped together' whatever he could get: 'the last man, the last artillery piece, the last machine gun'. The soldiers were issued the last rations of white bread, meat, cabbage, potatoes, tea, chocolate, and alcohol (as disinfectant). Every man was given a parka, sweater, fur vest, gloves, and leg wrappings. Habsburg forces were instructed not to launch frontal attacks and instead to seek flanking movements. The horrendous losses of Lemberg could not be repeated.[91]

On 28 September Hindenburg's Ninth Army attacked west of the Vistula, supported 3 days later by four Austro-Hungarian armies to the south. By 9 October the Ninth Army, relying once more on intercepts of 'clear' Russian radio transmissions, had advanced to the line of the Vistula River south of Warsaw. Then the temperature dropped suddenly. First rain and then snow turned Poland's dirt roads into quagmires, and streams and lakes rose to dangerous levels. Sixty Russian divisions counterattacked the 18 German divisions. In what the historian B. H. Liddell Hart has called 'perhaps the finest example of his art as well as one of the masterpieces of all military history',[92] Ludendorff conducted a skilful retreat, using his lateral railroads to fall back on Cracow, all the while destroying the countryside with a 'scorched earth' policy.[93] Even Conrad acknowledged the toughness of the German troops under fire during the Battle of Ivangorod.[94]

To the south of the German Ninth Army Conrad's forces, aided by intercepts from a single mobile wireless station that had been donated by an Austrian millionaire, had reached the besieged fortress of Przemyśl by 7 October. General A. A. Brusilov, head of the Russian Eighth Army, called on the fortress commander, General Hermann Kusmanek von Burgneustädten, to surrender. The bluff failed. Kusmanek refused to dignify Brusilov's demand with an answer. During 3 days of heavy fighting, in which Brusilov lost 10 000 men, the garrison at Przemyśl was freed from the Russian siege. Boroević's Third Army began the grisly task of clearing the great fortress's perimeter of 15 000 bloated corpses.

Then Conrad was checked by superior Russian forces at the San River, and forced to retreat over the same route along which he had just advanced. Przemyśl was left to its fate once more – after 15 000 wounded were evacuated. Losses soared: the Austro-Hungarian First Army's 5th and 12th Infantry Divisions each lost 4000, the 46th Infantry Division 4500, and the 43rd Infantry Division 7000 men. Overall, Dankl's First Army had lost 40 000 to 50 000 combatants.[95] Deeply depressed and shocked by yet another major setback, Conrad informed Vienna that the Russians enjoyed a superiority of 432 battalions and demanded the immediate transfer of 20 to 24 German divisions from France to Poland.[96] For the first time since the start of the war, Conrad noted the financial cost: nearly 4 billion Kronen to date (compared with a defence budget of 609 million Kronen in 1912).

Rumours circulated at Austrian headquarters early in November 1914 that a unified eastern command was in the works. While Hindenburg would maintain control of the German Ninth Army, Archduke Friedrich would assume overall command of Austro-Hungarian and German forces, with Ludendorff as his chief of staff (and thus the real power in the east). Conrad, 'sick and tired' of the 'egotistical ally', submitted his resignation. He refused, as he put it, to lead Habsburg forces under this 'young general of a foreign, even if allied, power'.[97] The resignation, as expected, was rejected in Vienna. Conrad conveniently forgot that his bungled mobilization and the division of his forces into two nearly equal parts at the start of the war in large measure had led to his predicament. He was convinced that German command of the Austro-Hungarian Army would destroy its independence – and perhaps that of the Dual Monarchy as well. Franz Joseph agreed, but noted: 'How on earth can we pursue even a tolerable foreign policy when we fight so badly?'[98]

In the end, Hindenburg was promoted to the rank of field marshal and on 1 November appointed Commander-in-Chief of the German Eastern Front (*OberOst*), with Ludendorff serving as his chief of staff. Conrad, for his part, was forced to relocate his headquarters still further behind the front at Teschen, in Austrian Silesia. Archduke Friedrich's castle and the nearby Albrecht High School served as his headquarters from 9 November 1914 until his dismissal by Kaiser Karl on 1 March 1917. Life for the staff was made easier by three levels of Court table service, coffee houses, stables, and tennis courts – and by the arrival in October 1915 of Conrad's new wife, his beloved 'Gina'. Kageneck, the German military plenipotentiary and a staunch Catholic, was outraged that Conrad shared a villa with 'his divorced, ten-year flame'. In his view, Conrad, who rapidly became the object of derisive jokes on the part of junior staff, had become 'senile' and displayed 'bad taste'.[99]

At *OberOst*, Hindenburg, Ludendorff, and Hoffmann next devised a bold scheme to deliver Grand Duke Nikolai Nikolaevich a crushing blow. Emboldened by Falkenhayn's promise of 12 new army corps – half of them from the Western Front – the triumvirate proposed to denude East Prussia and Silesia of troops and to hurl every available man against the Russian right flank at Łódź and Warsaw. If all went according to plan, the Russian Second Army would be crushed and the remaining Russian forces gathered up behind the Vistula River in a giant pincer movement.

But Hindenburg and Ludendorff refused to wait for the promised new army corps. Instead, between 11 and 25 November they launched the regrouped German Ninth Army, now commanded by General von Mackensen, up the Vistula against the joint of the two Russian armies guarding Nikolai Nikolaevich's northern flank. The Ninth Army, using concentration and mobility to paralyze a much greater force, drove a wedge between the Russian First and Second armies around Łódź, nearly annihilating Rennenkampf's First Army and driving the Second Army 80 miles back to Warsaw. Rennenkampf was relieved of command and sent home to face a commission of inquiry. The German Ninth Army took 136 000 Russian prisoners.

In the glow of apparent victory, Berlin and Vienna immediately renewed the debate concerning control of the future 'Congress Poland' and Galicia. While the Hohenzollerns sought outright annexation of Poland's industrial areas, the Habsburgs demanded Poland's personal union to the Monarchy. But Hungarian Prime Minister Tisza rejected such a trialistic solution out of hand, and instead demanded that Poland be added 'subsidiarily' to the Austrian lands. The debate dragged on without formal resolution for 4 years. Above all, it was premature. By 21 November the front had stagnated. Temperatures plummeted (to −13 degrees Celsius), resupply was tenuous at best, and snow storms as well as frostbite ravaged the weary troops.

Nikolai Nikolaevich, thrown off balance by the German Ninth Army's bold stroke, cancelled his planned offensive and withdrew behind the Russian frontier, leaving behind the burning town of Łódź. German losses in the Battle of Łódź amounted to 35 000 men; Russian casualties have been conservatively estimated at 90 000, or nearly 70 per cent of the combat strength of the Second and First armies. Much of the credit for the German strategic withdrawal belongs to General Reinhard von Scheffer-Boyadel, whose XXV Reserve Corps had stormed through the gap between the two Russian armies – only to face a determined counterattack by General P. A. Pleve's Russian Fifth Army from the south and by an improvised army from the north. General Ruzsky, Commander-in-Chief of the Russian northwest front, sought to annihilate what he called the 'rag-tag XXV Reserve Corps'. Surrounded and outnumbered, Scheffer-Boyadel refused to surrender. Over 9 days in subzero weather the XXV Reserve Corps instead broke out of the Russian ring and captured 16 000 prisoners and 64 guns; it suffered only 4500 casualties, including 1000 killed. On 25 November Scheffer-Boyadel even brought back his 2000 wounded.[100]

In the south Conrad once more found himself in dire straits. A new attack by the Russian Ninth Army drove Archduke Joseph Ferdinand's Fourth Army back south of Cracow. Concurrently, the Russian Third and Eighth armies pressed Boroević's Third Army in Galicia and General Karl von Pflanzer-Baltin's army corps in the Bukovina deep into the Carpathian Mountains. Losses climbed to between 70 000 and 80 000 men.[101] A 70-mile gap developed between the two Habsburg armies. The Russian Third and Eighth armies were poised to drive through this corridor and over the Uzsok, Dukla, Lupkov, and Tylicz passes into Hungary and Bohemia. Ludendorff grudgingly dispatched the German 47th Reserve Division to Conrad, who managed by 17 December to halt the Russian Third Army at Limanowa-Lapanów – but not before complaining bitterly to Vienna of the 'egotistical ally' in Berlin who failed to appreciate that Habsburg forces to date had held back the storm of 'half of Asia'.[102] In return, the German plenipotentiary at Teschen warned Falkenhayn that the Habsburg Army was a 'brittle' instrument: infantry divisions were down to between 5000 and 7000 and companies to 50 men. 'The lack of officers is a calamity.' Freytag-Loringhoven doubted even the 'defensive power' of Conrad's forces.[103] Hindenburg informed Wilhelm II of the impossible task of having to deal with an 'indecisive Austrian army command' and an 'inferior Austrian Army'.[104] Archduke Friedrich was promoted to the rank of field marshal for the victorious battle.

The winter battles in the east in November and December 1914 had taken a heavy toll on both sides. The German Ninth Army suffered 100 000 casualties. The Russians conceded that they had lost 530 000 troops, that the officer corps of many units had been reduced by 70 per cent, and that the 1.4 million new recruits raised had been sent to the front often without rifles.[105] According to Russian sources, more than 60 000 Austro-Hungarian (against only 2000 German) prisoners of war had been taken, while cholera and typhus had ravaged 6500 troops. Winter finally forced an end to the fighting.

A glum Conrad informed General von Bolfras in Vienna that the enemy in the east now enjoyed a two-to-one superiority: 120 Russian divisions, each with 16 battalions, against 60 Austro-Hungarian and German divisions, each with only 12 battalions. Conrad also warned Foreign Minister Berchtold that Wilhelm II would conclude a separate peace with Tsar Nicholas II at Austria-Hungary's expense.[106] Hindenburg, Ludendorff, and Hoffmann, for their part, took perverse pleasure in heaping further verbal abuse on the 'incompetent' Austrians.[107] Recriminations broke to the surface once more. While Conrad took malicious pleasure in Ludendorff's rebuff at Łódź, the German charged that Conrad's lacklustre advance had cost him a second 'Sedan'.[108]

The two allies, commonly referred to as the Central Powers, finally met at Breslau on 2 December to discuss the war in the east. The meeting brought no agreements either on a unified command or a common strategy. Instead, Wilhelm II, in Conrad's words, played 'theatre' and regaled his audience with mendacious musings: 'My ideal, indeed my dream, would be to arrange an understanding with France and to capture the English Army'. The only common ground reached, apart from Falkenhayn's promise to transfer nine infantry division to the Eastern Front, was a determination 'to continue the war'.[109] Kurt Riezler of the German Foreign Office out of desperation suggested to *OberOst* that Grand Duke Nikolai Nikolaevich, 'the soul of [Russian] resistance', be assassinated![110]

In the Balkans Potiorek invaded Serbia for a third time. At dawn on 6 November General von Frank's Fifth Army drove south from the Save–Drina triangle while Potiorek's Sixth Army pushed west across the Drina and the Jagodjina Plateau. Despite heavy rains and rugged terrain, fate seemed at last to favour Potiorek: Valjevo fell on 15 November and the drive to the Kolubara River was crowned with success. Franz Joseph showered Potiorek with compliments, cities made him an honorary citizen, and Sarajevo named a street after him (perhaps to overcome the shame of 28 June 1914?).

Potiorek drove his men, still clothed in summer uniforms, forward through the mud in the valleys and the snow above. The Serbs fell back on Kragujevac. Soon, Habsburg units were out of food and ammunition. Egon Erwin, a private with the VIII Corps, noted: 'The terrain is horrible, we have no reserves, the soldiers are thinking of suicide'.[111] Potiorek whipped them forward. On 24 November he appointed General Stefan Sarkotič 'governor of Serbia'. On 2 December, the anniversary of Franz Joseph's 66th year on the throne, Potiorek, ever the courtier, informed Vienna that he was laying 'town and fortress Belgrade' at 'His Majesty's feet'. The left wing of his Fifth Army had taken the Serbian capital without a major struggle. Potiorek was ranked equal with Prince Eugen(e), and in Vienna flags flew, regimental bands played, and torch-light parades celebrated Belgrade's fall.

Potiorek's piece of archaic chivalry backfired almost immediately. Field Marshal Putnik, knowing that the Austrians had been bogged down by snow in the mountains, rains below, and impassable roads, counter-attacked with four armies of 200 000 men and forced the exhausted and dispirited 80 000 Austro-Hungarian troops to abandon Belgrade. Many Habsburg battalions had shrunk to company strength. By 9 December the Serbians separated the Habsburg Fifth Army at Belgrade from the Sixth Army at Šabac. Six days later Putnik threw both armies 60 miles back behind the Drina–Danube line, where gunboats of the Danube flotilla pro-tected them from further pursuit. The Serbs reentered Belgrade on 15 December.

Conrad spoke of an unexpected 'thunder bolt' from the south and acknowledged that the Balkans had been lost. Potiorek's reckless offen-sive had not achieved any of its major objectives – to knock Serbia out of the war, to induce Bulgaria to join the Central Powers, and to convince Romania permanently to remain neutral. The savage fighting cost Potiorek virtually half his original army of 450 000 men, including 28 000 dead and 122 000 wounded.[112] The Habsburg Fifth and Sixth armies were merged into a single Fifth Army of 95 000 men. A total disaster was avoided only because the Serbian Army had also suffered horrendous casualties: 22 000 dead, 91 000 wounded, and 19 000 captured or missing. Dysentery, cholera, and typhus ravaged both armies. The Austro-Hungarian official history of the war concludes that defeat by Serbia con-stituted 'politically a serious diminution in the Dual Monarchy's prestige and self-confidence'.[113]

Potiorek was relieved of command at Peterwardein on 22 December for 'this most ignominious, rankling and derisory defeat'.[114] He was replaced by Archduke Eugen, partly in the hope that the name alone would suffice to restore Habsburg forces to the glory days of Prince Eugen(e). Therewith, the Habsburgs completed their emulation of the Hohenzollern tradition of appointing members of the royal house to command army groups. General von Frank was relieved of command of the Fifth Army.

Conrad was fully aware that his forces were at the breaking point, using the term 'pumped dry' to describe their state of exhaustion. In the span of 5 months his armies had marched 100 miles to the front, attacked the Russians twice, and retreated twice. No Habsburg Army since 1809, Conrad lectured Vienna, had ever been asked to undertake such strenuous combat.[115] But the cost had been high. One entire army group guarding the snow-covered Carpathian passes had been ground down to 900 men and reorganized into two battalions of the 3rd Infantry Division! The Third Army's 20th *Landwehr* Division had been reduced from 13 100 to 2615 soldiers in just 6 days of fighting. All too much valuable equipment had been abandoned on the battlefields. German officers attached to the *AOK* reported that Škoda's and Böhler's production of 50 to 60 howitzers and 2000 shrapnel shells and Weiss' output of 90 000 rifles per month fell far short of replacement needs.[116]

On 21 December Conrad briefed Berchtold on the sad state of his Army. 'The best officers and non-commissioned officers have died or been removed from service, likewise the core of the rank and file.' The reserves were of poor quality, 'partly young, partly old men'. Austria–Hungary could not win a war of attrition, given the Russian superiority of 600 battalions of 500 000 rifles. There was but one alternative: a desperate sortie against the Russian Vistula positions in the new year. Failure to defeat the Russians by mid-February 1915, Conrad warned the Foreign Minister, would mean that the Dual Monarchy 'could no longer master the military situation'.[117] Conrad remained firm that the war could be decided only in the east.

General von Falkenhayn was of a radically different opinion. He decided after the debacle at the Marne to 'pull victory from the jaws of stalemate'[118] by outflanking the Allied armies in Flanders. In what has inaccurately been termed the 'race to the sea', each of the two opposing armies desperately tried to turn the flank of the other. In the process they slogged 170 miles through the rain-soaked fields of Flanders before halting at the English Channel, heavily bloodied and exhausted.

Falkenhayn was born the son of an impoverished West Prussian estate owner at Castle Belchau, near Thorn, in 1861. After Cadet School, he attended the War Academy in Berlin and graduated third in his class in 1890. Six years later he toured China on assignment to the General Staff (enemies said to escape embarrassing debts), served as an instructor at the Chinese Military School at Nankow, and took part in the suppression of the Boxer Rebellion. Falkenhayn's reports from China found favour with Wilhelm II and his career was assured: staff work with the XVI and IV Army Corps, command of the prestigious Fourth Foot Guards in 1911, and Prussian War Minister at the age of 51 in 1913. Tall, slender, aloof (if not downright arrogant), Falkenhayn seemed the epitome of the Prussian staff officer. His closely-cropped hair and his 'clever but sarcastic eyes' conjured up visions of precision, sharpness, and action.[119] His detractors claimed that he had spent too many years in China and not enough with the General Staff in Berlin.

On 5 September 1914 Falkenhayn maliciously had noted Moltke's dilemma at the Marne. 'Our General Staff has completely lost its head.

Schlieffen's notes do not help any further, and so Moltke's wits come to an end.'[120] Falkenhayn had hit the mark. As *de facto* Chief of the General Staff after 14 September, he tried to resurrect the Schlieffen plan by reinforcing the depleted right wing with the Seventh and Sixth armies to roll up the Allies' left flank in Flanders. His goal was straightforward: 'to achieve the decision of battle on the Army's right wing as soon as possible and with forces as strong as possible'.[121] Falkenhayn sought to return to the offensive and to seek the decision in the west. The Ninth Army on the Vistula would serve as a 'Chinese Wall' to cover operations in Flanders.

Like Moltke before him, Falkenhayn quickly ran foul of logistics. It took 140 trains to shift a single army, and only one double-rail line existed between Metz and the four armies on the right wing of the German Army. Falkenhayn sought to distract his adversaries by mounting a diversionary action against Verdun, which netted the St Mihiel salient but denied the critical right wing sufficient forces to turn the Allied flank in the north. Falkenhayn curtly rejected the suggestion of his railroad expert, General Wilhelm Groener, that six army corps lying idle in the south be transferred to the right wing. Bitter fighting in Picardy (22–6 September) and Artois (27 September–10 October) resulted in draws. Behind the front, Maubeuge surrendered on 8 September; Antwerp by 9 October. The Belgian Army escaped to fight alongside Anglo-French forces in Flanders. Thereafter, Ghent, Lille, Bruges, and Ostend fell within a week. The Kaiser recovered his spirits and was reported 'full of lust for battle', albeit, 'from a distance of 1000 yards'.[122]

Falkenhayn organized four of the six army corps freed from Maubeuge and Antwerp into the Fourth Army under Duke Albrecht of Württemberg, and ordered it into what became the final actions of the 'race for the flank' between 18 October and 24 November. Fourth Army was to attack along the sea and to destroy the enemy at the Yser; at the same time, Crown Prince Rupprecht's Sixth Army was to advance from Lille westward to the Flemish coast.[123] At stake were the vital Channel ports. Joffre countered this new German threat with the BEF and French forces under General Foch. The spiral movements of this giant leapfrogging ended in stalemate – as well as in the loss of 80 000 soldiers killed and wounded for the German Fourth and Sixth armies. A final French attempt to break through in the Champagne (20 December) likewise ended in a draw. This notwithstanding, Joffre in November rejected a proposal to outfit French soldiers with steel helmets, arguing that he would wring 'the Boche's neck' before 2 months were up!

The fighting in the rich clover, beet, and grain fields of Flanders was anything but that envisaged by Schlieffen. General Karl von Fasbender, commander of the First Bavarian Reserve Corps, likened it to the siege warfare predicted in 1895 by Quartermaster-General Köpke. Villages little more than a mile apart and interconnected by tree-lined roads and rock fences constituted a natural defensive network. Their French defenders offered only token resistance along the village perimeter, thereafter falling back to defend the old stone homes. 'The village battles are truly terrible. . . . We have to conquer the houses one by one, drag the enemy out of cellars and storage sheds, or kill them by throwing hand-grenades down at them. The casualties are always high.' The Bavarians found that newly-developed trench mortars, or *Minenwerfer*, which the British with ironic affection dubbed 'Minnies', were highly effective at close range.

Fasbender informed the *OHL* of the horrendous collateral damage occasioned by this type of fighting:

> All churches, including their steeples, are destroyed, all roofs torn off, walls caved in, entire houses bared to the elements; human beings and animals lie about, the barns are empty, cows roam about lowing, horses stand stupidly in the middle of roads; none [of the cows] are fed, watered, or milked because no one has remained in the village.

Fasbender's battalions shrank to company strength, often led by sergeants-major because their officers had been killed. French flyers constantly harassed the Germans by dropping shrapnel bombs loaded with 'thick knife blades and sharp hooks' that ripped limbs from bodies. By the time the Bavarians had stormed the French second and third lines, 'our energy is burned out, we are without officers, and companies number between 60 and 80 men. Thereafter we sink deeper and deeper into the soil, eye-to-eye with the enemy. Thus we lie opposite one another for weeks, indeed for months, by and large motionless'. Morale plummeted due to 'general exhaustion'. Fasbender concluded: 'We no longer know days, only months of continuous fighting. Open field warfare has degenerated into a sort of siege warfare – without really being siege warfare'.[124]

German soldiers attested to the 'face of battle' in their letters home. Stefan Schimmer, a Württemberg farmer, put it simply: 'Those who are only at home cannot possibly imagine [the nature of the war]. There is no day, no night, no Sunday, no weekday'. The killing fields refused to stop for anything. The painter Ernst Nopper committed to diary his experiences with the 121st Infantry Regiment near Longwy: 'Horrible impression; one cannot describe these abominable atrocities. Mankind is an animal of the vilest sort, pitiless'. Nopper marched through the burned-out village of Romain, side-stepping piles of corpses. 'Horses, hogs, cows have in some cases been burned or shriek; where left tied-up [they stand] and shriek mercilessly out of hunger and thirst'.[125]

Germany's second bid for victory was costly and it inaugurated static (trench) warfare. It was also marked by the sad spectacle of *Landwehr* veterans as well as fresh volunteers, many of them German Youth Movement and university students who previously had escaped military service, seeking to compensate for their lack of training and experience with enthusiasm and vigour. On 10 November these battalions of the 206th Reserve Infantry Regiment, without wire cutters or spades but allegedly singing *Deutschland, Deutschland über alles*, ran across wet clay fields against battle-hardened British infantry entrenched behind barbed wire with machine guns near Langemark (actually Bixchote). They were cut to ribbons. As many as 7000 remained on the battlefield; 13 000 were evacuated to field hospitals. With their officers killed or lost, short on ammunition and out of food, the reservists fled in panic. Some sang the national anthem to distinguish 'friendly' from hostile fire. Some units lost 70 per cent of strength in what German nationalists thereafter celebrated as the 'march of honour to Langemark'.[126] Adolf Hitler received his baptism of fire near Langemark and claimed to have heard the singing as the 206th marched to the front; he would return to the site in triumph on 2 June 1940. Youth, sacrifice, and idealism became the myth of Langemark. The *OHL* called the battle off on 18 November. The Fifth and Sixth armies had sustained 23 500 additional casualties.[127]

Falkenhayn was morally shaken by the Flanders debacle. He informed the Kaiser as early as 13 November that the Army was exhausted and that the campaign in the west probably had been lost. Falkenhayn used the example of Napoleon in 1812 to dismiss as utopian suggestions that he shift the war's centre of gravity to the east. Having lost faith in total victory, he developed a political strategy to escape the military disaster: a separate peace with Russia. Using logic that he would resurrect in the winter of 1915–16 in planning the Verdun campaign, Falkenhayn stressed that Great Britain was the 'archenemy', Germany's 'main adversary' and 'most dangerous opponent'. France and Russia were but 'tools' of 'perfidious Albion'. Thus the only apparent strategy was to come to terms with Russia to pursue the war to the bitter end against Britain.[128]

Falkenhayn presented his proposal to an agitated and highly alarmed Bethmann Hollweg on 18–19 November. He informed the Chancellor that victory lay beyond reach. 'As long as Russia, France and England hold together, it will be impossible to beat them to such a point where we can come to a decent peace. Rather, we would run the danger of slowly exhausting ourselves.' In sober, realistic terms, Falkenhayn argued for a negotiated peace with Russia leading to a desire for peace on the part of France. Germany would demand from Russia 'war indemnities but no major territorial concessions'. France would only have to demobilize the fortress of Belfort.[129] Falkenhayn found it amusing with regard to Albert Ballin's attempted peace feelers through Danish intermediaries that 'the first dove of peace had appeared with a *crooked beak*' – a comment that 'obviously pleased' the Kaiser.[130]

For the first time in German history, a Chancellor was asked by a Chief of the General Staff to take charge, to make the necessary political decision, and to end the war. For the second time (since the Marne) Bethmann Hollweg chose not to do so. He undoubtedly realized that the Wilhelmian ruling elite would not over night accept that the war had been lost and instead insisted that Germany come out of it with major gains, including Poland as a 'pawn' for future negotiations. Already in late September Bethmann Hollweg had vetoed Falkenhayn's desire to issue a formal bulletin apprising the nation of the setback at the Marne for fear that this would unsettle the national psyche. Now in November he again declined to face reality, and informed Falkenhayn that he was prepared to fight to the bitter end, no matter how long it might take. By rejecting the advice of the only person who had a clear appreciation of Germany's strategic situation at the end of 1914, Bethmann Hollweg became morally culpable for the continuing slaughter. Privately, he denounced Falkenhayn as a 'gambler' as well as an 'execrable character', and decried the General's actions in Flanders as those of a 'blood sucker'.[131] The Allies' decision at London on 4 September never to conclude a separate peace severely limited Falkenhayn's options.

Bethmann Hollweg's refusal to end the war stemmed in large part from the fact that on 9 September, at the height of the Battle of the Marne and fully expecting an imminent German entry into Paris, he had drafted a war-aims programme that foresaw German domination of Central Europe 'for all imaginable time'. France was to be reduced to a second-class power, Luxembourg annexed outright, Belgium and the Netherlands transformed into German 'vassal states', Russia reduced to its borders under Peter the Great, and a German economic union forged from Scandinavia to Turkey and from the Atlantic Ocean to the Caspian Sea, augmented by a vast German colonial empire in Central Africa.[132] Falkenhayn's pessimistic vision of a compromise peace had no place in this grand scheme. The German nation, Bethmann Hollweg asserted, needed 'rewards for its incredible sacrifice'. War aims now became an integral part of German strategy. For Bethmann Hollweg a return to the *status quo ante bellum* after 9 September would translate into a major political defeat.

At this critical juncture Zimmermann, Under-Secretary at the Foreign Office, not for the last time exerted a powerful influence on German decision-making. On 14 November he presented the Chancellor with a dazzling blueprint for victory.[133] Germany, in alliance with the Ottoman Empire, Romania, Bulgaria, and Sweden (!), was to mount a war of annihilation against Russia. Should that scheme fail, Zimmermann proposed that Serbia be crushed, Russia humiliated, and the Balkan states as well as the Porte attracted as allies against Britain. Bethmann Hollweg was not the statesman to remain deaf to such geopolitical musings.

Disappointed in Falkenhayn, the Chancellor on 6 December turned to the duumvirate of Hindenburg and Ludendorff. He found exactly what he was seeking: reassurances that the war was not lost, provided that the Army was given more men and supplies. Bethmann Hollweg, who knew nothing about military affairs, was impressed by Hindenburg's and Ludendorff's grasp of military detail. The two eastern leaders, for their part, saw the Chancellor as a welcome ally in their fight against the 'Westerner', Falkenhayn. Ludendorff equated Falkenhayn's call for an end to the war with 'treason'.

Bethmann Hollweg returned to Berlin determined to sack Falkenhayn and to replace him with Ludendorff at the first opportune moment. But Falkenhayn pressed his case, warning the Chancellor that the German Army was a 'decimated instrument' and that the fronts could at best be stabilized. Victory was not in the offing. Falkenhayn was saved from disgrace by the Kaiser, who so disliked Ludendorff that he brazenly informed his Chancellor that Ludendorff's 'great deeds' had been mere suggestions, formally 'approved and recommended' by the Supreme War Lord![134] The dispute paralysed German decision-making and prompted charges that Berlin was without a cohesive concept of the war, simply trying to 'muddle through' (*Wurschtelei*) to an unknown resolution.

Falkenhayn, embittered by the Chancellor's turn to Hindenburg and Ludendorff, decided that all that was left was to stabilize the Western Front. He now ordered the preparation of several parallel defensive lines 100 to 200 yards from enemy positions that were eventually extended in the shape of a shallow 'S' about 475 miles from Nieuport on the English Channel to Bec de Canard on the Swiss border. It was of paramount importance, Falkenhayn stressed, that all occupied territory be held and that any land lost be recaptured at once through vigorous counterattacks.[135] On 14 November he informed Field Marshal Colmar von der Goltz, governor of occupied Belgium, of the new maxim in the west: 'Hold on to what you have and never surrender a square foot of that which you have won'.[136] Flexibility, one of the hallmarks of German military doctrine, was another victim of the war.

Christmas Eve 1914 came on Thursday, a cold, clear night. Suffering from frostbite, pneumonia, rheumatism, and trench feet after 3 months of slogging through the mud of Flanders, they were determined to celebrate the birth of the 'prince of peace'. German soldiers lit Christmas trees, sang carols such as 'Silent Night', and exchanged cigarettes, caps, and badges for British bully beef, jack-knives, sheepskin jackets, and preserves. On Hill 108 in the Aisne sector, Captain Bohner von Emmich celebrated Christmas Eve Yule at 4 p.m. in the field hospital, followed 1 hour later by a church service, and at 6 p.m. by an exchange of gifts. His regimental commander played Santa Claus. On Christmas Day, a beautiful cloudless day, the French opened up with an artillery barrage and aerial bombing. Then both sides remembered the sanctity of the day. 'Fraternization with the French in front of the trenches in [sectors] 74 and 91.'[137] Dirty, mud-caked, and bearded *poilus* (hairy ones) made common cause with German *Frontschweine* (front pigs). In the British sector, Christmas Day was spent sorting out the corpses in No Man's Land.

Nor were such Yuletide celebrations restricted to officers. That same 24 December, Sergeant Schlubeck of the 31st (Hamburg) Division enjoyed an afternoon feast of chicken breast and stewed beef, chocolates and nuts, sardines, goat cheese, and rum for grog, all presents from home. The Division sang Christmas carols at 7 p.m. 'Naturally, the true Christmas spirit did not come.' The next day Schlubeck enjoyed coffee and hot sausages and received mail from home. 'Other than that, it was a day like any other.'[138] There would be fewer presents and no 'fraternization' the next Christmas. At home, the police reported that the Christmas spirit had been dampened by the large numbers of women dressed in black.

Germany had suffered 800 000 casualties – including 18 000 officers – and the Allies an equal number between September and December in what was to go down in history as the bloodiest fighting of the war. The Reich had lost 116 000 young men killed – compared with 45 000 in the war of 1870–1. The one bright side was that Germany – unlike Austria–Hungary – could call on a ready reserve of 2 million men who had not been mobilized in August. And on another 3 million who had escaped military training due to personal or occupational exemptions.[139] The BEF, that 'army of non-commissioned officers', as Falkenhayn put it to Conrad,[140] had sustained 86 237 casualties (among 110 000 combatants). Battalions that had started the war with 1000 men were down to 30 commanded by a single officer. The 7th Division in 4 weeks went from 12 000 men to 2500, and from 400 officers to 50.[141] To find replacements, the British Army lowered its minimum height requirements from 5′8″ in August to 5′5″ in October and to 5′3″ in November 1914. The British official history poignantly notes: 'The old British Army was gone past recall, leaving but a remnant to carry on the training of the New Armies'.[142]

The Austro-Hungarian Army was nearly eliminated as a fighting force. War Minister von Krobatin calculated losses at 692 195 soldiers; in reality, the figure stood closer to 1 million. More than 189 000 officers and men had died, 490 000 had been wounded, and 278 000 taken prisoners of war. Officer casualties alone were set at 26 500. In December 1914 the Dual Monarchy fielded only 303 000 combatants against the Russians.[143] German observers at Teschen noted that Conrad 'had lost faith in his own troops', and that a dangerous 'fatalism' permeated the *AOK*.[144] Conrad, in turn, ruminated sarcastically about 'our secret enemies, the Germans, and . . . the German Kaiser, the comedian'.[145] In Vienna, Professor Josef Redlich wondered 'what dark doors would open in the next year? Whatever happens, the Europe that has been around since 1870 will no longer exist'.[146] Surely, the time had come to reassess the war.

Chapter 3 Notes

1. Reichsarchiv, *Der Weltkrieg 1914 bis 1918*. 1: *Die Grenzschlachten im Westen* (Berlin, E. S. Mittler & Sohn, 1925), p. 69. See also Arden Bucholz, *Moltke, Schlieffen, and Prussian War Planning* (New York and Oxford, Berg Publishers, 1991), p. 278.
2. Evelyn, Princess Blücher, *An English Wife in Berlin: A Private Memoir of Events, Politics, and Daily Life in Germany throughout the War and the Social Revolution of 1918* (New York, E. P. Dutton,1920), p. 14.
3. Jagow's report of 26 August 1914 in *Dokumente aus geheimen Archiven*. 4: *Berichte des Berliner Polizeipräsidenten zur Stimmung und Lage der Bevölkerung in Berlin 1914–1918,* eds Ingo Materna and Hans-Joachim Schreckenbach (Weimar, Hermann Böhlaus Nachfolger, 1987), pp. 4–5.
4. Otto Riebicke, *Was brauchte der Weltkrieg? Tatsachen und Zahlen aus dem deutschen Ringen 1914/18* (Berlin, Kyffhäuser-Verlag, 1936), p. 15, places the figure at only 120 million Marks.
5. Count von Lerchenfeld's report of 16 August 1914. BHStA, MA 3076 Militärbevollmächtigter Berlin.
6. Walter Görlitz, ed., *The Kaiser and His Court: The Diaries, Note Books and Letters of Admiral Georg Alexander von Müller Chief of the Naval Cabinet, 1914–1918* (New York, Harcourt, Brace & World, 1959), pp. 26, 40.
7. Görlitz, ed., *The Kaiser and His Court*, pp. 22–3.
8. Christoph Führ, *Das K.u.K. Armeeoberkommando und die Innenpolitik in Österreich 1914–1917* (Graz, Vienna, and Cologne, Hermann Böhlaus Nachf., 1968), pp. 116–18.
9. Edmund Glaise von Horstenau, *Die Katastrophe: die Zertrümmerung Österreich-Ungarns* (Vienna, Amalthea-Verlag, 1929), p. 66.
10. Volker Hoettl, 'Die Beziehungen Conrads von Hötzendorf zu den deutschen Generalstabschefs 1914–17 auf politischem Gebiet', unpubl. diss., Vienna University 1968, p. 5.
11. Rudolf Hecht, 'Fragen zur Heeresergänzung der gesamten Bewaffneten Macht Österreich-Ungarns während des Ersten Weltkrieges', unpubl. diss., Vienna University 1969, pp. 8 ff.
12. Führ, *Das K.u.K. Armeeoberkommando*, p. 92.
13. Gunther E. Rothenberg, *The Army of Francis Joseph* (West Lafayette, Ind., Purdue University Press, 1976), p. 177. Professor Josef Redlich, visiting Conrad on 26 August 1914, also noted the lackeys, three-course meals washed down with draft Pilsner beer and white and red wines as well as 2-hour breakfasts. Fritz Fellner, ed., *Schicksalsjahre Österreichs 1908–1918. Das politische Tagebuch Josef Redlichs* (2 vols, Graz and Cologne, Hermann Böhlaus Nachf., 1953–4) 1, pp. 251–2.

14. See Marc Ferro, *The Great War, 1914–1918* (London, Routledge & Kegan Paul, 1973), pp. 147–9; and Pierre Renouvin, *La crise européenne et la première guerre mondiale*. 19: *Peuples et civilisations* (Paris, Presses universitaires de France,1962), pp. 263–86.

15. Wolfgang J. Mommsen, *Max Weber und die deutsche Politik 1890–1920* (Tübingen, J. C. B. Mohr, 1959), p. 208. Letter of 28 August 1914.

16. Cited in Holger H. Herwig and Neil M. Heyman, eds, *Biographical Dictionary of World War I* (Westport, Conn., and London, Greenwood Press, 1982), pp. 45–6.

17. BA-MA, Nachlass Tappen, N 56, vol. 2. Reichsarchiv to Tappen, 4 July 1921; Reichsarchiv, *Der Weltkrieg 1914 bis 1918*. 2: *Die Befreiung Ostpreussens* (Berlin, E. S. Mittler & Sohn, 1925), pp. 43, 45.

18. Reichsarchiv, *Der Weltkrieg 1914 bis 1918* 2, pp. 93, 101.

19. Reichsarchiv, *Der Weltkrieg 1914 bis 1918* 2, p. 107.

20. Reichsarchiv, *Der Weltkrieg 1914 bis 1918* 2, p. 609. Moltke's comments to his staff.

21. Reichsarchiv, *Der Weltkrieg 1914 bis 1918* 2, p. 114.

22. Hindenburg had incurred the Kaiser's wrath for having foiled one of Wilhelm II's cherished cavalry charges during annual manoeuvres with the comment: 'Had this been for real, Your Majesty would now be my prisoner'. BA-MA, MSg1/2512 Nachlass von Alten.

23. See their respective entries in Herwig and Heyman, eds, *Biographical Dictionary of World War I* , pp. 184–6, 231–3.

24. Cited in Richard W. Harrison, 'Alexander Samsonov and the Battle of Tannenberg, 1914', in Brian Bond, ed., *Fallen Stars: Eleven Studies of Twentieth Century Military Disasters* (London, Washington, and New York, Brassey's, 1991), p. 22.

25. Reichsarchiv, *Der Weltkrieg 1914 bis 1918* 2, p. 230.

26. BA-MA, Nachlass Admiral von Müller, N 159, vol. 4, p. 292. Entry for 4 September 1914. The reference is omitted from the published diaries (see note 2). This description of the Battle of Tannenberg owes much to Dennis E. Showalter, *Tannenberg: Clash of Empires* (Hamden, Conn., Archon Books, 1991).

27. Showalter, *Tannenberg*, p. 326.

28. Reichsarchiv, *Der Weltkrieg 1914 bis 1918* 2, pp. 316–17.

29. Reichsarchiv, *Der Weltkrieg 1914 bis 1918* 2, pp. 242–3.

30. See the recent work by Rudolf Jeřábek, *Potiorek. General im Schatten von Sarajevo* (Graz, Styria, 1991).

31. See Conrad von Hötzendorf, *Aus meiner Dienstzeit 1906–1918* (5 vols,Vienna, Leizpig, and Munich, Rikola Verlag, 1923) 4, p. 465.

32. Cited in József Galántai, *Hungary in the First World War* (Budapest, Akadémiai Kiadó, 1989), p. 91.

33. Bundesministerium für Landesverteidigung, *Österreich-Ungarns Letzter Krieg 1914–1918*. 1: *Das Kriegsjahr 1914* (Vienna, Verlag der Militärwissenschaftlichen Mitteilungen, 1931), p. 152.

34. BA-MA, MSg 1/1914 Tagebuch Kageneck. Notes of 14 September 1914. One of Conrad's few critics within the senior Habsburg military command, General Alfred Krauss, as late as 24 August wrote in his diary Conrad's obsession 'to knock Serbia out quickly and then to turn against Russia with all [available] forces'. Cited in 'Der Feldzug gegen Serbien und Montenegro im Jahre 1914', *Österreichische Militärische Zeitschrift*, Special Issue, 1 (1965), p. 22.

35. Graydon A. Tunstall, Jr., *Planning for War Against Russia and Serbia: Austro-Hungarian and German Military Strategies, 1871–1914* (New York, Columbia University Press, 1993), p. 201.

36. See *Österreich-Ungarns Letzter Krieg 1914–1918* 1, pp. 163–4.

37. BA-MA, MSg 1/1914 Tagebuch Kageneck. Notes of 7 and 17 August 1914.

38. *Österreich-Ungarns Letzter Krieg 1914–1918* 1, pp. 173–8.

39. BA-MA, MSg 1/1914 Tagebuch Kageneck. Notes of 29 August 1914.

40. BA-MA, PH 3/328 Oberste Heeresleitung. Berichte Freiherr v. Freytag-Loringhoven 1912–1915. At Königgrätz, Austrian infantry in tight formation had charged Prussian troops armed with the Dreyse needle-gun; these shock tactics resulted in 43 000 casualties on 3 July.

41. Conrad, *Aus meiner Dienstzeit* 4, p. 564. Entry of 28 August 1914.

42. Conrad, *Aus Meiner Dienstzeit* 4, p. 648.

43. Conrad, *Aus Meiner Dienstzeit* 4, p. 787. Colonel Alexander Brosch von Aarenau faced his fate stoically, having predicted on 1 July that he would go to war 'as a resigned combatant who will see the black steamroller, which will obliterate us, approach, but who cannot stop it'. Rothenberg, *Army of Francis Joseph*, p. 177.

44. Tunstall, *Planning for War*, pp. 248, 250.

45. *Österreich-Ungarns Letzter Krieg 1914–1918* 1, pp. 263–4.

46. Fellner, ed., *Schicksalsjahre Österreichs* 1, p. 270. Diary entry of 9 September 1914.

47. BA-MA, PH 3/328 Berichte v. Freytag-Loringhoven, 2 September 1914.

48. Kageneck's notes on a conversation with Conrad on 11 September1914. BA-MA, MSg 1/1914.

49. See Hecht, 'Fragen der Heeresergänzung', pp. 8 ff.

50. ÖStA-KA, Militärkanzlei Seiner Majestät (MKSM) 1914, 38-2/2. Report of October 1914.

51. ÖStA-KA, Nachlass Kövess, B/1000, entry for 7 September 1914.

52. Peter Broucek, ed., *Ein General im Zwielicht. Die Erinnerungen Edmund Glaises von Horstenau* (2 vols, Vienna, Cologne, and Graz, Böhlau, 1980) 1, p. 279.

53. ÖStA-KA, Nachlass Boroević, B/4, entries for 6 and 16 September 1914.

54. Wilhelm Czermak, *In deinem Lager war Österreich. Die österreichisch-ungarische Armee, wie man sie nicht kennt* (Breslau, W. G. Korn, 1938), p. 51; *Österreich-Ungarns Letzter Krieg 1914–1918* 1, pp. 319–20.

55. ÖStA-KA, Nachlass Kövess, B/1000. Militärische Korrespondenz im Ersten Weltkrieg.

56. Cited in Rothenberg, *The Army of Francis Joseph*, p. 181.

57. Bolfras to Conrad, 25 September 1914. Conrad, *Aus meiner Dienstzeit* 4, p. 875.

58. Hoyos' memorandum of 17 September 1914. HHStA, PA VII Gesandschaft Berlin 196.

59. Conrad's memorandum of 4 November 1914. ÖStA-KA, MKSM 1914, 69-8/8. Conrad 's memoirs, *Aus meiner Dienstzeit* 4, are laced with bitterness concerning the German ally: see pp. 576, 608, 624, 670, 672, 681, 689, 703, 704, 707, 708, 737.

60. Cited in Tunstall, *Planning for War*, p. 249.

61. Conrad to Bolfras, 5 September 1914. Conrad, *Aus meiner Dienstzeit* 4, p. 647. Russian troops eventually slaughtered the Kaiser's prized stags at Rominten with machine-gun fire.

62. Conrad, *Aus Meiner Dienstzeit* 4, p. 894. Conrad to Auffenberg, 30 September 1914.

63. BA-MA, MSg 1/1914 Tagebuch Kageneck. Entry for 21 September 1914.

64. BA-MA, MSg 1/2515, Kageneck's entries for 11 and 17 September 1914; and BA-MA, PH 3/328, Berichte v. Freytag-Loringhoven, entry for 11 September 1914.

65. For the organization of the German armies in 1914 see Wilhelm Dieckmann, *Die Behördenorganisation in der deutschen Kriegswirtschaft 1914–1918* (Hamburg, Hanseatische Verlagsanstalt, 1937).

66. Relative strengths from *Der Weltkrieg 1914 bis 1918* 1, pp. 646, 654, 656.

67. *Der Weltkrieg 1914 bis 1918* 1, p. 651.

68. This was agreed upon as one of the causes of failure between Generals Hans von Plessen and Moltke on 30 April 1915. BA-MA, Nachlass Moltke, N 78, vol. 6, pp. 10–11.

69. BA-MA, Nachlass Moltke, N 78, vol. 37, p. 31. Moltke's comments to his son, Adam.

70. John Horne and Alan Kramer, 'German "Atrocities" and Franco-German Opinion, 1914: The Evidence of German Soldiers' Diaries,' *Journal of Modern History* 66 (1994), p. 22.

71. Figures from the official French and German histories of the war: *Der Weltkrieg 1914–1918* 1, p. 646; *Les armés françaises dans la grande guerre.* Tome 1, vol. 1: *La bataille de la Marne* (Paris, 1931), p. 589.
72. Reichsarchiv, *Der Weltkrieg 1914 bis 1918.* 3: *Der Marne Feldzug. Von der Sambre zur Marne* (Berlin, E. S. Mittler & Sohn, 1926), pp. 138–40.
73. Reichsarchiv, *Der Weltkrieg 1914 bis 1918* 3, p. 220.
74. Martin van Creveld, *Supplying War: Logistics from Wallenstein to Patton* (Cambridge, Cambridge University Press, 1977), p. 140. See also the diary entries for August and September in BA-MA, W-10/50631 Tagebücher Beseler (First Army).
75. Jehuda L. Wallach, *The Dogma of the Battle of Annihilation: The Theories of Clausewitz and Schlieffen and Their Impact on the German Conduct of Two World Wars* (Westport, Conn., and London, Greenwood Press, 1986), p. 110.
76. *Der Weltkrieg 1914–1918* 3, pp. 403–11.
77. See BA-MA, PH 5 II/119. First Army Retrospect.
78. Reichsarchiv, *Der Weltkrieg 1914 bis 1918.* 4: *Der Marne-Feldzug. Die Schlacht* (Berlin, E. S. Mittler & Sohn, 1926), pp. 139–40.
79. Gotthard Jäschke, 'Zum Problem der Marne-Schlacht von 1914', *Historische Zeitschrift,* 190 (1960), p. 336.
80. Cited in *Der Weltkrieg 1914 bis 1918* 4, p. 144.
81. See *Der Weltkrieg 1914 bis 1918* 4, pp. 222–330, 526–33.
82 *Der Weltkrieg 1914 bis 1918* 4, p. 524.
83. BA-MA, PH 3/60 Generalstab. Ruling of 24 May 1917. Hentsch had requested the inquiry to clear his name. Ludendorff later tried to revoke his signature.
84. BA-MA, Nachlass Müller, N 159, vol. 4. Diary entry of 13 September 1914. Again, this passage was not included in the published diary.
85. Görlitz, ed., *The Kaiser and His Court,* p. 32; and Karl-Heinz Janssen, *Die graue Exzellenz: Zwischen Staatsräson und Vasallentreue. Aus den Papieren des kaiserlichen Gesandten Karl Georg von Treutler* (Frankfurt and Berlin, Propyläen, 1971), p. 167.
86. Cited in Liddell Hart, *The Real War,* p. 101.
87. Alfred von Schlieffen, *Gesammelte Schriften* (2 vols, Berlin, E. S. Mittler & Sohn, 1913) 2, p. 441.
88. Moltke to Plessen, 2 May 1915. BA-MA, Nachlass Moltke, N 78, vol. 6, pp. 12–15.
89. BA-MA, MSg 1/1228 and 2511 Nachlass v. Alten. Tieschowitz's letters to his wife, Ellie, dated 15 September and 10 October as well as one undated (probably October 1914).
90. The concept apparently was first popularized by Gustave Babin in *L'Illustration* on 11 October 1915.
91. Conrad, *Aus meiner Dienstzeit* 4, pp. 819, 846–7, 888–9; *Österreich-Ungarns Letzter Krieg 1914–1918* 1, pp. 345–8.
92. B. H. Liddell Hart, *Reputations: Ten Years After* (Boston, Little, Brown, 1928), p. 188.
93. Reichsarchiv, *Der Weltkrieg 1914 bis 1918.* 5: *Der Herbst-Feldzug 1914* (Berlin, E. S. Mittler & Sohn, 1929), pp. 489–91.
94. Conrad, *Aus meiner Dienstzeit* 5 (1925), p. 110.
95. *Österreich-Ungarns Letzter Krieg 1914–1918* 1, p. 470.
96. Conrad, *Aus meiner Dienstzeit* 5, pp. 301, 377.
97. Conrad, *Aus Meiner Dienstzeit* 5, pp. 382–3, 393–4, 543. See also Reichsarchiv, *Der Weltkrieg 1914 bis 1918.* 6: *Der Herbst-Feldzug 1914* (Berlin, E. S. Mittler & Sohn, 1929), pp. 49, 53.
98. Cited in Gary W. Shanafelt, *The Secret Enemy: Austria-Hungary and the German Alliance, 1914–1918* (New York, Columbia University Press, 1985), p. 48.
99. The Austrian official history glosses over Conrad's move to and life at Teschen: *Österreich-Ungarns Letzter Krieg 1914–1918* 1, p. 512. See BA-MA, MSg 1/2517 Tagebuch v. Kageneck, entry for 21 October 1915.

100. *Der Weltkrieg 1914 bis 1918* 6, pp. 169–88, 201.
101. *Österreich-Ungarns Letzter Krieg 1914–1918* 1, p. 554.
102. Cited in *Der Weltkrieg 1914 bis 1918* 6, pp. 247–8.
103. BA-MA, PH 3/328 Berichte von Freytag-Loringhoven, dated 27 November and 14 and 28 December 1914.
104. Cited in *Der Weltkrieg 1914 bis 1918* 6, p. 256.
105. *Österreich-Ungarns Letzter Krieg 1914–1918* 1, p. 594.
106. HHStA, PA VII Gesandschaft Berlin 196, Separat Akten; Conrad, *Aus meiner Dienstzeit* 5, p. 611.
107. See Rothenberg, *Army of Francis Joseph*, p. 181.
108. BA-MA, MSg 1/1914 Tagebuch Kageneck. Entries for 12 October and 6 and 20 November 1914.
109. Cited in Conrad, *Aus meiner Dienstzeit* 5, pp. 655, 911. See also *Der Weltkrieg 1914 bis 1918* 6, p. 285; and *Österreich-Ungarns Letzter Krieg 1914–1918* 1, p. 598.
110. Kurtz Riezler, *Tagebücher, Aufsätze, Dokumente,* ed. Karl Dietrich Erdmann (Göttingen, Vandenhoeck & Ruprecht, 1972), p. 235. Entry for 23 December 1912.
111. Cited in Manfried Rauchensteiner, *Der Tod des Doppeladlers. Österreich-Ungarn und der Erste Weltkrieg* (Graz, Vienna, and Cologne, Verlag Styria, 1994), p. 185.
112. *Österreich-Ungarns Letzter Krieg 1914–1918* 1, p. 759.
113. *Österreich-Ungarns Letzter Krieg 1914–1918* 1, p. 762.
114. Winston S. Churchill, *The Unknown War: The Eastern Front* (New York, Charles Scribner's Sons, 1931), p. 269.
115. BA-MA, MSg 1/2515. Kageneck's diary entry for 18 October 1914.
116. BA-MA, PH3/328. Freytag-Loringhoven's report of 23 November 1914.
117. Conrad, *Aus meiner Dienstzeit* 5, pp. 731, 753, 852–4, 926.
118. Colin Gray, *The Leverage of Sea Power: The Strategic Advantage of Navies in War* (New York, Free Press, 1992), p. 195.
119. See Falkenhayn's entry in Herwig and Heyman, eds, *Biographical Dictionary of World War I*, pp. 145–6.
120. Cited in Hans von Zwehl, *Falkenhayn* (Berlin, E. S. Mittler & Sohn, 1936), p. 66.
121. *Der Weltkrieg 1914 bis 1918* 5, p. 63.
122. Görlitz, ed., *The Kaiser and His Court*, p. 40.
123. *Der Weltkrieg 1914 bis 1918* 5, p. 285. Falkenhayn's orders of 14 October.
124. BHStA-KA, HS 2112. Auszug a. d. Kriegs-Tage-Buch des Gen. d. Inf. Karl Ritter von Fasbender. Entries for the period 3 October to 7 November 1914.
125. Cited in Gerhard Hirschfeld, Gerd Krumeich, Irina Reuz, eds, *Keiner fühlt sich mehr als Mensch . . . Erlebnis und Wirkung des Ersten Weltkriegs* (Essen, Klartext, 1993), pp. 201, 205.
126. See Karl Unruh, *Langemarck. Legende und Wirklichkeit* (Koblenz, Bernard & Graefe, 1986), pp. 151 ff. It is interesting that the 206th regimental history was not written until 1931. The famous Army report of this slaughter was dated 11 November: 'West of Langemarck, youthful regiments stormed the first lines of the enemy trenches and took them, singing "Deutschland, Deutschland über alles"'. The *OHL* preferred the more 'Germanic' name of Langemarck to Ypres or Bixchote.
127. *Der Weltkrieg 1914 bis 1918* 6, p. 25. The German official history is strangely silent on Langemarck!
128. See Holger Afflerbach, *Falkenhayn. Politisches Denken und Handeln im Kaiserreich* (Munich, R. Oldenbourg, 1994), pp. 198–203.
129. BA-MA, MSg 1/1228 Nachlass v. Alten. Diary of Major Hans von Haeften (*OberOst*), 18–21 December 1914. See also *Der Weltkrieg 1914 bis 1918* 6, pp. 406–7.
130. BA-MA, W-10/50656 Tagebuch v. Plessen, entry for 24 November 1914. Ballin, head of the Hamburg–America Line, was Jewish.

131. See Afflerbach, *Falkenhayn*, p. 247.

132. Fritz Fischer, *Griff nach der Weltmacht. Die Kriegszielpolitik des kaiserlichen Deutschland 1914/18* (Düsseldorf, Droste Verlag, 1961), pp. 113 ff.

133. See Karl-Heinz Janssen, *Der Kanzler und der General. Die Führungskrise um Bethmann Hollweg und Falkenhayn (1914–1916)* (Göttingen, Musterschmidt, 1967), pp. 43, 45, 56; and *Der Weltkrieg 1914 bis 1918* 6, pp. 409–10.

134. See Gerhard Ritter, *Staatskunst und Kriegshandwerk. Das Problem des 'Militarimus' in Deutschland* (4 vols, Munich, R. Oldenbourg, 1964) 3, pp. 59–65.

135. Militärgeschichtliches Forschungsamt, *Handbuch der deutschen Militärgeschichte* (5 vols, Munich, Bernard & Graefe Verlag, 1979) 5, p. 505; Erich von Falkenhayn, *General Headquarters 1914–1916 and its Critical Decisions* (London, Hutchinson, 1919), p. 36.

136. *Der Weltkrieg 1914 bis 1918* 5, p. 585.

137. BA-MA, MSg 2/4705 Emmichs Tagebuch.

138. BA-MA, MSg 2/65 Schlubeck's Tagebuch, p. 13.

139. *Der Weltkrieg 1914 bis 1918* 6, pp. 444–5.

140. Conrad, *Aus meiner Dienstzeit* 5, p. 819. Wilhelm II never referred to the *BEF* as 'that contemptible little army'; the term was coined by Sir Frederick Maurice of the War Office in London, who tagged it on the Kaiser.

141. Trevor Wilson, *The Myriad Faces of War: Britain and the Great War, 1914–1918* (Cambridge, Polity Press, 1986), pp. 48–9.

142. James E. Edmonds, ed., *History of the Great War: Military Operations, France and Belgium, 1914* (14 vols, London, Macmillan, 1925) 2, p. 465.

143. ÖStA-K, MSKM 69-8/9, 'Betrachtungen über die Verluste im jetzigen Kriege', 31 March 1915; and Hecht, 'Fragen der Heeresergänzung', passim. The butcher's bill was as follows: 115 284 dead; 357 726 wounded; 212 611 sick; 259 233 'missing '; for a total of 1 253 800 casualties. If one deducts from this figure 658 446 new recruits added to the armed forces, one arrives at a net reduction of 595 354 men, or close to Krobatin's adjusted figure. ÖStA-KA, MSKM 69-8/6. Military Chancery statistics for 1914 losses.

144. BA-MA, MSg 1/1914 Tagebuch Kageneck. Entry for 26 November 1914.

145. Cited in Josef Stürgkh, *Im Deutschen Grossen Hauptquartier* (Leipzig, Paul List Verlag, 1921), p. 116. Entry for early 1915.

146. Fellner, ed., *Schicksalsjahre Österreichs* 1, p. 295. Entry for 31 December 1914.

4

Towards Industrialized War, 1915

The higher civilization rises, the more vile man becomes.

General Karl von Einem, April 1915

The winter of 1914–15 brought no reevaluation of German strategy. Wilhelm II moaned about having no choice but to 'die with honour', yet he called no war council to reassess Germany's options in the wake of the failed Schlieffen plan. His Chief of the General Staff simply adopted a siege mentality. Like the Austrian garrison besieged at Przemyśl, the German Empire could only hunker down and try to survive. 'Hold what you have and never surrender a square foot of what you have won.'[1] Falkenhayn even mused whether a 'future war', a 'second Punic war' might not be needed to defeat 'perfidious Albion'. On the other hand, German industrialists demanded continuation of the war out of fear that a 'bad peace' would bring 'the revolution'.[2] Bethmann Hollweg likewise spoke of the need 'to stick it out' (*durchhalten*) to obtain a victor's peace. But the word victory and the vision of a grand parade down the Champs Elysées had disappeared at the *OHL*. Field Marshal Gottlieb von Haeseler, activated for field duty in July 1914 at the tender age of 78, almost alone among the German military elite admitted that the Great Gamble of 1914 had failed. 'It seems to me that the moment has come in which we must try to end the war.'[3]

German leaders at least were secure in the knowledge that the nation had rallied behind the war effort. Millions of volunteers – mothers, wives, children – offered their services for the war. When the Red Cross in Berlin organized a First Aid course, it received 40 000 applications rather than the requested 3000. The Reichstag mounted exhibitions on how to care for the wounded. Church attendance rose and pastors and priests thundered from the pulpit about the righteousness of Germany's cause. War subscriptions were well received: Mosse Publishers in Berlin alone netted 122 million Marks in August 1914 in one such private drive.[4]

Patriotism abounded. The intendant of the Royal Theatre in Berlin announced that he would produce only patriotic plays and offer these to the public at reduced prices. Actors agreed to take a wage cut. 'Modern English and French plays disappeared without a trace from the program.'[5] Concert halls likewise concentrated on 'Germanic' works. Professors lectured the public on the just cause of the war. Friedrich Meinecke, Professor of History at Berlin University, compared the present conflict to the Prussian wars of liberation against Napoleon in 1806–13. Children played street games in which 'German soldiers' routinely routed their 'English' or 'Russian' opponents. Not even the rapid loss of the Reich's far-flung colonial possessions dampened the patriotic spirit. Australian, British, and Japanese forces had overrun Germany's South Sea islands by Christmas 1914. Togo in Africa had surrendered as early as 27 August; Kiaochow in China fell to the Japanese on 10 November.[6]

Most Germans spent the first Christmas in the firm belief that victory was just over the horizon. The Army routinely put out news bulletins of victories and advances, forts stormed, and enemy losses. The nation was informed neither of the defeat at the Marne nor of the dismissal of General von Moltke as Chief of the General Staff. Nor was it allowed to see the terrible casualty lists that emanated from the Marne, Aisne, Yser, and Vistula. Few even in high government positions had any inkling of the nature of the Schlieffen plan, and hence none but a handful of the militarily initiated understood that the German recipe for victory in the west had already failed. Most Germans still expected imminent news of victory. After all, many of the elderly recalled, it had taken the Elder Moltke 6 months to defeat the imperial armies of Napoleon III and the republican forces of Thiers in 1870–1. Could one expect more of the untried nephew?

The terrible losses at the fronts and the high intensity of public feeling brought to the surface a new and meaner side of war. In Hungary, Prime Minister Tisza announced that his government would show 'strength' in keeping the non-Hungarian population quiescent. Since November 1912, the Hungarian police had maintained a secret list (Cs-1) of possible enemies of the state (mainly Serbs, Croats, and Romanians living near the borders). 'Suspicion of espionage' sufficed to allow the police to undertake mass arrests 'on the day of mobilization'.[7] In Germany, shortly after the storming of Liège in mid-August 1914, Moltke issued an order establishing capital punishment for persons participating in 'any form of unjustified war activity'. Such offenders were to be treated as 'terrorists'. Hindenburg and Ludendorff at the Eastern Front on the last day of 1914 spelled out precisely what constituted 'unjustified war activity': possession of firearms of any kind; destruction of roads, telegraphs, and telephones; illegal listening to long-distance telephone calls; signalling news to the enemy; and any activity that gave 'advantage' to the adversary.[8] In March 1915 *OberOst* informed Vienna that it planned to burn two villages in Russian Poland for each German settlement destroyed in East Prussia – much to the delight of the Austrians, who hoped that the Poles would thereby be driven into their camp.[9]

The severity of *OberOst*'s measures was a direct result of revelations of Russian terror in East Prussia during August and September 1914. Despite official *Stavka* and individual army orders to eschew plunder and malicious destruction, especially Russian rear-guard and train personnel as well as Cossacks undertook a systematic campaign of terror against the German population. Entire villages – Domnau, Abschwangen, Ortelsburg, and Bartenstein, among many others – had been burned to the ground after the Battle of Gumbinnen on 20 August. A Russian soldier recorded the fate of Schirwindt (1300 inhabitants): 'In a few hours the town was totally plundered; everything that was not groceries or money was given over to the flames and total destruction'. Twenty people were summarily executed at Santoppen for ringing a church bell (a suspected signal) during a burial service. Women and girls particularly suffered during the occupation. Polish Jews were suspected of having encouraged the theft of household and farming goods for resale and personal gain.

The Russian retreat after the Battle of Tannenberg exacerbated the civilian horror. The Russians took with them about 10 000 draft-eligible men (but also women) as 'hostages'; countless bridges as well as rail and communications facilities were destroyed; and factories and utilities installations were rendered inoperable. East Prussian authorities estimated that the Russian occupation armies killed 1620 civilians, destroyed 17 000 buildings, and stole or slaughtered 135 000 horses, 250 000 cows, and 200 000 pigs.[10] 'Pillage, like death', as the historian John Lynn noted of an earlier struggle, 'arrives hand in hand with war'.[11]

The same story held true for Galicia, which Russian forces evacuated in the summer of 1915. The Ministry of the Interior at Vienna reported widespread devastation and destruction by the initial wave of 'undisciplined, robber-like Cossacks' who had 'plundered, robbed, killed, and committed innumerable acts of terror' against the indigenous population, of whom 500 000 had fled westward. More than 70 000 square kilometres of arable land from Brody to Cracow had been ravaged and lay fallow. Seven million farmers were ruined financially and millions of agrarian labourers reduced to beggars. Hundreds of thousands of cattle had been slaughtered by the Russians, this strange mix of 'Finns and Tartars'. At least 100 000 cows would be needed just to begin to restock the herds. Shell craters and abandoned trenches scarred the landscape. Thaddäus von Cienski was but one of countless nobles victimized by the Russians: his ancient castle at Pieniaki had been razed, more than 1000 hectares of forest burned, and countless villages levelled. 'The situation of this land is truly hopeless.' Pogroms had devastated Galicia's Jewish population of 650 000.[12]

The Ballhausplatz was concerned that Russian Orthodox Church priests had forcefully converted 30 000 Catholics in East Galicia ('the Tyrol of the East') alone. It also lamented that the Russians had closed all Polish schools and 'Russified' Lemberg University. Most disturbingly, much of the Habsburg gendarmerie had readily offered their services to the Russian secret police, with the result that tens of thousands of anti-Russian Poles and Ruthenes had been deported to Siberia. While some Jews had 'conducted magnificent business' with the Russians, most had remained loyal to the Habsburgs and as a result had lost all their worldly possessions. Polish farmers, long treated as 'little more than cattle' by their noble overseers, had used the invasion to ransack aristocratic residences, to chop down grand forests, and to claim noble land as their own. Poles had been set against Ruthenians and vice versa. Racial hatred abounded. Tens of thousands of Ruthenians and Poles had been hauled off by the retreating Russians as 'hostages'. 'The land bleeds from a thousand wounds.'[13]

Horrendous war losses affected the domestic spirit in Austria–Hungary. Habsburg armies in Galicia lost about a million men between September and December 1914, and the *AOK*'s stubborn (if futile) winter campaigns in the Carpathian Mountains took another 600 000 to 800 000. For the first 4 months of the war, a more rigorous application of the draft brought in 800 000 new recruits[14]: more than a third of these were added to the armed forces in September and October alone. Gypsies were now 'permitted' to serve the Empire, and military authorities recalled the 2.3 million men deemed unfit between 1901 and 1912 in the hope of reclassifying several thousand for front-line duty. Only the physically handicapped, civil servants, priests, farmers, and war-industries producers escaped service. Early in 1915 much of the Austro-Hungarian cavalry dismounted and spent the rest of the war as 'foot cavalry' because the loss of 150 000 horses could not be ameliorated.[15] Heavy draft animals for the artillery were in short supply.

Perhaps the most critical loss was that of infantry officers. Suicidal frontal attacks against the Russians had resulted in high death rates among long-term professionals. To remedy this loss of leaders, the military in 1914 undertook a number of *ad hoc* measures. Instruction at the military academies was turned over to civilians and retired or invalided officers, thus freeing up able-bodied officers for the front. Police forces as well as military bureaus throughout the Monarchy were screened for suitable officer material.[16]

The Military Chancery in Vienna conceded that the quality of its peacetime officer corps had left much to be desired when it came to fighting a major war. In November 1914 General von Bolfras' staff evaluated combat experience to date. It concluded that in future the officer corps needed to be raised in terms of its social niveau by 'attracting the nobility and the better bourgeois elements'. Especially the Prussian practice of ennobling deserving middle-class officers needed to be applied with greater rigour in Austria-Hungary. Bolfras' staff also recommended that the 1868 division of the armed forces into three distinct components (Joint Army, Austrian *Landwehr*, and Hungarian *Honvéd*) be scrapped and that one unified army be created. The imperial and royal bureaucracy needed to be staffed to a greater extent with military personnel so that it would develop a better understanding of the Army's needs. The antimilitarism fashionable especially in Viennese academic and professional circles was to be rooted out. And the multicultural and multi-ethnic character of the Empire's administration needed to be 'regenerated'.[17] But the octogenarian Franz Joseph was hardly the person to reenact the reformist zeal of Joseph II (1780–90).

Many Austrians developed draft evasion into a fine art. Military doctors at recruiting depots recorded increasing cases of self-inflicted gunshot wounds, self-induced mild poisons to simulate heart and liver ailments, and severe skin infections caused by the application of poisonous weeds. Countless Viennese resorted to the eternal practice of bribery to evade military service. Others went on hunger strikes upon receiving their draft notices. Young Jews overnight developed a thirst for rabbinical studies (and hence draft deferment on religious grounds). By 1915 the Army reacted with beefed-up military police patrols at railroad stations to catch draft evaders and with a tight cordon between the front and rear echelons. Still, the ever-mounting losses could not be made up. Civil–military relations declined as officers competed with bureaucrats and managers for manpower.

The German command system implodes

As 1914 gave way to 1915, the German command system faced a severe internal crisis. While most historical accounts of the Supreme Command concur that the 'silent dictatorship'[18] of the General Staff came about only after August 1916, when Hindenburg and Ludendorff replaced Falkenhayn, documentary evidence[19] suggests instead that the leadership crisis came already by January 1915. Its moving spirit was a major in the General Staff; its 'victims' ranged from Falkenhayn to Wilhelm II, and eventually to Bethmann Hollweg. At its heart was a bitter dispute about strategy.

In December 1914 Ludendorff discovered that the General Staff was creating four new reserve army corps and that these would be ready for deployment by 20 January 1915. He at once demanded that they be sent to the Eastern Front and promised to end the war against Russia early in 1915 if given the new formations. Allies quickly appeared. Conrad von Hötzendorf briefed Falkenhayn that Austria–Hungary could prosecute the war only until the spring of 1915, and that failure to concentrate against Russia would force the Dual Monarchy to conclude a 'disgraceful peace' with the Tsar.[20] Moltke, recently appointed to the largely ceremonial post of Deputy Chief of the General Staff in Berlin ('put in the corner like a used umbrella'),[21] spied a chance to regain his former post were Falkenhayn to be brought down. And Bethmann Hollweg, like Ludendorff convinced that Falkenhayn's conduct of the war would not lead to total victory, was more than ready to exploit the divisions within the *OHL* for his own political gain. The Chancellor immediately recruited two influential Bavarian politicians, Minister President Georg von Hertling and Ambassador Hugo von Lerchenfeld-Koefering, to the anti-Falkenhayn camp.

Since there existed no central agency where different military-political strategies could be debated, it is not surprising that the various sides resorted to public lobbying and backstairs intrigue to push their programmes. Each had an alternative to the failed Schlieffen plan: Falkenhayn pursued a policy of war 'with limited means' to bludgeon the Allies into ending the conflict, while Hindenburg and Ludendorff sought a grand battle of envelopment to annihilate the Tsarist armies in Poland. The eastern commanders found a ready and willing lobbyist in their press officer, Major Hans von Haeften,[22] who concurrently served as Moltke's adjutant. Through Haeften, Hindenburg and Ludendorff maintained almost daily telephone contact with Moltke – as well as with General von Plessen, Moltke's personal friend and the Kaiser's military adjutant. Falkenhayn, for his part, could count on the support of General von Lyncker, Chief of the Military Cabinet, and Lyncker's deputy, Colonel Ulrich von Marschall. The latter, who claimed credit for replacing Moltke with Falkenhayn, regarded his champion as the 'saviour of the fatherland' after the Marne debacle.

No love was lost between Falkenhayn and Ludendorff, which gave the affair a painful personal dimension. When Falkenhayn received glowing reports of the Battle of Tannenberg from Haeften, he deleted all positive references to the leaders of *OberOst*. Ludendorff unsurprisingly developed a visceral personal dislike of Falkenhayn. 'I can only hate and love, and I hate General von Falkenhayn; it is impossible for me to work together with him.'[23] Ludendorff's aide, Hoffmann, denounced Falkenhayn to staff in the east as 'the fatherland's evil angel.'[24] Falkenhayn's enemies, with Ludendorff at their head, resurrected the tale of his gaming debts as a young officer, and with intended double meaning now openly referred to him as the 'gambler'. The stage was set for confrontation.

Major von Haeften undertook a tour of the Western Front as Moltke's adjutant during the first week of January 1915 to promote *OberOst*'s plea that the war's centre of gravity be shifted to the east. On 3 January Bethmann Hollweg petitioned Wilhelm II to replace Falkenhayn with Ludendorff. Falkenhayn thereupon assumed the offensive and on 8 January, in an effort to separate Hindenburg from Ludendorff, transferred the latter to the Carpathian front where Ludendorff was to become chief of staff to a composite German-Austro-Hungarian 'South Army' (*Südarmee*) under General Alexander von Linsingen. Hindenburg was furious and gave Haeften carte blanche to act as 'broker' on behalf of *OberOst*.

By 11 January Haeften had recruited Major Max Bauer, Court Chamberlain Elard von Oldenburg-Januschau, Grand Admiral von Tirpitz, and Crown Prince Wilhelm to the eastern *fronde* against Falkenhayn. Hindenburg, recently stripped of much of his command by the creation of Army Group Leopold Prince of Bavaria and the General Government of Warsaw, spent the entire night drafting a letter to the Kaiser. Therein, Hindenburg, as the oldest active general, demanded 'in the name of the German people and Army' that Falkenhayn be fired and Moltke restored to his erstwhile post. In case Wilhelm II was of a different mind, Hindenburg threatened that neither he nor Ludendorff would remain at their posts. Hindenburg closed the meeting by citing Martin Luther: 'So! Here I stand, I can do no other, God help me. Amen!'[25]

That very day, 11 January, Falkenhayn travelled to Breslau to remind Ludendorff of his duty to Army and nation. The meeting rapidly degenerated into personal rancour. Hindenburg, once more acting as 'the Army's most senior general', informed Falkenhayn that the Army no longer had confidence in its chief and demanded that Falkenhayn resign. Haeften and Oldenburg-Januschau headed west later that same day: the former to brief Moltke on the proceedings at Breslau and Posen; the latter once more to rally the Crown Prince to the cause.

Haeften spun a devious web in Berlin. He alerted Eugen Schiffer, a National Liberal parliamentary deputy, to the split in the Army and then sought out Karl Helfferich, a director of the powerful Deutsche Bank and designated Secretary of the Treasury. Helfferich at once joined the plot. As a prominent spokesman for heavy industry, he demanded a German strike against Britain in Egypt – so that the Berlin–Baghdad Railway could be completed and a trunk line laid to the Suez Canal. Helfferich informed Haeften that Falkenhayn's grand strategic horizon did not go beyond 'the trenches in France'. Once in power at the Treasury, Helfferich brought King Wilhelm of Württemberg and King Ludwig III of Bavaria into the pro-Hindenburg camp. Oldenburg-Januschau reported that the Crown Prince as well as his chief of staff, General Constantin Schmidt von Knobelsdorf, and army group commander General Max von Gallwitz endorsed Falkenhayn's removal from office. Moltke, of course, was still on board. 'I rise and fall with you', he informed Hindenburg.

By 18 January the ubiquitous Haeften had rallied another of the Kaiser's sons, Joachim, as well as Empress Augusta Victoria to Hindenburg's cause. He now used the term *'Führerfrage'* with reference to the Army's leadership crisis. Finally, Haeften took several divisional staff officers at *OberOst* into his confidence. General Adolf Wild von Hohenborn, Falkenhayn's deputy, became so alarmed over the military *fronde* that he issued a gag order to staff officers on the Western Front.

On 20 January an irate Wilhelm II summoned Haeften to imperial headquarters at Mézières-Charleville. Highly agitated by the revolt both within the Army and the imperial family, the Kaiser threatened to convene a court-martial to deal with Hindenburg (and possibly Moltke). The head of *OberOst*, in the Emperor's words, had taken on the role of 'Wallenstein'.[26] Wilhelm II again ruled out operations in the east – 'the Russians will take evasive action and we will undertake a thrust into air' – and lectured Haeften that he, the Kaiser, would not 'do General Joffre the favour of being forced to remove his Chief of the General Staff every few weeks'. Above all, Wilhelm jealously guarded his exclusive 'right to command' (*Kommandogewalt*) and lectured Haeften that the withdrawal from the Marne in September 1914 had been his personal work. Pathetically, Wilhelm II argued that to remove Falkenhayn from power now would allow the General no option other than 'to put a bullet through his head'.[27]

In the end, Falkenhayn remained at his post; Wild von Hohenborn assumed the office of Prussian War Minister; Ludendorff returned to Hindenburg; three new army corps were sent east; and Haeften was transferred from *OberOst* to the military district of Cologne. Before leaving Charleville, however, Haeften had to answer five questions submitted by the Kaiser – much as a schoolboy might be asked to account for his class-room indiscipline. While some political leaders suggested that Falkenhayn replace Bethmann Hollweg, the General rejected such a course out of fear that it would bring Ludendorff the top spot at the General Staff.

Most critically, the entire sordid affair failed to bring about a strategic decision whether to concentrate against France or Russia. As far as Conrad von Hötzendorf was concerned, the Germans would continue their debilitating policy of half measures. '*Ni l'un, ni l'autre.*'[28] The affair also introduced a new element into Hohenzollern military affairs. Never in the history of the Prussian Army had a theatre commander demanded the dismissal of the Chief of the General Staff, much less under threat of resignation. And never in the annals of that institution had an army com-mander registered a vote of no confidence in the Chief of the General Staff with the monarch.[29] Ominously, the affair introduced a deep and abiding lack of trust among the Chancellor, the Chief of the General Staff, and the two eastern commanders.[30] Bethmann Hollweg survived the cri-sis, but only so long as Falkenhayn and Hindenburg-Ludendorff contin-ued their animosity. His senior political councilor, Riezler, lobbied co-workers in the Chancellery to abandon their 'wild' campaign against Falkenhayn.[31]

The greatest loser – apart from the German war effort – was Wilhelm II. On 15 January the Supreme War Lord begged Hindenburg to remain at his post. To offset this, he promoted Falkenhayn to the rank of General of Infantry. The Kaiser 'solved' the insurgency of two senior generals by submitting a major to a written loyalty test. Instead of restoring order to a rebellious generalcy, Wilhelm II, 'depressed' and 'upset', resorted to cut-ting wood, reading novels all night, and berating headquarters with laments about 'friends who had stabbed him in the back'.[32] He stalked the nearby battlefield of Sedan, where his grandfather had defeated Napoleon III in 1870, perhaps hoping thereby to escape the nightmare of stalemate in 'his' war.

What little remained of Wilhelm II's titular role as Commander-in-Chief now disappeared entirely. Numerous generals detected the Kaiser's fear that Hindenburg already 'overshadowed the monarch's position' as Supreme War Lord.[33] Bethmann Hollweg set the 'leadership crisis' in his-torical perspective: 'Eventually, one forgave the young Kaiser for dis-missing Bismarck; the mature [Kaiser] would not survive Hindenburg's dismissal'. Ludendorff maliciously informed Moltke that while Hindenburg still spoke about an omnipotent 'Kaiser', he, Ludendorff, preferred the word 'fatherland'.[34] In any event, no alternative to the Schlieffen plan emerged.[35] The Army's flag officers worked from now on not with one another but against one another – and at best independent of one another.

Wars of 'limited means'

While the 'real' war raged at German headquarters, both Conrad and Ludendorff planned great campaigns in the east. Ignoring the exhaustion of their men after the battles of 1914 and the harsh winter of early 1915, each drove the troops on to prove the value of his strategy. On paper, the January offensive took on Napoleonic dimensions: while Hindenburg's old Eighth Army and General Hermann von Eichhorn's Tenth Army would strike east from the Masurian Lakes in East Prussia, Boroević's Austro-Hungarian Third Army would seek to relieve Przemyśl at the same time as Linsingen's composite 'South Army' would advance northward through the Carpathian Mountains against Lemberg; the Habsburg Seventh Army under Pflanzer-Baltin would act as a support force.

There was little or no coordination between Habsburg and Hohenzollern staffs. Once again, each ally conducted its own campaign with little regard for the other. The two respective General Staff chiefs declined to converse even by telephone. On the last day of January, the German Ninth Army undertook a feint in the direction of Warsaw, designed to distract Russian attention from the main efforts elsewhere. The Battle of Bolimow was not a success. Sub-zero weather negated the first use of poison gas (xylyl bromide)[36] by the Germans – which the Russians failed to report to their western allies. The Russians committed 11 divisions to defend the 6-mile-wide front, losing 40 000 men in just 3 days.

To the north the German Eighth and Tenth armies were more successful, scoring some initial gains against the Russian Tenth Army, despite advancing in a blizzard. Eichhorn's Tenth Army rolled up its right flank, and by mid-February the Russians had been driven into the Augustov forest. Russian artillery once again rode away from the battle, leaving infantry to its fate. The Russian Tenth Army lost 92 000 prisoners of war and nearly 300 guns, while the XXI Corps suffered 5700 casualties in the last 3 days of fighting alone. It surrendered on 21 February. But a concerted Russian counterattack by the Twelfth Army the next day brought the German advance to a halt.[37] The Tsar's armies had lost another 200 000 men; German casualties were not revealed.

The Winter (or Second) Battle of the Masurian Lakes, while one of countless tactical successes scored during the Great War, brought no strategic relief. The Russian front was not broken. German lines were extended 70 miles further east, thereby making resupply more difficult. Perhaps Falkenhayn had been right in stating that no decisive battle could be fought in Russia.

Conrad's offensives in the Carpathians and in Galicia were designed to eliminate the Russian threat to Hungary, to deter a possible Italian entry into the war, and to relieve the great fortress of Przemyśl on the San River. Russian General A. N. Selivanov's Eleventh Arm invested General Kusmanek's 127 800 soldiers, 18 000 civilians, 1000 Russian prisoners of war, and 14 500 horses.[38] Przemyśl's loss would deal a major blow to the Dual Monarchy's prestige and Conrad was determined to rescue its garrison. In the south he sent Army Group Pflanzer-Baltin against the Russians in the direction of Czernowitz as a feint; the main thrust on 23 January was a frontal assault by Boroević's Third Army and Linsingen's 'South Army', centred on three German divisions. Once again Conrad's blue and red arrows on staff maps looked impressive; once again terrain and weather militated against success.

The Carpathian mountain chain along the Hungarian–Polish border was about 60 miles wide and alternated in height from 1000 yards in the northwest to 1500 yards in the east. Short on winter equipment and artillery but long on promise and hope, Habsburg troops moved through the high passes in deep snow against well dug-in Russian forces, who controlled the high ground and delighted in rolling barrels filled with explosives down into enemy trenches. Snow storms and dense fog all but eliminated accurate artillery fire. Supplies had to be dragged in by sleds or on pack animals. The troopers' hands and guns had to be thawed in warm water before every attack. Men sank up to their elbows in the deep snow drifts, and nightly temperatures rarely rose above −15 degrees Celsius.[39] Troops that fell asleep usually froze to death – or were devoured by wolves. Life expectancy was calculated between 5 and 6 weeks, after which a soldier was either killed, captured, or severely wounded. Many committed suicide.

Colonel Georg Veith of the Third Army left a graphic description of the bitter fighting. 'It is decimating', he wrote, 'to read the reports.' 'Hundreds freeze to death daily; every wounded soldier who cannot get himself back to the lines is irrevocably sentenced to death. Riding is impossible. Entire lines of riflemen surrender in tears to escape the pain.' Day after day, the troops were 'without food in −25 degrees Celsius; the emergency rations which they carry had frozen solid'. And even when a temporary thaw set in late in January, conditions hardly improved. 'Suddenly thaw and rain. Everything soaked down to the skin. No chance to dry off. And at night the men freeze and their clothes turn into ice armour.' Veith concluded that only those with 'iron constitutions' survived in the Carpathians; the others simply broke down.[40]

Pflanzer-Baltin's troops eventually captured Czernowitz – and 60 000 Russian soldiers – but in the Carpathians Boroević's Third Army suffered 89 000 casualties, or half its ready strength, in 2 weeks. The 2nd Division, for example, was reduced from its peacetime strength of 8150 men to a mere 1000 between 23 January and 2 February. Conrad, undeterred as always, resumed the offensive on 27 February by sandwiching his Second Army between the Third Army and the *Südarmee*. The result was the same: 40 000 of its 95 000 men were captured or lost in the snow and 6000 incapacitated by hostile fire. The 'South Army' was down to one-third of its strength. Nearly 800 000 casualties attested to the severity of the fighting in the east early in 1915.

The Carpathian offensive cost Conrad the last of his experienced offi-cers and noncommissioned officers. The Austrian official history refers to the Army after February 1915 as a '*Landsturm* and militia army'.[41] The mood at Conrad's headquarters was reported 'below zero'. Kaiser Wilhelm II, in one of his less lucid moments, chided the Austrians for the Carpathian fiasco during his birthday celebration at Charleville on 27 January. Germanic soldiers, he suggested, were better trained to fight on level ground than in the mountains. And had not Bismarck, Wilhelm II lectured Austrian General Stürgkh, always cautioned that 'the Carpathians [*sic*] were not worth the bones of a Pomeranian musketeer [*sic*]'?[42]

Przemyśl was now without hope. Desperate sorties by the Austro-Hungarian Fourth and Third armies to relieve the great belt fortress failed. A final bid to reach General Kusmanek early in March cost the Second Army 51 000 casualties. Colonel Veith once more captured the severity of battle:

> On 1 March fog and heavy snow falls, we lose all sense of direction, entire regiments get lost, catastrophic losses are the result. On 6 March a complete change in weather: clear skies, thaw by day and –20 degrees by night; with the result that all slopes are iced over. . . . On 20 March a snow storm breaks over us with a ferocity found only in glacial regions. Every forward move-ment ceases; no wounded can be evacuated; entire lines of riflemen are cov-ered [as] with a white cloth. The icy ground, sanded smooth by the storm, is impassable; digging in is impossible; the infantry stands without cover and unable to move in front of the enemy's defensive works; the artillery is sev-eral days' marching behind.[43]

On 19 March Kusmanek burned 700 000 Kronen paper money and over the following 2 days butchered his horses for food. On 22 March he demolished all train installations, fired off most remaining heavy artillery shells, and then blew up Przemyśl's guns with overloads. Finally, Kusmanek destroyed the remaining defensive works and burned his last

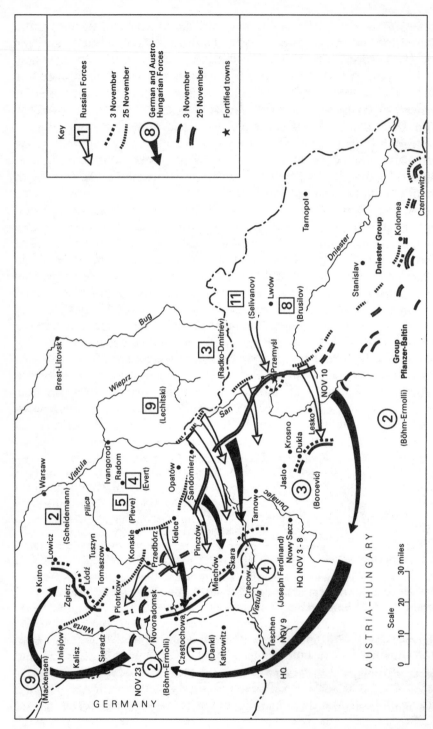

Map 4. Galicia, Przemyśl, the Carpathians, 1914–15

supplies. At 9 a.m. on 23 March the garrison raised white flags over the battered fortress in brilliant sunshine: nine generals, 93 senior staff officers, 2500 officers, and 117 000 enlisted men became Russian prisoners of war.[44] Kaiser Franz Joseph broke into crying fits on hearing of the fortress's surrender. Historians have compared its fall to the surrender of the German Sixth Army at Stalingrad in 1943.

Stavka used three divisions of the Eleventh Army released by the end of the siege of Przemyśl to take the war into Hungary. General Ivanov captured Dukla Pass early in April. Most ominously, two battalions (1800 soldiers) of the Czech 28th Infantry Regiment, officers and men, with banners flying and regimental band playing, surrendered to the Russians without resistance at Zboró. On 17 April Franz Joseph dissolved the regiment at General von Boroević's request.[45] Loyal Czech soldiers were distributed among four Austrian regiments. Conrad immediately placed Bohemia under military control and prepared a fighting retreat to Budapest, then Vienna, and finally Innsbruck. Instead, in what by now had become a regular rhythm of the war in the east, a hastily assembled German rescue force, the *Beskiden Korps* under General Georg von der Marwitz, halted the Russian advance in the Labourcza Valley, stabilizing the Habsburg front. The Hungarian House of Representatives hastily passed a bill extending the age span for military service from 19 and 42 to 18 and 50 years.

The War Ministry in Vienna noted the endless lists of war casualties and especially the alarming statistics which revealed that Habsburg officer losses were out of proportion to those of other armies, both allied and enemy. War Minister von Krobatin informed his government that 'missing and lost' officers constituted 48 per cent of total strength – compared with 16 per cent in Germany and 25 per cent in Russia. He was almost embarrassed that the tally of officers killed (8.7 per cent of total armed forces) was too low – again compared with Germany (16–18 per cent) and Russia (25 per cent). It was most disconcerting that three out of every four officers killed, wounded, or missing out of the total of 19 396 in 1914 alone were lieutenants and captains. Suicidal frontal assaults had decimated these largely infantry (96 per cent) ranks; other causes were special Russian sharpshooter squadrons detailed to kill officers, aided and abetted in their deadly work by the distinctive and colourful uniforms of the *k.u.k.* armies. Subaltern officers from the reserves – who served mainly at the company level – suffered disproportionately more (400 per cent) than those from the Joint Army,[46] suggesting a lack of realistic prewar training. The War Minister wondered how long the haemorrhaging could go on.

Colonel von Kageneck, the Reich's military plenipotentiary with the *AOK* and a staunch defender of Conrad for much of 1914, finally despaired of the Habsburg military. On 6 April he reported that Conrad's forces were 'rotten and decayed' through and through. Conrad, Kageneck informed Falkenhayn, had 'lost contact' with the front. His staff used their talents not to prosecute the war but to shuttle their women to and fro between Vienna and Teschen. A devout Catholic from Baden, Kageneck noted 'godlessness among the officers of the Catholic religion'. In Berlin restaurants, Bavarian General Maximilian von Hoehn had informed Kageneck, diners jeered when the band struck up the Austrian anthem, *Oh du mein Österreich*. On 31 May Kageneck warned: 'This land can no longer be helped'.[47] Hindenburg acidly noted that Habsburg units had always held off superior Russian numbers – until real soldiers arrived![48] That same month Conrad informed Falkenhayn to count Austro-Hungarian divisions as no more than brigades.

The *OHL* now had no choice but to concentrate on the east. However much Falkenhayn remained a 'Westerner' at heart, it was clear that Austria–Hungary would collapse without major German assistance. Italy was again demanding 'compensation' for its continued neutrality. Bulgaria and Romania were sitting on the fence, closely watching Rome's actions. And news reached Falkenhayn that the Allies were marshalling naval and land forces in the Mediterranean Sea; the Turkish Straits seemed the most likely venue for an amphibious assault. All in all, the Central Powers' situation seemed desperate and the mood at Charleville was dour, to say the least.

Falkenhayn refused to face the obvious: that Vienna's attempt to reestablish Habsburg power through war had foundered on its lack of military strength. Instead, he decided take swift action to shore up the Eastern Front, the Habsburg ally, and in the process the major neutrals at Rome, Sofia, and Bucharest. But the decision was not an easy one: the Allies' 112 divisions in the west surpassed Falkenhayn's 97, while in the east the two opposing armies numbered about 112 divisions each. Yet there was political capital to be gained in the east. Falkenhayn readily appreciated that General von Mackensen chafed under Ludendorff's control and sought an independent command. The nation demanded new deeds from Hindenburg. Falkenhayn therefore decided to launch what became Germany's third bid to win the war: a major offensive in the Polish salient designed to rout, or at least ruin, the Russian Army. But where to find the troops?

Colonel Ernst von Wrisberg of the Prussian War Ministry in February 1915 had convinced Falkenhayn that German forces could be expanded through reorganization of the armies in France. By March Wrisberg had created a large combat-experienced reserve by denuding every division on the Western Front of its fourth infantry regiment and every artillery battery of two of its six tubes. The troops and guns thus released were reformed into 14 reserve divisions while the affected units in France received 2400 men each to strengthen the remaining three infantry regiments.[49] Using this new reserve army as well as the monthly intake of 180 000 fresh recruits and convalesced veterans, Falkenhayn scraped together eight divisions for the east, appointed Mackensen head of a new Eleventh Army, and assigned a brilliant staff officer, Colonel Hans von Seeckt, to assist him. Falkenhayn moved imperial headquarters from Mézières-Charleville on the Meuse to Castle Pless in Silesia, an hour removed from Conrad's base at Teschen.

But once again Falkenhayn clashed with Hindenburg and Ludendorff over strategy. While *OberOst* demanded that a dozen army corps be released to them by shortening the Western Front to a line Nieuport–Lille–Maubeuge–Metz–Strassburg and that these forces be used for a giant 'Cannae' via Kovno and Vilna to drive Tsarist armies into the Russian swamps, Falkenhayn favoured a more modest drive bypassing Warsaw in the direction of Siedlce (the old concept of August 1914). In the end, using a plan attempted earlier by Conrad, Falkenhayn opted to break through the Russian front between Gorlice and Tarnów, where the Germans enjoyed a momentary numerical advantage of 357 000 against 219 000 troops and 1500 versus 700 medium and heavy guns. Thereafter, he planned to head north, trapping substantial portions of the Russian armies against Hindenburg's Eighth Army west of Warsaw. Falkenhayn kept Conrad in the dark as long as possible and only on 13 April, 3 weeks before the operation, requested that the Habsburg Third and Fourth armies protect Mackensen's flanks. If all went well, Falkenhayn would satisfy the national clamour for success in the east, create an inconvenient rival to Ludendorff, and relieve the pressure on Hungary. Falkenhayn ignored the critical question whether the Austro-Hungarian Army, having been nearly destroyed in August 1914 and again in January 1915, could sustain another campaign.

Mackensen struck at 6 a.m. on 2 May along a 30-mile front after a 4-hour hurricane bombardment that pulverized the Russian trenches and destroyed their wire.[50] The Austro-Hungarian Third and Fourth armies launched a simultaneous assault from the south. It was the first time that mixed Austro-Hungarian-German units fought under a unified command. Within 48 hours, six divisions of General Ivanov's Third Army had been shattered and the breakthrough accomplished. In 3 days the Germans overran the Tsar's defensive positions. The Russian X Corps lost 29 000 soldiers; the XXIV Corps nearly its entire force of 40 000 men.

General von François, commander of the German XLI Reserve Corps at Gorlice, later recalled the intensity of the offensive:

Six o'clock! The 12 cm gun on Hill 696 gives the signal shot and all batteries, from the field guns to the heavy mortars, fire their first salvo on cue at the Russians. It is followed by thunder and booming, slamming and banging, as 700 guns open fire and hurl hissing iron and steel through the air. The shells explode in the ground on the other side, throwing earth, wood splinters, and other defensive works yards-high into the air.

Villages were levelled, Russian oil tanks set on fire. Enemy soldiers ran from their trenches by the thousands – only to be massacred by ensuing German shrapnel and low-trajectory artillery fire. Thereafter, the mortars began their work. François recalled:

> Trees break like matches, huge trunks are hurled through the air, the stone walls of houses cave in, fountains of earth rise from the ground. Ten o'clock! The mortar fire subsides, the artillery advances its barrage. Shrill whistles. The first assault wave breaks over the trenches against the enemy.[51]

Mackensen caught the Russians by surprise. *Stavka* had shifted the bulk of its 1.8 million combat troops to the Carpathians fronting Habsburg units, in the process granting Mackensen a temporary advantage of three divisions over the Russian Third Army near Gorlice.[52] Once his front had been ruptured, General Danilov at *Stavka* ordered Ivanov 'categorically' not to undertake 'any retreat whatsoever'.[53] The order was superfluous. Advancing at the rate of 10 miles a day, Mackensen threatened to cut off Russian forces still entrenched at the base of the Carpathian Mountains; they ran for the cover of the San. Thousands drowned swimming the river or were machine-gunned by the Germans. The Russian X and XXIV Corps ceased to exist as the salient in Poland quickly crumbled. In a week, the Russians had lost 210 000 men, including 140 000 prisoners of war.

A combined Austro-Hungarian-German force advanced against Przemyśl and on 3 June Bavarian units entered the fortress. Captain Otto Kohler of the 9th Pioneer Company, Bavarian 11th Infantry Division, remembered the assault that dawn in bright sunshine. His men advanced over fields littered with dead soldiers, their guns and their kits. The troopers of the 11th Division decorated themselves with oak leaves and made bouquets in the Bavarian blue-white colours from corn-flowers and wind-flowers. Unfurling their regimental banners and the Bavarian flag, they entered Przemyśl lustily singing. The remaining German residents threw flowers at their feet.[54] Mackensen was promoted to the rank of field marshal. Maliciously copying Potiorek's failed action with regard to Belgrade in 1914, Mackensen, in a gesture much resented in Vienna, cavalierly 'laid Przemyśl' at 'Kaiser Franz Joseph's feet'.[55]

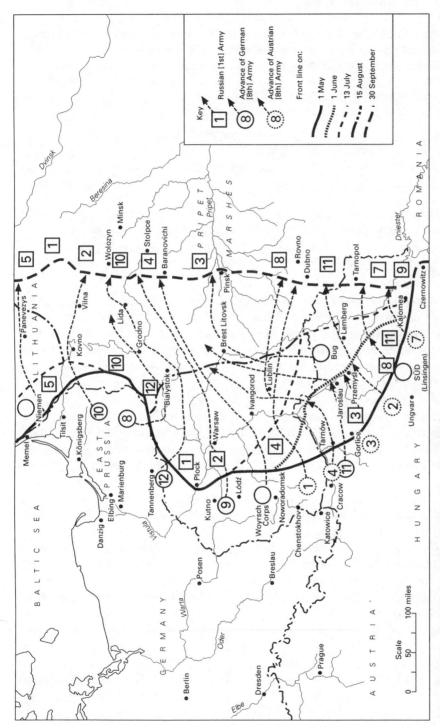

Map 5. German breakthrough, Gorlice–Tarnów, 1915

Elsewhere, the German advance rolled on relentlessly as the tactical breakthrough became a strategic success. By mid-May Russian armies had been hurled more than 100 miles back from the Carpathians to north of the Vistula River. Falkenhayn was ecstatic and informed Bethmann Hollweg: 'The Russian Army is ruined'.[56] On the Austro-Hungarian side, 31 officers and 1543 men of the Czech 36th Infantry Regiment deserted to the Russians. The unit was dissolved and its remaining members scattered among eight Hungarian regiments.

But nothing could halt the German advance. Lemberg fell on 22 June and Wilhelm II celebrated with a victory dinner and a bottle of champagne. This time, unlike the retaking of Przemyśl, Mackensen allowed the Habsburg Second Army to enter Lemberg first. Flags were raised, church bells pealed, and hymns of gratitude were sung in Vienna. Ruthenian labour battalions buried the dead and retrieved tons of war equipment and expended shells from the battlefield. Conrad was promoted to the newly-created rank of colonel-general.

The Russians had lost 412 000 men in May 1915 alone.[57] Still, General Ivanov vowed to hold every square foot of ground. But the Russian 'Great Retreat' continued unabated. The Germans crossed the Dniester River on 27 June. On 13 July *OberOst* mounted another major offensive: Hindenburg attacked in Russian Poland from the northwest, Mackensen from the south, and Woyrsch from the west. Early in August General von Gallwitz's new Twelfth Army stormed Lublin, Cholm, Ivangorod, and Warsaw. Thereafter, German units crossed the Bug River, took Brest-Litovsk (25–6 August) and Grodno (2 September), before halting their 300-mile advance in Vilna (19 September). General Yanushkevich, the Russian chief of staff, informed St Petersburg that his armies were 'melting like the snow' before the German onslaught.[58] More than 850 000 Russian soldiers had been captured by the Germans in what would become their greatest victory in the war. Autumn rains finally rendered the Russian roads impassable.

Falkenhayn immediately renewed his earlier calls for a separate peace without annexations with Russia. Surely, Tsar Nicholas II would now recognize the futility of continuing the war. Conrad von Hötzendorf shared Falkenhayn's views and declared that 'golden bridges' would have to be built to St Petersburg.[59] Moreover, the *OHL* realized that the overall military situation remained precarious for the Central Powers. France and Britain still enjoyed a superiority of 600 battalions in the west. German supply lines were stretched to the breaking point in the east. Once more the Russian armies had been beaten but not destroyed. Falkenhayn requested that Russia be offered Poland as a 'pawn' in return for a separate peace. He avoided the larger question of Vienna's ability to carry on the war.

But Bethmann Hollweg refused to accept this advice. The Chancellor declined to enter into direct negotiations with the Russians for fear that this could be interpreted as a sign of weakness by Britain and France as well as the Right in Germany. Moreover, he coveted a 'Polish border strip' twice the size of Alsace-Lorraine as 'effective protection against the Russian, Pan-Slavic tide'. And whereas Falkenhayn refused to celebrate the capture of Warsaw on 4 August for fear of thereby offending the Russians, Bethmann Hollweg repeated his calls for 'necessary strategic border corrections in Poland'.[60] The German annexationist camp remained strongest in Berlin rather than at Pless.

The issue was settled when Nicholas II informed the Danish intermediary Hans-Niels Andersen that he would not dishonour his pledge to Britain and France of 5 September 1914 not to conclude a separate peace. The decision eventually cost the Tsar his throne, his family, and his life. On 21 August Nicholas II relieved his uncle, Grand Duke Nikolai Nikolaevich, and personally took charge of the war, with General M. V. Alekseev as chief of staff. The Tsar obviously feared diplomatic isolation and possible hostile reactions by Britain and France in case of a separate peace with Germany. Student strikes in the Russian capital greeted the change in command.

The Central Powers' line in Russia stabilized from Riga in the north to the east of Pinsk and south to Tarnopol and Czernowitz by the end of 1915. Although the Russians had suffered 2 million casualties that year, Falkenhayn's strategy of bludgeoning Russia into a separate peace had suffered shipwreck. Still, Gorlice-Tarnów would be Falkenhayn's greatest – and last – victory. On 2 August Professor Hans Delbrück of Berlin University travelled to Pless and awarded the General an honorary doctorate.

The nature of the fighting on Poland's dusty plains in late summer 1915 was captured by Private Wilhelm Schulin of the German 26th Infantry Division, just north of Brest-Litovsk:

> Exertions, privations, very heavy knapsack, neck and shoulder pain from the rifle and long, difficult marches; extremely tired feet and body. Bad roads – either uneven asphalt or deep sand – and always the uneven fields, marching up and down deep furrows. Often in double time, and usually no water or at best stinking water, no bread for days on end. When we do get food, it is little or bad, hardly any meat at all. Nothing but freezing and freezing, and back pains.

The Württemberg troops lived off the land as best they could – 'potatoes, carrots, radishes, pears' – and constantly advanced across Poland's broad plains. 'Blisters on our feet.' When the men of the 26th Division were finally allowed to rest, there was little pleasure in it. 'Washing, delousing, hair cut, shaving. Afternoon we ate lamb . . . dried tobacco (one smoked willow leaves or whatever else grew). Gathered "tea" and coffee grounds. Cooked pears, damsons, turnips, every kind of fruit core. Many a day cold potatoes at night. Hard bread; gathered bread crumbs.'[61] One can only imagine the feelings of the millions of Russian peasant soldiers as they retreated in defeat.

Relief and joy abounded at Conrad's headquarters as the moral effect of victory was almost greater than its military connotations. At last there was good news to report to Vienna. General August von Cramon, the new German military plenipotentiary at Teschen, caught the mood well: 'Only someone who has lived through the deep depression following the Carpathian campaign can truly understand what Gorlice meant: liberation from an almost unbearable pressure, relief from the greatest worries, renewed confidence, and the sudden hope of victory'.[62] But Conrad, in his heart of hearts, was hardly elated by these spectacular German successes. 'I cannot at all express how distasteful the infiltration with German troops is', he wrote Bolfras at the Military Chancery in Vienna, 'but the heart has to follow the head'.[63] Berlin was rapidly becoming the senior partner in the alliance in the east and the *OHL* demanded an ever greater voice in the war. Mackensen and Seeckt had been formally placed under the *AOK* during the Battle of Gorlice-Tarnów, but the two German commanders had controlled the campaign and Conrad had been instructed not to issue orders without 'due consultation' with Falkenhayn. In addition, Falkenhayn pressured Conrad to encourage Vienna to make territorial concessions to Romania (Transylvania) and Italy (the Trentino) to keep both states neutral.[64]

In fact, Conrad was caught in a vicious circle of his own making. Unable to score major victories against Russia or Serbia, he became ever more the junior partner in the alliance. After each new defeat, Conrad was forced to call on Germany for help. Yet each German soldier, gun, and victory not unnaturally prompted the *OHL* to demand a greater voice in the east in general and in Poland in particular. Vienna had fallen from instigator of war in 1914 to satellite in 1915. This was resented by Conrad, who developed a personal animosity toward the ally. Increasingly, he equated a German victory with the end of Austria-Hungary's independence and great-power status. Yet as a soldier committed to victory, he could not muster the fortitude to demand a negotiated peace – which perhaps alone might have preserved the Habsburg Monarchy.

In late August 1915 Conrad did what he always did when confronted by crisis: he planned a grandiose Habsburg 'black-yellow' offensive in the direction of Rovno and Kiev designed, with some German cooperation, to encircle 25 Russian divisions! Men born in 1897 were drafted and all available reservists called to the colours. Conrad assured his staff that his armies were simply starting out from the same positions but with a better plan than in August–September 1914. Round two was at hand. But the Army of 1915 was not that of 1914. In 1 year it had suffered 57 000 officers and 2.5 million men killed or wounded. One in eight officers and one in 10 men had died. More than 730 000 soldiers were prisoners of war or listed as 'missing'; 928 000 had been seriously wounded.

This notwithstanding, Conrad launched his great offensive on 26 August. Fourteen Habsburg divisions charged eight Romanov divisions. Within a week they had stormed Grodno and Lutsk. But Russian forces refused to be encircled and instead conducted a skilful withdrawal behind the Styr River. Conrad's commanders proved as in 1914 to be a miserable lot. General Paul Puhallo von Brlog, in charge of the First Army, and General Joseph von Roth, head of his own army group, wasted their forces in endless frontal assaults and failed to appreciate that the operation had been designed as a pincer movement. Division, corps, and army commanders ignored orders, failed to inspire through energetic leadership, and developed no initiative. Conrad was furious. His Italian expert, Major Karl Schneller, commented on 3 September: 'This entire operation belongs among the most shameful in the annals of what we have been able to accomplish in leadership. An entire army is held up by two brigades . . . .'[65] The Russian Eighth Army retook Lutsk on 23 September, in the process capturing enough abandoned firearms to equip two corps. Falkenhayn dispatched two German divisions to the east to stabilize the Habsburg front – on condition that the Austro-Hungarian Fourth Army be commanded by the German General von Linsingen. Conrad followed the operation from a single Hughes teleprinter; he declined to visit the front.

The 'black-yellow' offensive quickly earned the nickname 'autumn swinery' (*Herbstsau*) from Conrad's staff.[66] Unflattering comparisons were made between Conrad in Russia in September 1915 and Potiorek in the Balkans in September 1914. Even his adjutant, Colonel Rudolf Kundmann, noted Conrad's bitter disappointment: 'Chief says: with our troops one cannot plan an offensive. Something as simple, as certain as this offensive we never had in the war, and even this we screwed up'.[67] The truth is that Conrad once again had asked too much of his armies and ignored climatic conditions. Uninterrupted rains turned the fields into quagmires. The troops were exhausted: the 3rd Infantry Division, for example, had marched nearly 600 miles eastward between May and September. Units were under strength, supplies below acceptable norms. More than 231 000 men were lost – including 100 000 prisoners of war!

Czech and Ruthenian units of the 19th Infantry Division ran over to the Russians almost to a man. The Fourth Army reported that 33 per cent of its officers had been taken prisoners of war; the comparable German figure for the east in 1915 was 5.2 per cent! Charges that Conrad had failed before 1914 properly to train his officers for war resurfaced in Vienna.[68]

The *Herbstsau* once more revealed Vienna's total reliance on Berlin and in the process again called into question Austria–Hungary's ability to preserve its independence and great-power status. Most grating of all to Conrad, Ludendorff heaped fresh scorn on the Austrians. He chided German prewar military representatives to Vienna for not having 'told the whole truth' about the sorry state of the Habsburg military and disparaged of Austrian generals as 'childish military dreamers' for whom he had nothing but 'contempt'. The Austrians, Ludendorff informed Moltke in April 1915, were a 'wretched people'; the Dual Monarchy would never again be a 'power factor' in Europe; and the 'arrogance and incompetence' of the Austrians knew no bounds. Eventually, Germany would have to gain 'dominance over Austria' in order to become the new 'bulwark against the Slavs'.[69]

Nor was Ludendorff better disposed toward his own Chief of the General Staff. He badgered Falkenhayn with remonstrances that Russia could have been defeated in 1915 if only the *OHL* had given *OberOst* more troops and artillery and developed some strategic insight. Specifically, Ludendorff argued long and loud that his own plan – the broad enveloping movement by Hindenburg's forces from East Prussia in the north and by Mackensen's units from Galicia in the south through Kovno against Vilna and Minsk – would have trapped the Russian armies in the Polish salient. He refused to accept Falkenhayn's argument that the Gorlice-Tarnów campaign had been designed first and foremost to force Russia to the peace table by occupying Russian Poland and that Germany simply lacked the forces to conquer and hold all of European Russia.[70] Indeed, it was Ludendorff and his sycophants and not Falkenhayn who failed to heed Clausewitz's sage counsel that 'the vast expanse of Russia' meant that 'an invader's strength could be worn down to the bone in the course of five hundred miles' retreat'.[71]

War aims once more united Chancellor and *OberOst* against Falkenhayn. Ludendorff sought nothing less than to create his own 'kingdom' in the Baltic states on the slender support base of their ruling German upper class, secure in the knowledge that his annexationist plans were grist to the mills of the Pan-Germans, the academic community, and the various industrial lobbies, all of which had bombarded Bethmann Hollweg with sweeping war-aims plans between March and July 1915. The Chancellor, for his part, vetoed Falkenhayn's suggestion that Moltke be named governor of the General Government of Warsaw, created on 24 August, and instead engineered the appointment of General Hans von Beseler. Falkenhayn replied by placing the General Government not under Hindenburg and Ludendorff but rather directly under Wilhelm II. In the process, Hindenburg lost his function as 'supreme commander' of all German troops in the east.

The Gorlice-Tarnów campaign had important consequences for the future conduct of German operations. Both Falkenhayn and Ludendorff strengthened their beliefs in frontal assaults designed by way of tactical breakthroughs to bring about strategic success. Falkenhayn would apply the lesson learned to Verdun in 1916; Ludendorff to northern France in 1918. But Hindenburg and Ludendorff in alliance with Bethmann Hollweg continued their fight with Falkenhayn over the direction of the war, depicting the Eastern Front as the decisive theatre. Intellectually Ludendorff never rose above the level of an infantry colonel[72] and remained blind to the broader realities of the war: Italy's entry on the side of the Allies, the British attack on Gallipoli, and the Anglo-French assaults against a weakened German line at Ypres, Artois, and in the Champagne.

The Italian 'snake'

Italy's statesmen and soldiers had watched the World War unfold with great interest. Having dishonoured their 32-year-old alliance with Austria–Hungary and Germany in August 1914, the Italians sat back and played the role of a reluctant bride, awaiting a wealthy suitor.[73] They did not have long to wait. Potential suitors stormed the proverbial doors, each offering what it did not possess. Former German Chancellor von Bülow arrived early in 1915 as a special envoy with 'offers' of the Austrian Trentino, Gradisca, and the west bank of the Isonzo River – as well as the suggestion that Trieste be turned into a 'free port' and that Italy be accorded a free hand in Albania.[74] Paris and London, of course, could offer much more (of territory that neither possessed): the Trentino, the South Tyrol, the Isonzo frontier, Trieste, Istria, the Dalmatian coast, Albania, the Dodecanese Islands in the southeastern Aegean Sea, and parts of the Ottoman Empire.

Not surprisingly, Vienna was outraged over Berlin's ready offers of Habsburg lands. Why did Wilhelm II not return Belgium to independence and Alsace-Lorraine to France, they queried the Wilhelmstrasse, or surrender parts of East Prussia and Silesia to Russia? After all, Alsace-Lorraine had been Hohenzollern only since 1870; the Trentino had been

Habsburg for 500 years. Franz Joseph and Conrad von Hötzendorf adamantly informed Berlin that they refused to preside over the dissolution of the Dual Monarchy. Reacting to the suggested cession of the Trentino, Franz Joseph stated that he would not 'allow himself to be pulled to pieces like an artichoke'.[75] Conrad asserted that the Austrians should rather 'go to ruin and drag Germany along with them, than to give in to more of such blackmail'.[76] Italy's 'perfidy', Conrad lectured Count Burián, who had replaced Berchtold on 13 January 1915, would have to be avenged at some point. Perhaps one could offer Rome immediate, generous territorial 'concessions', which could then be retaken after defeating France and Russia. Or, one could grant Bucharest parts of the Russian Bukovina to entice it to side with the Central Powers. Conrad now ranked Italy above even Serbia on his list of enemies.[77]

Austria–Hungary's dilemma over the issue of national territories was perhaps best put by Franz von Matscheko of the Foreign Ministry:

> The ceding of the Trentino to Italy would call into question the very principle upon which Austria–Hungary rests. The Monarchy's right to exist rests on the fact that the peace of Europe would be exposed to perpetual convulsions if in those areas where the great European races – German, Romance, North and South Slav – intermingled with one another, there did not exist a mighty Great Power that in the course of centuries had been created and firmly established to tie together these contiguous peoples and the isolated Hungarian block.

Matscheko reminded the Ballhausplatz that in light of this 'great European necessity', the Monarchy's various ethnic groups would have to renounce, or at least bridle, their nationalist aspirations.[78] One would be hard-pressed to find a clearer statement of the Habsburg mission in Europe.

Still, Burián, along with his mentor, Hungarian Prime Minister Tisza, was willing to give away Austrian German lands such as the South Tyrol and the Trentino, provided that Hungary lose no part of Transylvania to Romania and that it be 'compensated' with Sosnowiec in Galicia and parts of Russian Poland. In short, Vienna was divided on the issue of possible territorial concessions to Rome in return for Italy's continued neutrality.[79] And it received little help from Berlin. Bethmann Hollweg in February 1915 toyed with giving Austria–Hungary parts of 'Prussian Silesia' in return for Vienna offering Italy the Trentino, but irate reactions by his Prussian Cabinet replete with references to the memory of Frederick the Great quickly scotched the idea. Nor could the Chancellor persuade Falkenhayn to front the exchange. As a Prussian aristocrat, Falkenhayn was hardly positioned to undo the work of Frederick II. And while Falkenhayn regarded 'no sacrifice on the part of the Central Powers too great' to maintain Italy's neutrality, he also wished to maintain a 'free hand' in future to extract 'revenge' for Italy's 'criminal politics' by way of a 'definitive reckoning' with Rome.[80] In the end, all that Bethmann Hollweg could offer Vienna as 'compensation' for the Trentino was the Russian coal basin of Sosnowiec.

On 26 April, the day after the Allied landing at Gallipoli, Italy struck a deal with France and Great Britain on the basis of Prime Minister Salandra's generous definition of the nation's *Sacro egoismo* (sacred egoism): the South Tyrol, Trieste and Istria, the line of the Julian Alps, central Dalmatia, Valona, and the Curzolari and Dodecanese islands. In return, Italy promised to take the field within a month. War Minister General Vittorio Zupelli, who had replaced Dino Grandi, promised the Allies that he could put 1 million men in the field within 23 days of mobilization. Rome formally abrogated its alliance with Berlin and Vienna on 4 May 1915. General Cadorna, the Italian chief of staff, did not learn of the existence of the Treaty of London until 2 weeks after its signing – and then by chance. The Cabinet was not informed until 7 May. Italy formally declared war on Austria–Hungary on 23 May. Conrad railed against 'Italy's perfidy' and likened Italy to 'a snake whose head had not been crushed in time'.[81] Franz Joseph quietly wept at Schönbrunn. Wilhelm II's military entourage had already declared its solemn will to fight on, 'even if we all go down to defeat as a result'.[82] Rome published a *Green Book* in which it documented its territorial negotiations with Vienna – but not those with Paris and London. The secret treaty became public only 2 years later when published by the Bolshevik paper *Izvestia*.

The Italian General Staff had drafted a war plan against Austria–Hungary as early as September 1914! Cadorna proposed a main attack from Friuli across the Isonzo River, a defensive posture around the Austrian Trentino salient, and secondary attacks in the direction of Toblach and Carinthia. Three months later, Cadorna informed his government that the first battles of the war would take place 2 or 3 days' march inside the Austrian frontier, to be followed within 45 days by a decisive battle on the Ljubljana plain, from where he would launch his final assault on Vienna. In April 1915 Cadorna repeated his assurance that he would be in Trieste and threatening the heart of the Austro-Hungarian Empire within a month of the outbreak of war. What the military historian John Gooch has called Cadorna's 'amazing strategic vision of a march on Vienna' and 'complete disregard of the realities of trench warfare' were seconded by Victor Emmanuel III's Order of the Day on 27 May, wherein the King expressed complete faith in his Army's 'unquenchable dash' to overcome the Austrians.[83]

Cadorna was every bit a match for Conrad. Both ignored terrain and weather. Both underestimated supply. Both stressed the will to fight. Both devised grandiose strategies that bore little relation to ready strength. And both insisted on their own infallibility. In May 1915 Cadorna quite forgot that his million soldiers lacked modern rifles and artillery, and that they were drastically short of uniforms. The General overestimated his staff's ability to mobilize the Italian Army: that task took 48 rather than the pre-scribed 23 days. Additionally, he was ignorant of the problems of supply-ing such a large army even on Italy's borders – much less during its proposed march to Vienna. And Cadorna's grand strategic vision of Italy, in unison with Russia, Serbia, and possibly Romania, orchestrating a mul-tifront campaign to dismember the Habsburg Monarchy was quite beyond his own talents as well as those of Italian statesmen. Rome failed to coor-dinate its entry into the war either with Serbia or with Romania, and by the time that it signed a military convention with Russia on 21 May, the Tsar's armies were reeling backward before Mackensen's Gorlice-Tarnów campaign. Nor had the Allied expedition to Gallipoli knocked Turkey out of the war.

Cadorna also underestimated the psychological aspect of the war against Austria–Hungary. Vienna may have forgiven Königgrätz (1866); never Solferino (1859). In a curious way, Italy's 'felony' revitalized Austria–Hungary. Italy was a traditional, hereditary enemy whose mea-sure had been taken in the past by great Austrian captains such as Prince Eugen(e), Radetzky, and Albrecht. Croats, Slovenes, Slovaks, and even Czechs fought well against what Conrad termed the 'Italian thieves'. The Tyroleans, whose homeland was on the Allies' auction block, unsurpris-ingly fought tenaciously, even though some of their regiments consisted of as much as 31 to 48 per cent Italians. Even Ludendorff conceded that Habsburg troops 'fought well against Italy'.[84] Vienna removed 114 000 Italians from the new fighting front in the Trentino to cut down on poss-ible espionage; the measure was superfluous as Cadorna distrusted all espionage. He could not, of course, have known that Colonel Karl Egli, the head of Swiss military intelligence, routinely passed information on Italian forces on to Colonel William von Einem, the Habsburg military attaché to Bern.

Above all, Cadorna blithely ignored the terrain he had chosen for his major offensive. The South Tyrol and the Trentino, stretching east from Switzerland, constituted a deep salient in northern Italy, whose high ground almost everywhere was held by enemy forces. To the east the Julian and Carnic Alps sealed the battlefield off against external interfer-ence. Cadorna's major theatre of operations was thus reduced to a 50-mile plateau between the Adriatic and the pre-Alpine foothills, through which the Isonzo River cut a deep gorge. The plateau was swept by rain, sleet, and snow in the autumn and winter; heat and lack of water plagued the troops during the summer. In this 'howling wilderness of stones as sharp as knives' Cadorna sought quick victory.[85] Most troops dug into vile rock and ice caverns where the air was constantly contaminated by smoke, gas, dust, human excrement, and decaying flesh; suicides were a popular escape from the horror.

What became the first of more than a dozen 'battles of the Isonzo' began on 23 June 1915. Enjoying numerical superiority – 18 Italian against eight Austro-Hungarian divisions – Cadorna's 460 000 soldiers of the Second and Third armies charged Archduke Eugen's Austrian positions along the Isonzo. The fighting in what Conrad called Italy's 'cowardly, despicable, treacherous predatory raid' quickly degenerated into savage hand-to-hand combat, some of it on frozen Alpine peaks in subzero temperatures. Both sides attacked and counterattacked, mined and countermined. Neither achieved a breakthrough. Cadorna lost 15 000 men during the First Battle of the Isonzo in June and July, and a further 42 000 during the Second Battle of the Isonzo in July and August.[86] Another 200 000 Italian soldiers were reported either prisoners of war or simply 'missing'. The diary of an unknown Habsburg subaltern officer captured the brutality of the conflict: 'The artillery fire became terribly intense during the night. I am done for, I thought, and prepared myself to die as a brave Christian. I am done for. An unparalleled butchery. A horrible bloodbath. Blood is running everywhere and all about the dead and pieces of corpses lie in a circle. . . '.[87] The men suffered terribly from thirst in the barren rock wastes, and what little water could be gathered after rain or thaw was contaminated by the bloated dead soldiers. Appetites slackened noticeably. Cadorna, like Conrad the previous fall, blamed the lack of success on timid commanders; 27 Italian generals were removed from command in the first few weeks of the war alone.

German military leaders, pleased that Italy had not declared war on Berlin in May 1915, refused Conrad's by now customary pleas for help.[88] The Prussian War Minister, Wild von Hohenborn, perhaps put the feelings of many of his colleagues most brutally: 'Basically, it does not matter a hoot to us whether Italy hacks another piece off the tail of the dying camel Austria'.[89] Falkenhayn calculated that it would take 25 divisions, which Conrad could not raise and which Germany could not spare, to defeat Italy. Moreover, Falkenhayn was fully committed to the Gorlice-Tarnów campaign and doubted the wisdom of Conrad's Cannae-like strategy of allowing the Italians to advance to the Carinthian-Carniolan plain, where Conrad planned to destroy Cadorna's entire army. The *OHL* was willing at most to send one division of Bavarian mountain troops, the *Alpenkorps*, with orders not to cross the Italian border. The Germans thereby forced a defensive posture on Conrad. In fact, Falkenhayn's attention by summer 1915 had drifted from the Isonzo to the Danube and the Drina.

'The bones of a Pomeranian grenadier'

For much of 1914 and 1915, Falkenhayn was concerned that the north-west corner of hostile Serbia and neutral Romania blocked the Central Powers' ability to ship war supplies down the Danube and across the Black Sea to their Turkish ally.[90] Allied spies along the Danube even unearthed German attempts to smuggle artillery shells to the Straits in barrels marked Bavarian beer.[91] Falkenhayn became alarmed in the spring of 1915 when British leaders such as Churchill, the First Lord of the Admiralty, and Lloyd George, the Chancellor of the Exchequer, opted for an amphibious assault in the Turkish Straits. Their arguments were hard to reject. Turkey's entry into the war in November 1914 had cut off the Allies' vital supply route to Russia via the Turkish Straits. Conversely, interdiction of this trade artery deprived Britain and France of Ukrainian grain shipments. London in 1915 decided to restore the supply line to Tsarist Russia, which became ever more dependent on western war materials as the conflict dragged on. In the process, a vituperative and lasting debate ensued over the efficacy of peripheral operations: while B. H. Liddell Hart favoured such a 'strategy of the indirect approach', J. F. C. Fuller decried it as a 'strategy of evasion'.

Grand Duke Nikolai Nikolaevich demanded an Allied 'demonstration' at the Dardanelles to relieve the pressure on Russia created by the German assault out of East Prussia and the Ottoman attack on the Russian Army of the Caucasus. Although General Enver Paşa's Third Army was ravaged in the Armenian mountains by hunger, frostbite, disease, and hostile fire,[92] Churchill and Lloyd George hoped that an operation to force the Straits would threaten Constantinople, bring Greece into the war on the Allies' side, and topple the Turkish government.

On 19 February Admiral Sir Sackville Carden was ordered to bombard the outer forts of the Dardanelles; the following month he broke down from the strain. On 18 March Admiral Sir John De Robeck, his successor, decided to have a 'real good try' at the forts. De Robeck fared little better: more than one-third of his heavy ships (*Irresistible*, *Bouvet*, *Gaulois*, *Suffren*, and *Ocean*) were put out of commission by shore defences and mines. This notwithstanding, on 25 April General Sir Ian Hamilton stormed the beaches at Cape Helles and Gaba Tepe at the southern tip of Gallipoli with the 70 000-man Mediterranean Expeditionary Force.

Hamilton was confident of victory. 'Let me bring my lads face to face with Turks in the open field, we *must* beat them every time because British volunteer soldiers are superior individuals to Anatolians, Syrians and Arabs and are animated with a superior idea and an equal joy in battle.'[93] Hamilton's British, French, Australian, and New Zealand troops, five divisions in all, managed a foothold on the beaches but never dislodged the defenders from the heights above them.

The entire undertaking, which Lloyd George likened to 'knocking the props from beneath Austria–Hungary', while a brilliant strategic idea, had been abysmally planned.[94] Hamilton had left London with an elementary 1912 handbook on the Turkish Army, the 1913 *Manual of Combined Naval and Military Operations*, and not even his own choice of a staff chief. There was no plan for disembarking, no reliable maps, no one with knowledge of the terrain, no water ships, all too few engineers and signals personnel, and insufficient medical facilities to handle the cases of infectious disease that soon plagued the invaders. Guns and ammunition had been assigned to separate ships in Britain, thus necessitating a month-long reloading at Alexandria, Egypt.

In July Hamilton received an additional five infantry divisions and by October had established another beachhead at Suvla Bay. But the Cabinet quickly lost confidence in the side show and the War Office was asked to dispatch General Sir Charles Monro to Gallipoli to assess the local situation. In Churchill's biting words, 'He came, he saw, he capitulated'.[95] Hamilton was peremptorily removed from command on 15 October. Early November chills took the lives of roughly 200 men and frostbite afflicted an additional 5000. In all the Allies lost 252 000 men at Gallipoli, including 142 000 battle casualties; the Turks set their own battle losses at 165 000.[96] In what was the single bright page in the history of the campaign, General Birdwood evacuated about 100 000 soldiers in January 1916. Prime Minister Asquith, First Sea Lord Fisher, and Churchill all fell from power as a result of the Dardanelles debacle. In Greece the Germanophile King Constantine used the fiasco to 'sack' his pro-western Prime Minister, Eleutherios Venizelos, who had hoped to use a successful Gallipoli campaign as a springboard for his 'Greater Greece' expansionist ambitions.

Turkish defences at Gallipoli had been well established by the German General Otto Liman von Sanders, commanding 80 000 men of the Turkish Fifth Army, and his young Ottoman colleague, Colonel Mustafa Kemal (the future Kemal Atatürk), in charge of the 19th Division. Given Romania's decision in October 1914 to close its borders to all Central Power war shipments, the Dardanelles defenders were short of ammunition and other supplies. But roughly 700 German sailors under Admiral

Guido von Usedom arrived at the Straits and overhauled its much-neglected defences. When Carden first shelled the Gallipoli heights, he was answered by a steady bombardment from 100 medium and heavy Turkish-German guns. Eleven mine belts and an anti-submarine net further impeded British naval progress. Germany transported U-boats in sections by rail to the Habsburg naval bases at Pola and Cattaro in the Adriatic, where they were reassembled and towed to the Dardanelles. A U-boat torpedoed the British battleships *Triumph* and *Majestic*.

Liman von Sanders deployed the Turkish Fifth Army, reinforced to a strength of 150 000, in an active defence from Bulair in the north to Besika Bay in the south. He used Mustafa Kemal's division at Gaba Tepe to launch vicious counterattacks against the Allied invaders from the Straits' heights. Enfilading machine-gun fire took a horrendous toll of the untried Australian and New Zealand troops, none of whom advanced more than 600 yards inland.[97] German officers were impressed that the Turkish troops fought tenaciously despite suffering constant hunger and epidemics, and often going months without pay. Part of the reason was that the Turks were well aware that British and Anzac troops carried their pay with them into battle![98] As the Turks ringed the constricted beachheads, Hamilton's men were forced to resort to trench warfare for the next 3 months. His only advice to the troops was to 'dig, dig, dig, until you are safe'.[99] All in all, it was a creditable performance by the tiny contingent of German military advisers and their Ottoman surrogates.

Most importantly, the desperate defence of the Straits alerted Falkenhayn to the need to reopen Danube shipping to Turkey. In the process the entire Balkan question, which Bismarck had deemed not worth 'the bones of a single Pomeranian grenadier', resurfaced. Bulgaria and Romania were still neutral, Greece still leaning toward the Allies; and Serbia still a thorn in Vienna's side, having defeated Austria–Hungary twice in 1914 and controlling the railroad that led to the Porte. Thus Falkenhayn approached Conrad in March 1915 with a suggestion that the Central Powers undertake a quick joint strike against Belgrade to reopen the road to Turkey.

For once Conrad was not interested in opening up another front. His forces were disastrously engaged in Galicia and Italy was making ominous noises about entering the war. Falkenhayn thereupon upped the ante, dangling before Conrad the vision of Sofia joining Berlin and Vienna on the condition that Turkey secured Bulgaria against possible Romanian and Greek intervention. While fearing that a Berlin–Sofia pact might give Germany a dominant role in the Balkans, Conrad nevertheless became interested. Grand strategic visions began to dance before his eyes: an offensive with Bulgaria against Serbia, he informed Foreign Minister

Burián, might have highly desirable results and could prompt Romania to join the war on the side of the Central Powers. While Burián worried more about Italy's aggressive posture towards Vienna, he also saw merit in the proposal – provided that only Habsburg troops were used against Serbia. This astonishing misunderstanding of the state of Habsburg forces in 1915 prompted a sarcastic rejoinder from Conrad: 'But with what?'[100] But Hungarian Prime Minister Tisza, Burián's mentor, also let it be known that only Habsburg troops should be sent against Serbia. 'Austria–Hungary's influence in the Balkans is destroyed forever if we call on the Germans for help.'[101] In Berlin Bethmann Hollweg's advisor, Riezler, marvelled at the constant 'ups and downs in Vienna between bravado and despair'.[102]

In the end, Conrad had little choice but to agree to Falkenhayn's Serbian proposal. The German victory at Gorlice-Tarnów and the Allies' failure to force the Turkish Straits encouraged Romania to maintain its neutrality, and Berlin spent the summer of 1915 negotiating Bulgaria's entry into the war. Offers of immediate cession of Turkish lands (Thrace) and future gains at Serbia's and possibly Greece's expense (Macedonia) led Tsar Ferdinand, the 'Balkan Richelieu', to conclude a military convention with the *OHL* on 6 September.[103] Turkey joined the alliance 8 days later.

The problem of unified command once again brought a deep chill to Austro-Hungarian-German relations. While Falkenhayn and Bulgarian War Minister N. T. Zhekov insisted on overall German command (Mackensen), Conrad demanded that the operation be conducted by the *AOK*, and possibly led by a member of the imperial house. The outcome, once again, was an unsatisfactory compromise: Mackensen was appointed commander of the Serbian campaign, but the two General Staffs agreed jointly to decide all major issues and to have the *AOK* from Teschen issue such orders.[104] Conrad's plan for a broad battle of envelopment in Serbia yielded to Falkenhayn's more modest strategy of using Habsburg troops in Bosnia–Herzegovina and Bulgarian units in the south to tie down Serbian forces while Mackensen drove straight down the major valleys to Belgrade.

Mackensen attacked Serbia on 5 October. The Germans, for one of the few times in the Great War, enjoyed numerical superiority (75 battalions) in a major theatre. In the north four divisions of Kövess' Habsburg Third Army and 10 divisions of Gallwitz's German Eleventh Army crossed the Save–Danube border; in the south Zhekov sent two Bulgarian armies with six divisions west into southern Serbia 6 days later, with the important First Army heading for Nis. Serbian Field Marshal Putnik met the attack by frontal and flanking forces double his own strength (330 000) by a series of skilful retreats, barely escaping envelopment. Mackensen entered Belgrade on 9 October.[105] The German Eleventh Army at about the same time crossed the Danube near Temes Kubin – site of the alleged 'battle' in July 1914. Putnik's only hope was that the Allies would dispatch an expeditionary force in time to save Serbia before Mackensen and Zhekov joined up.

It was not to be. The Allied divisions hastily despatched to the Balkans by Paris and London early in October failed to arrive in time. Paralleling the German violation of Belgian neutrality in 1914, British and French divisions invaded and occupied parts of neutral Greece. French General Maurice Sarrail's grandiosely named Army of the Orient moved from Greek Salonika up the Vardar Valley, only to be repulsed by Bulgarian forces. British General Sir Bryan Mahon got no further than the Bulgarian border. The original Allied contingent of 150 000 soldiers at Salonika was later reinforced by Italian and Russian troops to a strength of 500 000 soldiers, but, apart from the capture of Monastir in November 1916, it remained a force in being. While the Bulgarians pressed Berlin to drive the Allies out of Salonika, the Germans were content to leave the garrison under Bulgarian guard. The *OHL* jokingly referred to Salonika as its 'largest internment camp'.[106]

By mid-November Putnik's situation had become critical as the Bulgarians controlled Skopje and the road to Salonika. On 25 November the aged *Vojvode* ordered what became an epic fighting retreat over the snow-covered Albanian mountains to the Adriatic Sea. The terrain was frightful: steep cliffs ringed narrow valleys whose clay soil had been turned into mud by the retreating troops; artillery could be moved only by teams of oxen; and all food had to be hauled by pack animals. Putnik was carried in a sedan chair and much of his supplies moved in ancient buffalo carts. All the while, General Kövess' Third Army pursued the 140 000 Serbian soldiers and civilian refugees (and Habsburg prisoners of war).[107] In time, the path to the Adriatic coast was littered with thousands of Serbian soldiers who had died of exhaustion, hunger, or cold.

The remnants of the once-proud Serbian Army reached Scutari on 7 December. Albanian irregulars viciously attacked King Peter's dispirited troops. At Valona the Italians not only refused to evacuate the Serbian soldiers, but sought to drive them back across the mountains. The French seized the Greek island of Corfu and transferred 133 000 Serbian survivors and volunteers there in February 1916. The Serbs eventually were regrouped, reequipped, and retrained under Field Marshal Živojin Mišić; they spent much of the remainder of the war as part of General Sarrail's Army of the Orient in Salonika, Greece.

All of Serbia was in Mackensen's hands. His forces had taken 124 000 prisoners of war and the Bulgarians another 50 000; more than 94 000

Serbs had either died or been wounded in the fighting. The Central Powers inherited about 600 pieces of Serbian artillery in addition to valuable stores of small arms; they sustained 67 000 casualties, including 12 000 German and 18 000 Austro-Hungarian soldiers.[108]

Yet relations between Conrad and Falkenhayn did not improve. The *OHL* throughout the Serbian campaign bypassed Teschen and issued orders directly to Mackensen.[109] Falkenhayn sarcastically noted that Habsburg units had 'found it difficult to overcome enemy resistance', implying that German forces had once again secured victory. Conrad reacted by ignoring Falkenhayn's order to halt at the Serbo-Montenegrin border and instead overran Montenegro, whereupon the *OHL* recalled 8 of its 11 divisions in Serbia and demanded that Conrad send two Habsburg divisions to the Western Front. On 11 January 1916 General Ignaz von Trollmann's 47th Infantry Division stormed the heavily fortified heights of Mount Lovćen, overlooking the Austrian naval base of Cattaro; 2 days later Conrad's forces occupied the capital. Montenegro capitulated on 17 January. King Nicholas I fled Centinje, but for good measure hung a portrait of Franz Joseph in his study! Austro-Hungarian units next moved into northern Albania – and in the process taxed their supply system beyond capacity.

Falkenhayn was furious over the land grab in Montenegro and Albania and informed the Austrians that he no longer had confidence in them. He curtailed communications with Teschen for an entire month.[110] Ever suspicious, Conrad suspected that the Germans planned to create their own satellite state at Belgrade and accused the Bulgarians of harbouring secret ambitions to annex southern Serbia. Interallied relations reached an all-time low in the winter of 1915: while Conrad temporarily halted German armaments shipments to Bulgaria, Tsar Ferdinand returned his medals and decorations to Vienna and threatened to declare war on the Dual Monarchy! Conrad confided to his staff that he found it 'physically painful' to deal with Falkenhayn, whom he depicted as being 'slippery as an eel, clever, and never upright'. He instructed his entourage constantly to remind the Germans of their 'defeat at the Marne' and of the fact that Austria–Hungary in 1914 had saved 'Prussian Silesia' and Berlin from Russian occupation. 'The time has finally come', Conrad crowed, 'to speak plainly with them.'[111] Instead, Conrad and Falkenhayn refused to communicate with one another between 22 December 1915 and 19 January 1916 – the very weeks in which the former finished plans to crush the Italian 'snake' while the latter put the final touches on a major offensive in France 'in the direction of Verdun'.

This personal animosity notwithstanding, euphoria reigned in Vienna and Budapest. Conrad immediately demanded that Austria–Hungary annex Serbia, Montenegro, and Albania. He placed Serbia under military administration as a first step toward creating a South Slav union under Croat leadership within an expanded trialistic Monarchy. In a secret memorandum on war aims to Kaiser Franz Joseph and Foreign Minister Burián, Conrad insisted that Austria–Hungary's future rested with the creation of a 'central European bloc' in alliance with Berlin, which alone could guarantee the 'existence of the Monarchy and its prosperity'. 'Asia Minor is the natural field of expansion for the Monarchy's economic ambitions.' Conrad lectured the Ballhausplatz that Russia 'is and remains the Monarchy's most dangerous enemy', seeking nothing less than its 'total destruction'. Italy 'is and remains the Monarchy's natural and most vindictive adversary' because the Habsburg Empire blocked Italy's expansion into the Balkan peninsula as well as across the Adriatic and Mediterranean seas. Serbia and Montenegro, long taken 'in tow by Russia', remained 'bitter enemies of the Monarchy'. In short, all three opponents could be held down only if Vienna acted in unison with Berlin.

Conrad demanded 'natural borders' as security for the future. In the east the line needed to be extended to the Bug River (at minimum to the Vistula), thereby adding most of Poland to the Habsburg realm. In the south Conrad demanded 'Serbia's total incorporation into the Monarchy'. A land-locked Montenegro could remain 'independent' under Viennese control. Finally, Conrad argued that the border with Italy be redrawn along the lines of 1866: Tyrol had to be moved south to the Piave and Tagliamento rivers, while elsewhere the Monarchy needed to move its frontier stakes to the line Po–Mincio south of Lake Garda. Italians living in these regions would be drafted into 'military construction battalions' already in peacetime.[112] Over and over, Conrad lectured Count Burián that Serbia's total eradication from the map of Europe alone could justify 'the present war with its immense sacrifices of blood and treasure'.[113]

Foreign Minister Burián seconded Conrad's call for the annexation of Serbia – but to Hungary. In Budapest, Tisza raised the issue of war aims in parliament for the first time in October 1915. Assuming that Vienna planned to incorporate Congress Poland (along with Galicia) into Austria proper, Tisza asked that Hungary receive Bosnia–Herzegovina and Dalmatia. At a Common Council at Vienna in January 1916, Tisza, seconded by War Minister von Krobatin, demanded that Hungary annex northern Serbia and 'colonize' it with politically 'reliable Hungarian and German farmers', thereby 'driving a wedge between the Serbs in rump Serbia and the Dual Monarchy'. Belgrade would become a 'Hungarian provincial town'.[114] Tisza suggested that reparations to be paid by the conquered states be shared equally between the German Reich and the Dual

Monarchy. But the Hungarian magnate would have nothing to do with Conrad's plans for a South Slav state.

That same month Tisza brought about a revision in the Monarchy's coat of arms to stress its dualistic character. The combined arms of the hereditary lands of the imperial Austrian crown, placed side-by-side with the arms of the royal Hungarian crown, replaced the former double-headed imperial eagle. Bosnia was not included in the new design: had Tisza already 'annexed' it in his mind? Within a year a new flag combining the imperial Austrian black and yellow with the royal Hungarian red-white-green further reflected the shared duality of power between Vienna and Budapest.[115]

The Germans also took stock of the future after the heady victories in Russia and Serbia. General von Seeckt mused about Germany's freedom to 'play with crowns and thrones', and spun grandiose 'dreams of a German imperium stretching from the Atlantic to Persia'.[116] Foreign Secretary von Jagow argued that Austria-Hungary's abysmal performance in the war had shown that state to be no longer viable and suggested that the time had come to reorder the Multinational Empire. Its German lands, or Cisleithania, Jagow suggested, should fall to Prussia-Germany; Hungary should become an independent state; and a semi-independent Poland should be tied to Germany economically. Jagow continued to couch the war in racial terms. The struggle between 'Slavic-Mongolian' Russia and the 'Germanic-Romance peoples of the West' remained eternal; the 'Russian nightmare' would have to be pushed back behind the Bug River. Jagow rejected all talk of a separate peace with St Petersburg.[117]

Falkenhayn liked the idea of a German-controlled *Mitteleuropa* – what he called a 'combine' of the four Central Powers (Austria-Hungary, Bulgaria, Germany, and Turkey) perhaps joined by Greece, Sweden, and Switzerland – and compared it to the United States of America. 'The Kaiser as President!', aided by a 'Senate'. But he rejected Jagow's geopolitical musings by arguing that the Habsburg Army was a 'cadaver' that could offer little to Prussia-Germany. Falkenhayn and Bethmann Hollweg were united in the belief that, while the Dual Monarchy had to be maintained for lack of an acceptable alternative, the lion's share of war gains would have to go to Germany.[118]

Yet, as Falkenhayn's most recent biographer has shown, there was a major division of opinion over the *Mitteleuropa* concepts of the two German leaders. Whereas the Chancellor desired its creation as a war aim that he had stubbornly clung to since September 1914, the Chief of the General Staff saw it as a means of ending the war. Put differently, whereas Bethmann Hollweg cherished *Mitteleuropa* as an end in itself,

Falkenhayn sought to create a blockade-safe military and economic Central Europe primarily as a means to break the Entente's will to pursue the war, as a strategy aimed first and foremost at the 'archenemy' Britain.[119] In October 1915 Friedrich Naumann gave intellectual direction to the debate by publishing his highly popular book *Mitteleuropa*; in Budapest, Tisza proclaimed that such musings would not be acceptable to Hungary.

While soldiers and statesmen dreamed in continents, the average soldier saw the Serbian campaign as welcome relief from the dreary killing fields of Galicia. Hans Hartinger, an Austrian noncommissioned officer with the 3rd *Landsturm* Regiment of General Kövess' Third Army, left a remarkable diary account of the action against Serbia. Hartinger's unit was stationed at Sarajevo as part of the mainly Slovene 26th Alpine Brigade. Sarajevo, Hartinger exclaimed, was a delight, exotically distant from Austria, 'like Constantinople'. The Turkish bazaar (Carsjya) featured pastries made with honey and sugar, broiled meats, and candied fruits. A German brewery offered good beer at reasonable prices. The city's brothel with its system of lights to indicate levels of service made a lasting impression on the *Landsturm* warrior. 'Red was for soldiers and common people. Green was the so-called better house. There the price of flesh had been pegged higher. The home marked by a blue lantern was very fine and only for officers and high civil servants.' A buffet, Turkish coffee and German beer restored the brothel's customers to full strength.[120]

But Hartinger noted that the war and military rule had brought hardships to Sarajevo's poor. Those unable to care for themselves – about 35 000 indigents – had been rounded up by the gendarmerie, herded with canes to the railroad station, there to wait for days on end for cattle cars that would remove them to the Bosnian hinterland. 'The screams of the children and mothers were frightful.' Hartinger recorded the negative impact of the Habsburg policy: 'This was one of the worst ways to inject the population with love for the dynasty'.

The 26th Alpine Brigade was a ragged unit, for it had endured months of trench warfare. The soldiers' shoes were torn from countless marches and countermarches, as well as from too many hours of standing in water-filled trenches. Coats were threadbare and filthy from the mud. Rifles were in a 'godforsaken condition'; foresights had been bent or broken from randomly stacking them in piles. The brigade had only six machine guns and its artillery was antiquated and short of ammunition. On 5 October Hartinger saw his first German regiment at Ruma. 'Snappy as if on the parade square. Officers and men singing ("The Watch on the Rhine").'

Early in October Hartinger's unit moved out as part of Field Marshal von Mackensen's Serbian operation. From Sarajevo it headed north to Karlovac and Sisak, then turned southeast and followed the Save to Ruma, Brestać, and Ašanja, where it crossed over to the river's southern shore. Thereafter the regiment pointed due east and advanced to Zabrežje, a town located in the big bend of the Save River just southwest of Belgrade. *Vojvode* Putnik's Serbian soldiers put up a tenacious defence. 'The shrapnel register shells burst high above us and showered us with a hail of lead. . . . We lie down and let the fire go over us.' At night Serbian spotlights probed the darkness to enable snipers to target the attackers. Heavy rains and equally heavy rifle fire impeded further progress. 'The Serbian bullets whistled past our ears', Hartinger noted, 'every other minute, a soldier cried out and collapsed. . . . We were up to our ankles in mud.'

Corporal Hartinger's 3rd *Landsturm* Regiment mounted its first assault on Zabrežje on 10 October. Six companies carrying only their ammunition and one day's rations stormed Serbian lines. Several companies were 'decimated'; the regiment lost four dead and 32 wounded. Numerous soldiers had refused to leave their trenches. Further infantry wave assaults were ordered on 11 and 12 October – 'the crazy idea of a General Staff officer'. The regiment suffered another nine dead, 77 wounded, and 32 missing. The rain continued unabated. 'Filth and mud runs down our necks. Miserable food and cold as hell. Rain. Rain. Rain.' Ground water from the Save began to rise in the trenches. Hartinger described his unit as looking like 'meandering dirt crusts'.

German artillery arrived on 16 October and took Zabrežje under fire. Hartinger's regiment advanced across the previous No Man's Land. It was a sobering experience. The meadow was littered with bodies, infantry mowed down by Serbian machine guns, some sited in trees for better command of the flat terrain. 'Countless worms covered the wounds and a disgusting stench of decaying corpses forced us on.' The dead had been picked clean of all possessions. Hartinger entered Zabrežje on 17 October after German artillery had forced the Serbs to evacuate the town. 'All the houses were in ruins, the streets torn up. Our 30.5 cm howitzers were especially effective. There were craters in the clay soil in which whole groups found cover; we used them to bury the corpses.' Hartinger found shelter for the night in a shot-up tavern. Delousing was first on the agenda. 'Whoever felt like it, counted them [lice] by the thousands.'

By late October the regiment had moved to the tranquil Kolubara Valley. 'Liquor in abundance; also fowl. We eat to our heart's content and sleep without care all night long.' Only a lack of salt put a momentary damper on the celebration. 'Animals [are] simply beaten to death, skinned, and the still warm meat boiled without salt in kettles.' For Hartinger, the Serbian campaign was over.

Strategically, Serbia's defeat gave the Central Powers control over a huge belt of *Mitteleuropa* stretching from the North Sea to the Dardanelles, and even beyond to the Tigris River. Pan-German dreams of a Berlin to Baghdad connection had been realized: the first train from Berlin arrived at Constantinople on 17 January 1916. Militarily, Berlin and Vienna had consolidated their interior position. Romania remained neutral. Italy had been repulsed along the Isonzo front. Russia had been driven back 300 miles and its army ruined. Turkey had thwarted the Anglo-French attempt to seize Gallipoli. Only the Western Front continued in bloody stalemate.

Deadlock: The western front

The first few months of 1915 brought several massive but inconclusive French attempts to dispel the German Army from the lands it had occupied in 1914. From 1 January to 30 March General Joffre, enjoying an overall advantage of 150 Allied against 100 German divisions, or 2.45 million men versus 1.9 million, mounted a major effort to drive the Germans from the Noyon salient and the area between Reims and Verdun. These battles scored limited gains, but then were repulsed by counter-attacks conducted by General von Einem's Third Army. A simultaneous British attempt to break through north of La Bassée was similarly repelled by Crown Prince Rupprecht's Sixth Army at Neuve Chapelle. French casualties for the winter battles of 1914–15 reached 400 000. Unperturbed, 'Papa' Joffre confidently assured his government: 'We're nibbling [*grignotage*] at them', which was, in the words of the military historian B. H. Liddell Hart, like mice nibbling at a steel safe.[121] A separate French attack against the north side of the St Mihiel salient in April 1915 was also blunted with heavy losses.[122]

The fighting on the Western Front had taken on a deadly regularity: attackers stormed enemy trenches in waves, only to be mowed down by hostile machine-gun fire and artillery as they tried to cut the wire entanglements that protected the earthworks. Few officers failed to note the debilitating effect of such 'storms of steel' on their men. Captain Werner von Blomberg of the 16th Infantry Division in February 1915 described the mood of his men as 'somewhat breathless, very pessimistic. . . . We cannot continue like this! . . . The soldiers are finished. . . . And the losses!' Colonel Hugo von dem Bergh, Blomberg's commander, painted a similar picture of the fighting in the Bémont sector of the Champagne: 95 000 artillery shells had rained down on the division in three days; some of its battalions reduced to 116 men. 'The most fantastic imagination cannot comprehend this cauldron of [steel] rain.' Bergh informed family at home that the German word for both battle and butchery, *Schlacht*, was 'terrible but suitable'.[123] But the nature of land operations was changing. Already in January 1915 Colonel von Seeckt had revised standard procedures at Soissons: defensive artillery and infantry pinned down the attacking enemy, thereby preventing resupply and reinforcement, and morally destroying the assault. Thereafter, infantry counterattacked a demoralized enemy.[124]

Four months later the Germans captured a French document at La Ville-aus-Bois detailing a novel elastic defence-in-depth consisting not of a rigid line but rather of an outpost zone, a battle zone, and a rearward zone. The new defence forced the enemy to expend its forces against several echelons of troops arranged in depth; counterattack infantry supplied the resiliency, or elasticity, of the system. Defensive units deployed on reverse slopes wherever possible; artillery was incorporated into the defence and commanded at the divisional level; and all combat arms were fully integrated into the defence units.[125] Allied soldiers found from this time on that they charged into a deadly killing ground: entrenchments and barbed wire, protected by enfilading concrete machine-gun posts and artillery echeloned in depth. Even if the attackers penetrated the first line, they were cut down by fire from machine guns sited in the second line, and then by artillery placed beyond the range of their own guns.

The war evoked charges of lack of material. On 14 May Colonel Charles à Court Repington, aided and abetted by Field Marshal French, commander of the BEF, caused a public furore with a front-page story in the London *Times*: 'Need for Shells. British Attacks Checked. Limited Supply the Cause'. Repington brazenly informed the British public that it was 'certain that we can smash the German crust if we have the means'.[126] Lloyd George spied the main chance to scale the slippery political ladder and allayed the public uproar by heading a Cabinet Munitions of War Committee. Similar cries for more material on the part of journalists, politicians, and generals in Berlin, Paris, and Vienna brought committees to investigate the 'shell crisis'. The feeling abounded that if just enough men and guns were concentrated at a vital point of the front, the static war of the trenches could yet be returned to the glorious wars of movement of the past.

Field Marshal Kitchener in London was the first senior commander to realize that the war would not be over by Christmas 1914, and that Britain would have to mobilize a million men. As the BEF bled heavily at Mons, Le Cateau, and Ypres, the Secretary of State for War worked to raise New Armies of 70 divisions: 175 000 volunteers streamed in by 5 September and another 600 000 by the end of the month.[127] Posters with Kitchener's extended finger pointing at Britain's young men carried the message 'Your Country needs YOU' to the corners of the Empire. It drew the epitaph 'the great poster' for Kitchener from the Prime Minister's wife, Margot Asquith.

Austria–Hungary recognized the need for enhanced war production perhaps most immediately because of the severity of its defeats in Galicia and Serbia. During the winter of 1915–16, War Minister von Krobatin completely reequipped the field artillery. Antiquated 8 cm M-99 field guns were removed from service and replaced with state of the art M-14 field guns as well as with the new 15 cm M-15 howitzer. With nearly 90 tubes, *k.u.k.* divisions finally caught up in fire power to both allies and adversaries. The heavy artillery received mobile 24cm M-16 howitzers and more of the renowned 30.5 cm howitzers that the Germans had used against Liège in 1914. At the Daimler Works in Wiener Neustadt, Ferdinand Porsche drew up plans to produce a massive 38 cm *Autohaubitze* and an experimental 42 cm tractor-drawn super howitzer. But the Dual Monarchy, basically limited to two major producers, Steyr in Austria and Škoda in Bohemia, could never match the other major combatants in output. Production of light machine guns rose by only 1400, allowing but four per battalion; early prototypes of flamethrowers proved deficient; gas shells remained on the drawing boards; no serviceable tanks were ever developed; and even after adopting German designs, only 400 aircraft were produced in 1915–16.[128]

Repington's alarm concerning a 'shell crisis' found a ready echo in Germany. In April 1914 Moltke had stated that the artillery was supplied for 30 or 40 days of fighting with 1000 shells per gun, but wondered whether an extra 500 rounds per tube might not be prudent. War Minister von Falkenhayn warned as early as 22 October that the Army would soon run out of shells, given its high rate of fire. Aware that private industry supplied only 40 per cent of the Army's needs, Falkenhayn convened a national conference of producers to coordinate private-sector output. He established a target of tripling or quadrupling ammunition production and warned that the availability of '*unlimited* amounts of ammunition' had become a 'question of life and death for the Army'. Falkenhayn was especially irate that Krupp continued to fulfil foreign orders while German units in France and Poland suffered from a shortage of shells. One year later, as Chief of the General Staff, Falkenhayn demanded further increased production, rejected the War Ministry's lamentations that shell output had become a 'screw without end', and lectured Berlin that victory would fall to the side that could 'tighten the screw of ammunitions (and weapons) production the most'.[129]

German monthly production of field artillery rose from 100 tubes in early 1915 to 800 by autumn 1916. The output of guns for heavy artillery went from 38 to 330 units per month during the same period. Shells for steel guns, produced at Siegburg, Spandau, Ingolstadt, and Dresden, rose dramatically: 147 333 in August 1914, 398 953 by December of that year, and 486 755 by February 1915. The figure climbed to more than 1 million in June 1915 and to nearly 3 million by February 1916. Ammunition output escalated 400 per cent by December 1914; in October 1915 it stood 1300 per cent above the level of August 1914. Already in 1914 the Army had added 18 firms beyond Krupp and Ehrhardt to the list of weapons producers. By war's end 654 new companies had entered gun and ammunition production.

Walther Rathenau, head of Germany's largest electrical conglomerate, General Electric (AEG), was shocked during a visit to the Prussian War Ministry early in August 1914 to learn from Colonel Heinrich Scheüch that no provisions had been made to coordinate the supply and distribution of vital raw materials either in Germany or in occupied Belgium. Scheüch arranged a meeting between Rathenau and Falkenhayn on 9 August to discuss economic mobilization for war. Rathenau recalled his discussion:

Your Excellency, you have prepared the military mobilization meticulously and carefully. You have lists for every man, every horse, every gun and their destination. Have you likewise also prepared the economic mobilization? The war can last a long time [and] what will you do if the raw materials that are indispensable for conducting the war – such as zinc, copper, aluminum, etc. – are exhausted? Do you also have lists for these?[130]

Unable to respond positively, Falkenhayn on 13 August appointed Rathenau along with Colonel Karl Oehme to head a special War Raw Materials Section within the Prussian War Ministry.[131] Ably assisted by the AEG engineer Wichard von Möllendorf, probably the author of the *Kriegsrohstoffabteilung* concept, Rathenau established a central system to purchase, store, and distribute raw materials, and to break down the barriers between the various German federal states that hindered the allocation of raw materials to industry. Within a few weeks, Rathenau created War Raw Materials Corporations, run as private stock companies and granted trust status within the War Ministry, in the chemical, metallurgical, and wool industries. Additionally, Rathenau set price ceilings on certain war-related goods to prevent excessive price speculation. A new Chemicals Section overcame the potentially fatal loss of Chilean saltpetre resulting from the British naval blockade by building nitrogen-fixation plants, while a War Chemicals Corporation regulated the supply of glycerin.

Nor did Falkenhayn ignore the human dimension of war. Under his stewardship the General Staff created 11 new army corps of 15 200 officers, 600 000 noncommissioned officers and men, and 130 000 horses – a force one-quarter the size of the Regular Army of August 1914 and one that almost completely swallowed up all available reserve formations. In 1915 the General Staff called up two cohorts of young men (those born in 1895 and 1896), and the following year another two cohorts (those born in 1897 and 1898). The critical shortage of qualified officers – 20 000 in 1915 alone – forced the General Staff to extend officer training from 2 to 3 months for the influx of reservists, students, and former garrison and administrative personnel. Improved military medicine also did its part to maintain force strength: wound mortality fell from 8.8 per cent in 1914 to 1.8 per cent by the end of 1915; conversely, the percentage of wounded returned to duty rose by 20 points (to 93 per cent) during the same period.

But Falkenhayn also harboured more radical reforms. In June 1915 he conceded to Gustav Krupp that the complaints of many front-line soldiers concerning war profiteering by workers at home were justified. All too many draft-eligible young men, Falkenhayn argued, 'were sitting at home, earning a lot of money, and living well while the others carried the burdens of the war alone'. He was alarmed by what he termed the 'unhealthy rise in wages' and the unwillingness especially of young workers to 'sacrifice'. While the Army had drafted nearly 2 million workers for front-line duty at the start of 1915, Falkenhayn nevertheless felt frustrated that he could not recruit more of the 1.68 million industrial workers in Germany fit for service late in 1916 for fear of thereby jeopardizing the supply of war material. General Franz von Wandel, the Prussian Deputy War Minister, rejected Falkenhayn's suggestion that armaments plants be 'militarized', that is, placed under military law, for fear of thereby antagonizing the Reich's 2.7 million trade unionists and interrupting the free flow of labour and goods.[132] The measure remained a dead letter until 1916–17.

This new flood of men and material allowed the *OHL* to contemplate renewed offensives along the Western Front. In the spring of 1915, Falkenhayn launched a surprise attack against the Allies at Ypres. While failing to dislodge the enemy from its strategic cornerpost in Flanders, the assault made world headlines on 22 April through the release of compressed chlorine gas from more than 5000 storage cylinders at Steestraten-Pilkem. The wind carried the 6-kilometre-wide, dense green-yellow clouds into the lines of the French 45th and 87th Divisions, incapacitating somewhere between 200 (German estimates) and 625 (French calculations) enemy soldiers.[133] Newspaper estimates ranged as high as 5000 Allied soldiers killed.

French authorities, tipped off to the coming use of 'asphyxiating gas' by a German deserter on 13 April, had failed to act on the information. While the strange gas opened a wide gap in the Allied lines and caused a hasty withdrawal from the affected front, the Germans failed to exploit their revolutionary advantage. Falkenhayn had merely sought to use the new weapon to distract attention from the planned eastern offensive at Gorlice-Tarnów, and thus had not counted on such immediate and dramatic results. Thus the *OHL* had no ready reserves with which to burst through enemy lines. On 25 April Falkenhayn used similar tactics against Canadian units at St Julien. The Canucks could only wet handkerchiefs, bandoliers, and towels to ward off the gas. The London *Times* condemned this 'atrocious method of warfare . . . a diabolical contrivance'. Scholars have debated its 'inhumanity' and 'illegality' ever since.

A first point to be made is that the Second Battle of Ypres did not, as is often claimed, witness the first use of gas. The French had fired primitive ethyl bromo-acetate rifle projectiles (*cartouches suffocantes*) as early as 1914 and stepped up their use in the Argonne sector in March 1915. The following month they introduced a new chemical (chloracetone) hand-grenade, the 'Bertrand No. 1'. And, as discussed earlier, the Germans had fired around 18 000 xylyl bromide shells against the Russians near Bolimow.[134]

The *OHL* had decided to explore more systematically the possibility of chemical warfare after the defeat at the Marne in 1914. Complaints from the front concerning the shortage of ammunition and the failure of high-explosive shells to dislodge enemy soldiers from their trenches drove Falkenhayn in this direction. By January 1915 the chemist Hans Tappen, whose brother Gerhard was Chief of the Operations Division of the General Staff, had tested 15 cm chemical shells for the Army. Fritz Haber, director of the Kaiser Wilhelm Institute for physical chemistry in Berlin and future Nobel Prize winner for his prewar work on the synthesis of ammonia, advised the military that chlorine gas, a potent 'lung irritant', might be most effective in penetrating enemy trenches and thus perhaps breaking the deadlock on the Western Front. Countless lives, Haber argued, could be saved and the war ended almost overnight by use of this novel weapon. Haber was confident that the Allies lacked the technology to develop similar gases. Given the bottleneck in German shell production, Haber suggested that the gas be moved to the front in industrial cylinders and released when favourable wind conditions permitted. Future Nobel laureate scientists such as James Franck, Gustav Hertz, and Otto Hahn rallied to the war effort.

The *OHL* also addressed the legal and moral aspects of gas warfare. As a signatory to the Hague Peace Conference of 1899, the Reich was pledged not to use 'poison or poisoned weapons', or 'arms, projectiles, or material calculated to cause unnecessary suffering', or 'projectiles' designed for the 'diffusion of asphyxiating or deleterious gases'.[135] The Army in 1915 resorted to legalistic sophistry to convince itself that it was acting within the Hague conventions. The prohibition of 'poison or poisoned weapons', it argued, applied only to the deliberate poisoning of food and water and the use of projectiles steeped in poison. Given that the matter of 'asphyxiating or deleterious gases' was dealt with in another provision, German soldiers argued that the first clause did not pertain to 'gas' warfare *per se*. Falkenhayn suggested that since Tappen's so-called T-shells contained both a gas-producing compound and an explosive charge to produce fragmentation, they could be said to serve a dual purpose. Last but not least, the generals argued that the release of chlorine gas from cylinders did not involve the use of 'projectiles'.[136] Thus they concluded that they acted within the letter of the law in releasing gas from industrial cylinders. Disingenuously, Falkenhayn code-named the Ypres operation 'Disinfection'.

The first use of gas by Duke Albrecht of Württemberg's Fourth Army at Ypres did not go off without major hitches. Early in March 1915 special engineering troops assisted Haber by night in embedding 5500 cylinders of chlorine gas (code-named 'F batteries') under a layer of earth in the sector held by General Berthold von Deimling's XV Corps. Repeated ill winds, which in Flanders mostly blew from a westerly or southwesterly direction, delayed release of the gas. Some cylinders leaked; others were punctured by random enemy shells or bullets. German infantry, unprotected against the gas, ironically became the first victim of this nascent chemical warfare.[137]

Several senior army commanders did not share Falkenhayn's faith in gas warfare. Crown Prince Rupprecht, commanding the Sixth Army south of Duke Albrecht's Fourth Army, informed Falkenhayn and Haber that he considered the plan both morally distasteful and militarily questionable. If the operation proved successful, the Allies, with their superior industrial plant, would quickly copy it. And given that the prevailing winds in Flanders blew east off the Atlantic, the Allies would be able to use gas at 10 times the German rate.[138] General von Einem, head of the Third Army in the Champagne, shared Rupprecht's concerns, adding that Germany's first use of gas would cause a 'tremendous scandal in the world'. Einem especially resented the industrial-scientific nature of the weapon. 'War has nothing to do with chivalry anymore', he wrote to his wife the day after the release of chlorine at Ypres. 'The higher civilization rises, the more vile man becomes.'[139] Wilhelm II was of a different mind: he awarded Fritz Haber the Iron Cross I Class and promoted Tappen to the rank of major-general (celebrated with a bottle of the Kaiser's favourite pink champagne) for the Ypres action. Within a year, German scientists added phosgene, a highly toxic pulmonary agent, to their chlorine discharges. In time, both sides developed smoke-making devices to simulate gas and therewith provide cover for advancing infantry.

The Austro-Hungarian Army now developed an interest in gas and in September 1915 despatched Captain Max von Ow to the German Ninth Army for information. Ow reported that the Germans used lead piping to hook up in series batteries of 20 cylinders each filled with liquid chloride and 20 per cent phosgene; on average, one cylinder of gas was required per yard of front. It was best to release the gas in the morning, when it was cool; the wind had to blow steady toward enemy trenches. It was impossible to release the gas during rain and difficult in heat. Ow noted that the Germans fired gas in artillery shells, which exploded above the ground and allowed the vapour, which was heavier than air, to seep down into the trenches. But on 15 September Franz Joseph ruled that his forces would not use gas.[140]

Habsburg commanders pleaded with the Kaiser to reconsider his decision and to allow gas to be added to the *k.u.k.* arsenal. Specifically, Archdukes Eugen (Southwest Front), Friedrich (Commander-in-Chief), and Joseph (VII Corps) as well as War Minister von Krobatin and General von Boroević (Fifth Army) requested permission to use gas, arguing that it was less 'barbaric' than high-explosive shells and that the mere threat of using it would act as a 'deterrent'. But the Kaiser remained firm, agreeing only to reconsider his decision 'the minute that our enemies should use this weapon against us'.[141]

The British harboured no such reservations about the use of gas. In fact, the fears raised by Rupprecht and Einem about enemy response to the release of gas at Ypres were soon realized. The Allies between September and December 1915 renewed the offensive in Artois and the Champagne. While the French mounted a major, though unsuccessful, effort to retake Vimy Ridge, the British at Loos for the first time countered with Kitchener's New Armies – and with gas warfare. At dawn on 25 September Haig's First Army released deadly chlorine gas from about 5000 cylinders, each weighing 200lbs, augmented by smoke candles to produce the first 'smoke screen' of the war. Six British divisions, armed with home-made, small cotton-wool-pad respirators, were poised to charge through the anticipated gap in the German lines. Haig released gas as part of a major breakthrough attempt.

Britain's use of gas at Loos was premature. While Haig's engineers had warned that the winds were too weak and unpredictable to warrant release, General Sir Hubert Gough, commanding I Corps, had overruled them in the belief that once committed, the British could not call off the attack. As the gas clouds drifted slowly toward the German lines on Gough's right, the wind on his left flank changed and poisoned unprotected British soldiers. Infantry, comfortable in the belief that the enemy had been gassed, advanced across No Man's Land, only to be cut down by ungassed German machine gunners. Subsequent assaults by Kitchener's new 21st and 24th Divisions led to such slaughter that German machine gunners stopped shooting out of a sense of pity. Nothing seemed to go right for the British at Loos: a military policeman halted the advance of the 72nd Brigade at Béthune because its commander did not have a proper pass to enter the area.[142] Haig's First Army suffered 60 392 casualties in the Third Battle of Artois; the Germans one-third that number. French was relieved of command of the BEF in favour of Haig. The latter overlooked experienced officers in France for his staff chief and instead brought his old friend, Sir Launcelot ('Kigg') Kiggell, over from London.

The year 1915 ended with the Third and Fourth Battles of the Isonzo, fought between 18 October and 14 December. Winter came early. Snow between 6 and 8 yards deep covered up natural caves and trenches hacked into the rough rocks, with the result that troops on both sides sought 'safety' in defensive works made of ice and snow. Life at the front became a living hell. Snow and ice storms as well as almost unbearable cold ravaged soldiers huddled in makeshift shelters at 2000 to 3000 yards altitude – only to be offset by warm Mediterranean winds that turned valleys and roads into raging streams and rampaging mud slides. Avalanches were a constant danger. Pack animals hauled 37 million cartridges, 706 000 artillery shells, and 76 000 hand-grenades up to the front. By the time the fighting was ended by total exhaustion on both sides, Boroević's Fifth Army had suffered 71 691 casualties, the Italians 116 000.[143]

The butcher's bill for 1914–15 was staggering: more than 2 million Russian, 2.1 million Austro-Hungarian, 1.3 million French, 612 000 German, 279 000 British, and 180 000 Italian men. While the Eastern Front had featured a classic war of movement on a grand scale, ranging from the Masurian Lakes in the north to the Carpathian Mountains and Serbia in the south, the Western Front remained stagnated in a deadly killing ground. Not even the introduction of gas warfare had changed its static character. Few soldiers looked forward to the new year with great expectations.

Chapter 4 Notes

1. Falkenhayn to Field Marshal von der Goltz, 16 November 1914. Reichsarchiv, *Der Weltkrieg 1914 bis 1918*. 5: *Der Herbstfeldzug 1914* (Berlin, E. S. Mittler & Sohn, 1929), p. 585.
2. Lerchenfeld to Hertling, 21 March 1915. BHStA, Geheimes Staatsarchiv, Politisches Archiv, VII. Reihe, vol. 50.

3. Arnold Rechberg, *Reichsniedergang. Ein Beitrag zu dessen Ursachen aus meinen persönlichen Erinnerungen* (Munich, Musarion Verlag, 1919), p. 21.
4. See Laurence V. Moyer, *Victory Must Be Ours: Germany in the Great War 1914–1918* (New York, Hippocrene Books, 1995), p. 95.
5. BA-MA, PH 1/3 Mobilmachung 1914.
6. German South-West Africa capitulated in July 1915, and the Cameroons in February 1916. Colonel Paul von Lettow-Vorbeck in German East Africa alone held out to the bitter end with 2700 European and 11 400 native troops against British/Dominion forces twice his strength.
7. József Galántai, *Hungary in the First World War* (Budapest, Akadémiai Kiadó, 1989), pp. 95–6.
8. BA-MA, PH 2/114 A.O.K. East. Order of 30 December 1914.
9. Hoyos to Hohenlohe, 21 March 1915. HHStA, PA 7 Gesandschaft Berlin 204, Separat Akten.
10. Reichsarchiv, *Der Weltkrieg 1914 bis 1918*. 2: *Die Befreiung Ostpreussens* (Berlin, E. S. Mittler & Sohn, 1925), pp. 325–30.
11. John A. Lynn, *The Bayonets of the Republic: Motivation and Tactics in the Army of Revolutionary France 1791–94* (Urbana and Chicago, University of Illinois Press, 1984), p. 113.
12. ÖStA-Verwaltungsarchiv der Republik, Vienna, Präsidium K.K. Ministerium des Innern Nr. 453 19/3. Wirtschaftliche und politische Verhältnisse in Galizien unter Einwirkung der Kriegsereignisse, Statthalter Korytkowski, 29 November 1915.
13. HHStA, PA I, Liassa Krieg 1064. Report by Baron Leopold Andrian, 26 July 1915.
14. Bundesministerium für Landesverteidigung, *Österreich-Ungarns Letzter Krieg 1914–1918*. 2: *Das Kriegsjahr 1915* (Vienna, Verlag der Militärwissenschaftlichen Mitteilungen, 1931), pp. 9–10.
15. Rudolf Hecht, 'Fragen zur Heeresergänzung der gesamten Bewaffneten Macht Österrich-Ungarns während des Ersten Weltkrieges', unpubl. diss., Vienna University 1969, passim.
16. *Österreich-Ungarns Letzter Krieg 1914–1918 2*, p. 12.
17. ÖStA-KA, Militärkanzlei Seiner Majestät (MKSM) 1914, 38-2/1. 'Auswertung der Kriegserfahrungen', 26 November 1914.
18. Martin Kitchen, *The Silent Dictatorship: The Politics of the German High Command under Hindenburg and Ludendorff, 1916–1918* (New York, Croom Helm, 1976).
19. All letters and telegrams to and from Falkenhayn during his period as Chief of the General Staff were marked 'confidential' and sealed by the General Staff, thereby confounding historical investigators until after the Second World War.
20. This analysis of the leadership crisis is from BA-MA, MSg 1/1228 Nachlass v. Alten. The two major pieces of documentary evidence are the diary and letters of Major Hans Tieschowitz von Tieschowa, adjutant to Generals Moltke and Falkenhayn, and Major Hans von Haeften, press officer at *OberOst* and adjutant to Moltke. See also Karl-Heinz Janssen, *Der Kanzler und der General. Die Führungskrise um Bethmann Hollweg und Falkenhayn (1914–1916)* (Göttingen, Musterschmidt, 1967), pp. 68–79; and Heinz Kraft, *Staatsräson und Kriegführung im kaiserlichen Deutschland 1914–1916. Der Gegensatz zwischen dem Generalstabschef von Falkenhayn und dem Oberbefehlshaber Ost im Rahmen des Bündniskrieges der Mittelmächte* (Göttingen, Musterschmidt, 1980).
21. Cited in Egmont Zechlin, 'Ludendorff im Jahre 1915. Unveröffentlichte Briefe', *Historische Zeitschrift* 211 (1970), p. 319.
22. Interestingly, after the war Haeften became first Director of the Historical Division and then President of the Reichsarchiv in Potsdam.
23. BA-MA, Nachlass Groener, N 46, vol. 63. See also Dorothea Groener-Geyer, *General Groener. Soldat und Staatsmann* (Frankfurt, Societäts-Verlag, 1955), p. 373.

24. Zechlin, 'Ludendorff im Jahre 1915', p. 322.

25. Hindenburg to Moltke, 11 January 1915. BA-MA, Nachlass Moltke, N 78, vol. 4.

26. Count Albrecht Wallenstein raised and maintained an Imperial Army with his own funds from 1625 until 1634, when he was assassinated, probably with the connivance of Emperor Ferdinand, for known ambitions and suspected treachery. The affair left a deep scar on the Habsburg Army.

27. BA-MA, W-10/50656 Tagebuch v. Plessen, entry dated 15 January 1915.

28. Conrad von Hötzendorf, *Aus meiner Dienstzeit 1906–1918* (5 vols, Vienna, Leipzig, and Munich, Rikola Verlag, 1925) 5, p. 919. 'Neither the one, nor the other.'

29. Gerhard Ritter, *Staatskunst und Kriegshandwerk. Das Problem des 'Militarismus' in Deutschland* (4 vols, Munich, R. Oldenbourg, 1964) 3, pp. 68–9.

30. Ekkehart P. Guth, 'Der Gegensatz zwischen dem Oberbefehlshaber Ost und dem Chef des Generalstabes des Feldheeres 1914/15. Die Rolle des Majors v. Haeften im Spannungsfeld zwischen Hindenburg, Ludendorff und Falkenhayn', *Militärgeschichtliche Mitteilungen* 35 (1984), p. 85.

31. Kurt Riezler, *Tagebücher, Aufsätze, Dokumente,* ed. Karl Dietrich Erdmann (Göttingen, Vandenhoeck & Ruprecht,1972), p. 244. Entry for 25 January 1915.

32. Walter Görlitz, ed., *The Kaiser and His Court: The Diaries, Note Books and Letters of Admiral Georg Alexander von Müller Chief of the Naval Cabinet, 1914–1918* (New York, Harcourt, Brace & World, 1959), p. 57. Entry for 23 January 1915.

33. BA-MA, Nachlass Groener, N 46, vol. 63.

34. Cited in Zechlin, 'Ludendorff im Jahre 1915', pp. 323, 346.

35. The strategic alternatives for 1915 are detailed in Volker Ullrich, 'Entscheidung im Osten oder Sicherung der Dardanellen. Das Ringen um den Serbienfeldzug 1915', *Militärgeschichtliche Mitteilungen* 32 (1982), pp. 45–63.

36. Reichsarchiv, *Der Weltkrieg 1914 bis 1918. 7: Die Operationen des Jahres 1915* (Berlin, E. S. Mittler & Sohn, 1931), p. 166. The gas would not vaporize in sub-zero temperatures.

37. Reichsarchiv, *Der Weltkrieg 1914 bis 1918* 7, p. 267.

38. *Österreich-Ungarns Letzter Krieg 1914–1918* 2, p. 114.

39. *Der Weltkrieg 1914 bis 1918* 7, p. 91.

40. *Österreich-Ungarns Letzter Krieg 1914–1918* 2, pp. 142–3.

41. *Österreich-Ungarns Letzter Krieg 1914–1918* 2, p. 271.

42. Josef Stürgkh, *Im Deutschen Grossen Hauptquartier* (Leipzig, Paul List Verlag, 1921), p. 114. Statement of 27 January 1915.

43. *Österreich-Ungarns Letzter Krieg 1914–1918* 2, p. 203.

44. *Österreich-Ungarns Letzter Krieg 1914–1918* 2, pp. 215–16.

45. ÖStA-KA, MKSM 1915, 52–4/16.

46. ÖStA-KA, MSKM, 69–8/9 'Betrachtungen über die Verluste im jetzigen Kriege'. Krobatin's calculations dated 31 March 1915.

47. BA-MA, MSg 1/2516 Tagebuch v. Kageneck. Entries for 9 January, 6 and 12 April, and 31 May 1915.

48. See Manfried Rauchensteiner, *Der Tod des Doppeladlers. Österreich-Ungarn und der Erste Weltkrieg* (Graz, Vienna, and Cologne, Verlag Styria, 1994), p. 209.

49. *Der Weltkrieg 1914 bis 1918* 7, p. 303.

50. *Der Weltkrieg 1914 bis 1918* 7, pp. 378–9.

51. Hermann von François, *Gorlice 1915. Der Karpathendurchbruch und die Befreiung von Galizien* (Leipzig, K. F. Koehler, 1922), pp. 47–8.

52. See *Der Weltkrieg 1914 bis 1918* 7, pp. 365–443.

53. Cited in Norman Stone, *The Eastern Front 1914–1917* (New York, Charles Scribner's Sons, 1975), p. 139.

54. BHStA-KA, HS 1972, Nr. 23.

55. ÖStA-KA, Nachlass Kundmann, B/15, vol. 2. Entry dated 3 June 1915.

56. Cited in Janssen, *Der Kanzler und der General*, p. 117. Dated 10 May 1915.
57. Reichsarchiv, *Der Weltkrieg 1914–1918*. 8: *Die Operationen des Jahres 1915* (Berlin, E. S. Mittler & Sohn, 1932), pp. 178–87, 236–37; *Österreich-Ungarns Letzter Krieg 1914–1918* 2, p. 451.
58. Cited in *Österreich-Ungarns Letzter Krieg 1914–1918* 2, p. 440.
59. Conrad to Falkenhayn, 21 July 1915. ÖStA-KA, AOK 512.
60. See Holger Afflerbach, *Falkenhayn: Politisches Denken und Handeln im Kaiserreich* (Munich, R. Oldenbourg, 1994), pp. 300–5.
61. BA-MA, MSg 2/4537 Tagebuch Schulin, pp. 19, 21.
62. A[ugust] von Cramon, *Unser österreichisch-ungarischer Bundesgenosse im Weltkriege. Erinnerungen aus meiner vierjährigen Tätigkeit als bevollmächtigter deutscher General beim k.u.k. Armeeoberkommando* (Berlin, E. S. Mittler & Sohn, 1920), p. 15.
63. Conrad to Bolfras, 10 April 1915. ÖStA-KA, Conrad Archiv, Flügeladjutant B, vol. 7.
64. See especially Andreas Hillgruber, 'Die Erwägungen der Generalstäbe für den Fall eines Kriegseintritts Italiens 1914/15', *Quellen und Forschungen aus italienischen Archiven und Bibliotheken* 48 (1968), pp. 346–64, for the positions of Conrad and Falkenhayn on the possibility of Italy entering the war.
65. ÖStA-KA, Nachlass B/509, vol. 2, Tagebuch Schneller; entry for 3 September 1915.
66. ÖStA-KA, Nachlass B/509, vol. 2, Tagebuch Schneller; Diary entries for 17, 22, 23, 27 September and 2 October 1915.
67. ÖStA-KA, Nachlass B/15, Nr. 2, Tagebuch Kundmann; entry for 13 September 1915.
68. Rauchensteiner, *Der Tod des Doppeladlers*, p. 290, claims that the 'dilletantism' of Habsburg officers in the 'autumn swinery' was 'shamefully covered up' in subsequent Austrian military history.
69. Ludendorff to Moltke, 1, 5, and 27 April 1915. BA-MA, Nachlass Moltke, N 78, vol. 35. These views were shared, albeit in milder form, by German diplomats. The Bavarian envoy to Berlin, Hugo von Lerchenfeld, informed his government of the unreliability of Habsburg forces on 14, 24, and 28 September 1915. BHStA, MA 3079, Militär Bevollmächtigter Berlin.
70. The bitter debate is summarized in *Der Weltkrieg 1914–1918* 8, pp. 269–77.
71. Carl von Clausewitz, *On War*, ed. Michael Howard and Peter Paret (Princeton, Princeton University Press, 1976), p. 615.
72. Dennis E. Showalter, *Tannenberg: Clash of Empires* (Hamden, Conn., Archon Books, 1991), p. 344.
73. See especially Alberto Monticone, *Deutschland und die Neutralität Italiens 1914–1915* (Wiesbaden, Franz Steiner, 1982).
74. Gary W. Shanafelt, *The Secret Enemy: Austria–Hungary and the German Alliance, 1914–1918* (New York, Columbia University Press, 1985), p. 67. Under Article VII of the Triple Alliance Treaty of 1882, Italy was entitled to request 'compensation' in case of territorial gain by Austria–Hungary in the Balkans. No such gain had been made.
75. Report of Minister Klemens von Podewils-Dürniz, 19 January 1915. BHStA-Geheimes Staatsarchiv, Politisches Archiv, VII. Reihe, vol. 68.
76. Cited in Shanafelt, *The Secret Enemy*, p. 64.
77. Volker Hoettl, 'Die Beziehungen Conrads von Hötzendorf zu den deutschen Generalstabschefs 1914–17 auf politischem Gebiet', unpubl. diss., Vienna 1968, pp. 51, 62.
78. Memorandum of 21 December 1914, cited in Rauchensteiner, *Der Tod des Doppeladlers*, pp. 222–3.
79. See Heinz Lemke, *Allianz und Rivalität. Die Mittelmächte und Polen im ersten Weltkrieg (bis zur Februarrevolution)* (East Berlin, Akademie-Verlag, 1977).
80. Falkenhayn to Jagow, 10 April, and Falkenhayn's memorandum of 25 April 1915, in AA-PA, Bonn, Deutschland 128, Nr. 1 geheim, vols 49 and 51.

81. See his comments at an audience with the Emperor at Schönbrunn on 8 March 1915 in ÖStA-KA, Conrad Archiv, A Nachlass Conrad, vol. 6; and *Protokolle des Gemeinsamen Ministerrates der Österreichisch-Ungarischen Monarchie (1914–1918)*, ed. Miklós Komjáthy (Budapest, Akadémiai Kiadó, 1966), pp. 228–9. Italy entered the war against Germany only in August 1916.
82. BA-MA, W-10/50656 Tagebuch v. Plessen, entry dated 8 January 1915.
83. John Gooch, *Army, State and Society in Italy, 1870–1915* (New York, St Martin's Press, 1989), p. 170.
84. Erich Ludendorff, *Meine Kriegserinnerungen 1914–1918* (Berlin, E. S. Mittler & Sohn, 1919), p. 132.
85. See Gunther E. Rothenberg, *The Army of Francis Joseph* (West Lafeyette, Ind., Purdue University Press, 1976), pp. 187–8. The 'howling stones' description is by Sir James Edmonds.
86. *Österreich-Ungarns Letzter Krieg 1914–1918* 2, pp. 744, 762. Conrad's comment is in ÖStA-KA, Nachlass Kundmann, B/15, vol. 2, Conrad to Bolfras, 17 May 1915.
87. Cited in Rauchensteiner, *Der Tod des Doppeladlers*, p. 251.
88. See Hermann Wendt, *Der italienische Kriegsschauplatz in europäischen Konflikten. Seine Bedeutung für die Kriegführung an Frankreichs Nordostgrenzen* (Berlin, Junker und Dünnhaupt, 1936).
89. Helmut Reichold and Gerhard Granier, eds, *Wild von Hohenborn. Briefe und Tagebuchaufzeichnungen des preussischen Generals als Kriegsminister und Truppenführer im Ersten Weltkrieg* (Boppard, H. Boldt, 1986), p. 60. Dated 13–14 April 1915.
90. Turkey had joined Austria–Hungary and Germany in October 1914, after Admiral Wilhelm Souchon brought the cruisers *Breslau* and *Goeben* to the Porte in August. Both ships joined the Turkish Navy as *Midilli* and *Sultan Yavuz Selim*, while Souchon became supreme commander of the Turkish fleet. See Ulrich Trumpener, 'The Escape of the *Goeben* and *Breslau*: A Reassessment', *Canadian Journal of History* 6 (1971), pp. 171–86.
91. Count von Lerchenfeld's report of 8 July 1915, based on information received from Kurt Riezler at the Wilhelmstrasse. BHStA, MA 3078.
92. See Ulrich Trumpener, *Germany and the Ottoman Empire 1914–1918* (Princeton, Princeton University Press, 1968), p. 79.
93. Ian Hamilton, *Gallipoli Diary* (2 vols, London, Edward Arnold, 1920) 1, p. 304. Entry for 15 June 1915.
94. See the recent assessment of Gallipoli in Eliot A. Cohen and John Gooch, *Military Misfortunes: The Anatomy of Failure in War* (New York, Free Press, 1990), pp. 133–64.
95. Cited in B. H. Liddell Hart, *The Real War 1914–1918* (Boston, Little, Brown, 1930), p. 123.
96. See Reichsarchiv, *Der Weltkrieg 1914 bis 1918. 9: Die Operationen des Jahres 1915* (Berlin, E. S. Mittler & Sohn, 1933), p. 192.
97. *Der Weltkrieg 1914 bis 1918* 9, pp. 173–81.
98. Report by Baron von Schoen, 21 September 1915. BHStA, MA 3079.
99. Cited in John Lee, 'Sir Ian Hamilton and the Dardanelles, 1915', Brian Bond, ed., *Fallen Stars: Eleven Studies of Twentieth Century Military Disasters* (London, Washington, and New York, Brassey's, 1991), p. 42. For the German defence see Reichsarchiv, *Der Weltkrieg 1914 bis 1918. 10: Die Operationen des Jahres 1916* (Berlin, E. S. Mittler & Sohn, 1933), pp. 173–93; and Carl Mühlmann, *Der Kampf um die Dardanellen*, vol. 16 of *Schlachten des Weltkrieges* (Oldenburg, Gerhard Stalling Verlag, 1927).
100. Rothenberg, *Army of Francis Joseph*, p. 190.
101. Cited in Shanahan, *The Secret Enemy*, p. 69.
102. Riezler, *Tagebücher, Aufsätze, Dokumente*, p. 271. Entry for 16 May 1915.

103. See Anne C. Holden, 'Bulgaria's Entry in the First World War: A Diplomatic Study, 1913–1915', unpubl. diss., University of Illinois 1976.

104. See Cramon, *Unser österreichisch-ungarischer Bundesgenosse*, pp. 31–3; and Gerard E. Silberstein, *The Troubled Alliance: German-Austrian Relations 1914–1917* (Lexington, Ky., The University of Kentucky Press, 1970), pp. 291-3.

105. *Der Weltkrieg 1914–1918* 9, pp. 211-13.

106. Liddell Hart, *The Real War*, p. 139.

107. See Bundesministerium für Landesverteidigung, *Österreich-Ungarns Letzter Krieg 1914–1918* 3: *Das Kriegsjahr 1915* (Vienna, Verlag der Militärwissenschaftlichen Mitteilungen, 1932), pp. 187–337.

108. *Der Weltkrieg 1914 bis 1918* 9, p. 276; *Österreich-Ungarns Letzter Krieg 1914–1918* 3, p. 336.

109. A[ugust] v. Cramon and Paul Fleck, *Deutschlands Schicksalsbündnis mit Österreich-Ungarn. Von Conrad von Hötzendorf zu Kaiser Karl* (Berlin, Verlag für Kulturpolitik, 1932), p. 112. Serbian losses according to Oskar Regele, *Feldmarschall Conrad. Auftrag und Erfüllung, 1906–1918* (Vienna and Munich, Verlag Herold, 1955), pp. 269–309, 363.

110. *Der Weltkrieg 1914 bis 1918* 9, pp. 308–9; and Cramon, *Unser österreichisch-ungarischer Bundesgenosse*, p. 45.

111. ÖStA-KA, Conrad Archiv, B 8/22, p. 112, memorandum dated 14 January 1916; ÖStA-KA, Nachlass Schneller, B/509, vol. 2, dated 17 December 1915; and Afflerbach, *Falkenhayn*, pp. 254, 349.

112. 'Denkschrift über das Kriegsziel', 10 October 1915. Conrad presented these views to Franz Joseph on 22 October 1915. ÖStA-KA, MKSM 1915, 25–1/5.

113. Conrad to Burián, 21 December 1915. ÖStA-KA, MKSM 1915, 25–1/5–5.

114. *Protokolle des Gemeinsamen Ministerrates*, pp. 353–81. Krobatin demanded that Serbia 'be erased from the map of Europe'.

115. See Galántai, *Hungary in the First World War*, pp. 152–4.

116. Friedrich von Rabenau, ed., *Seeckt. Aus seinem Leben 1866 bis 1917* (Leipzig, Hase & Köhler, 1938), pp. 249, 255.

117. Jagow's memorandum of 2 September 1915 in *L'Allemagne et les problèmes de la paix pendant la première guerre mondiale. Documents extraits des archives de l'Office allemand des Affaires étrangères*, eds. André Scherer and Jacques Grunewald (4 vols, Paris, Presses Universitaires de France, 1962–78) 1.

118. See Fritz Fischer, *Griff nach der Weltmacht. Die Kriegszielpolitik des Kaiserlichen Deutschland 1914/18* (Düsseldorf, Droste Verlag, 1961), pp. 249–54; and Janssen, *Der Kanzler und der General*, p. 169.

119. Afflerbach, *Falkenhayn*, pp. 321–4.

120. The following account is from ÖStA-KA, B 428, Nachlass Hartinger, pp. 36–75.

121. B. H. Liddell Hart, *Reputations: Ten Years After* (Boston, Little, Brown, 1928), p. 29.

122. The fighting in the west is detailed in *Der Weltkrieg 1914–1918* 8, pp. 34–98.

123. BA-MA, MSg 1/2512 Nachlass v. Alten. Blomberg's observations of 25 February 1915; Bergh's of 18 February 1915 and January 1916.

124. See Militärgeschichtliches Forschungsamt, *Handbuch zur deutschen Militärgeschichte* (5 vols, Munich, Bernard & Graefe Verlag, 1979) 5, p. 507; and Bruce I. Gudmundsson, *Stormtroop Tactics: Innovation in the German Army, 1914–1918* (New York, Westport, and London, Praeger, 1989), pp. 30–2.

125. Holger H. Herwig, 'The Dynamics of Necessity: German Military Policy during the Great War', in Allan R. Millett and Williamson Murray, eds, *Military Effectiveness* (3 vols, Boston, Allen & Unwin, 1988) 1, p. 95.

126. Paul Guinn, *British Strategy and Politics 1914 to 1918* (Oxford, Clarendon Press, 1965), pp. 76–7.

127. Bethmann Hollweg and the *OHL* thought Kitchener's armies to be composed of brave but ill-trained and poorly-led soldiers; 'nothing much can be done with this army'. BHStA, MA 3079, Count von Lerchenfeld's report of 5 October 1915.
128. See Rothenberg, *Army of Francis Joseph*, p. 193; *Österreich-Ungarns Letzter Krieg 1914–1918* 2, pp. 14–18.
129. BA-MA, PH 2/86 War Ministry, Reichstagsmaterial.
130. Cited in Afflerbach, *Falkenhayn*, p. 173.
131. Harmut Pogge von Strandmann, *Walther Rathenau: Industrialist, Banker, Intellectual, and Politician. Notes and Diaries 1907–1922* (Oxford, Clarendon Press, 1985), pp. 187–9.
132. *Der Weltkrieg 1914 bis 1918* 9, pp. 368–77; Afflerbach, *Falkenhayn*, pp. 316–20.
133. This analysis is based on Ulrich Trumpener, 'The Road to Ypres: The Beginnings of Gas Warfare in World War I', *Journal of Modern History* 47 (1975), pp. 460–80; and *Der Weltkrieg 1914 bis 1918* 8, pp. 39–41.
134. See *Der Weltkrieg 1914–1918* 8, p. 134. Gas warfare has recently been analysed by L. F. Haber, *The Poisonous Cloud: Chemical Warfare in the First World War* (Oxford, Clarendon Press, 1986).
135. See *The Reports of the Hague Conferences of 1899 and 1907*, ed. James B. Scott (Oxford, Clarendon Press, 1917), pp. 126 ff, 170 ff, and passim.
136. Trumpener, 'The Road to Ypres', p. 468. See also *Der Weltkrieg 1914 bis 1918* 8, pp. 35–48, for the use of gas at Ypres.
137. See BHStA, MA 3077. Count von Lerchenfeld reported on 27 April that five German soldiers had been killed by their own gas.
138. Crown Prince Rupprecht, *Mein Kriegstagebuch*, ed. Eugen von Frauenholz (3 vols, Berlin, Deutscher Nationalverlag, 1929) 1, pp. 304–5.
139. BA-MA, Nachlass Karl v. Einem gen. v. Rothmaler. Letter to his wife, 23 April 1915.
140. ÖStA-KA, MKSM 1915, 69–5/10. Report dated 14 September 1915.
141. ÖStA-KA, MKSM 69-5/10–2. Franz Joseph's decision of 18 November 1915.
142. Liddell Hart, *The Real War*, p. 195. For losses in the Champagne battles, see *Der Weltkrieg 1914 bis 1918* 9, p. 98.
143. *Österreich-Ungarns Letzter Krieg 1914–1918* 93, pp. 366–7, 510, 514.

5

Dual Defeats: From the Meuse to the Sereth, 1916

Dulce et decorum est, pro patria mori.

Horace

General von Falkenhayn could well be pleased with the military situation at the end of 1915. The Eastern Front had stabilized to Germany's advantage after the Battle of Gorlice-Tarnów in May, for Russia had lost 151 000 killed, 683 000 wounded, and 895 000 prisoners of war. Thereafter the Russian 'Great Retreat' ensued. In the Balkans Army Group Mackensen had overrun Serbia and taken 150 000 prisoners in October; by November it guarded Hungary against a possible Romanian entry into the war on the side of the Allies. Bulgaria had joined the Central Powers in September. In the process, Austria–Hungary had been spared defeat and occupation. Even the Italian front had stabilized after four savage but indecisive battles along the Isonzo River. And the Allied debacle at the Dardanelles had given new life to the Ottoman Empire. Not surprisingly, Falkenhayn now redirected his attention to the Western Front, where he enjoyed a momentary near-parity of forces: 94 German divisions (with 26 in reserve) were ranged against 'only' 91 Allied divisions (with 59 in reserve).

Falkenhayn had discussed his options with Chancellor von Bethmann Hollweg as early as 31 August 1915. 'The Russian Army has been so weakened by the blows it has suffered that Russia need not be seriously considered a danger in the foreseeable future.' The General equated Russia's position in 1915 to that of France in 1871 – except that Russia did not possess France's industrial base or its resilient statesmen. Germany's real enemies, Falkenhayn lectured Bethmann Hollweg, were Lord Kitchener and Britain, whose strategy was to involve Germany in a 'war of exhaustion'.[1] The Reich could not accept such a course under any circumstances.

Late in November Falkenhayn again aired his grand strategic thoughts to Bethmann Hollweg. He admitted that the chance had passed to conclude a separate peace with Russia and allowed that he no longer possessed faith in the Allies' willingness to conclude a general peace. The war had degenerated into a simple yet deadly 'struggle for survival'. Germany had no choice but to bludgeon especially France into submission. Britain remained the 'archenemy', and it would regard any German peace offensive as a sign of weakness.[2]

By 8 December 1915 Falkenhayn reached a decision: to mount Germany's fourth bid for victory by destroying the French Army and/or French will by a campaign of attrition. Falkenhayn and his chief of staff, General Gerhard Tappen, in mid-December entrusted the operation to the Fifth Army and debated it for 3 days with Crown Prince Wilhelm and the latter's chief of staff, General Constantin Schmidt von Knobelsdorf. Although the Crown Prince felt uncomfortable with Falkenhayn's frequent references to a desire to 'bleed' the French Army 'white', he nevertheless consented to the operation. Thereafter, Falkenhayn set out for Potsdam to brief the Kaiser on the offensive. The critical Crown Council took place on 21 December. While there is good reason to believe that Falkenhayn committed the so-called 'Christmas Memorandum' to paper only after the war, it nevertheless reflected his innermost thoughts in December 1915.[3]

Falkenhayn gave his Supreme War Lord a grand *tour d'horizon*. With an eye toward his tempestuous dealings with *OberOst*, he ruled out major operations in the east. Capture of St Petersburg, 'with its million inhabitants', would only burden Germany with victualling a major urban population; an attack against Moscow 'takes us nowhere' as it would disperse the German Army over the vast expanse of Russia; and a drive into the 'rich territory of the Ukraine' and toward Odessa necessitated the cooperation (or occupation) of Romania. Falkenhayn also ruled out operations against Italy, as desired by Conrad von Hötzendorf. Even a great victory against Italy along the Po River would not decide the war. Nor was Falkenhayn interested in peripheral operations. An offensive from Turkey against Egypt, Iraq, Persia, and India – what the General satirized as a 'crusade à la Alexander' – similarly was dismissed as it would not be decisive.

That left the west. The Allied offensives at Ypres, Artois, and in the Champagne in 1915, Falkenhayn argued, had proved the senselessness of frontal breakthroughs. 'Attempts at a mass breakthrough . . . cannot be regarded as holding out prospects of success against a well-armed enemy, whose *morale* is sound and who is not seriously inferior in numbers.' Flanking fire threatened to transform any minor breakthrough into a 'slaughterhouse'. German reserves were at low ebb and this further militated against a major penetrating assault. Nor were gigantic flanking operations designed to envelop entire armies any longer possible in a war in which there were no flanks but only endless red and blue and green defensive lines along vast fronts. Obviously, a new approach was required.

At the political level, Falkenhayn informed Wilhelm II that France was no longer a player. 'France has been weakened militarily and economically to the point of exhaustion.' Rather, Great Britain was the 'archenemy' that held the crumbling Anglo-French-Russian coalition together. 'Perfidious Albion' was willing to fight to the last Frenchman and quite prepared to finance the war as long as necessary. 'The history of the English wars against the Netherlands, Spain, France, and Napoleon is being repeated.' But a direct blow against Britannia was out of the question: the German fleet was too weak to risk a decisive battle at sea, and the island empire could not be 'reached by our troops'.

Therewith Falkenhayn came to his main point. Germany would have to strike at Britain indirectly, not via Egypt and India as Alexander the Great and Napoleon I had sought to do, but by 'knocking its best sword', France, 'out of its hands'. German policy 'would have to be nothing less than to drive the English completely from the Continent'. Hand in hand with this assault against France, 'England's tool on the Continent', Falkenhayn offered a maritime strategy: German U-boats would conduct unrestricted warfare to deny the British much-needed overseas succour, and act as an irritant to force them into a battle of annihilation. War with the Americans ('England's secret allies') as a result of unrestricted submarine warfare would have to be taken into the bargain because the United States 'cannot intervene decisively in the war in time'. The psychological moment was right. France was tired of war, drained of reserves, and demoralized. Further carnage would force Paris 'to lose any desire to continue the war'. In short, Britannia would be defeated by bleeding French forces white on the Western Front.

But how and where to deliver the main blow? Falkenhayn ruled out Schlieffen's encirclement panacea for having failed first along the Marne in September and then in Flanders in November 1914. He also rejected a permanent defence in the west because the Anglo-French alliance was superior both in manpower and material resources. Thus Falkenhayn settled on what he termed 'an operation limited to a narrow front', that is, a conventional assault hurling men against entrenched positions. He dismissed Alsace, the Champagne, Compiègne, and Arras as suitable targets, and likewise vetoed arguments for an attack against the fortress of Belfort as it lay too close to the Swiss border and thus restricted manoeuvrability. Instead, Falkenhayn chose Verdun – mainly for its historic and psychological significance.

There, in the Treaty of Verdun in August 843, Charles the Bald and Louis the German had divided Charlemagne's Frankish empire between them. In the eyes of German nationalists, the kingdom of the eastern Franks had been founded at Verdun. And there, Sebastian de Vauban had constructed for Louis XIV an ancient fortress salient.

Verdun, Falkenhayn argued, was an object 'for the retention of which the French General Staff would be compelled to throw in every man they have. If they do so, the French will bleed to death. . . '. By concentrating the attack against the forts guarding the eastern heights – Douaumont and Vaux – Falkenhayn hoped to lure French forces into a deadly field of artillery fire 'in which not even a mouse could live'.[4] If, on the other hand, the French refused battle, 'then the moral effect' of this on France 'will be enormous'. It was 'immaterial', Falkenhayn assured Wilhelm II, 'whether we reach our goal', Verdun. The main objective was to 'bleed' the French Army 'to death' (*Blutabzapfung*). Above all, Germany needed to maintain the initiative.

Falkenhayn later admitted that he never intended to capture Verdun. Indeed, his imprecise instructions to army commanders spoke only of an offensive 'in the direction of Verdun'. If all went according to plan, Verdun would become a gigantic 'suction cup' designed simply to 'drain' the French lifeblood. Germany would be 'perfectly free to accelerate or draw out its offensive' throughout the campaign, 'to intensify it or to break it off from time to time, as suits its purpose'. The moral aspect was decisive. Victory would be achieved not against the soldiers of the Meuse, but against the politicians in Paris. Undoubtedly buoyed by recollections of the political turmoil engendered by defeat in 1870–1, Falkenhayn cheerily predicted political collapse in the French capital by summer 1916. In short, the operation was to be much more than mere attrition – *Ermattungsstrategie* as the German military historian Hans Delbrück called it – but rather an elite strategy designed to destroy elite control in the enemy's capital.

Falkenhayn fully expected a carnage. Clausewitz's dictum that men defensively employed in well-fortified positions enjoyed an inherent advantage over attackers notwithstanding, Falkenhayn forecast a favourable kill ratio of five French soldiers to every two German. The 'Meuse mill', as he termed it, would eventually 'bleed to death' the French forces deployed in its defence. And the more the better. As Schlieffen had hoped to sweep up an anticipated British Expeditionary Force in Belgium along with the main French Army, so Falkenhayn considered it advantageous were General Haig to allow his forces to be sucked into the meat grinder. It would be optimal if the British also committed their New Armies being trained at home to the 'Meuse mill'.

Falkenhayn gave the operation the code name *Gericht*, or Court of Justice. Crown Prince Wilhelm's Fifth Army was given 41.5 divisions of infantry supported by 1521 heavy guns; 15 divisions of infantry and a further 100 heavy guns were held in reserve. On 12 January 1916 more than 200 ammunition trains began hauling shells up to the front. Once underway, the attack would require an additional 34 trains per day to supply the artillery massed before Verdun. The assault was set for 12 February, but 5 days of hail, snow, and rain forced repeated postponements.

Verdun: 'the heart of France'

At 8:12 a.m. on 21 February, a cold, clear, dry day, 1200 German artillery pieces concentrated along a 12-mile front rained a 'storm of steel' down on the French defenders encamped along the 400-yard high escarpment on the east bank of the Meuse River that protects Paris from invasion via the plain of Lorraine.[5] Falkenhayn hoped that the artillery barrage would demolish French barbed-wire barriers and trenches, and permit his infantry to cross No Man's Land with relative impunity. Both sides hurled 10 million artillery shells – or 1 350 000 tons of steel – at each other between February and December 1916. The German Fifth Army alone in a single day expended 17.5 railway wagons of shells at Verdun, including those from the 38 cm rail-mounted 'Long Max' naval coastal guns and the 42 cm 'Big Bertha' batteries. The craters created by the massive shells transformed the battlefield into a lunar landscape. US General John 'Black Jack' Pershing estimated that each opening artillery barrage on the Western Front cost $75 million. What the German General Staff termed the Verdun 'cauldron' was to be pulverized by massed artillery. A French aviator, looking down on the rain-soaked field, compared it to 'the humid skin of a monstrous toad'.[6]

Eight hours after the artillery barrage that 21 February, 10 divisions of infantry charged the French positions in waves. The Brandenburg III Reserve Corps assembled its band to give the troops a spirited send-off. Wilhelm II rushed to Fifth Army headquarters at Stenay on 25 February to witness the fall of Verdun. He soon tired of the indecisive human-wave assaults and, undoubtedly feeling superfluous, returned to his quarters at Charleville. The Germans eventually committed 48 divisions to Verdun, while the French rotated 259 of their 330 front-line battalions through the salient under the *noria*, or 'bucket brigade' system. The list of German Verdun combatants included the legendary Manfred Baron von Richthofen, the future tank advocate Heinz Guderian, two eventual leaders of the Nazi party, Rudolf Hess and Ernst Röhm, and the novelist Arnold Zweig.

The Battle of Verdun reached its climax early in March. On 4 March Crown Prince Wilhelm called on his Fifth Army to take Verdun, 'the heart of France'. After 2 days of intensive shelling, the Fifth Army stormed French positions; but by 9 March Wilhelm acknowledged that his troops had failed to storm the vital Côte de Poivre guarding Verdun. Instead, German forces came under a withering French artillery fire from the west bank of the Meuse; a belated attempt to storm these hostile positions broke down in the face of well-prepared French defensive positions. This notwithstanding, Falkenhayn continued the assault for another 9 months. 'The object', he lectured Schmidt von Knobelsdorf, 'is not to defeat but to annihilate France'.[7] In continuing the battle, Falkenhayn experienced first-hand Clausewitz's postulate concerning the 'diminishing force of the attack'. His staff began to speak derisively of a 'second Ypres' in reference to the 1914 disaster in Flanders.

Almost immediately Verdun became enshrouded in mythology. The French christened it a 'sacred city'. Field Marshal von Hindenburg spoke of it as 'a beacon light of German valour'.[8] Verdun, more than any other battle, became a synonym for the slaughter of the Great War. Casualty figures for Verdun are legendary. Visitors to the battlefield today are told of 1 million dead, of 250 000 *poilus* entombed behind the glass windows of the ossuary alone. The novelist Alistair Horne claims 350 000 casualties per side. In fact, the German Fifth Army reported 81 668 men either killed in battle or missing in action between February and September 1916.[9] Still, this figure was 300 per cent greater than that for the Franco-Prussian War.

Another myth pertains to *La tranchée des baionettes* – a dour and squat concrete monument replete with bayonets sticking out of the ground, allegedly still clutched by fallen French soldiers. In truth, *la tranchée* was the creation of an eccentric American millionaire. Upon discovering in 1921 that a French detachment had surrendered to a Bavarian unit on this spot on 12 June 1916 and simply had abandoned their rifles, the American decided to create a macabre shrine. And still another myth: General Henri Pétain is widely credited with the immortal line, *'Courage, on les aura!'*, but the phrase was 'coined' by his trusty aide, Captain Bernard Serrigny, who, in fact, had taken it from a trench newspaper.

Of course the *mentalité* that is Verdun cannot be denied. It remains omnipresent. In 1919 the Versailles Treaty stipulated that French crosses were to be white (for purity) while German crosses were to be black (for shame); that French graves were to be individual and sited in villages and towns, whereas German graves were to be massed and placed in remote areas. Poignantly, when the German commander in France in World War II, General Carl-Heinrich von Stülpnagel, was implicated in the attempted

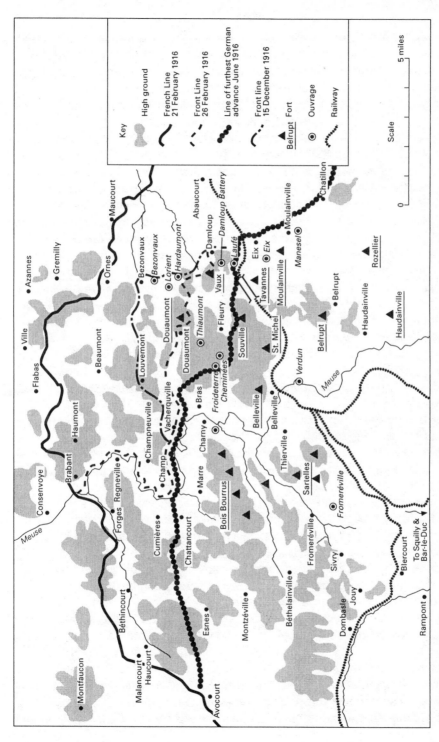

Map 6. *Verdun, 1916*

assassination of Adolf Hitler in July 1944, he returned to his 1916 post at Verdun and tried to commit suicide. As late as 1966 Charles de Gaulle, a captain at Verdun, could still not bring himself to invite either Germans or Americans to the 50th anniversary celebrations at this sacred *national* shrine. It remained for French President François Mitterand and German Chancellor Helmuth Kohl to break the taboo in 1984.

What, then, is the reality of Verdun 1916? The details of the campaign are sufficiently well known; hence it is hardly necessary to trudge it hill by hill and fort by fort. Rather, it seems more rewarding to select several interesting aspects and themes to shed light on the German experience.

Verdun was not coordinated with planners in Berlin and Vienna. Neither Conrad at the *AOK* in Teschen nor Bethmann Hollweg in Berlin were apprised of the offensive. The secretive Falkenhayn did his best to keep Verdun hidden from the Austro-Hungarians right up to February 1916, going so far as to feed Conrad's military plenipotentiary, General Klepsch-Kloth von Roden, disinformation concerning the German buildup.[10] Nor were German army and corps commanders included in the planning by Falkenhayn, who as late as 7 January still insisted that he had not yet decided where to attack! As a result, Falkenhayn was sarcastically referred to as the 'python of Charleville', the site of the *OHL*, by the German brass hats.

The ancillary unrestricted submarine campaign proved elusive. At a Crown Council on 4 March, Bethmann Hollweg declined to stake Germany's future on a single roll of the dice and reminded Falkenhayn that Frederick the Great had made Prussia a great power during the Seven Years' War without 'defeating even one of his enemies', simply by refusing to give in to 'a desperate situation'. Three weeks later, the Chancellor informed both the Reichstag Budget Commission and the German federal states that Great Britain probably could not be starved into submission with a dozen U-boats, and that the United States would enter the war against Germany in reaction to such a bold move.[11] On 10 March Wilhelm II postponed the final decision to 4 April.

Falkenhayn declined to inform Germany's ruling military and political elite of the connection between the U-boat campaign and the Verdun offensive. Grand Admiral von Tirpitz, who by now was shunned by the Kaiser and his entourage owing to his vacillating and often contradictory statements on the strength of the U-boat force, offered his resignation. The Kaiser formally accepted it on 15 March with the comment: 'He is leaving the sinking ship'.[12]

On 24 April, after a U-boat had torpedoed the unarmed French liner *Sussex*, resulting in a sharp American protest note, the Kaiser ordered that the submarine campaign be conducted by prize rules. Thereby, U-boats were to sink ships only after having previously warned them of their impending fate. Falkenhayn was irate and, perhaps in an effort to share the bloodbath before Verdun with Bethmann Hollweg, insisted on *both* the war of attrition along the Meuse and the unrestricted submarine campaign against Britain. Neither Kaiser nor Chancellor fell for this line of reasoning and on 2 May Falkenhayn tendered his resignation in protest. But Wilhelm II was not about to let the architect of Verdun slip out of the limelight so easily and Falkenhayn, well knowing that Hindenburg and Ludendorff were waiting for precisely such an opportunity, withdrew his resignation.

The element of surprise had evaded Falkenhayn. Rumours of 'a large operation against Verdun' circulated in Berlin as early as November 1915, and German officers spoke openly of having lost the advantage of surprise after the first cancellation of the attack on 12 February.[13] Although Falkenhayn opted not to use 'jumping off' trenches close to the French lines to increase the chance of surprise, two German deserters had leaked news of an impending attack to the French on 16 and 25 January. French civilians employed by the Germans in rear-echelon supply units throughout January 1916 informed Paris of large troop concentrations along the Meuse. German staff officers, who should have known better from their own interceptions of Russian telephone transmissions, used 'clear' telephone lines with uncoded messages detailing even the most minute preparations for the offensive – down to the fact that every man was to carry 110 rounds into battle. In all fairness, however, it should be pointed out that the French were not much better, broadcasting 'clear' radio messages concerning high-level staff decisions from the transmitter atop the Eiffel Tower.[14]

To be sure, intelligence is only as good as the use to which it is put. The French *Deuxième Bureau*, fresh from having bungled prewar intelligence concerning the Schlieffen plan, dismissed the numerous reports that it received of an impending German assault on Verdun. It argued against such an offensive because French aerial reconnaissance had detected no 'jumping off' trenches being dug before Verdun. Most importantly, the Second Bureau informed General Joffre that what fragmentary information it had received concerning a possible German assault simply did not fit into its projections. French military intelligence knew well that Joffre as early as 8 December 1915 had planned his own assault, and that on 10 February 1916 he had pressed the British to commence that attack on 1 July. Thus, *Deuxième Bureau* reassured the French commander that the Germans could not possibly launch an offensive before April. It was a classic case of mirror imaging, as each level in the chain of command reflected what the next level up wished to know.

Verdun was not of decisive strategic importance. The surrender of the fortresses of Liège and Namur to the Germans in 1914 had convinced Joffre that stone citadels were useless in modern warfare. Hence, when Verdun came under his control in August 1915, Joffre had ordered the French Army to dismantle its forts: 40 batteries of artillery and 128 000 shells were 'recovered' for use with the main armies in the north. Verdun was defended by only nine infantry divisions on 21 February 1916. The magnitude of the German attack was not readily recognized, and French headquarters at Chantilly remained convinced that it was only a feint designed to disguise the real blow expected in the Champagne.

On the other hand, Falkenhayn's strategy of attrition proved correct: the French High Command *was* prepared to 'bleed' its forces 'to death' to defend this historic and psychologically important position. General Pétain, who arrived at Verdun on 26 February to take command from General Frédéric Georges Herr, admitted that victory would most likely go to the side that had 'the last man left'. He was not far off the mark. The French official history lists 377 231 casualties at Verdun. And while this was roughly equal to overall German casualties, the French claim of 162 308 killed and missing in action, twice the corresponding German count, is staggering.

Verdun brought a number of new tools of war.[15] Phosgene, a novel, colourless, asphyxiating gas, was first used at Verdun – fired at the rate of 110 000 shells during the first week of its introduction in June. Wilhelm II learned of its use through German newspapers. Gradual improvements were also made in gas masks. Fritz Haber tested various models at the Kaiser Wilhelm Institute at Berlin-Dahlem. He found that the Russian masks, which consisted of muslin soaked with two-thirds sodium-thiosulfate and one-third soda and held against the face by a rubber band, were the worst. British hooded masks, which were fastened under the chin and which boasted glass eye-covers, were the best; a double layer of cotton was soaked with a mixture of 7 per cent glycerin, 3.5 per cent phenol, 8 per cent soda, and 14 per cent soap and renewed every fortnight. Armed with this testing data, Haber developed a superior mask that used granules of potassium carbonate coated with charcoal dust. It came in various sizes to accommodate beards and eyeglasses, and it had a special tin cylinder to house the cotton soaked in the British manner. The model 11–1 mask, introduced at Verdun, accorded the wearer 40 minutes of protection against gas – with the exception of the carbon monoxide produced by detonating artillery shells. Soldiers were trained to breathe through the masks like mountain climbers at high altitudes and to disinfect them after a gas attack with steam for 6 hours and air for another 18 hours.[16]

The Germans also deployed flamethrowers – initially tested in February 1915 in Malancourt Forest – in large quantities for the first time in the passageways of the Verdun forts. The new weapon consisted of a cylinder of oil and a steel tube, from which the oil was lit and fired at high pressure. It gave a special air to combat in the citadel's caverns. One German veteran recalled his experience: 'The air was suffocating. A mixture of the horribly sweet smell of putrefaction, of phenol and iodoform, the stench of human excrement, explosive gases and dust took our breath away'.[17] In July the flamethrower units were given the death's head (the future symbol of the SS) as a special insignia. While the Germans used flamethrowers as assault weapons, the French deployed their *lance-flammes* mainly in mopping-up operations.

Steel helmets, actually made from a chrome-nickel-steel alloy and weighing 3 lbs, were first used by mass formations at Verdun. The *Stahlhelm* had been developed in the fall of 1915 by an anonymous engineer at the Technical University of Hanover, but Friedrich Schwerd later claimed to have devised it from a fourteenth-century knights' model. Initially, there were too few available, with the result that subsequent waves of attackers had to claim the helmets of their predecessors, without proper fit being guaranteed. In the next 2 years, 11 German firms produced 7.5 million steel helmets for their own forces and 486 000 for Austria–Hungary as well as 170 000 for Turkey.[18] The success of steel helmets engendered experiments with steel arm shields and eventually with complete steel body suits as the knights of old.[19] The Germans also adopted a French rifle capable of firing grenades. And the famous 'storm troopers' of 1917–18 were already on the scene. Captain Willy Rohr led his *Sturmbataillon* – a 10-man section armed with semi-automatic weapons, hand-grenades, and flamethrowers – into action at Verdun.

The battlefield was a nightmare of sounds and sights. French farmers in the area became unwilling spectators (and at times participants) of the endless artillery bombardments and human-wave assaults. Soldiers caught in the barbed wire or hit by shrapnel lay screaming for hours in No Man's Land before overworked medics could reach them. Many bled to death. Horses especially suffered in the mud and the sleet and snow of early 1916, easy prey for both artillery and snipers. Many combatants retained images of horses with belly wounds still kicking their legs in deep shell holes 5 and 6 days after being shot. The lunar craters turned grey and brown as men and material filled them. The fields soon reeked of decaying human flesh. At Fort Douaumont, the bodies were stacked between layers of lime chloride to aid decomposition. Rats ate well and often. When a Württemberg unit encamped at Montfaucon – where the German poet Johann Wolfgang von Goethe had stopped en route to Valmy in 1792 – the soldiers counted no less than 25 000 rodents.

The German campaign failed in large measure due to excellent French reactions. Joffre initially dallied and refused to heed the warnings from War Minister Galliéni and Lieutenant-Colonel Émile Driant, Deputy for Nancy and a military writer, that Verdun was not prepared to repel a major German assault. The French generalissimo rejected such sage warnings as being 'calculated to disturb profoundly the spirit and discipline in the Army'.[20] But Joffre, paralleling his initial failure of August 1914, eventually recovered. He issued a stern order threatening to court-martial 'every commander who gives an order for retreat'.[21] He then chose a 60-year-old bachelor who had started the war in the grade of colonel, having spent 7 years as lieutenant and 10 as captain, to defend Verdun. At 3 a.m. on 25 February General Pétain was tracked down by Captain Serrigny to the Hotel Terminus at the Paris Gare du Nord. While Pétain struggled into his pants, Serrigny consoled his sobbing companion with the assurance: 'France's existence is at stake'.[22] Thus was Pétain apprised of his new command.

Pétain appreciated two things: the decisive influence of fire power and the need to keep defenders as fresh as possible. Using his superb *soixante-quinze* (75 mm) guns to deadly effect, Pétain systematically destroyed the Austrian 30.5 cm and the massive Krupp 42 cm howitzers by counter-battery fire. French artillery also blew up the German artillery park at Spincourt, destroying 450 000 heavy shells, which strangely had been kept fused. With regard to manpower, Pétain mitigated the strain and stress of constant battle by rotating 66 divisions through the 'Meuse grinder' up to 1 July.

Perhaps the most salient feature of the Battle of Verdun was logistics. A single German infantry division of 16 000 men and 7000 horses included 15 batteries of artillery; the latter required 36 ammunition trains stretching 35 miles in length. Each ammunition train carried from 2000 heavy howitzer to 26 880 light field artillery shells.[23] The Germans used railroads – both standard track and hastily-installed special narrow-gauge field rails – to move this enormous quantity of material. The French were denied this 'luxury' because the Germans had cut the two rail lines that served Verdun. Pétain turned to trucks. In the 10-day period from 24 February to 6 March alone, 3500 trucks hauled 190 000 troops and 23 000 tons of ammunition along the winding 47-mile road from Bar-le-Duc to Verdun, the legendary *voie sacrée*, as Maurice Barrès called it. At the height of the resupply, a vehicle passed every 14 seconds at any given point along the 7-yard-wide road, maintained by a host of colonial reserves.[24]

Air power also played a role, albeit peripheral, at Verdun. The French at first dominated the skies and directed their murderous artillery fire from

Nieuport aircraft and tethered balloons. On 22 June the French bombed the city of Karlsruhe, killing 154 children attending a circus performance. Most German aircraft were of inferior quality and could only fire their machine guns backwards or sideways. But by April the Germans had brought six squadrons of six planes each to Verdun and within a month Anthony Fokker had outfitted the new monoplanes with two machine guns each, synchronizing their fire with the spinning of the propeller by way of an interruptor gear and thereby allowing forward shooting.[25] Two of Germany's most renowned 'aces', Oswald Boelcke and the 'Red Baron', Richthofen, fought in the skies over Verdun.

There were as yet no distinct 'fighter' and 'bomber' units. The same plane dropped (20 or 30 lbs) bombs or sharpened steel arrows, took aerial reconnaissance photos, and spotted for the artillery. The Germans divided their air forces into troop, fighter, and bomber squadrons only in the summer of 1916. Parachutes were available but were frowned on as being 'dishonourable'. Their use was restricted to spotters in tethered balloons, who tended to use them at the earliest sign of an approaching aircraft. The French proved more adept at aerial reconnaissance for their artillery, while the Germans failed to appreciate and hence did not try to interdict the steady traffic on the *voie sacrée* from the air.[26] By and large they deployed their planes as fighter interceptors.

Most Verdun veterans recalled the deadly effectiveness of massed artillery. It killed in great numbers, but in the end it was neither accurate nor decisive. Artillery was deadly mainly due to its sheer weight. The massive high-angle-fire 'Big Berthas', named for Krupp heiress Bertha (who did not appreciate this 'honour'), when first tried at Manonviller in August 1914, scored only three hits out of 159 shots at 8-mile range. They were used at Verdun for the second time. It took five steam-driven tractors and 250 men to haul each of the 70-ton behemoths to the forest of Spincourt; the guns' barrels had to be rebored after 50 to 100 rounds.

But even regular field artillery was slow: it took 60 men and 24 horses to move a single heavy gun. Once engaged, artillery proved surprisingly inaccurate. Not even a daily hail of 2000 artillery rounds fired for 18 days managed to destroy Fort Souville in July. The constant bombardments wore out the barrels: the Germans discovered that their 13 cm guns (range up to 14 400 yards) deviated from their calibrated targets as much as 600 yards after extensive use.[27] The truth is that subterranean tunnels and ancient stone forts proved incredibly resilient and almost impervious to modern artillery. There can be no question, of course, concerning the overall devastation of the constant artillery pounding: Hill 304 in 3 months became Hill 297 as 7 yards of earth were blasted off its crown. Artillery accounted for 58 per cent of all German deaths during the Great War – compared with only 8.4 per cent during the Franco-Prussian War.

Clausewitz's notion of the 'fog of war' bedevilled the German attackers. At Fort Douaumont – which they dubbed 'death head', 'coffin lid', and 'Golgotha Hill' – companies ran into each other in wild confusion during the initial twilight assault. Officers either were quickly killed by machine-gun fire or got lost in the din and chaos of smoke, gas, and heavy shelling. Some attackers laid down to rest on reaching the last wire barricade, while others struggled on through – only to arrive at the outer perimeter of the fort 90 minutes early. And since German artillery fired according to predetermined tables, these men were subjected to so-called 'friendly' fire. Battery leaders often could not discern the progress of their own troops as night set in, and signal flares either failed to ignite or, when they did, could not be read on the smoke-enshrouded battlefield. Telephone lines between battalion and division commands were shot to pieces, and field runners required hours to make the trip – if they made it at all. The few exhausted troops that finally reached Fort Douaumont withdrew again when they found no officers to issue further orders.[28]

The fort was eventually 'stormed' in a classic *coup de main*. On 25 February three officers of the 24th Brandenburg Regiment made their way through the driving sleet to the very walls of Douaumont – and discovered the fort's drawbridge down. Without a map and under constant bombardment by their own artillery, which again failed to recognize flares calling for a halt to the barrage, they boldly entered the citadel and surprised its two dozen defenders asleep, deadbeat from exhaustion. The German Army, in the best tradition of *opéra-bouffe*, awarded its highest decoration, the *Pour le mérite*, to First Lieutenant Cordt von Brandis – not for taking the fort, wherein he had no role, but simply for telephoning the news to the General Staff![29] School children in Germany received a day off to celebrate Douaumont's fall.

Verdun also witnessed the first mass-scale distribution of medals. At the start of the war, Wilhelm II had immediately reinstituted the Iron Cross I and II Class of 1813 for distinguished soldiers and officers alike. The *OHL*, in an attempt to maintain morale, during the Great War awarded 5.2 million Iron Crosses – including 2.2 million I Class – to the troops as well as to civilians at home. Nor did the Weimar Republic show any restraint in this regard, showering veterans with a further 746 000 Iron Crosses between 1918 and 1924. General Staff officers routinely joked that one could escape the Iron Cross II Class only through suicide![30] The *Pour le mérite* was awarded to 687 officers.

Command and control could be practised but sporadically in such a crowded, confused, and devastated zone, one in which there existed a

German division for every 1100 yards of front. By and large, the 'front' ended at the regimental level; most soldiers saw only their company leader and battalion chief, at best, and only on occasion the regimental commander. Crown Prince Wilhelm, commander of the Fifth Army, spent his days 30 miles distant from the front in what he termed his 'personal sacrifice' in the 'godforsaken hole' of Stenay, playing tennis, riding horses, occasionally tossing cigarettes to the troops paraded on review for him, and chasing pretty mademoiselles. His staff, from the divisional level on up, saw the war abstractly via situation reports, telephone calls, and casualty reports.[31] Communication was by flares, semaphores, and carrier pigeons. Verdun also saw the first major use of dogs (mainly German shepherds but also Doberman pinschers and Airedale terriers) as message carriers; more than 20 000 died on this dangerous assignment during the war.

Falkenhayn kept a tight grip on the campaign. All plans of attack, redeployment, and eventually withdrawal had first to be cleared with him. Front-line commanders were encouraged not to develop initiative and thus sacrificed the famous *Auftragstaktik* (mission-oriented tactics) of 1870–1. The well-known hostility in every war between staff and front was revealed clearly when one of Falkenhayn's aides visited Verdun and asked a shivering soldier: 'Are you freezing? Only masturbators, drunkards, and whoremongers freeze!'[32]

Why, one may well ask, did the men go on fighting? Grenadier Rudolf Koch, injured storming Hill 304 on Easter Sunday, reflected on the matter while convalescing in hospital. Some feared the 'shame of ridicule' of their comrades or punishment from their officers if they deserted; others stayed in the line 'from a simple sense of duty'; 'most of us from habit'. In simple but mature terms, Koch encapsulated his experience at Verdun. 'We never understood the sense of the entire operation. . . . The soldier does his duty and does not question why. It was duty alone that kept us together and held our courage up. At such a place, one cannot speak of enthusiasm; everyone wishes they were a thousand miles away. . . .'.[33]

Dominik Richert, an Alsatian soldier, provided another sober assessment. 'In truth, courage has nothing to do with it. The fear of death surpasses all other feelings and terrible compulsion alone drives the soldier forward.' Richert was motivated to go on fighting by 'the damned discipline' of the Prussian Army, the occasional threat of being shot by his commanding officer, and the simple feeling that 'the terrible must be done'. Had there been a choice, 'not a man would have remained voluntarily at the front'.[34]

With the notable exception of Falkenhayn, who had staked his career on Verdun, Germany's premier soldiers soon questioned the operation.

The endless slaughter did not force the Parisian politicians to capitulate. The French Army fought valiantly. And the British, as will be discussed next, did not desert their 'continental sword'. Whereas Falkenhayn had predicted a kill ratio of three French soldiers to every German, battlefield casualties were almost even (1 German to 1.1 French). Germany's strategic reserve on the Western Front fell from 25.5 divisions in February to a single division by August. In the end, the Germans achieved the worst possible result: a half-victory. They scored initial triumphs and stormed Fort Douaumont but in the process advanced their lines to untenable positions under the guns of the French. Pride militated against a strategic withdrawal. The carnage went on.

As early as mid-March, Wilhelm II grew pessimistic: 'One must never utter it nor shall I admit it to Falkenhayn, but this war will not end with a great victory'.[35] Two months later, the Crown Prince seconded his father's sentiment and berated Falkenhayn for destroying the Fifth Army before Verdun. General Groener, who would succeed Ludendorff in 1918, spoke of Falkenhayn's 'homeopathic tactics' of committing reserves bit by bit into the Meuse meat grinder, and bluntly denounced Verdun as 'erroneous strategy'.[36] Crown Prince Rupprecht, head of the Sixth Army in Flanders, allowed that Falkenhayn's obsession with detail had caused him 'to lose the big picture'.[37] Perhaps the best comment belongs to General von Gallwitz, commander of Meuse Group West, whose forces advanced just over 2 miles in 4 months at a cost of 69 000 men. At the end of April 1916 Gallwitz sarcastically noted that given the present rate of progress, 'we will be in Verdun at the earliest in 1920'.[38]

Falkenhayn's strategy – if one dare use the word for Verdun – was too dogmatic, mechanical, and rigid. Millions of men were thrown into the 'Meuse mill' in the hope that somehow the Germans would have the last men left standing. Or that the enemy would suffer moral collapse. Casualty lists took the place of surprise, deception, concentration, and manoeuvre. Slide-rule body counts absorbed staff officers. Falkenhayn committed unit after unit to the slaughter with grisly determination, unable or unwilling to see that his strategy of attrition affected the German Army as much as it did the French. The Württemberg General Otto von Moser after the war lamented that the *OHL* had paid more attention to 'figures' than to 'heart'. 'Our highest leaders failed to develop a proper sense of what could be expected of the troops.' Too many staff officers were far removed from the front and planned operations from the comfort of their drawing boards. The troops began to question decisions to hold every yard of territory regardless of the cost.[39]

Throughout the operation, Falkenhayn kept Bethmann Hollweg in the dark concerning the monthly death rates. The Prussian War Minister as late as October 1916 informed the Reichstag that the French had, indeed, been 'bled to death' at Verdun.[40] But to his wife Wild von Hohenborn confessed that he was shocked by the callous carnage. 'Slowly one almost gets accustomed to looking at the deep wounds that this war inflicts in purely mercantile terms.' The General admitted that he glanced at the monthly tally sheets of losses and replacements 'much as a business man looks at his balance sheets. This sounds gruesome; but that is just what this war is'.[41]

The Verdun operation wound down in mid-August 1916 with a bitter split between the *OHL* and the Fifth Army. Crown Prince Wilhelm and Schmidt von Knobelsdorf, obviously fearful of losing their army, bombarded Falkenhayn with requests to end the infantry assaults against Verdun. The Fifth Army's commanders were no longer willing to sacrifice men for little or no gain. Falkenhayn reacted disingenuously. On the one hand he reminded the Fifth Army that the object of the campaign was not to seize the fortress but to 'bleed to death' the French armies and demanded continued attacks against Verdun. On the other hand he acknowledged that the Allied superiority in men and material allowed no course other than to create a defensive 'iron wall' along the Western Front. Falkenhayn left the final choice between offensive or defensive operations with the Fifth Army – and dismissed Schmidt von Knobelsdorf. The German official history claims another first in Prussian military practice: never before had an army staff chief uninvited presented the Chief of the General Staff with briefs flagrantly opposing official instructions.[42]

Not surprisingly, Verdun brought to a close Falkenhayn's stormy tenure as Chief of the General Staff. Militarily, the end came after Brusilov's offensive in Galicia of 4 June and Haig's assault along the Somme on 1 July. Politically, it came after Germany's decision not to undertake unrestricted submarine warfare against British maritime commerce owing to a lack of U-boats[43] and Romania's entry into the war on 27 August as a direct consequence of the Verdun debacle.

Wilhelm II was badly rattled by Falkenhayn's failure to read Romania's designs and declared that the war was lost.[44] Bethmann Hollweg spied his chance to drive a wedge between the Kaiser and Falkenhayn. Already shocked and disillusioned by Falkenhayn's attrition tactics at Verdun – 'where does incompetence end and criminality begin?' – the Chancellor instructed the Kaiser that the war could only be decided in the east and that ruling circles in Vienna had lost confidence in Falkenhayn.[45] Bethmann Hollweg was playing a fool's game. He hoped to harness the magic of Hindenburg's name: first to topple Falkenhayn or at least to send him back to his post as Prussian War Minister; and secondly to bring an end to the war by way of a negotiated (but annexationist) peace, covering this admission of less than total victory with Hindenburg's mantle. That neither Hindenburg nor Ludendorff shared this vision and instead sought power in order to win the war on the battlefield apparently never dawned on the Chancellor.

This notwithstanding, Bethmann Hollweg quickly gathered additional allies. General von Plessen, the Kaiser's military adjutant, joined in the assault. Crown Prince Rupprecht bluntly informed Wilhelm II that Falkenhayn no longer enjoyed the confidence of the Army.[46] The old *fronde* of January 1915 was thus reconstituted. Not even Falkenhayn's protector, General von Lyncker, Chief of the Military Cabinet, could stem the tide against his erstwhile protégé. In fact, even War Minister Wild von Hohenborn, who owed his position to Falkenhayn, had secretly abandoned him in favour of Hindenburg.

Falkenhayn sought to save his position by warning the Kaiser that he would cease to exercise 'command authority' under Hindenburg-Ludendorff. While the appeal hit the mark, Wilhelm II nevertheless began to waver in his support of Falkenhayn. Undoubtedly realizing that his job was in jeopardy, Falkenhayn on 23 August draughted a lengthy defence of his actions. With regard to Verdun, Falkenhayn reminded Wilhelm II that the object had never been 'to force France to sue for peace', but rather to force it to 'bleed to death' defending the fortress, or else to suffer 'internal demoralization' by surrendering it. In a bold-face lie, the General assured the Kaiser that the French had lost 'at least a quarter of a million veteran soldiers' more than Germany (!) before Verdun. Finally, with veiled reference to certain 'dilettantes in field grey' – read, Hindenburg and Ludendorff – Falkenhayn cautioned Wilhelm II not to pay heed to those who were unable 'to appreciate the true division of strengths' between the east and the west and admonished the Supreme War Lord not to chase the 'unrealistic dreams' of the military duumvirate in Russia.[47]

On 29 August 1916, the second anniversary of the Battle of Tannenberg, Wilhelm II replaced Falkenhayn with Hindenburg and Ludendorff. Leopold Prince of Bavaria, aided by Colonel Hoffmann, took command of *OberOst*. Falkenhayn left Pless by train at 1:16 p.m. Only General Groener, head of the General Staff's railway section, paid his respects at the railway station.

The 'crime of Verdun', as Falkenhayn's opponents put it, was thus 'avenged'. Bethmann Hollweg perhaps put the national mood best: 'The name Hindenburg puts terror into our enemies, electrifies our army and people, who have complete confidence in him'. Still ignorant of Hindenburg's and Ludendorff's plans to pursue the war to a victorious end, the Chancellor crowed that Hindenburg's reputation in Germany was such that he alone could sustain a lost battle or a negotiated peace.[48] Too late, Bethmann Hollweg realized the extent of his political blundering, and lamented to his inner circle: 'With Falkenhayn, Germany risks losing the war strategically – with Ludendorff, politically'.[49]

The German public and press shared the Chancellor's celebratory mood – as did most army leaders (Einem, Gallwitz, Groener, Lossberg, Crown Princes Wilhelm and Rupprecht of Bavaria). Conrad von Hötzendorf was delighted to see Falkenhayn go but apprehensive about his successors. Most observers agreed that the change was more than symbolic.

Falkenhayn's tenure as Chief of the General Staff has only recently been reexamined on the basis of new material. Holger Afflerbach divides Falkenhayn's rule into four distinct periods. From the time that Falkenhayn assumed office in September until November 1914, he sought victory in the west by outflanking the enemy armies in Flanders. Thereafter, Falkenhayn informed Bethmann Hollweg that the war could only be ended by a separate peace in the east. When that hope proved illusory, the General tied his colours to a war of attrition before Verdun designed to defeat the French materially and psychologically. Fourthly, after Verdun Falkenhayn was left with no option but to defend indefinitely in the west. His overall concept remained clear and consistent: the primacy of the Western Front; the belief that Britain was the 'archenemy'; and the conviction that Russia could be bludgeoned into concluding a separate peace. Falkenhayn greatly underestimated the ability of the French to sustain heavy losses at Verdun and overestimated the power of his own artillery and infantry. His greatest failure was that he did not coordinate a joint strategy with Conrad for 1916; on 29 August this cost Falkenhayn his post.[50] One wonders whether he remembered his flippant remark from November 1914: 'Even if we go under as a result of this, it still was beautiful'.

On 2 September Hindenburg and Ludendorff formally ended the German offensive 'in the direction of Verdun'. But determined French assaults ensued until the middle of December and resulted in the recapture of Forts Douaumont and Vaux. The *OHL* conceded 'serious tactical defeats' during these months, removed several army and corps commanders, instituted courts-martial proceedings against still others, and vetoed all recommendations for decorations higher than the Iron Cross. A terse General Staff order reminded officers of their duty to maintain morale and discipline. The 'hell of Verdun' had lasted roughly 300 days.

Verdun became (and remains) a symbol for the routine, almost monotonous slaughter of the Great War. The German official history uses the term 'system of temporary expediency' to describe Falkenhayn's 'strategy' in

1916 and speaks of 'the catastrophe of the tragedy of Verdun', noting that it constituted a stinging defeat with far-reaching consequences.[51] But what choice did Falkenhayn have? Twice in 1914–15 he had informed Bethmann Hollweg that the war could not be won and had demanded a separate peace with Russia. Twice the Chancellor had rebuffed his initiatives.

The German Army was heavily bled at Verdun: 48 divisions had gone through the 'Meuse mill'. Many of the *Landser* lost faith in their leaders. Discipline for the first time began to break down. Desertions mounted. 'Police measures' were instituted to maintain discipline. The harmonious 'spirit of 1914' was crushed. Who still remembered that in February the first regiments of the Brandenburg III Corps had stormed French positions to the ringing sounds of the *Yorck March*, *Hohenfriedberg*, and *Prussia's Glory*? The Army, in a vain attempt to dispel the broad public perception that Operation *Gericht* constituted a major defeat, suggested that Verdun, as the apex of modern industrial warfare, had rendered meaningless traditional concepts of 'victory' and 'defeat'. But Kurt Riezler, a senior councillor at the Chancellery in Berlin, appreciated that Verdun stood out among the battles of the Great War. 'How good it is that fog envelops the combatants. . . . Too much tragedy, too gigantically massive. It dulls the senses.'[52]

Ernst Toller – Jew, publicist, and war volunteer – eloquently described how Verdun transformed the spirit of the common soldiers. 'The great patriotic feelings turn dull, the big words small; war becomes commonplace, service at the front day's work; heroes become victims, volunteers slaves; life is one hell, death is a mere trifle; we are all screws in a machine that wallows forward, nobody knows where to.'[53] Nor was Toller alone in his feelings. After the war, Crown Prince Wilhelm sadly reflected on the destruction of his Fifth Army before Verdun: 'The Meuse mill ground up the hearts of the soldiers as much as their bodies'.[54] In November 1942 Adolf Hitler, a veteran of the Great War, assured the Nazi Old Guard at Munich that Stalingrad would never become 'a second Verdun'.[55] The German Sixth Army surrendered to the Soviets 2 months later.

Perhaps the final word should go to a recent scholar of the German Army in the twentieth century. Michael Geyer in his contribution to the new edition of *Makers of Modern Strategy* aptly summarized the meaning of Verdun: 'More than any other battle, Verdun showed the military impasse of World War I, the complete disjuncture between strategy, battle design, and tactics, and the inability to use the modern means of war. But most of all, it showed, at horrendous costs, the impasse of professional strategies'.[56]

The Somme: 'battles of material'

Not surprisingly, the French turned for relief to their allies. As early as 6 December 1915 British, French, Italian, Russian, and Serbian generals had met at Chantilly to plan a massive concentrated attack against the Central Powers on all fronts. Specifically, French forces were to spearhead an assault along the Somme River. The German operation against Verdun of course preempted that plan – and shifted the main burden from the French Army to the BEF. General Haig was quite prepared to show the Germans 'the fighting will of the British race'. On 26 May 1916 General Joffre met with Haig at Beauquesne and chose the salient from Beaumont-Hamel down to the marshes of the Somme River for a joint Anglo-French counterattack. Plans for the assault were formalized 5 days later in President Poincaré's Pullman car south of Amiens.

The British Fourth Army of General Henry Rawlinson and the Third Army under General Edmund Allenby, with 14 infantry divisions and four in reserve, would attack north of the Somme on 1 July. Concurrently, French General Foch's Army Group of the North with five infantry divisions (and six in reserve) would strike out from its position south of the river. Opposing them were seven divisions of General Fritz von Below's German Second Army. The BEF and the French had a three-to-one superiority (386 versus 129 craft) in the air and virtual artillery supremacy: 1655 to 454 light, 933 to 372 medium, and 393 to 18 heavy guns. A 7-day artillery barrage, which rained down 1 ton of steel per square yard, was designed to 'soften' German positions before the infantry stormed the enemy trenches.

An intelligence failure at German headquarters partly accounts for the French dominance at the Somme. Falkenhayn refused to believe that the French would attack from their position astride the river as they were desperately tied down around Verdun. When he received reports of French preparations, Falkenhayn dismissed them as a feint designed to conceal the main point of attack. As late as 25 June he reiterated his conviction that the French would not be able to mount an attack 'for several days', and hence sited only three infantry divisions south, but six north of the Somme.[57] Additionally, the French enjoyed an eight-to-one superiority in artillery and not only minimized German counter-battery fire, but also destroyed enemy wire, machine guns, and deep trenches.

Zero hour came at 7:30 a.m. on a beautiful and soon to be hot 1 July. Following the greatest bombardment of the war in which 55 000 British gunners in 5 days showered German lines with 12 000 tons of explosives and steel, the first wave of about 66 000 men of the BEF leaped out of their trenches and headed toward the German defences.[58] Laden down

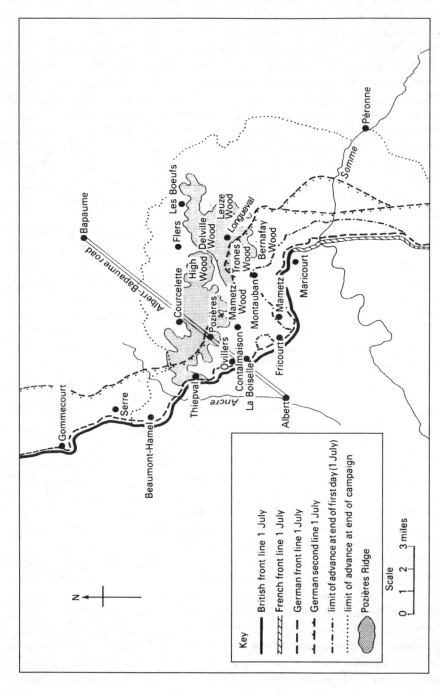

Map 7. The bloody Somme, 1916

Key

— British front line 1 July

╱╱╱ French front line 1 July

– – – German front line 1 July

–⊢–⊢ German second line 1 July

–·–·– limit of advance at end of first day (1 July)

········ limit of advance at end of campaign

▨ Pozières Ridge

Scale

0 1 2 3 miles

Gommecourt

Serre

Beaumont-Hamel

Thiepval

Ancre

Ovillers

La Boiselle

Contalmaison

Albert

Fricourt

Mametz

Maricourt

Montauban

Mametz Wood

Poziéres

Courcelette

High Wood

Delville Wood

Trones Wood

Bernafay Wood

Longueval

Leuze Wood

Flers

Les Boeufs

Bapaume

Albert–Bapaume road

Somme

Péronne

with 66 lbs of barbed wire coils, steel posts, and shovels with which to consolidate their hold on captured German trenches, the soldiers advanced slowly over No Man's Land. Artillery with clockwork precision lifted its mammoth rolling barrages 100 yards ahead of the men every 2 minutes. The assault was predicated on exact timing. The 36th Ulster Division, for example, had to cover 3000 yards precisely by 10:08 a.m. The campaign was to be a textbook operation: the plan of attack designed for the VIII Corps alone consisted of 76 pages, with a 365-page supplement appended for individual divisions.

As so often happened in the Great War, theory quickly yielded to reality. The BEF sustained 57 470 casualties (including 19 240 men killed) on 1 July – a figure that, according to the historian Martin Middlebrook, exceeds the total British losses in the Crimean, Boer, and Korean wars. About 50 per cent of the men engaged at the Somme on 1 July became casualties, including three out of every four officers. Two generals died that day; nine Victoria Crosses were awarded. The Germans suffered about 40 200 casualties during the first 10 days of the offensive.

What had gone wrong in what British officers called the 'Big Push' and the troops the 'Great Fuck-Up'? At the top of the chain of command, Haig sought to attack 'the whole of the enemy's lines of defence' by way of a quick, hurricane bombardment, followed by a breakthrough led by strong infantry patrols, to be exploited by the cavalry. Rawlinson, Fourth Army, had a distinctly different vision: a limited objective featuring a 'bite and hold' plan whereby the BEF would use artillery to 'bite' off chunks of territory and then consolidate and 'hold' them with infantry against expected counterattacks.[59] The two men obviously had conflicting perceptions of the operation.

The attack started too late. The early-morning mists of the Somme marshes, which might have hidden an assault at daybreak, were evaporating by 7:30 a.m. Thirdly, while the German official history stresses that British artillery shattered the batteries of the 12th Division and the 28th Reserve Division north of Mametz and Montauban, it did not destroy the infantry in their deep trenches. Not only had Haig failed to concentrate guns and infantry, but British guns proved 25 per cent defective. Many shells were duds, there was a shortage of both high explosive and gas shells in favour of shrapnel, and the artillery barrage moved too fast ahead of the advancing troops. Thus the German machine gunners waited for the barrage to roll over them, then came out of their trenches, and calmly massacred British infantry with fire from their higher-ground positions.

Indeed, the machine gun – which Haig continued to view as 'a much overrated weapon' – probably did more damage at the Somme than in any other battle of the Great War. Many veterans recalled the hissing and cracking of the machine guns on 1 July. The British 34th Division of Tyneside Irish and Scots suffered 6380 casualties at La Boiselle as it advanced wave after wave across a mile of open ground. At Gommecourt the 56th Division managed to take the German first line of trenches, but by nightfall had been driven back to its own lines. The 1st Newfoundland Battalion, crossing 300 yards of open ground at Beaumont-Hamel, was cut to pieces by a withering enfilading machine-gun fire; the unit lost 91 per cent of its men in 40 minutes. A private from the neighbouring 1st King's Own Scottish Borderers was horrified by the scene: 'I cursed the generals for their useless slaughter, they seemed to have no idea what was going on'.[60]

Undaunted, Haig pushed on at Bapaume, Péronne, and Nesle in what was now called *la guerre d'usure* (the wearing-out battle). The idea was to draw in and use up German reserves, and then deliver the decisive blow. At 3:25 a.m. on 14 July, after a 5-minute hurricane barrage, Rawlinson sent six assault brigades against the enemy at Longueval. While they advanced 6000 yards to the German second line, undue caution, misinformation, and weak artillery–infantry cooperation denied Fourth Army a breakthrough. Again, on 15 September Haig mounted an assault at Flers-Morval-Les Boeufs with three corps in hopes of breaking through to Bapaume and then Miraumont. And again, insufficient artillery–infantry cooperation, ignorance of the terrain, and misinformation bedevilled the operation.

Artillery pulverized the Somme landscape, but the strategy of the wearing-out battle and the decisive blow had not succeeded. Fresh assaults mounted on 3 and 20 September were repulsed at horrendous costs by Below's First Army and Gallwitz's Second Army, both part of Army Group Crown Prince Rupprecht. Falkenhayn, like Joffre at Verdun, reminded Below 'that the first tenet of trench warfare must be not to surrender a foot of territory, and, should that foot nevertheless be lost, to commit every last man to an immediate counterattack'.[61] Thus, Below threatened to court-martial any officer who gave up an inch of ground and vowed to retake it no matter the cost.

A British experiment with 49 'tanks' near Bapaume in September was premature; 13 of the 'land battleships' broke down en route to the front lines, a further 11 failed to cross No Man's Land, and only 11 engaged in battle.[62] German artillery accounted for most tanks destroyed, while hand-grenades and well-aimed sniper fire against fuel lines immobilized several units. The 28-ton tanks for the most part were underpowered and unreliable as well as too few in number to allow a breakthrough for infantry to exploit. 'Somme mud' finally ended Haig's offensive in mid-November.

The German Second Army was badly knocked at the Somme. Air superiority allowed the British to site their artillery accurately, to harass German counter-battery fire by shooting down its spotters in tethered balloons, and to strafe enemy trenches almost at will. One German staff officer noted that corps were bled regularly 'like lemons in a press'. German soldiers were required to carry small bags of chloride of lime to sprinkle on the corpses they passed. The Battle of the Somme witnessed the first instances of blatant fragging.[63]

Below's 100 anti-aircraft guns could do little against the oppressive Allied superiority, and German air command exacerbated the situation by dividing its scant forces between interception and bombing missions. Nor could German resupply keep up with the high demand for shells – the Reich's armies fired 11 million artillery shells in July and August 1916, and replaced 1600 light and 760 heavy guns worn out or damaged during that same period. Army Group Gallwitz alone required five ammunitions trains daily for the field artillery and another four for its howitzers.

Colonel Rüdiger von der Goltz, commanding the 10th Grenadier Regiment of the 11th Infantry Division, identified the keys to the British assault at the Somme in a report to the *OHL*. The week-long bombardment, well directed from spotter aircraft, had rained down a 'decimating fire' of heavy shells and howitzers on the defenders. Numerically inferior German artillery and aircraft had been 'as good as eliminated', meaning that no counter-battery fire was possible for the first few weeks of the campaign. Inaccurate bombardment and sweeping artillery fire was all that was left the defenders. Above all, the Germans had kept their infantry in the first line during the seven days of shelling, so that on 1 July the Second Army lost not only the trenches but also many of the men and material in them.[64] Goltz thought that an elastic defence-in-depth would have served the Germans better at the Somme.

Private Wilhelm Schulin of the 119th Württemberg Grenadier Regiment, 26th Infantry Division, kept a careful diary of the Somme fighting. A cobbler, he used his talents throughout July and August to reinforce the German trenches, some 10 yards deep, with rough boards and to cover the mass graves with stones. Enemy aircraft constantly harassed the German troops in their trenches. The only relief was to evacuate the front lines for parks and forests. But life there was not much better:

Into the tents, then, where it rains. Eat; write; search the knapsack for something. No water with which to wash hands in this mud. And then the lice plague. And everything always in a state of excitement, all done in haste: bathing, delousing; not comfortable, not like civilian life. And always more equipment, always something added: it is almost beastly how much we have to carry.

The chalky soil and the marshes of the Somme denied the men decent drinking water. Schulin's troops lost their gear and eventually their way in the chaos of the battlefield. 'We asked where we were, said we were lost. Laughed at. Scared. Sweat.'[65] Schulin was greatly relieved when Haig scaled down his assault.

The butcher's bill was frightening. The British lost 190 000 soldiers, the French 80 000 and the Germans 200 000 at the Somme in July and August alone. Over the course of the entire campaign, the BEF suffered 420 000 casualties, the French Army 200 000, and the Germans 465 000. The Somme, in the words of one of its veterans, the future military historian B. H. Liddell Hart, 'proved both the glory and the graveyard' of Kitchener's Armies.[66] It became grist for the mills of 'war poets' such as Siegfried Sassoon, Robert Graves, David Jones, and Wilfred Owen. The German Army lost its last small-unit leaders; it would never be the same instrument again. After Verdun and the Somme, military writers spoke of *Materialschlachten* (battles of material) that pitted machines and material against men. Lieutenant Gerhard Ritter, future military historian, fought at the Somme and was shocked by what he termed its 'monotonous mutual mass murder'.[67] Ernst Jünger, another veteran of the Somme, depicted the soldiers as 'workers of war'. The Austro-Hungarian psychologist Stephan Máday used the term 'workers of war', and the Frenchman Henri Barbusse the phrase 'workers of destruction'. No romance. No sport. No adventure.

Lutsk: 'lack of luck'

Conrad von Hötzendorf was undeterred by alarming casualty rates. His staff informed him that the Austro-Hungarian Army had lost 170 000 men per month in the east in the spring of 1915, and 200 000 in Galicia in September alone; for the entire year 1915, the Army had suffered 2 118 000 casualties, including 775 000 prisoners of war. But about half of the wounded had been returned to the front and nearly 3 million young men had been drafted. As a result, many Habsburg divisions late in 1915 boasted strengths of about 11 000 rifles.[68] Conrad once more was ready to plan major operations.

Beginning on 10 December 1915, Conrad peppered Falkenhayn with pleas for men and supplies to allow him to 'trample the snake's head', that is, Italy.[69] He confided to an aide that ever since his days as a divisional commander at Trieste 17 years ago, he had nurtured the 'dream' of one day attacking Italy out of the Trentino and thereby dashing its great power aspirations. 'And now I hope that my dream of beating these dago dogs will be fulfilled.'[70] Falkenhayn, about to mount his own offensive against Verdun, was not interested. He informed Conrad at a meeting at Pless on 3 February that an operation against Italy would not enhance the overall war effort but serve only the narrow interests of Austria-Hungary, that sufficient forces were not available for the undertaking, and that it would be difficult to supply a drive out of the Alps.[71] Falkenhayn refused 9 days before the start of the Verdun campaign to inform Conrad of his plans. No sooner had Conrad departed Pless, than the *OHL* moved its headquarters to Mézières-Charleville in the west. Kageneck, the German military attaché at Teschen, tersely noted this latest lack of coordinated planning: 'Divergent goals. Verdun-Italy'.[72] When Kageneck pressed Conrad's Italian expert for information on the *AOK*'s plans, Lieutenant-Colonel Schneller gleefully confided to his diary: 'Simply just plain lied to him'.[73]

Conrad would not be denied. On 6 February he had Archduke Friedrich issue the order to prepare an offensive against 'perfidious' Italy. Conrad next transferred six of his best combat divisions from Galicia to the Alps – at the very moment that Falkenhayn also denuded German forces in the east in favour of Verdun – and informed the Germans that he 'needed only to push the button in order to open fire'.[74] On 25 March Conrad took personal charge of the Italian theatre from his headquarters in Austrian Silesia – more than 600 miles from the front. He bypassed the local commander, Archduke Eugen, and refused a request by the latter's chief of staff, General Alfred Krauss, to come to Teschen to discuss the planned operation. Nor did Conrad or Schneller bother to visit the front in Italy.

Conrad planned to hurl Dankl's Eleventh Army (nine divisions) and General Kövess' Third Army (five divisions) across the 12-mile-wide high plain of Lavarone-Folgaria against the 'honourless' Italians. He eschewed diversionary feints and forbade any flanking attempts in favour of a frontal assault 'with all possible force'.[75] The grandiose *Strafexpedition* (punitive expedition) was designed to break the Italian front, penetrate the northern Italian plains via Thiene and Bassano, seize the key rail centre of Padua, and envelop Italian forces in Carnia and along the Isonzo River. Grand Admiral Anton Haus declined to support the offensive by sea because he lacked escort craft for the capital ships; Conrad testily replied that he would remember this in future budgetary discussions! The German ally was kept in the dark until 9 May.

In theory the operation looked simple. Conrad had sketched it out on a single piece of paper: a bold arrow divided into six parts pointed from the South Tyrol to Venice; each stroke represented a single day's march of 12 miles.[76] But once again Conrad neglected to take climatic conditions into consideration: deep snow in the mountains, combined with alternating periods of frost and thaw, sun and sleet, delayed the attack in the Trentino for 5 weeks until 15 May. Only one in every three supply trains reached the front. Trucks, largely with iron tires, skidded off mountain roads. Men bogged down in 12-foot snow drifts. More than a thousand Habsburg soldiers were buried by avalanches.[77] Conrad used the delay to design new uniforms, flags, and coats of arms, to ponder a new national anthem, and to launch a campaign to get his Chief of Operations, Colonel Metzger, promoted and decorated.[78] In the meantime, the Italians hauled reinforcements to the front. By the time Austro-Hungarian forces attacked in mid-May, they had lost the element of surprise. In fact, a barber in Vienna gave out the exact date for the offensive from information he had received through one of his clients, a department head at the Ballhausplatz.[79]

Habsburg artillery subjected the Italians to a two-hour bombardment on 15 May and then 157 000 soldiers advanced in deep snow against 114 000 Italians. Conrad's units scored initial gains, taking Arsiero and Asiago, the gates to the northern Italian plains, by the end of May. They then overran the Italian First Army, headed since 8 May by General Guglielmo Pecori-Giraldi, a commander sacked in 1911 for incompetence in Italy's desert war in Libya. Flushed with success and nurturing visions of victory, Conrad through Archduke Friedrich presented Vienna with a shopping list of war aims. Congress Poland and Galicia were to be 'annexed'. Montenegro was to share a similar fate. Serbia, which had caused this 'most gruesome of all wars', was to lose its independence. It was an 'axiom' of Austria–Hungary's 'self-preservation', the *AOK* informed the Military Chancery, that the Serb state be 'crushed and conquered', and that its citizens be 'pacified' and forced to become loyal Habsburg subjects through the imposition of a 'military regime' at Belgrade for at least a decade.[80]

General Cadorna, fully expecting a simultaneous Austro-Hungarian attack along the Isonzo River, was panic-stricken by the enemy's initial success in the Trentino. Beginning on 19 May, he repeatedly begged the Russians to mount an offensive in Galicia or the Bukovina to draw off Habsburg units. Italian headquarters made plans to evacuate the Isonzo and to destroy all roads and bridges as units retreated southward; Cadorna even toyed with the notion of flooding the Po River valley to delay Conrad's advance. On 10 June the Italian parliament passed a vote of no confidence in Salandra's government because the Premier had suggested that Cadorna might better have defended the nation's northern frontier.[81] Salandra was replaced by a coalition government headed by Paolo Boselli.

But once again Conrad had asked too much of his troops. The advance bogged down in rain and snow. Supplies failed to reach the troops. The artillery could not be moved up in the mud. Cadorna reinforced the battered Italian First Army and hastily assembled a new Fifth Army. On 6 June Cadorna counterattacked, grinding the Austrian operation to a halt. Much of the territory seized after 15 May had to be evacuated. On 16 June Conrad ordered his forces to stand on the defensive.[82] Both armies were exhausted by the bitter Alpine fighting: Italy lost 147 000 men, Austria 81 000.

Conrad blamed the lack of success on his subordinates. Specifically, he accused Dankl of having mismanaged the assault and in June accepted the irate General's resignation as head of the Eleventh Army. At the same time, Conrad fired Dankl's staff chief, General Kletus Pichler. But Conrad could no longer dispose of commanders as he had done with such consummate ease in Galicia in 1914. General Krauss dispatched a lengthy treatise on Alpine warfare to the Military Chancery in Vienna, wherein he indirectly lectured Conrad that successful Alpine assaults had to be launched down valleys and not across mountain crests! Worse still, Archduke Karl, the heir to the Habsburg throne who had commanded the XX Corps at the Battle of Asiago, accused Conrad of having failed to take local geography into account in crafting his grand scheme.[83] Most devastating, Conrad learned at the height of the Austro-Hungarian assault on Asiago on 4 June that his eastern front had collapsed before General Brusilov's massive assault.

The French, hard pressed by the Germans at Verdun, twice in the spring of 1916 appealed to Russia for aid. For the last time in the war, Russia sacrificed lustily for France. On 18 March *Stavka* at Mogilev, confident that it enjoyed a numerical superiority of 600 000 to 800 000 men on the northern front, ordered General A. E. Evert to mount a two-pronged attack against Hutier's German XXI Army Corps at Lake Narocz. It was a dismal failure. Evert began the battle with an unprecedented (for the Eastern Front) 2-day heavy artillery barrage but then failed to coordinate field artillery with infantry charges. Almost a foot of water and slush covered the half-frozen lake and Evert's men bogged down. Ten thousand *muzhik* (peasant) soldiers surrendered and as many as 100 000 more became casualties of the campaign; the Germans lost roughly 20 000 men.[84]

Almost unnoticed at the time, Lieutenant-Colonel Georg Bruchmüller introduced the notion of an accurate *Feuerwalze* (creeping barrage) to German operational doctrine. In place of the customary prolonged artillery shelling, which denied the attacker the element of surprise, Bruchmüller surprised the Russians at Lake Narocz with a hurricane-like brief barrage that pitted accurate artillery fire against previously identified targets. Bruchmüller used aerial photographs to select the targets and a 'highly centralized' firing command instructed each battery throughout the barrage.[85]

The key to the 'creeping barrage' was the closeness with which infantry followed it. Once soldiers accepted that there was advantage to be gained by advancing behind a curtain of exploding shells at only 50 yards, their confidence was increased to the point where they willingly followed their leaders into battle. Bruchmüller's objective was not simply to destroy the enemy physically, but rather to suppress his artillery with a mixture of shrapnel, high explosive, and gas fired by heavy guns and howitzers at long range, and to prevent him from moving his reserves by showering them with a similar mix of shells fired by light field guns, howitzers, and mortars.[86]

The French, beleaguered around Fort Vaux, sent another desperate cry for help to St Petersburg. On 11 May the Italians, led by King Victor Emmanuel III and the General Staff, bombarded *Stavka* and Nicholas II with peremptory calls for help in the Tyrol. General Alekseev, the Tsar's chief of staff, appealed to his front commanders to mount an offensive to help the French; most declined to answer the call. Only the fiery new head of the southwestern front, Brusilov, responded positively. Foregoing the usual days-long artillery bombardment as well as painstaking massing of regular and reserve units, Brusilov on 4 June attacked the Austrians along a 200-mile front with 600 000 infantry and 58 000 cavalry troops of the Russian Eighth, Eleventh, Seventh, and Ninth armies. Opposing him, from north to south, were roughly 620 000 soldiers of the Austro-Hungarian Fourth, First, and Second armies; a mixed Austro-Hungarian-German *Südarmee*; and the Habsburg Seventh Army. In fact, two-thirds of all Russian forces – 1400 battalions – still faced Hindenburg's armies in the north. With Conrad's attention riveted on Italy, nominal command of Austro-Hungarian-German forces in the east fell to the German General von Linsingen.

Aleksei Alekseevich Brusilov was probably Imperial Russia's best officer of the Great War. Born at Tiflis in 1853, the son of a noble general, Brusilov spent most of his career with the cavalry. In August 1914 he received command of the Eighth Army in Galicia and in March 1916 replaced the ineffectual Ivanov at the southwestern front. Brusilov proved an imaginative front commander. The old cavalry officer set his staff to pondering ways to end the static slugging match that had come to characterize the war even in the east: he reined in his querulous staff, no mean feat for a Russian army leader in 1916; and he was sufficiently flexible to change the monotonous and predictable rhythm of preceding every infantry charge with massive artillery bombardments. Moreover, Brusilov dug sapper trenches to within 250 yards of enemy lines and concealed his reserves in deep dug-outs (*platsdarmy*). Almost for the first time in the war, Russian armies used aerial photography to identify and target each Austrian artillery battery.[87] Two entire corps of Brusilov's Eighth Army were armed with Austrian rifles captured during the 'autumn swinery' of 1915.

At dawn on 4 June Brusilov launched his four field armies against the enemy units opposite him around Lutsk in the Bukovina. Artillery fire and infantry assaults were coordinated, a rare phenomenon in the Russian Army. Reserves were concentrated (and hidden) at each of the major points of attack, ready to exploit any breakthroughs. Outnumbered by almost 132 000 men at the critical centre of the front, Conrad's position at Ocna crumbled like a pastry shell. By the evening of 4 June, the Russians had overrun the first three lines of trenches and punched a gaping hole 20 miles wide and 5 miles deep into the front of Archduke Joseph Ferdinand's Fourth Army. In 3 days Brusilov took 200 000 prisoners, enough to man two armies.

At first, Conrad was not concerned about what he believed to be a minor breakthrough of his front. He refused to interrupt a 'gala dinner' at Archduke Friedrich's castle at Teschen. After all, 4 June was the Archduke's birthday and Archduchess Isabella ('the real field marshal') was in attendance. Brusilov's advance, Conrad assured his staff, was nothing serious; the Russians would be repelled in quick order. 'At most we will lose a few hundred yards [of] land.'[88]

In rapid order, the First and Fourth armies on the northern flank were rolled up and routed at Volhynia. Pflanzer-Baltin's Seventh Army, which formed the southern flank, was driven out of the Bukovina and hard up against the Carpathian Mountains. Felix von Bothmer's *Südarmee* almost alone stood its ground, but eventually collapsing neighbouring armies forced it to protect its flanks by retreating along the line Brody–Lemberg–Kovel. A furious German counterattack by Linsingen against the northern edge of Lutsk on 16 June finally stabilized Bothmer's position on the Styr River. Brusilov received little or no help from the adjoining two Russian army groups throughout the campaign. In July and August the Russian supply system broke down under the strain of supplying Brusilov's advance, which came to a halt on the Carpathian slopes. Brusilov had lost 1 million men in and around Lutsk.

The disaster at Lutsk was a blow from which the Habsburg Army never recovered. The Austro-Hungarian official history of the war lists losses of 464 382 men and 10 756 officers;[89] more recent estimates set the figures as high as 750 000 soldiers, including 380 000 prisoners. Conrad's failure to recognize the danger and his obsession with Italy tarnished what little lustre still remained to his reputation. Not only had he denuded the east of six infantry divisions for his pet project in Italy, but as late as 1 June had assured Franz Joseph that there was no danger of an attack in the Bukovina. Thereafter, in stark panic, Conrad had sought to evacuate his

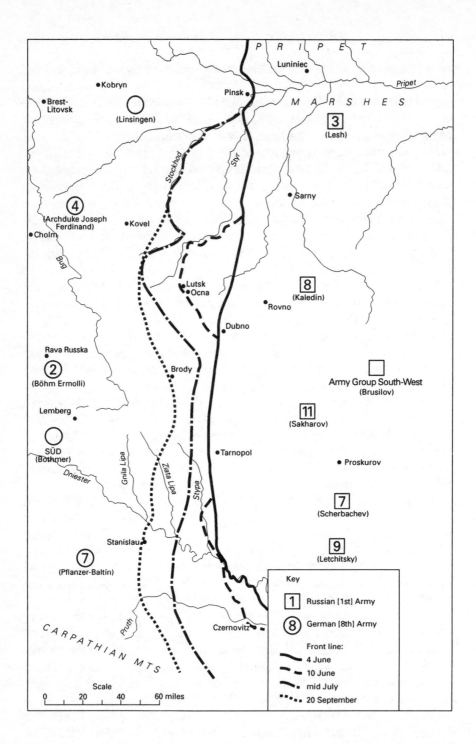

PRIPET

Luniniec

Kobryn

•Brest-
Litovsk

Pinsk

MARSHES

(Linsingen)

3
(Lesh)

Pripet

Stochod

Styr

•Sarny

4
(Archduke Joseph
Ferdinand)

•Kovel

•Cholm

Bug

•Lutsk
•Ocna

8
(Kaledin)

•Rovno

•Dubno

Rava Russka

2
(Böhm Ermolli)

•Brody

Army Group South-West
(Brusilov)

Lemberg

11
(Sakharov)

SÜD
(Bothmer)

Dniester

Gnila Lipa

Zlata Lipa

Stypa

•Tarnopol

•Proskurov

7
(Scherbachev)

Stanislau

9
(Letchitsky)

7
(Pflanzer-Baltin)

Key

1 Russian [1st] Army

8 German [8th] Army

CARPATHIAN MTS

Pruth

Czernovitz

Front line:

4 June

10 June

mid July

20 September

Scale

0   20   40   60 miles

Map 8. *The Brusilov offensive, 1916*

new wife, 'Gina', from Teschen. He lamely informed the Kaiser that he had been 'completely surprised' by the Russian offensive and begged for '10 to 14 days of patience and calm nerves'.[90] Colonel Schneller charged that 'winter sleep, females, hunts, and tennis' had incapacitated Conrad and his staff.[91]

On 8 June a humbled Conrad rushed to Berlin – 'like a bad schoolboy facing the reproaches of his teacher' – and begged Falkenhayn to stabilize the Eastern Front. A week later he wrote to the German that nothing less than 'the decision in the world war' stood in the balance. Falkenhayn finally replied by mobilizing his railway experts. During the first week of July, the General Staff dispatched four divisions from France and five from *OberOst*'s reserve in 494 troop trains as well as 98 artillery trains to Kovel, Cholm, and Vladimir-Volynski to prevent Brusilov from seizing the Carpathian passes. Falkenhayn later added the 11th Bavarian Infantry Division to the relief force. Conrad rushed four divisions from the Italian theatre to the Eastern Front.[92] In the process, he lost the last shred of independence vis-à-vis the German ally. Conrad informed his staff that he would rather receive 'ten slaps in the face' than to have to beg Falkenhayn for help again.[93] Schneller put the situation bluntly on 12 June, the day that General von Seeckt took control of the Seventh Army: 'We are now totally and completely under the thumb of the Germans'.[94] To make matters worse, German troops commanded by General von Woyrsch at the same moment shattered a Russian assault by General Evert's Fourth Army north of the Pripet marshes.

What the Austrians called the Battle of Olyka-Luck along the Sereth River between 4 and 7 June 1916 offers insight into the demise of Habsburg armed forces. At the top of the chain of command, Archduke Joseph Ferdinand, the Kaiser's godson, was an abysmal failure. The Archduke spent much of his time hunting with aristocratic friends, taking boat trips on the Styr, and debauching himself in the company of noble playboys such as his brother, Heinrich, and René Prince of Bourbon-Parma. As a result, he had little time to evaluate valuable military intelligence, which had reported the arrival of new Russian troops, the digging of sapper trenches right up to Austro-Hungarian lines, the building of the *platsdarmy* for the reserves, and the news from deserters that the troops had been issued clean underwear for an attack (which had prompted many to desert).[95]

The Austrians revelled in the glow of supreme confidence, having built an impressive in-depth defensive line in the Bukovina since fall 1915. Three positions of earthworks, reinforced with wood, had been built above ground; the ubiquitous ground water of the Styr River precluded deep trenches as found on the Western Front. Each of the three lines of defences, buttressed by concrete bunkers and enfilading machine-gun positions, gave a sense of safety and invincibility. In short, the Austrians expected Brusilov's attack and were well dug in and prepared to repel it.

Reality proved otherwise. Beginning at dawn on 4 June and lasting through the night, Brusilov subjected his adversary to an artillery 'drum-fire of unequalled intensity', whereafter the Eighth Army from Rovno charged Archduke Joseph Ferdinand's Fourth Army. Concurrently, the Russian Ninth and Seventh armies hit hard against Pflanzer-Baltin's Seventh Army on both sides of the Dniester River. Russian 18 cm heavy howitzers were especially lethal, shattering many of the enemy earthworks and tearing their barbed-wire entanglements to shreds. Close examination revealed that the Austro-Hungarian Army had used the abundant local wood not to reinforce their second and third lines but rather to build lavish officer quarters.[96]

The battle became deadly for the Fourth Army around Olyka-Luck at 6:20 a.m. on 5 June. Heavy smoke and dust whipped up by Russian mortar and artillery shells in the still, hot air obscured the battlefield. An asphyxiating gas swept across Austrian lines. Soldiers of the Russian Eighth Army quickly carried the first line of trenches. By 9:45 a.m. they had thrown part of the Habsburg X Corps back on to its second line. At 10:30 a.m. the Austrian 13th Infantry Division staged a desperate counterattack at Olyka. It was a disaster. Artillery, which had been concentrated between the first and second lines, could not support the attack. In fact, it had been overrun early on in the battle, and most gunners had dashed to the rear to save their lives, leaving the infantry to its fate.

Brusilov steadily pumped his reserves into the battle and mounted a new offensive by 10:45 a.m., and still another at 1:15 p.m. Linsingen warned Austrian commanders not to commit their reserves 'drop by drop', but they refused to heed his sage counsel. Instead, one reserve unit after another was rushed to the front to plug holes ripped into the lines by Brusilov's determined fighters – only to be pinned down in their own dugouts by Russian artillery fire and then taken by infantry charges. The staff of the 13th Division literally was 'blown up by artillery fire'. Staffs of other divisions dispersed and could not be reformed until late afternoon. By 6:35 p.m. the X Corps had fallen back on its third line.

Chaos ensued. The retreat degenerated into a rout.[97] Regiments became lost in the confusion or, as in the case of the Czech 8th Infantry, surrendered to the Russians *en masse*. Thousands of men rushed the pontoon bridges to flee across the Styr. Others impaled themselves on their own wire in the mad dash to escape destruction. Countless others, allegedly mainly Czechs and Ruthenians, ran for the cover of nearby woods. Telephone lines were destroyed, thereby disrupting command

and control on the battlefield. The artillery was separated from its ammunition. Everywhere, men left their equipment and fled the killing ground, in the process exposing the flanks of neighbouring units to Russian attacks. Linsingen lectured Conrad about the 'failure of a decisive leadership' among his armies. On 6 June Conrad relieved Archduke Joseph Ferdinand of command of the Fourth Army – the first time that a Habsburg archduke was dished in the middle of a battle – and replaced him with the Hungarian General Carl von Tersztyánsky. By 9–10 June, however, Brusilov had also caved in the front of Pflanzer-Baltin's Seventh Army. Habsburg forces once more streamed back to the Carpathian Mountains.

Losses were appalling. The Fourth Army was reported 'deeply shaken': it had sustained 71 000 soldiers wounded, lost, or surrendered – 54 per cent of its original strength. One month after the start of Brusilov's offensive, it consisted of a mere 20 000 soldiers organized into five (!) divisions. Pflanzer-Baltin described the Seventh Army, composed mainly of seasoned Hungarian and Croat units, as having been 'ruined': losses amounted to 133 600 men, or 57 per cent of original strength.[98] The 11th and 13th Infantry Divisions were completely shattered; the 24th Infantry Division was reduced from 16 000 soldiers to 3500. Even the toughest corps commanders, such as Alexander von Szurmay, were overrun by the Russians. Conrad estimated that he lost 2400 officers and 204 800 men (including 150 000 prisoners) at Lutsk. Not a single general died in battle.

Military leaders in Vienna attributed the defeat to a failure in the 'lower command posts' and to 'lack of luck'.[99] Conrad liked the phrase and in the Common Council soon spoke of Lutsk as an 'aleatoric moment', one obviously beyond his control.[100] Not surprisingly, Falkenhayn rejected Conrad's incredible suggestion on 18 June that the Central Powers annihilate Russian forces in a giant battle of envelopment east of Lemberg![101] Instead, the *OHL* 4 days later hurled its last 70 000 reserves against Fort Souville at Verdun.

The disaster at Lutsk to all intents and purposes marked the end of Austria–Hungary as a great and independent power. Within 2 weeks, Conrad advised the Ballhausplatz to reach quick agreements with the Germans over war aims and the future division of conquered territories. In July 1916 Archduke Friedrich apprised Foreign Minister Burián of the sad state of military affairs in the east. Raising his original estimate of losses to 300 000 men, the Archduke asserted that 44 German and Austro-Hungarian divisions of 450 000 combatants now faced 57 Russian divisions of 800 000 in Galicia alone. The *k.u.k.* Army was incapable of further offensives. If things remained as they were, the 'simple, mathematical result' would be that the 'inferior numbers [of the Central Powers] would succumb' to the greater Russian numbers.[102] In plain language, the war could no longer be won.

Viennese statesmen spied their chance to move against Conrad. Musulin, the diplomat who had drafted the ultimatum to Serbia in July 1914, warned Burián that the Russians would simply repeat their spring offences year after year, *ad infinitum*, until the Dual Monarchy was ground into the dust. From Berlin, Hohenlohe-Schillingsfürst instructed his government that it no longer had 'the strength to overcome the difficult operation posed by the war'. An 'irresistible fate', the Ambassador suggested, now loomed over the Monarchy; its present leaders had been reduced to 'be gravediggers of the old Austria and to shovel the grave for the new Austria-Hungary'.[103] He warned Burián of the growing dependence on Germany, noting that the Monarchy already owed 2.5 billion Marks in war loans. The diplomat cautioned Vienna that it would be years before an economically recovered Habsburg Empire would possess the 'hobnailed boots' with which it could risk stepping on 'Prussian cuirassier boots'.[104] Burián quietly conceded the accuracy of these reports: 'Once more only German help can save us, our dependence is increasing'.[105]

The deadliest critique came from Conrad's old nemesis, the Foreign Ministry, whose delegate at Teschen, Friedrich von Wiesner, led the charge. In a 'top secret' report to Burián on 25 June Wiesner accused Conrad of lacking 'seriousness, thoroughness, and especially responsibility' in his planning. The Italian campaign had been conducted against the wishes of Franz Joseph and Archduke Eugen, the theatre commander. Campaign after campaign had been based on fantasies and wishful thinking. What Wiesner termed 'the legend of treasonous Bohemian and Ruthenian regiments' was 'pure nonsense'. Conrad had 'lost touch with the troops' due to his ostentatious lifestyle at Teschen, 300 miles removed from the front. Conrad, Wiesner informed the Foreign Ministry, needed to be reined in and placed 'under guardianship' by Viennese authorities.

The most damaging part of Wiesner's brief pertained to Habsburg–Hohenzollern relations.[106] The German General Staff would immediately have to be accorded 'decisive influence' within the alliance. 'Brave but ill-trained' Habsburg forces, Wiesner lectured Burián, could regain their credibility and fighting ability only in 'closest contact' with German units and led and trained by German officers.[107] That Conrad remained in office was due in large part to the fact that there existed no suitable successor.

Wiesner's counsel was neither isolated nor without effect. Hungarian opposition leaders such as Julius Andrássy the Younger, long tired of what they considered to be Conrad's dominance, welcomed the chance to place a German commander over the *AOK*. 'People and army in Hungary would view a supreme command under Hindenburg as salvation.'[108] On 27 July the Field Marshal was given supreme command over the northern part of the Eastern Front: Army Group Leopold of Bavaria, the mixed Austro-German Army Group Linsingen, and the Habsburg Second Army (Böhm-Ermolli). That same day, the Russians crushed Puhallo's First Army; 24 hours later they caved in Tersztyánsky's Fourth Army. The arrival of German units alone prompted Brusilov to call off his attack. Archduke Friedrich, who had been summoned to Pless to witness Hindenburg's elevation, felt that he had been led to the 'butcher's block'. Conrad, who had been surprised by the news while sipping coffee with 'Gina', recoiled at what he termed the creation of a 'Hindenburg front from the Baltic Sea to the Romanian border'.[109] But few in Vienna cared to listen: on 6 September Wilhelm II assumed leadership of an overall 'United Supreme Command' in the east.

Real power, of course, rested with Hindenburg and Ludendorff. In fact, Wilhelm II's main concern during a visit to the Eastern Front was how he could 'supply Japan with ammunition in its war with America'![110] For many officers the Kaiser had become an embarrassment. Major Albrecht von Thaer of the IX Reserve Corps recalled a troop inspection in the summer of 1916. 'His Majesty looked well, was gracious, and spoke generally of world affairs. What he said about the war should better not be repeated. . . . I wonder if His Majesty has any idea what is at stake for him in this war, that it is about sceptre and throne, even for the Hohenzollerns?!'[111]

After September 1916 the only independent Austro-Hungarian unit was Archduke Karl's Army Group – a concession to the dignity of the House of Habsburg – but even there actual command was in the hands of its German chief of staff, Seeckt. Conrad's staff compared the military situation in 1916 to that after the Battle of Solferino in June 1859.[112] The *AOK* was deprived of its broad powers by the debacle at Lutsk – and therewith the Monarchy lost one of its main pillars. In short order, German staff and line officers, a battery or two of German artillery and machine guns, and several Prussian sergeants-major ('corset staves') were inserted into Austro-Hungarian formations to restore their fighting abilities.[113] Conrad begged Vienna in vain not to place Habsburg units under German command.[114] After all, German control would disrupt Habsburg plans to bring Poland into the Empire, prevent Conrad from moving troops to his pet theatre, Italy, and bar Austria–Hungary from concluding a separate peace with Russia – perhaps by the transfer of German Silesia. News that the Austro-Hungarian Fifth Army had lost another 100 000 men between 14 September and 4 November 1916 during the Seventh, Eighth, and Ninth Battles of the Isonzo hardly brightened Conrad's prospects.

The Battle of Lutsk also put an end to the so-called Austro-Polish solution, whereby Austria sought to place Archduke Karl Stephan on the throne of Congress Poland, in return for which Hungary would claim Bosnia–Herzegovina and Dalmatia. The wrangling over Poland's future had become so entangled that wags in Vienna claimed that whichever side lost the war should receive Galicia.[115] But Germany's preeminence within the Berlin–Vienna axis was so great by the fall of 1916 that it simply announced that all former Russian Polish territories would become a German vassal state, with the capital at Lublin. Statesmen in Vienna put the best slant on this by agreeing to a joint declaration on 5 November 1916 calling for the creation of an independent Polish constitutional monarchy. In Berlin Foreign Secretary von Jagow almost alone favoured the Austro-Polish solution as it would protect Germany from a flood of 'Jewish masses' from the east.[116] Ludendorff hoped to raise a million Polish soldiers.[117] More realistic estimates set a target of 15 Polish divisions by the spring of 1917; in fact, about 4700 Poles volunteered at Lublin and Warsaw. Count Burián lamely announced that he was content to annex a few Italian, Romanian, Russian, and Serbian border areas as well as to place an 'independent' Albania under Habsburg protection.[118] Conrad, too weak militarily to resist German pressures for command of the Eastern Front, once more committed his poisonous pen to battle. He informed the Military Chancery that what he called 'Ludendorff Inc.', for which Hindenburg was but the front man, would bring a return to the days of 'Bismarckian disregard' for Austria's vital interests. Ludendorff, Conrad warned Vienna, sought nothing less than 'the Monarchy's subjugation to German rule in the military as well as in the political realm'. The Germans were 'cold, ruthless calculators'; the command agreement was 'superfluous'. The *AOK*'s representatives at *OberOst* agreed that Germans in general and Ludendorff in particular viewed Austria as their 'prize for victory in this war'. Conrad could not resist a favourite barb: the present military misery was a 'consequence of the decades-long neglect of the Army' by politicians and bureaucrats at Budapest and Vienna. He warned that Bethmann Hollweg was anything but the 'disinterested partner' of the Dual Monarchy that he made himself out to be. Instead, the German Chancellor was cut from the same cloth as Ludendorff, whom he now sought to use to shore up his shaky position within Germany. 'Hegemony over the Dual Monarchy' was the goal that both men pursued.[119]

The Military Chancery circulated Conrad's venomous report to Franz Joseph as well as Foreign Minister Burián. The Ballhausplatz had already learned from its representative at Teschen that Conrad continued to preach that 'our only real enemy is still Germany'.[120] News from Italy that Austria-Hungary had suffered 40 000 casualties and lost Görz during the

Sixth Battle of the Isonzo hardly raised Conrad's stock.[121] But Franz Joseph refused to accept Conrad's letter of resignation and instead ordered the Chief of the General Staff to remain at his post.

Lutsk destroyed Conrad's reputation. In September 1916 Ambassador von Tschirschky sent his government a devastating assessment of Conrad's generalship, which Berlin passed on to the other federal states. 'Although General von Conrad develops beautiful theoretical plans, he lacks the forces, the requisite familiarity with actual conditions at the front, and most importantly any and all personal knowledge [of the area] in order to enact the plans.'[122] The Germans were appalled that 60 per cent of Habsburg casualties consisted of deserters – 226 000 by September. Politically, the new unified command under Wilhelm II not only cemented the German ascendancy in the Berlin–Vienna alliance, but also militated against Habsburg political initiatives. Financially, Vienna was indebted to German bankers to the tune of 2.5 billion Marks; borrowing continued at the rate of 100 million Marks per month.

The Romanian detour

Hindenburg and Ludendorff had assumed command at the *OHL* at a time of great crises. The Austro-Hungarian Army had been shattered at Lutsk; the German Fifth Army had been 'bled to death' before Verdun; and the German Second Army had been battered at the Somme. In August 1916 the new men at Supreme Command were confronted with a new crisis: Romania's entry into the war and the creation of yet another front. On 17 August Romania, following Italy's example from the year before, had concluded a secret accord with the Allies whereby London and Paris recognized Bucharest's claims to Transylvania, the Bukovina, and part of the Banat of Temesvár. Austro-Hungarian radio operators had intercepted Bucharest's radio traffic with the Entente as early as 19 August and had passed these intercepts on to an, albeit skeptical, Falkenhayn. Romania declared war on Austria–Hungary on 27 August; Germany declared war on Romania the next day, whereupon Italy extended its war to Germany.

Romania, Hindenburg noted, offered relief from the monotony of trench warfare in the west. 'Let us rejoice that we will once more have an adversary that is not mired down in trench warfare. I do not know today where and how we will defeat him. But I assure you that we will defeat him.'[123] The *OHL* also grasped that the nation needed 'a tactical success' to offset Verdun. And like Prussia's Frederick II before them, Hindenburg and Ludendorff escaped possible destruction because their enemies failed to coordinate their strategies. 'Had Romania started its attack six or only four weeks earlier', the Austrian military historian Rudolf Kiszling claimed, 'a military catastrophe could hardly have been avoided.'[124]

The Russians shifted the 'Brusilov offensive' – as well as almost one-third of their armies – south for the last 3 months of 1916. General A. M. Zaionchkovsky was given three divisions – the so-called Dobruja Detachment – to protect this fertile region along the Black Sea against Bulgarian invasion. Three-fourths of Romania's 623 000 largely illiterate soldiers, organized into 23 infantry and two cavalry divisions of General Constantine Prezan's Fourth and General Alexandru Averescu's Second armies, were concentrated in the north against the Central Powers. On 27 August, 369 000 Romanian soldiers invaded Hungary and immediately seized the old Saxon city of Kronstadt in coveted Transylvania. But General Arthur Arz von Straussenburg, a native of Transylvania, rallied the roughly 30 000 soldiers of his First Army – mainly reservists, Alpine militia, and customs police – and halted the Romanian offensive.[125] On 6 September Hindenburg and Ludendorff appointed Falkenhayn to command a new Ninth Army. Throughout that month German railway experts sent 1500 trains through Hungary – about the same number that Conrad had managed to muster against Russia in August 1914. Within 3 weeks of Romania's declaration of war the *OHL* assembled 200 000 soldiers, half of them German, in Transylvania.

The opposing plans of war were clear. German and Austro-Hungarian forces, nominally under the command of Archduke Karl, ably assisted by General von Seeckt, would first hold and then attack through Transylvania in the north, while Bulgarian units would mount an assault in the undulating corn and wheat fields of the Dobruja along the Black Sea. Oxen and buffalo carts were the only reliable means of transportation. Conrad's grand scheme to envelop Bucharest from Romania's north-western passes was dismissed out of hand as being beyond the capability of forces on the ground. The Romanians, for their part, planned to cross the Danube and invade Bulgaria with a Southern Army Group of 15 divisions under Averescu; at the same time, Zaionchkovsky's composite force of three Russian and six or seven Romanian divisions would drive the Bulgarians out of the Dobruja. Beyond Romania, 14 Anglo-French-Serbian divisions from Salonika in Greece would tie down Field Marshal von Mackensen's seven divisions in Bulgaria, and Russian troops under General Evert would attack Habsburg troops before Kovel in the Ukraine.

Sound in theory, the plan quickly degenerated in practice. The attack from Salonika was a total failure. While French General Sarrail's 'gardeners of Salonika' battled mosquitoes and the pest, an entire Greek army corps surrendered *in toto* and was interned by the Central Powers in Silesia for the remainder of the war. As a result, Mackensen, although outnumbered three-to-one, was free to move against the great Romanian belt fortresses of Turtukai and Silistria on the Danube early in September. Turtukai's commander vowed that the fortress, protected by 15 earthen works, would become Romania's Verdun. Instead, he hoisted the white flag on 6 September – within 1 day of sighting Mackensen. Three generals and 27 000 men of its garrison of 39 000 surrendered and the rest, led by its commander, fled. Both sides lost about 7000 soldiers.[126]

At Kovel, southwest of the Pripet Marshes, Evert throughout August, September, and October mounted one costly attack after another against the Austro-Hungarian Fourth Army, which had barely recovered from its near annihilation at Lutsk that summer. On 28 July three Russian infantry and cavalry divisions routed General von Tersztyánsky's Fourth Army, seizing 15 000 prisoners, and then broke through the front of General Walter von Lüttwitz's X Corps. But Evert, abandoning Brusilov's innovative tactics, with General Alekseev's approval resorted to lengthy bombardments (the 'phalanx' system) that tore up the Stokhod marshes – over which Evert then sent his infantry in waves. German and Austro-Hungarian high-explosive artillery shells, traversing machine-gun fire, and massed rifle fire broke 17 separate charges by the Russian Guards between 1 August and 16 September.[127] The bloated Russian corpses lying by the tens of thousands in the marshes became an effective, if malodorous, barrier for the Central Powers against further enemy attacks.[128]

Nor did the Allies fare better in Romania. Zaionchkovsky quickly despaired of the military quality of his Romanian allies in the Dobruja. Asking them to fight a modern war, he asserted, was like requesting a donkey to dance the minuet. And when Romanian units surrendered to the Russians, believing them to be Bulgarians, what little patience Zaionchkovsky possessed evaporated. His soldiers plundered Romanian wine cellars, laid estates waste, butchered farmers' beasts, and drowned drunken soldiers in vats of burning spirits for much of the campaign. A motley force of German, Bulgarian, Austrian, and Turkish soldiers under Mackensen drove Russo-Romanian forces out of the Dobruja. General Tappen, Mackensen's staff chief, recalled the misery of the advance: 'Bad roads. Large herds of water buffalo, oxen, horses. Many buzzards. Dust, heat. Then tropical rains.'[129] The vital port of Constanza on the Black Sea surrendered intact with its great stores of grain and oil. British agents burned the Romanian oil fields at Ploesti before the town was taken by the Bavarian 12th Infantry Division.

In the north Falkenhayn and Arz von Straussenburg defeated the Romanians first at Herrmannstadt between 26 and 29 September and then at Kronstadt between 7 and 9 October. By the end of October they had recaptured Transylvania. On 11 November Falkenhayn crossed the 6000-feet

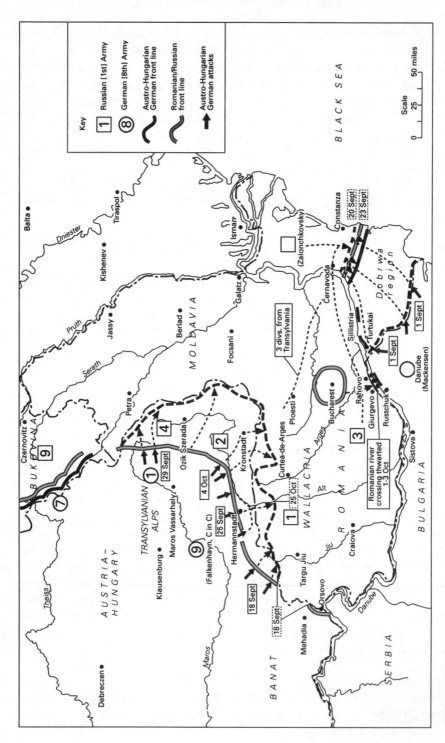

Map 9. The Romanian detour, 1916

Key

1 Russian [1st] Army
8 German [8th] Army
Austro-Hungarian German front line
Romanian/Russian front line
Austro-Hungarian German attacks

Scale
0   25   50 miles

BLACK SEA

Balta

Dniester

Tiraspol

Kishenev

Pruth

Jassy

Sereth

Berlad

Ismar

Galatz

MOLDAVIA

Focsani

(Zaionchkovsky)

Constanza

20 Sept
23 Sept

Cernavoda

D o b r u j a   r e g i o n

Sillistria

Turtukai

1 Sept

1 Sept

1 Sept

3 divs. from Transylvania

Ploesti

Rahovo

Giurgevo

Danube (Mackensen)

Rustchuk

Czernovitz

BUKOVINA

9

7

Petra

4

1

29 Sept

Ozik Szerada

2

4 Oct

Kronstadt

Curtea-de-Arges

Bucharest

3

Romanian river crossing thwarted 1-3 Oct

Sistova

TRANSYLVANIAN ALPS

Klausenburg

Maros Vassarhely

(Falkenhayn, C in C)

9

25 Sept

Hermannstadt

18 Sept

18 Sept

Alt

Arges

1

25 Oct

W A L L A C H I A

Jiu

R O M A N I A

Targu Jiu

Craiova

BULGARIA

Debreczen

A U S T R I A - H U N G A R Y

Theiss

Maros

B A N A T

Mehadia

Orsovo

Danube

S E R B I A

high Transylvanian Alps through the Szurduk Pass near Targu Jiu, just as the first heavy snows came, and then descended onto the Wallachian plains. The harshness of the campaign was recorded by Corporal Friedrich Wörlen, a signal corpsman of 2nd Company, Bavarian Life Guards Infantry Regiment, attached to General Konrad Krafft von Dellmensingen's Alpine Corps. By 6 October Wörlen's unit had reached Red Tower Pass in the Transylvanian Alps. Wind gusts reached 60 miles per hour and bitter cold forced the troops to stay in their tents 'packed like sardines'. Heat from fires filled the tents with smoke. The men ate requisitioned lamb and beans. Two weeks later the Life Guards headed south through Murgaso Pass in wind and snow. Pack animals had to be tied together and led over the pass; others had to be dragged over it with ropes and sleds. Countless horses slipped over steep mountain ledges; others froze to death or died from exhaustion.

For the troops this was a blessing in disguise. Wörlen's company, which had exhausted its meagre supply even of bread, at once built fires and roasted the horse meat in lamb fat. 'It was somewhat tough, but it tasted absolutely delicious. We then took along a few raw chunks to roast on spits the next night. It was very tasty and juicy.' The Bavarians lived off the land for the most part: chicken, geese, hogs, cows, and unleavened bread taken off dead Romanian soldiers. Late in November the Life Guards reached Curtea-de-Arges, site of King Carol's family castle and burial crypt. Bands played and officers sipped champagne. On Christmas Eve 1916 the Bavarians established permanent camp at Bisoca on the Wallachian plain. The company commander gave a Christmas address and led the men in singing *Silent Night*, followed by tea without sugar, and little else. 'We have never had such a miserable Christmas so far from home. There was not even bread.'[130]

The Romanian campaign was decided late in November. The German 109th Infantry Division crossed the Alt River on 26 November; Falkenhayn linked up with Mackensen's forces; and, protected by Austrian Danubian monitors, Mackensen crossed the 1000-yard wide Danube in snow and fog at Sistovo and Belene between 23 and 25 November. Thereafter, German forces headed for Bucharest. In desperation, the French despatched a military mission to Romania headed by General Henri Berthelot, Joffre's chief of staff during the Marne campaign in 1914. Unsurprisingly, Berthelot decided on a 'Balkan Marne': as the Germans advanced against Bucharest, Romanian forces would strike them in the flank at the Arges River. Instead, Falkenhayn and Mackensen defeated General Prezan's new Southern Army Group between 30 November and 6 December.

Romania's peasant soldiers thereupon went home. Of the nation's erstwhile 25 divisions, six had disintegrated, two had been captured, and the rest mustered a mere 90 000 soldiers. In 25 days of combat, Romania had lost 17 000 men killed, 56 000 wounded, 147 000 taken prisoner, and 90 000 missing. The Central Powers had captured 293 000 rifles, 346 machine guns, and 359 artillery pieces.[131] Most of Romania's remaining soldiers, organized into General Averescu's Second Army, withdrew behind the Sereth River into the wild regions of Moldavia. Nearly 40 Russian divisions were rushed south to secure the border. Mackensen entered Bucharest on 6 December. To the Central Powers fell the spoils of conquest: more than a million tons of oil, 2 million tons of grain, 300 000 head of cattle, pigs, and goats, and 200 000 tons of timber.

Vienna was struck by a dark thunderbolt amidst this jubilation: His Imperial and Apostolic Majesty Kaiser Franz Joseph died on 21 November 1916. During his last few months alive, the 86-year-old Emperor had lost all hope of military victory and become resigned simply 'to see if we can last out the winter'.[132] Franz Joseph had been on the throne since 1848, a strong (and perhaps the only) cohesive force in the Dual Monarchy almost by habit and longevity alone. Few Habsburg subjects could remember any other ruler; most remained loyal to his person, if not to his Empire. Those bonds of habit and affection were broken in November 1916.

Chapter 5 Notes

1. Baron von Schoen's report to his government in Munich of 31 August 1915. BHStA, MA 3078 Militärbevollmächtigter Berlin. Hans v. Zwehl, *Erich v. Falkenhayn, General der Infanterie. Eine biographische Studie* (Berlin, E. S. Mittler & Sohn, 1926), is the only biography based on the General's papers, which did not survive the Third Reich and the Second World War.
2. Falkenhayn to Bethmann Hollweg, 29 November 1915. Cited in Reichsarchiv, *Der Weltkrieg 1914 bis 1918*. 10: *Die Operationen des Jahres 1916 bis zum Wechsel in der Obersten Heeresleitung* (Berlin, E. S. Mittler & Sohn, 1936), pp. 1 ff.
3. The memorandum is reproduced in *Der Weltkrieg 1914 bis 1918* 10, pp. 2–16; and Erich von Falkenhayn, *General Headquarters 1914–1916 and its Critical Decisions* (London, Hutchinson, 1919), pp. 209–18. Its originality is closely examined in Holger Afflerbach, *Falkenhayn. Politisches Denken und Handeln im Kaiserreich* (Munich, R. Oldenbourg, 1994), pp. 543–5.
4. Helmut Reichold and Gerhard Granier, eds, *Wild v. Hohenborn. Briefe und Tagebuchaufzeichnungen des preussischen Generals als Kriegsminister und Truppenführer im Ersten Weltkrieg* (Boppard, H. Boldt, 1986), p. 120. Diary entry of 11 December 1915.
5. See *Der Weltkrieg 1914 bis 1918* 10, pp. 72 ff.
6. Cited in Alistair Horne, *The Price of Glory: Verdun 1916* (New York, Penguin, 1962), p. 173.
7. Cited in *Der Weltkrieg 1914 bis 1918* 10, p. 277. Discussion on 26 February 1916.
8. Paul von Hindenburg, *Aus meinem Leben* (Leipzig, Hirzel, 1920), p. 140.
9. The Fifth Army's 10-day casualty reports from 21 February to 10 September list 572 855 men dead, wounded, or missing. Of these, 75 000 were returned to the front from field hospitals, and a further 275 770 from temporary aid stations; hence, the popular figure of

350 000 casualties. How many of the 81 668 'dead and missing' opted to surrender rather than to die in combat will never be known. Official histories were most reluctant to admit the number of men who chose internment over death. See Hermann Wendt, *Verdun 1916. Die Angriffe Falkenhayns im Maasgebiet mit Richtung auf Verdun als strategisches Problem* (Berlin, E. S. Mittler & Sohn, 1941), p. 243.

10. ÖStA-KA, AOK-Akten, vol. 600. Klepsch's report of 14 February 1916 complaining about the Germans who 'nervously keep all their reports secret'. See Peter Broucek, 'Der k.u.k. Delegierte im Deutschen Grossen Hauptquartier Generalmajor Alois Klepsch-Kloth von Roden und seine Berichterstattung 1915/16', *Militärgeschichtliche Mitteilungen* 15 (1974), p. 114.

11. Bethmann's speech to the Reichstag of 28–9 March 1916. BHStA, MA 3080.

12. Walter Görlitz, ed., *The Kaiser and His Court: The Diaries, Note Books and Letters of Admiral Georg Alexander von Müller Chief of the Naval Cabinet, 1914–1918* (New York, Harcourt, Brace & World, 1964), pp. 142–3; Alfred von Tirpitz, *Politische Dokumente. Deutsche Ohnmachtspolitik im Weltkriege* (Hamburg and Berlin, Hanseatische Verlags Anstalt, 1926), pp. 508 ff.

13. See the reports of the Bavarian military envoy to Berlin, Count von Lerchenfeld, of 9 November 1915 in BHStA, MA 3079; and 12 February 1916 in BHStA, MA 3080.

14. This discussion of Verdun owes much to the most recent German account by German Werth, *Verdun. Die Schlacht und der Mythos* (Bergisch-Gladbach, Gustav Lübbe Verlag, 1979).

15. See Hans Linnenkohl, *Vom Einzelschuss zur Feuerwalze. Der Wettlauf zwischen Technik und Taktik im Ersten Weltkrieg* (Koblenz, Bernard und Graefe, 1990).

16. War Ministry memorandum on gas warfare, Spring 1916. BA-MA, PH 2/119.

17. See Werth, *Verdun*, pp. 202–6.

18. Otto Riebicke, *Was brauchte der Weltkrieg? Tatsachen und Zahlen aus dem deutschen Ringen 1914/18* (Berlin, Kyffhäuser-Verlag, 1936), pp. 72–3.

19. See Albrecht von Thaer, *Generalstabsdienst an der Front und in der O. H. L. Aus Briefen und Tagebuchaufzeichnungen 1915–1919*, ed. Siegfried A. Kaehler (Göttingen, Vandenhoeck & Ruprecht, 1958), p. 98. Entry of 16 November 1916.

20. Cited in B. H. Liddell Hart, *The Real War 1914–1918* (Boston, Little, Brown, 1930), p. 218.

21. Liddell Hart, *The Real War*, p. 221.

22. See Horne, *The Price of Glory*, pp. 145–6.

23. *Lehnerts Handbuch für Truppenführer. Kriegsausgabe* (Berlin, E. S. Mittler & Sohn, 1917), p. 197.

24. Ferdinand Otto Miksche, *Vom Kriegsbild* (Stuttgart, Seewald, 1976), p. 98.

25. *Der Weltkrieg 1914 bis 1918* 10, p. 147.

26. Werth, *Verdun*, pp. 196–9.

27. *Der Weltkrieg 1914 bis 1918* 10, p. 186.

28. Werth, *Verdun*, p. 162.

29. Werth, *Verdun*, pp. 116–17. Interestingly, the German official history fails to mention this.

30. Josef Stürgkh, *Im Deutschen Grossen Hauptquartier* (Leipzig, Paul List Verlag, 1921), p. 101. See also Riebicke, *Was brauchte der Weltkrieg?*, p. 130; and Gerhard Ritter, *Der Schlieffenplan. Kritik eines Mythos* (Munich, R. Oldenbourg, 1956), pp. 41 ff.

31. Werth, *Verdun*, pp. 184–5.

32. Cited in Werth, *Verdun*, p. 185.

33. Cited in Werth, *Verdun*, p. 209.

34. Dominik Richert, *Beste Gelegenheit zum Sterben. Meine Erlebnisse im Kriege 1914–1918* eds Angelika Tramitz and Bernd Ulrich (Munich, Knesebeck & Schuler, 1989), pp. 31, 50, 67, 70, 170, 324.

35. Walter Görlitz, ed., *The Kaiser and His Court*, p. 145. Entry for 10 March 1916.

36. Wilhelm Groener, *Lebenserinnerungen. Jugend, Generalstab, Weltkrieg*, ed. Friedrich Baron Hiller von Gaertringen (Göttingen, Vandenhoeck & Ruprecht, 1957), pp. 284, 300, 304.
37. Crown Prince Rupprecht, *Mein Kriegstagebuch*, ed. Eugen von Frauenholz (3 vols, Berlin, Deutscher Nationalverlag, 1929) 1, p. 436.
38. Max von Gallwitz, *Erleben im Westen 1916–1918* (Berlin, E. S. Mittler & Sohn, 1932), p. 19.
39. Cited in Gotthard Breit, *Das Staats- und Gesellschaftsbild deutscher Generale beider Weltkriege im Spiegel ihrer Memoiren* (Boppard, H. Boldt, 1973), p. 71.
40. Count von Lerchenfeld's notes on Hohenborn's address to the Reichstag Budget Commission on 2 October. BHStA, MA 3081.
41. Cited in Reichold and Granier, eds, *Wild v. Hohenborn*, p. 79. Dated 5 August 1916.
42. *Der Weltkrieg 1914 bis 1918* 10, pp. 401–2, 420, 422.
43. In mid-March 1916 Germany possessed only 48 submarines; of these, a mere 29 were in west European waters. See *Der Weltkrieg 1914 bis 1918* 10, pp. 291–309.
44. *Der Weltkrieg 1914 bis 1918* 10, pp. 644 ff.
45. *Der Weltkrieg 1914 bis 1918* 10, p. 560; Karl Heinz Janssen, 'Der Wechsel in der Obersten Heeresleitung 1916', *Vierteljahrshefte für Zeitgeschichte* 7 (1959), p. 539.
46. Crown Prince Rupprecht, *Kriegstagebuch* 1, p. 520.
47. See Afflerbach, *Falkenhayn*, pp. 443–4.
48. Cited in Gerhard Ritter, *Staatskunst und Kriegshandwerk. Das Problem des 'Militarismus' in Deutschland* (4 vols, Munich, R. Oldenbourg, 1964) 3, p. 227.
49. Cited in Janssen, 'Der Wechsel in der Obersten Heeresleitung', p. 371.
50. Afflerbach, *Falkenhayn*, pp. 451–6.
51. Reichsarchiv, *Schlachten des Weltkrieges 1914–1918* 15 (Berlin, Verlag Gerhard Stalling, 1927), p. 200.
52. Kurt Riezler, *Tagebücher, Aufsätze, Dokumente*, ed. Karl Dietrich Erdmann (Göttingen, Vandenhoeck & Ruprecht, 1972), p. 360.
53. Ernst Toller, *Gesammelte Werke* (5 vols, Munich, Hanser, 1978) 4, p. 72.
54. Crown Prince Wilhelm, *Meine Erinnerungen aus Deutschlands Heldenkampf* (Berlin, E. S. Mittler & Sohn, 1923), p. 218.
55. Max Domarus, ed., *Hitler. Reden und Proklamationen 1932–1945* (4 vols, Munich, Süddeutscher Verlag, 1965) 4, p. 1933.
56. Michael Geyer, 'German Strategy in the Age of Machine Warfare, 1914–1945', in Peter Paret, ed., *Makers of Modern Strategy from Machiavelli to the Nuclear Age* (Princeton, Princeton University Press, 1986), p. 536.
57. *Der Weltkrieg 1914 bis 1918* 10, pp. 344–5.
58. *Der Weltkrieg 1914 bis 1918* 10, pp. 349 ff.; and Martin Middlebrook, *The First Day on the Somme: 1 July 1916* (London, Penguin, 1972), pp. 122 ff.
59. Middlebrook, *First Day on the Somme*, pp. 69–73.
60. Middlebrook, *First Day on the Somme*, p. 189. See also Tim Travers, 'The Somme July 1, 1916: The Reason Why', *MHQ: The Quarterly Journal of Military History* 7 (1995), pp. 63–73.
61. *Der Weltkrieg 1914 bis 1918* 10, p. 355.
62. See Reichsarchiv, *Der Weltkrieg 1914 bis 1918. 11: Die Kriegführung im Herbst 1916 und im Winter 1916/17* (Berlin, E. S. Mittler & Sohn, 1938), pp. 68–9. The tanks were divided into 'males' (with two cannons and three machine guns) and 'females' (with only five machine guns).
63. Thaer, *Generalstabsdienst*, pp. 80, 86, 92. Diary entries of 2 and 24 August and 13 October 1916.
64. *Der Weltkrieg 1914 bis 1918* 10, p. 383. In 1918 Goltz spearheaded the German move into Finland; after the war, he continued to command German Free Corps units in the Baltic states.

65. BA-MA, MSg 2/4537 Tagebuch Schulin, p. 60.
66. Liddell Hart, *The Real War*, p. 226.
67. Ritter to Hermann Witte, 16 May 1917. Klaus Schwabe and Rolf Reichardt, eds, *Gerhard Ritter. Ein politischer Historiker in seinen Briefen* (Boppard, H. Boldt, 1984), pp. 202–3.
68. Bundesministerium für Landesverteidigung, *Österreich-Ungarns Letzter Krieg 1914–1918*. 4, *Das Kriegsjahr 1916* (Vienna, Verlag der Militärwissenschaftlichen Mitteilungen, 1933), pp. 86–7.
69. Conrad's comment at a ministerial council at Schönbrunn, 8 March 1915. ÖStA-KA, Conrad Archiv, A Nachlass Conrad, vol. 6. See also Hans Jürgen Pantenius, *Der Angriffsgedanke gegen Italien bei Conrad von Hötzendorf. Ein Beitrag zur Koalitionskriegsführung im Ersten Weltkrieg* (2 vols, Cologne and Vienna, Böhlau, 1984).
70. Cited in Afflerbach, *Falkenhayn*, p. 355. Dated 5 March 1916. Conrad used the German term '*Hunde von Katzelmachern*'.
71. Falkenhayn, *General Headquarters*, pp. 246–7.
72. BA-MA, MSg 1/2517 Tagebuch Kageneck. Entry for 27 April 1916.
73. ÖStA-KA, Nachlass Schneller, B/509, vol. 2. Entry for 28 February 1916.
74. *Der Weltkrieg 1914 bis 1918* 10, p. 303.
75. *Der Weltkrieg 1914 bis 1918* 10, p. 574.
76. Manfried Rauchensteiner, *Der Tod des Doppeladlers. Österreich-Ungarn und der Erste Weltkrieg* (Graz, Vienna, and Cologne, Verlag Styria, 1994), p. 330.
77. *Österreich-Ungarns Letzter Krieg 1914–1918* 4, pp. 194–5.
78. ÖStA-KA, Nachlass Schneller, B/509, vol. 2. Entry dated 29 March 1916.
79. Stürgkh, *Im Deutschen Grossen Hauptquartier*, p. 130.
80. Archduke Friedrich to General von Bolfras, 31 May 1916. ÖStA-KA, MKSM 25–1/4.
81. *Der Weltkrieg 1914 bis 1918* 10, pp. 585–6.
82. *Österreich-Ungarns Letzter Krieg 1914–1918* 4, p. 348.
83. See Gunther E. Rothenberg, *The Army of Francis Joseph* (West Lafayette, Ind., Purdue University Press, 1976), p. 195.
84. *Der Weltkrieg 1914 bis 1918* 10, p. 437. He quickly earned the sobriquet 'Breakthrough Müller' (*Durchbruchmüller*).
85. See David T. Zabecki, *Steel Wind: Colonel Georg Bruchmüller and the Birth of Modern Artillery* (Westport, Praeger, 1994).
86. Bruce I. Gudmundsson, *Stormtroop Tactics: Innovation in the German Army, 1914–1918* (New York, Westport, and London, Praeger, 1989), pp. 113–14.
87. See Holger H. Herwig and Neil M. Heyman, eds, *Biographical Dictionary of World War I* (Westport, Conn., and London, Greenwood Press, 1982), pp. 100–1; and *Österreich-Ungarns Letzter Krieg 1914–1918* 4, pp. 365-6.
88. ÖStA-KA, Nachlass Schneller, B/509, vol. 2, entry of 4 June 1916.
89. *Österreich-Ungarns Letzter Krieg 1914–1918* 4, p. 663.
90. *Österreich-Ungarns Letzter Krieg 1914–1918* 4, p. 485. German headquarters was outraged by the marriage. 'A scandal! In such dire times such stupidity at age 61'. BA-MA, W-10/50656 Tagebuch v. Plessen, entry dated 18 September 1915.
91. ÖStA-KA, Nachlass Schneller, B/509, vol. 2. Entry dated 8 June 1916.
92. *Österreich-Ungarns Letzter Krieg 1914–1918* 4, p. 439.
93. BA-MA, MSg 1/2517 Tagebuch Kageneck. Entry of 19 July 1916.
94. ÖStA-KA, Nachlass Schneller, B/509, vol. 2.
95. Norman Stone, *The Eastern Front 1914–1917* (New York, Charles Scribner's Sons, 1975), p. 241.
96. Wilhelm Czermak, *In deinem Lager war Österreich. Die österreichisch-ungarische Armee, wie man sie nicht kennt* (Breslau,W. G. Korn, 1938), p. 91.
97. See *Österreich-Ungarns Letzter Krieg 1914–1918* 4, pp. 375–8, 382–94, 410–15.

98. *Österreich-Ungarns Letzter Krieg 1914–1918* 4, p. 464.
99. Archduke Friedrich's after-action report to Kaiser Franz Joseph, 21 June 1916, ÖStA-KA, MKSM 1916, 69-4/20-4; and analysis of the Battle of Lutsk by General Otto Berndt, chief of staff of the Fourth Army, for Archduke Friedrich, 26 November 1916, ÖStA-KA, MKSM 69–6/37.
100. *Protokolle des Geheimen Ministerrates der Österreichisch-Ungarischen Monarchie (1914–1918)*, ed. Miklós Komjáthy (Budapest, Akadémiai Kiadó, 1966) p. 454. Entry for 22 January 1917.
101. *Österreich-Ungarns Letzter Krieg 1914–1918* 4, pp. 518, 520.
102. Archduke Friedrich to Count Burián, 8 July 1916. ÖStA-KA, MKSM 1916, 69–6 /23–4.
103. Cited in Gary W. Shanafelt, *The Secret Enemy: Austria-Hungary and the German Alliance, 1914–1918* (New York, Columbia University Press, 1985), p. 87.
104. HHStA, PA III Preussen Berichte, vol. 172. Report of 13 September 1916.
105. Cited in József Galántai, *Hungary in the First World War* (Budapest, Akadémiai Kiadó, 1989), p. 189.
106. See especially Rudolf Jeřábek, 'Die Brussilowoffensive 1916. Ein Wendepunkt der Koalitionskriegsführung der Mittelmächte', 2 vols, unpubl. diss., Vienna University 1982.
107. HHStA, PA I/1499 Krieg geh. XLVII/17, vol. 499.
108. Cited in Karl-Heinz Janssen, *Der Kanzler und der General. Die Führungskrise um Bethmann Hollweg und Falkenhayn (1914–1916)* (Göttingen, Musterschmidt, 1966), p. 231.
109. Oskar Regele, *Feldmarschall Conrad. Auftrag und Erfüllung 1906–1918* (Vienna and Munich, Verlag Herold, 1955), p. 283.
110. BA-MA, MSg 1/2517 Tagebuch Kageneck. Entry of 6 December 1916.
111. Thaer, *Generalstabsdienst*, p. 69. Entry of 15 June 1916.
112. *Österreich-Ungarns Letzter Krieg 1914–1918* 4, p. 563.
113. Bundesministerium für Landesverteidigung, *Österreich-Ungarns Letzter Krieg 1914–1918. 5: Das Kriegsjahr 1916* (Vienna, Verlag der Militärwissenschaftlichen Mitteilungen, 1934), p. 219.
114. See Conrad to Bolfras, 8 November 1916. ÖStA-KA, MKSM 1916, 69–23/3.
115. Fritz Fellner, ed., *Schicksalsjahre Österreichs 1908–1919. Das politische Tagebuch Josef Redlichs* (2 vols, Graz and Cologne, Hermann Böhlaus Nachf., 1953–54) 2, p. 7.
116. Jagow's memorandum of 2 September 1915. *L'Allemagne et les problèmes de la paix pendant la première guerre mondiale. Documents extraits des archives de l'Office allemand des Affaires étrangères,* eds André Scherer and Jacques Grunewald (4 vols, Paris, Presses Universitaires de France, 1962–78) 1, pp. 174–6.
117. See Fritz Fischer, *Griff nach der Weltmacht. Die Kriegszielpolitik des kaiserlichen Deutschland 1914/18* (Düsseldorf, Droste Verlag, 1962), pp. 288–300, 340–3.
118. HHStA, PA I 536, Botschaftsarchiv Berlin. Burián's notes of November 1916.
119. Conrad to Bolfras, 14 October 1916. ÖStA-KA, MKSM 1–3/200.
120. Cited in Galántai, *Hungary in the First World War*, p. 189.
121. *Österreich-Ungarns Letzter Krieg 1914–1918* 5, p. 102.
122. Count von Lerchenfeld's report of 9 September 1916 to his government at Munich. BHStA, MA 3081.
123. A[ugust] von Cramon and Paul Fleck, *Deutschlands Schicksalsbund mit Österreich-Ungarn. Von Conrad von Hötzendorf zu Kaiser Karl* (Berlin, Verlag für Kulturpolitik, 1932), p. 149.
124. Rudolf Kiszling, *Österreich-Ungarns Anteil am Ersten Weltkrieg* (Graz, Stiasny Verlag, 1958), pp. 50–1.
125. *Österreich-Ungarns Letzter Krieg 1914–1918* 5, pp. 246, 298–311.
126. *Österreich-Ungarns Letzter Krieg 1914–1918* 5, p. 275; *Der Weltkrieg 1914 bis 1918*

11, p. 204. A good account remains Ernst Kabisch, *Der Rumänienkrieg 1916* (Berlin, O. Schlegel, 1938).

127. *Der Weltkrieg 1914 bis 1918* 10, pp. 543–6.

128. Stone, *The Eastern Front*, pp. 271–2.

129. BA-MA, W-10/50661. Kriegserinnerungen v. Tappen. Diary entry of 10 September 1916.

130. BHStA-KA, HS 2156. Kriegstagebuch von Friedrich Wörlen.

131. *Österreich-Ungarns Letzter Krieg 1914–1918* 5, pp. 625–6; *Der Weltkrieg 1914 bis 1918* 11, p. 306.

132. Cited in Albert von Margutti, *Kaiser Franz Joseph: Persönliche Erinnerungen* (Vienna, Manz'sche Verlags- und Universitätsbuchhandlung, 1924), p. 458.

6

The Long-War Reality, 1915–16

A strategy of attrition will not do if the maintenance of millions [of men] requires billions [of Marks].

Alfred von Schlieffen, January 1909

Christmas 1915 brought little joy. The lavish food parcels of 1914 were noticeably absent at the front. Department-store packages contained harmonicas rather than food and the only luxury in the trenches was at best a small barrel of beer donated by the regimental commander. Soldiers home on leave also noted more spartan fare. Christmas trees were too expensive for most and thus graced few homes. In Stuttgart bakers produced only two modest forms of Christmas cake, while in Berlin a mayoral decree forbade fruit cakes. Pancakes and fritters (*Berliner*) fell victim to the fat shortage. Since Christmas Eve came on a Friday, a 'meatless' day, restaurants could offer only vegetarian dishes. Even traditionally festive Christmas Markets took on sad appearances: artificial flowers replaced chocolates and gingerbread while 'Hindenburg' vases and 'Mackensen' cups substituted for wooden toys and tree ornaments.[1]

Evelyn Princess Blücher caught the mood of Christmas 1915 in her diary. Berlin for weeks had been 'enveloped in an impenetrable veil of sadness, grey in grey', an appropriate setting for the 'white-faced, black-robed women who glide so sadly through the streets'. Some bore their sorrow proudly, 'as a crown to their lives', while others seemed 'bent and broken under a burden too heavy to be borne'.[2]

Gertrud Bäumer, head of the Federation of German Women's Associations, reduced the numbing effect of the cold killing statistics to human dimensions. She recalled the Christmas season of 1915 in Stuttgart vividly. A military band, playing Chopin's sombre funeral march, escorted a military cortege through the town. At the city limits, the coffin was transferred to a simple farmer's cart drawn by two draft animals; beside the animals stood a farmer and a young boy, both brushing tears from their eyes. Thus they led home the son who had died for Kaiser and King.[3]

Nor did the new year bring better cheer. In Austria–Hungary Franz Joseph had departed and little was known about his grand-nephew and successor, Kaiser Karl Franz Joseph I in Austria and King Karl IV in Hungary. The young man had not been included in the inner circles of decision-making before his accession to the throne and hence had a great deal to learn. Unfortunately, Karl brought to the throne a strange combination of idealism, inexperience, obstinacy, and personal prejudices; he was 'volatile, lacking in balance and experience, and strangely unable to make and stick with decisions'.[4] Karl's overall programme was to seek an end to the war, to consolidate the Monarchy by way of internal reforms, and to shake off German suzerainty. His well-intended but ill-conceived decision to pardon several political traitors, his unwillingness to swear to the Austrian constitution, and his refusal to receive the sacred crown of St Stephen from the hands of the Calvinist Hungarian Prime Minister Tisza hardly augured well for the future.

Militarily, Conrad von Hötzendorf's *Strafexpedition* against Italy had bogged down along the Isonzo, and in the east General Brusilov's break-through offensive at Lutsk had shattered what remained of the old Imperial and Royal Army. More and more, German 'corset staves' not only shored up the Army but increasingly meant German control over it. Food and fuel shortages dominated the home front; enhanced war production translated into ever scarcer consumer goods; and few families remained untouched by the ongoing carnage at the fronts.

In Germany Falkenhayn had yielded to Hindenburg and Ludendorff after Verdun. It was more than a mere change in personnel. A new spirit and a new concept of the war dominated the *OHL*. Ludendorff, with Hindenburg in tow, sought through a 'strategy of annihilation' to bring the war to a victorious end and to force his adversaries to sign a peace that included monetary indemnities and vast territorial annexations. Assured of almost universal popular support, the military duumvirate could dictate policy to the government, knowing that neither the Chancellor nor the Kaiser could afford to arouse their ire.

The German Army desperately needed a period of calm to refit and regroup. The new men at the *OHL* thus decided to straighten out the Western Front by withdrawing from advanced salients and by construct-ing massive defensive fortifications, soon to be known as the Hindenburg (or Siegfried) Line. They then took a hard look at two operational options: retraining the Army along the lines of Captain Rohr's *Sturmbataillonen* and unrestricted submarine warfare. Above all, Hindenburg and Ludendorff sought to gear the German economy wholly toward war production so as to allow the Reich to conduct 'total war' by 1917–18. Victory could only come by better war management, greater production, and escalated fighting.

Wartime economic policy, in the words of Bertrand Russell, became 'maximum slaughter at minimum expense'.[5] In short, Imperial Germany staked its survival on operational effectiveness: more arms and more men to fight more battles. But would its Habsburg ally be able to survive the disasters of 1914–16?

Austria–Hungary: on the brink

The peacetime Imperial and Royal Army had been destroyed on the battlefields of Galicia, the Bukovina, the Carpathian Mountains, and along the Isonzo River. In March 1916 Conrad apprised the Military Chancery that he commanded but a 'militia army'. On paper, things looked good: 30 000 officers and 2.3 million men, 700 000 horses and 40 000 cavalry, and 4500 field guns as well as 3000 machine guns. But the active fighting force had shrunk to less than 900 000 combatants, many of whom were poorly equipped, ill fed, and badly led. Losses between August 1914 and the end of 1915 had been staggering: 10 238 officers and 377 022 men killed; 22 503 officers and 978 423 men wounded; 30 372 officers and 853 379 men sick; and 11 642 officers and 906 379 men missing or prisoners of war. Total casualties stood at 74 755 officers and 3 115 203 men. Taking into account soldiers who had recovered from wounds and been returned to the Army, Conrad still came up with net losses of 37 062 officers and 2 082 649 men.[6]

The financial cost of the war was hard to pin down. When Foreign Minister Burián in April 1915 demanded to know what the Germans were spending on the war, Ambassador zu Hohenlohe-Schillingsfürst replied that Berlin was unable to present him with an accurate financial picture. Rough estimates from the Imperial Treasury suggested that the Reich had spent 10 billion Marks on the Army and 500 million Marks on the Navy for the first 8 months of the war. When Burián pressed his own Finance Ministry for an estimate, he was informed that Vienna had laid out 7143 million Kronen on the Army and 60 million Kronen on the Navy during the same period. However, Finance Minister von Biliński reported that roughly 395 million Kronen—about two-thirds of the last peacetime defence budget – had been tucked away in the Monarchy's so-called 'regular' budget.[7] Germany estimated that Austria–Hungary had spent 20 to 22 billion Kronen (16 billion Marks) on the war between August 1914 and December 1915.[8] Much of the money was raised in two war bond drives in the fall of 1914 (2.2 billion Kronen) and May 1915 (2.6 billion Kronen); the rest was covered by monthly German subsidies of 100 million Marks. War bonds were bought two-thirds by Austrians and one-third by Hungarians. Viennese ruling circles expected that they would be liquidated by indemnities and reparations.

To finance the war, Austria–Hungary relied on modest customs receipts, government war bonds, loans from Germany, and currency inflation. Tax increases were slight and public borrowing covered about 45 per cent of military expenditures. Like the Confederacy during the American Civil War, the Dual Monarchy bridged the growing gap between income and outlay by printing ever more paper money. This artificially stimulated the economy, engendered higher prices, and eroded 'hard' capital.[9] The Krone fell 40 per cent on the New York money market and 50 per cent on the Zurich exchange by the end of 1915.

But money mattered little to the generals who fought the war. They left it up to the politicians to secure capital and instead concentrated on war-industries production. Hindenburg and Ludendorff set the pace and in the fall of 1916 informed the *AOK* that Germany had created 33 new divisions that summer alone. Each division was now provided with nine batteries of artillery, each infantry battalion with six heavy machine guns and four light howitzers, and each German company with six light machine guns and two trench mortars.[10] How well, they wanted to know, was Teschen doing in this regard?

Conrad lamely replied that he had formed 24 new infantry divisions of four regiments each since August 1914, and that he was adding 200 000 men (75 per cent new recruits, 25 per cent convalescents) per month to the Army. Therewith, Conrad lectured Hindenburg, 'the Monarchy's [war] capacities had been stretched to their limits'. All available men between the ages of 18 and 50 had been drafted; no new formations were envisaged. (In reality, 75 per cent of all eligible males were drafted by the *end* of 1916; about 1.2 million draft-eligible men remained mainly in war industries at home while 400 000 soldiers had been removed from the front and assigned to war-related industries.[11]) With regard to material, Conrad stated that the Dual Monarchy had also reached its limits. The number of Schwarzlose 07/12 machine guns per battalion had been doubled to four; air companies had been increased from 11 to 35; and ammunition output stood at 3.5 million bullets and 60 000 artillery shells per month.[12] The Steyr-Mannlicher rifle M 95 remained standard.

Given the unprecedented scale of the Dual Monarchy's war effort, Conrad throughout 1915 and 1916 sought to tighten the Army's grip on both manpower and material reserves under the umbrella of the War Supervisory Office. Convinced that civilian authorities in Vienna were far too lenient in dealing with subversive actions and attitudes, Conrad wanted the military to police border areas, to control the schools and their curricula, and to purge the bureaucracy of suspected unreliable elements.

Conrad had reason to be concerned. Desertions and acts of treason, fuelled by repeated defeats, had increased dramatically. In June 1915 Conrad revived an ancient law, abolished in 1803, that allowed the state to seize the property of deserters and traitors and to use this collateral to cover courts-martial costs and damages. In Hungary the state simply seized the property of deserters. At the urging of Böhm-Ermolli, commander of the Second Army, Conrad used the money secured in this manner to establish a fund for widows of veterans as well as sick and wounded soldiers. But he could do little more. Politicians in Budapest and Vienna could not even agree that deserters and traitors deserved to lose their citizenship for fear that this would remove them from the draft lists! The *AOK* bitterly noted that while criminals caught and tried during the war were sentenced to death, deserters repatriated after the war would be liable to no more than 5 years incarceration.[13]

In November 1915 the Army tackled the thorny issue of a common language (*Staatssprache*). Commanders on the southwestern front argued that enforced use of German alone could combat what they termed Italian linguistic 'irredentism'. The *AOK* readily agreed – as did the Ministries of Justice, War, and the Interior – but Prime Minister Stürgkh was far too cautious to chance open discussion of such a politically suicidal issue.[14]

The *AOK* demanded that all frontier areas come under direct military rule. Specifically, on 10 November Conrad requested that a 15-mile zone be established along the borders with Russia, Romania, Serbia, Montenegro, and Italy, and that resident 'foreigners' and politically unreliable inhabitants be removed forcefully. The lands thus depopulated could be settled with invalids and veterans. Conrad's scheme resembled the old 'military border' that the Monarchy had maintained against the Turks in Slovenia, Croatia, and Transylvania. While Interior Minister Konrad Prince Hohenlohe-Schillingsfürst was enthusiastic about the proposal, Hungary vetoed it with the same argument used in 1869 to abolish the 'military border': it was not in Budapest's interest, Tisza declared, to create a new 'black-yellow Institute for Germanization' in the Empire.[15]

More realistically, in October 1915 Conrad in three separate notes addressed the issue of food conditions both at home and at the front. Rationing had led to skyrocketing prices which, in the *AOK*'s view, the government had failed to curb. As a result, morale had plummeted at home as well as in the trenches; countless troops expressed concern about the economic plight of their families. Discipline suffered as soldiers were less willing to risk life and limb for the Monarchy. Conrad demanded that the Army be allowed to oversee the distribution of bread and other food-stuffs in the large industrial centres.

But Vienna was reluctant to allow Conrad greater influence in political affairs. Stürgkh and Hohenlohe-Schillingsfürst informed Conrad in December 1915 that while they were sympathetic to his argument, they could not allow the *AOK* to expand its control over civilian populations. The government's brief, penned by Johann von Eichhoff, Interior's dele-gate to Teschen, concluded that military supervision of the food supply would only complicate the process. Conrad next sought to increase the rations and pay for miners and factory workers in Austrian Silesia and Moravia, but this time did not even receive a reply from Vienna. The General had to be content with accusing the government of bowing to the special interests of big business.[16] Vienna's reluctance to address the dete-riorating food supply was politically motivated: since Hungary supplied the 10 000 freight cars of wheat required to feed the Army as well as the 45 000 tons of green feed (oats and barley) for its horses, public debate over the food supply could only mean greater political clout for Tisza and the Magyars.

Given Conrad's well-known penchant for exaggerating negative situa-tions in official memoranda, the question of accuracy arises. For once Conrad cannot be accused of hyperbole. Shortly before leaving Vienna at the end of September 1916, Ambassador von Tschirschky sent Berlin a sobering analysis of the Viennese ally. 'The longer the war lasts', he stated, 'the more acute becomes the anxious question of how much longer the Austro-Hungarian Monarchy will be able to endure the struggle, eco-nomically as well as militarily'. Manpower reserves had been exhausted, morale was low, and complaints against the officer corps universal. Budapest and Vienna worked at cross-purposes. Economic conditions were 'simply wretched'. Finances were on the brink of collapse. Attempts to mobilize the economy for war had foundered on political infighting, corruption, favouritism, and the renowned Austrian *Schlamperei* (care-lessness). Bethmann Hollweg passed the report on to Wilhelm II with the tart comment: 'I am afraid that Herr von Tschirschky does not paint too blackly'.[17]

Conrad's basic problem was that he attempted to conduct what he termed a 'war of factories' with inadequate tools. On paper the Empire of nearly 51 million people and industrial strongholds in Bohemia and Moravia as well as Austria and Hungary should have been able to field

5 million combatants with ease and to mount a creditable war-production effort. But, as previously stated, Austria–Hungary for political reasons before 1914 had neither exploited its manpower reserves for military training nor tapped its tax base for military procurement. Traditional and deeply entrenched inertia by both the Crown and the imperial and royal bureaucracy militated against mobilization of men and material for fear that reform could usher in the long-expected demise of the Dual Monarchy. While Austrians and Hungarians eyed each other with suspicion over every Krone spent and wrangled over every ton of grain or coal produced, Czechs and Poles, Ruthenians and Romanians, Croats and Serbs, Slovenes and Slovaks, Italians and Moslem Slavs increasingly questioned their commitment to the Empire. Any attempt to put 51 million subjects on a 'total war' footing, bureaucrats in Budapest and Vienna agreed, was out of the question. And yet the war demanded ever greater amounts of blood and treasure.

Conrad's most pressing concern was manpower: Austro-Hungarian regiments of about 6000 men required each one battalion-strength reinforcement of 1000 men per month in 1914–15. The Army set a target of 2.2 million new soldiers and looked for means to reach it. Convalescents were a ready source as were officers still in administrative posts at home or in rear echelons. Conrad quickly rounded up 34 000 officers and 938 000 men in this manner, and in May 1916 – seven months ahead of schedule – called to the colours the cohort of males born in 1898, thus bringing 1.4 million replacements to the Army. Roughly 953 000 draft-eligible soldiers in war industries remained untouchable as their departure would jeopardize armaments production. Additionally, 13 million agricultural workers were deemed critical for the food supply and remained exempt from the draft – as did countless finance officials, ships' crews, communications employees, border police, and miners. More than 45 000 civilians as well as 301 000 prisoners of war already served at the front in logistical areas. Each year the Army had to release almost 800 000 soldiers to assist farmers during planting and harvesting. Still, Conrad managed to stock divisions with between 8000 and 10 000 men each.[18]

This was the last reserve – until the cohort of 1899 could be called up. The recruitment screw had been turned about as tightly as it could. Service in the *Landsturm* had been extended to all males between the ages of 18 and 50; noncommissioned officers with educational background and combat medals had been promoted to the rank of lieutenant under special decrees called *Sabelchargenerlässe*; artillery as well as supply and medical officers had been reassigned to the infantry in large numbers; and cavalry had been dismounted.

But the demand for soldiers continued unabated. Conrad finally executed a number of *Austauschaktionen* (exchange actions) whereby about 90 000 elderly soldiers were sent home annually in 1915, 1916, and 1917 and replaced by 6600 officers and 368 000 men previously spared or exempted from front-line service.[19] Teachers were deemed excellent non-commissioned officer material and trained for combat; their places in the schools were taken by invalids. Bureaucrats in the administrative and legal branches likewise were sent to the front in exchange for wounded veterans. Soldiers previously declared invalided or somehow 'unfit' for service were reexamined by military doctors and often reclassified 'fit' for duty. And the Army ordered all cadets and subaltern officers (lieutenants and captains) employed in rear-area training depots to report to the front.[20]

While the *Austauschaktionen* brought quantitative relief they did not always meet qualitative expectations. Lieutenant-Colonel Gustav Zieritz of the 5th Infantry Division was but one of many front-line officers who complained to the War Ministry about the quality of the new troops. He described their condition as 'inferior' because the Army had lowered its physical standards and because the men were 'elderly, undernourished, at other times also very young'. Food rations at training centres were so poor as to prohibit rigorous physical exercise, and the policy of granting the men leave during the planting and harvesting seasons 'disrupts their training and is deleterious for the maintenance of discipline'. Instructors by and large were of 'inferior calibre'. As a result, the men were often sent to the front with what Zieritz described as 'inadequate training'.[21] And whereas infantry regiments before 1914 had equal numbers of regular and reserve officers, by 1916 the latter outnumbered the former by factors of five and six.

Given that the majority of Hungarians worked as draft-eligible land labourers who could be replaced by Russian prisoners of war and that a far greater proportion of Austrians worked as draft-exempt industrial labourers who possessed special skills not found in most POWs, it is hardly surprising that a bitter quarrel over recruitment broke out between Budapest and Vienna. As early as September 1915, Prime Minister Tisza complained about the 'great disproportion . . . between Austria and Hungary regarding the burdens of war'. Specifically, Hungary with 40.95 per cent of the Monarchy's population supplied 43.43 per cent of the Army's soldiers. Thus a 'great disparity' of 3.58 per cent existed and Tisza demanded that Vienna immediately call 384 598 Austrians to the colours to equalize recruitment. Austrian Prime Minister Stürgkh pointedly countered that 26.6 per cent of Austria's peacetime territory, which included 1.5 million men of draft-eligible age in Galicia and the Bukovina, was currently occupied by Russia.[22] This haggling over body counts did little to improve either morale or fighting effectiveness.

Despite his personal distaste for the Germans, Conrad realized that he stood to benefit from their revised infantry tactics. The *OHL* agreed and by 1915–16 officers down to company commanders were exchanged between the two armies. German officers were also dispatched to Vienna to offer training courses, and their Habsburg counterparts went to the Western Front late in 1916 to be briefed on 'storm-troop' tactics – with the result that Austria established its first 'storm battalions' in February 1917. Reserves also underwent extensive months-long training using German gas, infantry, and artillery manuals. In time, the *AOK* compressed the seemingly bewildering plethora of German manuals into a number of its own.

The Germans tried to train their ally in the new methods of the defensive war 'in depth'. In the autumn of 1916, Austrian primary defensive positions were reinforced with belts of barbed wire augmented by trip wires, minefields, and mantraps. Secondary communications trenches were dug and outfitted with thick 'anti-shrapnel' roofs. Austria slowly began to appreciate the advantage of hiding its artillery from enemy view on reverse slopes, and to build reinforced concrete bunkers to house heavy machine guns. After much confusion the Austrians understood that when the Germans suggested creating 'hundred-yard zones' and then 'five-hundred-yard zones' they meant that defensive zones be deepened first to 100 and then to 500 yards! However, Conrad feared that such defensive works would provide too much comfort and security and thereby deprive the troops of their offensive drive.[23]

The technical modernization of the Army also occupied Conrad and his staff. As previously noted, the field artillery's old M-99 howitzers had been fired to the breakdown point and were being replaced with modern M-14 field guns and M-15 howitzers. Just under 2000 new guns arrived at the front in 1915 and another 1400 during the first half of 1916; by the end of 1916 the *k.u.k.* Army had 804 artillery batteries with 4018 tubes, about 1400 more than in 1914. Most divisions in 1916 had 60 pieces of artillery, with howitzers outnumbering field guns two-to-one. But Conrad's ambitious plan to reequip the Army with 13 300 new guns remained a mirage.

Strides were made, albeit slowly, in other areas as well. Gun production in 1914 was restricted to the Škoda Works in Pilsen, the Arsenal in Vienna, the Austrian Weapons Factory in Steyr, and the Weapons and Machine Factory in Budapest. Shell output was concentrated at the Munitions and Metalware Company in Enzensfeld, Škoda in Pilsen, the Munitions Factory at Wöllersdorf, the Hungarian Gun Factory at Györ, and the Manfred Weiss Munitions, Steel, and Metal Works in Budapest. Once the 'short-war illusion' proved to be just that, the War Ministry expanded its list of war producers to 575 Austrian firms, including Bros.

Böhler in Kapfenberg, M. Arthur Krupp in Berndorf, G. Roth in Vienna, and the Casings and Metalworks at Hirtenberg.[24] But the Steyr Works alone produced machine guns and despite their best efforts output rose only gradually from 180 to 320 units per month between 1914 and the end of 1916. Steyr raised its rifle production from 22 800 in October 1914 to 74 500 in April 1916, and the Hungarian Armory from 11 000 to 18 000 per month during the same period. Aircraft production remained the stepchild of Austria's war industry. For the first year of the war the *k.u.k.* Army remained wholly reliant on Germany, and even the six aircraft and seven engine plants built in 1915 produced only 408 airplanes and 512 motors – insufficient even to meet replacement and training needs. Anti-aircraft guns had barely come off the drawing boards by 1916.[25]

Germany also came to Conrad's assistance with the new 'machines' required for defensive warfare – gas, hand-grenades, and trench mortars. For much of 1915, Austro-Hungarian soldiers were provided with only the most primitive protection against gas: wool and oakum rags soaked in a calcium solution and pressed against nose and mouth. The first gas masks came from Germany at the end of 1915. Bells were mounted in trenches to warn of approaching gas but Austrian troops declined to use them in the firm belief that gas would not be deployed on the Eastern Front.[26]

Since Austrian 'corn cob' hand-grenades with timed fuses proved both cumbersome and unreliable, Berlin in 1916 began to supply Vienna with its stick and egg grenades, which a good infantryman could hurl 50 yards. And since Habsburg manufacturers had managed by early 1916 to develop but a single 9 cm trench mortar with an effective range of less than 600 yards and mounted on a sled pulled by dogs, Germany sent train-loads of its newest trench mortars with ranges up to 1300 yards. Late in 1916 the Germans decided to equip the Austro-Hungarian Army with steel helmets; the first 400 000 arrived by the end of 1917 and one million followed by July.[27] Finally, with German encouragement and loans, the Austrians in November 1916 sought to double their output of war material by investing 454 million Kronen in plant expansions for powder factories (Blumau, Pressburg, Magyaróvár), gun foundries (Brünn, Pilsen, Györ), and munitions plants (Wöllersdorf). Although well intentioned, the programme failed due to lack of capital, labour, raw materials, and transportation.

The outward appearance of Austrian soldiers changed radically. In late 1916 the traditional 'pike grey' (really, blue) uniform yielded to the green-tinged 'field grey' made from German cloth. Knickerbockers, cloth puttees, and lace-up boots (*Schnürschuhe*) replaced long pants tied at the ankles. Leather knapsacks gave pride of place to cloth rucksacks. A steel helmet weighing almost 3lbs replaced cloth caps. Even the old coloured regimental collar-tabs disappeared. *Kamerad Schnürschuh*, as the Germans dubbed their Austrian compatriots after their lace-up boots, was hardly recognizable from his 1914 predecessor.

War-material production and transportation bedevilled Conrad throughout 1916. In the early months of the war the *k.u.k.* Army had relied on horses to pull its artillery and transport wagons. But the debacles in Galicia and the Carpathians in 1914–15 had cost Conrad 320 000 horses – about half of all lost in the war. Lack of green feed caused the death of an estimated 45 000 horses. Motor transport was still in its infancy, and the production of 3000 trucks per annum by 1916 failed to meet the Army's demands. Lack of rubber meant that most units ran on iron rims covered with leather cloth.

Railroads remained the primary movers of men and goods. The 'short-war illusion' wreaked havoc in this area as well since 35 488 skilled rail-road workers (12 per cent of total force) were drafted in 1914 for what was to be a war over by Christmas; their places were taken by 31 499 women. Conrad's defeat in Galicia meant the loss of 15 000 freight cars, more than the entire national production. Lack of steel prevented the expansion of major lines into double spurs, while ersatz lubricating oils made from coal tar proved inferior to crude oil. The Dual Monarchy failed to appreciate the importance of locomotives: only 273 were built in 1914–15 and 395 in 1915, compared with an average of 5000 undergoing repair at any one time. Lack of copper forced the Monarchy to substitute cast-iron fire-boxes which, in turn, meant lower pulling power, reducing train loads from 657 tons in 1913 to 592 tons by 1917. The Finance Ministry vetoed foreign purchases as these would jeopardize Austria's postwar production. Disingenuously, it argued that the lower speeds prescribed in wartime would translate into less wear and tear and thereby further reduce the need for new locomotives![28]

Defenders of the transportation system point out that the Monarchy's trains in 1915 transported 8 million men and 647 000 horses to the front in 100 000 freight cars; and that another 100 000 cars moved the requisite supplies for these new formations. But such raw statistics, impressive as they are, fail to address the fact that rail needs always outstripped rail services. Comparisons with Germany were not flattering: the Reich managed in late 1916 to mount a rail-supply effort in a minor theatre (Transylvania) that was greater than the total Austro-Hungarian mobilization of 1914. Fighting, of course, destroyed much of the trackage, and the railroad sections of the War Ministry and the *AOK* worked feverishly in 1915 to extend the Austro-Hungarian rail network 1000 miles in the east beyond the Carpathians and to construct 600 miles of makeshift field track.[29]

Still, transportation remained the Achilles' heel of the war effort. More than 5000 firms were forced to close their doors already in 1914 and another 10 000 the following year due to lack of transport. By 1915 coal syndicates complained that they received only 69 per cent of the needed freight cars – despite a 'gift' of 5000 units from Germany. More than 5000 cars of rice – the Monarchy's total needs for a year – rotted at Trieste due to lack of trains. At the end of 1917 transport was down 50 per cent over the previous year as the mammoth logistical effort ground down the rolling stock and the declining steel production prevented its timely replacement. Late in 1917, Vienna's daily requirement of 300 freight cars of potatoes had dwindled to 20 to 50 due to the lack of trains. In 1918 Austrian railroads suffered a near-total collapse.

War industries were the *AOK*'s second major headache. Before 1914 Austrian industry had been centred in Bohemia and Moravia as well as around Vienna, with some development in western Hungary. After 1914 the Monarchy continued civilian control of industries – with the exception of steel and mining. The responsible ministries in Vienna (Trade, Agriculture, War) saw little need to centralize production as the war would be short. By and large they were content to establish oversight agencies manned by a single officer for the main branches of industry and mining; Hungary followed this example 1 year later to head off Austrian control. These 91 *Zentralen* functioned much like limited stock companies, providing capital, setting production quotas, and regulating the import of raw materials and finished products. The first agencies were established for non-ferrous metals as well as for hemp, flax, linen, rubber, and petroleum. The *AOK* controlled war-related production mainly in occupied and front areas: Galicia, the Bukovina, Austrian Silesia, and, after Italy entered the war in 1915, the South Tyrol, northern Italy, Dalmatia, Istria, Carinthia, Carniola, and Styria. Hungary successfully resisted domination by either the *AOK* or the Austrian government.

By late 1916 German pressure for increased industrial output brought added centralization. The Inspector of Technical Artillery had supervised all raw-materials procurement and industrial war production since 1914, but early in 1917 the War Ministry at Vienna was expanded by 11 departments to deal with specific problem areas such as coal, iron, steel, munitions, and powder. Reviving the War Productions Law of 1912, the War Ministry set production quotas, seized private factories and railroads for war production, and directed labour to these industries. The *Kriegsamt* also won the right to invest in or to expand existing factories, but the Cabinet was reluctant to interfere in the private sector out of fear for the postwar stock exchange. Hungary once again proved the exception as Tisza in 1915 readily helped himself to Austrian funds to expand the armaments plants at Györ and Disgyör. Kaiser Karl dismantled this centralized control system in March 1917 and replaced it with the Commission for War and Transitional Economy – which, as its name suggested, worked not to enhance war production but rather to prepare the economy for a return to peacetime market conditions.[30] Few in Germany noted the name change which, in fact, perfectly reflected Karl's burning desire to end the war at the first possible moment. The Austrian Krone fell 240 per cent on the Viennese exchange, thereby further aggravating industrial investment and expansion.

The Dual Monarchy was hamstrung throughout the Great War by its lack of vital raw materials. The textile industry collapsed after only a few months as the British, French, and Italian blockades cut Austria–Hungary off from its major suppliers of raw cotton (the United States, Egypt, and India). Wool became scarce, as did hides. Non-ferrous metals required for steel and gun production were especially hard to get. Abandoned zinc, tin, lead, and copper mines were reopened but shortages of copper, nickel, and lead arose early in 1915.

Vienna established a central agency to deal with raw materials, but it could not meet the monthly shortfall of copper, for example. Before the war, Austria–Hungary had produced 4000 tons of copper and imported 36 500, but by 1915 it could cover only 55 per cent of the Army's needs even after emergency supplies had arrived from Germany. By 1917 this figure fell to 37 per cent. To offset the shortfall Viennese authorities seized the copper stores of breweries and electrical suppliers. Iron replaced copper in electrical wires. In 1916 the government confiscated and melted down 3703 tons of copper church bells, followed by 9771 tons in 1917. By 1918 the shortage could not be alleviated even by seizing copper chandeliers, school, door and dinner bells, lightning rods, kitchen pots, door handles, and casings from store display windows. Lack of labour prevented full-scale gathering and remelting of empty shell casings from the battlefields.[31] The production of bronze gun barrels had ceased in favour of steel in 1915.

Nickel was also in short supply and caused a changeover to steel in gun production. As with copper, the shortage led to the wide-scale confiscation of nickel pots and pans as well as the introduction of iron in place of nickel coins. Less than half of the required amounts of lead and manganese were produced in 1915,[32] and soon iron replaced lead in shrapnels. Vast amounts of zinc were imported from Germany to make up for the lack of bronze and copper in fuses, grenades, and canteens. The exploitation of mines in Poland (1915) and Serbia (1916) failed to satisfy the need for vital raw materials, partly because Germany took two-thirds of all production from Serbia as reparations for its military aid. Only in bauxite for aluminum was Austria well supplied, with major mines in Laibach, Fiume, and Transylvania.

Iron and steel, of course, were critical to the war effort. Once again lack of planning and the 'short-war illusion' almost proved fatal. No attempt was made in 1914 to exempt steel workers from the draft, with the result that 37 per cent of Hungary's iron and 28 per cent of its steel workers joined the *k.u.k.* Army in Galicia and Serbia, where a good many died. Production fell 73 per cent in 1914 and recovered to peacetime levels only in 1915 after the forced closure of 15 000 non-war-related factories had released a large pool of skilled workers. At the start of the war, Austria relied on steel reserves on hand; thereafter it exploited its historic iron mines in Styria. By 1917 Vienna met the Army's needs only by importing 210 000 tons of Swedish steel provided by Germany. The War Ministry took control of the production of special steels (nickel, chromium, vanadium, molybdenum, and tungsten) in 1915, and 2 years later banned all housing and bridge construction using steel. Transport difficulties in the first half of 1918 forced a 23 per cent cutback in steel production.[33]

Coal became another choke point in war production. To be sure, Austria had ample coal fields in Bohemia and Moravia, which in 1913 provided 14 of the 18 million tons mined, but this was largely soft brown coal unfit for high-energy smelting plants. The Monarchy imported 43 per cent of its hard coal before the war and after 1914 its reliance on superior German hard coal grew. Again, confidence that the war would be over by Christmas had prompted the Army to draft 25 per cent of coal miners; the recruitment of women, children, and prisoners of war restored labour levels to their prewar state only in 1917. Wartime production of coal remained relatively steady at around 16 million tons per annum, but in 1918 fell off to 7 million tons. Trains were rendered idle as a result and the Prague Iron Industry Society's steel mills, to name but one example, shut down from May to August 1918 for lack of coal.[34]

Austria–Hungary did, however, enjoy a surfeit of oil. Although the Russians burned three-fourths of the Austrian oil fields in Galicia when they withdrew in May 1915, engineers had the fields back in operation by June. Private cars and trucks were denied petrol and oil in August 1915 as stocks were reserved both for the *k.u.k.* Army and the German ally (to help pay for food supplies and war materials). The government took control of oil production in October 1916, but then negated this by diffusing supervision among the Ministries of Agriculture, Trade, and War. And it failed to bring its two major refineries at Limanova and Drohobycz under state control.[35]

Even if Austria–Hungary had been a veritable treasure house of raw materials, its slender industrial base could not have met the Army's escalating needs. Conrad's staff at Teschen jealously noted that Germany produced four times more war materials. Specifically, Germany created 887 batteries of heavy artillery compared to Austria–Hungary's 182; its armourers monthly outproduced their Habsburg counterparts 160 to 43 in heavy artillery pieces, 5500 to 45 in trench mortars, and 29 000 to 3000 tons in barbed wire; and the Reich's monthly output of 250 000 artillery shells dwarfed the Monarchy's 60 000 shells.[36] In fact, the 60 000-shell figure of 1916 proved to be the high-water mark: by 1918 it fell to 29 000.[37] The shell shortage was aggravated by the fact that the *k.u.k.* Army, like its German counterpart, maintained a broad assortment of 29 gun models and required 100 different types of ammunition for its small arms and artillery.

The precarious state of Austro-Hungarian war industries and manpower notwithstanding – or perhaps because of them (?) – Conrad in January 1917 dusted off yet another operations plan. Forty per cent of his soldiers (328 000) were deployed in the southwest and Conrad decided to hurl them against Italy as the *AOK*'s 'last card'. Once more Conrad refused to allow reality to interfere with planning. Although outnumbered 60 to 29 divisions by the Italians, Conrad magically calculated that 45 divisions would suffice for victory; he asked the Germans to supply 13 and removed three from the Russian theatre (hopefully to be replaced by the Germans). Optimism once again reigned supreme at Teschen. Conrad planned to deliver a double blow against the Italians out of the Tyrol and along the Adriatic. While his Isonzo forces tied down the enemy in the east, the main attack centred on Tolmein in the north was designed to catch the Cadorna offguard, break his lines, and 'roll up the entire Julian [Alps] front'.

It was not to be. Not only did Hindenburg and Ludendorff refuse to put 13 German divisions at Conrad's disposal, but Kaiser Karl had no desire to risk his newly-acquired crown on another of Conrad's grandiose battles of encirclement. On 2 December 1916 – the day celebrated each year to honour Franz Joseph's accession to the throne in 1849 – Karl, who believed that he possessed military talents, announced that he would take personal control of the Army and reduce its power by way of a major reorganization. Bolfras yielded as head of the Military Chancery to the unctuous Ferdinand von Marterer. Archduke Friedrich, the armed forces' titular commander since 1914, was promoted to the rank of field marshal in November 1916 – and retired early in 1917. On 3–4 January Karl moved the *AOK* from Teschen in Austrian Silesia to Baden, a fashionable resort just south of Vienna, far removed from any front. General von Tersztyánsky quipped that visiting Kaiser Karl at Baden 'you hope to meet a thirty-year-old there, but you find a man with the appearance of a twenty-year old youth, who thinks, speaks and acts like a ten-year-old boy'.[38] Grand Admiral Haus died on 8 February and Karl replaced him with Vice Admiral Maximilian Njegovan.

On 27 February 1917 the 29-year-old monarch dismissed his 65-year-old Chief of the General Staff – just 2 months after promoting Conrad to the rank of field marshal. Conrad grudgingly accepted the Grand Cross of the Military Order of Maria Theresa. But his request to retire was rejected and, after a good deal of begging by Karl and Marterer, Conrad agreed to command the forces in his beloved Tyrol. Both Karl and Conrad undoubtedly knew that parting had become inevitable. While the Kaiser worked behind the scenes to initiate secret discussions to end the war, the General planned a grand battle of envelopment in the Tyrol. Above all, Karl aspired to command alone. As Conrad later put it, 'one does not happily take the governess from one's parents' home into a young marriage'.[39]

General Arz von Straussenburg, a relatively junior corps commander whom Karl earlier had found to be 'very adroit but not at the same heights of ability as Conrad',[40] became the new Chief of the General Staff. The German military plenipotentiary at Baden, Kageneck, described Arz as a 'little schnauzer' and attributed Conrad's fall solely (and incorrectly) to the Field Marshal's 'wretched marriage' to his former mistress 'Gina'.[41] The mediocre Alfred von Waldstätten took Metzger's place as chief of operations. The fiery War Minister, Krobatin, was dispatched to command the Tenth Army to make room for the pliable courtier Rudolf Stöger-Steiner von Steinstätten.[42] At the express demand of the Hungarian Prime Minister, Kaiser Karl created the special office of 'Chief of the Replacement Branch' and staffed it with Tisza's candidate, *Honvéd* Minister Samuel von Hazai, one of 25 Jewish or converted Jewish generals in the Imperial and Royal Army.[43] Conrad's protests against this diminishing of the *AOK*'s powers fell on deaf ears. And further to humble the General Staff, Conrad's locus of power, Karl created a special medal to be awarded to officers who had undergone 6 weeks' service at the front – that is, to field commanders only.

Kaiser Karl now had his team in place and was free to exercise his combined role of ruler, supreme warlord, and commander of the armed forces. Under the influence of his wife, Empress Zita of Bourbon-Parma, Karl halted strategic bombings of military targets if they endangered civilians; decreed that gas not be used without express imperial sanction; ended physical punishments such as chaining soldiers for up to 6 hours for acts of indiscipline; forbade summary executions of civilian and military persons even in war zones; and banned duelling in the Army. Therewith, the bonds of military discipline were loosened forever. Still more damaging, Karl met with radical Hungarian leaders such as Mihály Károlyi (which led to Tisza's dismissal in May 1917) and on 2 July, the name-day of his son Otto, granted amnesty to Czech nationalists Karel Kramár, Alois Rasin, Václav Klofac, and about 1000 others, who promptly returned to Prague to resume their seditious work.[44] Parliament, reconvened in May 1917, debauched in riot as these measures were announced. Since none had been discussed with government leaders, the Kaiser quickly earned the sobriquet 'Karl the Sudden' from Vienna wags.

Of men and machines: the third *OHL*

By late 1916 the Western Front had been transformed into what Paul Fussell has called 'a troglodyte world'. The French maintained about 6250 miles of trenches, the British another 6000, and the Central Powers just under 12 000 – an underground labyrinth sufficient to girdle the globe. At the height of static warfare in October 1916 the Reich had built roughly 1400 miles of front trenches. Given that its defensive systems generally boasted three successive trenches, the linear measure rose to 5200 miles; by adding the numerous communication, sapper, and support trenches, it doubled to more than 10 000 miles. Sixty million cubic yards of earth were excavated by the Germans, who by July 1916 weekly shipped 7000 tons of barbed wire to the front to maintain its subterranean labyrinth. German field telegraphs laid about 4 million miles of lines in all theatres.[45]

The preferred German trench system along the Western Front, based on the principle of the defence in depth, consisted of three parallel trench lines, each several thousand yards apart: front, support, and reserve. The front-line trench, protected by two barbed-wire belts, usually was 100 to 400 yards – but could be as close as 5 to 10 yards or as far as 1000 yards – from its enemy counterpart. It was either below ground or above as breastworks, or a combination of the two, depending on soil and drainage conditions. Firing trenches were dug in a zigzag pattern to protect against enfilade fire or shell blasts. Sandbags piled 2 or 3 high protected the soldiers from snipers and a fire-step two or three feet high allowed them to stand, fire, and hurl grenades. Machine guns and periscopes were concealed along the firing trenches at specified intervals. Special 'sap' trenches extended 20 or 30 yards from the firing trenches into No Man's Land as observation or advanced warning posts.

The second line of trenches usually was built 2000 to 3000 yards behind the front. These support trenches, also protected by barbed wire, featured deep dugouts where soldiers could either rest after prolonged fighting or seek shelter from artillery bombardments; they also housed support troops that could be called up to reinforce the front-line. And 2000 yards further back was the third, or reserve, line of trenches. There a garrison was deployed to reinforce the front and support trenches. The entire defence in depth was interconnected with lateral trenches along which rations, reliefs, ammunition, and communications moved. A line of machine guns 800 yards apart and sited in concrete strongholds about 1000 yards behind the front trenches swept the defensive position.

The Allies discovered during the Battle of the Somme that the Germans had developed rather sophisticated trenches, many of them 30 feet deep. They featured boarded or timbered floors, walls, and ceilings; sandbags, sticks, and corrugated iron supported unstable sand and chalk walls. Many had electric lights, kitchens, cupboards, water tanks, furniture, wallpaper, and bunk beds. Steel doors protected the soldiers from sudden attack or mortars. According to Fussell, German trenches were 'efficient, clean, pedantic, and permanent'; French generally 'nasty, cynical, efficient, and temporary'; and British 'amateur, vague, *ad hoc*, and temporary'.[46]

The trenches were vile at the best of times. Flies and fleas, mites and mosquitoes were a constant irritant, while lice and rats were lethal typhus carriers. Lice laid their eggs in the hair of soldiers, the seams of their garments, and the stuffing of chairs and couches. Habsburg *Landser* complained bitterly that every hut on the Eastern Front was infested with the vermin. French *poilus* claimed that the lice were so fertile that one born in the morning was a grandmother by night![47] The modern troglodytes tried to burn the lice with candles or cigarettes, to crush them between finger nails, or to overpower them with powders and pomades sent from home. The largest were given pet names: British favourites were Kaiser, Crown Prince, Ludendorff, and Hindenburg. Lice entered the English language: the word 'lousy', which originally had meant lice-infected, was applied by soldiers after the war to anything bad; and the word 'crummy', used by soldiers because a crumb often looked like a louse, also entered civilian usage. By 1915 the German Army had developed large, portable fumigating stations called 'lauseoleums' by the soldiers in which medical personnel used chemicals and soaps to clean several hundred men per day.

Rats the size of cats were noted in almost all reports from the front. Their dietary staples were leftover food and decomposing corpses, and they carried a host of potentially fatal diseases. Soldiers hunted rats with a passion and often proudly displayed their 'bag' strung up in rows along the trenches. The only beneficial side effect of gas was that it killed rats – at least for a time.

Major von Thaer, staff officer with the IX Reserve Corps on the Western Front, left a graphic description of German trenches. The foremost line was protected by 12-feet-thick roofs made of crisscrossed tree trunks filled in with earth and stone. In a few isolated places wood had yielded to concrete. Still, the IX Reserve Corps complained that the first line was routinely turned into a killing ground by artillery. Troops unearthed remains of former colleagues and adversaries alike when digging new trenches. Thaer's corps had laid roughly 700 miles of twin underground telephone cables that connected 800 field stations. Hastily-constructed narrow-gauge rail lines brought ammunition, blankets, drugs, food, and linen to the front lines. Much of this material had been requisitioned from the populace in Lille. Thaer's men were most appreciative of two distilleries and one brewery constructed for them by the Army. But the soldiers usually were denied one luxury accorded their French colleagues. In May 1915 Thaer noticed that after shelling of the French forward lines, 'a host of figures, mostly women in negligees', ran from the trenches. 'The French really are a warped people.' A former church welfare volunteer, Thaer was appalled that 'Parisian women take their patriotism to such lengths as to make life in the trenches more appealing for Turks and Moroccans'.[48]

Trench culture remains an intriguing but controversial subject. On the one hand, there is no question that the trenches were a killing ground. British sources claim that even in quiet times 7000 soldiers were killed or wounded each day in their 90 miles of front trenches − 'wastage' in the cold terminology of the General Staff. Yet there is a good deal of evidence to suggest that soldiers developed a certain 'ritualization of fire' and a 'live and let live' mentality that made life in the forward trenches almost bearable. Breakfast 'truces' became common in quiet sectors. Artillery generally remained silent when rations were brought up to the front, or after heavy rains had flooded the trenches. Snipers occasionally fired high. War weariness ('inertia') dampened the will to kill.[49] Once more military terms made their way into civilian usage: 'trench coat' and 'trench mouth', for example, took the place of raincoat and Vincent's infection, respectively.

In the autumn of 1916 Hindenburg and Ludendorff decided to end this primitive form of trench warfare in favour of a more sophisticated system of defences along the Western Front. Specifically, they opted to straighten out a 20-mile bulge along a 65-mile front in Army Group Crown Prince Rupprecht's sector and in the process create a great defensive arc along the line Lens–Noyon–Reims.

The *OHL* reached this decision after an exhaustive review of the Western Front. It estimated that in 1916 the Army had lost 350 000 soldiers killed and 1.4 million wounded − 800 000 alone during the period July to October. Hospitals were strained to the limit with roughly 3 million casualties. The Supreme Command set its own manpower at 5.1 million soldiers, of whom 2.85 million were deployed in 134 divisions in the west against seven Belgian, 57 British, and 111 French. Neither Ludendorff nor Hindenburg had great faith in the 1.6 million Austrians in the east or the 1.1 million in the south. 'Where German soldiers stand, the situation is secure; where Austrians stand, it will always be problematic'.

The new *OHL* studied the Battle of the Somme and sent its findings to all army commands. It found that the heaviest losses had occurred wherever infantry had been massed in the front lines, that attacks had been most easily repelled where artillery and machine guns had been placed well behind the front line, and that counterattacks had succeeded only when carried out by small units immediately upon penetration of the line. Lessons emerged. The armies were to man their front lines lightly, similar to an outpost line; barrage fire was to be limited to 3 minutes and supported by trench mortars and machine guns; enemy artillery was to be 'beaten down' by its counterpart; defensive positions were to be extended 'in depth'; and 'new technical means' were to be deployed to save soldiers.[50]

These findings resulted in the 'Principles of Command for the Defensive Battle in Position Warfare' of 1 December 1916. Drafted by the Bavarian Captain Hermann Geyer, they stated that the aim was to 'allow the enemy to exhaust itself and to bleed itself' heavily, 'but to husband one's own forces'. German defensive positions were not to feature 'the deployment of the greatest possible number of live bodies' but rather 'preponderantly machines (artillery, trench mortars, machine guns, etc.)'. Possession and defence of land were no longer to be regarded as cardinal tenets of warfare. And defences were to be constructed 'in depth'.[51]

The *OHL* abandoned the linear trench system roughly 1 mile in depth described earlier in favour of a killing zone that ranged between 6 and 8 miles in depth. Such an extended defensive network would deny enemy artillery the ability to shell the first and second lines simultaneously. The mass of German machine guns was to be located well behind the first line and housed in steel-reinforced concrete bunkers that could withstand 15 cm shells. Each half mile of the line was to receive five or six batteries of barrage fire and division fronts were to be reduced to 2500 to 3000 yards. The division was elevated to almost independent status and given control over the artillery in its area.

The 'defence in depth' received 'elasticity' insofar as the front lines (or outpost zone) were no longer to hold to the last man but to resist only as long as was reasonable and thereafter to 'evade' the main assault. The latter would then expend itself in the battle zone dominated by machine-gun nests with interlocking zones of fire. From the counterattack (rear) zone small groups of combined arms units would deal with further penetration of the lines and recapture lost ground. Hostile artillery would be engaged by guns sited on reverse slopes and directed by aerial spotters during the initial phase of the battle; after enemy penetration of the lines, artillery would concentrate against the attackers, who were beyond the range of their own support fire.[52]

Reserve formations were critical. The Supreme Command calculated that almost one-half of all reservists called to the front either failed to arrive on time or were 'diverted' by ancillary units. Few divisions had created storm battalions as ordered by the General Staff in the spring of 1916. On 2 September Ludendorff demanded eight new divisions, including five for the Western Front. The Prussian War Ministry agreed at once to release 72 000 men mustered fit for garrison duty only and promised another 57 000 in the near future. The *OHL* estimated that roughly one million draft-eligible males remained in war-related industries and that of these 740 000 were fit for military service. Of more immediate interest were the 310 000 males born in 1898, who normally would have entered the Army in December 1916. Ludendorff pressed them into service in September. By combining the men born in 1898 with those sent out by the War Ministry and those who had recovered from their wounds of the summer of 1916, the Army collected a reservoir of 1.3 million reservists.[53] From this it created an additional 13 new infantry divisions in the winter of 1916–17 and another 20 in April 1917, raising total paper strength to 197.

Organizational innovation helped the *OHL* expand its forces rapidly in what one Prussian general called the 'war of mutilated units'. Rather than attempt to maintain regional regiments, the Supreme Command as early as February–March 1915 had created new formations by mixing in equal portions front-line veterans, recruits, and convalescents. At the regimental and divisional levels it built new units around two or three battalions of seasoned veterans that it removed from the front and trained jointly with reservists and recruits. In the artillery branch the *OHL* built new batteries of six guns by taking two batteries out of the front lines to serve as a core for the four new batteries sent out from home.[54] While this system allowed for the rapid expansion of troop formations, it destroyed the old sense of camaraderie and friendship built over years of mutual training and combat.

The quantity of shells expended at the Western Front continued to alarm: the rate of fire had climbed from 643 000 shells in August 1916 to 907 000 just the following month.[55] The War Ministry informed the *OHL* that ammunition trains for the field artillery alone had risen from 157 in July 1915 to 235 in July 1916, shells from 3.2 to 4.5 million, and powder from 906 to 2436 tons.[56] Army Corps VII, for example, reported that it fired one million artillery shells per month during an offensive – with an effectiveness of one enemy casualty per 100 rounds.[57] Field Artillery Regiment 79 calculated that it fired 677 100 rounds in 1181 days – more than the entire artillery during the Franco-Prussian War.[58] Industry could not meet – nor would the General Staff condone – such a waste of shells.

Given this dire picture of manpower and material reserves, Hindenburg ruled out major operations in the west for 1917. He also informed Conrad von Hötzendorf that Germany was in no position to spare 16 to 20 divisions for yet another offensive in the Tyrol. Defence was all that remained; attacks would have to await future developments. Meanwhile, special refresher courses and schools to instil the new defensive warfare into front commanders were deemed 'indispensable'.[59] The first 3-months training courses for division and corps commanders were immediately established.[60]

The Western Front remained 'the decisive theatre'. The *OHL* expected a period of relative calm after Verdun and the Somme. Britain and France, it estimated, would not renew their spring offensives before 1 March and Russia was likely to remain quiet until 1 May. In fact, Allied commanders had met at Chantilly on 15 November 1916 and sketched out a coordinated strategy to pressure the Central Powers on all fronts in the coming year. And they had made major political and military changes. On 7 December Lloyd George, until then Minister of Munitions, replaced Prime Minister Asquith and formed a national coalition government. An inner 'War Cabinet' of five directed the war in place of the cumbersome full Cabinet of 23. Concurrently French Premier Aristide Briand moved in the Chamber of Deputies' *Comité secret* to curb General Joffre's almost unlimited powers by recalling him to Paris as special advisor to the *Comité de guerre*. Joffre declined this 'promotion' on 26 December, whereupon Briand elevated Joffre to the rank of Marshal of France – and then replaced him with Robert Nivelle.

Convinced that the Allies would mount major offensives in the spring of 1917 and deeply shaken by the experience at the Somme, the Supreme Command debated the best course of action for 1917. Army Group Crown Prince Rupprecht (Sixth, First, and Seventh armies), which had taken the brunt of the fighting at the Somme, in December 1916 and again in January 1917 informed the *OHL* that the soldiers were 'exhausted' and 'used up'. Rain had turned the low-lying regions of Flanders into slime and the men found little comfort in the shell craters that they used as dugouts. Nor did the prospect of Allied renewed attacks supported by an expected 800 British and 1200 French tanks allow room for optimism. Rupprecht, supported by his staff chief, General Hermann von Kuhl, repeatedly requested permission to withdraw to new defensive positions along the line Arras–Laon. Especially the First Army's exposed bulge at the 'Ancre knee' between Arras and Soissons invited Allied attack. A strategic withdrawal, which could be undertaken over 3 months, would shorten the front and release 11 divisions for duty elsewhere.[61]

Ludendorff toured Rupprecht's positions in January 1917. On 4 February he officially endorsed a strategic withdrawal, arguing that this would free up 13 divisions as well as 50 batteries of heavy artillery. While there would be some 'negative political fallout' as a result of this 'retreat', Ludendorff reminded his staff that the British had survived the withdrawal from Gallipoli and his own armies that from Warsaw in 1915. The 'top secret' move was to be executed in March and codenamed *Alberich* – after the malicious king of the dwarfs in the ancient Germanic *Nibelungen* saga.[62] The *OHL* moved from Pless in the east to Kreuznach in the west to supervise the undertaking.

Operation *Alberich* became the war's greatest feat of engineering. For 4 months 370 000 German reservists, civilian workers, and Russian POWs toiled on the new defensive barrier; 170 000 additional construction workers prepared the building materials well behind the front; and 1250 supply trains of 40 freight cars each hauled concrete and steel to the construction sites. The 300-mile-long 'line' actually consisted of five major defensive positions.

Work on the Flanders Line between the English Channel and Lille began in February 1917 as a defensive position for the Fourth Army 2 to 6 miles behind the front. East of Armentières and on the right flank of the First Army, the Wotan Line was also begun in February for the Sixth Army; it was to be 10 miles behind the existing front north of Péronne. The Siegfried Line ran behind the left wing of the Sixth, First, and Second armies and the right wing of the Seventh Army from Arras to St Quentin and the Chemin des Dames. It crossed 'Wotan' at Quéant and was the only project finished on schedule. The Hunding Line began from the 'Wotan' position at Péronne and was to run via La Fère (where it crossed 'Siegfried') northeast to Verdun. Designed for the Second, Seventh, Third, and Fifth armies, little of it was completed in the spring of 1917. Later that year part of the Hunding Line was renamed Brunhild Line and given over to the Third Army, while another part was retitled Kriemhild Line and assigned to the Fifth Army. The Michel Line was to protect the St Mihiel salient as an extension of 'Hunding' south to Metz.[63] Much of the construction was done at night to hide it from Allied spotters, but Crown Prince Rupprecht was shocked to learn on 9 February that Berlin knew the details of *Alberich*. 'It is really scandalous.'[64]

Captain Friedrich Schinnerer of the Royal Bavarian Army, one of the engineers on the Siegfried Line, left a detailed memoir. The initial defence consisted of a large antitank trench, 3 yards deep and 4 yards wide, that took 3 weeks to dig. The first formal line of defence behind this ditch was a series of at least five barbed wire barriers, each 4 yards deep and 20 yards apart. This 100-yard wide zone was interconnected with perpendicular wire cross-fields each 4 yards wide. The wire was supported by metal posts screwed into the ground 2 yards apart. Gangs of 16 men and one noncommissioned officer carried out the work; daily quotas averaged 960 square yards.

Allied troops who successfully crossed first the ditch and then the wire would next run up against the major killing ground consisting of what Schinnerer called *Panzer-Mebu*: small steel-reinforced concrete forts or blockhouses, each housing two machine guns as well as the spotter and gunner crews in subterranean bunkers. Construction gangs could build five *Panzer-Mebu* per day in each of the five sites that the Bavarians controlled. Each sector daily consumed 30 to 40 tons of steel and 100 cubic yards of concrete. The only problems with the forts were that noises echoed loudly and the concrete tended to shift during heavy artillery bombardments.

The second and final major barrier, sited 200 yards behind the first, consisted of a system of zigzag trenches, each 6 to 10 yards long before undertaking a 120-degree turn to prevent enfilading fire. The trenches for the Siegfried Line alone took 4.5 months to build. They stored ammunition and food, served as emergency medical stations, and were equipped with electricity and telegraphs. Their roofs were covered with 6 to 8 yards of dirt and were never penetrated by howitzers or bombs. Two lines of artillery were sited in the German rear zone – on reverse slopes, if at all possible, or later in trenches and tunnels.[65]

Operation *Alberich* formally commenced on 9 February and the first troop withdrawals came on 15 March. War material, tools, and food were removed at night by 900 trains hauling 37 100 carloads. Ludendorff, who well remembered the Russian 'scorched-earth' policy in Poland in 1915, decided that all territory abandoned was to be laid waste – insofar as artillery and bombs had not done so already. The Allies were 'to find a totally barren land, in which their manoeuvrability was to be critically impaired'. Ernst Jünger left a graphic description of the destruction:

Right up to the Siegfried Line, every village was reduced to rubble, every tree felled, every street mined, every well poisoned, every creek dammed up, every cellar blown up or studded with hidden bombs, all metals and supplies taken back to our lines, every rail tie unscrewed, all telephone wire rolled up, all combustible material burned; in short, we transformed the land into which the enemy would advance into a wasteland.[66]

The Allies later saw the actions as typical of 'Hun' behaviour; former Premier Viviani demanded 'reparations' for the destruction. By the end of March the Siegfried Line had been manned by 21 German divisions, or one for each 4 miles of front. The *OHL* calculated that the Siegfried Line alone freed up 10 divisions and shortened the front by nearly 30 miles.[67]

Alberich constituted a daring gamble. No general on either side attempted anything quite like it during the war. With one bold stroke Ludendorff surrendered 1000 square miles of territory won with the blood of tens of thousands of soldiers over the past 3 years. In the process, he also abandoned Falkenhayn's hallowed principle enunciated during the Battle of Flanders in November 1914: 'Hold on to what you have and never surrender a square foot of that which you have won'. Incredibly, the operation was carried out over weeks under the eyes of superior enemy air forces. General Groener deemed Operation *Alberich* brilliant, perhaps the 'masterpiece' in Ludendorff's art of operations.[68]

While the Army executed the great withdrawal, Ludendorff carried out a major reorganization of existing formations. The division was divided into three regiments of three battalions each; the battalions, in turn, into four infantry companies and one heavy machine-gun company. Each division thus was armed with 54 heavy machine guns (MG 08) as well as 108 light (MG 08/15) – well below the British average of 64 heavy machine guns and 192 light, and the French figure of 88 heavy machine guns and 432 light *fusils mitrailleurs*. Four of the 11 cavalry divisions on hand in 1914 were dismounted late in 1916.[69]

The *OHL* appreciated that its soldiers needed to be retrained to fight with the new 'machines' of war. Hindenburg conceded that the Army of 1914 had been content to leave 'technical weapons' in the hands of a few specialists and that the Allies had passed the Germans in the deployment of 'machines of war'. He also acknowledged that Falkenhayn had recognized the effectiveness of the special 'storm troopers' – Renaissance mercenaries, in the words of Jünger.

In May 1916 Falkenhayn had trained two officers and four noncommissioned officers from each division of the Third Army for 14 days at Beuveille. Impressed with the results, he suggested that every division train and equip a battalion of storm troops,[70] and in June ordered Jäger battalions changed to storm battalions. Each was to consist of 20 officers and 1052 noncommissioned officers and men organized into a staff, four storm companies, one machine-gun company, one artillery battery, one section of 24 men for flamethrowers, and one section of 105 soldiers for trench mortars. Mostly volunteers under the age of 25, the men were outfitted with steel helmets, mountain boots, Alpine pants with leather seats

and knees, spades, axes, hatchets, picks, wire cutters, and field telephones. Officers received automatic pistols; the men carbines and the rifle
71/84. Training courses designed for 10 officers, 20 noncommissioned
officers, and 20 men at a time were established at Leboncourt/Seboncourt.
Captain Rohr trained the storm battalions for Army Group Crown Prince
Wilhelm.[71]

Ludendorff quickly built on these modest beginnings. In September
1916 the *OHL* relocated the depot battalions of every division assigned to
train raw recruits behind the lines and there gave special attention to
retooling company-level commanders in defensive warfare. Early in
October it established 1-month-long instruction courses for all company
and battalion commanders. Next came special 'war schools' where the
best and brightest officers of army groups received advanced instruction
in 5- or 6-month refresher courses. The first 100 officers and 100 noncommissioned officers from Army Group Crown Prince Wilhelm
received instruction early in November.[72] Within a few weeks Army
Group Crown Prince Rupprecht dispatched its first 80 regimental and
divisional commanders as well as staff officers to a leadership school at
Solesmes (and later Valenciennes). Crown Prince Wilhelm countered with
a *Führer-Kursus* at Sedan. In all cases instruction centred on the General
Staff's 'Principles of Command for the Defensive Battle in Position
Warfare'.

In November 1916 Lieutenant-Colonel Max Bauer, the General Staff's
expert on artillery and fortresses, drafted new instructions on the role of
infantry in position warfare, attack, defence, and withdrawal on the
Western Front. Bauer stressed the need for soldiers to become acquainted
with machine guns, howitzers, trench mortars, and flamethrowers. Above
all, he emphasized the centrality of battle. 'Battle is the proving ground
for the inner value of all soldiers. *Infantry* is the *primary weapon.*' Its only
thought should be but one: '*Forward against the enemy, cost what it may*'.
Infantry, the queen of battle, needed to abandon entrenched notions of
combat, to expect the unexpected, to learn to fight by night and with the
new 'machines of war', to train as combined arms units, to learn the ways
of the storm battalions, and to use aerial photographs of enemy positions
to simulate battle conditions.[73] Bauer encouraged officers to make 3-week
rest and recuperation furloughs available to all soldiers – during which
their bodies could be replenished with extra rations and hardened by way
of individual and team sports.

Ludendorff shared Bauer's emphasis on the centrality of battle. Too
many staff officers at division level were mired in administrative matters
pertaining to ammunition, housing, food, and medical care; in the process
they had forgotten their primary mission of planning for battle. Too few of

those on the General Staff had been to the killing ground and there talked to front-line commanders. Most preferred to dictate battle 'down to the minutest of details' from headquarters by way of 'an avalanche' of memoranda. 'Individual initiative' and 'love of responsibility' were being sacrificed. Ludendorff insisted that staff officers accompany line officers into battle rather than remain behind to redraw their beloved battle maps.[74]

Convinced that Rohr's storm battalions had proved their value at Verdun and the Somme, Ludendorff intensified their creation and training. By November the new 'workers of war' had been outfitted with special vests to carry hand-grenades, gas masks, bread sacks, field flasks, daggers, and light machine guns. A typical storm battalion, led by a captain and four lieutenants, consisted of 24 light machine guns, 8 trench mortars, 8 light mortars, 8 flamethrowers, 4 light artillery pieces, heavy machine guns, and a signal horn.[75] Fire stability and accuracy were enhanced by light tripod mounts for the heavy machine guns and mobility by wheeled carriages for the light trench mortars. Late in December 1916 Ludendorff ordered training courses for storm battalions to begin in January 1917. The courses initially were run for 5 or 6 days, and later extended to 4 to 6 weeks.[76] Ludendorff sited an artillery school at Mouzon to train his artificers in the art of laying down rolling barrages to cover infantry's advance on the battlefield. By spring 1917, eight additional artillery schools had been established on the Western Front.

The *OHL* shared its training with the Austro-Hungarian Army. Officer exchanges began in mid-September 1916 and by the end of October agreement had been reached concerning common training of infantry and artillery as well as storm battalions. But these good intentions brought few results. The vast expanse of the Eastern Front as well as the proclivity of Habsburg officers to seek security in large fortresses negated the very principle of the 'elastic defence in depth'. In the east divisions often held sectors 12 to 19 miles wide, which in the west would have been manned by six or eight divisions. General von Seeckt, 'supreme staff chief' assigned to various army groups, noted that many Habsburg commanders eschewed the German methods due to 'psychological considerations'.[77] Seeckt eventually recommended that Austrian storm battalions be dissolved for lack of competent instructors.[78] Italy copied the storm troops with 'detachments of fearless soldiers' (*reparti di soldati arditi*), France with *grenadiers d'élite* or *groups francs*, and Russia with special 'shock battalions'.

'Total war': reality and myth

Having adopted a defensive strategy for 1917, withdrawn to the Siegfried Line, and established major training programmes, the *OHL* next tackled the issue of war supplies. In the winter of 1914 Rathenau had created a special Raw Materials Section within the Prussian War Ministry, but in the spring of 1915 had yielded to Major Josef Koeth. The latter attempted to enhance war production by exploiting existing resources within the Reich as well as occupied lands, by expanding established industries, and by founding new ones with state subsidies. Thereby Koeth introduced a clean division between domestic and military needs and priorities.[79]

But the war demanded more material than anyone had imagined. Whereas Germany had produced 1200 tons of gunpowder per month in August 1914, 6 months later it needed 6000. And whereas the Army had required but 15 artillery tubes per month at the start of the war, by Christmas 1914 it needed 100. By the end of 1915 armouries had made 3500 new guns, including 800 of heavy artillery. About 750 artillery barrels had also been re-bored – no mean feat, given 50 different models and calibres. The number of machine guns delivered to the front had increased from 1000 in 1914 to 6100 in 1915.[80]

This intensified production devoured ever greater amounts of raw materials. While Germany was self-sufficient in coal from the Ruhr, Saar, and Silesia and low-grade iron ore from Lorraine, Luxembourg, and Peine, it lacked the high-grade iron ore and rare metals to produce special gun steels. These metals – manganese, chromium, copper, brass, tungsten, and nickel – had largely been imported before the war. Moreover, low-grade iron ore had first to be cleansed of phosphorous impurities through the Thomas process, an expensive and time-consuming undertaking. Low-grade steel translated into lower-quality fuses, shell casings, artillery jackets, and driving bands, which, in turn, meant reduced life expectancy for the guns. The vital components for powder and dynamite – glycerin, saltpetre, cotton, phenol, and toluene – had also been imported before 1914. And since Germany had depended on overseas for 100 per cent of its cotton and 95 per cent of its silk, wool, and other fibrous materials, the British blockade denied the Reich the requisite raw materials for uniforms, blankets, and civilian clothing.

At first Germany managed to get by with supplies on hand in military depots, then with those requisitioned from nonwar chemical industries, and finally with stocks seized in Rotterdam's bustling port in 1914. But soon shortages developed and the hunt was on for alternate sources. Consumer-related industries were closed. Old slag heaps were combed for recoverable metals. Chemical industries had to surrender their vital stocks for war production. Barns were scraped to recover nitrates. Neutrals and allies alike were pressured to supply raw materials: Norway and later Serbia and Bulgaria for copper; Hungary and Serbia for manganese; and Sweden for 4 million tons of high-grade iron ore in 1915 alone. Machines and workers were requisitioned from occupied lands. An aluminum industry, using Austrian bauxite, was created by the Prussian War Ministry almost overnight.

Germany, like Austria–Hungary, appealed to its citizens to surrender vital raw materials: telephone wires, water and steam pipes, kettles and tubs from refineries, breweries, and distilleries; door knobs and brass ornaments from homes; and copper bells and roofs from churches and city halls. The Old Prussian Synod alone 'donated' 10 312 church bells to the war effort – a total probably matched by Protestant churches in the rest of Germany. Evelyn Blücher was bemused by this war effort:

> It is an interesting sight, though, to see cartloads of old pots and kettles and candlesticks, door-handles, chandeliers, etc., being driven along the street, and a poor woman or schoolboy carrying a copper kettle or brass lamp to the collecting offices to be weighed and paid for.

Even more amusing to the English-born Princess were German bureaucrats attempting to explain that there was no copper shortage, that the Reich merely wanted to inventory existing stocks![81]

Scientists rallied to the war effort as they had not done since the French Revolution. Fritz Haber invented a system for extracting nitrogen from the air, thereby alleviating the Reich's prewar reliance on Chilean saltpetre (nitrates). Ersatz became the rage. Nitrate crepe paper made from wood cellulose took the place of gun cotton; synthetic camphor replaced imported natural camphor; glycerin was manufactured from sugar rather than fats; gypsum yielded sulphur; a host of flowers and weeds were processed to produce alcohol for ammunition; and rosins and gums were extracted from a plethora of coal derivatives.

Transportation perhaps was the most vexing problem. The Army after 1914 combed the Reich for 1.4 million horses as well as several hundred thousand donkeys and mules. Roughly 400 000 horses were killed by hostile fire and 500 000 died of illness due to malnutrition.[82] As a result, Germany turned to motorized transport: the number of trucks increased fivefold to 10 400 during the first year of the war and eventually reached a total of 40 000. But it possessed neither rubber plantations nor oil fields. Petrol and rubber on hand in 1914 quickly ran out. By 1915 the monthly need of 15 000 rubber tyres and 25 000 pneumatic tubes could no longer be met. Trucks were reduced to 80 per cent of normal load capacity to save wear and tear on rubber tyres, and trailers were forced to use iron 'tyres'. By 1917 wooden 'tyres' were prescribed. Attempts to produce synthetic rubber (*Kautschuk*) proved slow and unrewarding.

Romanian oil deliveries covered the Reich's monthly needs of 4655 tons of petrol and 322 tons oil in 1914, but these dried up with Bucharest's entry into the war in August 1916. For a while Germany stretched its supplies with 'gasohol' (*Benzolspiritus*), a mixture of 75 parts petrol to 25 parts distilled alcohol, but the need to reserve grains and potatoes for the food supply put severe limits on this innovation. The reconquest of Galician oil fields in the spring of 1915 partly alleviated the dire petrol shortage; Austria began to deliver 6000 tanker cars of refined oil semi-annually by 1916. Industry developed ersatz lubricants by extracting oils from coal tar and brown-coal slags.[83] But, as became dramatically evident by 1917, no amount of ersatz could hide the Reich's painful shortages of oil and rubber.

The Imperial Treasury quickly discovered that the war exceeded all fiscal projections. In 1913 the Reich had collected a mere 2.3 billion Marks in receipts while the various states (*Länder*) had taken in 3.3 billion – enough to cover the costs of the war for about two months by 1915. Whereas the entire Franco-Prussian War had cost 1551 million Marks, by 1915 the Reich spent 2000 million Marks *per month* on the Great War. Each army corps *daily* fired artillery shells in the value of 4–5 million Marks. Great expectations that 'contributions' from conquered states would offset war outlays proved illusory: whereas Brussels agreed to pay 50 million francs and Belgium 590 million for occupation costs and indemnities, by Christmas 1914 the Treasury had collected but 15 million.[84] Helfferich, who in February 1915 left his post as director of the Deutsche Bank to become State Secretary of the Treasury, put the war effort at home on a par with that at the front. 'We must make clear to the German people that this war, more than any other, will be fought not only with blood and iron but also with bread and money.' Military duty needed to be supplemented by 'a duty to save and to pay'.[85]

Stock markets remained closed from 1914 until 1918. Copper and silver coins gave way to iron and aluminum. Novel ideas to raise funds for war widows came into vogue. On 28 August 1915, the first anniversary of the Battle of Tannenberg, a 28-ton statue of Hindenburg was raised in the Königsplatz next to the Reichstag. For a small donation Berliners could drive nails into the 'wooden titan' – 90 000 common and 10 000 silver nails the first week alone – and thereby turn Hindenburg into a gleaming armor-clad knight.

Fiscally, Germany began the war on 31 July 1914 when the Reichsbank refused to exchange gold for paper notes. Four days later the Treasury established a two-tiered system of war financing. So as not to undermine the Bank Law of 1875 which stated that paper currency be covered one-third by gold and the rest by a positive balance of trade, the Treasury established special banks of issue to print paper notes against collateral in the form of goods and securities. These 99 so-called 'loan banks'

(*Darlehenkasse*) created the cash necessary for private industry and allowed the Reichsbank to concentrate on war finances. But the Reichsbank quickly passed an amendment to the Bank Law allowing it to hold cash reserves not only of gold but also of the new paper money issued by the loan banks and government Treasury Bills. In short order, an unrestricted supply of paper money flooded German financial markets: by the end of 1918, note circulation in Germany had increased by 1141 per cent over late 1913.

The German taxpayer had underwritten the war to the tune of 22 billion Marks by the summer of 1915. Nine war loans in the form of bonds at 5 per cent return were floated in March and September of every year by national subscription.[86] Eventually the Reich raised 98 billion Marks in this way. The proceeds surpassed the short-term debt up to the fourth loan in March 1916, but after the 'battles of material' at Verdun and the Somme, the loans, beginning with the fifth drive in September 1916, failed to keep pace with the rapidly escalating national debt. War costs topped 3 billion Marks per month in October 1916, 4 billion in October 1917, and ended in October 1918 at just under 5 billion Marks. The debt solely in terms of outstanding Treasury Bills doubled in the second half of 1916 to 13 billion Marks; then doubled again to 28 billion Marks by the end of 1917; and ended at 50 billion Marks by war's end. Taxes collected by Berlin barely covered the interest on the debt.[87]

Year	Expenditures	Receipts	Deficits
		(in million Marks)	(in million Marks)
1914	8620	2351	6269
1915	25 694	1735	23 959
1916	27 732	2029	25 703
1917	52 003	7830	44 172
1918	44 020	6795	37 225
TOTAL	158 068	20 741	137 327

Small subscriptions (under 2000 Marks) mainly from the ranks of middle-class civil servants, small shopkeepers, and store employees, which liquidated peacetime bonds and savings for the war effort, fell from 17 to 8 per cent between 1914 and 1918. Conversely, large subscriptions (more than 1 million Marks) almost doubled from 19 to 34 per cent during the same period. Workers by and large ignored the subscription. It is interesting that the poster for the seventh war loan in September 1917 – that is, after Verdun and the Somme – depicted not tanks, aircraft, machine guns, or flamethrowers, but an idealized, semi-naked Thor with hammer and anvil!

German taxpayers also had to reach deep into their collective pockets to keep the allies at Vienna, Sofia, and the Porte afloat. Helfferich readily conceded the dangers of tying Berlin's financial wagon to that of Vienna, but saw no alternative. 'If Austria–Hungary collapses', he confided to Bethmann Hollweg in April 1915, 'our enemies will doubtless slice the hunks that suit them off the cadaver'.[88] Helfferich in 1915–16 extended credits of 800 million Marks to Vienna so that it could pay for its purchases in Germany. By October 1917 Austria–Hungary's debt to Germany had risen to more than 5 billion Marks.

Taxes covered little of the German war effort. The first 6 months of the war, for example, cost 8.65 billion Marks; taxes paid for 7.4 per cent of this.[89] In fact, taxes covered only 6 per cent (9 of 157 billion Marks) of the war's costs in Germany, compared with 20 per cent in Britain and 23 per cent in the United States. One problem was that the federal government could raise only indirect taxes. Yet revenues from the postal, telegraph, and telephone services as well as the railroads and the excise duties collected from Alsace-Lorraine steadily dwindled under wartime conditions. The British blockade halted the inflow of taxable luxury goods such as coffee, tea, and cocoa. So-called 'sin taxes' on alcohol disappeared as grains were withheld from breweries and the sale of brandy for personal use was banned because alcohol was needed for munitions production. Direct taxation – levies on personal and corporate income – were the prerogative of the *Länder*, but their rates and effectiveness were so different from state to state as to defy centralization in Berlin, even had the requisite political goodwill existed.

Berlin, like Paris where the Banque de France issued 23 billion paper francs during the war, geared up its printing presses to produce vast quantities of paper money. In the process, the national debt rose from 5 billion Marks in 1914 to roughly 157 billion by war's end.[90] Helfferich in July 1915 convened a meeting of federal and state finance ministers to address the mounting debt – then listed at 30 billion Marks for past military expenditures as well as 30 billion Marks for future claims by widows and invalids. The best that could be wrung from the Reichstag in December was a 10 to 50 per cent 'war profits tax' on excess profits that industries had made due to the war – above and beyond their average profits for the last 5 years of peacetime. Helfferich bleakly predicted that payment for the war constituted 'the greatest problem that the world has ever faced'.[91] In August he openly admitted that the war was being fought on the premise that the loser(s) would pay 'the leaden weight of billions'[92] in debt through indemnities and reparations.

To make certain that Germany would not be among the latter, the *OHL* undertook two steps to place it on what Ludendorff later called a 'total war' footing. On 31 August 1916 Hindenburg instructed the War Ministry dramatically to increase war production. 'Men – as well as horses – must be replaced more and more by machines.' While conceding that war production was a 'screw without end', he avowed that victory would go to the power that turned 'the screw up the most at the proper moment'. With regard to human resources, Hindenburg demanded that the 'wounded, prisoners of war, women, and minors' be recruited and trained for work in war industries. He offered to release 'several thousand highly-qualified specialists' from the Army to stimulate production. Sunday work would have to be introduced and remaining non-war-related industries shut down. The public would have to be informed about the need to mobilize the home front – the genesis of the programme of *Vaterländischer Unterricht* (patriotic instruction) launched in July 1917. Using August 1916 production as a base, Hindenburg on 31 August demanded that industry double the monthly output of powder to 12 000 tons and of light artillery to 3000 pieces, and triple that of machine guns to 7000. Targets for aircraft production were later set at 1000 engines and 1000 planes per month. Colonel Bauer, when asked by industry how long these quotas were to remain in effect, coolly responded: not past May–June 1917, as 'the war would have been ended by then'.[93]

Secondly, on 5 December 1916 the Reichstag by a vote of 235 to 14 passed the Auxiliary Service Law designed to mobilize the nation's human resources. All males between the ages of 17 and 60 not serving in the armed forces or employed in agriculture, forestry, and war-related industries were to work for the war effort. The War Office was to oversee the Law and to punish anyone who refused labour assignment with incarceration not to exceed one year and fines not to exceed 10 000 Marks.[94] Shortly after passage of the Law, Hindenburg decreed that skilled workers could not be drafted without permission from employers, and that specialists currently in German occupation armies at once could be recruited for industry. He acknowledged that both measures were based on Britain's Ministry of Munitions, created in May 1915, and the Munitions Act of July 1915, which controlled the free movement of labour. The *OHL*, which initially had wanted to promulgate the reforms by imperial decree, insisted that both measures be passed into law by the Reichstag both to ensure popular support and to include parliament in enforcing them.

Belgium's prewar industries were a ripe target for labour exploitation. The Central Powers by summer 1916 had 'recruited' 12 000 workers for German munitions works as well as for Hungarian weaving mills and Bohemian glass-blowing plants. Still, almost 600 000 Belgian workers remained unemployed and Ludendorff, immediately after establishing the

Hindenburg Programme, in October demanded that 20 000 Belgian workers per week be deported. But German industries were not geared to receive such vast numbers, and the intake slowed to 2000 per week in December. And when it became apparent that Belgian workers could not be forced to undertake skilled work in German munitions plants, the deportations were halted in February 1917.[95]

The *OHL* rounded off its reform programme by overhauling the Prussian War Ministry. On 1 October it replaced the Ordnance Master's Office with the Weapons and Munitions Procurement Agency (WUMBA) within the War Ministry. On 1 November Wilhelm II signed into law the 'War Office' under General Groener as a super agency charged with the 'direction of all matters pertaining to the recruitment, deployment, and feeding of workers as well as the procurement of raw materials, weapons, and munitions for the overall war effort'. Numerous departments within the War Ministry were abolished as WUMBA assumed command over the nation's coal, iron, and steel.[96]

As was to be expected, the reforms brought an avalanche of criticism down on the General Staff. Bethmann Hollweg was concerned that the traditional workers' freedom of employment was being replaced by a system of compulsory labour direction, and he feared that the draconian reforms would have little effect since most skilled workers had already shifted from lower-paying consumer to higher-paying war industries. Nor did he favour Hindenburg's demand that women be forced to work. Wild von Hohenborn seconded Bethmann Hollweg's concerns. The War Minister deemed compulsory employment of men and women to be unnecessary and potentially damaging to industry and raised concerns about the forced recruitment of invalids, youths, prisoners of war, and workers from occupied lands.[97] But in the end neither Bethmann Hollweg nor Wild von Hohenborn was able to influence a policy deemed vital to the nation by the General Staff and heavy industry.

While the Chancellor regarded both the Hindenburg Programme and the Auxiliary Service Law as infringements on his political authority, the Prussian War Ministry saw the creation of the War Office – headed by a south German no less – as a vote of no confidence in its management of the war. As early as 25 December, General von Wrisberg, director of the General Department, informed Deputy War Minister von Wandel that 'dark clouds' and 'rolling thunder' were breaking over the *Kriegsamt*. The *OHL* had created the War Office without even informing the War Ministry; its production quotas were 'impossible' and the costs would haunt the nation well after the end of the war; the myriad of new training courses could not be staffed; and the Auxiliary Service Law was a 'wild-goose chase'. Wrisberg concluded: 'It hardly surprises that the *OHL* turns its attention to everything and demands so many – often unbelievable – changes that one can only shake one's head. In essence, everything has been turned on its head and new staffs created daily'.[98] In time the War Ministry accused Groener of 'moving too far to the Left' in his treatment of workers and respect for collective bargaining, of being unable as a Württemberger to understand Prussian affairs, and of nurturing a 'love of organizational matters'.[99]

There was some truth to these charges. As early as February 1917, Rathenau lamented what he termed 'the progressive destruction of our war production industry' through 'overly rigid organization, human and material mistakes, loss of direction'.[100] He calculated that it would take 150 000 bureaucrats just to administer the Hindenburg Programme. The Reichstag, by adding 12 paragraphs to the General Staff's original four, created loopholes in the Auxiliary Service Law that exempted a host of workers such as students, civil servants, pastors, priests, health technicians, farmers, and women. In truth, there hardly existed a labour pool to be tapped.

Above all, Hindenburg and Ludendorff could not overnight overcome either the inertia of the bureaucracy or the prejudices of many German and Prussian agencies against greater centralization. Prussian Minister of the Interior Clemens von Delbrück opposed in principle all government involvement in economic and industrial planning. Helfferich at the Treasury was apprehensive that unlimited armaments expenditures would jeopardize an already severely strained budget. While the Treasury argued that victualling the home population was a matter to be regulated by the German states, the *Länder* replied that it was a purely military concern. Most Bavarian, Prussian, and Saxon agencies feared even the suggestion that federal bureaus be allowed to cut into the states' fiscal 'fat'. No formal channels existed either between the public and the private sectors or between the federal government and the various states to coordinate war planning.[101]

By allowing private producers to work on a cost-plus-profit margin rather than negotiated fixed-price contracts, the Hindenburg Programme encouraged generous labour settlements and generated an explosive wage–price spiral as firms simply passed the costs of higher wages on to the government. When Groener in July 1917 demanded limits on profits and wages, Ludendorff unceremoniously pushed him out of office. Moreover, the Auxiliary Service Law stipulated that plants employing 50 or more workers were to establish 'conciliation committees' to mediate between management and labour, that unions were to have a seat in the new War Office, and that 15 Reichstag deputies constituted as a special oversight committee were to monitor the Auxiliary Service Law.

Ironically, Hindenburg and Ludendorff thereby allowed German trade unions, long marginalized, to open the doors to the inner chambers of heavy industry.

Industrial leaders (Hugenberg, Kloeckner, Kirdorf, Stinnes) soon discovered that their workers made extensive use of the new freedoms: whereas only 10 per cent had changed jobs before August 1916, thereafter 40 per cent took advantage of this right. The captains of industry met at the Hotel Esplanade in Berlin in February 1917 to protest against the new job mobility – and to remonstrate that the Auxiliary Service Law had brought them 'no new workers'. Fearing that the radical labour legislation could remain on the books after war's end, the *OHL* and industry warned Bethmann Hollweg that the Auxiliary Service Law had become 'the weapon of choice in the so-called workers' rights' movement. 'This situation can not be tolerated permanently; it must be opposed, *otherwise we will be destroyed by it and by other domestic concessions.*'[102] Ludendorff, who was one of the first to don the new Merit Cross for War Service, soon regretted its creation and stated that he wore it with a 'certain sadness' as the Auxiliary Service Law had proved a deep disappointment.

How effective were the Hindenburg Programme and the Auxiliary Service Law? Documents long buried in the Soviet Union and East Germany and only made available to researchers after German 'accession' in 1990 allow a fresh interpretation. The Reichsarchiv, responsible for the official history of the war, in the 1920s combed the (still extant) files of the General Staff, the Prussian War Office, and Groener's War Office to assess the *OHL*'s war production and labour reforms. Interestingly, its findings were not included in the official history but have survived as separate studies.

The Reichsarchiv team concluded that especially the Hindenburg Programme was largely smoke and mirrors, an ambitious reform programme designed for public consumption.[103] It noted with regard to the alleged 'doubling' of powder to 12 000 tons per month that the *Kriegsamt* had already raised the quota from 6000 to 8000 tons in December 1915, and then again to 10 000 tons in July 1916. Thus, the Hindenburg Programme in effect called for a mere 33 per cent increase of 2000 tons, which the War Office deemed '*technically fully feasible*'. With respect to light artillery, the Reichsarchiv discovered that the War Office had already raised monthly output to 2000 pieces; hence, again, the demand for 3000 per month comprised but a modest 33 per cent increase. 'Without being fully aware of the fact that two-thirds had already long ago been ordered', Ludendorff and Hindenburg crowed about doubling and tripling production.

Concerning rifle production, the Reichsarchiv noted that output had risen from 3600 rifles per month in 1914 to 250 000 by August 1916. With more than 100 specialized factories mass-producing the 67 parts required for a Mauser, there was in fact a surfeit of rifles. Likewise, machine-gun output, which had stood at 200 per month in 1914, had soared to 2300 by August 1916. Whereas the Hindenburg Program demanded a 'tripling' to 7000 per month, existing War Office orders already called for (and attained) 7200 units per month by July 1917; in autumn 1917 that figure rose to 14 400. In fact, the Army was so short of men by winter 1917–18 that the new artillery, trench mortars, and machine guns rusted on loading docks.

Finally, the Auxiliary Service Law failed to meet the General Staff's expectations. Instead of the 200 000 civilians that Groener hoped to place in military agencies, only 60 000 had reported for duty by April 1917. And of the 118 000 civilians recruited by the end of May, 75 000 were women and 4000 youths and old men.[104] The *OHL* released 1.2 million workers from the Army in September 1916 and a further 1.9 million in July 1917 to meet the new production quotas and in the process reduced battalion strength especially on the Western Front. The transportation system, already strained to the limit, could not handle the added tasks of moving vast amounts of raw materials, labour, and finished goods between home and front. Shortages of rolling stock and coal as well as railroad bridges and yards proved bottlenecks to increased production. In short, the attempted mobilization of the nation for 'total war' was well beyond the means of the Wilhelmian state. For Bethmann Hollweg it was political dynamite as it would have threatened the delicate socio-economic fabric of society.

It could be argued in defence of Ludendorff and Bauer, the true architect of the 1916 reforms, that they demanded the impossible in order to realize the possible. Gerald Feldman, a student of the German military-industrial complex in the First World War, calls the Hindenburg Programme and the Auxiliary Service Laws ambitious failures. But Michael Geyer, a more recent scholar of the Third *OHL*, sees the 1916 reforms as an 'explosive fusion', as a 'symbiosis between the military and industry' in which machines replaced men as the primary agents of state-organized violence. Ludendorff's and Bauer's efforts in 1916, Geyer suggests, catapulted the German military into the twentieth century by 'fusing' the new 'frontline mentality' of soldiers with the equally novel 'machine culture' of workers.[105]

Geyer has a point – aside from the fact that industry never surrendered control, initiative, or profits to the military. Hindenburg, Ludendorff, and Bauer sought nothing less than to restructure German military–industrial–labour relations from the ground up. They appreciated what the German Army had avoided facing up to before 1914: that modern industrialized wars fought by millions of soldiers and fuelled by the labour of millions of workers could not be conducted with the organizations and tools of the Napoleonic era. They *attempted* to mobilize the nation's manpower and material reserves for 'total war', to erase all distinctions between the military and home 'fronts', and to create a 'symbiotic' relationship between the suppliers and the 'workers' of war. But neither labour nor industry nor government in Imperial Germany was ready in 1916 for such a radical restructuring of traditional social, economic, military, and political relations.

The *OHL* based its demands not on sound military planning or rational economics but on a theoretical image of 'total war'. Thus Hindenburg in September 1916 had demanded that military service be extended to age 60; that schools and factories introduce military training for boys over the age of 16; and that urban youths be sent to the country for 'health reasons' before coming to the armed forces. Hindenburg repeatedly drew attention to the 'screaming injustice' that existed between the group of men that risked life and limb for the Fatherland daily at the front and the group that enjoyed the security of home and raked in war profits.

The Chief of the General Staff was even more caustic with regard to women. 'Untold thousands of childless soldiers' wives,' he suggested, were idle and 'just cost the state money'. Uncounted others pursued 'useless' occupations. The principle, 'He who does not work shall not eat', was justified 'more than ever before' with regard to women. Even 'dispensable' women – that is, asocials and prostitutes – were to be harnessed for the war effort. Hindenburg argued that universities, with the exception of medical schools, be closed for the duration of the war so that 'men incapable of military service and women' would not usurp 'the positions of students now at the front'. With reference to the wild-cat strikes of 55 000 workers for peace and bread in Berlin and other large urban centres in the summer of 1916, Hindenburg demanded that the government suppress the rights of these 'screamers and agitators' to protest publicly while pursuing their 'search for profit and pleasure'. Therewith, he gave concrete expression to the front-soldiers' bitterness over the gulf that separated them from workers at home. 'The entire German people', Hindenburg concluded, 'should live only in the service of the Fatherland'.[106]

Although the government successfully resisted these drastic suggestions, they nevertheless reveal the thinking of the men around Hindenburg. Turning Clausewitz on his head, Ludendorff suggested that in time of war politics be subordinated to military considerations. Bauer used Ludendorff's authority to demand a voice in domestic matters and spun effective ties to industrial leaders. Perhaps the task of organizing the nation for 'total war' was beyond the capabilities of any man. By summer 1917 Bauer expressed concern that 'too much rests on Ludendorff: all domestic and foreign policy, economic questions, the matter of the food supply, etc. He is greatly overtaxed, usually totally exhausted, also oftentimes nervous'.[107]

Two decades after the Great War, Harold Lasswell published a seminal article on what he termed the 'emergence of the military state under present technical conditions'. Lasswell noted the rise of authoritarianism and the concomitant decline of democracy in the West. The new emerging 'garrison state', wherein the specialists of violence had surfaced as 'the most powerful group in society', was highly centralized and bureaucratized. 'With the socialization of danger as a permanent characteristic of violence,' Lasswell wrote, 'the nation becomes one unified technical enterprise'. Its outward hallmarks were a 'reliance on propaganda as an instrument of morale', 'compulsory labour service', and an 'energetic struggle to incorporate young and old into the destiny and mission of the state'. The new 'body of specialists' had unleashed the 'stupendous productive potentialities of modern science and engineering' in war.[108] The degree to which Lasswell had the wartime actions of Hindenburg, Ludendorff, and Bauer in mind unfortunately must remain an open question. In 1916 it also remained an open question whether German citizens – men and women alike – were ready for such a radical redefinition of their lives.

Chapter 6 Notes

1. See Laurence V. Moyer, *Victory Must Be Ours: Germany in the Great War 1914–1918* (New York: Hippocrene Books, 1995), p. 135.
2. Evelyn, Princess Blücher, *An English Wife in Berlin: A Private Memoir of Events, Politics, and Daily Life in Germany throughout the War and the Social Revolution of 1918* (New York, E. P. Dutton, 1920), p. 100.
3. See Gertrud Bäumer, *Heimatchronik während des Weltkrieges* (Berlin: F. A. Herbig, 1930), pp. 35–6. Entry for 17 December 1915.
4. Guenther E. Rothenberg, *The Army of Francis Joseph* (West Lafayette, Ind., Purdue University Press, 1986), p. 201.
5. Cited in Gerd Hardach, *The First World War 1914–1918* (London, Allen Lane, 1977), p. 53.
6. Conrad's report of 9 March 1916. ÖStA-KA, MKSM 1916, 87-1/14.
7. Report of 22 April 1915. HHStA, PA I Deutschland 1918. Liassa Krieg, 841.
8. Reichsarchiv, *Der Weltkrieg 1914 bis 1918*. 9: *Die Operationen des Jahres 1915* (Berlin, E. S. Mittler & Sohn, 1933), p. 365.
9. Arthur J. May, *The Passing of the Hapsburg Monarchy 1914–1918* (2 vols, Philadelphia, University of Philadelphia Press, 1966) 1, pp. 340–1.
10. Hindenburg to Cramon, October (?) 1916. ÖStA-KA, MKSM 1916, 69-4/51.

11. Reichsarchiv, *Der Weltkrieg 1914 bis 1918*. 11: *Die Kriegführung im Herbst 1916 und im Winter 1916/17* (Berlin, E. S. Mittler & Sohn, 1938), p. 24.
12. Conrad to Hindenburg, 8 October 1916. ÖStA-KA, MKSM 1916, 69-4/51.
13. Christoph Führ, *Das K.u.K. Armeeoberkommando und die Innenpolitik in Österreich 1914–1917* (Graz, Vienna, and Cologne, Hermann Böhlaus Nachf., 1968), pp. 99–115.
14. Führ, *Das K.u.K. Armeeoberkommando*, pp. 144, 146.
15. Führ, *Das K.u.K. Armeeoberkommando*, pp. 150–4. Black and yellow were the official Austrian colours.
16. Führ, *Das K.u.K. Armeeoberkommando*, pp. 123–5.
17. Cited in Gary W. Shanafelt, *The Secret Enemy: Austria–Hungary and the German Alliance, 1914–1918* (New York, Columbia University Press, 1985), p. 97.
18. Bundesministerium für Landesverteidigung, *Österreich-Ungarns Letzter Krieg 1914–1918*, 6, *Das Kriegsjahr 1917* (Vienna, Verlag der Militärwissenschaftlichen Mitteilungen, 1936), pp. 48–9.
19. Bundesministerium für Landesverteidigung, *Österreich-Ungarns Letzter Krieg 1914–1918*. 5: *Das Kriegsjahr 1916* (Vienna, Verlag der Militärwissenschaftlichen Mitteilungen, 1933), pp. 88–9.
20. See Rudolf Hecht, 'Fragen zur Heeresergänzung der gesamten Bewaffneten Macht Österreich-Ungarns während des Ersten Weltkrieges', unpubl. diss., Vienna University 1969, passim.
21. Report of 6 August 1917. ÖStA-KA, Kriegsministerium 1917, 5A/61-191 'Durchhalten über Winter 1917/18'.
22. Hecht, 'Fragen zur Heeresergänzung'; and József Galántai, *Hungary in the First World War* (Budapest, Akadémiai Kiadó, 1989), p. 135.
23. *Österreich-Ungarns Letzter Krieg 1914–1918* 4, pp. 123–9.
24. Robert J. Wegs, *Die Österreichische Kriegswirtschaft 1914–1918* (Vienna, A. Schendl, 1979), p. 118.
25. *Österreich-Ungarns Letzter Krieg 1914–1918* 6, pp. 93, 97–8, 101–02.
26. *Österreich-Ungarns Letzter Krieg 1914–1918* 6, p. 130.
27. *Österreich-Ungarns Letzter Krieg 1914–1918* 6, pp. 52–6.
28. Wegs, *Die Österreichische Kriegswirtschaft*, pp. 106–10.
29. *Österreich-Ungarns Letzter Krieg 1914–1918* 6, pp. 104–8.
30. Wegs, *Die Österreichische Kriegswirtschaft*, pp. 24–38.
31. Wegs, *Die Österreichische Kriegswirtschaft*, pp. 66–73.
32. *Österreich-Ungarns Letzter Krieg 1914–1918* 6, p. 61.
33. Wegs, *Die Österreichische Kriegswirtschaft*, pp. 52–62.
34. Wegs, *Die Österreichische Kriegswirtschaft*, pp. 64, 84.
35. Wegs, *Die Österreichische Kriegswirtschaft*, p. 90.
36. *Österreich-Ungarns Letzter Krieg 1914–1918* 6, pp. 61–2, 67.
37. Otto Riebicke, *Was brauchte der Weltkrieg? Tatsachen und Zahlen aus dem deutschen Ringen 1914/18* (Berlin, Kyffhäuser-Verlag, 1936), p. 42.
38. Cited in Mark Cornwall, *The Last Years of Austria–Hungary: Essays in Political and Military History 1908–1918* (Exeter, University of Exeter Press, 1990), p. 118.
39. Cited in A[ugust] von Cramon, *Unser Österreichisch-Ungarischer Bundesgenosse im Weltkriege. Erinnerungen aus meiner vierjährigen Tätigkeit als bevollmächtigter deutscher General beim k.u.k. Armeeoberkommando* (Berlin, E. S. Mittler & Sohn, 1920), p. 172. See also Helmut Hoyer, *Kaiser Karl I. und Feldmarschall Conrad von Hötzendorf. Ein Beitrag zur Militärpolitik Kaiser Karls* (Vienna, Notring, 1972).
40. *Der Weltkrieg 1914 bis 1918* 11, p. 496.
41. BA-MA, MSg 1/2517 Tagebuch Kageneck. Diary entry of 2 March 1917.
42. Stöger-Steiner's habit of wearing all his military decorations even in his office caused one parliamentarian to describe him as a 'sort of cultivated Chippewa Indian' in appear-

ance. Fritz Fellner, ed., *Schicksalsjahre Österreichs 1908–1919. Das politische Tagebuch Josef Redlichs* (2 vols, Graz and Cologne, Hermann Böhlaus Nachf., 1953–54) 2, p. 215.

43. *Österreich-Ungarns Letzter Krieg 1914–1918* 6, pp. 68–72.
44. Rothenberg, *Army of Francis Joseph*, pp. 203–4; Cramon, *Unser Österreichisch-Ungarischer Bundesgenosse im Weltkriege*, pp. 95, 113–14, 133.
45. Riebicke, *Was brauchte der Weltkrieg?*, pp. 73–6, 79.
46. Paul Fussell, *The Great War and Modern Memory* (London, Oxford, and New York, Oxford University Press, 1975), p. 45.
47. Modris Eksteins, *Rites of Spring: The Great War and the Birth of the Modern Age* (Boston, Houghton Mifflin, 1989), p. 149.
48. Albrecht von Thaer, *Generalstabsdienst an der Front und in der O.H.L. Aus Briefen und Tagebuchaufzeichnungen 1915–1919,* ed. Siegfried A. Kaehler (Göttingen, Vandenhoeck & Ruprecht, 1958), pp. 25, 29, 35, 37, 39, 42, 46.
49. See Tony Ashworth, *Trench Warfare 1914–1918: The Live and Let Live System* (London, Macmillan, 1980).
50. Reichsarchiv, *Der Weltkrieg 1914 bis 1918*. 12: *Die Kriegführung im Frühjahr 1917* (Berlin, E. S. Mittler & Sohn, 1939), pp. 33–4.
51. *Der Weltkrieg 1914 bis 1918* 12, pp. 39–40.
52. *Der Weltkrieg 1914 bis 1918* 12, pp. 40–51.
53. *Der Weltkrieg 1914 bis 1918* 12, pp. 4, 10.
54. Josef Stürgkh, *Im Deutschen Grossen Hauptquartier* (Leipzig, Paul List Verlag, 1921), pp. 126–7.
55. See *Der Weltkrieg 1914 bis 1918* 11, pp. 14–16, 79.
56. BA-MA, PH 2/88 Feldart. Munition.
57. Report of 14 May 1917. BA-MA, PH 6I/28 7. AK (Gallwitz).
58. Riebicke, *Was brauchte der Weltkrieg?*, p. 43.
59. Hindenburg's memorandum of 22 November 1916. BA-MA, PH 3/26.
60. Edict of 12 October 1916. BA-MA, PH 3/25.
61. See the relevant memoranda of 15, 28, and 19 January 1917 in *Der Weltkrieg 1914 bis 1918* 1I, pp. 511–13.
62. *Der Weltkrieg 1914 bis 1918* 11, pp. 515–16.
63. *Der Weltkrieg 1914 bis 1918* 12, pp. 62–3.
64. Kronprinz Rupprecht von Bayern, *Mein Kriegstagebuch,* ed. Eugen von Frauenholz (3 vols, Berlin, Deutscher Nationalverlag, 1929) 2, p. 97.
65. BHStA-KA, HS2695. Vortrag über den Bau der Siegfriedstellung.
66. Ernst Jünger, *In Stahlgewittern. Ein Kriegsbuch* (Berlin, E. S. Mittler & Sohn, 1926), p. 139.
67. *Der Weltkrieg 1914 bis 1918* 12, pp. 120–33.
68. BA-MA, N 46 Nachlass Groener, vol. 63.
69. *Der Weltkrieg 1914 bis 1918* 12, p. 5. The light machine gun weighed 43 lbs, had a wooden shoulder stock and water-cooled barrel, and was mounted on a bipod.
70. Falkenhayn's memorandum of 15 May 1916. BA-MA, PH 3/305 Sturmabteilung.
71. Falkenhayn's memorandum of 27 June 1916. BA-MA, PH 3/305 Sturmabteilung.
72. *Der Weltkrieg 1914 bis 1918* 12, pp. 53–4.
73. Bauer's memorandum of 13 November 1916 with undated attachment. BA-MA, PH 3/28. See also Fritz von Lossberg, *Meine Tätigkeit im Weltkriege 1914–1918* (Berlin, E. S. Mittler & Sohn, 1939), pp. 295–304.
74. Ludendorff's memoranda of 17 and 22 April as well as 11 July 1917. BA-MA, PH 3/25. It is estimated that German staff produced about 775 million maps during the war. Riebicke, *Was brauchte der Weltkrieg?*, p. 80.
75. BA-MA, PH 3/305 Sturmabteilung.

76. Ludendorff's order of 29 December 1916. BA-MA, PH 3/305 Sturmateilung.
77. *Der Weltkrieg 1914 bis 1918* 12, pp. 60–1.
78. Seeckt to Hindenburg, 11 September 1917. BA-MA, PH 3/305 Sturmabteilung.
79. Reichsarchiv, *Der Weltkrieg 1914 bis 1918*. 8: *Die Operationen des Jahres 1915* (Berlin, E. S. Mittler & Sohn, 1932), p. 13.
80. *Der Weltkrieg 1914 bis 1918* 9, pp. 383–92.
81. Blücher, *An English Wife in Berlin*, p. 83.
82. Riebicke, *Was brauchte der Weltkrieg?*, p. 87.
83. *Der Weltkrieg 1914 bis 1918* 9, pp. 351–2, 392, 456.
84. Memorandum of 12 November 1914 by Baron v. d. Goltz, Brussels. BA-MA, PH 1/3 Mobilmachung 1914.
85. Cited in *Der Weltkrieg 1914 bis 1918* 9, p. 362. Reichstag speech of 10 March 1915. See also John G. Williamson, *Karl Helfferich 1872–1924: Economist, Financier, Politician* (Princeton, Princeton University Press, 1971), Ch. 4, 'Financial Warlord'.
86. See Riebicke, *Was brauchte der Weltkrieg?*, pp. 89–90; and Hardach, *The First World War*, pp. 159–60.
87. Figures by Manfred Zeidler in Wolfgang Michalka, ed., *Der Erste Weltkrieg. Wirkung, Wahrnehmung, Analyse* (Munich and Zurich, Piper, 1994), pp. 418–27.
88. Cited in Williamson, *Karl Helfferich*, p. 259.
89. *Der Weltkrieg 1914 bis 1918* 9, p. 361.
90. Lothar Burchardt, 'Die Auswirkungen der Kriegswirtschaft auf die deutsche Zivilbevölkerung im Ersten und im Zweiten Weltkrieg', *Militärgeschichtliche Mitteilungen* 15 (1974), pp. 88–9.
91. Cited in *Der Weltkrieg 1914 bis 1918* 9, p. 365; see also Williamson, *Karl Helfferich*, pp. 129–31.
92. Germany, *Verhandlungen des Reichstages. 13. Legislaturperiode, 2. Session*, vol. 306 (1916), p. 224.
93. BA-MA, W-10/50397 'Hindenburgprogramm und Hilfsdienstgesetz'. See also Erich Ludendorff, *Urkunden der Obersten Heeresleitung über ihre Tätigkeit 1916–18* (Berlin, E. S. Mittler & Sohn, 1920), pp. 63–5. The relevant documents have been reprinted by Wilhelm Deist, ed., *Militär und Innenpolitik im Weltkrieg 1914–1918* (2 vols, Düsseldorf, Droste Verlag, 1970) 2, pp. 482–536.
94. *Der Weltkrieg 1914 bis 1918* 12, pp. 38–40. The text is in *Ursachen und Folgen. Vom deutschen Zusammenbruch 1918 und 1945 bis zur staatlichen Neuordnung Deutschland in der Gegenwart*, eds Herbert Michaelis and Ernst Schraepler (15 vols, Berlin, Dokumenten-Verlag Dr. Herbert Wendler, 1958) 1, pp. 17–22.
95. Reports of the Austro-Hungarian Commissioner, Brussels, 22 October and 4 December 1916; and 6 March 1917. HHStA, PA I Deutschland 1918. Liassa Krieg 841. See also Hardach, *The First World War*, pp. 68–9.
96. *Der Weltkrieg 1914 bis 1918* 12, pp. 40–1.
97. *Der Weltkrieg 1914 bis 1918* 12, p. 37; Ludendorff, *Urkunden*, pp. 70–6.
98. Letter of 25 December 1916. BA-MA, N 564 Nachlass Wandel, vol. 10.
99. War Minister Stein to Wandel, 28 June 1918. BA-MA, N 564 Nachlass Wandel, vol. 11.
100. Rathenau to Wandel, 14 February 1917. BA-MA, N564 Nachlass Wandel, vol. 11.
101. See Holger H. Herwig, 'Industry, Empire and the First World War', *Modern Germany Reconsidered, 1870–1945*, ed. Gordon Martel (London and New York, Routledge, 1992), pp. 66–9.
102. BA-MA, W-10/50397. Italics in the original.
103. BA-MA, W-10/50397. The materials now are at the Bundesarchiv-Militärarchiv in Freiburg.
104. Gerald D. Feldman, *Army, Industry, and Labor in Germany, 1914–1918* (Princeton, Princeton University Press, 1966), pp. 303–4.

105. Michael Geyer, *Deutsche Rüstungspolitik 1860–1980* (Frankfurt, Suhrkamp, 1984), pp. 90–105.
106. Ludendorff, *Urkunden*, pp. 65–7, 78–81.
107. BA-MA, W-10/50652 Kriegstagebuch v. Kuhl. Entry for 2 July 1917.
108. Harold D. Lasswell, 'The Garrison State', *The American Journal of Sociology* 46 (1941), pp. 455–68.

7

Survival

*When . . . England declared war our country became a
beleaguered fortress. Cut off by land and cut off by sea it was
made wholly self-dependent; we were facing a war the
duration, cost, danger, and sacrifices of which no one could
foresee.*

Walther Rathenau, December 1915

Few leaders, civilian or military, in Austria–Hungary or Germany had
given much thought prior to 1914 to the eventuality – much less the conduct – of a protracted war. To be sure, several right-wing writers such as
Professor Dietrich Schäfer of the Pan-German League and General
August Keim of the Navy League had demanded the creation of an 'economic general staff' in the last years of peace, but their clarion calls had
gone unanswered. Neither the War Ministry nor the vast majority of
Prussia's generals had any desire to conduct a war of attrition that would
have entailed mobilization of the nation's manpower and material
reserves. Conrad von Hötzendorf at Vienna had shared this firm faith in a
brief, albeit apocalyptic, war. The ruling elites in Berlin and Vienna had
taken comfort in the 'short-war illusion'. Militarists as well as pacifists
believed that modern industrial societies with their interwoven economies
and trade, and their vast hordes of urban industrialized workers, could not
sustain another Seven or Thirty Years' War.

History seemed to support this view. Prussia's war with Austria in 1866
had lasted but 7 weeks and even the Franco-Prussian War of 1870–1 had
ended in just under 6 months. Europe's soldiers learned little from the
American Civil War, which they dismissed as a struggle between amateur
civilian soldiers lacking the expert training of staff colleges. Similarly,
they ignored the lessons of the Russo-Japanese War since it was seen as
an uneven conflict between a moribund and corrupt European feudal

empire and an upstart Asiatic power using the knowledge and training that it had acquired from its German military and British naval advisors.

War to most Europeans remained the sport of kings, run by elite aristo-cratic cabinets. Few paused to contemplate US General Philip H. Sheridan's comments, made while an observer with the Prussian Army during its war against France in 1870–1, that Bismarck had failed to understand the nature of modern warfare. Sheridan had wished to see 'more smoke from burning villages' and 'so much suffering that [the French] must long for peace and force the government to demand it. The people must be left nothing but their eyes to weep with after the war'. While Prussia knew like no other power 'how to defeat an enemy', Sheridan noted that it had not yet learned 'how to annihilate one'.[1]

Austria–Hungary and Germany set out in August 1914 to fight a short war. Both hurled their million-men armies of regulars and reservists into the conflict with reckless abandon. In Galicia and northern France they ran lemming-like to their destruction. Civilian populations accepted tem-porary unemployment – which reached 21 per cent in Germany late in 1914 – as a necessary side-effect of mobilization. Food supplies were abundant after a good harvest. Industries were left alone to produce the tools of war. Finances were ignored in the expectation that the vanquished would pay for the conflict via indemnities and reparations. There was almost an over-consumption of foodstuffs and consumer goods in the autumn of 1914. Daily intakes of 3400 calories – divided among 90 g. of protein, 120 g. of fat, and 400 g. of carbohydrates – seemed assured per-petually. In Germany, leaders stressed that farmers produced 90 per cent of the nation's food needs – but omitted to point out that they did so only with the help of more than 2 million tons of foreign nitrogenous and phos-phatic fertilizers, 6 million tons of hard fodder such as barley, corn, and oats, and 1 million foreign seasonal workers. Without these, domestic production soon fell to 70 per cent of national needs. It plummeted even further in Austria.

Hunger: Austria–Hungary

The outbreak of war had been greeted with popular enthusiasm in most parts of the Habsburg Empire. Crowds waved flags, sang anthems, and demanded a quick punitive strike against Serbia. Vienna's Cardinal Piffl detected the 'voice of God' speaking to Austrians through the 'roar of the guns' and admonished his flock to smite down 'the enemies of God'. The Social Democrat Viktor Adler, echoing Karl Marx and paralleling his comrades in Berlin, endorsed the war to keep the Tsar's dreaded hordes out of Brünn, Budapest, and Vienna. Newspaper editors throughout the realm detected a new 'Austrianness, a new Hungarianness' as political squabbles were set aside in favour of a new sense of purpose and a spirit of regeneration.[2]

A willingness to sacrifice abounded. The late Crown Prince Rudolph's widow showed the way by converting her castle into a 200-bed hospital. Franz Joseph's companion, Katharina Schratt, likewise offered her villa in Vienna as a hospital. The Kaiser's youngest daughter visited recovery wards. The grandmother of Archduke Karl, the new heir to the throne, founded an institution to rehabilitate the blinded. And when news reached Franz Joseph that 'certain Viennese circles' refused to quarter Jewish refugees from Galicia, the Kaiser by way of example offered his summer residence at Schönbrunn. Less charitably, Austrian Prime Minister Stürgkh trumpeted that his government's greatest success was to have turned the Reichsrat (parliament) on the Ring into a hospital!

Vienna also rose to the occasion. Public buildings, schools, and the great Rotunda at the Prater amusement park were transformed into military hospitals. Libraries, museums, and theatres were neither heated nor lit to save fuel. The city's mayor, Richard Weiskirchner, combated food 'hoarding' by buying up available stocks of food and fuel and reselling them at cost. A giant wooden 'Iron Guardsman' – soon to be copied in Berlin by a massive wooden statue of Hindenburg – was raised at Schwarzenberg Square, and affluent Viennese were invited to drive nails into it for a contribution to the widows' and orphans' fund. Women exchanged gold wedding rings for iron to help pay for the war. An Imperial Organization of Austrian Housewives knitted socks and sweaters for the troops, wrapped bandages, and helped young brides care for their infants. Thousands of Viennese answered the call to collect wool, pans, newspapers, and tobacco for the 200 000 refugees who streamed into Vienna after the military disasters in Galicia. Doctors went from door to door to vaccinate against smallpox. Prominent surgeons developed artificial limbs for the growing army of amputees. And the city opened a special section of the venerable Central Cemetery, where its greatest writers, musicians, and composers were honoured, to bury the legions of war dead.[3] Hastily constructed breastworks topped with barbed wire around Vienna's periphery, however, were a constant and stark reminder of the closeness of the war.

Public morale was maintained in part by a steady stream of atrocity stories – later published in two *Red Books* – concerning Serbian ritual murders of Austrian women and children and Russian Cossack cruelties perpetrated against Habsburg soldiers. And by the wholesale distribution of medals. Civilians who ministered to the poor, sick, and hungry received a Service Cross, while soldiers at the front were showered with 3 million Courage Medals – which, cynical wags noted, could have been better used to produce war material. High-ranking officers were rewarded in large numbers with the Great Cross Order of Leopold and the Order of Stephen; some with the Knight's Cross of the Order of Maria Theresa; and a very few with its august Grand Cross.

But the initial sense of *Gemeinschaft* collapsed when food shortages began to arise in the larger cities by October 1914. The first 10 000 horses were butchered to offset the government's ban that same month on slaughtering calves. By December bakers were instructed to add 30 per cent barley, rye, corn, and potato meal to wheat flour. Ration cards for the coarse 'war bread' were introduced in Vienna and other urban centres in April 1915. In short order, other cards and vouchers followed for coffee, fat, milk, and sugar. On 11 May 1915 Vienna experienced its first food riots as women stormed and then plundered stores. At the same time, the government introduced 2 'meatless' days per week (extended to 3 in 1916). Beer brewing was sharply curtailed to save cereal grains. More than 1000 women stormed government buildings in Linz in October to protest food shortages and high prices.

Vienna ran out of flour, potatoes, and fat by autumn 1915, while milk and butter could be obtained only at exorbitant prices. An American observer that year noted the poor quality of what he called the 'heavy, unappetizing bread . . . made of a mixture of potato flour, corn-meal, rye and a very little wheat'. One year later an officer at the American Embassy reported on the desperate plight of workers in the Favoriten district:

> I noticed strings of poorly dressed women and children held in line by police . . . waiting for milk, vessel in hand. . . . Latecomers went home empty-handed, while lucky ones obtained only half as much as they expected. Similar lines . . . can be observed standing in the morning hours in front of the bakers' shops and stores where coffee, tea, and sugar is [sic] being sold.

Potatoes 'not fit for consumption' were all that was available at the public markets.[4]

The truth is that the Dual Monarchy had made no plans for a protracted struggle. In peacetime the two halves of the Empire had complemented each other: Hungary was the breadbasket of the Habsburg realms while Austria, Bohemia, and Moravia constituted their industrial base. Beyond that, Galicia was a major producer of grains and oil while Transylvania was rich in mines and timber. The Empire of 51 million people had seemed well positioned to undertake a modest war of short duration.

The wholly unexpected grain shortage that plagued the Empire had several immediate causes. The drain of farm labour to the armed forces had dramatically reduced the 1914 harvest in Austria and Hungary, and the Russian occupation of Galicia (one-third of all arable land in the Austrian half of the Empire) and the Bukovina eliminated southern Poland as a source of grains and oil. Cereal crops in both halves of the Dual Monarchy between 1914 and 1916 fell from 91 to 49 million quintals (220 lbs each) in Austria and from 146 to 78 million in Hungary. Budapest banned food exports to Austria at the start of 1915, which drew sharp cries of Magyar 'disloyalty' from Vienna. Shortages of corn and oats for horses and cattle led to their widescale slaughter. Conditions simply worsened from year to year. Whereas the Monarchy estimated that it was 9.8 million quintals short of its grain needs in 1914, that figure leaped to 37.1 million quintals by 1916 – despite the fact that the Army released 90 000 soldiers to help bring in the harvest. Hoarding, a dearth of artificial fertilizers, requisitioning of draught horses from farms, government mismanagement, lack of effective market controls, and the Army's indiscriminate drafting of agrarian labourers accounted for much of the food misery during the early period of the war.[5] By 1916 Austrian provinces, districts, and villages virtually became self-contained economic zones which raised trade barriers against each other. Peasants despised price controls and kept products from market.

Urban dwellers flocked to the countryside to exchange jewels and silks for food. Austrian gendarmes by and large turned a blind eye to the flourishing black market, which many Austrians regarded as the new national sport. 'War gardens' flourished as amateur gardeners and children turned flower beds and lawns into grain and potato fields. Even the stately gardens of the Schwarzenberg Palace in Vienna were turned over to food production. Franz Joseph created 1000 family plots to raise food in the city's Prater garden. By 1917 more than 34 000 Viennese cultivated allotment gardens (*Schrebergarten*); 1 year later the figure reached 157 300 small holdings.[6]

The year 1916 was especially disastrous. The potato harvest came in at a dismal 50 million quintals, 72 million below the last peacetime figure. As a result, potatoes were rationed at 2.2 lbs per person per week. The Army's monthly slaughter of 147 000 cows stood in stark contrast to the 48 700 bovines provided for the civilian population in 1916. And the 160 g. of meat allowed each person per week sufficed to purchase one cutlet for a Sunday *Wiener Schnitzel* – provided the fat to fry it in was available.[7] Massive slaughters of horses set in to satisfy the growing demand for meat.

Austrians turned to ersatz to meet food shortages. Roasted acorns, chicory, and beechnuts replaced coffee; later in the war, 'coffee' was stretched with caramel-flavoured raw sugar and beet flour. 'Tea' consisted mainly of roasted barley, grasses, and wild flowers. Plant fats replaced animal fats in most diets. Stockyards saved the blood from slaughtered animals as 'mixer' for ersatz foods such as the infamous 'war sausage' which working women equated to 'a mouthful of sawdust'. Bouillon cubes were made 70 to 90 per cent of cooking salt rather than meat extracts. Special 'potato dryers' were imported from Germany to start up 120 Austrian food-processing plants hastily built to render potato flour edible. Alcohol consumption was limited to 1 per cent of peacetime volume and enterprising distillers used wood, sawdust, and sulphide byproducts to produce what must have been an unappetizing and potentially lethal *Schnaps*. Cooking oil was extracted from corn. Oil and sunflower 'cakes' replaced corn and oats as feed for horses; rape, poppy, and mustard 'cakes' took the place of green feed for cattle. The shortage of artificial fertilizers was partly offset by hordes of volunteers who combed the caves of Galicia and Hungary for pigeon droppings. Paper and nettle fibres took the place of cotton in textiles; wood and paper that of leather for shoe soles.[8] When ersatz tobacco made from plant fibres proved too vile, wealthy Viennese, such as Sigmund Freud, drew their cigars entirely from the black market. Karl Kraus, the Austrian satirist, is widely credited with the apothegm that while conditions in Berlin were serious but not hopeless, in Austria they were hopeless but not serious.

Shortages were everywhere accompanied by skyrocketing prices: food prices jumped 600 per cent in Vienna in the first 2 years of the war. Profiteers became the object of visceral hatred. Leather speculators reaped gains of 200 per cent in a single year. Vienna alone added 400 millionaires to its rolls during the war. Nor were city fathers immune to profiteering: the capital's stockyard and processing plants, which had a monopoly on the sale of meat, in 1915 pocketed net profits of 350 per cent – 10 times the peacetime rate.

Food riots forced the government to rescind plans to raise maximum prices for bread and flour on 1 January 1916 within 7 days. In May and September 1916 women and children smashed windows and pillaged shops to protest bread shortages and rising prices. Viennese police used fire hoses to disperse angry crowds of mothers protesting the lack of food. City Hall set up soup kitchens to alleviate the hunger; 54 000 people daily frequented them in search of cheap food. Special 'soup and tea institutions' serviced another 10 000 residents each day. Trams printed recipes for boiling water, vegetables, potatoes, and grasses on the back of fare tickets. The phrase 'Vienna sickness' was coined as poor nutrition caused a tuberculosis epidemic (10 000 reported cases).[9] The Army's attempt to alleviate the capital's food shortage by slaughtering 4000 goats taken from the Balkans was little more than an act of good will. Food riots lasting several days ravaged the land from St Pölten to Graz.

Lack of fuel plagued not only military transport and industrial output. Railway travel for civilians was banned in 1914. Streetcar service in Vienna by 1916 was curtailed during the day and suspended after 9 p.m. Street lighting was cut down to dim illumination or was eliminated entirely. 'Daylight saving time' was introduced in May 1916 to conserve fuel. In the winter of 1916–17 city households were allowed to heat only one room – with the result that water pipes froze by the thousands and water had to be dispersed from fire hydrants. Churches, schools, public offices, and theatres went without heat entirely. Late in 1916, coal production daily fell 20 000 tons short of needs. Since the Army took 81 per cent of all iron produced there was none left to repair urban infrastructures – much less to undertake new construction. Horses were by then so feeble from lack of green feed that dogs increasingly pulled the small four-wheeled carts that moved most urban goods.

An exasperated Friedrich Adler, son of the socialist leader, murdered Prime Minister Stürgkh in a Viennese restaurant on 21 October 1916 partly to protest the abysmal plight of his fellow citizens. Allen W. Dulles, a young official in the American Embassy, reported on living conditions in Vienna. The people, he concluded, were hungry and discouraged. Food shortages were chronic. Bread was an indigestible, soggy 'black concoction' desired by few. Restaurants had not served butter for months and their chefs had precious little fat or milk for cooking.[10] Consular reports from Prague, Karlsbad, and Vienna told a similar story.

Conditions in the lands of the Hungarian Holy Crown were marginally better. Since only one-fourth of peacetime trade had been with states other than Austria, Hungary was little affected by the British and Italian blockades. But Prime Minister Tisza was well aware that food shortages could lead to urban riots, which might threaten the Magyars' political stranglehold over a country in which they were outnumbered by Slavs. Tisza kept the parliament at Budapest in session both as a control on Vienna and the *AOK*, and as a lightning rod to deflect internal dissent. Early in 1915 he reduced grain shipments to Austria from 23 to 4 million quintals (!) to assure the domestic supply. Hungary sold surpluses to Germany for hard currency or much-needed industrial goods and raw materials. Tisza understood that Hungary's agricultural productivity lagged behind that of Austria – it took two Hungarian farmers to feed a single city dweller whereas one Austrian farmer fed two urban residents – and hence was careful not to deplete his food supply.[11] Displeased by the escalating conscription of Hungarian peasants into the *k.u.k.* Army, Tisza used food supplies to protest this action.

But Hungary could not entirely escape the food misery that plagued the Central Powers. Fish and meat were scarce by 1915 and prices rose 200 to 400 per cent. The cost of potatoes nearly doubled. Beer output was cut by 60 per cent to save grain. Cereal crops fell to 60 per cent of peacetime levels. Ration cards were introduced and price ceilings set on basic goods. In 1916 2 'meatless' days and 1 'fatless' day per week were imposed. The consumption of horse and dog meat rose as veal and beef disappeared from markets. Butter, milk, and sugar often were not available and daily diets for most of Hungary's poor consisted of cornmeal, cabbage, and dark bread. The birthrate fell to less than half its prewar level, in large measure due to poor nutrition and health care. In 1916 a disastrous harvest brought in only half the usual crop, and coal shortages idled many of Hungary's 25 000 steam-driven harvesters.

On 27 February 1917 Tisza finally bowed to repeated Austrian demands to create a Joint Food Committee. But General Landwehr von Pragenau's super ministry, which was placed directly under Kaiser Karl not to arouse Hungarian constitutional hackles, only had the power to suggest and to persuade, not to command.[12] Tisza continued to sell Hungarian surplus grains primarily to the *AOK* and thus denied cereal crops to the Austrian civilian populace. In the process, the Magyar leader drove Vienna ever closer toward total dependence on Berlin.

Both Austria–Hungary and Germany hoped to alleviate shortages by exploiting conquered territories. In December 1916 they raised great expectations of mammoth grain and oil deliveries in the wake of the occupation of Romania: Germany was to receive five-eighths and the Dual Monarchy three-eighths of the anticipated spoils of war. Deliveries began to materialize by late 1916: 54 000 rail cars of grain and 1000 tons of oil per day. Concurrently, Serbia was 'relieved' of 170 000 head of cattle, 190 000 sheep, and 50 000 hogs. Albania supplied 50 000 turtles to Austrian and German tables. Poland in 1916–17 surrendered 6000 freight cars of grain, 14 000 of potatoes, 300 000 of coal, and 2000 of green feed for cattle and horses as well as 1.9 million eggs, 19 000 horses, and 1.7 million cubic yards of wood.[13] Devalued currency paid for most of the products.

But even this largesse failed to meet the demands of more than 100 million Austro-Hungarian-German civilians. The high hopes for Romanian deliveries were dashed due to a near complete breakdown of that country's markets and transport. In 1916 General Landwehr estimated that the shortfall in flour in Austria-Hungary amounted to 100 wagons per day, with the result that flour rations were reduced to 120 g. per week.[14] The prewar per-capita consumption of 493 g. of potatoes was cut to 118.

The war also ravaged Hungarian finances, which suffered on a par with those of Austria. Tisza's economic advisor, János Teleszky, projected that under a complex formula whereby Hungary assumed 36.4 per cent of the cost of the war, Budapest expended 15 000 million Kronen between 1914 and 1917. Only a small portion of this amount was raised by new income and war profits taxes. Like Austria and Germany, Hungary raised funds by way of war loans and courted inflation by increasing the amount of money in circulation. Somehow it would all be settled at war's end – hopefully by indemnities and reparations to be exacted from the vanquished.

Hungarian industries, which were mainly centred in the western regions around Győr, survived relatively better than those in Austria. Coal and iron-ore production remained at about 90 per cent of peacetime levels. The major downturn came in the textile industries, where the Allied blockade by 1916 cut imports to 21 per cent of prewar levels. The loss of industrial workers among Hungary's 700 000 war casualties by late 1916 was compensated by the employment of women, the extension of the working week up to 85 hours, and the recruitment of children as young as 8 years for factory work.[15]

Above all, Austria–Hungary used prisoners of war to make up for the mounting human losses. By the summer of 1915, almost 100 000 Russian POWs cultivated the land or built roads in each half of the Monarchy; only 2500 were fit for the highly-skilled mining industries. Only the large estates could afford to use POWs due to the costs of guarding them. Prisoner of war camps were built at Theresienstadt and Eger in Bohemia and at Győr in Hungary. By 1917 the POW total had risen to 1.1 million. Officials from the American Embassy at Vienna toured the camps and found them to be well run. A camp at Linz housing 90 000 Russians, for example, consisted of a 'town' laid out in squares with 'comfortable buildings', kitchens, Orthodox churches, running water, and garden plots. The only problem was that Russian and Serb soldiers constantly engaged in murderous feuds.[16]

Industry benefited less as few of the POWs possessed machine or tool skills. As a result, Habsburg officials maintained far stricter military control over their workers than was the case in Germany, where labour boards allowed them to transfer freely to higher-paying industrial jobs. In time, inflation, food shortages, and price hikes militated against industrial tranquillity. Teleszky calculated for Hungary that while workers' wages rose on average 50 per cent between 1914 and 1916, food prices tripled. Living costs for a Hungarian worker's family of five increased 225 per cent during the same period.[17]

In Austria, the state held the upper hand. Trade unions were weak in comparison to those in France and Germany. The Social Democratic Party had succumbed to war euphoria in 1914, admonishing its 'veterans of class warfare' to rally 'behind the flag to their last breath'. A War Productions Law from December 1912 allowed the state to recruit for war production all men under the age of 50 declared unfit for military duty. Put in force on 25 July 1914, the Law forbade workers under age 50 to quit their employment. Heavy fines and imprisonment up to 1 year – and in severe cases transfers to the front – faced workers who agitated against their employers. The ban on Sunday work was rescinded on 30 July. Workers who had been called to military service but who remained at their industrial jobs by order of the Army until July 1916 were paid a military rather than an industrial rate. Civilian workers who demonstrated for higher wages or better food could as punishment be shifted to the 'military' (*Landsturm*) list, with greatly reduced pay. Factories where workers demanded change were 'militarized', that is, placed under Army discipline. The establishment of so-called 'wages and complaint commissions' in March 1917 did little to assuage the workers. In industrial border regions under the direct control of the *AOK*, labourers were forbidden even to assemble peacefully.[18] Pubs were closed by 9 p.m. to prevent heated discussions of wartime conditions.

Like its counterparts in France and Germany, the Austrian military in 1914 had conscripted legions of industrial workers in the firm belief that the war would be over in a matter of weeks. In August the number of skilled workers in the north Bohemian metal industry, for example, dropped from 24 887 to 9706. The Prague Iron Industry Society (PEIG) lost 21 per cent of its workers and 24 per cent of its non-factory employees, and the Austrian Alpine Mining Society 18 per cent of its labourers at the start of the war. To make up for this loss of skilled labour, many factories demanded double shifts and instituted 110-hour working weeks (16 hours per day for 7 days).[19]

By the end of 1914 the *AOK* realized its error in conscripting workers from war-related industries and gradually began to 'repatriate' 1.3 million Austrian labourers to their erstwhile workplaces. The closure of luxury and clothing industries in 1914 also freed up large numbers of skilled workers for war industries; more than 10 000 labourers entered first unemployment rolls and then munitions factories in Vienna alone. Women, of course, were another potential source of labour. In 1913 they constituted only 14.5 per cent of the Austrian machine industries' employees, but made up nearly half of the labour force in munitions plants such as Manfred Weiss in Budapest and the Munitions Factory at Wöllersdorf. A 1911 law that precluded night work for women was lifted in October 1914, and the War Office routinely pressured industry to employ women.

The results were mixed at best. Many women preferred work on the land where they were at least assured food and shelter. Labour leaders remonstrated that women were not physically up to the demanding work required of them in mines and factories – and undoubtedly feared that they might permanently take the place of males at the front. Entrepreneurs opposed the employment of women because they could not be threatened with transfer to the front and thus were free to demonstrate for higher wages and to foment strikes. Coking plants, for example, employed only 15 per cent women in 1916; the following year they reduced the figure to 7 per cent by replacing women with Russian POWs. By comparison, females comprised 35 per cent of coking and smelting plants in France and Germany. In Vienna, on the other hand, the percentage of women in metal and machine industries rose from 17.5 in 1913 to 42.5 in 1916. In Graz, Budapest, Pressburg, and Vienna, women were employed in great numbers as trolley drivers and conductors, working average shifts of 12 to 14 hours.

Women in factories were paid between one-third and one-half the wages of males; most worked 11-hour days augmented by 1 or 2 hours of overtime (without additional pay). Remuneration for piece work was reduced to prevent women from 'enriching' themselves from the war: the pay for producing three grenades at the Heinzenfeld Munitions Plant, for example, fell from 1 Krone 20 Heller to 90 Heller (pennies) between 1914 and 1918. Škoda tied the wages it paid women to those they received in agriculture, traditionally the lowest-paying sector.

There is no question that women were willing to work. Their numbers in munitions plants directly controlled by the War Office rose to between 45 and 50 per cent of the work force as the *Kriegsamt* actively encouraged their employment. Still, whereas the French steel industry by 1918 consisted of 35 per cent women, the Austrian figure was 9 per cent. Copper and zinc industries likewise never had more than 11 per cent women in their ranks. Most entrepreneurs continued to consider the home the proper place of employment for females and feared that their presence in factories would lead to industrial unrest. Adolescents were recruited in large numbers mainly for zinc mines and smelters, where they comprised 11 per cent of all workers; elsewhere their proportion rarely surpassed 5 per cent.[20] Most youths worked between 60 and 70 hours per week.

Housing for female workers was abysmal. In Wiener Neustadt 72 people huddled together in a three-room house; 36 slept by day and an equal number by night. The Roth AG powder factory housed its employees in a former weaving factory. Women and children slept on the ground floor; soldiers on the floor above. Beds consisted of rough wooden planks covered with straw sacks. There was no soap, no linens, few brooms, and even fewer sinks. Most toilets consisted of holes dug into the ground. The children were dirty and unkempt. Lice ruled the factory. Most of its

20 000 occupants preferred to sleep outside in the summer. Showers could at best accommodate 1000 people per 24-hour day. Toxic fumes in the armaments plants raised the incidence of amenorrhea from 2 per cent in peacetime to 25 by 1917. Promiscuity and prostitution among the so-called 'gunpowder girls' were frequent. It is estimated that 35 000 women worked the world's oldest trade in Vienna alone, charging between 20 and 40 Kronen per 'trick'.[21]

Initially, Austrian industry kept industrial wages and bonuses low so as not to set a dangerous precedent for the postwar period. But by February 1915 it was forced to supplement these low wages with special food and cost-of-living adjustments. A female head of a household in Innsbruck received 1.5 Kronen per adult per day; in Vienna 1.32 and in Galicia 0.86. Children received half the adult sum. By the end of 1915, inflation was so rampant that a litre of milk cost 72 Heller – 6 more than a child of 8 received in government subsidies per day.[22]

In August 1916 the government created special 'wage commissions' in an attempt to index wages to the cost of living. In fact, nominal wages rose gradually between 1914 and 1916. The scales for miners and mill workers at Leoben, for example, shot up 46 and 65 per cent, respectively. But inflation quickly ate up the extra funds, and in 1917 wages throughout Austria had to be doubled just to keep pace with higher food costs and inflation. While wages rose two or threefold during the course of the war, the cost of food and housing increased twelvefold. In real wages, a metal worker's income of 40 Kronen per week in 1914 had dropped to 6.84 by 1918. And wages fluctuated wildly from industry to industry. Whereas textile workers received 12 to 16 Kronen per week at the end of 1916, their comrades in iron and steel industries were paid 35 to 40 per week.

Still, labour remained calm throughout the first 3 years of the war. The number of strikes per annum actually declined from 104 in 1914 to just 19 in 1915, and 15 in 1916. The average length of strikes during the war stood at 5 days – compared with 16 for the period between 1904 and 1913. Part of the reason was that the metal industry in July 1916 persuaded the War Ministry to pay civilian and *Landsturm* workers on the same industrial scale. The government also offered workers the option of taking Sundays off or receiving overtime pay. Rents for workers' flats were frozen at peacetime levels while those of others were left free to float on the market. Workers received extra food rations and many firms paid them in foodstuffs. The Steyr munitions works and numerous coal mines contracted directly with agrarian cooperatives for food deliveries.

In March 1917 Vienna created 'complaints commissions' to regulate labour–industry relations. In large industrial centres, the government set up three separate committee systems for mining, metal industries, and other industries. The committees were composed of representatives from labour and industry and chaired by a delegate from the *AOK*. In this they had much in common with Benito Mussolini's later 'corporations' in Italy – and like them had little power. Bitter acrimony among labour and industry reduced the commissions to debating societies, and late in 1917 the government withdrew their powers to set minimum wages and to conclude collective bargaining agreements.[23] Interestingly, the military representatives generally took the side of workers against employers. Their preindustrial and patrimonial mentality may have been better attuned to the hardships of labourers and biased against the profit-driven considerations of capitalists. In the end, the latter triumphed by pressuring the government to remove 'uncooperative' military delegates from the committees.

The increasing misery caused by inflation, food shortages, and skyrocketing prices reached crisis proportions in the spring of 1917. The Ballhausplatz informed Berlin in March that 'the Monarchy is at the end of its endurance'. The food supply was 'critical' and hunger epidemic in Bohemia and Dalmatia. Stores were without meat. Raw materials for industry sufficed only until the autumn. The Romanian harvest was 30 to 40 per cent below expectations.[24]

The political consequences came quickly. In May labour unrest exploded in the metal and munitions industries at Wiener Neustadt and the Arsenal in the capital. Sympathy strikes broke out at Škoda in Pilsen, Witkowitz, and Märisch-Ostrau. By 24 May more than 42 000 metal and machine workers had walked off their jobs. Police hauled workers out of their beds at dawn and escorted them back to work. On 8 July the government placed all industrial plants under military law and swore their workers into the *Landsturm*. Industrial order was restored when the government introduced the 52.5-hour working week. Civilian courts found that their workloads multiplied tenfold to 23 000 cases per year as domestic unrest translated into public violence. The May strikes were mainly for higher wages and more food, although for the first time they brought to the surface demands for an end to the war. Little wonder that Kaiser Karl launched his secret diplomacy to end the war at the height of the strikes.

Beleaguered fortress: Germany

The first food shortages also appeared at German markets by late 1914. The Army continued to purchase what it needed without regard for civilian requirements; food prices rose sharply as supplies dwindled. The government quickly established maximum prices on a host of food items such as potatoes and sugar, but in January 1915 the Social Democrats and their trade unions demanded price ceilings for all goods and foodstuffs as well as production controls. Otherwise, the labour movement warned, it would unilaterally terminate the domestic truce (*Burgfriede*) of August 1914.

Berlin at once moved to head off possible labour unrest. It nationalized wheat and rationed bread at 5 lbs per person per week (January). Next it established maximum prices and production quotas for butter and fish (October), milk and pork, fruits and vegetables (November). And it forbade farmers to feed their livestock with cereal grains. The Federal Chamber decreed that starting on 1 November, Tuesdays and Fridays were to be 'meatless' and 'fatless' days; that restaurants were not to prepare dishes made with fat on Mondays and Thursdays; and that no pork could be served on Saturdays.[25] By 1916 the German people were reduced to a meagre and monotonous diet of black bread, fatless sausage, 3 lbs of potatoes per person per week, one egg per week, and turnips. Plant foods replaced meat. Few Germans understood fully the complex causes of their predicament.

In the first place, the Army consumed copious amounts of food and fodder. A single corps of 35 000 soldiers *monthly* devoured 1 million lbs of meat, 660 000 loaves of bread, 189 000 lbs of fat (or 242 000 lbs of canned meat and 121 000 lbs of marmalade), and 73 000 lbs of coffee; its horses needed 7 million lbs of oats and more than 4 million lbs of hay. The XVIII Army Corps, for example, estimated that it needed 1000 wagons extending for 9 miles to haul its monthly allotment of bread; its butchers slaughtered 1320 cows, 1100 hogs, and 4158 sheep every month. Taken as a whole, the German Army *weekly* demolished 60 million lbs of bread, 131 million lbs of potatoes, and 17 million lbs of meat.[26] No one in the government or the General Staff had given serious considerations to such mammoth needs for a period of 4 years.

Secondly, the highly decentralized nature of the Bismarckian state militated against tight controls over the nation's food supply. The special interests of state governments often clashed with those of the Reich. Royal Prussian ministers especially were reluctant to take orders from imperial German secretaries. The devolution of political and economic power to the Deputy Commanding Generals of the Reich's 24 army corps under the Prussian Law of Siege enacted in August 1914 further diffused the federal government's powers. Some of these generals behaved in almost comical fashion. In October 1916, at the height of the food crisis, the deputy commander of the VII Army Corps at Münster devoted all of his energies to enforcing a recent ban on renting out hunting and fishing rights to foreign residents in Germany.[27]

Thirdly, soldiers and statesmen pursued separate strategies with regard to labour. While the Chancellor sought to hold the line on wages and prices, the *OHL* was quite content to raise workers' wages in order to enhance productivity. This, in turn, gave industrialists ample excuse to hike prices and to broaden profit margins. The workers, for their part, developed a keen sense of their intrinsic value to the new 'garrison state'. In the process, economic and social distinctions were magnified and the sense of *Gemeinschaft* disappeared; the war became a business proposition, an industry unto itself.[28]

Mismanagement and lack of prewar planning contributed significantly to the vicissitudes of the national food supply. Cut off from overseas supplies of fodder by British naval power, Germany experienced a grave shortage of green feeds as early as the winter of 1914–15. Average weights for dressed hogs fell by 40 lbs and for cattle by more than 200. Farmers responded by (illegally) feeding their animals cereal grains and potatoes, thereby removing these commodities from markets. The government thereupon created a Wheat Corporation to oversee grain supply in November 1914, followed by an Imperial Export and Exemptions Office to regulate cereal grain consumption in January 1915. It also seized the national supply of potatoes and oats and forbade the 'waste' of grains and potatoes on animals. A bewildering plethora of imperial agencies to regulate food production and supply quickly came into being: the Imperial Cereals Office (1915), the Food Controls Office (1916), and the War Food Office (1916), to name only a few. But mismanagement continued to haunt Berlin bureaucrats: in February 1915 they ordered the troops on the Western Front to plough under French and Belgian sugar-beet fields for fear that these products would drive down the price of beets at home![29]

The three-way war among farmers, consumers, and government quickly escalated. When farmers refused to abide by the government's injunctions against using grains and potatoes for animal feeds, Berlin in the spring of 1915 ordered the wholesale slaughter of hogs. Perhaps as much as 35 per cent (9 million) of Germany's pigs were killed in what the public dubbed the great *Schweinemord* (hog murder). Not surprisingly, the reduced pork supply immediately translated into steep price hikes at local markets and the Federal Chamber in November was forced to institute maximum prices on about 700 staples to protect consumers. Tit for tat, farmers withheld hogs from markets: the number slaughtered fell from 61 000 to 17 000 in the span of two weeks.[30] Meat rationing cards were hurriedly ordered to complement bread cards, first introduced at Berlin in February 1915.

Panic set in among bureaucrats as the public mood turned ugly. The Federal Chamber sought to head off food riots by ordering all inhabitants of towns larger than 5000 to lay in a store of canned meats – without defining either how many cans or where they were to come from. In March 1915 Berlin ordered a national count of both potatoes and farm animals, which on 12 April led to the creation of an Imperial Potato Office. The new agency was empowered to buy up available stocks to ensure the summer's supply. And when it undertook another national survey of potatoes, it found that stocks far exceeded earlier estimates. Not only had the mass slaughter of hogs been unnecessary, but the government, fearing that the potatoes would spoil, immediately lifted its ban on distilling them for domestic 'brandy'.[31] While this undoubtedly satisfied many imbibers, it did little to assure the populace that the government was in control of the food situation.

Public outcries against rising prices and war profiteering mounted. In July 1915 the government established special commissions to investigate flagrant cases of war profiteering and in September ordered all cities with more than 10 000 inhabitants to create formal price-control agencies. As was to be expected, the 1000 control boards established throughout the Reich quickly bogged down in mountains of paperwork. The first food riots were recorded at Berlin-Lichtenberg in October. Thereafter, women in many parts of Germany plundered food shops and showered city halls with stones to protest the lack of food. The Berlin police estimated that food prices rose 130 per cent in the first year of the war.

The crisis in the German food supply can also be traced to the illegal British naval blockade that commenced with the onset of hostilities in August 1914. Great Britain had signed two critical international agreements pertaining to blockade. The Declaration of Paris (1856) stipulated that a blockade, to be 'obligatory', had to be 'effective', that is, 'maintained by a sufficient force really to prevent access' to any part of an enemy's coast. And in February 1909 Whitehall had inked the London Naval Conference that divided materials into three distinct categories: 'absolute contraband' for goods (arms, munitions, military equipment) used for war only; 'conditional contraband' for goods (food, fodder, fuel, clothing) used in both civilian and war industries; and noncontraband items (cotton, rubber, fertilizers, metallic ores) used only in the civilian sector.[32] As early as May 1912 the Royal Navy had worked out a policy of 'distant blockade' whereby it could control Europe's imports and exports from the English Channel and the Norway–Shetlands straits.

Britain quickly reneged on these agreements. It violated the Declaration of Paris when the Royal Navy failed to blockade Germany's Baltic Sea ports. And it voided the protocols of the London Naval Conference through a steady and unlimited expansion of the contraband list. Specifically, two British Orders in Council of 10 August and 29 October 1914, while paying lip service to the 1909 agreement, made foodstuffs 'absolute contraband' and threw overboard the doctrine of 'continuous voyage' whereby ships bound for neutrals such as the Netherlands, Denmark, Norway, and Sweden could not be subjected to search and seizure. When Germany planted mines off the British coast, London reacted on 2 November 1914 by declaring the North Sea a 'military area' – a move which prompted Germany on 4 February 1915 to proclaim the waters surrounding Great Britain and Ireland a 'war area'. Britain escalated the maritime war on 11 March with yet another Order in Council prohibiting neutral vessels from calling at German ports, abolishing all distinction between contraband and noncontraband cargoes, and demanding that neutrals subject themselves to British search and seizure.[33] 'Guilty until proven innocent' became the 'new law of the sea'.[34]

The first German effort at submarine warfare between February and September 1915 was ineffective. The 27 U-boats available for duty managed to sink only 21 of 5000 ships travelling to and from Britain. This notwithstanding, Grand Admiral von Tirpitz of the Navy Office and Vice Admiral Gustav Bachmann of the Admiralty Staff assured the *OHL* that Britain could be forced to 'yield' to German demands within 6 weeks. Instead, the political fallout from the U-boat offensive proved both immediate and significant. On 7 May *U-20* torpedoed the 30 400-ton British liner *Lusitania* off the coast of Ireland with the loss of 1201 passengers, including many women and children, and 128 Americans. On 19 August a similar fate at the hands of *U-24* befell the 15 800-ton British steamer *Arabic*; this time 44 passengers including 2 or 3 Americans were killed. Sharp protest notes from President Wilson forced Germany to impose such tight restrictions on the U-boats that the underwater campaign ended for all intents and purposes on 18 September. Just under 800 000 tons of shipping had fallen prey to the U-boats since August 1914 – a mere fraction of the 12.4 million tons available to Britain and the Empire.

The spiralling violence of the war at sea aroused bitter hatred on both sides of the North Sea. On 23 December 1915 Britain issued the Trading with the Enemy Act which established a 'statutory black list' of firms – friendly or neutral – that traded with the Central Powers.[35] Germany responded on 12 February 1916 with its second U-boat offensive against shipping bound for the British Isles. Once more, German U-boat captains reported difficulties in distinguishing between neutrals and belligerents. They also reported that British ships used neutral flags to confound them and armed decoy (Q) ships to trap them. On 24 March *UB-29* torpedoed (but did not sink) the 1300-ton French steamer *Sussex* with the loss of 55 passengers including several Americans. Yet another protest note from Washington forced the Reich to rescind the U-boat campaign on 24 April after a total bag of 899 000 tons in 3 months.

Britain and Germany were now locked in an economic death grip. On 23 February London created a Ministry of Blockade under Lord Robert Cecil; France followed suit with its own Ministry of Blockade and Italy with a Blockade Committee. Yet another British Order in Council on 7 July officially voided the Declaration of London, thereby formalizing the reality of the past 20 months. Europe's neutrals were compelled to conclude 'forcible rationing' agreements with London whereby they were allowed to import just enough food and material to sustain their own populations. On 6 October 1916 Germany reacted with its third attempt at submarine warfare. It deployed 82 U-boats in the Atlantic Ocean and the Mediterranean Sea, where they destroyed an average of 325 000 tons of shipping per month.

Germans in all walks of life soon felt the effects of what they called the British 'hunger blockade'. At the outset of the war German merchant ships unfortunate enough to have been caught in British, French, and Russian ports had been seized and 623 German freighters had interned themselves in neutral harbours. After August 1914 the Reich retained less than 36 per cent of its merchant fleet. Its foreign trade collapsed almost overnight, falling from $5.9 billion in 1913 to a mere $800 million by 1917.

Domestic production had to take up the slack. To compensate for imported textiles, Berlin ordered the planting of flax and hemp; to increase yields of raw wool, it prohibited the slaughter of sheep. Berlin encouraged textile industries to seek substitute fibres from wood by-products, cellulose, and paper; to develop artificial silk; and to extract fibres for clothing from free-growing stinging nettles, peat, reeds, and bullrushes. But demand far outstripped production. Retail clothing prices rose meteorically between October 1915 and October 1918: woollen materials by 800 to 1700 per cent, cotton goods by 900 to 1400 per cent, and cotton stockings by 1000 per cent.[36]

Germany next turned to ersatz products in the civilian realm as it had in the industrial sector. Lack of farm labour due to the war and a shortage of artificial fertilizers due to the Army's demand for nitrates reduced the rye, wheat, barley, oats, and potato harvests to between 50 and 60 per cent of prewar levels. As early as January 1915, federal authorities ordered potato flour to be added to wheat in the production of so-called 'K' (for war or potato) bread. In quick succession barley, oat, and rice meals entered bread production – as did ground bean, pea, and corn meal later in the war.

Nor was the use of ersatz limited to bread. Butter was replaced by a concoction of curdled milk, sugar, and food colouring; cooking oil by a mixture of red beets, carrots, turnips, and spices; salad oil by 99 per cent mucilage; meat soup cubes by flavoured brine; and eggs by yellow-coloured corn or potato flour. Wheat flour was stretched by adding powdered hay. Enterprising housewives replaced luxury goods such as chocolates and cocoa with ground cocoa shells, and mixed pure pepper with 85 per cent ash to make it go further. Ground European beetles (cockchafers) and linden wood replaced fats. Sausage, a German staple, was formed of wondrous mixtures of water, plant fibres, and animal scraps. More than 11 000 ersatz products reached German stores during the war. Patents for ersatz goods were granted for 6000 varieties of beer, wine, and lemonade; 1000 kinds of soup cubes; 837 types of sausage; and 511 assortments of coffee.[37] Princess Blücher, an English observer in Berlin, suffering from influenza in March 1916, jokingly suggested that she had succumbed to 'Ersatz illness'. 'Everyone is feeling ill from too many chemicals in the hotel food. I don't believe that Germany will ever be starved out, but she will be poisoned out first with these substitutes.'[38]

As wheat production fell from 4.4 million tons in 1913 to 2.5 million by 1918, German consumption of potatoes leaped from 7660 g. to 21 8000 per month. Conversely, by 1916–17 that of meat had fallen to 31 per cent, of butter to 22, and of vegetables to 14. Milk was restricted to infants and small children as output fell from 24 to 9 million litres between 1914 and 1918. After the introduction of rationing in 1916, the weekly entitlement for a German adult consisted of 160 to 220 g. of flour, 120 g. of fish, 100 to 250 g. of meat, 60 to 75 g. of fats, 200 g. of sugar, 270 g. of a jam and artificial honey 'spread', 0.7 litres of milk, and one egg (when available).[39] Even these rations, already below subsistence level, often were not available on the open market.

The black market thrived for those able to barter clothing, coal, and jewels for food. Lieutenant-Colonel von Thaer, offspring of a Silesian estate owner, termed the farmers' refusal to submit to national food decrees and price ceilings 'passive resistance'. The farmers ground their grains 'black', sold their butter 'black', and butchered their livestock 'black'. 'They eat it themselves or sell it at great profit to the rich.'[40] By 1918 one-half of all egg, meat, and fruit production, one-third of milk, butter, and cheese output, and one-seventh of the grain, flour, and potato supply passed through the black market at prices often 10 times the pre-war level.[41] The black market by 1917 was beyond the reach of civil servants, clerks, and rentiers; by 1918 also of most industrial workers. The government's failure to suppress the black market demoralized countless otherwise loyal Germans.

Rumours that farmers were hoarding food spread like wildfires in the cities. Smuggling became a national passion. Perhaps as much as 50 per cent of all food reached consumers illegally. Hoarding, bartering, and black marketing not only undermined the national 'controlled economy' but also corrupted moral order. Those who had nothing to exchange for food suffered terribly. Those who could play the black market often made fortunes but were constantly exposed to its consequences. Princess Blücher recorded a typical occurrence at the Breslau train station:

> A well-dressed, dignified-looking lady appeared at the luggage-room with the object of checking her trunk. Her flurried mien, and the obvious nervousness with which she hurried on the porter to weigh her trunk, aroused the suspicion of the station-master. The trunk was promptly opened, and to the surprise of the amused onlookers a whole pig was discovered in it. It was confiscated and sold in the town at the official price, to the great discomfiture of the stately lady.[42]

Police searched the knapsacks of urban dwellers returning from their 'hamster' tours to the countryside. Bavaria set up border controls to make sure that its produce did not fall into 'foreign', that is, non-Bavarian, hands. Not even the exploitation of conquered Romania's resources late in 1916 brought much relief. Bucharest's deliveries of 1.8 million tons of foodstuffs, while impressive on the surface, amounted to less than 6 per cent of the total volume on the Reich's grain market.

Draconian government controls rudely enforced by an army of police alienated many Germans. Butcher shops were often closed for 2 or 3 weeks while the government debated maximum meat prices. Ration cards were required to buy fruit, vegetables, syrup, sauerkraut, tinned fruit, marmalade, and dried vegetables; priority vouchers were needed for dresses, coats, stockings, shoes, gloves, and washing. Soap was limited to 1 lb per month. An underground market of forged or stolen ration cards flourished. Whatever the commodity, it was precious and scarce. In May 1916 Princess Blücher recorded her impressions of shopping in Berlin:

> Long processions of women waiting for hours before the butchers', grocers', and bakers' shops were to be seen everywhere. . . . These women often get up in the middle of the night, to be the first on the scene, and took camp-stools with them, working or knitting. . . . One industrious woman was even said to have taken her sewing machine with her!

The euphoric 'mood of 1914' was a thing of the past. 'Now one sees faces like masks, blue with cold and drawn by hunger, with the harassed expression common to all those who are continually speculating as to the possibility of another meal.'[43] Britain and France did not ration bread and sugar until the spring and summer of 1918.

Many Germans resented that the Kaiser whiled away his time at headquarters playing at war. Few appreciated or cared that Wilhelm II maintained only a modest dinner table, that he forwent most luxuries, and that he even bridled his passion to hunt. General Alfred von Lyncker of the IV Army Corps in October 1916 warned the War Ministry of the growing rift between monarch and people. 'The Kaiser does not know the mood of the people; it is damned agitated and I suspect that no one has the courage any more to inform him of it.'[44] Police noted that the long food lines became crystallization points of public dissatisfaction, protests, and rumours.

Censors in the summer of 1916 intercepted a letter by Lina Dorstewitz of Leipzig to her brother in Britain, wherein she described everyday life in Saxony. The food supply had become 'horrendous' and civil war appeared in the offing. 'No one has money any more; in any case one cannot buy anything with it.' The state doled out every bite to eat; ration cards were all-decisive. Dorstewitz received a daily ration of 1 lb of potatoes; and weekly rations of 2 lbs of bread and 400 g. of flour, one-quarter lb of sugar and an equal amount of salt, and one-sixteenth of a lb of butter – sufficient to bake two rolls per week. Infants and children under the age of 2 received one-quarter litre of milk per day. Cheese had disappeared in November 1915, vegetables had been unavailable for a year, and meat was limited to 500 g. per week. Eggs, restricted to two a week, cost 30 pennies each (up from 8 before 1914). Dorstewitz had lost 37 lbs since August 1915.[45] The censors filed the confiscated letter under the rubric 'anti-German activity'.

Theodor Wolff, editor of the *Berliner Tageblatt*, also noted the mounting misery. In October 1916, 371 smugglers and profiteers including 126 fruit and vegetable sellers were arrested in Berlin. Special 'profiteering courts' (*Wuchergerichte*) handled up to 4000 cases per month. By November coal shortages forced stores, restaurants, and theatres to close early. A harsher than normal winter brought temperatures of –30 degrees Celsius. For the first time in 100 years, schools closed for lack of heat. Berliners wrapped their feet in newspapers against the cold. Maîtres d'hôtel at fashionable restaurants such as Hotel Esplanade, Horcher, Richards, and Hiller & Wagner sold meat dishes to regular customers who possessed no meat rationing cards; a public outcry forced the police to close these establishments. Food, Wolff noted, had become the only topic of discussion.[46] The government had sought to diffuse the tense mood in May 1916 by appointing Adolf Tortilowicz von Batocki-Friebe head of a national War Food Office, combining in this East Prussian's hands the old wheat, potato, and food agencies. It was a classic case of too little too late.

The dismal harvest of autumn 1916 ushered in the so-called 'turnip winter' of 1916–17. Heavy rains, an early frost, and a shortage of field hands reduced the potato harvest by 50 per cent to just 25 million tons.

Turnips, whether boiled, baked, or dried, became the national staple. The *Kohlrübe* was a stringy, coarse root crop, tasteless and bland at the best of times. Sailors with the German High Sea Fleet reported that their diet had been reduced to what they termed *Drahtverhau* (literally, wire entanglement) – a nauseous concoction of '75% water, 10% sausage, 3% potatoes, 2% peas, 1% yellow turnips, and small amounts of beef, fat, and vinegar'.[47] The writer Ernst Glaeser noted that the 'turnip winter' had brought the war home. 'Hunger destroyed our solidarity; the children stole each other's rations. . . . Soon the women who stood in pallid queues before shops spoke more about their children's hunger than about the death of their husbands.' What Glaeser termed a 'new front' had been created. Its battles were fought by legions of women against an army of police. 'Soon a looted ham thrilled us more than the fall of Bucharest.'[48] The *OHL* toyed with the idea of creating large numbers of mobile field kitchens, dubbed 'goulash guns' by Berlin wags, to race from town to town to feed the hungry civilian populace. The war had become 'total' for the home front.

The police reported with increasing frequency on the number of angry public protests, food riots, and plundering of grocery stores mostly by women and youths. In April 1916 striking Krupp workers demanded higher wages to 'buy foodstuffs at the prices which the well-off population pay'.[49] In May more than 55 000 Berlin metal workers stayed off their jobs for three days to protest the arrest of the radical socialist Karl Liebknecht for an anti-war speech at the Potsdamer Platz on 1 May.

The year 1917 brought renewed and intensified labour unrest. When the government reduced the flour ration for workers on 15 April, 'hunger strikes' broke out in about 300 factories. More than 40 000 Krupp workers demanded higher wages and 75 000 coal miners in Rhineland-Westphalia struck for better food. The Austrian Ambassador, Hohenlohe-Schillingsfürst, informed his government on 26 April that 149 000 Berlin workers in critical war industries such as Siemens & Halske, Siemens-Schuckert, Schwartzkopf, Zeppelinwerke, and the Royal Munitions Factory had rioted for better food and the vote in Prussia. The total would soon double. Two months later the Ambassador informed Vienna that food riots and looting in Cologne had involved Belgian and Russian forced labourers. In July Hohenlohe sent news of food riots by coal miners in Gelsenkirchen and Dortmund.[50] Workers in Hamburg, Leipzig, and the Saar demanded an end to the war. The Army eventually restored order by subjecting many factories to 'militarization' and by sending workers' leaders to the front.

The cost per pound of most food staples doubled at least during the course of the war: bread from 14 pennies to 25; flour from 20 pennies to 50; meat from 90 pennies to 2 Marks; potatoes from 4 pennies to 12; and salt from 10 pennies to 20.[51] In 1915, for example, prices rose more than they had during the 45 years since unification. Incomes, on the other hand, climbed in widely divergent fashion. Most industrial wages increased by 90 per cent during the war, but those in the highly-skilled chemical, electrical, machine, and metal industries increased by 150 per cent. Real wages actually fell 25 per cent between 1914 and 1918. Salaries of government bureaucrats failed to keep in step with the rising cost of living: military employees received salary boosts of 15 per cent during the first 2 years of the war and civil servants barely 10 per cent. Real income for junior-rank officials between 1914 and 1918 fell to 70 per cent and that of middle- and senior-rankers to 50 per cent of prewar levels. Salaried employees, the backbone of the Prusso-German state, saw wartime inflation destroy their savings and erode their real incomes. The Mark, in peacetime a symbol of stability and strength, fell 75 to 100 per cent in value. Inflation by war's end reached 250 per cent.

Hardest hit were those who depended on the government for relief: children, the aged, and the wives (increasingly the widows) of men called to military service. By the end of 1915, about 4 million families of 11 million people received some form of war-related support; by 1918 the figure had risen to almost one-third of all city dwellers. Prussia alone paid 4.1 billion Marks support to so-called 'war families' between 1914 and 1918. But the price of food, which comprised half the outlay of most working-class households, simply outraced the level of state aid. Whereas it cost 60 (inflated) Marks to feed a worker's family of four in 1916, family support came to only 37.50 Marks.[52] By 1916 most working women in Hanover did not earn enough to purchase more than a dozen eggs; half a chicken cost twice as much as they could earn in a single day. In farm-rich Bavaria 5 lbs of butter in 1918 cost as much as most women earned in a week.[53] The war benefited only industrialists and their highly-skilled workers; it impoverished most lower-middle-class and semi-skilled labourers.

The labour market remains difficult to pin down. In 1914 the Army drafted roughly 28 per cent of the male workforce in the expectation that the war would be short. By 1916 it had called up one-half of all elementary school teachers in Prussia. When the 'short-war illusion' proved to be just that, males were called to the colours in ever greater numbers: 8.2 million by September 1916 and 13.25 million by war's end. The number of male workers in Prussia by 1917 had declined 24 per cent to 2 558 000 (including POWs and foreign labourers!); concurrently, the number of female workers had increased 76 per cent to 1 392 200. Throughout Germany, the war brought 1.2 million new female employees into the labour market.[54]

Women worked up to 80 per cent of the small farms in Germany as husbands and sons were called to serve, or left the homestead for high-paying

jobs in armaments industries. Some farm relief was provided by the
300 000 mainly Polish agricultural workers caught in Germany by the
outbreak of war, and thereafter by about 800 000 Russian POWs. But the
latter were often less than enthusiastic about working German farms, their
productivity was low, and they required armed overseers, which few
small farms could afford.

The urban labour market is difficult to assess. Most consumer and
almost all luxury industries were closed at the start of the war and their
workers directed either to the Army or to war-related industries. The textile industry, for example, lost three-quarters of its prewar male and two-
fifths of its female labour force. Mining and metalworking held their own
in terms of the number of employees while the chemical industry doubled
its male and quadrupled its female workforce. Night shifts became compulsory as did Sunday work. Hours of work were constantly extended and
safety regulations relaxed. Rebellious male workers were threatened with
'the trenches', that is, military service.

According to Marie-Elisabeth Lüders, head of the special Women's
Labour Centre within the War Office, machine shops recruited more than
400 000 and ammunition plants roughly 600 000 women. In the Krupp
works, where no women had been employed before the war, 30 000
females were added to its 80 000 males by 1918. Railroads recruited
100 000 women as baggage handlers, porters, ticket agents, conductors,
stokers, and yard personnel while the postal service took another 30 000.
Roughly 20 000 women worked in military rear echelons servicing
trucks, airplanes, and tractors; hauling ammunition and food; and staffing
stables and veterinary units. Untold thousands worked at home as seam-
stresses producing uniforms, gas masks, shoes, rucksacks, and other items
of clothing for the military. An attempt in 1918 to recruit some of the 5000
female university and high-school students for national work, on the other
hand, was met with indifference.

Numerous problems accompanied the mobilization of females. Most
employers saw women only as temporary replacements, and guaranteed
soldiers their former jobs after the war. Government leaders such as State
Secretary of the Interior Delbrück also reminded the women that they
were to return to home and hearth once the war was over in order not to
upset the 'normal' labour market. Although the Army estimated that
female replacements released 64 000 male factory workers for front duty
and produced 90 to 99 per cent of grenades and mines, Ludendorff and
Bauer nevertheless considered women to be too weak for heavy manual
jobs. Male workers and shop stewards resented the women's intrusion
into traditional high-paying 'male' jobs, denied them technical education,
and reminded them that soldiers at the front were paid a paltry 1 Mark per

day! The 400 000 POWs who toiled in German factories by 1917 often saw the women, many single and in their thirties, as being readily available.

Poor working conditions, lack of equal pay, and long hours rounded out this bleak picture. While women's average daily earnings rose by 138 per cent – compared with 112 for men – during the war, they were paid 63 to 71 per cent less than males in electrical, chemical, and machine industries. Daily wages of between 1.45 and 2.40 Marks barely covered food costs of roughly 2 Marks. Seventy per cent of female factory workers put in between 51 and 60 hours per week and almost 30 per cent between 66 and 75. Night work doubled during the war. Housing consisted mainly of over-crowded barracks, huts, and barns. Children were left unattended during the day. Poisons used in the manufacture of shells and canisters reduced the birth rate among women in armaments plants by half. No statistics seem to have been kept on birth defects as a result of these toxins in the workplace. In the final analysis, there was no 'emancipation' of female workers.

The employment of adolescents revealed an equally dismal picture. Forced to contribute to household incomes constantly eroded by inflation and seduced by high industrial wages, roughly a quarter of a million youths between the ages of 14 and 17 took employment in war-related industries between 1914 and 1918. Their numbers rose 225 per cent in the chemical branch, 97 in steel plants, and 59 in machine industries, where 15-hour working days were not uncommon. Many of the youngsters abandoned formal schooling as well as promising apprenticeships in traditional consumer-oriented industries. Training programmes were abandoned for much of the war. Weekly instruction in Prussia slipped to 12 hours per week as 51 000 of its 98 000 teachers had been drafted by 1915. The police became alarmed that many youths, with their fathers at the front and their mothers working long hours in factories, gained an independence that bordered on lawlessness. In 1917 half a million indigent children were sent to farms on 'holidays', soon followed by 75 000 students (*Jungmannen*) to work the land. The next year the Prussian War Ministry marched them out of schools to unload railway cars.[55]

Malnutrition in general and the lack of foods high in protein and carbohydrates in particular exerted a terrible toll on the populace. The average diet between 1914 and 1918 was reduced from 3400 to 1000 calories; weekly meat consumption from 1050 g. to 135. Doctors recorded the first instances of 'food edema' – swelling of the arms and legs – in the spring of 1917. The wartime mortality rate among civilians increased by 37 per cent. Postwar estimates that the 'hunger blockade' alone was responsible for the deaths of 800 000 civilians and the loss of 1 million births[56] may be inflated, yet recent studies suggest that women's mortality rose 51 per cent and that of children under the age of 5 50 per cent. Women's deaths from tuberculosis, 'a key indicator of social conditions', increased by two-thirds; the national birthrate fell by half to just 15 per 1000.[57]

Whatever yardstick is applied, the war ravaged the home front in both economic and social terms. The middle class was destroyed by inflation leading to poverty. Industrial workers gained at the expense of non-skilled labourers. Urban dwellers fell prey to the greed of agrarian producers, who, in turn, lagged far behind the income and power of heavy industry. War producers raided the labour force of consumer and commodity producers and destroyed the latter in the process. The concentration of armaments plants in Prussia came at the cost of the south German states. And the notion of a national *Volksgemeinschaft* put forth after 1900 by German youth, liberal imperialists, anti-Semites, and military enthusiasts, and reinforced by the 'ideas of 1914', was by 1916–17 at best a mirage.[58]

Death, disease, and doctors

Death and disease were the hallmarks of front-line experience. No one escaped them. Few survived them. And yet the German Army's medical corps was probably the best prepared among the major combatants. As early as the Franco-Prussian War, surgeons were assigned to head individual units from battalion to regiment, division to corps, with a Chief Surgeon for the Regular Army. The wounded were evacuated from first-aid stations at the front via field ambulances to dressing stations and field hospitals, while the more serious cases graduated to evacuation hospitals and finally to base hospitals at home. By 1900 surgery had reached legitimacy as a scientific revolution transformed the Army's erstwhile barbers and bloodletters into modern practitioners of medicine. Ether and chloroform for anaesthesia had been introduced in 1847, surgical antisepsis followed in 1867, steam sterilization of surgical instruments was practised by 1886, and X-rays came on the scene in 1895. Further strides in medicine were achieved during the Great War: sterilized gauze, rubber gloves, motor ambulances, mobile laboratories featuring diagnostic bacteriology, lighter X-ray machines, intravenous saline transfusions, blood transfusions, clinical thermometers, improved retractors and hemostatic forceps, surgical lighting, and the hypodermic syringe.[59] In short, the Prussian-German Army pioneered in applying medical breakthroughs on the battlefield.

Roughly 70 per cent of Germany's 25 000 doctors worked at the front or in rear-echelon medical facilities during the Great War. Each month they treated 175 000 wounded at field hospitals, 66 600 at evacuation hospitals, and 86 300 at base hospitals. Almost 70 per cent of battle wounds were caused by secondary missiles and exploding artillery shot, and 64 per cent of wounds affected arms and legs.[60] Smokeless powder propelled rifle and artillery shells at higher velocities and for greater distances than ever before. A 9 mm bullet from a British Lee-Enfield Mark III rifle with a mass of approximately 150 grains fired at 2500 feet per second could traverse 8 inches of bone and tissue in 0.00033 seconds, releasing 1330 foot-pounds (or 7200 horsepower) of energy.[61]

About half a million soldiers underwent amputations and teams of German orthopedic engineers developed 30 different types of arms and 50 types of artificial legs. The fighting in 1914 alone crippled 30 000 soldiers and the Reich constructed 138 special homes for them. A crafts school in Düsseldorf retrained 2000 amputees by the end of 1916; Adler in Frankfurt and Mignon in Berlin developed Braille typewriters for soldiers blinded by gas.[62] Thousands suffered horrible facial wounds. There were no surgeons trained in general plastic surgery, so artists were recruited to paint masks so that those with maxillofacial injuries could hide their 'disfigurement'. Whereas the government by the end of 1914 had ordered newspapers to cease publishing lists of soldiers killed, there was no censorship with regard to amputees and those otherwise 'disfigured' – of whom there were 2.7 million by the end of the war. In 1916 more than 60 firms proudly held a 'Special Exhibition of Artificial Limbs and Accessories for War Wounded, Accident Victims, and Cripples' at Berlin-Charlottenburg.

Fortunately, a report of German surgical practice has survived, and it deserves full treatment. Its author, Dr B. Hallauer, a gynaecologist from Berlin, served as staff surgeon of the third medical company of the III Army Corps near Verdun. On 6 May 1916 Hallauer, noting that his medical staff was losing two of every five wounded soldiers during transport from Fort Douaumont to the evacuation hospital 4 miles away, established a temporary dressing and forward surgical station within the citadel. It quickly grew into a four-room complex featuring separate rooms for *triage*, dressing, operating, and evacuation.[63]

At 5 a.m. on 8 May Fort Douaumont was shaken by a tremendous blast, followed by three further explosions. The Germans spied unidentifiable, black-powder-covered riflemen running through the corridors. Panic-stricken at the thought of confronting French African troops, they screamed, 'The blacks are coming!' Hallauer, probing the dark passages of his station, was met at once by 'a thick cloud of smoke and sulphur fumes' and the 'cries and groans' of the wounded. He alleviated their suffering by restarting the fort's ventilation system, releasing oxygen from metal flasks, and offering caffeine to those suffering from shock and injury. Among the living, Hallauer noted an immediate blueing of the lips and the onset of dizziness and tiredness. Several soldiers dragged Hallauer out of the citadel to clear air.

Once recovered, Hallauer reentered Fort Douaumont and explored its vaulted passageways. There he came upon several hundred young reservists 'in a pathetic state'. The men cowered in the dark amidst countless 'wounded, dazed, and mentally deranged soldiers'. The passageways were filled with dirt and corpses, 'many of them hideously deformed. Arms, legs, and body trunks lay everywhere; between them, smashed war material. The bodies of many of the dead, heaped three and four high, had been ripped open'. Beds, helmets, and rifles had been flung through the air by the pressure of the detonations. In one of the dead-end passages in the fort's lowest level, Hallauer found dozens of corpses, charred and covered with black-powder dust, broken against the stones, 'as though shot through a rifle barrel'. The surgeon set the death toll at between 700 and 800 men.

Hallauer later defined the principal causes of death. The majority of men had died as a result of the pressure from the explosion ('blood from nose and mouth'). The second cause of death was bodies flung by the blast against stone walls ('broken bones'). Third on the list was shrapnel ('pieces of explosives, stones, chalk, rifle parts, grenade splinters'). Others had burned to death. Still others had died of asphyxiation and smoke inhalation ('smoke-blackened face, no blood in mouth or nose'). A sixth cause of death was from an unknown gas ('faces and bodies relatively free of smoke, fresh colour, good tension in the eyeballs'). 'The dead appeared as though they were asleep.' One officer had shot himself through the head.

Perhaps the most sobering part of Hallauer's official report to the commander of the 5th Infantry Division was headed 'nervous symptoms'. It reflects the psychological trauma of the desperate struggles in Douaumont's catacombs:

> Nervous disorders could be observed in great quantity. Shock, confusion, loss of speech, hysteria, cramps, delirium, and other various psychoses, among which I especially noted amentia [imbecility]. The horrible scenes of mass carnage in the dark passageways of the fort (filled with powder and sulphur fumes), the picture of horribly decimated corpses combined with the moaning of the wounded, the death-rattling sounds of the dying, the screaming and ranting of the mad – all this heightened the horrors after the catastrophe to the edge of human resistance.

Hallauer later discovered the cause of the explosions. Soldiers had heated their coffee with oil taken from flamethrowers and powder retracted from hand-grenades – in barbettes housing 100 French 15 cm shells. The oil and powder had caught on fire, burning many of the coffee makers, who thereupon had hurled their flaming pots and burning clothes against the shells. Others, seeing the 'blacks' before them and mistaking them for French Senegalese, had thrown hand-grenades at their own men. The result was the inferno visited by Hallauer. Most of the dead were buried in the fort's passageways simply by closing these off with brick walls.

The diary of Staff Surgeon Gerlach, German Alpine Corps, gives insight into the workings of two field hospitals at Romagne sous les Côtes, behind the front near Verdun. Dr Gerlach arrived at the hospitals on 4 July 1916 and discovered that the entire surgical staff consisted of three doctors. The facilities were primitive. 'Barracks, tents, and the village church stood at our disposal.' Water had to be hauled daily from Montmédy by an improvised narrow-gauge field railroad; water wagons distributed the precious liquid within Romagne. Bandages and hospital linens were washed daily by Russian POWs; all other laundry was carted twice weekly to Longyon. French prisoners dug latrines and garbage dumps.[64]

The wounded were evacuated from Fort Douaumont at night, carried out by litter-bearers just over a mile to the terminus of a field railroad, usually under hostile fire. Doctors at a clearing station near the train stop at Romagne attended to minor injuries such as broken limbs and clean shot wounds. Serious head and belly wounds immediately went to one of the two field hospitals. The convalescents, once recovered from surgery, were hauled in medical trucks specially equipped with litters to another railroad station, from where they were taken in medical trains to evacuation hospitals in Montmédy and, if need be, to base hospitals in Germany. Those able to walk were directed to a forest camp named 'German Cliff', from where yet another improvised railroad took them to the main artillery park at Spincourt – and eventually back to their units at the front.

The countryside around Romagne had a deadly pallor to it. 'If it rained, all was quickly transformed into a deep, stubborn morass; if it was dry, a fog of fine chalk dust hovered over the entire region.' Tetanus infection was a major problem. The soil was unclean: cultivated, fertilized, and defiled for centuries by the excreta of animals, it was laden with pathogenic bacteria. Combined with hasty and inadequate initial first-aid treatment, this led to horrendous rates of amputation and infection with deadly gas gangrene. Wound mortality ran between 30 and 40 per cent. Tetanus antitoxin vaccines reduced the rate of tetanus infection to less than 1 per cent by war's end.[65]

Trench fever, caused by parasites in the fecal matter of lice, produced hundreds of thousands of casualties. Delousing became an art form.

Special stations at Romagne were established for bathing and steam disinfection, thereby almost eliminating typhus and trench fever. As in the case of tetanus infection, new vaccines drastically reduced typhoid rates by 1918. The doctors at Romagne also noted 'billions of flies', the cause of widespread digestive problems, the so-called 'Verdun fever'. Gerlach developed his own remedy against the flies and fever, avoiding fresh fruits and vegetables and taking a shot of rum or arrack every morning, noon, and night. '*Probatum est*', he proudly noted in his diary. Hostile aircraft strafed and bombed the area around the convalescent park ('German Cliff') almost daily, further complicating the surgeons' efforts.

The field hospitals took only those cases requiring immediate surgery. Survival rates were relatively low: Gerlach estimated that he lost six to eight patients per day on the operating table. Surprisingly, the most serious cases rarely developed fever. 'The heavily strained body apparently no longer had the power or the means with which to fight the infectious germs.' After hours of standing at the operating tables cutting off arms and legs, the surgeons fell into comas in which they wanted 'prophylactically to amputate every organ'. In fact, the traditional practice of amputation for all compound fractures lasted well into 1917 before improvements in wound surgery and reduced infection lowered the amputation rate. The frequently long delays between when a soldier was shot and when he was surgically treated accounted for all too many deaths. The surgeons worked 'till late into the night, into the morning, every single day'. There was no relief from death.

The two hospitals also had a mortuary – a 'corpses hall' (*Leichenhalle*) in graphic German terminology – that consisted of a barn directly behind the operating rooms. Due to the oppressive July heat, the bodies were interred within 24 hours; whoever died during the night or in the morning was buried that same afternoon. 'And yet – the countless rats were soon at their horrible, despicable work of destruction.' While most hospitals had hectographic machines to mass-produce death notices, Dr Gerlach still wrote individual letters to surviving family members. 'The list of relatives and dear comrades who fell [*sic*] before Verdun never ended. It seemed endless. . . . And so one day went like every other, work and more work.'

The sheer statistical magnitude of the doctors' task can perhaps be appreciated by a glance at the Fifth Army's 10-day casualty reports covering the first seven months of fighting at Verdun in 1916. Dressing stations handled 275 770 cases of light injuries; field hospitals returned 75 000 soldiers to duty. No one will ever know how many of the 81 668 deaths occurred on the operating table or in recovery units. Wound mortality for the entire war was approximately 8 per cent.

By contrast, the Austro-Hungarian Army's medical corps – like those of the other combatants – was utterly unprepared for the Great War. In August 1914 the Army drafted medical students to assist surgeons in the field. While this brought its complement of doctors to 1500 – or two for every 1000 soldiers – it also meant that there was no resupply of doctors on the way after 1914. The Habsburg Army lost 331 doctors (16 dead, 68 wounded, 118 missing, and 129 prisoners of war) in 1914 alone. It quickly combed the home front for available surgeons, with the result that by early 1917 it possessed 7392 doctors (2.1 per cent of forces), still only two doctors for every 1000 soldiers. One-year volunteers with four semesters medical study were hastily promoted Medical Lieutenants. Still, most infantry regiments had only two or three rather than the stipulated five doctors.

Despite the critical shortage of doctors, the surgical recovery rate was 78 per cent in field hospitals and 77 in evacuation hospitals; the death rate on the operating table was 3.69 per cent. The medical corps returned 106 000 officers and noncommissioned officers (of 118 000 wounded or sick) as well as 2 858 000 soldiers (of 4 600 000 wounded or sick) to the front after treatment between August 1914 and January 1918.

The Army entered the war with only 191 military hospitals of 17 708 beds, but by 1918 those figures had increased to 874 and 95 000, respectively. Already at the end of 1916, 133 medical and 60 surgical 'trains' (of 65 doctors each), 266 field hospitals, two dozen mobile surgical groups, 151 bacteriological laboratories, and 200 permanent epidemics hospitals had been established. As a result, the ravages due to epidemics declined precipitously. Quarter-annual statistics reveal that between 1914 and 1917 cholera fell from 25 000 cases to 1000; abdominal typhoid fever from 50 000 to 7000; and dysentery from 65 000 to 15 000. Typhus, scurvy, and smallpox were erased by 1916. General cases of pestilence fell from 15 000 in 1914 to 1000 in 1915. Only malaria proved stubborn in low-lying regions near the Adriatic Sea; the 47th Infantry Division in Albania, for example, reported 10 000 men (of whom one-quarter died) down with the disease in 1916 alone.[66]

Death was omnipresent. Initially, the Army decreed that only officers were to be buried in single graves; soon that regulation was extended to highly-decorated soldiers. Enemy dead were not identified, and were interred in mass graves. Architects vied with one another to design grandiose 'death castles' on the Kahlenberg near Vienna and in the Wachau on the Danube, but lack of building materials and funds delayed these projects. The home front was denied knowledge of the immense slaughter as journalists were barred from the killing grounds; instead, the journalists concocted largely idealized versions of the fighting from the safety of rear-echelon areas.

The politics of 'total' war

The government in Berlin tried to rally the home front with promises of indemnities, reparations, and annexations to make the suffering bearable. Late in the war it also held out promises of constitutional reform to maintain industrial calm. The calculus behind war aims was simple: the more the war cost in blood and treasure and the longer it went on, the greater the clamour for postwar gains. The conservative regimes of the Central Powers feared that failure to bring home vast indemnities and annexations would endanger their near-exclusive rights to rule. Victory at all cost was their maxim.

To be sure, Berlin and Vienna were not alone in dangling war aims before their populations. The Russians hoped to annex Austrian Galicia and East Prussia, thereby moving their border west to the Vistula River. In the south, they set their sights on the Dardanelles and the northern Turkish provinces of Erzerum, Trebizond, and Ardahan. Great Britain, which already had an Empire of 250 million Indians and 50 million Africans as well as Australia, New Zealand, and Canada, could not justify territorial expansion and hence centred its demands on the restoration of Belgium, the creation of a South Slav state of Serbs, Croats, Slovenes, and Montenegrins, the surrender of the German fleet and merchant marine, and control over the oil-rich provinces of the Ottoman Empire. London also on occasion gave vague promises to 'liberate the Italians, Slavs, Romanians, and Czecho-Slovaks from foreign rule'. The most boisterous imperialists, demanding gains from the monthly war debt of £120 million, hoped to realize their dream of a Southern British World that ran from Cape Town through Cairo, across Asia Minor to Baghdad and Calcutta, and finally across the South Seas to Sydney and Wellington. His Majesty's Government on occasion could rival the Germans in war-aims rhetoric. Two months after the outbreak of the war, the Russian Ambassador in London instructed St Petersburg that Britain aimed to seize the German colonies, either to neutralize the Kiel Canal or to hand it (along with Schleswig) over to Denmark, to destroy the German fleet, to give German Frisia to Holland, and to demand substantial indemnities after the war.[67]

French war-aims enthusiasts, led by President Poincaré and organized into extra-parliamentary lobbies such as the *Action française*, *Ligue des patriotes*, and *Comité des forges*, cried out for vast reparations and indemnities. Specifically, they demanded the 'return' of Alsace-Lorraine, the annexation of the coal-rich Saar, part of the Palatinate and the left bank of the Rhine, and the inclusion of Belgium and Luxembourg in a French 'orbit'.[68] The Belgians coveted Luxembourg, Aachen, and strips of the

Netherlands. Italy's *sacro egoismo* demanded Cisalpine Tyrol, Trieste, and Dalmatia as well as colonial gains in Africa and Asia Minor. Belgrade's 'Greater Serbia' aspirations included Bosnia–Herzegovina, Montenegro, Albania, and parts of Greece. The Hellenist Kingdom countered with its dream of a 'Greater Greece' at the expense of Bulgaria and the Ottoman Empire. Romania lusted after Transylvania. The poet J. C. Squire recognized the magnitude of the task awaiting the postwar settlement: ' "My God", said God, "I've got my work cut out".'[69]

Germany had first defined its war aims during the euphoria of September 1914, when it seemed that its armies were about to enter Paris. Government leaders ranging from the Imperial Chancellor to the Prussian Minister of the Interior, from the influential Centre Party to powerful extra-parliamentary lobbies such as the Pan-German League and the German Colonial Society, agreed that a 'central European economic union' under German leadership needed to be established and that this *Mitteleuropa* include Austria–Hungary, Belgium, Denmark, France, the Netherlands, and Poland – possibly also Italy, Norway, and Sweden. France was to be reduced to the status of a minor power and Russia deprived of its non-Russian populations; Belgium was to become a German 'economic province'; and a German central African colonial empire was to be carved out of existing Belgian, French, and Portuguese possessions.[70]

In May 1915 German industrial leaders put forth their own demands, followed in July by a petition of 1347 German intellectuals, including 352 professors, demanding German territorial expansion. Naumann's popular *Mitteleuropa* book, published that year, bridged the war-aims aspirations of German officialdom, industry, and academia. The Bavarian military plenipotentiary in Berlin, Lerchenfeld-Koefering, by October 1915 had grasped the basic dynamic that war aims merely intensified and prolonged a conflict that was fundamentally 'unpolitical [but] based on national hatred, envy, and jealousy'.[71] Late in the war, German royal clans such as the Hohenzollerns, Wettiner, Wittelsbach, and Urachs were reduced to haggling over thrones in Finland, the Baltic states, Poland, and Romania – at a time when their own thrones were being threatened by defeat and revolution!

Austria–Hungary also developed a war-aims programme but, given its repeated military setbacks, this was neither as ambitious nor as rigid as the German blueprint. In December 1915 as well as July and October 1916, Foreign Minister Burián, fearing that Berlin might ignore Austro-Hungarian vital interests in a future peace, demanded that the Habsburg Empire be confirmed in its borders of 1914 – but with the addition of 'strategic border improvements' at the expense of Italy, Russia, Romania, and Serbia. Burián also expressed an interest in annexing Montenegro and establishing a protectorate over Albania. Serbia was to be allowed to exist, but only on a vastly reduced scale.[72]

War aims took a giant leap with Hindenburg and Ludendorff. Their decision to put the nation on a 'total war' footing and the accompanying national sacrifice required that the German *Volk* have a clear understanding of what it was fighting for. To this end, the *OHL*, in the wake of victory over Romania, presented its own war aims complete with colour-coded maps. In the west, it demanded that iron-rich Longwy-Briey as well as Liège and Luxembourg be annexed outright, and that Germany establish a 'marshalling area' west of the Meuse River. In the east, it sought a 'safety zone' against Russia by annexing western Poland, Courland, Latvia, and Lithuania as well as by taking control of Romanian Wallachia as a sort of 'Roman province'. The *OHL* spoke of eastern annexations as future 'colonization lands'. Hindenburg announced that these demands, formulated by Ludendorff, were absolute minimal war aims.[73]

The Navy also established a comprehensive war-aims programme – at the very moment that it pressed for unrestricted submarine warfare. On 26 November and 24 December 1916, Admiral Henning von Holtzendorff laid down a sweeping design that left no doubt that Germany intended to supplant Great Britain as the world's premier naval power after the current conflict. In Europe, the Chief of the Admiralty Staff wanted to annex the Belgian coast with the harbours of Bruges, Ostend, and Zeebrugge as well as the Baltic coast with Libau and Windau. The Danish Faeroe Islands, 160 nautical miles west of the Shetlands, would give Germany a flanking base against Britain. In the Atlantic, Holtzendorff desired naval bases at either Dakar or the Cape Verde Islands and at the Azores as the forward bastions of Germany's central African colonial empire. In the Far East, he hoped to gain Tahiti; in the West Indian Ocean, Madagascar along with one of the major East African ports; in the East Indian Ocean, one of the large Dutch islands; and in the Mediterranean Sea, Valona on the Albanian coast along with a land connection to the Austro-Hungarian Empire.[74]

Holtzendorff, like Grand Admiral von Tirpitz before him, depicted the Great War as the opening round of a titanic Anglo-German struggle: a 'Second Punic War' would decide control of the world's great thoroughways. In January 1915 Admiral Harald Dähnhardt of the Navy Office crafted a 134-page document which called for doubling the naval budget to 980 million Marks to grant Germany parity at sea with Britain. Dähnhardt demanded that the fleet expand from 61 to 81 capital ships and from 72 to 280 U-boats by 1934.[75] Wilhelm II, Bethmann Hollweg, and

Hindenburg as well as Ludendorff quickly approved the Navy's war-aims programme, which remained in place with only minor additions until 1918.

The historian Fritz Fischer has argued that the winter of 1916–17 constituted both a major turning point in the history of the First World War and a 'caesura' in war aims.[76] In quick succession, Germany established Congress Poland as a vassal state (5 November 1916), floated a half-hearted 'peace offensive' by the Allied Powers (12 December 1916), and decided to resume unrestricted submarine warfare (9 January 1917). Almost as if to make certain that the United States would enter the war, Foreign Secretary Zimmermann on 16 January 1917 – that is, 1 week after the decision for submarine warfare and 2 weeks before Washington broke off diplomatic relations with Berlin – sent Mexico an offer via British-controlled submarine cables to join Germany (and Japan) against the United States in return for Arizona, New Mexico, and Texas![77] While Zimmermann dismissed the fateful episode simply as 'bad luck', Berlin bankers joked that the most lucrative business prospect was to start up a spittoon factory. '30 million spittoons – that would meet a pressing demand because the entire *Volk* wants to throw up.'[78]

Perhaps equally important, on 15 November 1916 the *OHL* released the matter of war aims for public debate. Therewith they rallied industry and nationalists against Bethmann Hollweg, and formally rent asunder the domestic *Burgfriede* of August 1914. War aims now became the litmus-paper test by which nationalists and the *OHL* measured the credibility of political leaders. In the process, Hindenburg and Ludendorff became deeply embroiled not only in economic and labour relations but also in constitutional reform. They tore up the last shreds of the fiction of the 'apolitical' German soldier in their elusive quest to manage 'total war'.

War aims were used as a bludgeon against the Chancellor's alleged 'weak' leadership and the Left's pronouncement on 19 April 1917 of a peace 'without annexations and indemnities'. Over and over, Conservatives, Pan-Germans, industrialists, and generals warned of impending revolution were the workers to return empty-handed from the front and handed the bill for the cost of the war as a result of a 'defeatist peace.' But war aims were no longer the placebo they had been in 1914–16. Few worker-soldiers in 1917 had the slightest interest in, or willingness to continue to fight for Courland or Wallachia or Liège. Few women who daily lined up for 150 g. of flour or an egg were willing to suffer hardships for a slice of Montenegro, Luxembourg, or Lithuania.

The Right's real agenda, of course, was continued control over the nation's political future, and to this end it even toyed with overthrowing Bethmann Hollweg and creating a 'Caesarian' regime under Ludendorff or Tirpitz. Ominously for Wilhelm II, 'state' began to replace 'monarchy' in nationalist rhetoric. In fact, talk about the need for a 'dictator' had appeared as early as 1914 and linked to Tirpitz. Over the next 2 years, a diverse spectrum of the ruling elite ranging from Crown Prince Wilhelm to General von Bernhardi, from Class to Colonel Bauer considered asking Wilhelm II either to go on 'sick leave' or to abdicate in favour of his eldest son. In the winter of 1916–17, three of Ludendorff's trusted aides – Bauer, Hoffmann, and Mertz von Quirnheim – floated Ludendorff's candidacy as wartime chancellor and spoke of the need for a 'military dictator'.[79] The conservative *fronde* was united in the belief that Bethmann Hollweg was too weak to lead the nation in wartime.

The Right badly maligned the Chancellor in the area of war aims. Bethmann Hollweg was neither the *Flaumacher* (defeatist, weakling) despised by his adversaries in 1917, nor the 'moderate' lauded by many historians today. His position on war aims can be gleaned from a candid conversation that he had on 16 March 1917 at the Ballhausplatz in Vienna. The German leader bluntly lectured Foreign Minister Czernin that he would never cede Alsace-Lorraine to France; that he demanded the return of all lost colonies; and that he would hold Belgium and northern France as 'pawns' to assure that his demands were accepted in peace negotiations. He further sought to annex Courland and Latvia and to control Congress Poland. When the 'moderate' Chancellor rejected as too demanding Czernin's plea that Vienna take Wallachia, Czernin was reduced to begging for Austria–Hungary's 'territorial integrity' and a few scraps of additional land as no government could survive 'were the Monarchy, which is bleeding from a hundred wounds, to go away with empty hands'.[80]

Once back in Berlin, Bethmann Hollweg walked a tightrope over the abyss of domestic politics. While his survival depended solely on the goodwill of the Kaiser, he nevertheless had to maintain a working majority in the Reichstag to gain passage of the semi-annual war loans. Whereas from spring 1915 until fall 1916 the Chancellor had used Hindenburg and Ludendorff as his 'trump card' against Falkenhayn, the appointment of the duumvirate to head the General Staff in August 1916 deprived Bethmann Hollweg of this 'trump card'. He now had no choice but to work with the new *OHL*. Step by step, the generals roped off the Chancellor's freedom of manoeuvre and worked to nail him to their standard.

In April 1917 Bethmann Hollweg, like a cornered animal, decided to tackle the conservative *fronde* head-on. He chose as his field of battle not the slippery slope of war aims but rather the comfortable turf of political reform. On 5 April he informed the State Ministry that he intended to introduce direct, secret, and equal male suffrage in Prussia, where the electorate for the last century had been divided into three voting 'classes' based on immovable property and wealth. Conservatives, led by Interior Minister von Loebell, treated this attempt to 'alter power relations in Prussia' as a call to arms. They lobbied both the Kaiser and the *OHL* to oppose the reforms, fully aware that universal male suffrage would cost them 75 per cent of their present seats in the Prussian Lower House – and conversely increase those of the Social Democrats 1300 per cent. They were successful: Wilhelm II's much vaunted 'Easter Message' of 7 April promised only to address (not reform) the Prussian suffrage question after the war. Ludendorff warned the Chancellor that reform was impossible without the consent of the '*Volk* in arms' – that is, the Supreme Command.[81] The Left cautioned Bethmann Hollweg that the promise contained in the 'Easter Message' was too little and too late. But the Social Democratic Party was itself no longer in control of the political agenda. On 11 March the first Russian revolution had broken out; 4 days later Nicholas II abdicated. And the SPD's own radical left refused to back the war any longer: at Gotha between 9 and 11 April 1917 it voted to cede from the party and to found the 120 000-member Independent Social Democratic Party of Germany (USPD). Within 2 weeks, Berlin and the Ruhr were rocked by workers' strikes and food riots. The politics of 'total' war had come home to roost.

In vain, Ludendorff persuaded the Munich publisher J. F. Lehmann to mass produce a pamphlet entitled 'Germany's Future under a Good and a Bad Peace'. A 'German peace' meant victory and a 'free *Volk*' with only minimal war debts of 5 billion Marks; a 'bad peace' would reduce the German people to 'loan slaves of England' with a whopping debt of 170 billion Marks. The General next tried to rally Vienna behind his war-aims programme. On 23 April and again on 17–18 May 1917 Austrian and German planners met at *OHL* headquarters at Kreuznach and committed to paper a war-aims programme that far surpassed any to date.[82] Bethmann Hollweg once more pursued a policy of inconsistency: he signed the Kreuznach Agreement and then described it to his inner circle as 'flights of fantasy'.

The political lines were drawn by the spring of 1917. On the one side stood the so-called 'moderate' Bethmann Hollweg seeking to maintain what by early 1917 was a fictional *Burgfriede* and to keep his options open for future peace negotiations. On the other side stood the *OHL* supported by Conservatives, industry, and extra-parliamentary pressure groups demanding a victorious peace with vast annexations and indemnities in order to stabilize the Prusso-German state. Both sides appreciated that their fates were tied to battlefield success in 1917.

Chapter 7 Notes

1. Cited in Michael Howard, *The Franco-Prussian War: The German Invasion of France, 1870–1871* (London and New York, Methuen, 1961), p. 380.
2. Arthur J. May, *The Passing of the Hapsburg Monarchy 1914–1918* (2 vols, Philadelphia, University of Pennsylvania Press, 1966) 1, pp. 287–9.
3. May, *Passing of the Hapsburg Monarchy 1*, pp. 310–13. See especially Marion Breiter, 'Hinter der Front. Zum Leben der Zivilbevölkerung im Wien des Ersten Weltkrieges', unpubl. diss., Vienna University 1991.
4. Cited in May, *Passing of the Hapsburg Monarchy 1*, p. 332.
5. Gary W. Shanafelt, *The Secret Enemy: Austria–Hungary and the German Alliance, 1914–1918* (New York, Columbia University Press, 1985), p. 98.
6. Ottokar Landwehr von Pragenau, *Hunger: Die Erschöpfungsjahre der Mittelmächte 1917–18* (Zurich, Leipzig, and Vienna, Amalthea, 1931), p. 72.
7. Landwehr, *Hunger*, pp. 113–16, 164–70.
8. Landwehr, *Hunger*, pp. 62, 74–9.
9. May, *Passing of the Hapsburg Monarchy 1*, pp. 333–4.
10. May, *Passing of the Hapsburg Monarchy*, pp. 347–8.
11. Landwehr, *Hunger*, pp. 24–5.
12. See Shanafelt, *The Secret Enemy*, p. 100.
13. ÖStA-KA, MKSM, Standort des AOK am 18. Juli 1917.
14. Landwehr, *Hunger*, pp. 31, 38, 93.
15. József Galántai, *Hungary in the First World War* (Budapest, Akadémiai Kiadó, 1989), pp. 192–3.
16. May, *Passing of the Hapsburg Monarchy 1*, pp. 128–9.
17. Galántai, *Hungary in the First World War*, p. 171.
18. Robert J. Wegs, *Die österreichische Kriegswirtschaft 1914–1918* (Vienna, A. Schendl, 1979), pp. 93–4.
19. Wegs, *Österreichische Kriegswirtschaft*, p. 95.
20. Wegs, *Österreichische Kriegswirtschaft*, pp. 95–7.
21. Sigrid Augeneder, *Arbeiterinnen im Ersten Weltkrieg. Lebens- und Arbeitsbedingungen proletarischer Frauen in Österreich* (Vienna, Europaverlag, 1987), pp. 60–9, 172–3.
22. Augeneder, *Arbeiterinnen im Ersten Weltkrieg*, pp. 24–5.
23. Wegs, *Österreichische Kriegswirtschaft*, pp. 99–101.
24. Protocol of a meeting between Foreign Minister Czernin and Chancellor von Bethmann Hollweg on 16 March 1917. HHStA, PA I Botschaftsarchiv Berlin 536.
25. See *Dokumente aus geheimen Archiven. 4: Berichte des Berliner Polizeipräsidenten zur Stimmung und Lage der Bevölkerung in Berlin 1914–1918,* eds Ingo Materna and Hans-Joachim Schreckenbach (Weimar, Hermann Böhlaus Nachfolger, 1987), p. 98.
26. Otto Riebicke, *Was brauchte der Weltkrieg? Tatsachen und Zahlen aus dem deutschen Ringen 1914/18* (Berlin, Kyffhäuser-Verlag, 1936), p. 78. The domestic social tensions in Germany have been analysed by Jürgen Kocka, *Facing Total War: German Society, 1914–1918* (Leamington Spa, Berg, 1984).
27. BA-MA, PG 6 I/255 VII Armeekorps Münster. Memorandum of 30 October 1916.
28. See C. Paul Vincent, *The Politics of Hunger: The Allied Blockade of Germany, 1915–1919* (Athens and London, Ohio University Press, 1985), pp. 16–19.
29. See Albrecht von Thaer, *Generalstabsdienst an der Front und in der O.H.L. Aus Briefen und Tagebuchaufzeichnungen 1915–1919*, ed. Siegfried A. Kaehler (Göttingen, Vandenhoeck & Ruprecht, 1958), p. 28. Entry for 23 February 1915.
30. Reichsarchiv, *Der Weltkrieg 1914 bis 1918. 8: Die Operationen des Jahres 1915* (Berlin, E. S. Mittler & Sohn, 1932), pp. 13–14; Lothar Burchardt, 'Die Auswirkungen der Kriegswirtschaft auf die deutsche Zivilbevölkerung im Ersten und im Zweiten Weltkrieg',

Militärgeschichtliche Mitteilungen 15 (1974), p. 67. Gerd Hardach, *The First World War 1914–1918* (London, Allen Lane, 1977), p. 115, questions the extent of the 'hog murder' and suggests that only one-tenth of the Reich's 27 million hogs were butchered.

31. Reichsarchiv, *Der Weltkrieg 1914 bis 1918.* 9: *Die Operationen des Jahres 1915* (Berlin, E. S. Mittler & Sohn, 1933), p. 355.
32. Marion C. Siney, *The Allied Blockade of Germany 1914–1918* (Ann Arbor, The University of Michigan Press, 1957), pp. 1–9.
33. Siney, *Allied Blockade of Germany*, pp. 21–2, 66–7.
34. Vincent, *Politics of Hunger*, p. 38.
35. *Der Weltkrieg 1914 bis 1918* 9, pp. 342–3.
36. *Der Weltkrieg 1914 bis 1918* 9, p. 352; Burchardt, 'Auswirkungen der Kriegswirtschaft', p. 70.
37. See Marie-Elisabeth Lüders, *Das unbekannte Heer. Frauen kämpfen für Deutschland 1914–1918* (Berlin, E. S. Mittler & Sohn, 1936).
38. Evelyn, Princess Blücher, *An English Wife in Berlin: A Private Memoir of Events, Politics, and Daily Life in Germany throughout the War and the Social Revolution of 1918* (New York, E. P. Dutton, 1920), p. 122.
39. Hardach, *The First World War*, p. 118.
40. Thaer, *Generalstabsdienst*, p. 121. Entry of 15 May 1917.
41. Hardach, *The First World War*, p. 120.
42. Blücher, *An English Wife in Berlin*, p. 180.
43. Blücher, *An English Wife in Berlin*, pp. 136, 162.
44. Lyncker to Wandel, 5 October 1916. BA-MA, Nachlass Wandel, N 564, vol. 10.
45. BA-MA, PH 2/17 Deutschfeindliche Bestrebungen.
46. Theodor Wolff, *Tagebücher 1914–1919*, ed. Bernd Sösemann (2 vols, Boppard, H. Boldt, 1984) 1, pp. 377, 453, 460, 479, 483–4.
47. Holger H. Herwig, *'Luxury' Fleet: The Imperial German Navy 1888–1918* (London and Atlantic Highlands, The Ashfield Press, 1987), p. 230.
48. Cited in Vincent, *Politics of Hunger*, pp. 21–2.
49. Cited in Richard Bessel, *Germany after the First World War* (Oxford, Clarendon, 1993), p. 41.
50. HHStA, PA IIII Gesandschaft Berlin 173. Reports dated 26 April, 30 June, and 4 July 1917. See also *Dokumente aus geheimen Archiven. 4: Berichte des Berliner Polizeipräsidenten*, pp. 190–4, 105.
51. Riebicke, *Was brauchte der Weltkrieg?*, pp. 90–1.
52. Burchardt, 'Auswirkungen der Kriegswirtschaft', pp. 82–5.
53. Bessel, *Germany after the First World War*, p. 33.
54. The following discussion is from Lüders, *Das unbekannte Heer*; and Ursula von Gersdorff, *Frauen im Kriegsdienst 1914–1945* (Stuttgart, Deutsche Verlags-Anstalt, 1969).
55. BA-MA, PH 6 I/27 VII Armeekorps Münster.
56. Riebicke, *Was brauchte der Weltkrieg?*, pp. 105–6.
57. Paul, *The Politics of Hunger*, pp. 137, 138, 146.
58. See Gunther Mai, 'Burgfrieden und Sozialpolitik in Deutschland in der Anfangsphase des Ersten Weltkrieges (1914/15)', *Militärgeschichtliche Mitteilungen* 22 (1976), pp. 21–50.
59. See Fielding H. Garrison, *Notes on the History of Military Medicine* (Hildesheim and New York, G. Olms, 1970), pp. 180, 200.
60. Friedrich Ring, *Zur Geschichte der Militärmedizin in Deutschland* (East Berlin, Deutscher Militärverlag, 1962), pp. 224–45.
61. Robert Weldon Whalen, *Bitter Wounds: German Victims of the Great War, 1914–1939* (Ithaca and London, Cornell University Press, 1984), p. 50.
62. See Gerd Krumeich, 'Verstümmelungen und Kunstglieder. Formen körperlicher

Verheerungen im 1. Weltkrieg', *Sozialwissenschaftliche Informationen* 19 (1990), pp. 97–102.

63. Dr B. Hallauer, 'Bericht über die Explosionskatastrophe im Fort Douaumont', 10 May 1916. I am indebted to German Werth, author of *Verdun* and a staff-member of German Radio in Berlin, for making this document available to me.

64. BA-MA, MSg 2/626 Aufzeichnungen eines Stabsarztes Feld. Laz. 201 (Alpenkorps). Verdun.

65. Richard A. Gabriel and Karen S. Metz, *A History of Military Medicine* (2 vols, New York, Westport, and London, Greenwood Press, 1992) 2, pp. 242–3.

66. ÖStA-KA, MKSM, 'Standort des AOK am 18. Juli 1917'; Bundesministerium für Landesverteidigung, *Österreich-Ungarns Letzter Krieg 1914–1918*. 7: *Das Kriegsjahr 1918* (Vienna, Verlag der Militärwissenschaftlichen Mitteilungen, 1938), pp. 88–9.

67. Benckendorff to Sazonov, 28 September 1914. Cited in Wolfgang Michalka, ed., *Der Erste Weltkrieg. Wirkung, Wahrnehmung, Analyse* (Munich and Zurich, Piper, 1994), p. 97.

68. See D. Stevenson, *French War Aims Against Germany 1914–1919* (Oxford, Clarendon Press, 1982); David French, *British Strategy & War Aims 1914–1916* (London, Allen & Unwin, 1986); and Horst Günther Linke, *Das zaristische Russland und der Erste Weltkrieg. Diplomatie und Kriegsziele, 1914–1917* (Munich, Fink, 1982).

69. Cited in Holger H. Herwig and Neil M. Heyman, eds, *Biographical Dictionary of World War I* (Westport and London, Greenwood Press, 1982), p. 47.

70. See Gerhard Ritter, *Staatskunst und Kriegshandwerk. Das Problem des 'Militarismus' in Deutschland* (4 vols, Munich, Verlag R. Oldenbourg, 1964) 3, pp. 36–47.

71. Lerchenfeld to Hertling, 24 October 1915. BHStA, MA 3079 Militär Bevollmächtigter Berlin.

72. Burián's notes of November 1916. HHStA, PA I Botschaftsarchiv Berlin 536.

73. Ritter, *Staatskunst und Kriegshandwerk* 3, pp. 352–3. War aims of 23 December 1916.

74. BA-MA, Nachlass Vanselow, F 7612, 'Kriegsziele der Marine'. See Holger H. Herwig, 'Admirals *versus* Generals: The War Aims of the Imperial German Navy 1914–1918', *Central European History* 5 (1972), pp. 214–16.

75. BA-MA, RM 3/11624, dated 26 January 1915.

76. Fritz Fischer, *Griff nach der Weltmacht. Die Kriegszielpolitik des kaiserlichen Deutschland 1914/18* (Düsseldorf, Droste Verlag, 1961), p. 425.

77. The Wilhelmstrasse tried to downplay its monumental blunder, assuring Vienna that it was 'relatively meaningless' given the likelihood of war with the United States over the U-boat campaign in any case. Hohenlohe to Czernin, 4 March 1917. HHStA, PA III Gesandschaft Berlin 175.

78. The banker Franz Andraede, Walther Rathenau's cousin, 5 March 1917. Cited in Wolff, *Tagebücher* 1, p. 485.

79. See Bruno Thoss, 'Nationale Rechte, militärische Führung und Diktaturfrage in Deutschland 1913–1923', *Militärgeschichtliche Mitteilungen* 42 (1987), pp. 28–47.

80. HHStA, PA I Botschaftsarchiv Berlin 536. Protocol of discussions, 16 March 1917.

81. Thoss, 'Nationale Rechte', p. 50.

82. See Fischer, *Griff nach der Weltmacht*, pp. 455 ff., 463 ff.

8

A Sea-Change, 1917

In war politics has to hold its tongue until strategy once again allows it to speak.

Kaiser Wilhelm II, December 1915

The year 1917, dubbed *'l'année troublé'* by French President Poincaré, proved to be decisive along political lines. Two developments determined not only the course of the war but subsequent world history: in April 1917 the United States declared war on Germany as a result of unrestricted submarine warfare, and in November 1917 Lenin and his Bolsheviks took Russia out of the conflict. The American action would tilt the balance in the stalemated war toward the Allies, and the draconian peace that Germany imposed on Lenin at Brest-Litovsk would make the Allies more determined than ever to prosecute the war to a victorious conclusion.

In January 1917 Germany embarked on its fifth bid for victory: unrestricted U-boat warfare. Hindenburg and Ludendorff, as discussed in Chapter 6, had evaluated their position in the winter of 1916–17 and opted for a defensive posture for the coming year. Accordingly, they had crafted detailed infantry manuals for the new elastic defence in depth, retrained the Army with the 'machines' of position warfare, built a massive system of fortifications along the Western Front, and mobilized the nation's manpower and material resources to put the nation on a 'total war' footing. They had also tried to rally the nation behind a sweeping catalogue of war aims. Vienna had been brought into line – despite its unpredictable young ruler, Kaiser Karl – and offered a share of the anticipated spoils of war. The stage was set for greatness. Victory in 1917, the argument ran, lay with the Navy's new technology: the U-boat.

U-boat warfare: playing *va banque*

On 22 December 1916 Admiral von Holtzendorff, Chief of the Admiralty Staff, penned a strategic paper that he later submitted to both the Chancellor and the General Staff. 'The war demands a decision by autumn 1917', Holtzendorff stated, 'if it is not to end with a general exhaustion of all parties and thus disastrously for us'. Like Falkenhayn the year before in his Christmas memorandum on Verdun, Holtzendorff identified Britain as the driving force behind the Allied coalition. 'If we can break England's backbone, the war is at once decided in our favour.' And Britain's 'backbone' was its 'shipping tonnage'. Thus, Holtzendorff argued, if Germany could launch a campaign of 'unrestricted submarine warfare' against all shipping bound for the British Isles by 1 February 1917 at the latest, the war would be over before the Allies brought in their next harvest – that is, by 1 August. The stakes were so high that Holtzendorff was prepared 'to accept the risk of a break with America'. After all, the Republic's lackadaisical performance against Spain in 1898 hardly instilled fear in German planners.[1]

Holtzendorff's proposal was enthusiastically endorsed by high-ranking naval officers, many of whom thirsted for action to justify the Navy's future existence. In March 1916 Grand Admiral von Tirpitz had been forced from office on account of his vacillating calls first for a major fleet action and then for unrestricted submarine warfare. 'He is leaving the sinking ship', Wilhelm II had noted.[2] Then on 31 May the German High Sea Fleet and the British Grand Fleet had collided in the Skagerrak off Denmark. While a tactical German victory – the British lost 14 ships of 111 000 tons to Germany's 11 ships of 62 000 tons – the Battle of Jutland nevertheless did not alter the strategy of the war at sea. Admiral Reinhard Scheer, the German fleet commander, in his after-action report to the Kaiser on 4 July pointed out that Britain's 'great material superiority' combined with Germany's 'disadvantageous military-geographical position' ruled out victory in this war. All that remained for the Germans, like the French after Trafalgar, was *guerre de course* – which for Scheer meant the 'defeat of British economic life, that is, by using the U-boats against British trade'. Scheer conceded that by playing what he called the U-boat 'trump', Germany would probably bring the United States into the war. He was willing to accept the risk.[3] Bethmann Hollweg, on the other hand, was shocked by what he termed the 'incredibly frivolous manner' in which Scheer at Jutland had risked the nation's existence on a single throw of the dice.[4]

The Chancellor was the key to the U-boat offensive. In the winter of 1916–17 he faced the second major crisis of his wartime rule. As in July

1914, inconsistency marked his behaviour. In fact, Bethmann Hollweg had developed a two-pronged plan. On 12 December 1916 he launched his famous peace offensive, hoping with the help of Wilson, reelected President on 7 November, to begin discussions to end the war.[5] The Chancellor was certain of the backing of the Kaiser and felt that he could bargain from a position of strength after Germany had occupied Bucharest on 6 December. Domestically, a peace offensive would gain him the support of the German people and the moderate parties in the Reichstag; diplomatically, it might sow dissension in the ranks of the Allies. It appeared to be a win–win proposition: if the Allies accepted his offer to mediate, Bethmann Hollweg could 'atone' for his ineptness during the July 1914 crisis[6] and regain his popularity; if the Allies refused to negotiate, he was free in good conscience to endorse unrestricted submarine warfare.

The 'peace offensive' was bound to fail, as Bethmann Hollweg well knew. Haughty in tone, the 'lean' peace contained not a single word about restoring Belgian or Serbian sovereignty. The Chancellor's well-known demands for annexation of the Baltic states and parts of Poland as well as Longwy-Briey and Liège, his call for a 'compact colonial empire in Africa', and his insistence that Belgium remain a German 'vassal state', raise troubling questions about the seriousness of his irenic actions in December 1916. The Russians rejected his note on 15 December, followed by Britain and France on 30 December. The Allies accompanied their letters of rejection to President Wilson on 10 January 1917 with a litany of German 'transgressions' ranging from the deportation of Belgian workers to the execution of Nurse Edith Cavell,[7] from bombing raids on London to submarine warfare. Britain and France were committed to Prime Minister Lloyd George's policy of delivering 'Prussian militarism' a 'knock-out' blow before going to the peace table. And the Entente made it clear that the dismemberment of the Habsburg Empire was likewise a firm war aim.

Bethmann Hollweg was also inconsistent on the U-boat question. In the company of trusted aides, he raised doubts about its efficacy and fears concerning its impact on the United States; in public, he consistently stated his willingness to endorse it as 'military necessity' if that were the wish of the General Staff. As early as 28 August 1916, for example, Bethmann Hollweg had informed the Prussian State Ministry that 'not a single day ought to be lost' if the Reich were to 'go over to unrestricted submarine warfare'. On 28 September he had played to the Reichstag galleries by stating that 'any German statesman deserved to be hanged if he shrank from using against this enemy every suitable weapon that would really shorten the war'. The following day he repeated this line of argument before the Budget Commission and on September 30 denied that submarine warfare was a 'policy of desperation'.[8] In November 1916 Bethmann Hollweg informed the Austrians that he endorsed U-boat warfare against unarmed merchant ships as being 'in every sense fully justified'.[9] Little wonder that few people understood the Chancellor's stand on submarine warfare – then or later.

War aims related directly to unrestricted submarine warfare. It is no coincidence that Holtzendorff had developed his annexationist programme on 26 November and 24 December 1916 – that is, at the very moment that he was pressuring Kaiser, Chancellor, and General Staff for the U-boat offensive. Few among the Wilhelmian political elite doubted that their continued stay in office depended on victory. Indemnities would pay for the war and territorial annexations justify its human cost.

Alfred Hugenberg, the Ruhr coal baron, as early as November 1914 had lectured fellow industrialists that the workers returning from the trenches would possess 'a very increased sense of power' and demand political influence. 'It would therefore be well advised, in order to avoid internal difficulties, to distract the attention of the people and to give phantasies concerning the extension of German territory room to play.'[10] Wolff, the Berlin journalist, early in 1917 likewise pointed to the tie between victory in the field and domestic dominance by the ruling elite in a discussion with the former Ambassador to the United States, Johann Heinrich Count von Bernstorff: 'One will no longer be able to rule in such a reactionary manner once the people return from the trenches'.[11] Rathenau, head of the AEG, agreed with Wolff and that July apprised Ludendorff of the 'necessity of raising the income of the lower classes by at least 50%' after the war. 'The trenches', Rathenau allowed in reference to the soldiers, 'cannot be paid for with a deterioration in the standard of living'.[12]

Certain mathematical calculations help explain Holtzendorff's faith in the U-boats. He estimated that Great Britain had about 11 million tons of shipping at its disposal, including neutral vessels trading to Allied ports. If Germany could destroy an average of 600 000 tons per month for a period of 6 months, and if about 1.2 of the 3 million tons of neutral shipping available to the Allies could be scared off the seas, then Britannia would lose 39 per cent of its tonnage, a 'final and irreplaceable loss'.[13] Britain's critical reliance on imported cereal grains and anticipated poor harvests in North America due to wheat rust seemed to play into his hands.

The Admiral ran his projections by the *OHL* on 8 January, the day before the decisive meeting at Pless. Hindenburg fully endorsed the Navy's initiative: 'It has to be. We expect war with America and have made all preparations [for it]. Things cannot get worse.' Admiral Eduard von Capelle, Tirpitz's successor at the Navy Office, had already assured Reichstag leaders that the military danger posed by the United States 'was zero'. Wilhelm II declared that U-boat warfare was purely a military decision, one which did not concern the Chancellor. Bethmann Hollweg at the last minute consulted the Imperial Treasury about the Navy's prognostications. Helfferich felt uncomfortable with Holtzendorff's figures and warned against taking precipitate action.

Bethmann Hollweg refused this advice. On 9 January 1917, after debating the possibility of revolution in Russia and the unlikelihood that Denmark and the Netherlands would declare war as a result of the U-boat offensive, the Chancellor came to the heart of the matter. The submarine campaign was Germany's 'last card'; the resolve to use it constituted a 'very serious decision'. President Wilson was certain to go to war over this issue, but Bethmann Hollweg promised 'to try to keep America out'. He deemed the overall 'prospects for unrestricted U-boat warfare very favourable'. Most critically, the Chancellor abrogated his political responsibilities. If military leaders 'consider the U-boat war to be necessary, then I am not in a position to speak against it'.[14] For the second time in the war – after July 1914 – he allowed a national issue to be decided by the General Staff along narrow military lines.

The meeting concluded with a discussion of the probable reaction of the United States. Captain Magnus von Levetzow 'guaranteed' victory for the U-boats 'with good conscience' on behalf of Admiral Scheer, and assured those present that war with America was 'of no importance to the Fleet'. Ludendorff stated that the Army 'needed to be spared a second Battle of the Somme', and that he was quite prepared 'to accept the risk' of war. 'I don't give a damn about America.' Hindenburg chimed in that any future American war effort was bound to be 'minimal, in any case not decisive'.

Wilhelm II closed the meeting by stating that he 'fully expected America's entry into the war', but that this was 'irrelevant'.[15] Concurrently, the Kaiser poured out his feelings concerning the nature of the war to Houston Stewart Chamberlain, the late Richard Wagner's son-in-law:

> The war is the struggle between 2 *Weltanschauungen*: the Germanic-German [one] for manners, right, loyalty a[nd] faith, true humanity, truth and real freedom; against the Anglo-Saxon [one for] service of mammon, power of money, indulgence, land hunger, lies, treason, deception, and, last but not least, insidious assassination.

Wilhelm II averred that there could be no compromise between the two systems: 'one must *win*, the other must *perish*!'[16] The order to resume unrestricted submarine warfare on 1 February went out later that night. The Kaiser sent champagne to Bethmann Hollweg's room.

Lieutenant-Commander Ernst von Weizsäcker almost alone in the Navy warned – albeit, to no avail – that the U-boat decision constituted a desperate gamble. 'It remains a *va banque* game of Germany against half the world.'[17] Princess Blücher in Berlin caught the public mood well: 'Every one is excited about the submarine question. We all know and feel that Germany is playing her last card; with what results, no one can possibly foretell'.[18] Bethmann Hollweg's political adviser, Riezler, appreciated the cruel nature of the decision. He termed it yet another 'leap in the dark' and surmised that the Hohenzollern crown rested on its success. '[Either] Wilhelm the Very Great or else Wilhelm the Last.' For Riezler understood that the decision had come down to the accuracy of the Navy's figures. 'One cannot believe the Navy, and [yet] one cannot deny it this belief.'[19]

Why did Bethmann Hollweg support a policy that he had once denounced as a 'game of dice whose ante is nothing less than Germany's existence'?[20] And why did he not resign to protest the measure? The historian Gerhard Ritter, one of Bethmann Hollweg's staunchest defenders, claimed that 9 January 1917 constituted 'the darkest hour of his political career . . . the literal capitulation of political authority before the military in the most decisive question of the entire World War'.[21]

Bethmann Hollweg probably hoped that the decision would lift public opinion during the 'turnip winter' of 1916–17 by holding out the promise of an end to the war within 6 months. The Chancellor, who preferred to rule through bureaucratic consensus, could hardly disavow the expert opinions of his own High Sea Fleet and Admiralty Staff without causing a serious crisis. The Reichstag caucus of the pivotal Centre Party in fact had demanded that the government accede to the wishes of the military in this matter. Thirdly, Bethmann Hollweg had little faith in his 'peace initiative' and once the Allies had rejected it, there remained no obstacles on the road to unrestricted submarine warfare. Nor did the Chancellor see any future in putting himself at the head of an anti-submarine parliamentary faction of Social Democrats. He was a product of the semi-authoritarian Wilhelmian system and in 1917 became its most prominent (self-incarcerated) prisoner. Perhaps Bethmann Hollweg still laboured under the illusion, held since the spring of 1915, that he could use Hindenburg's immense popularity to cover a negotiated peace. That he failed to appreciate Ludendorff's power within the Third *OHL* speaks volumes for the Chancellor's political sagacity. Finally, Bethmann Hollweg hoped that his bold stance would erase his negative image in Conservative circles as a weak and spineless leader (*Flaumacher*). He erred. Crown

Prince Wilhelm openly denounced him as a weakling in the tow of 'Jews and Social Democrats' and insisted that he be 'thrown out' of office. Within 24 hours of the Pless decision, Hindenburg demanded that the Kaiser fire Bethmann Hollweg for his insipid leadership.[22]

The decision made at Pless, Holtzendorff, along with the new German Foreign Secretary, Zimmermann, rushed to Vienna to convince Kaiser Karl and the Ballhausplatz to endorse the underwater campaign. It proved to be a hard sell. To be sure, Grand Admiral Anton Haus, War Minister Krobatin, and Conrad von Hötzendorf ('We must undertake total U-boat warfare, if we do not want to go down to defeat in 1917') endorsed unrestricted submarine warfare at once; Kaiser Karl as well as his new Foreign Minister, Czernin, Hungarian Premier Tisza, and the new Austrian Prime Minister, Heinrich Count Clam-Martinic, initially were 'negative' about its possible political ramifications.[23] Karl refused to entertain the two German envoys at Court. But Austria–Hungary was no longer a fully sovereign power given its dependence on German financial, material, and military aid. Zimmermann's argument that the Western Front could not be held without submarine warfare bowled over Czernin. On 23 January Kaiser Karl bowed to the inevitable and endorsed the U-boat campaign; 2 days later, accompanied by Conrad, he travelled to Pless to deliver the news to Wilhelm II as an early birthday present.[24]

Karl may have agreed to the German submarine campaign in part because he was about to launch his own secret negotiations with the French to end the war. In a risky act of personal diplomacy, the Kaiser on 17 March entrusted his brother-in-law, Prince Sixtus of Bourbon-Parma, with a delicate mission to French President Poincaré, wherein the last of the Habsburgs offered a negotiated peace at Germany's expense. Karl promised 'to support France and to exert pressure on Germany with all means available' to restore Belgian neutrality, to reconstitute the Serbian state, and to recognize France's 'just claims' to Alsace-Lorraine.[25] Apparently it dawned on few in Vienna that French war aims could hardly be satisfied simply by the 'return' of Alsace-Lorraine. The Germans learned of Karl's secret diplomacy from Foreign Minister Czernin – thus for the moment ending the 'Sixtus Affair'.[26] While there were few open charges of Habsburg treachery and infidelity, Berlin henceforth viewed Vienna with greater suspicion. One can only guess how the Germans would have treated Austria–Hungary in the wake of a successful U-boat campaign.

Germany's bid for victory was based on extensive research into British food and shipping requirements by a host of German military and civilian experts. For months the Admiralty Staff's special research office as well as academics and merchants such as Dr Richard Fuss, Hermann Lewy,

Henry Newman, and Hermann Weil had pored over newspapers, shipping statistics, Lloyd's Registry, and wheat tables to buttress their seemingly irrefutable prediction of Britain's demise by 1 August 1917. For the first time in history the government was confronted by massive data amassed by civilian experts. The gist of their argument was that the Reich could not let the opportunity slip by to deal its most dangerous enemy a decisive blow. The U-boat was a new weapon and deserved a chance to demonstrate its effectiveness. Modern economies could never absorb the strain of economic warfare *à outrance*. And the British 'national character' precluded recourse to rationing or wartime mobilization of domestic industries and agriculture.

Initial results from the unrestricted submarine campaign seemed to bear out the Admiralty Staff's experts. The U-boats destroyed 499 430 tons of shipping in February, 548 817 in March, 841 118 in April, 590 729 in May, 669 218 in June, and 534 799 in July.[27] German industrialists such as Ferdinand von Stumm spoke confidently of victory and envisaged 'one hundred billion Marks' in war indemnities to be paid by the Allies.[28] But in August the U-boat figure fell to 477 338 tons and in September to 344 789. Thereafter sinkings rapidly fell to below 300 000 tons per month. Conversely, U-boat losses, which had averaged four per month in the first half of 1917, rose to seven in the last half of the year.[29] The first of August came and went – without the promised British demise.

The reasons for the failure of unrestricted submarine warfare are many and diverse. In the first place, statistics can (and often do) prove whatever their authors wish. The Germans included only British shipping in their calculations, whereas they should have taken stock of total world shipping, including German vessels interned especially in the United States since 1914. Nor did they take into account the Republic's shipbuilding potential. By relying solely on wheat totals the Germans overlooked that the British could compensate for lower wheat imports by turning to other grains and by ploughing up grasslands for grain production. In fact, the British in 1917–18 turned 1.3 million acres of grass and common lands over to grains, thereby raising food output 31 per cent.

The experts also failed to appreciate that grain reserves on hand from the 1916 harvest in Australia, Canada, South America, and the United States more than sufficed to feed the Allies for much of 1917. Grains were so plentiful in Britain in 1917 that not even the corn and oats rations for race horses had to be lowered. Given the planners' flawed assessment of the British 'national character', they never imagined that London would institute rationing. The argument that U-boat sinkings would force insurance rates through the roof and thus render idle shippers was negated when London seized all available shipping and controlled insurance rates.

Another fatal flaw was the argument, endorsed by Ludendorff at Pless, that British coal mines would close for lack of pit-props as wood imports from Scandinavia would be interdicted; in fact, the British received all the wood they needed from their own forests by curtailing domestic housing construction as well as from Scandinavia, whose shipping they escorted with warships.[30]

Most importantly, the Germans ignored the simplest antidote of all: convoy, which Britain had instituted since the age of sail in the sixteenth century to protect imports against maritime raiders, and which the Germans had used since 1914 to convoy vital shipments of Swedish iron ore across the Baltic Sea. To be sure, British admirals at first were reluctant to institute convoy, arguing that the difficulties of assembling ships, keeping them in formation, sailing at the speed of the slowest ship in the group, and congestion at the port of destination militated against its use in the age of steam. But the Royal Navy instituted convoy: on 10 May 1917 more than a dozen ships reached Plymouth from Gibraltar with no losses. Almost 12 months passed before the U-boats attempted to attack a convoy. Escorts were outfitted with depth charges, explosive paravanes, hydrophones, antitorpedo nets, 'dazzle' paint, and guns.

Perhaps the greatest impediment to success was of the Germans' own making: lack of U-boats. Naval planners as early as 1914 had estimated that they would need at least 222 submarines to mount an effective blockade of Great Britain. On 1 February 1917 the Navy possessed 107 boats – of which a mere 30 were suitable for ocean duty. Given that one-third of the U-boats were always en route to the war zones and another third on the way home for repair and resupply, roughly 30 submarines (including only 10 large boats) were on station off western Britain at any given time. Construction barely kept pace with losses: 20 U-boats were destroyed in the first half of 1917 and 42 in the second half, while 87 were launched.[31] The risk percentage for Allied and neutral merchant shipping in the waters around the British Isles fell to 0.6 per cent by 1918.

The Germans reacted to this setback by training crews at the U-Boat School at Eckernförde to attack convoys, pooling information on Allied sailings, attacking convoys closer to shore where the larger escorts left the freighters, and extending the war zones around the British Isles in order to disperse escort craft. German naval leaders also toyed with the notion of hunting convoys with 'wolf packs', but Holtzendorff vetoed this novel idea by arguing that dispersal of U-boats translated into dispersal of escorts as well. Germany failed to establish a central U-Boat Office until December 1917 – almost a year after staking the Reich's future on submarines – and Ludendorff refused to release skilled labour from munitions plants to build more craft.

Technical problems also plagued the U-boats. German codes were frequently lost or broken. Wireless communications were of insufficient range on the surface and not developed under water. Air leaks from the torpedoes often provided ample warning to the intended victim, while similar air seepage from torpedo tubes revealed the U-boat's position to attack craft. And the boats were too slow both submerged (5 to 8 knots) and on the surface (12 to 16 knots) to be effective against fast destroyers.[32]

The political fallout from the U-boat campaign came quickly. The sinking of the USS *Housatonic* on 3 February prompted Washington to break off diplomatic relations with Berlin. On 2 April the House of Representatives passed a war resolution by a vote of 373 to 50; on 6 April the United States declared war against Germany. President Wilson, in his address to Congress, abandoned his 'peace without victory' formula of 22 January in favour of a crusade to make the world 'safe for democracy'. The President denounced the U-boats as 'pirates' and 'outlaws' and the campaign as one 'against mankind' and 'against all nations'.[33] Wilson believed that he could dictate the peace settlement he desired only by armed intervention in the war. The U-boats determined the timing of that intervention. On the lighter side, hamburgers were renamed 'liberty steak', sauerkraut 'liberty cabbage', and German measles 'liberty measles'.

War-weary Britain, France, and Italy took heart in the addition of the world's greatest neutral to their alliance as an 'Associated Power'. Yet in April 1917 the United States War Department had only 213 557 troops, including 127 588 active, on its roster. Its air forces consisted of 55 planes, of which 51 were considered obsolete. And its sea-lift capacity was ranked lower than that of Norway. But the U-boats did not sink a single eastbound troop transport in the Atlantic. The US Navy not only sent its entire destroyer force of 68 ships and 121 so-called submarine-chasers to Europe to assist in the fight against the U-boats, but attached its newest squadron of five dreadnoughts to Admiral David Beatty's Grand Fleet. By the summer of 1918, the United States shuttled 536 000 tons of supplies per month to France. Put differently, a troop transport or cargo vessel left the United States every 5 hours, with the result that seven soldiers and their equipment disembarked in France every minute of every day. By war's end the Republic had brought 1.97 million soldiers to the Western Front.

The decline of Germany's submarine campaign by late 1917 perhaps can best be reproduced from the logs of two U-boats. In April 1918 the submarine cruiser *U-151* (originally designed to be the mercantile carrier 'U-Oldenburg') was despatched to North America to harass the Admiralty's new HC ('Home from Canada') convoys emanating from

Halifax. Built in 1916–17, *U-151* displaced 1512 tons, carried a crew of 56, had a range of 2500 sea miles at 5.5 knots; best surface speed was 12.4 knots, submerged 5.2 knots. The boat was armed with two 15 cm and two 8.8 cm guns, carried eight G6 AV torpedoes as well as six mines with 200 pounds of TNT each on the upper deck for surface launch, and stored eight mines in the torpedo room for submerged launch. Its skipper was Lieutenant-Commander Heinrich von Nostiz; first officer was Lieutenant Martin Niemöller, who would later join Karl Dönitz and Wilhelm Canaris in the Adriatic Sea.

U-151 left Kiel on 18 April with orders to capture enemy prizes and cargoes and to lay mines and cut submarine cables off the eastern seaboard of North America.[34] From the Baltic Sea it passed through the Danish Belts, rounded the Shetland Islands, and entered the Atlantic Ocean. Mines and patrols in the English Channel dictated that one-half of all outbound and 90 per cent of all returning U-boats had to take the long route around Scotland. Unknown to Nostiz, decrypters at Operational Intelligence's 'Room 40' in London reported his departure to all Royal Navy units as well as to US Naval Operations. On the first practice dive Nostiz took the boat down to a depth of 20 yards in 1 minute. Lightly built with broad upper decks, the U-cruisers were highly unmanoeuvrable and ill-suited to attack convoys. *U-151*'s lack of seaworthiness quickly became apparent. On 2 May Nostiz spied a two-stack steamer north of the Azores. When it proved too fast at 13–14 knots for submerged attack, he surfaced in its keel water. A brief artillery duel ensued but the steamer, zigzagging, escaped in heavy rain and high seas. Thirteen days later *U-151*'s torpedoes misfired against the freighter *Huntress*. On 22 May another fast steamer escaped under the cover of darkness. The next day the cruiser finally arrived off Cape Henry and Cape Charles, Virginia. On 24 May Nostiz sowed the six mines from the upper deck in the entrance to Chesapeake Bay at 900 to 1000 yard intervals. It was a long-shot since mines are best deployed in saturation rather than in random drops. All the mines were later discovered by the Americans.

On 15 May *U-151* dispatched three sailing ships (*Hattie Dunn*, *Hauppauge*, and *Edna*) en route to the Overfall lightship in Delaware Bay. The actions were simple yet effective: *U-151* approached the target submerged, surfaced to fire a warning shot, boarded and interrogated the ships' crews, gave their skippers receipts for the lost ships and cargoes, and then destroyed them with scuttling charges. None of the ships had been warned that a German U-cruiser was in American waters; none was able to radio its position to shore. During the night of 26 to 27 May, *U-151* entered Delaware Bay, ably assisted by American beacons and lights. Swift eddies were its major concern. Shortly after midnight dense fog enveloped the U-cruiser, which used this cover to drop four more mines. Buffeted by rapid currents, Nostiz sought stability on the Bay's bottom and launched the last four mines through the forward torpedo tubes. On 3 June the American steamship *Herbert L. Pratt* (7145 tons) carrying crude oil from Mexico struck one of the mines and had to be beached.

Given *U-151*'s severely 'limited manoeuvrability and submerged operating characteristics', Nostiz decided to leave the Chesapeake Bay's dangerous currents for his second major mission. On 28 May, lying in 25 fathoms of water off Fire Island, he deployed the boat's pressure cutters and severed two cables emanating from New York City. Both were repaired within little more than a month.

Nostiz was now free to commence commerce raiding and did so with a vengeance, destroying 20 vessels between 1 and 28 June. *U-151*'s victims ranged from the 8173-ton British troop ship *Dwinsk* to the 124-ton Canadian schooner *Dictator*. Captured or destroyed cargoes ranged from copper to cotton, machine parts to salt. Noteworthy was the transfer at sea of 70 tons of pure 100 per cent electrolytic copper in bars from the Norwegian *Vindeggan*. On several occasions *U-151*'s torpedoes failed to detonate and Nostiz had to surface to dispatch his victims by artillery fire. At other times steamers proved too fast for *U-151* to attack on the surface, or else escaped under a dense screen of smoke and fog. Operations were conducted according to prize rules. Nostiz offered medical attention to those in need, secured crews in their lifeboats, and broadcast in English the positions of those who needed rescue to American authorities. Back home he would be chastised for his humane actions as being 'detrimental to the intended effect of U-boat warfare'.[35]

Nostiz left a graphic description of his first encounter, on 18 June, with depth charges. Tracking a four-funnelled steamer, he discovered that it was the 22 700-ton former converted German auxiliary cruiser *Kronprinz Wilhelm*, which had been interned at Newport News in April 1915 and refitted as an armed troop transport. Nostiz fired a first torpedo at 1400 yards. Then the hunter became the hunted.

> Detonations heard; probably depth charges. At once down to 40 m[etres]. Detonations now positively identified as depth charges. Come closer. Down to greater depth. At 65 m detonations close to boat. Assuming it was a depth charge, we go still deeper, to 82 m. Boat really water tight. Depth charge carried away fresh air in periscope. . . . In all, we heard 15 detonations, of which 8–10 were depth charges.

On 20 July *U-151* returned to Kiel after 94 days on patrol. It had destroyed 22 vessels of 51 929 tons, sown 14 mines, launched six torpedoes, and fired 288 rounds of 15 cm shells. Nostiz informed the Admiralty

Staff that naval patrols off the United States coast were weak and lacked air patrol, that ships sailed independently and without escort, and that traffic followed direct, well-established routes.

Armed with *U-151*'s intelligence, Lieutenant-Commander Otto Dröscher headed out of Kiel on 11 July bound for Canada and the United States in *U-117*, a 1200-ton minelayer refitted as a U-cruiser.[36] His mission was to lay mines and conduct cruiser warfare in the waters off Halifax, New York, and Cape Hatteras. If feasible, *U-117* was to shell shipyards and docks. In less than 2 weeks Dröscher experienced serious mechanical difficulties attributable to the poor quality of workmanship and materials in German yards. A faulty friction clutch frequently endangered dives; a malfunctioning evaporator impaired the availability of fresh water; and leaking fuel tanks reduced the cruiser's range and left telltale oil traces on the surface. The engineers had to overhaul both engines on patrol.[37]

This notwithstanding, Dröscher pressed on through the Danish Belts, passed to the north of the Shetlands, and entered the open Atlantic bound for Cape Race, Newfoundland. In heavy seas *U-117* unsuccessfully attacked two lone vessels, a cruiser, and a convoy of 22 ships. Problems with the clutch and the supply of fresh water were multiplied by a torpedo which simply spun in the tube. Fortunately for Dröscher, the errant torpedo 'finally [fell] out of its own accord'. On 10 August *U-117*, operating under prize rules, despatched nine fishing trawlers on Georges Bank off the coast of Maine.

Dröscher then turned south, sinking the 3875-ton Norwegian steamer *Somerstad* in thick fog off Fire Island. Bearing south, Dröscher on 13 August destroyed the 7127-ton American tanker *Frederick R. Kellogg*, inbound from Mexico with 7500 barrels of crude oil. He then laid his first series of mines off the Barnegat along the New Jersey coast, which 2 months later claimed the American steamer *San Saba* (2458 tons) as well as the Cuban freighter *Chappara* (1505 tons). On 14 August Dröscher destroyed the American five-masted schooner *Dorothy B. Barrett* near the mouth of the Delaware River, and then leisurely approached the Five Fathom Bank lightship to silence its SOS signals.

Instead, *U-117* crash dived at the approach of aircraft. Lying in 25 yards of water, Dröscher counted nine bombs in a span of 50 minutes, with each one getting closer. He wondered whether the light-grey colour of his hull could be seen through the shallow water, but feared that air bubbles or leaking oil might have betrayed his position. After several anxious hours on the bottom, *U-117* headed for the Fenwick Island Shoal lightship off the coast of Maryland, where it laid a second series of mines, and then for the Winter Quarter lightship, where it sowed a third minefield. The battleship USS *Minnesota* was severely damaged by these mines almost 6 months later; in November the empty troop ship *Saetia* (2873 tons) also fell victim to the mines.

Dröscher next destroyed the 1613-ton American schooner *Madrugada* by gunfire and then proceeded to Cape Hatteras, North Carolina, where he laid a fourth and final minefield. While mining Wimble Shoals off Hatteras, Dröscher sighted but failed to attack two fast convoys. Then luck favoured him. On 16 August he spied the British steamer *Mirlo* (6978 tons) slowly making its way through his mines. Dröscher torpedoed the vessel at 400 yards. Loaded with petrol, the *Mirlo* succumbed to a series of spectacular internal explosions.

But the *Mirlo* was to be Dröscher's last triumph in American waters. Suffering severe oil loss from its defective tanks – only 107 of 224 cubic metres remained – *U-117* was forced to march home via Nova Scotia and Cape Race. Sorry to forgo the pleasure of raiding target-rich Halifax due to the deteriorating oil supply, Dröscher none the less dispatched several small trawlers, schooners, and barques – albeit nearly coming to ruin when *U-117*'s bowplanes malfunctioned. Only one sinking was noteworthy – had Dröscher had the time to take note. On 24 August he attacked the Canadian schooner *Bianca* with gunfire and then set scuttling charges. Instead of sinking, *Bianca* miraculously remained afloat and three days later was found and towed into port by a Boston fishing schooner. *Bianca*'s cargo of tobacco from Brazil had swelled with incoming sea water and sealed the holes in the hull.[38]

U-117 limped across the Atlantic to the Faeroe Islands where it took on 19 cubic metres of oil from *U-140*. With the two boats lying 100 to 200 yards apart and rolling on a heavy sea, their crews improvised at-sea refuelling by stringing a hemp line, supported by sealed cartridge cases as floats, between the two U-boats. *U-140* then filled and sealed about 75 cartridge cases with oil one at a time, which the crew of *U-117* pulled over the makeshift flotation line. The machinists on *U-117* then drained the cartridge cases into the fuel tanks via long funnels. *U-117* put into port on 22 September.

Dröscher's after-action report was a sobering document. In 74 days he had travelled over 9000 nautical miles, consumed 13 tons of provisions and 14 000 litres of water, and expended 159 15 cm and 48 8.8 cm shells. Five of the nine torpedoes fired were duds. Machine failures had nagged *U-117* during the entire patrol and would require 5 weeks of repair in Hamburg. Since the U-cruiser was prone to list, gunfire, at the rate of a shell a minute, was inaccurate and potentially dangerous to the crew. The U-Boat Office, rather than appreciating the perilous conditions under which Dröscher had operated, rebuked him for timidity in general and for failing to press home attacks on merchant convoys in particular.

The German submarine service commissioned 391 U-boats during the First World War. Of these, 178 along with 3226 men were lost at sea; another 1908 men died in POW camps or were simply listed as 'missing'. Manpower losses amounted to almost half the submarine force. The boats destroyed 6394 ships of 11.9 million tons.[39]

The Nivelle offensive: à *Berlin* once more

While the nation anxiously awaited news of victory in the U-boat campaign, the *OHL* braced itself for the expected Allied offensives. Since autumn 1916, Ludendorff had increased the Army by 53 divisions to its highest total ever of 238 divisions. More than 4500 officers had been pulled out of administrative posts with industry or in rear echelons and sent to the front, and about 124 000 men fit for service 'combed out' of the home front in a 'general muster' in the winter of 1916–17. Roughly 310 000 men born in 1899 had been called to the colours ahead of schedule. Convalescents made up fully one-third of the monthly need of 250 000 men.

However, numerous problems accompanied this human mobilization. About 300 000 skilled workers had to be withdrawn from the front and sent back to factories under the Hindenburg Programme, raising the total number of soldiers 'repatriated' to industry to 1.5 million (of whom half were fit for front-line duty). Many young recruits were undernourished while the more elderly were physically substandard. Training had been cut to the bone in time and intensity. Isolated acts of indiscipline took place. In July 1917, for example, one-third of the 300 men dispatched to the Western Front by the Third Army Corps in Brandenburg were arrested after refusing to board trains. Almost 18 000 soldiers languished in Prussian garrisons under arrest for indiscipline.[40] According to Colonel von Thaer, nearly 30 000 deserters roamed the streets of Cologne alone.[41] Battalions were down to 750 men – compared with numerous British battalions of 1000.

The *OHL* was on the mark in its expectation of Allied offensives. At Rome on 5 January 1917, Britain's Lloyd George sought to send Anglo-French units to help the Italians knock Austria–Hungary out of the war, but when overruled instead underwrote a French plan to roll up the German front. The next month the Russians promised to attack the Germans on 1 May; *Stavka* massed 62 divisions by early March. The troops were equipped with 5500 light and 1900 heavy field guns and 15 000 machine guns supplied in large part by the Allies. French artillery instructors were attached to the Russian Army and French and British aircraft were also on hand for the attack.

The offensive never materialized. General Ruzsky, commander of the northern front, in mid-February reported that the morale of his troops was low, that units of the 4th Division had refused to leave their trenches, and that the Army had been reduced to a 'militia'. Coal was not available and the transportation system was near collapse.[42] Austrian observers at the front noticed the frequent appearance of red and white rags to signal discontent and revolt. Russian soldiers on occasion left their trenches unarmed to fraternize. Revolutionary pamphlets appeared in large numbers. Sailors with the Russian Baltic Fleet, immobilized by idleness and lack of food and tormented by brutal and senseless drill, refused to follow orders. Workers in Petrograd went on strike early in March.

On 11 March Prince George Lvov led a Cabinet revolt against the corrupt and inefficient entourage of Nicholas II. The Tsar was removed from power in favour of his brother, Grand Duke Michael, on 15 March – the very day on which the Petrograd Soviet called on soldiers to form 'councils' to represent them. By 27 March the Petrograd Workers' and Soldiers' Council challenged Prince Lvov's government for power. All the while, the Army disintegrated as its *muzhik* soldiers refused to follow orders. On 15 April tens of thousands of Russians left their trenches to join Austrians and Germans in Easter celebrations.

Lvov's government was unable to restore discipline in the Army or order at home. On 2 May a Provisional Government headed by the socialist War Minister Aleksandr Kerensky took control in Petrograd. As a measure of its goodwill, the government released all soldiers above the age of 43 from service – which merely overburdened an already strapped transportation system. Kerensky's decision to abolish the death sentence for desertion prompted 1 million soldiers to strike out for home. Workers refused to produce ammunition or to run trains. Soon millions of veterans streamed into rear echelons, causing utter chaos.

Allied prospects on the Western Front were brilliant in comparison. On 21 December 1916 General Robert Nivelle, the new Commander-in-Chief of the French Army, paid the British a visit. He brought Field Marshal Haig a Christmas present: a new French assault force (*masse de manoeuvre*) composed of 27 divisions organized in three army groups would launch a Napoleonic breakthrough (*percée*) to win the war in a flash. Boasting new artillery tactics perfected at Verdun, Nivelle offered a spring offensive against the broad German salient that stretched from Arras southward to Soissons and then eastward to Reims; in the process, the Chemin des Dames would be retaken and the British would extend their front to Roye.

Lloyd George was impressed not only that Nivelle was the only French general with whom he could converse in English, but also by Nivelle's promise of swift, decisive victory – and assurance that the French would break off the campaign should it prove too slow and costly in lives. While Haig loathed placing British forces under French command, the Prime Minister nevertheless subordinated the BEF to Nivelle at the Calais Conference on 26–7 February 1917.

Nivelle revamped his list of army group commanders to find generals more to his liking. The temperamental Foch was dispatched to the Swiss frontier and his Army Group North given to Franchet d'Esperey. Initially, Nivelle wanted to spearhead his assault with Pétain's Army Group Centre, but when he found Pétain to be too defensive minded, Nivelle took the Fifth Army from him and entrusted General Joseph Micheler with the critical *Groupe d'armées de Réserve*, dubbed by insiders as *Groupe d'armées de Rupture*. While Nivelle happily chatted about advancing almost 20 miles in 3 days, none of Pétain, d'Esperey, or Micheler had confidence in his recipe for victory.

To draw German reserves away from the main assault, Nivelle ordered Haig's right wing and his own Army Group North to attack with the First and Third Armies between Bapaume and Arras. Thereafter, Micheler's *Groupe* was to launch the main attack between Reims and Soupir. The Fifth and Sixth Armies were to crash through the German defences: the Fifth Army, aided by the Fourth Army east of Reims, would then turn to the right and advance along both sides of the Aisne River while the Sixth Army would turn to the left in the direction of Laon-St Quentin. Finally, the Tenth Army would follow between these two forces and mop up all remaining resistance toward Guise.[43] Nivelle concentrated 4800 guns against 2431 German and 1000 aircraft against 640 German along the Aisne and Ailette rivers. More than 1.4 million French soldiers gathered in 52 divisions stood ready to drive the enemy back to Berlin. The operation, which would have to advance through the territory recently laid waste by the Germans in Operation *Alberich*, was based on speed, surprise, and weight of artillery. General Charles Mangin of Sixth Army, for example, crowed that he would sleep in Laon on the evening of the first day of the assault.[44] Nivelle promised the *Comité de guerre* in Paris at least 200 000 German prisoners.

Nivelle had selected for his breakthrough one of the most difficult terrains on the Western Front. Mangin's assault infantry would have to cross the thickly wooded, 6-mile-deep German front at the rate of 100 yards every 3 minutes. The rise of the 600-foot-high Chemin des Dames, which the daughters of King Louis XV had favoured for their equestrian outings, dominated enemy positions from Bailly in the north via Chavonne-Soupir to Cerny en Laonnois and finally to Lauffaux in the south. The entire area was studded with steep tree-covered gorges cut into the sandy rock and punctuated by the swampy valleys of the Ailette and Oise rivers. The Germans occupied the heights and, wherever possible, had placed their artillery and much of their infantry on reverse slopes.[45]

Nivelle almost missed his chance for glory when General Micheler enlisted War Minister Paul Painlevé in a last-ditch attempt to call off the offensive. A defensive posture seemed propitious in the spring of 1917 in the wake of Russia's March revolution and the impending United States entry in the war. But President Poincaré was not about to sacrifice Nivelle so soon after pushing Joffre out of office. On 6 April Poincaré invited political and military leaders to a conference in his railroad car at Compiègne. Nivelle forced the government to choose between approving the planned offensive or accepting his resignation.[46] Poincaré gave Nivelle the green light. The French commander moved his headquarters as well as wine cellar and chefs to Chantilly, where he occupied a château that once had belonged to Marie Antoinette.

The day of the Compiègne conference, Haig launched his diversionary attack in wind and sleet near Arras with 15 divisions supported by 2800 guns and 400 aircraft. The British scored some early gains against the 10 German divisions in their sector, which only three weeks earlier had taken up stations in the partly completed Siegfried Line. Most Germans had not yet adopted the new defence-in-depth concept and were 6 hours' march from the front lines. On 9 April the Canadian Corps stormed Vimy Ridge following excellent counterbattery fire and a sustained attack barrage.[47]

After several delays due to foul weather, Nivelle on 16 April unleashed his artillery for 9 days and then mounted his infantry charge in driving rain. Reports from agents and French POWs had tipped the Germans of the coming offensive. Given the news of the offensive and the difficulty of the terrain, the Germans were able to halt the main attack before it got beyond their first line. Whereas Nivelle had forecast a penetration of 7 or 8 miles on opening day, the French rarely advanced more than 1 or 2 miles. Losses were horrendous. Whereas Nivelle had coldly predicted 10 000 casualties for the first day, the number was 10 times greater. After the war the historical service of the French General Staff placed casualties for the first 4 days of the offensive at 30 000 killed, 100 000 wounded, and 4000 missing.[48] Paris hastily despatched Pétain to the Aisne River to rein in Nivelle; on 15 May Pétain replaced the hapless Nivelle.

The reasons for Nivelle's disaster are many. The Germans had deprived the French of the element of surprise. Nivelle's faith in superior artillery failed to materialize as the German defenders were well entrenched in 5-mile-deep elastic defensive positions with their artillery sited on reverse slopes. As a result, German counterbattery fire was able to suppress the French artillery early on 16 April. Speed also eluded Nivelle as the steep wooded terrain impeded the progress not only of his infantry but also of his field artillery after the initial bombardment. The soft stone along the Aisne and Ailette rivers offered the defenders countless caves from which they deployed machine guns and light mortars. Finally, Nivelle's hurricane artillery bombardments were well-known to his old foe from Verdun – Crown Prince Wilhelm, who now opposed him at the Chemin des Dames.[49]

The Nivelle offensive sputtered on well into June. French losses were estimated at 271 000 men, German at 163 000.[50] Potentially more fatal was that numerous French units mutinied in the wake of the disastrous offensive. In February Nivelle had alerted Paris to the activities of what he called international revolutionaries, anarchists, and syndicalists and their attempts to foment unrest in the armed forces through strikes and sabotage. But the Minister of the Interior, Louis Malvy, stood close to these very circles and declined to act on Nivelle's information.

The first incidents of mutiny occurred on 3 May in two regiments of the 2nd Colonial Division. The unit had been badly battered at Heurtebise on the first day of Nivelle's offensive and refused to return to the trenches. Placards in the regiments' barracks demanded: 'Down with the War! Death to those who are responsible!' Specific grievances contrasted the soldiers' pay at 60 or 70 centimes per day to that of munitions workers back home at 15 to 20 francs.

On 20 May the mutiny spread like a wild brushfire. Soldiers of the XXXII Corps, singing the workers' *Internationale*, vandalized their commander's quarters. Thereafter, the insurrection spread to the Fourth, Fifth, Sixth, and Tenth armies – that is, to those formations most heavily mauled during the Nivelle offensive. In time, 115 regiments of 45 divisions from 16 army corps mutinied: 75 of infantry, 23 of *chasseurs*, and 12 of artillery. Sympathy strikes by civilians were widespread in Soissons, Fimes, Châlons, and the suburbs of Paris.[51] On numerous occasions military police were fired at or shot, and often cavalry had to be brought in to quell the revolts. The historian Guy Pedroncini in 1967 undertook the first study of the mutinies based on archival evidence and concluded that they were primarily a protest against 3 years of tried-and-failed offensives, culminating in Nivelle's Chemin des Dames debacle.[52] Fortunately for France, the Germans did not get wind of the mutinies as only two reliable regiments stood between Soissons and Paris in June 1917.

Pétain moved at once to redress potential grievances and to punish mutinous soldiers. His famous 'Directive Nr. 1' of 19 May promised to end unlimited offensives and to await the arrival of the Americans and the tanks. Pétain ordered officers to inspect their soldiers' mess, to appear in the trenches regularly, to upgrade barracks, to improve the quality and quantity of food, to regularize furloughs, and to grant extended leaves after long periods of combat. He further decreed that firepower was to be increased, the tank corps expanded, and tactical doctrine amended to permit only limited offensives to secure limited objectives. Finally, Pétain empowered special *conseils de guerre* to review the files of the suspected 23 000 mutineers. The *conseils* found 3427 men guilty of mutinous offences and issued between 500 and 600 death sentences; perhaps as many as 75 soldiers were shot and about 100 exiled to the colonies.[53]

Once more, the British were called upon to take the pressure off the French Army. In what has been described as the only true siege-warfare attack in a siege war, the British at 4:10 a.m. on 7 June blew up 19 mines stuffed with 600 tons of high explosives under the German first-line defences at Spanbroekmolen near Wytschaete (Messines). For almost a year, British sappers had constructed 21 horizontal mine shafts under enemy lines; the entire system eventually entailed 7300 yards of subterranean construction. Major Walter Kranz, a geologist serving with Württemberg forces, left a vivid description of the explosion:

> One saw 19 giant 'roses with carmine-red petals' or colossal 'mushrooms' slowly and majestically rise out of the ground. They burst apart with a muffled roar; immediately thereafter brightly-lit multicoloured columns of fire and smoke shot up [and] dark material flew through the columns of fire toward the sky.[54]

The earth moved visibly as far as 30 miles away and the furthest tremors were recorded 130 miles distant in London. The 19 craters on average measured 76 yards wide by 26 yards deep, enough to hold a five-storey apartment house. Army Group Crown Prince Rupprecht had recommended evacuation of the Wytschaete area as early as 30 April, but the local theatre commander (Fourth Army) had successfully warded off this suggestion by arguing that its defence was plausible.[55] British forces captured the German first line of defence almost intact and took 7000 prisoners.

But Haig nurtured far more ambitious plans. Nivelle's defeat in the Champagne allowed the British commander to undertake his pet scheme: an unlimited offensive in Flanders. Spurred on by Admiral Jellicoe, who wanted to seize the German U-boat bases in Belgium, and confident in his conviction that the French 'lacked both the moral qualities and the means for gaining victory', Haig planned to break out of the Ypres salient, march along the Belgian coast, and roll up the entire German Army – preferably before the Americans, whom Haig detested, arrived in force. Haig and his staff devised a three-stage offensive: the first attack would strike south of Ypres near Wytschaete; the second would advance between Dixmuiden and Ypres; and the third would crash against Passchendaele. Haig, who sought nothing less than to 'smash up the whole of the Bosche [*sic*] Army', blithely ignored Foch's warning not to undertake 'a duck's march through the inundations to Ostend and Zeebrugge', which Foch considered to be 'futile, fantastic, and dangerous'.[56] Lloyd George agreed to the offensive on 20 July for fear that failure to relieve the pressure on France after the Nivelle offensive – and the resulting mutinies, about which he was denied information – could cost London its second ally in 1917.

The brunt of the fighting for the Third Battle of Ypres fell on Gough's Fifth Army, supported by one corps of General Henry Plumer's Second Army. On 21 July more than 2300 British guns subjected General Friedrich Sixt von Arnim's Fourth Army, part of Army Group Crown Prince Rupprecht, to a 10-day artillery bombardment that claimed 30 000 casualties, including 9000 missing. At 4:50 a.m. on 31 July British gunners unleashed a thundering bombardment against enemy positions; at about 6:00 a.m. British troops under cover of a rolling barrage stormed the German first line. Tanks and low-flying aircraft supported the infantry. Haig happily reported capturing 6100 Germans.

Rain fell during the night of 31 July and continued through 6 August. Gough, known for his dash and 'cavalry spirit', spurred his men on across the Flanders swamps. The campaign quickly became a disaster. 'General Rain' proved unrelenting. For 50 months British artillery, convinced that quantity of shell rather than surprise and concentration was the key to victory, had mercilessly pounded and thereby destroyed the fragile drainage system of low-lying Flanders. In the summer of 1917 one million British soldiers trudged through the waist-deep mud. Their guns disappeared in the slime. Artillery rounds sank harmlessly into the mud. Shell craters and trenches became bogs. Men and horses drowned. Few units managed to penetrate German lines as far as a mile. Haig's Chief of Staff, Kiggell, broke down from 'nervous exhaustion' after visiting the front.

The Germans also encountered problems in Flanders. The Fourth Army had overstaffed its front lines with infantry and had rushed reinforcements to these forward positions at first contact with the enemy. General von Kuhl, Chief of Staff to Crown Prince Rupprecht, complained bitterly that the 'elastic defence' was too rigid and demanded 'greater freedom' for front commanders to abandon first-line defences. Sixt von Arnim readily agreed and ordered Fourth Army troops to occupy the foremost shell craters only as a 'thin outpost screen' from which they were free (after the initial clash) to withdraw to the main line of defence 500 to 1000 yards behind the craters. There, heavy barrage fire and machine guns were to halt the enemy advance.[57] In the 3 months since 11 July, the 63 divisions of Army Group Crown Prince Rupprecht had suffered 159 000 casualties in Flanders.

'Third Ypres' became forever associated with Passchendaele, in the words of Liddell Hart, 'a synonym for military failure – a name black-bordered in the records of the British army'.[58] On 12 and 26 October Haig ordered his Fifth and Second armies to mount a final push toward the ridge and village of Passchendaele. Stubborn to the core, Haig was determined not to let what once had been a mere post on the road to Berlin elude him. British artillery around Passchendaele enjoyed an advantage of 3000 tubes; intelligence reported that German reserves had been exhausted; and Haig described the shell craters that enemy infantry now used as forward echelon protection as 'simply the refuge of the destitute'.[59]

Haig's optimism was ill-founded. His men once again became stuck in the mud, easy targets for German snipers; their rifles became clogged with mud. On 6 November fresh forces of the Canadian Corps finally stormed Passchendaele. At the cost of 271 000 casualties – compared with 217 000 for the Germans – Haig indeed had taken Passchendaele Ridge, which he now depicted as a splendid observation post for a planned new offensive in 1918!

'Third Ypres' had been a bloody affair. Sixt von Arnim's Fourth Army had rotated 67 fresh divisions in and 51 exhausted divisions out of the battle between mid-July and mid-November 1917. In all, 73 German divisions had been engaged in Flanders against six French and 51 British, each almost twice the size of their German counterparts. The Fourth Army had fired 18 million rounds of artillery and estimated that the British had expended six times that amount.[60] Haig's deepest penetration along the 14-mile front was just 5 miles. The German submarine pens in Belgium remained beyond his grasp.

Crown Prince Rupprecht's defences in Flanders had held – but just. As a result of bitter experiences with overmanned forward lines in July and August, the Germans developed a system of thinly-held front outposts supported at a depth of 500 to 1000 yards by a main line of defence that consisted of concrete blockhouses and disconnected strong points. Reserves were massed in rear areas for swift counterattacks. The first extensive use of Yellow Cross (mustard) gas further enhanced the defence. Crown Prince Rupprecht gave full credit for the victory to the 'delightful rain, our most effective ally'.[61] But the human costs had been high: German battalions were reduced from 750 men to 700 after Flanders.

The year 1917 ended on the Western Front with a notable British success that was a harbinger of things to come. On 20 November Sir Julian Byng's Third Army launched a surprise attack at Cambrai that caught General von der Marwitz's Second Army in its Cambrai-St Quentin-La

Fère sector of the Siegfried Line off-guard. Enjoying an advantage of 1000 to 54 guns, Byng's forces at 7:15 a.m. emerged from behind a lifting and standing barrage of explosive, gas, and smoke shells that began without previous registration. Fourteen squadrons of the Royal Flying Corps observed, bombed, and strafed Marwitz's forces. German spotters were startled by the advance of 360 gigantic Mark IV tanks of General Hugh Elles' Royal Tank Corps that crashed through their wires and rolled over forward defences to an initial depth of 7000 yards.[62] German industry had not taken note of the American development of caterpillar tracks and instead had experimented unsuccessfully with broad-tyred tractors and engines; as late as 1916 the Reich possessed virtually no tanks. Nor had German factories, strained to the limits by the Hindenburg Programme, been able to produce an effective antitank gun; a special machine gun firing steel-core bullets could penetrate only the most lightly armoured tanks.

Six British divisions mauled the 54th Infantry Division. Numerous fresh artillery batteries had arrived at the front with new guns produced under the Hindenburg Programme – but without ammunition as the Army refused to endanger its remaining horses by hauling live shells. In quick order the British overran the German first line of defence, charged the second, and took 5000 prisoners. The German official history claimed that 70 tanks either broke down or were destroyed.[63] Church bells in London rang out in triumph for the first time during the war.

But the British had made no plans to exploit the tanks' advance either with cavalry or infantry. Nor had Haig developed any objectives for the attack – save 'to restore British prestige and strike a theatrical blow against Germany before the winter'. Once again, the attack had been pushed for too long. The wedge that the British had driven into the German lines invited counterattack: at dawn on 30 November 18 divisions of Marwitz's Second Army counterattacked with gas and smoke and hurled the British back to their original lines.[64] Unnoticed by the enemy, Marwitz tested new infiltration tactics whereby small, fast-moving groups of storm troops bypassed strong points, infiltrated open areas, and moved rapidly against artillery supports. Foreshadowing developments in 1918, German soldiers, undernourished by a steady diet of dark 'K' bread and turnips, frequently stopped their advance to loot bountiful British stores of food and rum.[65]

Triumph in the east

While the Army repelled the Nivelle and Haig offensives in the west, the General Staff scored two major victories – against the Russians in the east and Italy in the south. Working through Fritz Platten, Secretary of the Swiss Socialist Party in Bern, Ludendorff on 6 April 1917 struck a deal with Lenin: in one of history's most cynical designs, the *OHL* agreed to transport Russia's radical socialists to Petrograd to foment revolution. Two days later a special train carried 32 Bolsheviks, including Lenin, Karl Radek, G. Y. Sokolnikov, and G. E. Zinoviev, from Bern to Berlin to Sassnitz. A ferry took the group across the Baltic Sea to Malmö, Sweden, and then another train via Stockholm across Finland and on to Petrograd, where they arrived at the Finland station on 16 April. The *OHL* considered the train's occupants sufficiently important to hold up Crown Prince Wilhelm's personal train for 2 hours at Halle. Lenin's insistence that the train be granted extraterritorial rights and that no one enter or leave it gave rise to the legend of the 'sealed train' whereby Ludendorff exported revolution to Russia.[66] The *OHL* hoped to drive the 'devil' Nicholas II out with the 'Beelzebub' Lenin.

While Lenin introduced himself to Russian socialists and acquainted himself with conditions inside a country he had not seen for a decade, War Minister Kerensky decided on the gambler's last throw: an offensive against Austria–Hungary and Germany designed to show the Allies that Russia was still a trustworthy ally and a Great Power, to uphold Russia's claims for war compensation at Constantinople and in Poland, and to head off the forces of change and revolution at home. Kerensky chose General Brusilov to command Russia's last campaign. The victor of Lutsk chose to attack in the direction of Lemberg in the hope of retaking Eastern Galicia in general and the oil fields at Drohobycz in particular.

On 1 July Brusilov attacked in force during the so-called Kerensky offensive. His Seventh Army charged the Austro-Hungarian Second Army while his Eleventh Army tackled the Austro-German South Army; and his old Eighth Army was to join the battle later against the Habsburg Third Army along the Dniester River. At first it seemed that Brusilov would rekindle the victories of 1916: at Zloczów, Böhm-Ermolli's Second Army was driven back and more than 3000 men of its 19th (Czech) Infantry Division bolted; and at Stanislau, General L. G. Kornilov's Eighth Army caved in the front of Tersztyánsky's Third Army.

But then, in a repeat of the customary pattern on the Eastern Front, German General von Bothmer's *Südarmee* halted Brusilov's advance and decisively defeated his Eleventh Army. On 19 July nine Hohenzollern and two Habsburg divisions counterattacked Brusilov near Zloczów after only a brief hurricane artillery bombardment. For much of July, troops of the Central Powers under General Hoffmann advanced as rapidly through Galicia and the Bukovina as the Russians could retreat. Brusilov was forced to admit that he could not repeat the spectacular success of Lutsk in 1916 as his Seventh and Eighth armies also fell back before the advance. Within 3 weeks, deadly counterattacks by four German divisions forced the old cavalry officer to begin a long retreat that ended in defeat and revolution. Russian losses amounted to 40 000 soldiers killed, compared to 12 500 for the Central Powers.[67]

But for the Austrians there were danger signs amidst victory. The Russians had recruited heavily among their 300 000 Czech and Slovak prisoners of war and formed several so-called 'Hussite Legions' to aid the war effort. At Zboróv early in July the Russian Eleventh Army, comprised mainly of Finnish and Siberian troops but also with a good number of Czech and Slovak units, attacked Kaiser Karl's Second Army. For the first time in the war, Czechs were pitted against Czechs as a 'Hussite Legion' charged the Austro-Hungarian 19th (Czech) Division.[68] The latter's 35th and 37th regiments refused to obey orders. News of the Czech–Czech confrontation quickly spread throughout the Dual Monarchy, further exciting already heated national passions.

This notwithstanding, the German drive eastward continued unabated. Only lack of supplies and exhaustion finally ended the advance. By the end of the campaign, Bothmer's German forces and Kövess' Austro-Hungarian units had outrun their advanced rail heads by more than 60 miles. Destroyed bridges slowed the pursuit. Resupply became impossible. More than 45 000 horses collapsed from exhaustion. The country had been denuded of all sustenance by the retreating Russians. Summer heat added a further strain on operations, which more and more approached chaos as the Russian Army disintegrated before the eyes of its pursuers.[69] Neither the threat to shoot deserters on the spot nor the attempt to create special storm troops, female battalions, or so-called death troops could arrest its dissolution. German forces conquered Riga early in September and in a rare amphibious assault stormed the Baltic islands of Ösel, Moon, and Dagö in October. The Bolsheviks took advantage of the military debacle and seized power in Petrograd between 6 and 8 November 1917.

Ironically, Ludendorff, who in 1915 and 1916 had berated Falkenhayn for failing to allot him the necessary forces with which to seek a decision in the east, in the summer of 1917 was totally committed to the Western Front and refused to transfer forces to *OberOst* for a final blow against Russia. Instead, Germany entered into armistice discussions with Lenin's regime on 3 December. The talks reached fruition 12 days later, and on 21 December the two sides opened peace negotiations at Brest-Litovsk. King Ferdinand of Romania had no choice but to conclude an armistice with Berlin on 9 December. There remained Italy.

Caporetto: a cosmetic victory

In accordance with the Allied strategy laid down at Chantilly in the winter of 1916, the Italians attacked along the Isonzo River: the Tenth Battle of the Isonzo raged from 12 May to 6 June and was especially disastrous. General Cadorna hurled 280 000 combatants supported by 2200 guns and 1000 trench mortars against 173 000 Austrians. Cadorna gained 2 miles of barren rock; losses amounted to 36 000 killed, 96 000 wounded, and 27 000 captured. Most fell prey to Austrian artillery, which fired off 37 800 tons of explosives. Habsburg forces suffered 7300 men killed, 45 000 wounded, and 23 400 taken prisoners of war.[70]

Undeterred, Cadorna resumed the offensive on 18 August. In the Eleventh Battle of the Isonzo, he deployed 51 divisions and 5200 guns. The Italians advanced between 6 and 8 miles and seized the Bainsizza plateau, but failed to break the enemy front. Once more Austro-Hungarian artillery saved the day: its light guns fired 1.5 million rounds, its medium field guns 500 000, and its heavy howitzers 22 000. About 38 per cent of Austro-Hungarian guns broke down under the strain. Again, losses on both sides were horrendous. The Austro-Hungarian official history claims 40 000 Italians killed, 108 000 wounded, and 18 000 missing; it sets its own losses at more than 10 000 killed, 45 000 wounded, and 30 000 missing.[71]

Civilian as well as military leaders in Vienna appreciated that the Dual Monarchy could no longer achieve success on the battlefield without German help. The problem was that none wanted to accord Berlin a still greater role within the alliance. The Balkans had long been regarded as an exclusive Habsburg preserve; even to allow the Hohenzollerns into the South Tyrol was unthinkable. Thus, acrimony marked the intra-Germanic debate in the summer and autumn of 1917. Kaiser Karl let it be known that he equated a 'German peace' with the Monarchy's 'ruin'. Kaiser Wilhelm II countered that he would rather drop the alliance with Vienna than forgo annexing Liège. Hindenburg trumpeted that he would consider a triumphant German entry into Bohemia as the capstone of his military career. Lost in the debate was the fact that most Austrians and many Germans no longer cared about the war, that 'apathy and resignation' had replaced the thirst for 'annexations and deeds'.[72] But perhaps a joint military undertaking against Italy could plaster over the cracks in the alliance.

The Twelfth Battle of the Isonzo, better known as the Battle of Caporetto (Karfreit), began on 24 October. It ended 3 weeks later with a spectacular operational victory for the Central Powers – and with continued strategic stalemate in the south. Italy lost 700 000 men and 3000 guns, and experienced widespread demoralization in the ranks. In the end, the hasty transfer of 10 Anglo-French divisions from the Western Front stabilized the Italian lines. Karfreit was to be Austria–Hungary's last military success; it greatly enhanced the German Army's reputation for operational excellence.

Kaiser Karl, acutely aware that his armies could not sustain the loss of 100 000 to 150 000 soldiers per battle along the Isonzo – a region in which 'bleeding white' exceeded anything that had taken place at Verdun – turned to Berlin in August and suggested that a decisive offensive alone would allow him to 'master the difficult situation' against Italy. He appended a request for heavy artillery and relief of Austro-Hungarian units on the Russian front, proposing to undertake the attack 'only with my own troops'. The *k.u.k.* Army, Karl lectured Wilhelm II on 26 August, considered the war against Italy 'its war'. 'Since childhood, every officer has inherited from his forefathers the desire . . . to fight against the hereditary enemy.'[73] The *AOK* called to the colours the cohorts of 1897, 1898, and 1899 – 300 000 youths in all – to show its resolve to take the offensive.

General Arz von Straussenburg, Chief of the General Staff, revived Conrad's plan of 10 January 1917 to launch two simultaneous offensives from Astico and Brenta in the South Tyrol and from Tolmein and Flitsch in the Julian Alps[74] to catch Italian forces in a pincer movement around Cividale-Udine. A successful offensive, to be commanded by Archduke Eugen, would extend the front as far west and south as the Piave River. On 29 August General von Waldstätten, head of operations, travelled to Kreuznach and implored Hindenburg and Ludendorff to endorse the campaign.

But the *OHL*, apart from Major Georg Wetzell of the Operations Division, had little interest in a purely Austro-Hungarian assault. Politically, Ludendorff feared that Karl would use a successful campaign as the springboard to a separate peace with the Allies; militarily, he had little faith in the efficacy of Habsburg troops. Already in July, Ludendorff had requested Seeckt, the German Chief of Staff to Army Group Archduke Joseph, to analyse the Dual Monarchy's political-military situation. The report was hardly optimistic. The Kaiser, Seeckt reported, was confused in his ideas, wishes, and influences, and driven by 'fear of internal revolution', 'concern about the military situation' of his realm, and 'demands for peace'. In military matters, Karl was totally under the influence Waldstätten, who had convinced him that Habsburg forces should be independent of the *OHL*. German leadership would only 'evoke the appearance that *k.u.k.* generals were less able and [would] lower their fragile self-esteem'.[75]

Armed with this information and determined that the Army not remain totally on the defensive in 1917, Ludendorff insisted on a joint operation limited to a narrow 30-mile front westward from the Isonzo to the Tagliamento. The *OHL* committed seven divisions to the undertaking and appointed General Otto von Below commander of the new Fourteenth Army, with General Krafft von Dellmensingen, a Bavarian expert on Alpine warfare, as its chief of staff. Krafft von Dellmensingen had already scouted the upper Isonzo region for Ludendorff, and on 8 September informed the *OHL* that the Austro-Hungarian Army probably could not survive another attack. There remained no choice but to undertake a joint assault in the sector between Flitsch and Tolmein. In its centre stood the small village of Caporetto. The Bavarian rejected Conrad's customary practise of storming and then advancing along the Alpine ridges in favour of broad sweeps down the mountain valleys. The operation, Krafft von Dellmensingen informed Ludendorff, would be 'difficult, dangerous, and uncertain' – but possible. 'Undoubtedly we will also need luck.'[76]

Starting 20 September, Below transported his heavy artillery, howitzers, and air units from Riga on the Baltic Sea to Carniola and Carinthia. About 2400 military trains of 100 000 wagons, taxing one-third of the Dual Monarchy's entire railroad capacity, were used for the month-long assembly. Five Habsburg divisions from the Tyrol, Galicia, Volhynia, the Bukovina, and Romania joined the German Fourteenth Army on the north side of the Julian Alps, beyond the view of Italian airmen. General Richard von Behrendt, the Fourteenth Army's artillery commander, hauled 1800 guns and 420 howitzers as well as 1 million artillery rounds to the front. Archduke Eugen received 30 000 horses to transport war material from rail heads to front-line depots.[77]

By 22 October, Below had marched his forces in steady rain along four major roads to well-camouflaged jump-off positions on the southern slopes of the Julian Alps. The troops moved by night and over circuitous routes; wireless deception and close air cover largely hid their movements from Italian spotters. The Germans, honed for battle by gruelling training patrols and mock attacks in the mountains, were acclimatized for Alpine warfare. The final advance into jump-off positions was supplied by pack animals with muffled hooves. In place of the customary rigid attack schemes and lengthy artillery preparations, Below opted for surprise and hurricane saturation bombardment, followed by creeping barrages.

Below divided his forces into four assault groups: one German and three Austro-Hungarian divisions commanded by General Alfred Krauss in the north; mostly German units under the Bavarian General Hermann Stein and his Württemberg colleague, General Albrecht von Berrer, in the centre; a joint force headed by Habsburg General Karl Scotti in the south;

and the Austro-Hungarian Tenth Army under General von Krobatin in the Carnolian Alps. General von Boroević's Army Group (First and Second Isonzo armies) was to tie down the Italians along the lower Isonzo front, while Conrad's Tyrolean Army Group was to paralyse the Italians in the west. Overall, the Central Powers mounted 33 under-strength divisions against Cadorna's 41 full divisions; but in the decisive Flitsch-Tolmein-Karfreit assault sector, they enjoyed 100 per cent superiority. News of the impending attack relayed by one Czech and two Romanian deserters failed to impress the Italians, who were secure in the knowledge of their superior strength.

After 2 days of delay due to foul weather, at 2 a.m. on 24 October Below's Fourteenth Army unleashed a decimating Blue and Green Cross gas-shell attack from 2000 guns in dense, grey fog. For the first time in the war, the Germans deployed British 'Stokes'-type launchers to hurl gas canisters at enemy positions where they were detonated by electric fuses. The gas was highly effective in the fog-and-snow shrouded narrow Alpine valleys; primitive Italian gas masks were useless against the heavy clouds of deadly toxin. Thereafter, the German trench mortars switched to shell and wreaked great material and moral damage on the Italian first line. Around 6:30 a.m., after a 2-hour pause in the bombardment, Below concentrated heavy mortar fire against Cadorna's troops and machine guns between the first and second lines of defence.[78] Between 8 and 9 a.m., German and Austro-Hungarian infantry, spearheaded by General Arnold Lequis' Prussian 12th Infantry Division, advanced from Flitsch and Tolmein in thin columns behind a creeping barrage through the mountain valleys, stormed Caporetto, and seized the commanding 4000-feet heights above the enemy. Many units advanced more than 10 miles that day. General Luigi Capello's Italian Second Army of 26 divisions was routed in the opening phase of the battle.

The Austro-Hungarian official history describes the front as a barren 'stone wilderness'. Grey, sharp-angled limestone cliffs limited supply to pack animals and made rapid advances nearly impossible. The soldiers had to seek shelter behind only knee-deep stone barriers hastily scraped together. At best, using gimlets, the soldiers drilled holes into the limestone rock to plant posts which anchored makeshift shelters of sheet iron and cardboard to protect them against both icy winter storms and hot summer siroccos. Occasionally they were able to use motor drills and dynamite to blast 'caverns' into the rock. Most work had to be done by night out of view of enemy artillery: caverns were built, the wounded and dead were removed from No Man's Land, broken telephone lines were repaired, and wire as well as barbed-wire obstacles (so-called Spanish riders) were laid.[79]

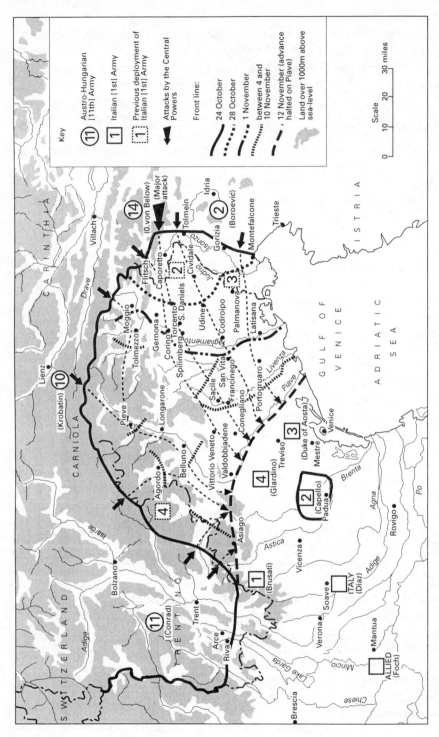

Map 10. German relief: Caporetto, 1917

Lieutenant Ludwig Streil of the 19th Bavarian Infantry Regiment remembered the struggle in the Julian Alps. His troops had moved slowly to the front lines in steady downpours throughout October, their morale maintained only by the 'thought of attacking'. Laden down with supplies, the men waded 'up to their chests' through the icy Upper Isonzo, while engineer battalions struggled to erect temporary bridges across its raging waters. About 30 000 Russian POWs daily hauled away tons of mud created by the rains and shored up the few existing roads with rock and shale. Enemy searchlights probed the nights to permit artillery to shatter the buildup. The Bavarians reached their assigned jump-off positions on 23 October. 'The only cover and quarters for the troops were provided by shell craters, narrow dirty trenches, and damp stinking caverns in the surrounding hills.'

Streil's advance from Tolmein in the direction of Cividale began with a howitzer barrage at 2 a.m. the following day in dense fog. Later that morning, the Bavarians charged the Italian front line with a mixture of fear and anticipation. 'Men splattered with mud and cowering in heaps stare out of craters and trenches with vacant, dull-witted eyes. Between them lie the dead and the wounded; help-imploring screams ring in the ears of those advancing.' The 19th Infantry Regiment stormed the first line of defence in 2 hours – mainly with the aid of hand-grenades, 'a wild hand-to-hand skirmish'. The Bavarians fought in small mixed-arms platoons. 'Each soldier becomes a leader himself.' By noon Streil's men had seized their first major geographical obstacle, Leisce Vrh (Mt Lisser), in cold rain and grey fog.

The Bavarians pressed their attack with vigour and by 5:30 p.m. had dislodged the Italians from neighbouring Hill 1114 – the 5000-feet high anchor point of Cadorna's defence system – and captured more than 1400 enemy soldiers. Everywhere the Italians waved white handkerchiefs in surrender. Streil's troops quickly developed a routine: they seized the high ground above the defenders and then raked their trenches with machine guns to murderous effect. By the evening of the first day, the Bavarians had taken 4760 prisoners and captured 40 guns and 10 howitzers. Following a cold, clear night in the field, Streil's units stormed Hills 110 and 1192 in bright sunshine. 'The number of prisoners became incalculable; thousands of Italians streamed in from all sides, all in the best of moods and in full gear including their machine guns. They were glad to have escaped with life and limb'. Pack animals and 2000 POWs were then used to haul supplies up the steep mountain slopes. For 4 days the Bavarians crossed the 'barren, cold mountains' until they spied 'a blue stripe on the left' – the Adriatic Sea. They ended their operation in Cividale on 27 October. 'Stone-pines and cypresses greet the victors.'[80]

Captain Erwin Rommel of the Württemberg Mountain Battalion recorded similar experiences. His regiment advanced from Carinthia to Tolmein after 18 October, and moved to its jump-off positions 4 days later. 'Huge searchlights . . . illuminated our way. Heavy artillery fire struck among us and the powerful and dazzling searchlight beams forced us to lie motionless for minutes at a time. As soon as they swept past us, we hurried through the endangered area.'[81] The Württembergers seized Monte Cragonza; 37 Italian officers and 1000 men threw down their rifles and surrendered at the sight of the enemy. With the Bavarian Life Guards Regiment by its side, the Württemberg Mountain Battalion next seized Monte Kuk, taking prisoner 43 officers and 1500 men of the 1st Regiment of the Salerno Brigade. Thereafter, 1200 soldiers of its 2nd Regiment laid down their arms before Rommel's men reached the 5400-feet summit of the Matajur.

Italian forces lost the commanding heights of Monte Maggiore in a blinding snow storm on 26 October. Ten regiments surrendered en masse. After receiving a disastrous situation report from General Capello, Cadorna decided to evacuate the Isonzo front and to seek shelter behind the Tagliamento River. A rout ensued. One million soldiers of the Second and Third armies, along with their gear, streamed backwards through a 30-mile-wide corridor. Cadorna in 4 days abandoned all the territory that he had seized in the past 30 months at the cost of 300 000 dead and 740 000 wounded. His entire 100-mile-wide defensive position between Monte Peralba and the Adriatic Sea was destroyed. More than 260 000 soldiers, including 200 000 prisoners, were lost; 1700 guns and innumerable trucks were abandoned.[82] General Luca Montuori replaced Capello as commander of the Second Army. Cadorna's escape behind the Tagliamento was made possible only by Boroević's inability to advance from the lower Isonzo to close the trap on the Italian Third Army.[83] All available resources had been showered on Below's Fourteenth Army; Boroević had to live off the land, requisitioning horses at every stop for both his supply and artillery trains.

On 2 November General Krauss' forces gained bridgeheads over the Tagliamento at Cornino and Pinzano. In the heat of victory, Below abandoned Ludendorff's orders not to pursue the Italians beyond the Tagliamento. Karl issued a ringing manifesto that same day, wherein he reminded his troops that he had taken his place in the long line of great captains from Franz Joseph to Archdukes Karl and Albrecht and Josef Radetzky. For 5 days, Austro-Hungarian and German units pursued the hapless Italians along the slopes of the Venetian Alps to the Piave River, 70 miles behind the original Isonzo front. Torrential downpours as well as the lack of cavalry and mechanized units hindered a more rapid advance to the Piave – and beyond.

The collapse of the Italian position along the Isonzo threatened the rear of General Nicolis di Robilant's Fourth Army in the Dolomites. After some initial hesitancy, Robilant began to withdraw southward to Fonzaso and Belluno during the night of 4–5 November, destroying magazines, bridges, and war material as he retreated. The next day five divisions of Tyroleans pursued him in the direction of Asiago. Conrad now demanded that the campaign's centre of gravity be shifted to his theatre. Instead, by 10 November Krauss' and Below's forces were poised to cross the Piave. The elderly battleships *Wien* and *Budapest*, augmented by the scout cruisers *Admiral Spaun* and *Aspern* as well as 12 torpedo-boats, stood by in Trieste to cover the crossing.

They waited in vain. The Italian collapse stampeded the British and French into action. London as well as Paris equated Karfreit with Gorlice-Tarnów. Foch, now Chief of the French General Staff, met Cadorna at Treviso on 30 October and announced the impending arrival of four divisions from the Western Front under General Denis Auguste Duchène. The next day, Sir William Robertson, Chief of the Imperial General Staff, likewise arrived at Treviso with the promise of two British divisions. Cadorna, who as late as 3 November obliquely suggested that Rome begin separate peace negotiations with the Central Powers, on 5 November was called to Rapallo, where British, French, and Italian officials resolved to hold the 80-mile-wide Piave line from Asiago to the Adriatic Sea at all costs. Three days later, the Allies agreed to found a Supreme War Council at Versailles to coordinate their various strategies.

The new Italian Prime Minister, Vittorio Orlando, seized the opportunity to reform his military. On 7 November Cadorna was despatched to Versailles and General Armando Diaz became the new army commander. Diaz promised a fighting retreat as far south as Sicily; Foch acidly suggested the Piave as a starting point. To stabilize the front, Orlando demanded 15 and Diaz 20 divisions; the Allies offered 12. A compromise of six French and five British divisions was reached eventually.

Between 14 and 18 November, General Krauss mounted an assault along the steep valleys of the 5800-feet high Monte Grappa near Bassano in the direction of the Piave River. Stiff resistance from 47 fresh Anglo-French-Italian battalions, supplemented by 24 batteries of heavy and 40 of light artillery, stemmed the advance. Once more Conrad was slow to support Krauss with attacks out of the Tyrol.[84] Ludendorff became worried over the British attack at Cambrai on 20 November and called for cessation of the fighting in Italy. Moreover, Clausewitz's notion of the 'diminishing force of the attack' dogged Below's offensive. His troops were exhausted from 3 weeks of steady marching and fighting; reinforcements were slow in coming; and bridging materials were still en route from Romania. Attrition had decimated the ranks. The crack Austrian Edelweiss Division, for example, was down to 2000 combatants. Heavy snows found Below's troops without winter clothing. On 29 November Ludendorff queried Baden anew whether the time had come to halt the offensive; on 2 December Kaiser Karl concurred.

The Battle of Caporetto was one of the Great War's most spectacular operational successes. What had begun as a limited campaign designed to relieve Italian pressure on the Austrians along the Isonzo had expanded into an advance of 80 miles in 17 days – and into a rout of the Italian Army, first to the Tagliamento and then to the Piave. In the process, the Central Powers' front with Italy had been narrowed by more than 200 miles. The Italian Army had sustained staggering losses: 10 000 dead, 30 000 wounded, and 293 000 prisoners of war along with 3150 guns and 1730 howitzers. More than 350 000 deserters and refugees roamed the Italian countryside. The Central Powers suffered 65 000 to 70 000 casualties.[85]

Karfreit, as the victors called the battle, momentarily alleviated the Dual Monarchy's food-supply problem as nearly-starved soldiers for days revelled in the bountiful Italian stores which they had captured. A massive traffic jam ensued behind the fighting lines as 10 000 wagons hauled away the captured booty, of which the Austrians kept six parts to every one given the Germans.[86] But relief was only momentary. More than 300 000 Italian POWs had to be fed. By the end of the year, the *k.u.k.* Army was once again down to barely 2 days of flour and vegetable rations, and 4 days of green feed for its horses. The Army's daily needs consisted of 240 wagons of flour, 40 of vegetables, and 250 of green feed; its actual consignments were 158 wagons of flour, 1–2 of vegetables, and 101 of green feed. Flour rations in some units were down to 280 g. per man per day;[87] in Vienna they were lowered from 200 to 165 g. per day. And few in the capital noted that the U.S. Congress declared war on Austria–Hungary on 7 December in reaction to Karfreit and public pressures to offer Italy relief.

For the Italians, Caporetto meant humiliation and shame. A postwar Commission of Enquiry probed the causes for the collapse. At the top, Cadorna had completely misread the situation. Ever the optimist, he had assured the British that he could hold out for 5 weeks in case of an enemy attack; in fact, in many places his front crumbled in 5 hours. The *Comando Supremo* had lived in splendid isolation from the troops and exacerbated an already existing morale problem by manning front lines with munitions workers from Turin conscripted as punishment for a strike in August 1917. Cadorna had also instituted a system of occupying only the foremost of his three lines of defence, that is, the extreme advanced line of his last offensive. The majority of combatants thus held the first line; the next two were to be defended with divisions scattered all along the front. Ammunition dumps, food depots, and repair facilities likewise were placed near the front line. Consequently, once the Central Powers had penetrated the Italian first line, there was little to stem their advance.

Morale – rather, the lack of it – had also plagued the Italians. The Commission of Enquiry found that entire divisions, along with their artillery, had simply disappeared from the field of battle. In other instances the artillery, with officers in the lead, had ridden away from the battle, leaving the infantry to its fate. German bayonet charges on numerous occasions had frightened the Italians. At Diagno on the Tagliamento, for example, the 26th Württemberg Division, charging only with cold steel, had taken 20 000 prisoners and captured an artillery park. The common practice of looting peasant food and cattle further demoralized the retreating Second Army, most of whose soldiers simply went home and donned civilian clothes. Roads were choked with 750 000 stragglers and refugees as well as with thousands of guns and army carts, making reinforcement and resupply impossible.[88] Cavalry and Carabinieri rounded up many of the stragglers and interned them in 'concentration camps' for reeducation; about 60 000 of the hardest cases were sent to France in April 1918 as forced labour.[89]

The morale problem can partly be traced to Cadorna's tendency to change commanders at the least sign of independence or unwillingness to charge enemy lines. Thus, in the 10 months before Caporetto, Cadorna had sacked 24 corps commanders; in the 11 Isonzo battles between June 1915 and October 1917, he had dismissed no fewer than 307 colonels and generals. The Italian 144th Infantry Regiment, for example, in October 1917 received its 41st commander since the start of the war.[90] Little wonder that few units had confidence in their senior officers.

Among the victors, recriminations about lost opportunities and what might have been quickly set in. Krauss accused Boroević of having failed to close the trap on the Italian Third Army from the south by not moving his Second Isonzo Army with sufficient speed. Numerous commanders felt that Conrad had dallied too long on the defensive in the Tyrol. Almost all *k.u.k.* generals later argued that Ludendorff had ended the offensive too early. General Heinrich Wieden of the Edelweiss Division accused the Germans first of looting and then of bad-mouthing the performance of Habsburg units.[91] The Germans replied in kind concerning the 'dash' and 'valour' of the Austrians.

In fact, the *OHL* had never viewed the Isonzo front as decisive. Ludendorff had agreed to the offensive for political and military reasons, both culminating in the fear that without a victory against the Italians, the Dual Monarchy would not survive another year. Karfreit served this purpose well. But Ludendorff was sufficiently astute to understand that a German advance even on Rome would not end the war as far as France, Britain, and the United States were concerned. Thus he had informed the *AOK* at Baden as early as 3 November that he was redirecting his attention to the Western Front.

L'année troublé provided roller-coaster highs and lows for the Central Powers. It began with their armies hunkered down on the defensive on all fronts, hoping at best to repel anticipated Allied offensives; it ended with the defeat of Russia and the operational brilliance of Caporetto. Along the way, the French Army was shattered by Nivelle's ill-conceived offensive in the Champagne, while Haig's British forces exhausted themselves in the mud and blood of 'Third Ypres'. In desperation, the Germans turned to a novel technology, the U-boats, to starve the British into surrender. Instead, the world's most powerful neutral, the United States, entered the war in 'association' with the Allies. The Petrograd revolution of March 1917 proved to be a bitter irony for Germany: it ended the war in the east for all intents and purposes at the very moment that the United States entered the conflict. Without the German U-boat gamble, Allied fortunes would have been bleak indeed in the wake of Tsarist Russia's collapse.

Above all, the war had brutalized political life. In Vienna, Professor Redlich reflected on the year past:

> The glance back is sad; the hopes for 1918 are even slimmer. Mankind has been rendered so soulless by technology, science, and capitalism that it probably no longer possesses the mental and physical strength to work its way out of this horrible war. [Friedrich] Nietzsche wanted to create an advanced form of 'human being': . . . Ludendorff today is the hero figure of the industrialist-capitalist-monist-military German.[92]

In Berlin, Foreign Office counsellor Riezler likewise saw little cheer at the end of 1917:

> Where is the world headed [?] I try to think about this in order to transform this nonsense of Europe's demise into some kind of sense. I do not succeed. The nonsense is too nonsensical. Only one thing is certain: Europe will either come to an understanding or it will go under. The first is impossible and so the second follows.[93]

Both agreed that the fate of the Central Powers, for better or for worse, rested with Ludendorff.

Chapter 8 notes

1. Reichsarchiv, *Der Weltkrieg 1914 bis 1918*. 11: *Die Kriegführung im Herbst 1916 und im Winter 1916/17* (Berlin, E. S. Mittler & Sohn, 1938), pp. 464–6.
2. Cited in Holger H. Herwig, *'Luxury' Fleet: The Imperial German Navy 1888–1918* (London and Atlantic Highlands, Ashfield Press, 1987), p. 165.
3. BA-MA, Nachlass Levetzow, N 239, box 19, vol. 2.
4. Cited in Herwig, *'Luxury' Fleet*, p. 188.
5. Reproduced in Erich Ludendorff, *Urkunden der Obersten Heeresleitung über ihre Tätigkeit 1914/18* (Berlin, E. S. Mittler & Sohn, 1920), pp. 311–12. See also Wolfgang Steglich, *Bündnissicherung oder Verständigungsfrieden. Untersuchungen zu dem Friedensangebot der Mittelmächte am 12. Dezember 1916* (Göttingen, Musterschmidt, 1958).
6. See Theodor Wolff, *Tagebücher 1914–1919*, ed. Bernd Sösemann (2 vols, Boppard, H. Boldt, 1984) 1, p. 490, for this line of reasoning. Bethmann Hollweg compared January 1917 to July 1914 in a speech before the Federal Chamber on 16 January 1917!
7. Cavell was executed for hiding Allied soldiers and nursing them back to health. General Traugott von Sauberzweig, the German military commander in Belgium, confirmed the death sentence to set an example to others and refused to pass Cavell's request for clemency on to the Kaiser. The Austrians deemed the execution a 'serious political mistake'. HHStA, VII PA Gesandschaft Berlin 204. Separat Akten. Report of 30 October 1915.
8. See Gerhard Ritter, *Staatskunst und Kriegshandwerk. Das Problem des 'Militarismus' in Deutschland* (4 vols, Munich, Verlag R. Oldenbourg, 1964) 3, pp. 322, 327, 329.
9. HHStA, PA I 536, Botschaftsarchiv Berlin.
10. Cited in Gerald D. Feldman, *Army, Industry, and Labor in Germany, 1914-1918* (Princeton, Princeton University Press, 1966), p. 136. Dated 7 November 1914.
11. Wolff, *Tagebücher* 1, p. 490.
12. Harmut Pogge von Strandmann, ed., *Walther Rathenau: Industrialist, Banker, Intellectual, and Politician. Notes and Diaries 1907–1922* (Oxford, Clarendon Press, 1985), p. 224. Discussion of 10 July 1917.
13. See Holger H. Herwig and David F. Trask, 'The Failure of Imperial Germany's Undersea Offensive Against World Shipping, February 1917–October 1918', *The Historian* 33 (1971), p. 619.
14. *Der Weltkrieg 1914 bis 1918* 11, pp. 467–9; Bernd Stegemann, *Die Deutsche Marinepolitik 1916–1918* (Berlin, Duncker & Humblot, 1970), pp. 71–5; Ludendorff, *Urkunden der Obersten Heeresleitung*, pp. 322–4. The protocol is in *Ursachen und Folgen. Vom deutschen Zusammenbruch 1918 und 1945 bis zur staatlichen Neuordnung Deutschlands in der Gegenwart*, eds Herbert Michaelis and Ernst Schraepler (15 vols, Berlin, Dokumenten-Verlag Dr. Herbert Wendler, 1958) 1, pp. 146–7.
15. Cited in Herwig, *'Luxury' Fleet*, p. 197. See also Schoen's report of 31 January 1917 for the King of Bavaria. BHStA, MA 3080. Militär Bevollmächtigter Berlin.
16. Cited by John C. G. Röhl, *Die Zeit*, 2 December 1994, p. 8. Dated January 1917. The reference to 'insidious assassination' pertained to the regicide of June 1914.
17. Weizsäcker to Rear Admiral Adolf von Trotha, 28 December 1918. Leonidas E. Hill, ed., *Die Weizsäcker-Papiere 1900–1932* (Berlin, Frankfurt, and Vienna, Propyläen Verlag, 1982), p. 234.
18. Evelyn, Princess Blücher, *An English Wife in Berlin: A Private Memoir of Events, Politics, and Daily Life in Germany Throughout the War and the Social Revolution of 1918* (New York, E. P. Dutton, 1920), p. 164.
19. Kurt Riezler, *Tagebücher, Aufsätze, Dokumente,* ed. Karl Dietrich Erdmann (Göttingen, Vandenhoeck & Ruprecht, 1972), pp. 395. 402, 404. Entries of 10 and 31 January 1917.

20. Cited in Hans Herzfeld, *Der Erste Weltkrieg* (Munich, Deutscher Taschenbuch Verlag, 1968), p. 175.
21. Ritter, *Staatskunst und Kriegshandwerk* 3, p. 382.
22. Walter Görlitz, ed., *The Kaiser and His Court: The Diaries, Note Books and Letters of Admiral Georg Alexander von Müller Chief of the Naval Cabinet, 1914–1918* (New York, Harcourt, Brace & World, 1959), pp. 212, 231. Entries dated 14 October 1916 and 10 January 1917.
23. BA-MA, MSg 1/2517 Tagebuch Kageneck. Diary entry for 14 January 1917. See also Volker Hoettl, 'Die Beziehungen Conrads von Hötzendorf zu den deutschen Generalstabschefs 1914–17 auf politischem Gebiet', unpubl. diss., Vienna University 1968, p. 199. The discussions of 22 January 1917 are in *Protokolle des Geheimen Ministerrates der Österreichisch-Ungarischen Monarchie (1914–1918),* ed. Miklós Komjáthy (Budapest, Akadémiai Kiadó, 1966), pp. 452–8.
24. *Der Weltkrieg 1914 bis 1918* 11, pp. 473, 495. Wilhelm's birthday was on 27 January.
25. Reichsarchiv, *Der Weltkrieg 1914 bis 1918*. 12: *Die Kriegführung im Frühjahr 1917* (Berlin, E. S. Mittler & Sohn, 1939), p. 171; Arthur J. May, *The Passing of the Hapsburg Monarchy 1914–1918* (2 vols, Philadelphia, University of Pennsylvania Press, 1966) 2, pp. 486–91; Gary W. Shanafelt, *The Secret Enemy: Austria–Hungary and the German Alliance, 1914–1918* (New York, Columbia University Press, 1985), pp. 128–30; and Ludendorff, *Urkunden der Obersten Heeresleitung,* pp. 369–94.
26. Interestingly, Czernin, who earlier had pursued his own programme to end the war, compared Kaiser Karl's peace bid to the act of a man who is so afraid of death that he commits suicide! Manfried Rauchensteiner, *Der Tod des Doppeladlers. Österreich-Ungarn und der Erste Weltkrieg* (Graz, Vienna, and Cologne, Verlag Styria, 1994), p. 490.
27. Bodo Herzog, *60 Jahre Deutsche Uboote 1906–1966* (Munich, J.F. Lehmanns, 1969), p. 111. Admiralty Staff figures were almost 300,000 tons per month higher. Henry Newbolt, *History of the Great War: Naval Operations* 5 (5 vols, London, New York, and Toronto, Longman, Green, 1931), pp. 424–40, gives totals on average 100 000 tons lower that those of Herzog.
28. Wolff, *Tagebücher* 1, p. 481. Entry for 14 February 1917.
29. Newbolt, *Naval Operations* 5, pp. 424–30; Herzog, *60 Jahre Deutsche Uboote,* p. 111.
30. Herwig, *'Luxury' Fleet,* pp. 197–8. I wish to thank Professor L. E. Hill of the University of British Columbia for unselfishly sharing his research on the German U-boat campaign.
31. Herzog, *60 Jahre Deutsche Uboote,* pp. 79–80.
32. Herwig, *'Luxury' Fleet,* pp. 226–9.
33. An Address to a Joint Session of Congress, 2 April 1917. Arthur S. Link, ed., *The Papers of Woodrow Wilson* (69 vols, Princeton, Princeton University Press, 1983) 41, pp. 519–27.
34. The following is from the cruiser's official war diary: BA-MA, RM 97/1114, KTB U151. I am inebted to Professor Michael Hadley for providing copies of the war diary. See also Michael L. Hadley and Roger Sarty, *Tin-Pots and Pirate Ships: Canadian Naval Forces and German Sea Raiders 1880–1918* (Montreal and Kingston, McGill-Queen's University Press, 1991), pp. 239 ff.
35. Hadley and Sarty, *Tin-Pots and Pirate Ships,* p. 244.
36. The following is from Dröscher's war diary: BA-MA, RM 97/1094 KTB U117. Once again, I am indebted to Michael Hadley for making this war diary available.
37. Hadley and Sarty, *Tin-Pots and Pirate Ships,* p. 273.
38. Hadley and Sarty, *Tin-Pots and Pirate Ships,* pp. 276–7.
39. Herzog, *60 Jahre Deutsche Uboote,* p. 113.
40. Reichsarchiv, *Der Weltkrieg 1914 bis 1918*. 13: *Die Kriegführung im Sommer und Herbst 1917* (Berlin, E. S. Mittler & Sohn, 1942), pp. 24–6.
41. Alrecht von Thaer, *Generalstabsdienst an der Front und in der OHL. Aus Briefen und*

Tagebuchaufzeichnungen 1915–1919 (Göttingen, Vandenhoeck & Ruprecht, 1958), p. 147. Entry of 4 November 1917.

42. Bundesministerium für Landesverteidigung, *Österreich-Ungarns Letzter Krieg 1914–1918. 6: Das Kriegsjahr 1917* (Vienna, Verlag der Militärwissenschaftlichen Mitteilungen, 1936), p. 88.

43. See Anthony Clayton, 'Robert Nivelle and the French Spring Offensive of 1917', in Brian Bond, ed., *Fallen Stars: Eleven Studies of Twentieth Century Military Disasters* (London, Washington, and New York, Brassey's, 1991), pp. 52–64.

44. *Der Weltkrieg 1914 bis 1918* 12, pp. 102–4.

45. *Der Weltkrieg 1914 bis 1918*, 12, pp. 307–8.

46. See Jere Clemens King, *Generals & Politicians: Conflict Between France's High Command, Parliament and Government, 1914–1918* (Berkeley and Los Angeles, University of California Press, 1951), pp. 156–9.

47. See Ian Brown, 'Not Glamorous, But Effective: The Canadian Corps and the Set-piece Attack, 1917–1918', *Journal of Military History* 58 (1994), pp. 421–44.

48. *Der Weltkrieg 1914 bis 1918* 12, p. 351.

49. *Der Weltkrieg 1914 bis 1918* 12, pp. 403–4.

50. *Der Weltkrieg 1914 bis 1918* 12, p. 410.

51. King, *Generals & Politicians*, pp. 172 ff.

52. Guy Pedroncini, *Les Mutineries de 1917* (Paris, Presses universitaires de France, 1967), pp. 71–89.

53. Pendroncini, *Les Mutineries de 1917*, pp. 194, 215. The mutinies have been analysed at the divisional level by Leonard V. Smith, *Between Mutiny and Obedience: The Case of the French Fifth Infantry Division during World War I* (Princeton, Princeton University Press, 1994).

54. Cited in *Der Weltkrieg 1914 bis 1918* 12, p. 453.

55. *Der Weltkrieg 1914 bis 1918* 12, p. 475.

56. Cited in David French, 'Who Knew What and When? The French Army Mutinies and the British Decision to Launch the Third Battle of Ypres', in L. Freedman, P. Hayes, and R. O'Neill, eds, *War, Strategy and International Politics: Essays in Honour of Sir Michael Howard* (Oxford, Clarendon Press, 1992), pp. 144–5.

57. *Der Weltkrieg 1914 bis 1918* 13, p. 80.

58. Basil Liddell Hart, *The Real War 1914–1918* (Boston, Little, Brown, 1930), p. 337.

59. Tim Travers, *How the War was Won: Command and Technology in the British Army on the Western Front, 1917–1918* (London and New York, Routledge, 1992), pp. 16–17.

60. *Der Weltkrieg 1914 bis 1918* 13, p. 95.

61. Cited in Herzfeld, *Der Erste Weltkrieg*, p. 107.

62. Travers, *How the War was Won*, pp. 19–30.

63. *Der Weltkrieg 1914 bis 1918* 13, pp. 130–1.

64. *Der Weltkrieg 1914 bis 1918* 13, pp. 139–47.

65. Bruce I. Gudmundsson, *Stormtroop Tactics: Innovation in the German Army, 1914–1918* (New York, Westport, and London, Praeger, 1989), pp. 139-45.

66. John W. Wheeler-Bennett, *Brest-Litovsk: The Forgotten Peace March 1918* (London, Macmillan, 1963), pp. 37–41; and *Ursachen und Folgen* 2, pp. 109–15.

67. *Der Weltkrieg 1914 bis 1918* 13, p. 156.

68. *Österreich-Ungarns Letzter Krieg 1914–1918* 6, pp. 236–52.

69. See Allan K. Wildman, *The End of the Russian Imperial Army: The Old Army and the Soldiers' Revolt (March–April 1917)* (Princeton, Princeton University Press, 1980).

70. *Österreich-Ungarns Letzter Krieg 1914–1918* 6, p. 181.

71. *Österreich-Ungarns Letzter Krieg 1914–1918* 6, pp. 484–6.

72. See the report of military censors on the public mood in Rauchensteiner, *Tod des Doppeladlers*, p. 493.

73. Cited in *Österreich-Ungarns Letzter Krieg 1914–1918* 6, p. 496.
74. *Österreich-Ungarns Letzter Krieg 1914–1918* 6, pp. 3, 5.
75. Seeckt to Ludendorff, 22 July 1917. BA-MA, Nachlass Seeckt, N247, vol. 33.
76. Report of 8 September 1917. *Der Weltkrieg 1914 bis 1918* 13, p. 221.
77. *Österreich-Ungarns Letzter Krieg 1914–1918* 6, pp. 502–3.
78. *Der Weltkrieg 1914 bis 1918* 13, pp. 30, 230–1. A good description is provided by Cyril Falls, *The Battle of Caporetto* (Philadelphia and New York, J. B. Lippincott Company, 1966), pp. 35 ff. See also Gudmundsson, *Stormtroop Tactics*, pp. 125–37.
79. Bundesministerium für Landesverteidigung, *Österreich-Ungarns Letzter Krieg 1914–1918. 5: Das Kriegsjahr 1916* (Vienna, Verlag der Militärwissenschaftlichen Mitteilungen, 1933), pp. 132–4.
80. BHStA-KA, HS 1958. Tolmein-Cividale, October 1917. Lt. Streil. Inf. Regt. 19.
81. Erwin Rommel, *Infantry Attacks* (Toronto, Stoddart, 1990), pp. 169–70.
82. *Der Weltkrieg 1914 bis 1918* 13, p. 276.
83. Rudolf Kiszling, *Österreich-Ungarns Anteil am Ersten Weltkrieg* (Graz, Stiasny Verlag, 1958), pp. 64–8. See also Eduard P. Hoffmann, 'Feldmarschall Boroevic von Bojna. Österreich-Ungarns Kriegsfront an den Flüssen Isonzo und Piave', unpubl. diss., Vienna University 1985.
84. See the verdict in *Österreich-Ungarns Letzter Krieg 1914–1918* 6, p. 666.
85. *Österreich-Ungarns Letzter Krieg 1914–1918* 6, pp. 712–13; *Der Weltkrieg 1914 bis 1918* 13, p. 308.
86. Ottokar Landwehr von Pragenau, *Hunger: Die Erschöpfungsjahre der Mittelmächte 1917–18* (Zurich, Leipzig, and Vienna, Amalthea, 1931), p. 138.
87. War Minister Stöger-Steiner to Kaiser Karl, 27 December 1917. ÖStA-KA, MKSM 1917, 93-2/78.
88. Falls, *Battle of Caporetto*, pp. 61–6.
89. Bundesministerium für Landesverteidigung, *Österreich-Ungarns Letzter Krieg 1914–1918. 7: Das Kriegsjahr 1918* (Vienna, Verlag der Militärwissenschaftlichen Mitteilungen, 1938), p. 212.
90. *Österreich-Ungarns Letzter Krieg 1914–1918* 6, p. 561.
91. Gunther Rothenberg, *The Army of Francis Joseph* (West Lafayette, Ind., Purdue University Press, 1976), p. 208.
92. Fritz Fellner, ed., *Schicksalsjahre Österreichs 1908–1919. Das politische Tagebuch Josef Redlichs* (2 vols, Graz and Cologne, Hermann Böhlaus Nachf., 1954) 2, p. 253. Entry of 31 December 1917.
93. Riezler, *Tagebücher*, p. 453. Entry of 3 October 1917.

9

The Last Levy, 1917–18

Basically, this war comes down simply to killing one another.

General Erich Ludendorff, April 1917

Albrecht von Thaer, about to be assigned to the staff of the Third *OHL*, on the last day of 1917 pondered Germany's situation. From the 'purely military point of view', Thaer averred, the Reich's position had never been so good since the start of the war. 'Russia, this gigantic military power totally defeated, begs for peace; Romania the same. Serbia and Montenegro have simply disappeared.' Italy had been soundly beaten, its 'best province' (Venetia) occupied; it survived merely at the pleasure of Britain and France. The latter two, while still willing to continue the struggle, were 'severely exhausted'. France was almost defeated. The U-boats continued to threaten Britain's overseas trade.

'Will America yet be able to turn the page of history?' Thaer did not think so since only 225 000 American soldiers had landed in Europe to date. While Germany's allies – especially Austria–Hungary – were 'worth little' militarily, all that was needed of them was to hold previously conquered territory. By comparison, Germany's prospects for 1918 were both simple and bright: 'We can now deploy our entire strength in the west'. The moment of decision had arrived. 'To be sure, that is our last card.'[1]

The Central Powers spent the winter of 1917–18 mobilizing their armed forces as well as home populations for one final, desperate effort to achieve victory before the Americans arrived in sufficient numbers to turn the tide. Ludendorff had abandoned any thought of a strategic break-through and had accepted attrition as the norm. 'Basically, this war comes down simply to killing one another'.[2] The *OHL* demanded that war output be increased, that workers yet again raise their productivity, and that civilians prepare for a last winter of hunger and cold. Ludendorff and his staff drew up draconian peace treaties for defeated Romania and Russia,[3] and dispatched troops to exploit their grain and oil reserves. While Kaiser Karl planned the postwar configuration of the Austro-Hungarian Army, Conrad von Hötzendorf prepared another assault against Italy out of the Tyrol. And while General Hoffmann's troops marched ever deeper into Russia, Hindenburg and Ludendorff worked frenetically on Operation *Michael*, an offensive named after Germany's patron saint and planned for France in early 1918. The home front was instructed to hold together for 'the last card'.

The hollow ally

In March 1917 Kaiser Karl had created the Commission for War and Transitional Economy to prepare for the postwar demobilization of industry and had, albeit unsuccessfully, approached France about ending the war. Thereafter, Karl turned his attention to the armed forces, that is, to prepare them for the postwar period. He was guided by two considerations: the decennial negotiations with the Hungarians about renewing the Compromise of 1867 were due, and the dramatic expansion of the Army after 1914 had created organizational chaos. Divisional artillery had been increased from 42 pieces to 76, and the number of Schwarzlose machine guns almost 400 per cent. Each year, nearly 2 million replacements had been sent to the front helter-skelter, with the result that some divisions had 15 or 18 battalions each and others but 8 or 9. Obviously affected by the Kaiser's rosy visions of an imminent peace, General Arz von Straussenburg decided in May 1917 to lay the foundations for the postwar army.

'However the war would end', the Chief of the General Staff minuted, 'one could not count on obtaining in peacetime the means necessary for the creation of a modern army'.[4] Thus, the time to restructure the Army was now, while funds were still available. Arz's plan, endorsed by Karl in May 1917, called for a force of 60 infantry and 12 cavalry divisions – 594 000 men in all, or 11 divisions more than had been at hand before the war. The new divisions were to be triangular rather than square with three regiments of three battalions each, thereby creating on paper 35 new regiments. Each division was to receive a mortar battalion, a special assault battalion, and an artillery brigade of 72 light guns and 24 heavy. Soldiers were to receive steel helmets, gas masks, and field-grey uniforms. The Army was to have a permanent supreme command and a joint sapper-engineer corps. Politically, it was to maintain the prewar triad of *k.u.k.* Joint Army, Austrian *Landwehr*, and Hungarian *Honvéd*.[5] The air arm was set at 82 squadrons.

But politics never went according to plan in the Dual Monarchy. In November 1917 the new Hungarian Premier Alexander Wekerle and *Honvéd* Minister Szurmay informed Karl that they demanded separate Austrian and Hungarian armies after the war as the price for renewing the 1867 Compromise. Hardly the man to make a decision on such a critical issue, Karl on 4 December called a meeting of military leaders. Szurmay reiterated the demand for a separate Hungarian army and informed those present that 'all groups' in Budapest were 'united on the issue of a Hungarian army'. General Sarkotić, the Croat wartime ruler of Bosnia-Herzegovina, countered that Szurmay's demands were inadmissible and instead argued for a 'small unitary army' designed to 'repress revolutionary subversions and coups'. This drew a sharp rebuke from Böhm-Ermolli, commander of an army group in Russia, who would not tolerate any suggestion that the Army was unreliable. War Minister Stöger-Steiner defused a potentially explosive situation by suggesting that Karl bow to the inevitable on the issue of a separate Hungarian army, but that he do so in such a manner as to turn its creation into a 'genuine coronation of dualism'. In any case, Stöger-Steiner lectured the council, such a step would have to wait until the end of the war. General Dankl, colonel of the *Leibgarden*, closed the meeting on a true Habsburg note by muttering 'later, much later' in support of the War Minister's decision to delay the issue.[6]

In fact, Stöger-Steiner had more pressing matters on his mind. In August 1917 he had sent the Kaiser a detailed memorandum on the 'Possibilities of Our Lasting Through the Winter of 1917/18', wherein he had concluded that it was 'possible', but just possible.[7] For more than 3 years, the War Minister lectured the Kaiser, the Dual Monarchy had fought the war without the benefit of a unified 'war office' such as existed in Germany under General Groener. Human losses had been catastrophic. 'We are at the end of our capacity with regard to officer replacements.' One million troops still stood at the various fronts, but most were ill-fed and poorly-clothed. After the 160 000 men fit for service from the cohort of 1900 had been conscripted in May 1918, only convalescents would be available. Reserves were physically inferior due to malnutrition; training was far below peacetime standards; and officers recruited from among managers of closed consumer industries were substandard. Rear-echelon units would run out of potatoes by May 1918. More than 70 000 horses had died recently due to lack of green feed and the use of surrogate feeds such as molasses and treacle had only partially alleviated the situation. The Army was forced to sell many of its horses to butchers so that the rest could survive.

Stöger-Steiner then turned to the military-industrial situation. Coal supplies were down to 24 days in Austria and 11 in Hungary – compared with the minimal norm of 28 days. In raw terms, Austria's monthly coal supply had been reduced from 2.7 to 1.8 million tons and Hungary's from 864 000 to 452 000. It was of 'eminent importance' to effect an 'equitable distribution' of coal among the civilian population. Railroad ties and rails lagged far behind demand. Trains would soon be ordered to reduce speeds to conserve existing tracks. About 500 miles of Alpine cable railways had been closed due to lack of replacement cables.

Rubber was in such short supply that the Army even requisitioned billiard pocket cushions. Copper, aluminium, and zinc were far below minimal levels. Wood was available in sufficient quantity, but there was neither the labour to harvest it nor the transport to move it. Petroleum supplies ran 33.3 per cent behind needs. All miners had been released from the Army to return to their former pits and food was to be allotted to them according to their needs. Textiles were at a premium. Wool had been mixed with paper fibres and cotton likewise diluted with nettle. Paper bandages had taken the place of cotton gauze. Some units had been issued paper underwear for want of cotton. Only an 'intensive exploitation' of occupied territories – especially Poland – could alleviate the shortages of raw materials. In fact, requisitions from Poland, measured against the previous winter, rose dramatically in 1917–18: cows from 13 200 to 56 600, hogs from 51 400 to 77 400, fowl from 290 500 to 446 900, and eggs from 59 to 69 million.[8]

Stöger-Steiner was slightly more optimistic with regard to war equipment. Machine-gun production could be raised from the present 1500 units per month to 3000 by the spring of 1918. The current output of 2.25 million shells per month could be maintained. Industry promised to raise aircraft production by 400 per cent early in 1918, but shortages of aluminium, nickel, and iron made him skeptical of its promises. Most importantly, the sad state of food supplies had led to 'dissatisfaction' among industrial workers and thereby created the 'breeding ground for strikes, unrest, and work stoppages that could jeopardize' the Dual Monarchy's 'ability to survive' the winter of 1917–18.

The final section of the document dealt specifically with food and morale. 'Human beings', the War Minister lectured his Kaiser, 'are our most precious commodity'. The Monarchy could not afford costly new offensives. 'Machines' such as flamethrowers, gas, machine guns, and trench mortars had, to the degree possible, already taken the place of men at the front. Workers at home had to escalate their productivity. Women needed to be brought into the workplace in greater numbers, and food supplies rationed equitably and sold at fair prices. The existing disparity between allegedly abundant supplies in Hungary and grave shortages in Austria only served to demoralize the home front. Even the armed forces had to tighten the belt. The tried and true adage, 'demand much in order to obtain a little', was now 'inappropriate and irresponsible'. Stöger-Steiner concluded that the availability of food and coal alone would determine survivability and morale.

Stöger-Steiner's memorandum was not unduly pessimistic. Internal assessments of Army morale that same August led the War Minister to inform General von Marterer, head of the Military Chancery, that the war had brought about 'unfortunate incidents of human weaknesses and moral lapses *even in high positions*'.[9] Stöger-Steiner pointed out that generals had profited handsomely by selling produce from their estates to the Army; that they acted as middle men in purveying other provisions to the armed forces; and that they routinely recommended only certain (friendly) firms for military procurement. He further noted that a number of generals had taken lucrative positions on the boards of banks and industrial firms and demanded 'decisively and trenchantly' that all flag-grade officers reveal at once such participation.

In a separate document, the War Ministry expressed concern about what it called a 'surplus' of 150 generals. It put forth four possible solutions. Generals serving in rear echelons could be forced into retirement to make room for younger talent. At least 12 corps commanders could be offered 4000 Kronen per year as a retirement incentive. Other commanders could be reassigned to largely honorific posts with the Guards, the Court, and the chanceries of Military Orders, where the Kaiser would have to assume their salaries. Railroads, banks, and especially war industries would have to be 'persuaded' to hire retired generals – as was the case in Germany. This step had two advantages: it would reduce the Army's payroll at the top levels, and it would give the military new and expanded influence in banking and industry. The War Ministry concluded optimistically that these former generals would then hire wounded officers and invalids, thereby further reducing military expenditures and expanding martial influence.[10] There is no record of an acceptance from any flag-grade officer.

In November 1917 the Army warned that 'lack of proper training' had reduced the quality of both its officer and noncommissioned officer corps. The rank and file suffered from lack of food and clothing.[11] The Chief of the General Staff pointed out that companies had been reduced from 175 men each to 145 due to lack of reserves; that the number of military doctors had fallen from 7392 in January 1917 to 5399 in January 1918; and that 28 300 military police were required just to hunt deserters. Transport at the front was paralysed due to lack of horses: despite the forced requisition of 57 000 mounts from Poland and 90 000 out of Ukraine, the Army's pool had fallen from 809 000 horses in June 1917 to 459 000

1 year later; the anticipated shortfall for 1918 was 80 000.[12] The lack of horses had forced the Army to dismount seven cavalry divisions by March 1917, to suspend riding courses for messengers, to purchase the private mounts of officers, and to deny company commanders horses.

General von Seeckt, Germany's senior adviser to the *k.u.k.* Army, informed the *OHL* in September 1917 that Arz von Straussenburg fully concurred with Stöger-Steiner's assessment. The shortage of officers was especially critical: too many staff officers were deployed in industries and rear echelons to supervise war production; platoon and company commanders (lieutenants and captains) were scarce; numerous officers roamed Poland requisitioning food and hence were lost to the front; and lack of staff officers kept the War Academy closed. But the creation of a 'war office' along German lines would 'completely bulldoze all customary and tried relations' in the Monarchy. On a positive note, the *AOK* was finally willing to requisition race horses! Troops were instructed to bring their own underwear and linens from home. Women and children were to repair roads and to work in industry.[13] Unsurprisingly, Seeckt found the Monarchy's commitment to 'total war' somewhat short of the mark.

But Austria–Hungary was at the end of its human and material tether by the winter of 1917–18. The last volume of Austria's official history of the war provides detailed testimony to support this conclusion. The Army's artillery consisted of 14 regiments of four batteries each, of which only half were sufficiently modern and mobile to be designated 'attack artillery'; two regiments in the Tyrol and one in Bosnia were ranked 'defensive artillery'; and two regiments in Pola and one at Cattaro were classified immobile 'coastal artillery'. Lack of horses greatly reduced the mobility of all artillery. The 176 batteries of artillery on hand in early 1918, while numbering an impressive 1800 tubes, ranged in calibre from 6 cm to 42 cm. Some units were motorized, others horse-drawn. Some batteries had standard army guns, others naval designs. Some guns were new, others were 30 to 40 years old.[14] Infantry regiments each had lost one of their four battalions.

Austro-Hungarian artillery was cannibalized to gain men and guns for the fighting fronts. Coastal defences in Montenegro and Dalmatia were turned over to local militia units and 13 500 of their regular crews transferred to Italy. Artillery units at Belgrade were disbanded. The garrisons of the great fortresses Cracow, Peterwardein, and Przemyśl were reduced to skeletal guard details. The Bug River–Carpathian Mountains defensive works were abandoned. Obsolete ships at Cattaro and Pola were placed out of service. These drastic measures allowed the Army to release a further 60 000 to 80 000 soldiers for front-line duty.[15]

Armaments plants had reached the zenith of their capabilities early in 1917 and output fell sharply thereafter. The production of rifles, for example, dropped from 113 000 in March 1917 to 9000 by February 1918; that of machine guns from 1900 in October 1917 to 350 by February 1918. Lack of coal and iron was chronic. Coal consignments to railroads, mines, food processors, armaments plants, and public utilities at the end of 1917 were reduced to 40 per cent of prewar levels. By 1918 only 24 of the 45 iron blast furnaces working in 1916 were operational. The immediate result was a severe reduction in munitions: heavy-artillery-shell output fell from 410 000 per month in the autumn of 1916 to 130 000 by the summer of 1917; and that of machine-gun bullets from a daily quota of 6 million to 1.5 million by early 1918.[16] Quality also declined: the number of duds rose from 2 to 5 per cent in peacetime to 10 per cent by 1917.

Aircraft industries were especially hard hit by the shortage of precious metals. In 1917 the Empire's seven plants produced 1740 airplanes – compared to 14 421 in Britain and 14 915 in France. Its six aircraft engine factories put out 1230 motors – compared with 11 536 in Britain and 23 092 in France. Given the average life of 4 months for an aircraft, production barely managed to keep 450 to 500 planes aloft. And given the annual loss of 100 per cent of pilots, the three aviator schools at Wiener Neustadt, Neumarkt, and Udine fell far short of providing the required 50 new pilots per month.[17] Shortages also affected gas warfare: all Blue and Yellow Cross gas shells came from Germany. Transport difficulties forced the *AOK* to dissolve many of its gas units early in 1918.

Transportation remained the Achilles' heel of the Habsburg war effort.[18] Each division required one supply train per day. In 1917 the Army had moved 230 000 men, 21 000 horses, and 7000 trucks and carts to the front every month – in addition to hauling grains and oil from Romania and Poland, bringing home the war booty after Caporetto, and transporting hundreds of thousands of former prisoners of war home from Russia as well as former Russian POWs to the Empire's eastern borders. These tasks lay far beyond the modest rail capabilities of its rail system. By the winter of 1917, almost 28 per cent of all locomotives were down for repairs and not even a German contingent of 250 engines brought much relief; military trains that usually required 4 days to reach the front now took up to 2 weeks. Congestion plagued the network as a result of slower speeds and expanded down-time: in February 1918 more than 4000 freight cars stood idle on the *Nordbahn* in Galicia alone, and that number would double by the end of the war. Personnel was equally ground down by the demands for transport: accidents rose from 1883 in 1914 to 4065 by 1917–18, collisions from 350 to 761 during the same period.[19]

Automobile and truck production reached its peak in mid-1917 with a monthly output of just 120 units.

The return of Habsburg soldiers from Russian POW camps in the spring of 1918 proved a difficult undertaking. More than 2 million men had been interned in camps in Siberia, Manchuria, and Turkestan, and of these roughly 500 000 had died due to hunger, disease, and mistreatment. The Dual Monarchy was woefully unprepared to receive the returnees – 380 000 by the end of April and 517 000 by the end of June. Neither field kitchens nor barracks, neither clothing depots nor field hospitals had been built. Nor had any debriefing centres been established – although it was well known that many of the soldiers had embraced revolutionary philosophy while in Russia. The Army decided that the men should swear a new oath of allegiance to the Kaiser, undergo 3 weeks of quarantine, return to reserve formations behind the front, and be interrogated concerning their capture. Only then would they be given 6 to 8 weeks of recuperation, followed by 4 to 5 months of retraining, before returning to the front. Temporary housing for the former POWs was hastily constructed in Russian Poland, eastern Galicia, the Bukovina, Transylvania, and Turkey.

But few returnees cherished service at the front and many took to the forests especially in the south of the Monarchy, where they formed so-called 'green cadres' that lived off the land by theft and extortion.[20] By 1918 roughly 200 000 deserters operated in Bohemia, Bosnia–Herzegovina, Dalmatia, Galicia, Lower Austria, Moravia, and Slavonia. As a result, Kaiser Karl in February 1918 reintroduced the punishments – such as tying to stakes and locking in irons – that he had abolished the previous year. The government now decreed that it would not grant amnesty to deserters.

A report on returning POWs by the Foreign Ministry's representative to the Governor-General in Poland in May 1918 is indicative of conditions in the east.[21] About 1500 former POWs attached to the 58th Infantry Regiment for retraining complained bitterly that they were to be returned to the front, that they had been stripped of the clothes they had purchased for dear money in Russia and put into 'old, badly damaged uniforms', and that they had to stand in line for hours to be served 'miserable and inferior food' from a single field kitchen. Above all, they resented the 'heartless, indifferent' reception that they received especially from officers.

On 18 May one of the erstwhile POWs was arrested for drunken and disorderly behaviour in a public house. His comrades stormed the guard house and released the man by breaking out the window frames. When General Anton Lipošćak asked the men for their complaints, a single soldier came forth: 'First and foremost we want to know why we are fighting this war without sense or purpose now for four years; then we want to know why we prisoners of war cannot finally go home'. Lipošćak became irate. 'We are fighting this war because His Majesty has so commanded and because we obey according to our oath of allegiance.' He ordered the soldier arrested, whereupon 50 or 60 mates, believing that the trooper was being led before a firing squad, seized their rifles and fired on the military escort. A storm battalion of the 106th Infantry Division was called in to quell the rebellion and arrest the POWs.

The Ballhausplatz's man in Lublin contrasted the treatment of former POWs in the Dual Monarchy to that in Germany. 'Returning prisoners of war are downright festively received [in Germany]; they are clothed in brand-new uniforms from head to feet; they receive 3 months holiday pay after a short time (ours only 4 weeks).' While Lipošćak eventually commuted a number of death sentences to prison terms, only better food and uniforms, and respect on the part of officers could defuse such explosive situations.

'Human beings', as Stöger-Steiner had reminded the Kaiser in his August 1917 memorandum, remained the Monarchy's 'most precious commodity'. The need to maintain a balance among draft-eligible males between combatants and war-production workers continued to prove troublesome. More than 1.26 million men laboured in domestic industries and 448 000 officers and men had been 'commanded' to managerial or oversight posts with state and private war industries. Of these 1.7 million, roughly 24 per cent worked on farms and in forestry, 40 per cent in the Monarchy's 7000 war-related industries, 22 per cent in the communication and transportation branches, and 14 per cent in the public-service sector.

After the Dual Monarchy's third 'exchange action' in April 1917 to resupply as well as rejuvenate the front, only soldiers under the age of 43 remained at the front. Those aged 44 to 46 had been reassigned to rear-echelon areas; and those 47 and over (the cohorts of 1865 and 1866) sent home to assist with planting and harvesting. The number of men released from the armies in the east came to only 8000; most served as carriage drivers and medical aides behind the trenches. 'Flying commissions' of military police were created to hunt down 'deserters and shirkers'. Special efforts were made to attract women into the Army's workforce: their numbers between August 1917 and the end of the war rose from 60 000 to 107 000 at home and from 27 000 to 33 000 in the field. Attempts to recruit military labourers from among the 4 million Poles under Habsburg administration came to naught as only 15 000 men came forth; forced recruitment was dismissed due to 'political considerations'.[22]

By 1918, as noted in the Austro-Hungarian official history of the war, the cup of human resources had been drained. More than 70 per cent of all draft-eligible males had been called to the colours: 8.42 of the 9.12 million men found fit for military service had been conscripted and 0.7 million held back in war industries. Almost half of the 4 million draftees had been rendered *hors de combat* mainly by death (0.78 million), capture (1.6 million), or severe wounds (0.5 million). The Army estimated that only 2.7 million men between the ages of 18 and 50 remained outside the armed forces, and that the majority of these had been classified unfit for service. The most optimistic guess was that perhaps 140 000 could be reclassified as militarily fit and deployed behind the front. General von Hazai, Chief of the Replacement Branch, managed to muster 25 000 formerly 'unfit' men in Austria, 20 000 in Hungary, and 5000 in Bosnia-Herzegovina. Of these, doctors found only 5000 – actors, waiters, furniture makers, jewellers, and the unemployed – fit for service. Even with the return of an estimated 500 000 convalescents, the Army still would fall 600 000 men short of needs in 1918. Standard divisions of 11 567 men were down to between 5000 and 8000; and regiments of 1275 paper strength to 832.[23]

An obvious point, but one worth repeating, is that the home front tied down an incredibly large number of soldiers. *K.u.k.* forces stationed in Austria and Hungary on 1 January 1918 stood at 1 487 000. These included 485 000 in hospitals; 324 000 in reserve for future deployment; 157 000 unfit for front duty; 114 000 just released from hospitals and not yet ready to rejoin their units; 90 000 being formed into reserve cadres; 70 000 working in military offices and staffs; and 35 000 listed as irreplaceable training personnel.[24] Similarly, only about a quarter of the Army's 2.3 million men in the field in 1918 were combatants: 400 000 in Italy, 150 000 in Russia, 50 000 in the Balkans, and about 18 000 in two divisions with the Germans on the Western Front. The *AOK* estimated that a mere 145 000 *Landser* remained from those called up in 1914.

The shortage of manpower in industry and on the land was equally critical. The only relief came in the form of 1.3 million POWs, including 908 000 Russians. About 362 000 POWs were used as labourers with the Army and 947 000 at home. Among the latter, 438 000 farmed the land, 105 000 toiled in industry, 127 000 worked on military posts, and the rest were assigned to state industries and forestry. About 219 000 POWs were unfit for work.[25] Yet not even these numbers sufficed, and the Army in January 1918 detailed 14 battalions to assist with food requisitioning in Hungary. Their efforts were largely responsible for the collection of 1300 wagons of grain that fed the Army in Italy that spring.

Last but not least, even nature seemed to be with the Entente. In Vienna, Professor Redlich recorded in his diary what he called 'a summer the likes of which our land has not seen in 50 years, a summer of searing heat which simply roasts vegetables, potatoes, and corn to death'. The city's vegetable and fruit markets were empty as the Army requisitioned whatever produce was available directly off the farms. Workers subsisted on pickled cucumbers, which caused an outbreak of intestinal illness. Prices doubled, then quadrupled. Hungary estimated that its harvest of cereal crops and potatoes would reach only half the prewar level. Redlich wondered whether Austria could survive a fourth winter.[26]

Strikes and mutinies

Hunger was the catalyst for the wave of strikes and mutinies that plagued Austria–Hungary early in 1918. Soldiers at the front received scarcely 100 g. of meat per day – one-fourth of what they had been allotted at the start of the war. In Austria civilians were down to 23 g. of meat per person per day; in Hungary they received about 10 g. more. General Landwehr von Pragenau, head of the Joint Food Committee, was fully aware that starvation haunted the populace. The consumption of potatoes had fallen to just 70 g. per person per day – compared with 357 in Germany and down from 493 in 1913. Meat ration cards had been issued in Vienna, where 3 'meatless' days per week remained the norm. Bread, flour, and potatoes were severely rationed in the capital; milk, fat, eggs, and vegetables were unavailable at markets. The Austrian half of the Empire received just 48 of the required 273 grain cars per day. And due to a near-total breakdown of transportation, only 11 890 of the 1 million cars of grain anticipated from Ukraine in 1917–18 as a result of the so-called the 'bread peace' of Brest-Litovsk actually arrived.

Special 'war kitchens' and 'people's kitchens' provided 184 000 meals per day at the end of 1916 in Vienna alone. For 60 Heller (pennies) workers and lower-middle-class employees were served a watery concoction of vegetables, potatoes, and animal rinds. But even this relief effort embraced only 15 to 20 per cent of the capital's population. In June 1918 Kaiser Karl and his wife Zita accompanied mobile soup kitchens to Viennese working-class districts to boost morale; the next month they organized a mammoth 'Children into the Country' movement that sent 100 000 Austrian child labourers for 2 months on to Hungarian farms.[27]

When the government announced on 13 January 1918 that it would reduce flour in Cisleithania from 200 g. to 165 per day per person, strikes erupted throughout the Dual Monarchy. The first strikes by 10 000 workers hit the Daimler Motor Works in Wiener Neustadt on 14 January; the next day they spread to the Vienna Locomotive works, Fiat plant, and state aircraft factories. From the capital, the labour unrest spread to Arthur

Krupp in Berndorf as well as to ammunition plants in Enzensfeld, Hirtenberg, and Wöllersdorf. On 16 January the movement took off in Vienna: 6600 workers walked off the job by breakfast, another 35 000 before noon, and by supper time more then 84 000 men and women were on strike. Across Austria – from St Pölten to Graz, Linz to Bruck – 600 000 labourers refused to report for work. Stores closed. Newspaper presses ground to a halt. Isolated street brawls turned into political demonstrations. A second major wave of strikes paralysed the naval dockyards at Pola and a third the Austrian Shipyards and Austrian Lloyd in Trieste. Györ and Magyaróvár in Hungary were also paralysed by strikes. By 17 January, more than 200 000 workers had walked off their jobs in Vienna, joined by other hundreds of thousands from Cracow to Trieste, Prague to Temesvár.[28] They demanded more food, an end to the militarization of industrial plants, and in many cases an end to the war.

The seriousness of the strikes can be gleaned from Ambassador Hohenlohe-Schillingsfürst's briefings in Berlin. On 16 January Hohenlohe shared Viennese police reports stating that 12 000 workers at the state locomotive plant, 2000 at the Fiat auto factory, and 1800 at Kofherr & Schrantz as well as at the United Rubber Works had walked off the job. Within 48 hours, Berlin promised 125 000 tons of grain and 8000 tons of wheat from Romanian depots. That same 18 January, Hohenlohe reported that leading Austrian Social Democrats were meeting with the government to discuss the strikes. Within 48 hours, the Bavarian government promised to reroute 2000 to 3000 freight cars of potatoes to Vienna. As late as 23 January, Hohenlohe allowed that 45 000 strikers were still off their jobs outside Vienna, including 11 000 workers at the Blumau munitions plant.[29] The *AOK* at Baden in February 1918 reported demonstrations in Prague, student riots in Lemberg, and sporadic strikes by coal miners in Ostrau, iron mongers in Witkowitz, and railroad workers in Oderfurt. Rail strikes in Bohemia forced Škoda to lay off 40 per cent of its workers.[30]

German statesmen took almost malicious delight in noting Vienna's plight. Ambassador Botho Count von Wedel informed Berlin that 600 000 workers were on strike and that the Dual Monarchy was at the end of its human and material strength. 'Whoever does not want to close his eyes must see that this Monarchy is lurching on the edge of the abyss.'[31] The Wilhelmstrasse used rather undiplomatic language to summarize the situation in Vienna. 'Now, when the misery is at its zenith, one finally begins to stir; [now], when the stable is already fully in flames, one thinks about rescuing the cow. Always the same old Austrian *Schlamperei.*'[32]

Official Vienna was well aware of the popular feeling behind the strikes. An army of 1000 censors each month monitored between 8 and 10 million postcards and letters. In January 1918 the censors apprised the government that 14 per cent of letter writers welcomed the strikes as a harbinger of peace, and that 33.3 per cent saw them as revolutionary acts. The public was war-weary and desperate for peace. Writers complained about the endless requisitioning of food and horses, the never-ending call-ups for military service, the lack of food at markets, the meteoric price hikes, and the inefficiency of governmental agencies. Many expressed the popular belief that 'only the poor carry the burdens of the war while the rich enjoy it'.[33] Rural villagers saw the Russian revolution as a sure sign of a 'religious-messianic prophecy' of the coming end of the world.

Still, the strikes caught Viennese bureaucrats by surprise. The police seemed powerless to end them and the loyalty of the capital's military garrison was questionable. The government eventually restored order by revoking the 13 January decision to reduce the flour ration, by promising electoral reforms, and by reopening the talks with the Russians at Brest-Litovsk, which had broken down in rancor and acrimony. The Army, for its part, enacted operations 'Mogul' and 'Revolver', whereby it despatched military patrols to arrest strike leaders and deployed seven infantry divisions under General Aloys Prince Schönburg-Hartenstein throughout the Empire. It arrested no fewer than 44 000 deserters in the first 3 months of 1918.[34] Vienna created a 'Counterpropaganda Bureau' to motivate the home populace as well as the soldiers through patriotic lectures, films, courses, and literature. And while some hoped that Schönburg-Hartenstein would proclaim military rule, the Prince was no Leon Trotsky and Kaiser Karl declined to turn power over to the Army.

The Vienna Police Directorate was profoundly shaken by the waves of strikes and in March 1918 compiled a lengthy analysis of events for Foreign Minister Czernin.[35] Food conditions in the capital had been horrendous at the start of the year. Flour was totally absent from stores and only ersatz products were for sale. Meat, vegetables, fruit, and potatoes were scarce, driving prices up by leaps and bounds; beets sold at 1000 per cent of their 1917 price. Food queues of 15 000 women and children were not an unusual sight. The black market flourished. Eighty persons had been arraigned in court for overcharging and hoarding early in January 1918. The public mood was 'the worst imaginable' and blamed government officials up to the Kaiser as well as Jews for the shortages.

More than 2000 women had rioted at Vienna's public markets on 11 January; 5 days later 25 000 stood in line at the main meat market. It was not unusual for buyers to line up at markets the night before; many fainted in the process. While the best hotels and butcher shops had beef and pork for sale to their regular (and wealthy) clients, the markets in the working-class districts had only horse meat on hand. Butchers there complained bitterly that they were forced to sell at fixed prices. Soup kitchens were besieged by patrons, many of them *Landser* on leave. Countless 'soldiers in rags' went door to door begging food. The capital's populace, in the words of the police, was on the point of starvation and rebellion. A top secret Army report of 21 January conceded: 'We are living from hand to mouth. . . . Exhaustion and malnutrition among the personnel, shortage of coal, . . . shortage of doctors'.[36]

News of strikes in the Empire's major cities quickly spread to the naval base in the Bocche di Cattaro on the Adriatic Sea. Equally plagued by hunger, cold, and lack of decent clothing, the sailors rebelled on 1 February. Shortly before noon, men on the armoured cruiser *Sankt Georg*, flagship of the cruiser flotilla, broke into the ship's arsenal, seized control of the vessel, and shot an officer and a noncommissioned officer. The rebellion quickly spread to the armoured cruiser *Kaiser Karl VI* and the depot ship *Gäa*. The 4000 rebels, led by Midshipman Anton Sesan, demanded more meat and vegetables in their diet, new uniforms and shoes, full bread rations of 500 g., longer shore leave, and less work and drill. On the second day of the uprising, they also put forth political demands: an end to the war 'without annexations', democratization of all governments, and the right to self-determination.[37] Government leaders in Vienna feared a repeat of the 1917 revolts of the Russian Baltic Sea Fleet and the Petrograd workers.

The mutiny reached its climax on the second day. General Oskar Guseck von Glankirchen, the harbour commander, ringed the base with coastal artillery and called the Third Battle Division of three *Erzherzog*-class battleships down from Pola to isolate the mutiny. Coastal artillery fired on and hit the harbour guardship *Kronprinz Erzherzog Rudolph* with 15 cm shells as it tried to leave anchorage at Porto Rose. The revolt collapsed at this first sign of armed resistance. Small units, led by the light cruiser *Novara* and the *Helgoland*, broke away from under the guns of the rebellious ships on the third day to show their loyalty to the Kaiser. German U-boats threatened to torpedo any of the mutineers' ships that tried to get up steam. Sesan fled to Italy by seaplane. Eight hundred rebels were removed from the ships, and 40 were ordered to stand trial on charges of insubordination and treason. At dawn on 11 February four seamen were executed by firing squad; 392 faced courts-martial for their roles in the revolt.[38] Admiral Maximilian Njegovan was replaced as fleet commander by Captain Miklós Horthy, hastily promoted to the rank of vice admiral. The end of the war put a halt to the trials and hearings for 348 rebels.

Austria was so desperate for food that General Landwehr on 30 April seized a convoy of barges on the Danube carrying 2455 cars of Romanian grain to Germany. The action precipitated a crisis within the alliance. While the barges were eventually returned to Germany, the grain was hauled away in 2455 freight cars and distributed to Austrian bakeries. Landwehr tried to dismiss the action as nothing more than 'simple street robbery'; Ludendorff wanted to declare war on Austria![39] In the end, the issue was resolved diplomatically: Austria–Hungary agreed to leave the economic exploitation of Ukraine solely in German hands.

The strikes of 14 January and the mutiny of 1 February 1918 were clear indications that the Empire's workers and sailors were no longer willing to continue the war indefinitely. Three years of war, hunger, cold, and deprivation had taken their toll. Army leaders at Baden wondered whether the troops at the fronts in the Balkans and Italy would hold and remain calm. Soldiers in Italy received between 125 and 500 g. of mainly inferior corn-meal bread per day; combatants were fed 160 g. of meat per day, those in rear echelons often none. When the men complained of maggots in their meat, the Army's Quartermaster-General lectured them that this constituted extra protein!

The men were mad with hunger. Tenth Army, for example, reported that it had yielded to the pleas of its troops not to destroy meat declared inedible by its quartermaster staff, and that it had treated it with salt and potassium permanganate to render it palatable. When once again declared inedible, the Tenth Army buried the meat along with stale bread – only to witness the starving soldiers in the dead of night digging up the meat and bread soaked in rancid blood. Fresh vegetables were unavailable; dried vegetables consisted mainly of corn meal and grits. Daily fat rations were down to 8 g. Horse meat had become a rare delicacy as many artillery batteries had already consumed half of their draught animals. On average, the soldiers weighed 120 lbs.[40] Most were without leather boots, decent uniforms, underwear, or sufficient ammunition. Those who favoured an offensive undoubtedly did so because this might allow them, as at Caporetto the previous October, to raid rich Allied stores of food, liquor, and tobacco. Archduke Joseph bluntly informed Baden that his men pleaded 'for an immediate offensive so that they would not die of hunger'.[41]

The *k.u.k.* army disintegrates

On 3 November 1917 the *AOK* had weighed its options for the coming year in the wake of the Russian collapse. It was not optimistic. In the east the Monarchy maintained 32 infantry divisions and 12 cavalry along a 325-mile front; the Germans 92 divisions on their 775-mile line. In Italy the Central Powers posted 37 Austrian divisions and eight German along a 290-mile front. Density ratios were one division per 8 miles in the east; and one per 6 miles in Italy. Most divisions were down to between 5000 and 8000 men. Dismounted cavalry divisions were at half strength. One-third of all artillery batteries lacked sufficient horses. Karl's staff posed the rhetorical question whether the *k.u.k.* Army could undertake offensive actions in 1918 and came to a quick and unanimous decision: '<u>No</u>, not by itself!'[42] At best, given immediate reinforcements of five or six divisions, the Army hoped to hold current lines. It ruled out even minor counter-offensives.

Conrad was of different opinion and decided once more to play *va banque*, victory or demise. On 30 January 1918 he sent Baden the first of numerous proposals for a major offensive out of the Sieben Gemeinden around Asiago and across the Etsch and the Piave rivers on to the Venetian plain, taking the main Italian Army in the flank. Eight days later, after receiving only a lukewarm reception for his plans from the *AOK*, the Field Marshal again proposed a thrust out of the Tyrolean Alps designed 'vitally to hit' the enemy's principal supply routes. Baden again reacted skeptically. On 22 March Conrad sent in yet another plan for a Tyrolean offensive. The main attack this time was to be launched from both sides of the Brenta River toward Pasubio-Vicenza-Cornuda and conducted with 31 infantry divisions and 3 cavalry. Short of 15 infantry divisions and 2 cavalry (!), Conrad brazenly asked Arz von Straussenburg to supply the missing forces.[43] The Chief of the General Staff, while paying lip service to this grand design ('I expect Italy's military destruction'), worked behind the scenes to deny Conrad the forces necessary to mount the operation.

As so often in the past, Conrad once more chose not to let reality interfere with his strategic designs. He ignored both the difficulty of the heavily-wooded and mountainous terrain and the 'terrible condition' of his own forces. Having devoured the abundant Italian food supplies captured after the Battle of Caporetto, daily rations were down to roughly 230 g. of flour per man; some regiments received but 125 g. of lumpy corn meal; and meat rations averaged 150 g. German deliveries of 30 000 tons of flour – against 35 000 cattle and 50 000 hogs from Hungary – alone allowed the *AOK* to contemplate an offensive.[44] *K.u.k.* soldiers were so undernourished and badly trained that the Army fully expected loss rates of 5 per cent per month during 'normal' (holding) operations. In March Karl out of a sense of pity ordered soldiers in their early fifties home.

Nor were the necessary 'machines of war' available. The 70th Artillery Brigade, for example, reported that it was short of 150 men and 300 horses. The 51st and 64th brigades stated unequivocally that they were immobilized by the lack of draught animals: individual batteries were down to only three or five horses; one had but a single animal to pull its guns.[45] And while the Army worked feverishly at its training schools at Brixen and Passariano to develop new manuals for the attack, these were not published until June.[46]

Most importantly, Austro-Hungarian military leaders from the Kaiser on down ignored the visible signs of rebellion among the troops especially in rear-echelon areas. Three weeks before the planned offensive in Venetia, War Minister Stöger-Steiner sent the Kaiser, the Ballhausplatz, and all senior commanders a report on seven recent mutinies.[47] On the night of 12–13 May, Slovenian reserves attached to the 17th (Kronprinz) Infantry Regiment at Judenburg had followed several noncommissioned officers 'like wild hordes' and for 6 hours plundered cafés, pubs, restaurants, merchant stores, silver and gold smiths, and a tobacco warehouse. The troops destroyed the local barracks and officers' mess, tore up railroad tracks, and riddled the train station and several cars with bullets, killing six soldiers and one civilian and injuring 17 others. Local machine-gun units were helpless against the marauders as they had no ammunition. Most of the mutineers disappeared into the nearby forests with thousands of pounds of flour and sugar taken from freight cars.[48] Eventually, loyal troops had to be brought in from Graz to put down the mutiny. Several rebels were shot; six ringleaders were summarily executed; 51 faced courts-martial; and most of the remaining 1200 eventually were rounded up. Two days later, some of the mutineers from Judenburg incited the 7th Jäger battalion at Murau to riot. Loyal units once more suppressed the rebellion and executed one of its leaders. A third outbreak, again marked by looting and plundering, affected the 80th Infantry Division at Rimaszombat. The fourth case, involving the 58th Infantry Regiment at Lublin, has already been mentioned.

On 20 May reserves of the 6th Infantry Division at Pécs rioted and killed two officers. It took loyal units 2 weeks to round up the mutineers. Four ringleaders were summarily executed while courts-martial awaited the remainder. In one of the largest uprisings, about 500 Czech soldiers of the 7th Reserve Rifle Battalion at Rumburg and Haida in northern Bohemia rioted for days; courts-martial awaited the ringleaders. Finally, several reserve units of the 97th Infantry Regiment at Radkersburg rebelled on 24 May, but their leaders were quickly arrested and placed before military tribunals.

Reserve units had instigated each of the revolts. Most had involved some of the 500 000 former Russian POWs detailed to rear-echelon formations.[49] Almost all of the mutineers – save the ringleaders – were disarmed and sent to the front. Not even the classic Habsburg practice of setting one ethnic group against another – in this case Hungarian against

Czech troops, and Czech and Bosnian against Hungarian – proved effective. The Foreign Ministry wryly noted that news of the mutinies had been leaked to the German press, and from there had found its way to the Entente. Could Conrad possibly have missed it?

In fact, Stöger-Steiner had failed to mention two other cases of insurrection. A bloody mutiny by the 71st Infantry Regiment at Kragujevac in Serbia was suppressed only with the aid of artillery and machine guns at the cost of 16 soldiers killed and 40 wounded.[50] And most of the Polish Auxiliary Corps had run over to the Russians; the rest were disarmed and the Corps disbanded on 19 February. More than 4800 Poles taken into custody by military police were sent to the Italian front, where in April they rioted against further fighting.[51] Laibach, Mostar, and Przemyśl also experienced military uprisings while the 'green cadres' continued to roam the countryside at will.

Yet the *AOK*, being without firm plans for 1918, was both embarrassed and paralysed by Conrad's operational barrages. Whatever one might say of Conrad, he at least was consistent in demanding an assault against the Italians out of his native Tyrol. In contrast, Field Marshal von Boroević, recently given his own army group consisting of the erstwhile Isonzo Army and a new Sixth Army (the former German Fourteenth Army), had developed a 'bunker mentality'. The Croat insisted on a defensive posture in Italy – especially when Vice Admiral Horthy denied his request for naval support. But, when pressed for an operations plan, Boroević came out for a suicidal frontal assault from Oderzo across the Piave in the direction of Treviso. Boroević had 14 divisions and wanted 23 or 24; Conrad had 16 and demanded 32. Neither apparently pondered on where they were going to get the 70 tons of food, 30 tons of ammunition, and 30 tons of fodder and other supplies that each division needed – while standing still! General von Waldstätten, Arz's deputy, favoured a broad offensive designed to pinch both Italian flanks, but with the main assault coming in the centre. He expected nothing less than a total collapse of the Italian front.

On 11 April, after having sent the *AOK* yet another operations plan, Conrad was summoned by the Kaiser to Baden. He at once decided to force a decision. Karl, who had advanced in just over 2 years from major to colonel-general and who fancied himself a military talent, revealed a glaring lack of strategic sense by decreeing that Boroević and Conrad were to launch two separate pincer attacks with 23 divisions each, one across the Piave and the other out of the Tyrol.[52] Karl thus ensured that neither attack would be decisive. The operations were codenamed 'Albrecht' (Boroević) and 'Radetzky' (Conrad) in honour of the two great Habsburg captains. The offensive by four armies was to be the largest in the course of the war.

Conrad had pressed his operational studies on the *AOK* suspecting that Ludendorff desired an Austro-Hungarian 'diversion' in the south while the *OHL* orchestrated an offensive on the Western Front. But whatever leverage the Dual Monarchy might have derived from this was quickly lost early in April, when Foreign Minister Czernin blundered into reopening the so-called 'Sixtus affair' of the previous year. In an important address to the Vienna Municipal Council on 2 April, Czernin stated that the French had been prepared for peace negotiations in 1917, but that these had foundered on Premier Georges Clemenceau's demand that Alsace-Lorraine be 'returned' to France. Czernin allowed that he had rejected the 'Old Tiger's' demands out of loyalty to Berlin.

Clemenceau was hardly the man to stand for this gross distortion: on 12 April he had *L'Illustration* print Prince Sixtus' letter in its entirety, thereby revealing to all the world Karl's written acknowledgment of France's 'just claims' to Alsace-Lorraine. Panicked by Czernin's suicide threats should he not declare on his honour that he had never sent the letter via Sixtus, Karl worsened an already dreadful situation by stating that the 'Sixtus letter' was a forgery! He informed the German Ambassador, Wedel, that 'he was as innocent as a newborn child'.[53] Few believed him. There was talk in Vienna of a regency under either Archdukes Friedrich or Eugen.

German leaders spoke openly of perfidy by the House of Habsburg, and made caustic references to Karl's role as a 'dual' monarch.[54] Patriotic Austrians in the Tyrol detected the hand of the 'Italian' Empress Zita behind the affair, and as newfound 'Bavarians' mounted public demonstrations of loyalty to Germany. The Czechs, fearing that a separate peace could translate into a German occupation of Bohemia, likewise protested about the Kaiser's diplomatic odyssey. Egged on by Zita, Karl forced a tearful Czernin to yield his post at the Ballhausplatz within 48 hours. Innsbruck and Salzburg were draped in black out of a sense of grief and shame. As his last act as Foreign Minister, Czernin fired off a communiqué stating that the 'Sixtus letter' was 'fictitious from beginning to end'.[55] Karl sought to save face with the Germans by blaming the affair on Czernin, and by assuring them that 'his cannons' would give the French the proper response along the Western Front. Clemenceau's 'Sixtus' bombshell convinced both the Allies and the Germans that the House of Habsburg could not be trusted. Karl's word was worthless. Brokers in London noted that aristocratic clans such as the Counts Clam-Martinic, Clary, and Czernin put their estates in Bohemia and Moravia on the market.

On 12 May Karl was forced to travel to German headquarters at Spa – the so-called pilgrimage to Canossa – to apologize for his actions. The

Germans demanded nothing less than a binding political, military, and economic alliance, thereby committing Vienna to what was now popularly called the 'German course'. Specifically, Hindenburg inked an agreement with Arz von Straussenburg calling on both Empires to mobilize their entire peoples; every eligible male 'must pass through the school of the Army'. Organization, training, and deployment of troops were to be coordinated between Berlin and Vienna, and weapons and munitions standardized. Officers were to be exchanged regularly, rail networks expanded by common consent, and preparations for war 'mutually arrived at'.[56] No one asked why this had not been the case in 1914.

Weakened by Clemenceau's revelations and recognizing the need to raise the Dual Monarchy's fortunes, Karl yielded to Conrad's operational bravado. The attack out of the Tyrol, originally scheduled for 28 May, was delayed two weeks due to transport difficulties. It also lost the element of surprise when deserters and wireless intercepts apprised the Italians, strengthened by five British and French divisions, of the impending assault. Snow in the mountains delayed supply: Conrad's staff estimated that 2 million artillery rounds remained in depots on the opening day of the attack; and more than 50 batteries of artillery were still struggling to move up to the front. Artillery and infantry were short roughly 6000 horses, with the result that soldiers routinely spent 4 to 6 hours per day hauling supplies on their backs up steep mountain paths. Troops had barely half of the requisite 3-days' provisions.[57] And on 5 June Italian artillery severely pounded Conrad's marshalling positions, destroying two artillery parks.

After almost a week of steady rain, Conrad's Eleventh Army on 15 June 1918 attacked along a broad 50-mile front between Astico and the Piave River. The artillery bombardment commenced at 3 a.m., and infantry stormed enemy positions four hours later. Conrad's troops, like those of Napoleon Bonaparte in 1796, pressed forward in hopes of raiding bountiful Italian food depots and garnering bounty money – 50 Kronen for a French prisoner of war, 500 for an enemy aircraft downed by ground fire, and 3000 for a hostile plane forced to land behind Austrian lines.[58] Conrad dreamed of entering Venice; Boroević wanted to reach Padua via Treviso. Conrad's forces made some initial progress, but by late afternoon were repulsed by the stiff Anglo-French defence. Allied artillery tore up Conrad's telegraph lines and completely overpowered his guns. By 16 June, the Eleventh Army was back in its original positions, low on food and ammunition, demoralized. It had lost more than 1000 officers and 45 000 men. The planned pincer envelopment of the Italians from the Tyrol and along the Adriatic Sea now gave way to the Battle of the Piave – a straight frontal assault across the river.

Field Marshal von Boroević, attacking in the direction of Oderzo-Treviso, opened his offensive with a gas-shell attack in dense fog and smoke at 3 a.m. on 15 June. At 5:30 a.m. he ordered his infantry to cross the Piave. The Sixth Army managed to establish a 15-mile-wide by 5-mile-deep bridgehead on the river, but then its waters rose suddenly to three times their normal level. Allied air forces destroyed the Croat's pontoon bridges by 18 June. Boroević's pilots reported that their water-cooled machine guns froze at high altitudes and that hostile phosphoric bullets ignited their linen-covered craft: the Austrians lost 269 of 382 airplanes. Low on supplies and demoralized, Boroević's troops faced certain Allied counterattacks. Peter Fiala, an Austrian historian of the June offensive, states that the evening of 15 June constituted the '*Götterdämmerung* of Austro-Hungarian strategy'.[59] The following day, Colonel Ottokar Pflug of the logistics branch reported that the last 29 supply trains had been sent to the front. There would be no more.

Panic-stricken, Karl raced his special train first to Conrad's headquarters to inquire into the demise of the Eleventh Army, and then toward the Piave to consult Boroević. On 19 June the Kaiser discussed the military situation with the Croat. 'General consternation' was recorded on both sides. Karl pleaded with Boroević: 'Hold your positions. I beg you to do this in the name of the Monarchy'.[60] Boroević reminded Karl that he had opposed Conrad's frontal assault out of the Tyrol from the start with the query, 'But one does not want to grab the bull by the horns?' To which Karl lamely replied: 'But Conrad wanted it'.[61] The next day, the Kaiser called off the attack. Boroević's forces were saved from annihilation only by General Diaz's failure to hurl his reserve of six Italian divisions against the Habsburg units struggling to recross the Piave.

The aborted offensive had been bloody. In the 9 days between 15 and 25 June, the Austro-Hungarian Army lost 142 550 men, including 11 643 dead and 24 474 prisoners of war; Allied losses were set at 84 830 soldiers, including 8030 killed.[62] Especially the infantry had suffered terribly due to lusty sacrifice and lack of artillery support. Food supplies had been exhausted and the expectations of plundering Allied depots disappointed. Karl dispatched two divisions as well as 46 batteries of heavy artillery to the Western Front to assuage the Germans.

Arz von Straussenburg sent the Military Chancery his confidential assessment of the battle on 14 July. He began with a patronizing defence of the operation, claiming that it had spared his troops an 'equally bloody, sacrificial defensive battle'. By tying down Allied forces on the Piave, he suggested, Vienna had in fact defended the Rhine! As to specific reasons for the defeat, Arz stated that gas shells had proved ineffective because the Italians had been outfitted with new British gas masks and because it had rained on 15 June. Deserters, including Czech officers from the 56th Infantry Regiment, had betrayed the time of the attack. The Chief of the General Staff failed to mention that rigidly-timed rolling barrages did not work either while fighting in the mountainous terrain of the Tyrol or while fording a major river in Venetia.

Finally, Arz argued that Austro-Hungarian soldiers simply were not as good as German. Officers lacked the 'originality' of their northern colleagues. Nor were they steeped in the 'Prusso-German military tradition'. With regard to the rank and file, each German soldier benefited from 'cultural development, moral power, and sense of duty'. The Germans, in short, were 'an organized people'; 'all for one and one for all'. By contrast, the very diversity of the Multinational Empire militated against the development of such military and cultural cohesion.[63]

The Chief of the General Staff's strange lamentations were given more substance after the war by the Austrian official history. It censured Conrad generally for once more having undertaken an assault without proper regard for terrain, and specifically for having launched a frontal attack against eight enemy divisions well-entrenched in a deep forest. 'There is hardly an example in military history . . . where an army has conducted an attack against a forest in closed formations according to plan.'[64] Equally, the official history condemned Boroević's decision to press across the Piave without sufficient numerical superiority or proper equipment. It failed to point out that the Allies, in addition to the extensive use of machine guns, flamethrowers, and trench mortars, had established an 'elastic defence' wherein the front lines were only sparsely manned and thus beyond the reach of Habsburg gunners.

A 'broken man', Conrad was dismissed on 15 July 1918 – and raised into the peerage with the title of count. The Magyar Archduke Joseph succeeded as commander in the Tyrol. Arz submitted his resignation to Karl both orally and in writing, but the Kaiser refused to admit poor judgment by sacking 'his Arz' as Conrad's successor. Boroević took the brunt of charges of military incompetence and even treason. Incredibly, on 21 July Arz's staff penned a new list of war aims that called for the annexation of Serbia and Montenegro. Line officers joked that Kaiser Karl had issued his ban on duelling to prevent them from killing General Staff officers!

Parliaments in both Budapest and Vienna railed against the military fiasco. Hungarian deputies again demanded a separate Magyar army, while their counterparts in Austria openly accused Empress Zita of treason. It was decided in the best tradition of bureaucratic obfuscation to establish a committee to investigate the origins of the defeat on the Piave. The report, finally submitted in December 1921 by two members of

Conrad's former staff, Glaise-Horstenau and Ratzenhofer, caused a storm of protest as it totally exonerated the *AOK*![65]

The Battle of the Piave, while not a decisive battle in terms of territorial gains or losses, nevertheless destroyed what remained of the *k.u.k.* Army. Within 3 months, the number of Habsburg troops in Italy melted from 406 000 to 238 900; that of combatants from 252 950 to 146 650. Conservative estimates are that 200 000 soldiers deserted and that their numbers doubled by September. The *Honvéd* Ministry in Budapest calculated that 200 000 deserters were on the loose in Transleithania alone. Military officials in Galicia claimed to be looking for 30 000 deserters, while the fortress commander at Przemyśl noted that 20 000 soldiers refused to report back from leave.[66] The seven infantry divisions posted in the interior to combat unrest and rebellion never returned to the front. While the War Ministry continued to list a paper strength of 57 divisions in Italy, in reality these had the combat strength of only 37 full divisions.[67] There can be no question that the Austro-Hungarian Army began to disintegrate immediately after Conrad's last offensive.

Germany: mutinies, strikes, and megalomania

Germany experienced turbulent political and social unrest in 1917–18. Buoyed by victory in the east, Ludendorff was in no mood to condone criticism or even independence of thought and action at home. He levelled his guns at Bethmann Hollweg and on 13 July 1917 forced the Chancellor to resign. Crown Prince Wilhelm deemed it to be the happiest day of his life.

No single issue brought about either the rupture or the resignation. In truth, a world separated Bethmann Hollweg from Ludendorff. While the latter was the classic self-made man who had risen from humble origins in Posen to run the General Staff, Bethmann Hollweg had been born into a life of easy wealth and power on the family estate of Hohenfinow on the Oder River. The offspring of Prussian nobility and Frankfurt banking money, Bethmann Hollweg had studied law and pursued a brilliant career in the Prussian civil service that ultimately led to the posts of State Secretary of the Interior (1907) and then Chancellor (1909). While Ludendorff saw the world in either–or terms of black or white, right or wrong, good or bad, friend or foe, Bethmann Hollweg dabbled in the grey regions of nuance, subtlety, and compromise. In the spring of 1915 both men had made common cause against Falkenhayn, whom both wished to remove from power. That having been accomplished in August 1916, little remained to hold this marriage of convenience together.

In the winter of 1916–17 Bethmann Hollweg had challenged some of the assumptions underlying both the Hindenburg Programme and the Auxiliary Service Law and had waffled on the issue of unrestricted submarine warfare. From the perspective of the *OHL*, he was too reluctant to take an unequivocal stand on annexations and indemnities and to demand that the war be fought to a victorious end. For example, while Ludendorff simply demanded vast annexations in the east as the spoils of victory, Bethmann Hollweg toyed with the notion of creating 'buffer states' east of the Vistula so as to square the circle between his promise of an 'honourable' peace with Russia and his pledge to oppose the Left's peace without victory. Moreover, the Chancellor had floated his own peace initiative in December 1916 and had promised Prussian constitutional reform at Easter 1917. Could he be trusted to lead the nation via 'total war' to a Carthaginian peace?

The Reichstag was due to reconvene and vote on war credits early in July 1917. Bethmann Hollweg and Hindenburg/Ludendorff exchanged a series of notes in June which left do doubt in the *OHL* that the Chancellor was drifting too far into the camp of the socialists, pacifists, and democrats. Ludendorff believed that Bethmann Hollweg was caving in to the forces behind the Russian revolution; Conservatives argued that the Chancellor's 'moderate' politics would end with a republic; and Hindenburg accused Bethmann Hollweg of 'unfortunately' nurturing 'gloomy views'. 'We will not go along with that.'[68] On 6 July the Centre Party leader, Matthias Erzberger, shocked the nation by stating that victory was no longer within reach; 24 hours later a parliamentary Main Committee consisting of Progressive, Centre, and Social Democratic deputies introduced a 'peace resolution' in the Reichstag calling for an end to the war 'without annexations and indemnities'. That same day Hindenburg openly questioned Bethmann Hollweg's right to rule; on 12 July he and Ludendorff submitted their resignations, refusing any longer to work with the Chancellor. Wilhelm II had no choice but to beg the two soldiers to remain in office.

While Bethmann as usual sought to steer a middle course between the 'peace resolution' and his own war aims and attempted to persuade the Kaiser to place himself at the head of a popular, plebiscitary monarchy (*Kaiser im Volksstaat*), Ludendorff demanded a clear choice between the *OHL* and the Chancellor. On the evening of 11 July, Crown Prince Wilhelm for the first time in Prusso-German history invited a cross-section of parliamentary leaders ranging from the Centre Party to the National Liberals, from the Social Democrats to the Progressives, to ascertain whether they supported the Chancellor. Ludendorff's alter ego, Colonel Bauer, hid in an anteroom and kept a record of the talks.[69] The following day the Crown Prince apprised his father of the unanimous feeling among the politicians that the Chancellor no longer served the national interest. Bethmann Hollweg, ever the loyal servant, resigned on 13 July.

Bethmann Hollweg had been a fervent advocate neither of a dictated victor's peace nor of a negotiated moderate peace. Instead, he had vacillated between the two poles represented by the *OHL* and the Social Democrats. Throughout his tenure in office, the 'German Hamlet' had fluctuated between hope and resignation. His stewardship at the Chancellery had lacked direction, firmness, and consequence. His enemies pointed out that in July 1914 he had plunged Germany into a war against a superior coalition, and that in January 1917 he had accepted war with the United States as the price for unrestricted submarine warfare. They charged that Bethmann Hollweg rejected long-term goals for short-term gains.

The Chancellor's critics from both Right and Left in July 1917 joined forces temporarily and accused him of having conducted an aimless, zigzag national policy. At times he had favoured a separate peace either with France or with Russia. At other times he had pursued a policy of accommodation and then again of firmness with regard to the major neutrals. Then again, he had favoured restoring Belgian and establishing Polish independence – only to cave in at the first sign of resistance by the military or heavy industry. And at various times, Bethmann Hollweg had spoken either for or against unrestricted submarine warfare. In the process, he had developed no firm base of support in the Reichstag or among the German people. His departure from office was mourned by few.

Wilhelm II found himself on the horns of a dilemma. The two most popular putative successors were Grand Admiral von Tirpitz and former Chancellor von Bülow. The Kaiser detested both: Bülow had 'betrayed' him in peace, and Tirpitz had committed 'treason' in war.[70] Thus, Wilhelm on 14 July went along with the *OHL*'s choice of Georg Michaelis, a colourless bureaucrat and since February 1917 state commissioner for the national food supply, to succeed Bethmann Hollweg. The Kaiser's total knowledge of his new Chancellor, the first non-aristocrat in that position, was that 'he is supposed to be short, a midget'.[71] One of Michaelis' first acts was to kill with faint praise the Reichstag's 'peace resolution', formally passed by a vote of 212 to 126 on 19 July, by promising to support it 'as I understand it'. On 19 September Michaelis rejected Pope Benedict XV's offer to mediate a peace. His handlers within the *OHL* demanded victory at any price, and Michaelis accepted their rationale.

These internecine manipulations resonated little among a general populace that was hungry, cold, and weary of war. Henrich von Oppen, Police President of Greater Berlin, informed the Ministry of the Interior that most people believed that it would be 'business as usual' under Michaelis. In a report that Oppen later censored for fear of its brutal honesty, he suggested that the public was gripped by a mood of 'despondency and fear of the future'. Women stormed food centres. Public kitchens could not meet the demand for meals. The 'food question' dominated daily life; 'all other [considerations] receive little attention'. Few Berliners were willing to make additional sacrifices, and many stated openly that any peace was better than continuation of the war. 'One fears the fourth winter of the war.'[72]

There was good reason to fear the future. Hunger and war weariness reached every sector of German society, but especially the industrial workers in its major ports. Kiel, a city of about 220 000 inhabitants, went without potatoes from the beginning of January to the end of March 1917. Workers at its two principal shipyards, Germaniawerft and Howaldtswerke, went on strike on 27 March; the next day, they were joined by their comrades at the Imperial Shipyard and the Torpedo Yard. The men demanded bread, potatoes, and meat. Attempts by the Germaniawerft to send 100 strike leaders to the front were rejected by the Prussian War Ministry.[73] Only immediate promises of extra food brought the workers back to the yards.

Germany's other naval port, Wilhelmshaven, experienced more serious revolts. By July 1917, morale on the capital ships of the High Sea Fleet had plummeted to deplorable levels. The last sortie against the Grand Fleet had been in October 1916 and idleness and boredom gnawed at the spirits of the sailors. Minor issues took on unwarranted proportions. Petty injustices, whether real or imagined, gave rise to heated debate. The steady diet of turnips and dehydrated vegetables, inadequate shore leave, and the transfer of the best subaltern officers to the U-boats combined to create an atmosphere of distrust and anger. Young cadets and reserve officers unaccustomed to command substituted petty drill for military readiness. In an attempt to assuage some of the food complaints emanating from the High Sea Fleet, Admiral von Capelle, State Secretary of the Navy Office, offered that the sailors could establish food supervisory committees on the ships. But when numerous officers refused to accede to this concession, passive resistance yielded to open mutiny.

On 2 August about 600 sailors of the battleship *Prinzregent Luitpold* left the vessel and headed for the little village of Rüstersiel to vent their displeasure with conditions on board. Men from other units, including the battleships *Friedrich der Grosse*, *Kaiser*, *Kaiserin*, and *Westfalen* as well as the cruiser *Pillau*, joined the revolt. Naval authorities in Wilhelmshaven called out police and shore patrols, placed the *Prinzregent Luitpold* under siege, and charged the rebellious sailors with mutiny and political conspiracy. The latter charge originated from reports that about 5000 men had recently joined the Independent Social Democratic Party (USPD) and that they had conferred with parliamentary deputies about the upcoming Socialists Congress in Stockholm.[74]

Germany's senior admirals quickly decided to strike not only against the rebellious sailors, but especially against the radical USPD. Admiral Franz von Hipper, Chief of Scouting Forces, detected what he termed an 'anarchist movement' afoot, and he demanded that the Navy 'ruthlessly put a few [mutineers] against the wall'.[75] Vice Admiral Georg Hebbinghaus of the Navy Office, sent by Berlin to investigate the mutinies, immediately saw the utility of using the uprisings as 'a weapon against the left-wing socialists', whom he denounced as 'scoundrels and traitors'.[76] Apparently the naval courts agreed: on 26 August they convicted five sailors of giving aid to a foreign power and of 'treasonable incitement to rebellion'. Admiral Scheer, Chief of the High Sea Fleet, reviewed the cases on 2 September, having let it be known previously that he was anxious for 'a few death sentences'. Two sailors were executed 3 days later; the other three received lengthy prison terms.

The mutinies might well have ended then and there had it not been for the Chancellor's political blundering. Informed – albeit, incorrectly – that one of the rebellious sailors had confessed the existence of a plot against His Majesty, Michaelis decided early in October to censure the USPD in the Reichstag. He informed parliament that the Independent Social Democrats 'threaten[ed] the existence of the German Reich'. Tumultuous scenes ensued. Admiral von Capelle, speaking for the Navy, was repeatedly interrupted by interjections and catcalls. Friedrich Ebert, head of the million-member Social Democratic Party (SPD), saw Michaelis' actions as nothing less than an attempt to set aside parliamentary immunity. He concluded his speech with an implicit threat: 'We shall be glad for every day sooner that the German people are freed from this government'.[77] Ebert did not have long to wait: faced by a solid Reichstag majority from the Catholic Centre Party to the USPD against him, Michaelis tendered his resignation on 31 October. He was replaced on 1 November by the septuagenarian Bavarian Catholic, Georg Count von Hertling.

The Reichstag debates revealed that the Navy had indeed been permeated with politics – but from the Right. In July 1917 Ludendorff, impressed with Britain's Department of Information, had ordered 'patriotic instruction' (*Vaterländischer Unterricht*) for all troops. Initially, the Navy's efforts were amateur: officers read their men heroic sagas of the

House of Hohenzollern. But in time the effort became more sophisticated: right-wing pamphlets and papers were brought on to ships and naval bases; civilians lectured about the evils of parliamentary government; a Picture and Film Office (BUFA) was established in Berlin; and Pan-German speakers railed about the need for expansion.[78] Unsurprisingly, many sailors turned to union workers in the large shipyards for socialist reading materials.

The Right's propagandistic efforts received a tremendous boost on 2 September, Sedan Day, when retired Grand Admiral von Tirpitz and the Prussian bureaucrat Wolfgang Kapp, the son of an 1848 liberal, founded the German Fatherland Party at Königsberg. German industrialists such as Stinnes lavishly financed the *Vaterlands-Partei*, which campaigned for victory and an annexationist peace, and against suffrage reform in Prussia as well as the Reichstag's peace resolution. Tirpitz's clarion call, 'Germany awake, your hour of destiny has arrived!', had great appeal: within 6 months of its founding, the Party boasted 1.25 million members, thereby surpassing the SPD as the Reich's largest political organization. Specifically, Tirpitz argued that a peace which did not leave Belgium in German hands translated into 'Germany's demise and the victory of Anglo-American capitalism'.[79] Military and naval authorities, in principle opposed to politicization of the armed forces, turned a blind eye to the activities of the Fatherland Party.[80]

By the winter of 1917, German politics were hopelessly polarized. On the Left stood the USPD and SPD, representing labour and seeking a 'Scheidemann peace'[81] without annexations or indemnities. On the Right stood the Fatherland Party as the political arm of the Supreme Command and the Monarchy, demanding a 'Hindenburg peace' with vast annexations and huge indemnities. Few political observers any longer paid even lip service to the *Burgfriede* of August 1914.

Unrest came to a head in January 1918, when a wave of strikes swept the Reich.[82] The strikes, like those earlier in the Dual Monarchy, were driven by three major concerns: hunger, cold, and war weariness. But, again as in the Austro-Hungarian case, the strikers also had political motives: suffrage reform in Prussia, speedy conclusion of peace negotiations with the Bolsheviks at Brest-Litovsk then being held up by German demands for territorial gains, and an end to the domestic 'state of siege' that had existed since August 1914. The strikes were to highlight the desperate plight of labour, not to simulate the Bolshevik example in Petrograd. They were led in the main by so-called 'revolutionary foremen' elected by workers in individual factories and not by leaders of either of the two socialist parties.

On 25 January the workers of the Torpedo Yard in Kiel walked off their jobs to protest the Navy's decision to send several of their 'foremen' to the front as punishment for public demonstrations for food. Within 72 hours, the number of strikers had reached 24 000. By 28 January they were joined by tens of thousands of workers in Berlin; 2 days later the police estimated the number at 185 000 from 299 factories.[83] Daily food consumption had fallen from 3000 calories in peacetime to just 1400 by 1918. The first violent confrontations between workers and police took place at Berlin-Moabit. Ambassador zu Hohenlohe's cables once more captured the anxiety of the moment. On 29 January he informed Vienna that at least 150 000 workers were on strike. Especially hard-hit around the capital were the German General Electric (AEG) aircraft plant in Reinickendorf and its gunpowder factory in Henningsdorf; the Daimler Motor factory in Marienfelde; the Rumpler Airplane Works in Johannisthal; Borsig in Tegel; and the Artillery plant at Spandau. Specific demands by the strikers included better food, an end to the 'state of siege', the release of all political prisoners, peace in the east, and the vote in Prussia for all men and women over the age of 20. The next day Hohenlohe informed the Ballhausplatz that 350 000 men were on strike in Berlin alone; on 31 January he reported that martial law had been declared in Hamburg and Brandenburg. The first instances of violence occurred on 1 February as trams were overturned, electric wires cut, police shot at (including one killed), and many government officials stoned in the streets.[84]

Consular reports supported Hohenlohe's claims. On 1 February the Habsburg Consul in Bremen cabled that one-third of the work force at the Weser AG yards, about 3000 men, had gone on strike, and that 8000 labourers in Lübeck likewise had walked off their jobs demanding better and more food. The Austro-Hungarian envoy at Cologne that same day reported strikes in eight metal factories as well as ancillary walkouts by about 4000 workers. But the Consul in Essen stated that only 400 employees of Friedrich Krupp's 11 000 had gone on strike; the vast majority remained on the job as they were well-paid and well-provisioned by the company.[85]

By 4 February, Ambassador zu Hohenlohe's reports took on a political tone. He informed Foreign Minister Czernin that the strikes constituted a 'pure political demonstration of the working classes'. Strikers in Hamburg, for example, demonstrated against the right-wing Fatherland Party. The deteriorating quality of life for German workers during the war now brought out 'with crass clarity' the 'development of class warfare as a result of the social upheavals of this war'.[86] The Ambassador had never before used – nor would he ever again use – terms such as 'class warfare' and 'political demonstration of the working classes' in his official communiqués.

The Prussian Army, which had received word of the planned walkouts on 25 January and thereupon alerted all commanders under the codename 'Start', played down the nature and size of the strikes. Most military leaders attributed them to 'Entente money' – 250 million Marks allegedly from President Wilson alone[87] – as well as the Bolshevik example. They also denied the role of local initiative and claimed that strike leaders came directly from the SPD and the USPD. Crown Prince Wilhelm and his staff demanded swift action: 'Dictatorship. Suppression of all revolutionary activity. Exemplary punishment for all deserters and shirkers, militarization of armaments factories, [and] expulsion of questionable foreigners'.[88]

On 5 February War Minister Hermann von Stein informed Wilhelm II that the workers had been led astray by 'external' impulses such as the Russian revolution and the Austro-Hungarian strikes earlier in the month. The General reported that on 28 January about 45 000 workers in Berlin's 38 most important armaments plants had walked off their jobs; by 30 January, their numbers had risen to between 150 000 and 180 000; and then they receded to 140 000 by the last day of the month. In Hamburg and Kiel, about 23 000 shipyard workers had gone on strike on 28 and 29 January, respectively; 3600 dock workers had also struck at Bremen. In the Ruhr and the Rhineland, roughly 20 000 metal workers and 15 000 miners had walked off their jobs. Almost 17 000 labourers had gone on strike at Halle and Magdeburg in central Germany, and 53 000 in the Nürnberg-Fürth region of Bavaria. Finally, 3500 men had refused to report for work in Saxony and 2500 (mainly youths) in Silesia. Smaller demonstrations had also occurred at Altona, Lübeck, Rostock, and Schwerin.

Stein vowed not to 'tolerate Soviets on the Russian model', and informed the Kaiser that seven 'radical' factories in Brandenburg had been placed under military law and their strike leaders sent to the front. The USPD deputy Wilhelm Dittmann had been arrested and sentenced by an extraordinary military tribunal to 5 years imprisonment for 'attempted treason'. Four battalions of *Jäger* released by the *OHL* supported local police and militia in keeping order. The War Minister claimed that the strikes were 'of no significant importance' to the overall war effort. Only work on three tanks was seriously jeopardized as all three factories producing tanks in Berlin had been struck. The Navy would receive about 140 torpedoes fewer in February, which 'has no immediate impact on the conduct of the war', and U-boat production would be slowed only by 8 days – that is, the duration of the strike.[89]

General Gustav von Kessel, Commander-in-Chief in Brandenburg, assured Wilhelm II as early as 6 February 'that the revolt can be regarded as having ended'. Kessel stated that the number of strikers had never surpassed 170 000, and that radical leaders had 'terrorized' most workers into participating. Like Stein the day before, Kessel vowed 'ruthlessly to suppress any attempt to introduce Russian conditions' in the Mark. The 'unenlightened masses' of workers understood only force. The 'primary result' of the strikes was that the workers, in contrast to Austria–Hungary, had resumed work 'unconditionally and without any concessions' by the government.[90] Regional commanders took similarly harsh stands against the distribution of socialist pamphlets, public speeches on behalf of strikes, demonstrations, and even the publication of strike numbers.[91]

While the size of the strikes remains disputed – ranging from the Army's figure of 170 000 to the SPD's counter of half a million in Berlin and an equal number outside the capital – the motives behind them seem relatively clear. In economic terms, the workers demanded more food at lower prices, an end to the black market, prosecution of war profiteers, and freedom to work wherever they chose. Politically, they demonstrated for an end to the war and the 'state of siege', suffrage reform in Prussia, and a speedy peace with Russia.[92] Neither the summary sentencing of Dittmann nor the closing of the SPD's newspaper *Vorwärts* could obscure the fact that the impetus for the strikes had come not from the two organized workers' parties, but rather from elected factory 'revolutionary foremen'. Ominously, in May soldiers in Erlangen and Munich rampaged through the streets and vandalized city halls to protest the war.

Ludendorff had instructed Chancellor von Hertling as early as 30 January to arrest the leaders of the Berlin strikes. Eventually, about 150 ringleaders were taken into custody and between 3500 and 6000 strikers sent to the front as a result of the 'militarization' of factories.[93] The Army had effectively broken the strike. Hohenlohe informed Vienna that 1 May, the traditional day of labour which fell within 4 days of the centenary of Karl Marx's birth, had gone by quietly. But he noted the same of 15 June, the 30th anniversary of Wilhelm II's coronation.[94]

In a strange, almost perverse way the strikes strengthened the *OHL*'s hand at a critical time. At Brest-Litovsk the Central Powers were negotiating a victor's peace with the Bolsheviks, while at Spa Ludendorff planned his great offensive in France for 1918. Few checks, if any, existed to curb the near-absolute 'silent dictatorship' of the Supreme Command. The Kaiser had long been relegated to the background, a pathetic figurehead. Colonel Bauer at the *OHL* had even suggested at the height of the January strikes that Wilhelm II be asked simply to resign 'for some time' as he had become superfluous to the war effort. Ludendorff stated openly: 'The German *Volk* stands higher with me than the person of the Kaiser'.[95] The 74-year-old Chancellor, Hertling, could hardly be expected to act as a brake on the Supreme Command. In fact, Hindenburg and Ludendorff in January made it abundantly clear to Hertling that they 'bore the responsibility before the German people for the conduct of the war and its end result'.[96]

Specifically, Hindenburg and Ludendorff brooked no opposition to their megalomaniacal plans for the east. They were not amused when Foreign Secretary Richard von Kühlmann, an experienced bureaucratic infighter, made common front with his Austro-Hungarian counterpart, Czernin, to obtain a quick 'bread peace' with Lenin that would entail only minor 'border revisions' at Russia's expense. The two diplomats wanted a separate peace with Russia and a general peace with the Entente. The two generals adamantly rejected a moderate settlement and instead demanded a victor's peace that would dismember Russia, annex its 'border states', and accord the Reich a favourable strategic position for a future war in the east. They saw especially the Baltic states of Latvia, Lithuania, and Estonia not only as 'settlement areas' for German soldiers and Russian Volga Germans, but also as a 'wall of German people against Slavdom'.[97] Both repeatedly threatened to resign should their wishes not become official policy.

The negotiations at Brest-Litovsk broke down in January 1918 in an almost Kafkaesque drama of posturing, manipulating, threatening surrealism. When Czernin warned the Germans that he would conclude a separate peace with the Bolsheviks should their demands be too extreme, Wilhelm II lowered Austria–Hungary to the rank of 'perfidious' Italy, while General Hoffmann of *OberOst* welcomed the suggestion with the sarcastic retort that this would free up 25 German divisions currently shoring up Austria's eastern front! And when Trotsky on 10 February announced that the Bolsheviks refused to surrender '18 governments of the Russian Empire' and that they would neither accept German terms nor renew the war ('no war, no peace'), Reich leaders convened at Bad Homburg 3 days later to chart their future course of action.

Few, if any, German statesmen and soldiers had taken note of President Wilson's sweeping peace proposal to a joint session of Congress on 8 January 1918. The Fourteen Points called, among other things, for an end to secret treaties and secret diplomacy, freedom of the sea, restoration of Belgium, creation of an independent Poland, surrender of Alsace-Lorraine to France, acceptance of the principle of self-determination, and establishment of a general association of nations 'for the purpose of affording mutual guarantees of political independence and territorial integrity to great and small nations alike'.[98] And few in Berlin were sufficiently astute to notice that Trotsky in December 1917 had already pre-empted Wilson's moralization concerning the self-determination of peoples by calling on Britain and France to apply the doctrine to Ireland, Egypt, India, Madagascar, and Indochina!

The Bad Homburg Crown Council of 13 February 1918, coming just four days after the Central Powers had imposed a so-called 'bread peace' on Ukraine, offers insight into the mindset of German leaders. Wilhelm II was in fine fettle and wished to dismember 'Greater Russia' into four lesser 'empires': Ukraine, Central Russia, Siberia, and a Union of the Southeast. Poland was to fall to the House of Württemberg, Lithuania to the House of Saxony, the rest of the Baltic states to the House of Hohenzollern, and Finland to his son Oskar (it later went instead to Friedrich Karl Prince of Hesse). The Kaiser demanded that the Bolsheviks 'be beaten to death'; perhaps encircled and shot down in a manner 'akin to a tiger hunt'.[99]

Hindenburg seconded this stance. 'We must defeat the Russians.' Claiming that he needed the Baltic states 'for the manoeuvring of my left wing in the next war', the Field Marshal proposed a policy of *divide et impera* and demanded that hostilities be resumed within the week. The decisive stance at Bad Homburg proved to be that of Ludendorff, who called for 'clarity' in the east. 'Clarity' meant that Estonia, Livonia, Finland, and Ukraine were to be truncated from 'Greater Russia' and the Bolsheviks, now that they had served their historic purpose, 'overthrown'. Later in the day, Ludendorff hinted that his annexationist demands ran as far east as Armenia, Georgia, and the Caspian Sea. Only after mopping up the Bolsheviks, he allowed, could the great offensive in France begin. The General put forth his ambitious programme secure in the knowledge that he enjoyed the support of German industrialists and bankers such as Hugo Bruhn, Karl Helfferich, Alfred Hugenberg, Emil Kirdorf, Peter Klöckner, and August Thyssen, among others, who promised 2 billion Marks to exploit the east.

Hertling and Kühlmann were aghast at the prospect of renewed fighting, and both flirted with tendering their resignations that day. Instead, Kühlmann tried to appeal to reason and history. The Bolsheviks, he suggested, should simply be allowed 'to fry in their own fat' while Germany moved 'every man and every gun' from Russia to the Western Front. The Foreign Secretary lectured Hindenburg and Ludendorff that Germany could no more retard the ideology of Bolshevism than 'Old Europe' had reversed that of the French Revolution in 1792–3. Bismarck's 'moderation' in dealing with defeated France in 1871 should serve as a model to policymakers in 1918. Above all, Kühlmann argued that Russia remain in the pentarchy of European powers and reminded the military duumvirate that one could not rationally proceed in the east 'with the pen in one hand and the sword in the other'. Last but not least, Kühlmann warned that Austria–Hungary could not survive the strains of a new war.

On 18–19 February more than 50 German divisions renewed the war in the east under the codename *Faustschlag*: a northern army composed of 16 divisions marched from Pskov to Narva; a middle contingent (Tenth Army and XLI Army Corps) headed for Smolensk; and a southern force occupied Ukraine. Concurrently, Turkish units marched into the Caucasus as far as Baku. General Hoffmann termed the military campaign nothing more than a leisurely stroll by train and car. Dvinsk fell to the Germans on the first day of operations, Narva by 26 February, and Kiev by 1 March. On 3 March Lenin agreed to terms at Brest-Litovsk – while German units stormed the Caucasus and the Crimea. An amphibious force took Helsinki on 13 April; German troops rounded up 25 000 Red Army soldiers and occupied Finland by the end of the month.

The Treaty of Brest-Litovsk, which Wilhelm II called one of the 'greatest successes in world history'[100] and which only the Independent Socialists opposed, sheds light on the terms that a victorious Germany would probably have imposed on the Entente. Russia was forced to recognize the 'independence' of Finland and Ukraine; Lithuania, Estonia, Courland, and Livonia were turned over to German 'police forces'; Poland was separated from Russia, awaiting final disposition between Berlin and Vienna; and Russian forces had to evacuate all 'border lands'. Russia lost about 90 per cent of its coal mines, 50 per cent of its industry, and 30 per cent of its population. Under a separate treaty negotiated on 9 February, Germany was to receive 30 per cent, Austria–Hungary 50 per cent, and Bulgaria and Turkey 20 per cent of Ukraine's grain reserves. And bilateral supplementary treaties concluded in August detached Estonia and Livonia from Soviet Russia, which was to pay 6 billion Marks in reparations.

On 7 May Germany signed the Treaty of Bucharest, whereby the Reich acquired 56 per cent and Austria–Hungary 24 per cent of a 99-year monopoly on Romanian oil fields. Hungary gained some strategic frontier posts in the Carpathian Mountains and Bulgaria obtained part of the Dobruja. Although Romania was allowed to keep the former Russian province of Bessarabia, it was effectively reduced to a German vassal state. The country was to be occupied until 'a date to be determined later', to pay all occupation costs, to demobilize one-third of its armed forces, and to hand all 'surplus grains' over to the Germans. Proponents of the *Mitteleuropa* concept were delighted that Berlin was on the way to economic hegemony in Europe on the basis of 'indirect' expansionism. Mackensen, the conqueror of Romania, was more blunt, noting that for once the pen had secured what the sword had won.[101] Both peace settlements were presented to the Reichstag for approval to grant them the stamp of parliamentary legitimacy.

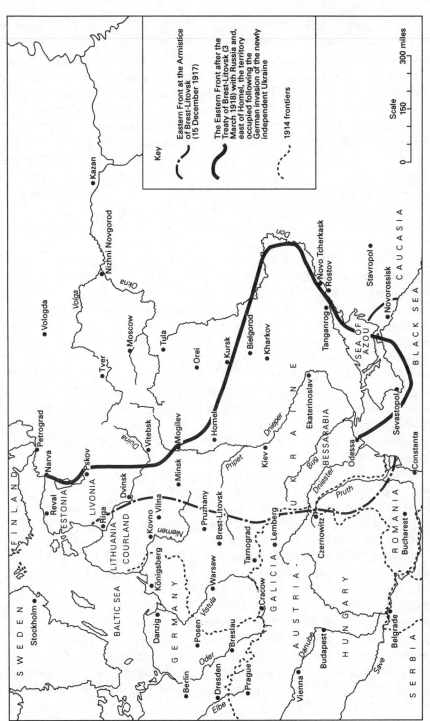

Key

⌇ Eastern Front at the Armistice
of Brest-Litovsk
(15 December 1917)

⌇ The Eastern Front after the
Treaty of Brest-Litovsk (3
March 1918) with Russia and,
east of Homel, the territory
occupied following the
German invasion of the newly
independent Ukraine

⌇ 1914 frontiers

Scale
0   150   300 miles

Map 11. Ludendorff's eastern empire, 1918

Brest-Litovsk accorded both Lenin and Ludendorff what each needed most: time. Lenin had surrendered space for time, and he used the breathing room not only to extend his rule beyond Petrograd, but also to bombard German workers and soldiers with repeated appeals to mutiny and to murder their commanders and Kaiser. Ludendorff had reduced his military fronts to only one and now concentrated on defeating Britain and France before the United States arrived in Europe in force. He also ordered his staff to draw up plans for Operation *Schlußstein*, a march via Petrograd to Murmansk designed both to remove the Bolsheviks from power and to drive Allied units out of northern Russia. It was Ludendorff's greatest hour: the *OHL* had taken advantage of the power vacuum presented by a Kaiser unable to fulfil his command role and a parliament not yet able to flex its legislative muscles to claim that it alone represented the will of the nation.

The Central Powers placed their greatest hopes and expectations in Ukraine. Visions of abundant grain depots and bountiful future harvests danced before their eyes. Archduke Wilhelm of Austria established a headquarters at Kiev in hopes of becoming its crowned ruler. Austrian monitors steamed up and down the Dniester and Bug rivers, while the Second Army was grandiosely retitled 'the *k.u.k.* East Army'. On 1 April Vienna opened the world's first commercial airline to haul mail between Vienna and Kiev. But the 250 000 Habsburg and 400 000 Hohenzollern soldiers stationed in Ukraine daily consumed 300 railroad cars of food. Grain exports amounted to barely one-tenth of expected volume.[102]

In fact, Ludendorff's megalomania required that 1 million troops remain in Russia to enforce the peace and to exploit its resources. The German official history of the war claims that 52 000 tons of grain and feed, 34 000 tons of sugar, 45 million eggs, 39 000 cattle, 53 000 horses, and 48 000 hogs and sheep were removed from former Russian territories by October 1918.[103] It studiously refused comment on whether the million soldiers might have been put to better use in France.

At home, Princess Blücher noted that Germans had returned to the ways of their ancestors as a result of the war's deprivations. 'The old forgotten arts' of spinning and weaving were again being cultivated. Many families kept two or three sheep for their raw wool. Virtually all peasants planted flax for spinning. Farm buildings were 'growing dilapidated'. Animals were being slaughtered for the lucrative black market at such a rate that stocks were threatened. Blücher's husband, 'as in the good old days (how good we never knew until now) of the dark ages', fed his family as well as city children sequestered with them by hunting 'wild ducks and roe-deer'.[104]

Rumours of an impending offensive in France raised spirits amidst the gloom and despair of the winter of 1917–18. Princess Blücher detected 'an almost insatiable craving for pleasure of any kind amongst every class of society'. There was just enough money to fill the theatres, cinemas, and concert halls. 'Artistes of the day' vied with one another to raise public spirits. 'Every one is anxious to forget the depression of the times and get rid of the heavy burden of sorrow and care which has so long been clogging and depressing public and private life.' Dances and balls, forbidden for much of the war, were again in full swing. The great hotels offered concert teas and mediocre food to packed houses at high prices. 'It is as if the long-repressed desire for amusement innate in human nature is now breaking forth stronger than ever.'[105] German society entered the final stage of the war with a certain sense of masquerade.

Chapter 9 Notes

1. Albrecht von Thaer, *Generalstabsdienst an der Front und in der OHL. Aus Briefen und Tagebüchern 1915–1919*, ed. Siegfried A. Kaehler (Göttingen, Vandenhoeck & Ruprecht, 1958), pp. 150–1. Entry of 31 December 1917.
2. BHStA, MA 3080 Militär Bevollmächtigter Berlin. Ambassador von Schoen's report of 17 April 1917.
3. Thaer, *Generalstabsdienst an der Front*, p. 159, found out on 20 January 1918 from his fellow staffer, Major Wetzell, that the final draft of the peace to be presented Russia had been 'ready in Wetzell's briefcase for 1.5 years'.
4. Bundesministerium für Landesverteidigung, *Österreich-Ungarns Letzter Krieg 1914–1918*. 7: *Das Kriegsjahr 1918* (Vienna, Verlag der Militärwissenschaftlichen Mitteilungen, 1938), p. 50.
5. *Österreich-Ungarns Letzter Krieg 1914–1918* 7, pp. 52–8.
6. Gunther E. Rothenberg, *The Army of Francis Joseph* (West Lafayette, Ind., Purdue University Press, 1976), pp. 209–10.
7. ÖStA-KA, MKSM 69-9/27. 'Ein Memoire August 1917', 26 pp.
8. ÖStA-KA, MKSM 25-1/9. 'Darstellung der materiellen Lage der Armee im Felde', 18 August 1918. General Arz von Straussenburg.
9. ÖStA-KA, MKSM 70-1/83-2. Memorandum of 4 August 1917.
10. ÖStA-KA, MKSM 70-1/83-2. Undated memorandum, probably late 1917.
11. ÖStA-KA, MKSM 69-6/26. 'Die militärische Lage im Frühjahr 1918', dated 3 November 1917.
12. ÖStA-KA, MKSM 25-1/9. General Arz von Straussenburg, 18 August 1918.
13. Arz to Stöger-Steiner, 23 September 1917. BA-MA, Nachlass Seeckt, N247, vol. 35.
14. *Österreich-Ungarns Letzter Krieg 1914–1918* 7, pp. 67–70.
15. Rudolf Hecht, 'Fragen zur Heeresergänzung der gesamten bewaffneten Macht Österreich-Ungarns während des Ersten Weltkrieges', unpubl. diss., Vienna University 1969, pp. 458 ff.
16. *Österreich-Ungarns Letzter Krieg 1914–1918* 7, pp. 72–3.
17. *Österreich-Ungarns Letzter Krieg 1914–1918* 7, pp. 75–7.
18. For a statistical summary see Robert J. Wegs, 'Transportation: The Achilles Heel of the Habsburg War Effort', in Robert A. Kann, Béla K. Király, Paula S. Fichtner, eds, *The Habsburg Empire in World War I: Essays on the Intellectual, Military, Political and Economic Aspects of the Habsburg War Effort* (New York, Columbia University Press, 1977), pp. 121–31.

19. Kann, Király, Fichtner, eds, *The Habsburg Empire in World War I*, pp. 82–5.
20. Kann, Király, Fichtner, eds, *The Habsburg Empire in World War I*, pp. 43–4, 95–7.
21. HHStA, PA I 818 Liassa Krieg. Interna. Report of 22 May 1918.
22. *Österreich-Ungarns Letzter Krieg 1914–1918* 7, pp. 38–40, 42.
23. *Österreich-Ungarns Letzter Krieg 1914–1918* 7, pp. 41–9.
24. *Österreich-Ungarns Letzter Krieg 1914–1918* 7, p. 49.
25. *Österreich-Ungarns Letzter Krieg 1914–1918* 7, p. 45.
26. Fritz Fellner, ed., *Schicksalsjahre Österreichs 1908–1919. Das politische Tagebuch Josef Redlichs* (2 vols, Graz and Cologne, Hermann Böhlaus Nachf., 1954) 2, p. 226. Entry of 20 August 1918.
27. General Ottokar Landwehr von Pragenau, *Hunger. Die Erschöpfungsjahre der Mittelmächte 1917-18* (Zurich, Leipzig, and Vienna, Amalthea, 1931), pp. 164, 170, 191, 229, 236; Sigrid Augeneder, *Arbeiterinnen im Ersten Weltkrieg. Lebens- und Arbeitsbedingungen proletarischer Frauen in Österreich* (Vienna, Europaverlag, 1987), pp. 142–7.
28. See Arthur J. May, *The Passing of the Hapsburg Monarchy 1914–1918* (2 vols, Philadelphia, University of Philadelphia Press, 1966) 2, pp. 654 ff.; Richard Georg Plaschka, 'The Army and Internal Conflict in the Austro-Hungarian Empire, 1918', in Béla K. Király and Nándor F. Dreisziger, eds, *East Central European Society in World War I* (New York, Columbia University Press, 1985), pp. 340–5; and Rudolf Neck, ed., *Arbeiterschaft und Staat im Ersten Weltkrieg 1914–1918* (2 vols, Vienna, Cologne, Stuttgart, and Zurich, Europa Verlag, 1964–1968) 2, pp. 185 ff.
29. HHStA, PA I 818 Liassa Krieg. Interna. Hohenlohe's reports of 16, 18, 20, and 23 January 1918.
30. HHStA, PA I 818 Liassa Krieg. Interna. Reports dated 9 February and 23 March 1918.
31. Wedel to Foreign Office, 21 January 1918. BHStA, MA 3084.
32. BHStA, MA 3084. Foreign Office minute of 23 January 1918.
33. Péter Hanák, 'Die Volksmeinung während des letzten Kriegsjahres in Österreich-Ungarn', in Richard Georg Plaschka and Karlheinz Mack, eds, *Die Auflösung des Habsburgerreiches. Zusammenbruch und Neuorientierung im Donauraum* (Munich, R. Oldenbourg, 1970), pp. 59, 62-3, 65-6.
34. József Galántai, *Hungary in the First World War* (Budapest, Akadémiai Kiadó, 1989), p. 299.
35. Police directorate to Count Czernin, 18 March 1918. HHStA, PA I 818 Liassa Krieg. Interna.
36. Cited in Manfried Rauchensteiner, *Der Tod des Doppeladlers. Österreich-Ungarn und der Erste Weltkrieg* (Graz, Vienna, and Cologne, Verlag Styria, 1994), p. 547.
37. See Richard Georg Plaschka, *Matrosen. Offiziere. Rebellen. Krisenkonfrontationen zur See 1900–1918* (2 vols, Vienna, Cologne, and Graz, Hermann Böhlaus Nachf., 1984) 2, pp. 192–7.
38. Plaschka, *Matrosen. Offiziere. Rebellen.*, pp. 273–5. See also Hans Hugo Sokol, ed., *Österreich-Ungarns Seekrieg 1914–18* (Zurich, Leipzig, and Vienna, Amalthea-Verlag, 1933), pp. 653–94.
39. Landwehr von Pragenau, *Hunger*, p. 191; Thaer, *Generalstabsdienst an der Front*, p. 199, entry of 5 May 1918.
40. *Österreich-Ungarns Letzter Krieg 1914–1918* 7, p. 184. See also Hecht, 'Fragen zur Heeresergänzung ', passim.
41. *Österreich-Ungarns Letzter Krieg 1914–1918* 7, p. 202.
42. ÖStA-KA, MKSM 69-6/26. 'Die militärische Lage im Frühjahr 1918'.
43. *Österreich-Ungarns Letzter Krieg 1914–1918* 7, pp. 186–90.
44. Peter Fiala, *Die letzte Offensive Altösterrreichs. Führungsprobleme und Führerverantwortlichkeit bei der öst.-ung. Offensive in Venetien, Juni 1918* (Boppard, H. Boldt, 1967), p. 12.

45. Fiala, *Die letzte Offensive Altösterreichs*, p. 203.
46. *Österreich-Ungarns Letzter Krieg 1914–1918* 7, pp. 90–1.
47. HHStA, PA I 818 Liassa Krieg. Interna. Memorandum dated 24 May 1918.
48. Foreign Office report of 3 June 1918 for the Bavarian government. BHStA, MA 3084.
49. See Otto Wassermair, 'Die Meutereien der Heimkehrer aus russischer Kriegsgefangenschaft bei den Ersatzkörpern der k. u. k. Armee im Jahre 1918', unpubl. diss., Vienna University 1968.
50. BHStA, MA 3084. Report of 5 June 1918. See also Fiala, *Die letzte Offensive Altösterreichs*, p. 15.
51. See Hecht, 'Fragen zur Heeresergänzung', passim.
52. *Österreich-Ungarns Letzter Krieg 1914–1918* 7, pp. 190–3; Fiala, *Die letzte Offensive Altösterreichs*, pp. 54–5. See also Eduard P. Hoffmann, 'Feldmarschall Boroevic von Bojna. Österreich-Ungarns Kriegsfront an den Flüssen Isonzo und Piave', unpubl. diss., Vienna University 1985.
53. Wedel to Foreign Office, 7 April 1918. BHStA, MA 3084. See also A[ugust] von Cramon, *Unser Österreichisch-Ungarischer Bundesgenosse im Weltkriege. Erinnerungen aus meiner vierjährigen Tätigkeit als bevollmächtigter deutscher General beim k.u.k. Armeeoberkommando* (Berlin, E. S. Mittler & Sohn, 1922), pp. 152–7.
54. May, *Passing of the Hapsburg Monarchy* 2, pp. 632, 634.
55. Gary W. Shanafelt, *The Secret Enemy: Austria–Hungary and the German Alliance, 1914–1918* (New York, Columbia University Press, 1985), pp. 190–1; Galántai, *Hungary in the First World War*, p. 301.
56. HHStA, PA I 536 Botschaftsarchiv Berlin. Agreement of 12 May 1918. In 1077 Emperor Henry IV had to perform penance before Pope Gregory VII at Canossa castle in Emilia, Italy.
57. Fiala, *Die letzte Offensive Altösterreichs*, pp. 78–9.
58. Rauchensteiner, *Der Tod des Doppeladlers*, p. 572.
59. Fiala, *Die letzte Offensive Altösterreichs*, p. 92.
60. *Österreich-Ungarns Letzter Krieg 1914–1918* 7, p. 276.
61. *Österreich-Ungarns Letzter Krieg 1914–1918* 7, p. 319; and especially ÖStA-KA, Nachlass Boroevic, B/4, 'Die Schlacht an der Piave Juni 1918'.
62. *Österreich-Ungarns Letzter Krieg 1914–1918* 7, pp. 338, 359.
63. ÖStA-KA, MKSM 69-6/14. 'Junischlacht in Venetien', 14 July 1918.
64. *Österreich-Ungarns Letzter Krieg 1914–1918* 7, p. 353.
65. Fiala, *Die letzte Offensive Altösterreichs*, p. 140.
66. Karel Pichlík, 'Der militärische Zusammenbruch der Mittelmächte im Jahre 1918', in Plaschka and Mack, eds, *Die Auflösung des Habsburgerreiches*, pp. 258, 263. The most exhaustive treatments of the military collapse of 1918 are Richard Georg Plaschka, *Cattaro-Prag. Revolte und Revolution. Kriegsmarine und Heer Österreich-Ungarns im Feuer der Aufstandsbewegungen vom 1. Februar und 28. Oktober 1918* (Vienna, Böhlau, 1963); and Richard Georg Plaschka, Horst Haselsteiner, and Arnold Suppan, *Innere Front. Militärassistenz und Umsturz in der Donaumonarchie 1918* (2 vols, Vienna, Verlag für Geschichte und Politik, 1974).
67. See Rothenberg, *Army of Francis Joseph*, p. 214.
68. Reichsarchiv, *Der Weltkrieg 1914 bis 1918*. 13: *Die Kriegführung im Sommer und Herbst 1917* (Berlin, E. S. Mittler & Sohn, 1942), pp. 5–8.
69. Gerhard Ritter, *Staatskunst und Kriegshandwerk. Das Problem des 'Militarismus' in Deutschland* (4 vols, Munich, R. Oldenbourg, 1968) 3, pp. 577 ff.; Fritz Fischer, *Griff nach der Weltmacht: Die Kriegszielpolitik des kaiserlichen Deutschland 1914/18* (Düsseldorf, Droste Verlag, 1964), pp. 523 ff.; and Wilhelm Deist, ed., *Militär und Innenpolitik im Weltkrieg 1914–1918* (2 vols, Düsseldorf, Droste Verlag, 1970) 2, pp. 782 ff. The text of the protocol is in Erich Ludendorff, *Urkunden der Obersten*

Heeresleitung über ihre Tätigkeit 1916/18 (Berlin, E. S. Mittler & Sohn, 1920), pp. 408–11.

70. Ambassador zu Hohenlohe's report dated 11 July 1917. HHStA, PA I 536 Botschaftsarchiv Berlin.
71. BA-MA, W-10/50656 Tagebuch v. Plessen, entry dated 13 July 1917.
72. Report of 21 July 1917 in *Dokumente aus geheimen Archiven*. 4: *Berichte des Berliner Polizeipräsidenten zur Stimmung und Lage der Bevölkerung in Berlin 1914–1918*, eds Ingo Materna and Hans-Joachim Schreckenbach (Weimar, Hermann Böhlaus Nachfolger, 1987), pp. 214–16.
73. See Wilhelm Deist, 'Kiel und die Marine im Ersten Weltkrieg', in Jürgen Elvert, ed., *Kiel, die Deutschen und die See* (Stuttgart, Franz Steiner, 1992), pp. 150–1.
74. Holger H. Herwig, *The German Naval Officer Corps: A Social and Political History 1890–1918* (Oxford, Clarendon Press, 1973), pp. 202–5. The pertinent documents are in Deist, ed., *Militär und Innenpolitik 2*, pp. 996 ff.
75. BA-MA, Nachlass Hipper, N 162, vol. 7. Entries for 3 and 7 August 1917.
76. Herwig, *German Naval Officer Corps*, p. 203.
77. Germany, *Verhandlungen des Reichstags. XIII. Legislaturperiode. II. Session*, vol. 310, p. 3794D. Speech of 9 October 1917.
78. *Der Weltkrieg 1914 bis 1918* 13, pp. 23–4. See also Herwig, *German Naval Officer Corps*, pp. 210–12; documents again in Deist, ed., *Militär und Innenpolitik 2*, pp. 321 ff. Propaganda had started in 1622 with Pope Gregory XV's *Congregatio de propaganda fide*.
79. HHStA, PA III Gesandschaft Berlin 173. Hohenlohe's report of 26 September 1917.
80. See, for example, the position paper of the Navy Office on the Fatherland Party of 1 February 1918 in BA-MA, F 7635 Reichstagsmaterial 1918, vol. 3. The documents pertaining to the genesis and founding of the Party are at the Hauptstaatsarchiv Stuttgart, J 47 Nachlass Haussmann, boxes 27 and 52.
81. Named after Philipp Scheidemann of the SPD, one of the architects of the Reichstag's 'peace resolution' of 1917.
82. See *Ursachen und Folgen. Vom deutschen Zusammenbruch 1918 und 1945 bis zur staatlichen Neuordnung Deutschlands in der Gegenwart*, eds Herbert Michaelis and Ernst Schraepler (15 vols, Berlin, Dokumenten-Verlag Dr Herbert Wendler, 1958) 1, pp. 242–55.
83. See the reports by Police President von Oppen in *Dokumente aus geheimen Archiven* 4, pp. 242–3, 256, 264–5.
84. HHStA, PA III Gesandschaft Berlin 174. Reports of 29, 30, 31 January and 1 February 1918.
85. HHStA, PA III Gesandschaft Berlin 174. Report of 1 February 1918.
86. Hohenlohe to Czernin, 4 February 1918. HHStA, PA III Gesandschaft Berlin 174.
87. Thaer, *Generalstabsdienst an der Front*, p. 161. Entry of 2 February 1918.
88. Cited in Karl Peter Rosner, ed., *Erinnerungen des Kronprinzen Wilhelm. Aus den Aufzeichnungen, Dokumenten, Tagebüchern und Gesprächen* (Stuttgart and Berlin, J. G. Cotta, 1922), p. 230.
89. Stein to Wilhelm II, 5 February 1918. BA-MA, PH 2/14 Kriegsministerium. 'Eingreifen der bewaffneten Macht bei Unterdrückung von Unruhen'.
90. Kessel to Wilhelm II, 6 February 1918. BA-MA, PH2/14 Kriegsministerium. The most important documents pertaining to the military and the strikes are in Deist, *Militär und Innenpolitik 2*, pp. 1139–73.
91. See BA-MA, PH 2/69 Kriegsministerium. Saarbrücken, 31 January 1918.
92. See, for example, the report of the Bureau for Social Politics in Saarbrücken to the War Ministry, 15 February 1918. BA-MA, PH 2/69. 'Streikbewegungen und Streikgefahren.'
93. Deist, *Militär und Innenpolitik 2*, p. 1169.

94. HHStA, PA III Gesandschaft Berlin 174. Reports of 1 May and 15 June 1918.
95. Discussion with Ludendorff on 14 June 1918. BA-MA, Nachlass Haeften, N 35, vol. 4, p. 5.
96. Ambassador von Lerchenfeld's report to the Bavarian government of 17 January 1918. BHStA, MA 3084.
97. Ritter, *Staatskunst und Kriegshandwerk* 4, p. 102.
98. See Arthur S. Link, ed., *The Papers of Woodrow Wilson* (69 vols, Princeton, Princeton University Press, 1984) 45, pp. 534–9.
99. All citations from the Crown Council are from Bundesarchiv Koblenz, Nachlass Schwertfeger, Nr. 119, vol. 2, pp. 73 ff.; and Zentrales Staatsarchiv Potsdam (formerly East Germany), Reichskanzlei: Grosses Hauptquartier 21, Beiheft, Handakten betr. grundlegende Besprechungen über Kriegsziele 2477. See also Holger H. Herwig, 'Tunes of Glory at the Twilight Stage: The Bad Homburg Crown Council and the Evolution of German Statecraft, 1917/18', *German Studies Review* 6 (1983), pp. 475–94; and Lilli Lewerenz, 'Die deutsche Politik im Baltikum 1914–1918', unpubl. diss., Hamburg University 1958.
100. Fischer, *Griff nach der Weltmacht*, p. 671.
101. See Winfried Baumgart, *Deutsche Ostpolitik 1918. Von Brest-Litowsk bis zum Ende des Ersten Weltkrieges* (Vienna and Munich, R. Oldenbourg, 1966), pp. 132 ff.
102. See Rauchensteiner, *Der Tod des Doppeladlers*, pp. 542–3.
103. *Der Weltkrieg 1914 bis 1918* 13, p. 399.
104. Evelyn, Princess Blücher, *An English Wife in Berlin: A Private Memoir of Events, Politics, and Daily Life in Germany throughout the War and the Social Revolution of 1918* (New York, E. P. Dutton, 1920), pp. 234–5.
105. Blücher, *An English Wife in Berlin*. Entry for February 1918.

10

Operation *Michael*: The 'Last Card'

I object to the word 'operation'. We will punch a hole into [their line]. For the rest, we shall see. We also did it this way in Russia!

Erich Ludendorff, Spring 1918

At 4 a.m. on 21 March 1918 the Western Front erupted in a hurricane of fire and thunder as 6608 guns and 3534 trench mortars announced the start of Germany's sixth bid for victory: the great *Michael* offensive in France.[1] At 9 a.m. the artillery changed over to a creeping barrage, and 40 minutes later 76 assault divisions supported by 1070 airplanes charged the Allied lines between Arras and La Fère.[2] Berlin was flagged and bells rang out in anticipation of victory. The *OHL* had played what many of its staff officers termed the 'last card'. With Russia, Romania, and Serbia defeated, the Supreme Command gambled Germany's future on victory on the Western Front to force Britain and France to their knees before the Americans arrived in strength.

The *OHL* codenamed the attack Operation *Michael* in honour of the Reich's patron saint; it has also been referred to as the Kaiser's Battle and the Peace Offensive. The German railroads orchestrated their greatest feat of the war as 10 400 full-length trains ran day and night moving men and material from rear echelons to the front between 15 February and 20 March.[3] Army commanders reported that morale was high, but added that the troops viewed *Michael* as the last roll of the dice.

Kurt Riezler, Chancellor von Bethmann Hollweg's political counsellor for the first 3 years of the war, appreciated what was at stake. 'All depends on the offensive – should it succeed completely, then we will have the military dictatorship that the public cheerily will put up with – should it not succeed, [then there will come] a severe moral crisis which probably none of the present government leaders has the talent to master peacefully.' Riezler noted that Germany was now being run by the 'barely veiled military dictatorship' of Hindenburg and Ludendorff. Wilhelm II had abdicated his role as Supreme War Lord for all intents and purposes; the *milites gloriosi* had taken his place.[4]

Tactical virtuosity

While Ludendorff had busied himself during the Brest-Litovsk negotiations sketching future borders on European maps with reckless abandon, his field commanders and staff had assessed Germany's prospects for 1918. They were not cheery. More than one million draft-eligible men remained in war-related industries at home, and the *OHL* estimated late in 1917 that it could at best pry loose 300 000 for front-line duty. Reserves were being called up at the rate of 58 000 trained and 21 000 untrained men per month and would cover needs only until January 1918. Thereafter, the cohort of 1900, not due to be called to the colours until the autumn, was all that remained. 'Seen from this point of view all operations that are not necessary should be avoided.' Ludendorff hoped that leaders in Germany would 'keep our nerves 10 minutes longer than the enemy'. General von Kuhl sadly noted that the U-boat war had turned into 'a wild-goose chase'.[5]

Kuhl's superior, Crown Prince Rupprecht, sent Ludendorff his appraisal of the military situation on 25 October 1917. The Bavarian ruled out major offensives in the west, claiming that his forces were capable only of 'limited counterattacks'. Time was running out. The anticipated arrival of the Americans in the autumn of 1918 would turn the numerical advantage against the Reich, which was in no position to 'do the enemy the favour of allowing ourselves to be destroyed bit by bit in battles of material'. Crown Prince Wilhelm seconded Rupprecht's analysis. Both agreed that men had to be spared; territory could more easily be lost. On 28 October Ludendorff 'generally' concurred with Rupprecht's views and merely raised the possibility of a limited offensive by the Fourth Army against the British in the area of Armentières-Bailleul 'to deflect the impact of the Americans'.[6] Like Kuhl, Ludendorff had lost faith in the U-boats. The only cheerful news was that deep divisions between the English and French peoples in Canada prevented that country from sending more troops to France.[7]

On 23 October Major Wetzell, the *OHL*'s head of operations, penned what became the critical position paper on its military alternatives for

1918. 'If we do not wish to succumb to false illusions', Wetzell stated, 'then we must count on the fact that the Entente will survive the winter . . . and that the Americans will have added significant forces to the western war theatre in the spring of 1918 (10 to 15 divisions)'. The Western Front remained decisive. The only viable strategy was 'to deliver an annihilating blow to the British before American aid can become effective'. The Army could be strengthened in two ways: shortening Army Group Crown Prince Wilhelm's front by withdrawing to the Gudrun Line would free up 20 divisions; and 15 more could be removed from the east. Within 24 hours, Ludendorff approved Wetzell's concept.[8] The collapse of Russia allowed the *OHL* to raise its estimates of reinforcements from the Eastern Front first to 31 infantry and cavalry divisions and then to 45. But Ludendorff's insatiable appetite for Russian lands reduced this figure to 33, with the result that there were still 40 infantry and three cavalry divisions in the east when the Army launched its great offensive in France.[9] Indeed, Ludendorff was caught on the horns of a dilemma of his own making: on the one hand, he wanted to get every soldier and every gun to the Western Front for the great Armageddon, but on the other hand he knew the low fighting value of these occupation troops and feared withdrawing too many lest the Russians – Red or White – seize the chance to retake the lands lost at Brest-Litovsk.

The need to force a decision in the west early in 1918 occupied military commanders throughout the winter of 1917–18. Army Group Crown Prince Rupprecht worked on a modest campaign in Ypres designed to break out of Armentières in the direction of Bullécourt-La Fère.[10] Army Group Crown Prince Wilhelm proposed a double-sided pincer movement against Verdun (!) designed to annihilate French forces in the region. Army Group Archduke Albrecht of Württemberg planned to shift the war's focus to Alsace. And Hindenburg favoured a direct assault against the British to throw Haig's forces back to the Channel. Yet a number of high-ranking commanders – Hoffmann, Seeckt, Schulenburg, Lossberg, Gallwitz, and Crown Prince Rupprecht – seriously questioned whether the Army could sustain a major offensive in the coming year.

On 11 November Ludendorff decided on the gambler's last throw of the dice. Wilhelm II was apprised of Operation *Michael* on 23 January 1918; on 10 March Hindenburg issued formal orders for infantry to charge enemy lines at 9:40 a.m. on 21 March.[11] Colonel von Thaer fully appreciated the immensity of the decision. 'Here in the west we stand before the future as before a dark curtain. The coming events will bring tremendous and for many horrible [things].' Using language similar to that which Falkenhayn had used at Christmas 1915 to describe his Verdun offensive, Thaer predicted that both sides would be subjected to a severe 'bloodletting' throughout the coming summer.[12] Thaer as well as countless colleagues used the term 'last card' to describe Operation *Michael*. Yet all agreed on the need for decisive action. General von Lossberg, staff chief of the Fourth Army, put it bluntly to Wilhelm II on the eve of *Michael*: if the war continued at its present pace, 'it can well last into 1920'.[13]

Ludendorff divided the forces for *Michael* into three categories: 44 'mobile' divisions with full-strength battalions of 850 each armed with machine guns, flamethrowers, and trench mortars and assigned the best supply horses available; about 30 'attack' divisions similarly equipped and designed as first-line replacement units; and finally more than 100 'trench' (*Stellungs*) divisions stripped of their best equipment and intended merely to hold the front.[14] Ludendorff stepped up training courses for his infantry throughout the winter of 1917–18. The captains and majors of the roughly 70 'mobile' and 'attack' divisions chosen to spearhead the initial assault underwent training in 80-men cohorts in special 8-day courses run by a staff of 18 instructors at Sedan (and then Valenciennes) as early as September 1917. Subjects taught ranged from tanks to antitank warfare, machine guns to gas, and artillery to air warfare.[15] The courses, which were quickly expanded to 4 weeks each, stressed rigid discipline, daily physical exercise, special instruction in the use of machine guns, and joint operations with artillery and air power. Artillery was trained to deploy high-angle howitzers against tanks.

The German front remained committed to an in-depth and elastic defence, with the third line holding 'the mass of troops in bunkers'. Enemy assaults were to be halted where possible at the first line 'with the last bullet and hand-grenade', but in the case of strong hostile artillery the troops were to withdraw to the second line of defence. German soldiers were drilled to accept that timely counterattacks were their best and only hope; the speed of the echeloned counterattack, the place chosen for it, and the coordination between machine-gun and artillery fire were critical. Units were instructed to reorganize the minute an attack had been repelled as enemy artillery was to be expected.[16]

Ludendorff calculated that the Army had sufficient seasoned officers available to command its battalions, but that it lacked veterans to staff its companies. All too often young and inexperienced officers, mainly from reserve formations, were rapidly advanced to command companies. Thus, training was critical to *Michael*'s success. The *OHL* also made sure that the assault divisions received sufficient food: 600 g. of bread, 200 g. of meat (served 5 days of the week), 50 g. of fat, and 100 g. of honey or marmalade per day. Still, the soldiers' caloric intake overall had fallen from

3100 in August 1914 to 2500 by early 1918. Dried cod and canned meats often substituted for fresh meat.[17]

The *OHL* lavished special attention on machine guns. It decreed that each infantry regiment was to have 30 heavy MG 08 guns and 72 light MG 08/15, but production bottlenecks cut the number of light machine guns in half. The MG 08/15 could be used in the first defensive line to repel an assault, but its true value lay as a counterattack weapon in forward positions beyond the range of friendly artillery; it was also deemed fit to use against tanks at close range. Machine guns were to be deployed in clusters of two or three and each crew carried 5000 rounds in belts, sufficient for four bursts of about 3 minutes each. The guns could fire at the rate of 400 to 500 shots per minute, but barrels tended to overheat quickly. The fine dust of the Champagne and Flanders (when dry) caused frequent jamming, and the troops were instructed to oil their weapons well and to use wet cloths to protect them from both dust and gas.

The heavy MG 08 gun was described as 'the weapon of intermediary terrain', that is, as the main killing tool between the first and second lines. While it could be used against enemy flyers, it was most effective against hostile troops that had overrun the first trench line. Teams consisted of one gunner and four assistants, which were most advantageously placed in reinforced concrete pill-boxes 7 to 10 yards deep with a firing platform 2 yards below the surface. Gunners were to move only by night and then to use rakes to erase their footsteps in the dirt to foil enemy reconnaissance by air. A school at Rozoy trained 20 machine-gun crews at a time. Austro-Hungarian and Turkish officers were invited to the courses.

Reconnaissance and communications received detailed attention. In good weather the pilots of tethered balloons could take pictures up to a range of 18 or 19 miles. Reconnaissance planes were outfitted with special radios and telephoto-lens cameras, allowing a pilot both to report his sightings and to photograph them. About 4000 cartographers on the ground developed and analysed the pictures. The Army found that dogs – 12 per regiment – remained the most reliable means of getting messages to and from the front. Each animal underwent 4 to 6 weeks of training with two trainers: one at the front and one in the rear to assure accurate runs. Each division had 120 pigeons housed in hermetically sealed cages to protect them against gas. The birds were tattooed under the wing for identification and had aluminum tubes attached to their legs to hold messages. They could go 48 hours without food. Howitzers were designed to fire special metallic message containers; smoke released on impact with the ground marked their whereabouts. Message runners remained the final recourse.[18]

The Supreme Command also beefed up its air forces for the great push in France. The number of aircraft on hand – not counting 1000 machines with reserve formations – had more than doubled from 1200 in 1917 to 2600 in 1918 under the auspices of the so-called 'America Programme'. On the eve of *Michael*, the German Air Force in the west consisted of 2000 active and about 1700 reserve aircraft organized into 80 attack squadrons of 12 planes each, 38 support squadrons of 12 craft each, and eight bomber squadrons of 18 machines each. An all-metal, single-wing Junkers craft constituted a significant advance over the usual wooden-framed aircraft that easily succumbed to fire. Reconnaissance craft could reach an altitude of up to 7000 yards in 45 minutes; fighters could do so in half the time at a speed of 100 miles per hour. Two-thirds of the Reich's 2000 anti-aircraft guns were also positioned on the Western Front.[19]

Alarmed by the increased activity of Allied spies early in 1918, the *OHL* in January instructed Army Group Crown Prince Rupprecht to alert all units that spies most frequently landed or parachuted behind its lines between midnight and dawn in captured planes. They dressed in German uniforms, used forged documents to fool patrols, carried about 2000 francs to bribe French civilians, and brought hot pepper to throw police dogs off the trail. Once on the ground, they switched to civilian garb. Railroads were the spies' primary objectives, and they sent their findings out by pigeons with messages scribbled in invisible ink.[20]

Ludendorff's staff developed a detailed 'decoy plan' to confuse the Allies concerning the actual deployments for *Michael*. On 24 February General von Lossberg instructed army-group commanders to increase their artillery bombardments, to send up additional observation balloons, to step up aerial reconnaissance and bombing, and to withdraw their front units a few yards to occupy the enemy's attention. Commanders were also instructed to send out numerous and meaningless radio messages, and to release hundreds of pigeons, including especially captured enemy birds, with false orders. Civilian populations were to be assembled in mass formations in non-assault areas behind the front to lead the Allies to believe that they were German reserves; elsewhere they were to be driven out of their homes for the same purpose. All front areas were closed to travel. Lossberg instructed his commanders to march their men in all conceivable directions by day to deceive enemy flyers, noting that this tactic was especially effective against 'the cunning English'.[21]

Tanks bedevilled the German Army throughout the war in two ways: it had neither developed an effective antidote nor built its own in numbers. Daimler in Berlin in the winter of 1914–15 had experimented only with light armoured personnel carriers with wheels designed for street use and ignored the American-designed caterpillar track. The *OHL* eventually realized the tank's potential, and on 30 October 1916 had ordered the first prototype built. The tank was to be manned by a crew of six and powered by an 80 to 100 horsepower motor capable of speeds of 7 or 8 miles per hour on roads and about 4 in open terrain. The unit was to weigh 4 tons and mount one machine gun each front and back as well as two on the side.

Thereafter, designers divided their attention amongst a heavier (150-ton) tank armed with four 7.7 cm and two machine guns, a medium (30-ton) tank mounting one 6 cm and six machine guns and flamethrowers, and a light (8.5-ton) model with only two machine guns. However, industry was fully taxed with producing ammunition, guns, and U-boats and never gave tank development full attention. The net result was that the Germans used mainly captured British and French tanks and put out only one model, the A7V. This medium tank had a best speed of 5 miles per hour on level surfaces, with a range of only 15 miles. The A7V tank lacked manoeuvrability and its crew of 12 proved too large for smooth operation of the vehicle. Daimler reported in February 1918 that it was still 8 to 9 months away from developing a new large tank, and that production could not start before 1919.[22] Moreover, Daimler's exorbitant prices – it demanded a 50 per cent increase in its car and tank costs in 1918 alone – in March forced the government after a bitter debate in the Reichstag to 'militarize' the firm, thereby further slowing tank production.[23]

The Army published its first manual for tank warfare in January 1918. It depicted the tank as an 'auxiliary weapon' incapable of deciding battle on its own; its major function was to assist infantry in reaching enemy positions.[24] On 18 January Ludendorff decreed that the few tanks on hand were to be used to reduce wires, to run over machine-gun positions, but thereafter to avoid enemy artillery fire by returning to their own lines. The tanks were not to spearhead infantry's advance, but rather to support the first assault wave as mobile field artillery. Iron-cross markings on the tops or sides were to identify friendly tanks. Some units, such as General Finck von Finckenstein's 4th Guards Infantry Division, painted white death's heads on the front of their tanks as signs of elite formations.[25]

This rather simplistic approach to tank warfare should not obscure the fact that lower commands were intensively experimenting with the new weapon. Around the start of *Michael*, the Commander of Armoured Vehicles, Division III (Bornschlegel), summed up experiences to date for front commanders. It required at least 10 days to prepare a tank assault. The vehicles were best deployed in pairs, were to move up slightly behind the infantry as mobile artillery, and were not to advanced more than 4 to 5 miles per day. Tank leaders were to train daily with infantry and to develop close communications with infantry leaders. Because signal lamps could not be read in fog and smoke, each tank was to be painted with numbers and flags for ready identification and be given a radio for communication. Canister-shot was most effective, but insufficient storage room for shells limited the tank's assault capability. Revolving periscopes were dismissed out of hand as the tanks pitched and rolled too violently for steady observation and firing; notched sights remained the norm. Unfortunately, the tanks were front-heavy due to the placement of the large gun; there were no gun weights to offset this; and the constant pounding that the tank took off-road loosened the bolts on gun placements.[26] Obviously, the tank required more development before it could play a decisive role in battle.

Antitank warfare also troubled the Germans. The first manual on how to deal with tanks was published in December 1916, and recommended machine-gun and howitzer fire against the mechanical monsters. In April 1917 Army Group Crown Prince Wilhelm encapsulated its experiences with British tanks during the Battle of Arras. The report, penned by Captain Bernhard Bronsart von Schellendorf, recommended close-support batteries as the best deterrent. Three to four shells sufficed to put a tank out of service; the best shots were through the side where they hit the lethal petrol tanks. Bronsart von Schellendorf bravely suggested that the German infantryman 'generally has nothing to fear from the tanks'.[27]

The Battle of Cambrai in November 1917, of course, proved otherwise and the search for an effective antitank weapon continued. In March 1918, two weeks before the start of the *Michael* offensive, the General Staff reminded soldiers that single hand-grenades were ineffective against tanks, and instructed them to tie several grenades together with wire and to hurl them at the tank's turret.[28] Roughly 200 former 2 cm anti-aircraft guns proved inadequate as tank defence, and hence the front received a new 13 mm antitank gun. It also remained of questionable value as single shots failed to puncture enemy armour. The gun was effective only if grouped with others and fired at close range (200 to 300 yards) as well as high angle (60 to 90 degrees) in order to penetrate the soft tops of tanks.[29]

Having trained the assault troops for *Michael*, Ludendorff next turned his attention to doctrine. Unsurprisingly, he called on Captain Geyer, the Bavarian officer in the operations section of the General Staff, who in December 1916 had crafted the 'Principles of Command for the Defensive Battle in Position Warfare'. In January 1918 Geyer completed 'The Attack in Position Warfare'; it became the manual for *Michael*. The Bavarian had studied the last 3 years of 'attacks with limited objectives' to devise a method to 'break through' the enemy trench networks and thereby to regain operational manoeuvre. The Army had spent the winter of 1917–18 systematically honing its tactical skills; the question now was how to rupture enemy lines and, more importantly, how to exploit that rupture.

First, Geyer acknowledged that the military instrument, in classic Clausewitzean terms, had been worn down by years of constant combat. Veterans in their thirties and forties, and especially *Landsturm* men in their fifties, would not do as 'attack' specialists or 'storm-battalion' troops. Geyer, following Ludendorff's suggestion, thus selected about 25 per cent of all soldiers – those between the ages of 25 and 35 – for special 'attack' divisions, and relegated the rest to 'trench' divisions comprised of older men with inferior equipment.[30] *Der Angriff im Stellungskrieg* stipulated that small units were to infiltrate (*durchfressen*) Allied lines, bypass centres of resistance, and 'penetrate quickly and deeply' into the enemy's rear. Reserves were to be kept in forward positions and detailed by the Supreme Command to exploit ruptures in enemy lines. Individual units were not to halt and await reinforcements, but to drive forward until exhausted. Fresh formations would then leapfrog ahead of them. Storm troopers would spearhead the attack. Artillery would lay down fast and accurate barrages designed to neutralize rather than to destroy hostile positions. Training, surprise, and uninterrupted forward movement were critical to success. 'The surprised adversary should not be allowed to regain consciousness.' Troops, in the words of General Hoffmann, were 'to test various positions' in the lines 'one after another in order to ascertain where one encountered the enemy's weakness', against which 'one would have to press the attack with all possible force'.[31] Tactical virtuosity had replaced strategy at the *OHL*.

The battle

The war had started in 1914 with Germany mounting an operation (the Schlieffen plan) designed to win a campaign (in France). It ended in 1918 with a campaign designed to win a war. Ludendorff refused to use the word strategy and cut short army commanders who questioned him about *Michael's* operational objective. 'I object to the word "operation". We will punch a hole into [their line]. For the rest, we shall see. We also did it this way in Russia!'[32] In doing so, Ludendorff was consistent with the objectives outlined in Captain Geyer's 'The Attack in Position Warfare'. The official history of the war later stated that 'the tactical breakthrough was and remained the initial goal'. Its success would determine all future actions.[33]

The German assault line in March 1918 consisted of 1 386 177 soldiers organized into 192 largely under-strength divisions: 61 of Army Group German Crown Prince were concentrated north of St Quentin and Reims down to the Argonne forest; 24 of the new Army Group Gallwitz consisting of the Fifth Army and Army Group C stood to the east of Crown Prince Wilhelm; and 83 of Army Group Crown Prince Rupprecht were deployed from Nieuport on the English Channel down to La Fère on the Oise River. Ranged against them were 178 full-strength Allied divisions: 12 Belgian formed the Allied left wing from the North Sea to Ypres; the British First and Second armies extended this line from Ypres about 120 miles south to the Oise, while General Byng's Third Army and General Gough's Fifth Army stood directly in the path of the main line of attack; and finally, 42 French divisions manned the remaining 340 miles of the front. There were also 287 000 Americans in France, but only three divisions were in the line and none of them near the battle zone.[34] The real German weakness lay in the number of 'machines of war': 3670 aircraft against 4500 Allied; 14 000 guns of all calibres against 18 500 Allied; 10 tanks against 800 Allied; and 23 000 largely iron-rimmed trucks against 100 000 Allied rubber-wheeled vehicles.[35]

Ludendorff's plan called for Crown Prince Rupprecht's left wing to open the campaign with an advance on both sides of the Scarpe River (*Mars*). Below's Seventeenth Army was to push toward Bapaume (*Michael I*), while von der Marwitz's Second Army was to advance southwest from Cambrai (*Michael II*). General Oskar von Hutier's Eighteenth Army had been attached to Army Group German Crown Prince in January, and these forces combined were instructed to drive forward on both sides of St Quentin (*Michael III*). The Seventh Army was to hold itself in readiness on the left wing of the attack south of the Oise (*Erzengel*).

If all went according to plan, the German Seventeenth, Second, and Eighteenth armies would crash through Field Marshal Haig's Third and Fifth armies in a pincer movement and trap British forces in the Cambrai salient. Thereafter, these German units would follow the Somme River northwest to Arras-Albert and throw Haig's remaining forces into disarray. Crown Prince Wilhelm's divisions would protect this advance from being outflanked by marching on its left wing toward the Somme and the Crozat Canal.

Depending on where the Germans encountered their greatest success, either the Fourth and Sixth armies were to destroy the British position in Flanders first, or the Seventh, First, and Third armies were to tackle the French Army Group North. This would result in the rupture of the entire Allied front from the Channel to Verdun. The main brunt of the offensive was to fall on Below's Seventeenth Army. Famed for his success at Caporetto in 1917, Below was to break through the British lines near Arras and then, while heading southwest, execute a difficult 90-degree turn northwest along the line of the Somme. Speed, surprise, and concentration were critical to his success.[36] In the 12 hours of daylight on the first day of the offensive, his troops were to advance 8000 yards across No Man's Land to the British artillery positions. They were to avoid strong positions whose reduction might slow them down.

The area chosen for the attack consisted mainly of flat sweeps of heavy clay soil, dissected by the swampy 50-yard-deep valleys of the Ancre and Somme rivers as well as the Crozat Canal heading south from St Simon. The nearly-completed Canal du Nord between Douai, Noyon, and Péronne constituted another major obstacle as it was partly filled with water and mud. The main attack zone between Albert and Montdidier had been devastated by the British in the summer of 1916 during their Somme assault as well as by Germans in the winter of 1916–17 during their withdrawal to the Siegfried Line. Hardly a building or tree remained. Villages, with the exception of Bapaume, Péronne, and Ham, had been levelled and foundation walls were now overgrown with weeds and brush. Forests had been cut down; vegetation consisted of small scrub brush. Shell craters and rusted barbed wire dotted the landscape. Rain would turn the clay into a quagmire. Early victories would require German railroad engineers to lay tracks across the desolate terrain to connect with existing French lines to the west.[37]

Were the troops ready for the great offensive? Lieutenant Hermann Pürckhauer of the 2nd Regiment, First Bavarian Infantry ('attack') Division, left a vivid diary of the weeks preceding *Michael*. Pürckhauer's regiment underwent thorough training in January 1918 at Machault in the Champagne, followed in February by a 3-week advanced course with the Eighteenth Army at Vervins. The first week was devoted to discipline, basic firing and advance, and terrain; the second to machine-gun and howitzer practice and coordination; and the third to field exercises at regimental and divisional levels. The last week included simulated manoeuvres with aircraft and (model) tanks, and featured division-level assaults. Men and horses were strengthened with excellent food and fodder. Officers were instructed to liaise with the rank and file.

On 16 March the First Bavarian Infantry Division started to move up to the front by night. No lights. No singing. No music. Each division was assigned its own road. All unit identification markers were removed in favour of coloured codes. Pürckhauer's regiment marched 9 miles the first night and 20 the second. On 19 March maps as well as firing tables for the creeping barrage were handed out to all officers down to the company level. The men were issued with ammunition, signal flares, gas masks, hand-grenades, and emergency ('iron') rations. At 9 p.m. on 20 March the Bavarians moved into their jumping-off trenches near Regny. Their goals were Jussy and the Crozat Canal.[38]

The proverbial 'fog of war' literally set in on 21 March: the battlefield remained enshrouded in dense fog until early afternoon. The region's soft, swampy soil, soaked by days of rain, slowed the men down. Colonel Bruchmüller's creeping barrage moved forward 100 yards every 2 or 3 minutes according to preset timetables rather than to the troops' actual progress. Soon the wall of explosives outpaced the men, whose progress it was designed to ease. Signal rockets fired by infantry commanders could not be read in the fog by artillery spotters and signal corps. Fog, gas, and smoke obscured the battlefield and countless soldiers succumbed to choking and tears.[39] Units became lost in the chaos of battle. The first line of enemy defences was overrun only around Croisilles-Doignies; most units advanced but 3 miles, half their assigned task. More than 78 000 Germans were wounded or killed – the highest casualty figure for any single day of the war. They included Ludendorff's son, an airman.

The nature of the fighting on 21 March was graphically caught by Lieutenant Edgar von LeSuire of the 1st Bavarian Infantry Regiment near Regny. Artillery had opened up around 5:40 a.m. 'It is mainly a whizzing and groaning, whistling and hissing. All are impatiently standing in the trenches that we have come to despise; they do not fit in with German manliness.' Then came the cry: 'Out of the trenches!' The Bavarians leaped from their lines – into a nightmare of fog, gas, and smoke. The first soldiers fell; the rest moved forward. 'There is still good German soldierly spirit in the men.' LeSuire's units stormed the enemy's first line of defence shouting 'Hurrah!'. British soldiers 'begged for quarter' and 'showered us with cigarettes, food, and the like'.

The Regiment advanced amidst enemy machine-gun and artillery fire to another British trench, which it found filled with 'dead Tommies' as a result of the German artillery barrage. Moving across a bit of open ground, LeSuire's men were suddenly without covering fire. 'Our creeping barrage has rushed ahead of us too fast.' To make matters worse, the protective fog began to burn off around noon. Bright sunshine broke through. LeSuire discovered that his artillery had not been able to keep pace with the morning's rapid advance. Officers had been separated from their men in the heat of battle. Units with gaping holes in their lines seemed confused and dazed. Stumbling upon the British second line, the Bavarians found that it had escaped artillery pounding almost completely as the creeping barrage had passed over it too quickly. 'The battle becomes coarser and more brutal.' A savage machine-gun duel ensued for much of the afternoon. Hastily reconstituted Bavarian companies pursued fleeing British forces through Cornet d'Or and Urvillers as night fell.

LeSuire and his fellow officers used the cover of night to track down units lost in the fog of battle. Then they took stock of the first day's

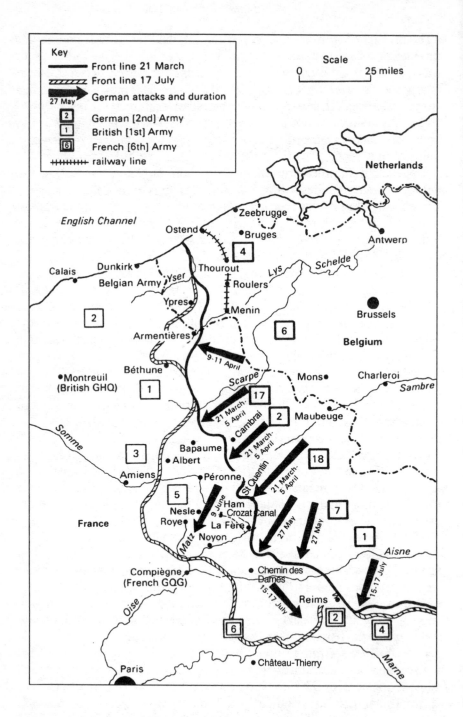

Map 12. *The last card: Operation* Michael, *1918*

fighting. Light howitzers and trench mortars had failed to leave the lines that morning and to follow the advancing infantry. Closer investigation revealed that in the excitement, their gunners had simply seized rifles and charged off to join the infantry! Telephone and telegraph wires had been shot to pieces by artillery; it had been impossible to read signals in the fog and smoke. As a result, there had been virtually no communication between infantry and artillery, and only a few runners had crossed the fields of fire.[40]

Ludendorff's armies pressed forward again on 22 March. Savage battles with hand-grenades, rifles, and bayonets raged in the heavily-manned British second lines, especially near Croisilles. Haig ordered his forces to withdraw to their third line of defence. The German Seventeenth Army linked up with the Second Army to advance in the direction of Bapaume (*Michael II*). Supported by attack aircraft, these forces broke through the British front and stormed the artillery lines, taking 10 000 prisoners and 200 guns. Haig's headquarters broke down in an avalanche of orders and counterorders. It also launched a series of extremely costly counterattacks supported by tanks.

Elsewhere, the Eighteenth Army (*Michael III*) crashed through the main British forward zone, seized the second lines of the 'Haig Position', and reached Foreste, taking 7000 prisoners and 90 guns. Wilhelm II showered Hutier and his staff with medals. Crown Prince Wilhelm rushed two bottles of Veuve Cliquot champagne to Hutier's headquarters. Ludendorff quickly fed reserves to the Eighteenth Army, which reached the Somme near Péronne on the morning of 23 March. Haig rushed reserves to the front with his motor transport fleet and cleverly utilized 'infiltration-resistant' obstacles such as the Crozat Canal to site his artillery and heavy machine guns in an indirect mode to harass the pursuing Germans.[41] In fact, Ludendorff's guns had put only one-sixth of enemy artillery out of action.

The nature of the fighting was once more captured by Bavarian diarists. Lieutenant Pürckhauer's 2nd Bavarian Infantry Regiment crossed the Crozat Canal on 22 March and spent the night in Jussy. Forty-eight hours later it captured Neuville with its 'rich booty of food and wine'. On 27 March the Bavarians reached Canny, where they literally ran out of food and supplies. The entire First Bavarian Infantry Division deployed defensively in echelon to a depth of 1 mile. The 'fresh, happy dash forward' had ended. Position warfare resumed.[42]

Lieutenant von LeSuire's 1st Bavarian Infantry Regiment resumed the advance at 9 a.m. on 22 March in heavy fog in the low-lying region of the Crozat Canal near Jussy and Essigny le Grand. Protected by the grey mist, the Bavarians marched to Essigny along open roads. The fog lifted shortly before noon. Sunshine brought a deadly hail of fire from British heavy machine guns. LeSuire's men took cover in an open gravel pit and in ditches by the side of the road. There they cowered from 11 a.m. until 6 p.m., pinned down by hostile fire. Fortunately for the Bavarians, a Prussian unit stormed Jussy, thereby relieving the pressure on the 1st Infantry Regiment. LeSuire's engineers spent the night building pontoon bridges on which the troops crossed the Crozat Canal in the morning of 23 March.[43] Both diaries end at this point. Were both officers killed soon thereafter?

In 2 days, Ludendorff's 'mobile' and 'attack' divisions had decimated Gough's Fifth Army and driven the British almost 40 miles behind the Somme and the Crozat Canal. Haig had lost 200 000 killed and wounded, 90 000 prisoners of war, and 1300 guns. Most importantly, his defences had been ruptured, a 50-mile gap driven through the lines. 'Open field' lay ahead of the Germans. The British had attempted to adopt the 'elastic defence in depth' without really understanding it, were not used to being on the defensive, and had failed to defend the marshy Oise region of Gough's thinly-deployed Fifth Army. But German losses had not been inconsiderable: Hutier estimated his casualties at 8 per cent, or 56 000 combatants out of 700 000.[44] Equally important, the 'open fields' drawn on staff maps in fact were studded with forests, rivers, towns, and canals, which took time and energy to storm or cross.

Wilhelm II rushed congratulations to the troops and admonished them to push on. 'Much has been accomplished; much more still remains to be conquered.'[45] The Kaiser ordered schools closed in Germany to mark the 'victory'. He presented Hindenburg with the Iron Cross with Golden Rays – last given to Gebhard Leberecht Prince Blücher for ridding Prussia of Napoleon I. And Wilhelm II informed his entourage over champagne that 'if an English delegation came to sue for peace it must kneel before the German standard for it was a question here of a victory of the monarchy over democracy'.[46] Ludendorff assured his Kaiser that the British Army had been defeated.

But on further reflection, Ludendorff had to concede that success had come unexpectedly in the south against the French rather than according to design in the north against the British. Without a strategic or even an operational plan, Ludendorff on 23 March was forced to choose where to drive home the next assault. Convinced that Hutier's offensive had been completely successful and that Gough's Fifth Army had been destroyed, he ordered the Seventeenth Army to head for Doullens and to attack in the direction of Arras-St Pol. The decisive push was to be made by the Second and Eighteenth armies south of the Somme toward Miraumont-Lihons and Chaulnes-Noyon. The units that had originally been designed as flank protection now became the campaign's centre of gravity (*Schwerpunkt*). The immediate aim was to drive a wedge between British and French forces and to push the former 'into the sea'.[47] Additionally, Ludendorff hoped to seize the vital rail junction of Hazebrouk – and perhaps the Allied Channel ports.

During the next 3 days, the three German armies moved forward steadily for nearly 20 miles. Haig's troops were driven back to their Somme redoubts of 1916. Chaos and confusion gripped British headquarters. While Haig suspected a French withdrawal southwest to guard Paris, General Pétain feared that the British might not stand on the Somme and instead head for the Channel – and home. But General Foch kept his nerves and correctly detected that Amiens was the key: if the Germans separated the British from the French at this vital rail link, the battle could be lost. The Allies, Foch warned, were not to retreat another foot. The remnants of Gough's shattered Fifth Army were taken out of the front and replaced with the British Fourth Army as well as French reserves. General Pershing, whose 'obstinate' and 'stupid' policy it had been, in Haig's words, to maintain a '*great self-contained American Army*' in France, on 28 March agreed to release American formations to plug the holes in the Allied lines.[48]

Suspecting a gap between the British and French lines at Amiens-Montdidier, Ludendorff decided to broaden the scope of his attacks. He ordered the Second and Eighteenth armies to turn the left flank of the French at Noyon to sever them from the British. Specifically, the Second Army was to take Amiens; the Eighteenth Army was to form the axis of this movement and later head toward Compiègne-Fontenoy; and Army Group German Crown Prince was to advance on both sides of the Scarpe and mop up remaining British forces. Therewith, Ludendorff totally overthrew his original plan. The new centre of gravity was now firmly shifted to the Second and Eighteenth armies fronting French forces in the south. German units were to fan out in a giant radiating movement across the region between the Oise River and the English Channel. Put differently, Ludendorff's original scheme to deliver a single, powerful blow against British strength gave way to a series of small attacks with limited objectives against both the British and the French. In the process, Ludendorff weakened the momentum of the entire assault.

In truth, Ludendorff asked too much of his exhausted and bloodied Army.[49] The renewed offensive stalemated as early as 27 March, and position warfare ensued north of the Somme. 'The offensive power of the troops', in the words of the German official history, 'naturally had suffered terribly in six days of fighting'. But since the 'trench' divisions were neither equipped nor trained to go on the offensive, Ludendorff as early as

24 March had ordered 'mobile' and 'attack' divisions to remain at the front, and to refit behind the lines only in 'exceptional cases'. Half of his reserve divisions had already been committed. One-third of all artillery had broken down or been destroyed. Neither horse-drawn artillery nor supply wagons were able to keep up with the infantry's advance across the scarred Somme battlefields of 1916. The enemy front had been pushed back, but not ruptured. The bag of prisoners of war and captured guns had hardly risen in 2 days. Hostile aircraft had gained supremacy in the sky, harassing German troops with machine-gun fire and bombs.[50] The military historian Gerhard Ritter, an officer with the Eighteenth Army in 1918, recalled the 'doubts' that his men harboured after 23 March concerning their ability 'totally to defeat' the enemy and to hurl the British 'against the sea'.[51]

On 29 March the British launched a deadly counterattack at Albert. Still, Ludendorff remained optimistic. He cheerily informed his staff 2 days later: 'We have overrun the great English defensive system from southeast of Arras to La Fère, have defeated or at least severely mauled about 41 English and 18 French divisions'. Untold British war equipment had fallen into German hands. 'The English Army at the moment is not capable of operating [in the field].'[52] Ludendorff's optimism momentarily obscured the fact that the Army had given its all and that *Michael* had run its course. After the war, Ludendorff admitted that he had misjudged the Allies' tenacity. But he refused to address the charge that his offensive had lacked a centre of gravity, or that he repeatedly had changed his operational plan. Ludendorff simply allowed that he declined to engage the enemy in a 'battle of attrition'.[53]

On 3 April General Foch was given command over Anglo-French forces, and 11 days later was appointed *Général en Chef des Armées alliées en France*. The German assault had finally forced unified command on the Allied and Associated Powers.

Michael officially ended on 5 April. The offensive had brought in 90 000 prisoners of war and 1300 guns; it had cost the British an additional 178 000 and the French 70 000 casualties. The Germans set their own losses at 239 000 men. The front had been dangerously extended from 56 miles to 93 and was open to flanking attacks. The British had not been driven 'into the sea'. The French had not collapsed. More than 90 German divisions, including virtually all 'mobile' and 'attack' divisions, were exhausted and demoralized. The 'mobile' divisions had been reduced to 'attack' divisions. Many were down 2000 men.[54] The Allies in April dropped more than 1 million pamphlets over German lines encouraging the troops to desert or to refuse to obey orders; another 24 million brochures followed from May to November.[55]

The Young Turks in the General Staff quickly pointed to the root cause of failure: absence of a strategic plan. Major Wilhelm von Leeb with Army Group Crown Prince Rupprecht, a future field marshal of the Third Reich, on 29 March percipiently noted Ludendorff's lack of an overall concept. '*OHL* has changed direction. It has made its decisions according to the size of territorial gain, rather than according to operational goals.' On 31 March Leeb recorded that Ludendorff had 'totally lost his nerves'. There existed no overarching concept of the campaign. 'According to Ludendorff we are to conduct *operations* wherever a tactical victory has been achieved; in other words, the OHL utterly lacks a definite plan of operations.' Two weeks later Leeb again lamented the lack of direction: 'We had absolutely no operational goal! That was the trouble'.[56]

Colonel von Thaer concurred. While Hindenburg lectured Thaer that troop morale was '*very* good, in fact brilliant almost everywhere', the Colonel, a veteran of the trenches, held no such illusions. 'Every battalion and company leader and therefore every rifleman and gunner', he stated, 'clearly understands that the hope [for victory] has been dashed'. There was 'little in the way of strategy' in *Michael*. When Thaer and several other staff officers reminded Ludendorff of his earlier claim that the fourth day of the operation would tell whether it had been a success,[57] Ludendorff acidly replied: 'What is the purpose of your croaking? What do you want from me? Am I now to conclude peace at any price?'[58] Obviously, war aims remained paramount to Ludendorff, who made it clear that politics stood above sober military calculations.

Nor was such critique restricted to the Young Turks. Lossberg, staff chief of the Fourth Army, accused Ludendorff of pursuing 'operational breakthroughs' wherever 'tactical breakthroughs' had been achieved, and decried the rigid and arrogant staff system that dominated the *OHL.*[59] Crown Prince Rupprecht noted with understatement: 'I get the impression as if the OHL is living from hand to mouth without acknowledging definite operational designs'.[60] His colleague, General von Kuhl, staff chief to Army Group Crown Prince Rupprecht, was of similar mind. Ludendorff continued to chase 'another Tannenberg'; there existed 'no great operational goal behind all the attacks'. Tactics had become an end in themselves. 'Such are the limits of Ludendorff's [military] abilities.'[61]

The German official history of the war, noted for its non-judgmental language, basically agreed. 'Overall one misses in the battles a clear centre of gravity.' Ludendorff had failed to concentrate against a single adversary (Britain), and instead had sent his reserves wherever a crack had appeared in the front. Moreover, he had failed to pull his fatigued 'mobile' and 'attack' divisions out of the line in time and to replace them with reserves. At the height of the battle against the British on 23 March, for example, the General had held four fresh divisions behind the Seventeenth Army, two behind the Second, and 11 behind the Eighteenth; furthermore, six unbloodied divisions remained in reserve in Flanders.[62] At the tactical level, the official history noted that *Michael* had been dogged by foul weather, slowed by the devastated Somme battlefields, and hampered by the difficulty of resupply. As at Tannenberg and the Masurian Lakes in 1914, Ludendorff in 1918 had placed supreme trust in his railroad system. But the armies had marched far beyond their railheads, and neither trucks nor horse-drawn wagons could bring up food or ammunition fast enough. Above all, the 'mobile' divisions had been ground down to the point of total fatigue. Many had lost up to 100 officers in the first month of combat.[63]

Few German commanders either in 1918 or later wished to admit that the assault had been impeded by the soldiers' desires to satisfy two basic needs: hunger and thirst. Yet General von Einem, commanding the Third Army, openly stated that '*one* of the motivating factors for the bravery of our infantrymen during the offensive is the craze to plunder'.[64] Crown Prince Rupprecht conceded that his Sixth Army had halted at Estaires, Merville, and Bailleul in April to quench their thirst from the ample wine stores, and that 'repulsive scenes of drunkenness' had ensued. Two months later he noted that the capture of Reims had been delayed by drunken soldiers. Discipline had collapsed. Wherever a village was taken, 'the troops search for food and wine'.[65] Thaer discerned similar developments. 'Entire divisions', he recorded', had '*totally* gorged themselves on *food* and *liquor*', and had failed to 'press the vital attack forward'.[66]

News of German troops stopping to slake their thirst and still their hunger on bountiful Allied supplies quickly reached Berlin. Princess Blücher heard rumours that German soldiers had found treasures in British trenches:

> Stacks and stacks of food, cases of biscuits, jam, tobacco, corned beef, milk
> – all that a poor starved German's imagination could desire in his wildest
> dreams. Then clothes, mackintoshes, leather waistcoats, silk socks, . . .
> wonderful waterproof trench boots, depots of leather goods, saddles, reins,
> bags; real English compact army outfits of every kind.[67]

After the war, Bavarian officers and military historians reading the 1918 reports of looting laconically questioned the critique of this activity by high-ranking commanders. After all, who could blame starving soldiers for halting to satisfy their hunger and thirst from captured supplies?

On the home front, morale had remained high during the opening weeks of the *Michael* offensive. The Deputy Commanding Generals of the Reich's two dozen army-corps districts noted in April that 'joy and jubilation' had met the reports of victories in France. The public mood seemed to have reached the giddy heights of 'the August days of 1914'. Military censors reported that civilians were delighted 'that especially England was feeling the sharpness and the full weight of the German sword'.[68] Seven million citizens, intoxicated with visions of victory, gave 15 billion Marks for the eighth war-bond drive – the largest amount ever collected. Few, if any, could know that the troops, exhausted by the all-out charges of late March, were keenly aware that the enemy had held – and that it was gaining strength.

Once more, several poignant diaries give insight into the changing tide of battle. Lieutenant Joseph Kübler of the 15th Bavarian Infantry Regiment was deployed at Moreuil on the Avre River during the first week of April. His unit, commanded by Major Franz Schaaf, was part of the Eleventh and Eighteenth armies' drive south of the Somme in the direction of Amiens. On 3 April Kübler noted that the enemy 'had brought up new reserves and that especially his artillery was being reinforced day by day'. Hostile flyers had gained superiority in the skies above Moreuil. German attacks were now being launched helter-skelter with little preparation. At 4 a.m. on 4 April his unit received orders to attack Génoville-Ferme at 8:10 a.m! There was no time to brief company leaders, to inform the men of their mission, or even to give them breakfast.

After a brief 2-hour artillery bombardment, Kübler's troops stormed enemy lines in fog and rain on schedule 'in deeply-echeloned waves, the platoons one after the other, just as we had learned in the quiet months beforehand'. The men pressed forward with reckless abandon 'and soon the prescribed distances [between platoons] became ever smaller and soon disappeared altogether, causing a scrambling and mixing of individual units'. The reserves detailed to exploit ruptures in the British lines were only 200 to 300 yards behind the advance.

Enemy machine guns immediately exacted a heavy toll. Kübler's men in desperation sought protection behind straw trusses – with the result that the field was soon littered with dead soldiers. 'This hillside of corpses and wounded was one of the most horrible sights that I saw in this war.' The wet, heavy clay soil delayed the arrival of about 30 friendly machine guns. Once they arrived, the Bavarians advanced again. Then they waited again for their guns. Then they advanced again. At 10 a.m. hostile artillery opened fire. The range was too far, but soon the exploding shells crept up to the Germans from behind. 'They literally chased us toward the enemy.' The Regiment's staff had been dispersed by the fire and Major Schaaf as well as his deputy wounded. All contact with the flanks as well as the rear had been severed. The men ran blindly forward, using handkerchiefs to direct their own machine-gun fire. Shortly after noon they reached

Anchin-Ferme. 'Unfortunately I had to witness the sad picture of our men plundering enemy knapsacks in order to still their hunger with a piece of white bread.'

Thereafter, the advance bogged down completely in the face of intensive British machine-gun and artillery fire. 'Our own losses became ever greater, the battle lines ever thinner; one could detect enemy reserves moving up to the front at a distance of about 1800 yards. The enemy's artillery fire intensified; our own was silent.' British machine guns sited in Rouvrel's buildings and church steeple repulsed the Bavarians' attempt to storm the village. 'At the front all was chaos and confusion; scrambled companies, scrambled regiments, even some people from another division.' Kübler's shattered forces were taken out of the front lines on the morning of 5 April. The 15th Bavarian Infantry Regiment had attacked with 1300 men. In 3 days it lost 37 officers and 1037 men (including 8 officers and 160 men killed).[69]

Lieutenant Willi Held, 9th Company leader in the 6th Bavarian Infantry Regiment, from hospital sent his brother his impressions of the fighting at Croisilles just south of Arras. Held's men spent the morning of 6 April 'rifle in hand in our jump-off trenches shivering in the hoarfrost. Our thoughts strayed home once more; we knew that many of us would not see the evening'. At precisely 4:50 a.m. their musings were rudely interrupted when the artillery laid down a deafening fire. 'A hurricane bombardment of gas such as one probably has not experienced on the Western Front. The sky was red with the muzzle flashes of countless batteries.' Some of the gas drifted back toward the German lines and forced the men to don gas masks. At 6:40 a.m. the artillery changed over to high-explosive shells. 'The sun rose blood-red; it could barely penetrate the powder smoke, the gas clouds.' Then came infantry's turn. '9:40 is zero hour. Finally. Finally!' The Regiment took heavy losses from British machine guns and flyers as its companies scattered across the landscape.[70]

Undaunted, Ludendorff renewed the attack in Flanders on 9 April with the Fourth and Sixth armies. By then, one-fifth of the 55 divisions were veterans of the original *Michael* attack. And since many of the 'mobile' divisions had been wasted, Ludendorff turned to 55 'attack' as well as a few 'trench' divisions for the so-called Lys offensive. With 400 horses on average fewer than the 'mobile' divisions and with inferior equipment, these units attacked along the Lys River between Warneton and La Bassée. Originally named *George*, the operation was scaled down and renamed *Georgette*.

It caught the British near Armentières by surprise. The Germans quickly infiltrated enemy positions to a depth of 5 miles and seized Kemmel Hill. Haig, enduring the rigours of warfare at the splendid

Château de Beaurepaire, sought to rally his troops on 11 April with a ring-ing appeal. 'With our backs to the wall and believing in the justice of our cause, each one of us must fight on to the end.'[71] British resistance even-tually stiffened appreciably, and Haig repelled Ludendorff's drive for Amiens between 24 and 27 April. *Georgette* ground to a halt by 29 April with a furthest advance of 12 miles south of Ypres. German artillery had already expended three times the ammunition that had been used during the Franco-Prussian War. On 21 April Germany's greatest 'ace', Richthofen, was shot down probably by ground fire over the Somme, shortly after scoring his 80th 'kill'.

Allied tanks had once again harassed the Germans. Lieutenant Robert Simm, an artillery specialist with the 5th Bavarian Infantry Regiment on Height 141 near Reims, described a tank action during the Battle of the Aisne. At 9 a.m. on 16 April the Regiment spotted French infantry mov-ing forward in dense fog. The mist lifted just before noon. At 1:50 p.m. Simm spied 28 French tanks approaching at intervals of 50 to 60 yards, followed by 'immense infantry formations'. Bavarian artillery opened fire in panic. The first three shots missed the lead tank at almost point-blank range; one shot fell short and two were wide. The breech on Simm's 13 mm antitank gun jammed already on the fourth shot due to heat. Fire was too slow as each iron shell case had to be removed by a swabber from in front of the gun. The French lead tank, a 13-ton Schneider-Creusot, opened fire, scattering Simm's artillery, whose artificers fell back on the battery behind them. Soldiers from the 50th Infantry Division were called up to charge the tanks with hand-grenades and machine guns. The combi-nation of artillery, machine guns, and grenades finally produced results. Four hostile tanks were hit and their petrol tanks and ammunition exploded before Simm's eyes. 'A grandiose picture. I see . . . burning crews lurch out of the tanks and collapse like flaming torches.' Bavarian headquarters offered 500 Marks for every tank destroyed.[72]

The *OHL* had monitored the progress of Operation *Michael* over the first 4 or 5 weeks, and on 17 April apprised army commanders of its findings. Best results were obtained where surprise, speed, and concentration were achieved. Coordinated gas and high-explosive artillery fire was best laid down in short, massive bursts designed not to destroy the enemy, but as '*moral decimation*' to be exploited at once by infantry. Lengthy preparatory bombardments were to be avoided as they merely gave the enemy time to prepare for an attack. The *OHL* favoured gas over high explosives as it could better neutralize machine guns. Creeping barrages were to be stag-gered at 100-yard intervals and to advance every 4 or 5 minutes strictly by predetermined timetables; only after the opening phase of battle were the barrages to be determined according to the actual situation on the ground.

Infantry, in the opinion of the *OHL*, was still too heavily massed in front trenches at a ratio of one division roughly per mile of front, and its deployment in dense formations militated against success. Instead, the troops were to be arranged in thin lines, which were then to be sent to probe enemy positions for possible breakthrough points. Once such points had been located, storm troops with machine guns and flamethrowers were to rupture the enemy line and exploit the situation. Storm battalions were to fight continuously for as long as 10 days, and were not to be relieved as this wasted valuable time. Reserves likewise were to bypass enemy points of resistance and to deploy wherever the adversary proved weakest. Tanks could 'easily be knocked out' by trench mortars, artillery, machine guns, and grenades bundled and placed under their caterpillar tracks. But Ludendorff's staff ominously counselled that military police, both mounted and on foot 'in large formations', be on the lookout for stragglers and deserters. They were also to use firearms against soldiers robbing enemy dead and wounded.[73]

The Prussian Army Gas School, which had already conducted more than 90 instruction courses, likewise issued new orders for the use of gas in combat. Chemical weapons were to be placed at the front, controlled at the corps level, and made mobile. Each division was to carry 1200 to 2400 gas shells weighing 12 to 14 tons. Only Green Cross (diphosgene) and Blue Cross (75 per cent explosives, 25 per cent diphenyl-chlorarsine) gas was to be used during an attack as it did not linger too long over the battlefield. Blue Cross was especially recommended against machine guns because it dissipated immediately after the explosive charge detonated. Yellow Cross (mustard) gas, on the other hand, was to target supply dumps or entire army corps, for it lingered in the air and clung to the ground and water for days and even weeks.[74]

The *OHL* was acutely aware that the offensive was rapidly grinding down the instrument with which it was being waged. The three main assault armies, in the cold terminology of the Army's Medical Reports, between 21 March and 10 April had lost one-fifth of their original strength, or 303 450 men. Some divisions in the Seventeenth Army were down one-third of combat strength. Ludendorff's Lys offensive in Flanders had been purchased at a terrible price: between 1 and 30 April the Sixth Army lost 63 469 of its 361 142 soldiers, and the Fourth Army 59 209 of its 421 221. Overall losses were 235 544 in March and 257 176 in April. The Sixth Army warned Ludendorff in mid-April: 'The troops will not attack, despite orders [to do so]. The offensive has come to a halt'.[75]

Having failed to separate the British from the French at Amiens, Ludendorff next shifted the campaign's centre of gravity to the Aisne

River. He concentrated 36 divisions – of which no fewer than 27 were veterans of the original *Michael* attack – against 24 French divisions between La Fère and Reims. The commanders of the three attacking armies – Marwitz, Below, and Hutier – were classmates from the Prussian cadet corps class of 1875. All three understood that reserves were at full ebb. As Hutier bluntly put it: 'If the pending operation does not have truly decisive success, then we are stuck'.[76]

The breakthrough battle of the Chemin des Dames (*Blücher*) on 27 May was designed to threaten Compiègne, Reims, and eventually Paris, in the process drawing French reserves away from Haig, the real target of Ludendorff's attention. *Blücher* constituted the single greatest German artillery effort in the war. Field railroads – a train 340 miles long if all cars were placed end-to-end – hauled 2 million shells to the front, and 1100 batteries fired off this entire supply in just 4.5 hours.[77] The 15 divisions of General Hans von Boehn's Seventh Army quickly rolled over Duchêne's Sixth Army at the Chemin des Dames and the Aisne River – the site of Nivelle's aborted offensive of 1917 – before halting at Fismes on the Vesle River on the evening of the first day of battle. Ignoring the experiences of 3 years of warfare, Duchêne defended with the bulk of his forces in forward positions.

The Allies were stunned. Ludendorff immediately exploited his tactical success by expanding the limited attack on the Chemin des Dames into the great Battle of Soissons-Reims. In five days the Germans advanced to Château-Thierry on the Marne River, just 56 miles from Paris. They took more than 50 000 prisoners and cut the vital Paris–Nancy rail link. Soissons fell on 29 May, but Reims remained in French hands. Early in June German soldiers were in many of the same positions that they had abandoned in September 1914. The Allied front had been driven back 30 miles. Paris once more seemed in danger, and as many as 1 million people left the capital in panic. The famous 'Paris' or 'Wilhelm' gun, a Krupp-modified 21 cm naval gun with a range of 75 miles, had taken Paris under fire from the forest of Crépy throughout this period – doing little damage but adding fuel to charges of 'Hun barbarity'. Still, Ludendorff, in the biting words of General von Kuhl, continued to lurch from one tactical success to another, without the slightest idea of how 'to end the war or to bring about a decision'.[78]

Ludendorff now faced what became his last major offensive decision in the war. Should he reorganize his forces to drive the British against the Channel – the original aim of *Michael* – or should he exploit his success by widening the Marne salient in order to march on Paris? Not surprisingly, Ludendorff chose the latter, more tantalizing option. His forces were now 90 miles beyond their railheads.

On 9 June Hutier's Eighteenth Army and Boehn's Seventh Army attacked (*Gneisenau*) between Noyon and Montdidier, just west of the Marne salient. After a 4-hour hurricane bombardment with gas and explosives, the infantry moved forward behind the creeping barrage at the rate of 100 yards every 3 to 6 minutes. Thick fog, hazy air, and lingering swaths of gas impeded the attack.[79] Ludendorff's forces advanced 6 miles on 9 June, but only two days later Foch launched a counteroffensive at Château-Thierry and Belleau Wood supported by tanks as well as the U.S. 2nd and 3rd divisions. General Pershing was delighted that his 'superior' troops were finally able to rescue 'the tired Europeans'.[80]

The German Army was halted once more just outside the gates of Paris. It was even more bloodied and exhausted than it had been in 1914. Overall losses for June were 209 435 men. The front from Verdun to the Flanders coast had been extended by another 75 miles. The Prussian War Ministry warned the *OHL* that the storm troops had been ground up in the fighting, and demanded that 13 battalions of 450 officers and 18 000 men be dissolved. Ludendorff concurred and amalgamated these forces with the remaining 'attack' divisions.[81] Hutier received reports of mounting cases of indiscipline; units of the Brandenburg Reserve Division had painted 'red guards' on numerous train cars. At home, the Berlin police warned the government that the populace was driven by one thought alone: an end to the war. 'In troubling numbers the voices demanding "peace at any price" increase . . . because all are afraid of another winter of war.'[82]

The *OHL* was keenly aware that the outcome of the war hung in the balance, and it brooked no civilian criticism of its actions. Thus, when Foreign Secretary von Kühlmann informed the Reichstag on 24 June of his conviction that the war could no longer be ended by 'military decisions alone', Hindenburg and Ludendorff forced Kühlmann out of office by 8 July.[83] It would be the duumvirate's last political triumph.

The turning point

Ludendorff, seeing 'the overpowering moral superiority in the attack', refused to be denied the pleasure of taking Paris. On 15 July he drove his dispirited and weary troops forward again in what was to be his last offensive. Hoping to draw British forces down from the north, Ludendorff changed theatres once more and sent 24 divisions of the Seventh and First armies against the eastern side of the Marne salient, striking against both the eastern and the western side of Reims. Wilhelm II came to the front to witness the so-called 'peace battle' in the Champagne. Although advanced units established a bridgehead across the Marne at Dormans, the campaign collapsed within 48 hours. Alsatian troops, as dispirited as the Germans, had betrayed the timing of the assault.[84]

Foch by now understood the precise nature of the German attack system with its creeping barrages and infiltration tactics, and countered with a sophisticated 'elastic defence'. The Allied generalissimo left only skeletal forces in his foremost trenches, marshalled his main units about a mile behind the front lines to absorb the brunt of the assault, and held fresh French and American divisions in the rear for quick counterattacks. In fact, 250 000 American troops now arrived in France every month, with the result that Pershing commanded 25 divisions and 1 million support troops. Ludendorff hastily abandoned plans for the cherished offensive in Flanders (*Hagen*).

Instead, Wetzell, Ludendorff's operations officer, drafted memoranda detailing offensives on the Western Front as well as combined German-Austro-Hungarian operations to 'obliterate the Italian Army' in the autumn of 1918. Ludendorff allowed himself even greater flights of fantasy, informing General Friedrich Kress von Kressenstein that even after defeating France, his troops would have to pursue the British 'to their most vulnerable spot, to India'! For the time being, Ludendorff felt secure that his attacks since 21 March had so damaged the French Army as to preclude an attack.[85]

In his obsession with total victory, Ludendorff refused to acknowledge the appearance of what the writer Kurt Tucholsky called 'the Spanish sickness', a virulent influenza that in March 1918 had come from South Africa via Spain to France. In July about half a million soldiers lay sick in their trenches and another 80 000 in hospitals. While it usually lasted only 4 to 5 days, the Spanish influenza nevertheless had devastating effects on combatants: fever of 40 to 41 degrees Celsius, slowed heart rate of 60 beats per minute, tiredness, weakness, chill attacks, irritant coughs, and head as well as joint, back, and neck aches. Doctors initially responded only with bloodletting and cold compresses; later with antipyrin and salvarson.[86] When army commanders informed the *OHL* that the troops were exhausted and that a sudden bout of Spanish influenza had laid low almost 400 000 men, Ludendorff curtly replied: 'The troops need to get used to weak battle strengths; and I do not know influenza'.[87]

In the early hours of 18 July, German forward listening posts heard motor noises and traffic hums through the rain and thunder. Two French deserters came out of the forest of Villers-Cotterêts, and informed the Germans that a major attack would come between 5 and 6 a.m. Before the information could be passed back to headquarters, massive enemy formations emerged from the mist and fog around 5:35 a.m. The Germans could see swarms of tanks advancing at the rate of 5 miles per hour from behind the cover of a creeping barrage. Without prepared defensive positions or even shell craters to hide in and with their vision impaired by the high stands of grain in the fields, they were no match for the Allied onslaught. Foch's forces quickly ruptured Ludendorff's front, penetrated deep behind his lines, and then rolled his infantry up from the rear.[88] British planes mercilessly strafed the fleeing soldiers.

The so-called Second Battle of the Marne, spearheaded by 19 French divisions and 4 American, 2100 guns, 750 tanks, and more than 1000 airplanes, caved in Ludendorff's front. General Mangin's Tenth Army and General Jean Degoutte's Sixth Army hurled the Germans back behind the Vesle River. Ludendorff could only express his fervent hope that 'the Good Lord will not desert us'. Hindenburg bravely informed the Kaiser that the present predicament reminded him 'of the situations that Frederick the Great had to suffer through – and still won'.[89] French Premier Georges Clemenceau ebulliently proclaimed: 'My foreign policy and my home policy are the same. At home I wage war. Abroad, I wage war. . . . I shall go on waging war'.[90]

Ludendorff was forced to order a general retreat within 48 hours of Foch's breakthrough. On 19 July Lossberg pleaded with Ludendorff, whom he found to be 'terribly nervous' and 'very depressed', to withdraw immediately to the Siegfried Line. But the First Quartermaster-General blamed all past failures on his operations chief, Wetzell, and refused to accept this counsel, still believing that the Army was sound and intact.[91] Rage, panic, and paralysis gripped Ludendorff. Crown Prince Rupprecht apprised the *OHL* of his 'concern about the increasing deterioration of morale among the troops' in general and among the elderly soldiers who had been sent to France from Russia late in 1917 in particular. It was not at all unusual, Rupprecht informed the Supreme Command, for 20 per cent of reserves sent to the front to fail to report for duty.[92] Cases of desertion skyrocketed in July and August. Some openly refused to obey orders; others lost any sense of discipline; still others wildly fired their weapons out of moving trains. All too many readily surrendered to the Allies.[93]

The German Army had given its all for *Michael*. Skeletal divisions manned by badly clothed and undernourished soldiers and powered by emaciated horses had driven the best-equipped and best-fed armies of Britain and the Empire, France, and the United States back to the very gates of Paris. Outnumbered and outgunned in the air and on the ground, Ludendorff's soldiers had fought like lions. That they halted to sack rich Allied food and clothing depots speaks volumes for their physical state of being. Yet all they had achieved, in the words of the German official history, were 'ordinary victories'. Nowhere had they possessed sufficient manpower to 'roll up' the enemy front. The lack of tanks and the inferior quality of their iron-rimmed trucks had denied them the ability to encircle large enemy units.[94]

General von Hutier readily conceded that his soldiers were exhausted. No petrol for trucks. No ammunition for the artillery. No reserves. Poor defensive positions. 'The situation is terrible.' For the first time, reserves coming up to the front were met with shouts of 'strike breakers' by hardened veterans. Hutier was upset that 'the OHL counts only the number of divisions, not their strength and their [fighting] value'. Some battalions were down from their normal strength of 900 men to just 100. British air strafed the trenches with such intensity that the soldiers could neither sleep nor rest. *Michael* had driven them to the limits of their moral and physical capabilities.[95]

But Ludendorff refused to admit that his final roll of the dice had come up a loser. The Army now fought its second stubborn retreat in 4 years from the Marne step by bloody step – at the horrendous cost of 420 000 dead and wounded as well as 340 000 captured and 'missing'.[96] Groener, who would succeed Ludendorff in October, recalled that Hindenburg's second in command was a physically and morally broken man after 18 July. Ludendorff, Groener argued, had been absent from the front too long to understand its plight, had overestimated the Army's resilience, and yet had refused to concede defeat 'for political reasons' – read, war aims. Ludendorff simply hoped and prayed that the enemy was equally exhausted.[97] He refused to recall his occupation forces from the east for fear of surrendering conquered lands. Groener after the war reiterated his firm belief that the tide had turned on 18 July, whereafter 'Ludendorff's entourage complained about his indecision and inability to see the larger picture. He really duped himself and, just like Falkenhayn in 1916 at Verdun, was at his wit's end'.[98]

General von Lossberg shared Groener's thoughts. In his opinion, also, Ludendorff had 'overestimated the internal cohesion of our Army' and as a result had lost the initiative to the Allies on 18 July. Whereas Ludendorff would later claim that 8 August – the day Rawlinson's British Fourth Army led by 456 tanks and 800 airplanes crashed through the six skeletal divisions of Marwitz's Second Army near Amiens and inflicted 27 000 casualties on the enemy – constituted the 'black day' of the German Army, Lossberg (and Groener) moved that date back to 18 July.[99] With historical hindsight, one can well argue that the tide had turned already by 29 March. Bavaria's diplomatic delegation in Berlin informed King Ludwig III that Operation *Michael*, much like the U-boat campaign of the previous year, had raised hopes too high, only to dash them. Few inside Germany any longer believed Army communiqués; most gave greater credence to Allied casualty and POW reports.[100]

The truth is that Ludendorff never rose above the intellectual level of a regimental colonel commanding infantry. He believed that it sufficed merely to break the enemy line somewhere, at some time for the Allied armies to disintegrate and then surrender. He never understood that holes in the line, no matter how wide, could be filled with fresh reserves quicker than they could be exploited by exhausted attackers. He was bewildered by the storm of protest that he raised after the war with his comment: 'Tactics had to be raised above pure strategy'. And he defended his statement to the official historians of the war in 1923 as follows: 'I always had only the one great goal of victory before my eyes. The means to accomplish this were dictated by the prevailing situation. . . . For the offensive I always asked, where do I best break through, where is the enemy's weakest point'.[101] In a word, strategy became reduced to tactics.

Nor did Ludendorff admit that the Army was at the end of its physical and psychological capabilities after 18 July. Repeated Allied blows sent it reeling along the ropes like a punch-drunk boxer: Amiens, Meuse-Argonne, Flanders, Sambre, and Scheldt. The Allies stormed the Siegfried Line. Tens of thousands of German veterans deserted. Other tens of thousands simply went 'missing'. Artillery became lost in the massive retreat, and many regimental histories later attested to the demoralizing effect of so-called 'friendly fire'. 'Slackers' and 'shirkers' simply melted into the confusion of humanity in rear areas and in Belgium. Trains hauling the wounded back to base hospitals were often commandeered by rebellious troops.[102]

Like a boxer feeling his last shot at the title disappearing, Ludendorff refused to accept defeat. Instead, he blamed setbacks on his staff and on front-line commanders. He demanded that officers use their side arms to deal with cases of disobedience, that military courts hand down more draconian sentences for any and all infractions of military law, and that deserters be summarily executed. Last but not least, he blamed the looming defeat on the sheer numbers of Americans arriving daily at the front – without apparently ever recalling the haughty ease with which he as well as Wilhelm II and Hindenburg had dismissed American power when deliberating unrestricted submarine warfare in January 1917.

The Allied summer offensive of 1918 finally drove home the value of the tank to the *OHL*. While Ludendorff barely managed to scrape together 20 mostly captured enemy tanks at the start of 1918, Foch commanded a fleet of 600 to 700. By war's end, 45 German front-line tanks ranged against 3500 Allied. And while Britain had 5000 and France 4000 units on order for 1919, Germany hoped to field at most 1000.[103] After Foch's great tank-led offensive of 18 July, Colonel von Thaer sarcastically mused that 'even Ludendorff' should now acknowledge the tanks' value. The 'demigods' on the staff of the *OHL* for too long had reassured Ludendorff that 'our infantry laughs about the tanks'. Thaer bitterly noted that he had heard no such 'laughs' while serving at the front; rather, the men had '*pleaded* for an effective antitank weapon'.[104]

Reports from the front confirmed Thaer's concerns. On 11 August, 3 days after the British tank-led triumph near Amiens, the German Ninth Army summarized its experiences with the mechanical monsters. It bravely admonished troops not to overestimate tanks, but to show 'cold blood' and 'fire discipline' in combating them. Tanks were to be allowed to advance to almost point-blank range for the 13 mm antitank guns to be effective. Hutier's Eighteenth Army had experienced success by simply letting the tanks pass through its lines and directing artillery in rear echelons to dispatch them. But lately the Allies sent their tanks not as isolated units, but in waves. Individual antitank guns and machine guns were useless against massed vehicles. Hand-grenades were effective only if bundled together and placed in the caterpillar tracks – unless one was brave enough to climb on to the tank, open its hatch, and drop a grenade inside!

The best antidote consisted of a number of measures which, when combined, might prove successful. The troops were to dig deep and wide antitank ditches, to flood existing bogs and streams wherever possible, to dismantle or destroy solid bridges and replace them with fragile wooden structures too weak to support tanks, and to fell trees across their paths of advance. Artillery was to be massed in batteries throughout the entire defensive zone. And the guns had to be mobile: all too often they were deeply dug into earthen emplacements and hence ineffective against moving targets.[105] The Army estimated that it destroyed 102 French tanks in July, and 887 Allied between 8 August and 11 November.[106]

Germany's only production model, the A7V, proved to be so unwieldy and unreliable that it was mothballed in the summer of 1918; the 80 remaining chassis were converted to field trucks. The German Army in France had only 20 A7V tanks; its main armour consisted of about 170 captured Allied vehicles in various states of disrepair. The German official history conceded that its new 13 mm antitank gun had found little favour with the troops as it proved to be unreliable and tedious to operate.[107]

Manpower, of course, proved to be by far the most critical concern. Between March and July, the ranks of the German Army had been thinned from 5.1 to 4.2 million men. By July, one-third of the 196 divisions attached to Army Groups Crown Prince Rupprecht and German Crown Prince were down from 850 to 600 men at the battalion level. The 700- to 800-men reserves of the 'mobile' divisions had been exhausted. Countless divisions had but 2000 combatants.

The *OHL* undertook one last, frantic search for able bodies to send to the front. Relatively 'safe' rear-echelon formations such as motor, railroad, and communications units were stripped of 62 700 men and their counterparts at home of another 2500 for service with the infantry. Occupation battalions in Russia were reduced from 800 men to 600. More than 132 000 soldiers were 'combed' out of rear-echelon support units, staffs, deputy staffs, and Belgian occupation forces. About 152 000 former German POWs were exchanged against Russians held by the Reich, but these could hardly be expected to serve in France in 1918. The 2.3 million men of the Home Army consisted mainly of indispensable staff, training officers, doctors, medical care workers, and superannuated *Landsturm* veterans unfit for front-line duty. Roughly 70 000 to 80 000 convalescents returned to duty each month. The only true reserve available was the cohort of 1900 – 400 000 youths of whom 300 000 could be expected fit for duty. 'Too bad about the [loss of this] young blood' was General von Hutier's terse comment.[108] No amount of juggling, however, could satisfy the Army's minimal demand for 200 000 replacements per month.

The *OHL* calculated that 1.3 of the 2.5 million men employed in war-related industries at home were fit for combat duty, but declined to conscript them for fear of thereby endangering armaments production. Nearly 4 million women as well as 130 000 Russian and 170 000 Belgian labourers already worked in German industry. None could be spared. In desperation, Hindenburg on 18 June demanded that the government enact his draconian proposals of the winter of 1916–17: forced direction of labour, reduction of wages and prices, restrictions on war profits, enforced female work, an end to job mobility, and the extension of war service to age 60. But Chancellor von Hertling had no desire to challenge either the Reichstag or trade unions on the matter, and on 1 July allowed it to lapse.[109]

The United States, in contrast, had no manpower problems. Unknown to the Germans, the Americans had laid plans for an 80-division Army of 4.3 million men to be ready in 1919.[110] But the presence of American units in the Allied lines as early as March had not escaped attention. Although Captain Willi Brüninghaus of the Navy Office brazenly informed German leaders as late as September that the U-war was on track and that the Americans arrived in Europe 'naked so to speak', without equipment or supplies,[111] in reality the United States had sent half a million men to France at the very moment (July) that the German Army had been reduced by a million. The Republic had built 1000 bulk-cargo carriers of 3 million tons in 1917–18, and by 1918 was sending 296 000 tons of shipping down slips every month. Allied new construction in 1918 outpaced U-boat sinkings by nearly 3 million tons. At the height of the supply effort in the summer of 1918, one cargo or transport ship left its eastern seaboard for France every 5 hours. German naval leaders never explained what had happened to their 'guarantee' that not a single American soldier would ever land in France.

President Wilson, while in principle opposed to the 'amalgamation' of American troops with British and French forces, in July had allowed Pershing to let the Allies use his 'doughboys' (infantrymen) to plug gaping holes punched in their lines by Ludendorff's offensives. But Pershing thirsted for his 'own' battle. Foch and Haig yielded to his demands and agreed with the American commander that the first battle of the American Expeditionary Forces (AEF) needed to be a certain victory. The St Mihiel salient, a German bulge in the French lines in the direction of Bar-le-Duc that truncated the vital rail link between Verdun and Nancy, seemed a suitable target.

At 1 a.m. on 12 September more than 3000 artillery tubes for 4 hours fired 1.1 million shells at the Germans – the greatest single artillery bombardment in the war.[112] Thereafter, nearly 20 divisions of the American First Army, supported by 267 light tanks under the command of Lieutenant-Colonel George C. Patton, Jr., as well as about 1400 Allied aircraft attacked the eight war-weary and understaffed German divisions of Composite Army C in the form of two sharp pincers of a set of forceps on both sides of the salient. Victory was never in doubt – especially since Ludendorff on 11 September, the day before the attack, had ordered Army Group Gallwitz to evacuate the salient in case of attack.[113] The Americans in effect 'relieved the Germans' in the St Mihiel salient.[114] The moral fibre of the Germans can be gauged by the fact that they received the newly-arrived Austro-Hungarian 1st and 35th divisions with cries of 'war prolongers'.

The AEF next joined British and French forces in the Meuse-Argonne region to deliver the Germans a 'knockout' blow. Brilliant staff work by Colonel George C. Marshall, Jr., moved about 600 000 doughboys roughly 60 miles from St Mihiel to the new sector. Basing their operational planning on the faulty assumption that the Argonne forest was impenetrable, the Allied and Associated Powers sought to hurl the Germans against this natural barrier, while at the same time cutting off all possible avenues of retreat. But the Argonne forest was not impenetrable, and the Germans hastily erected an 'elastic defence' consisting of deep trenches, concrete pill boxes, miles of barbed wire, and artillery to a depth of 6 miles in and around the Kriemhild Line. On 26 September the great American assault, supported by 3000 guns and 189 tanks, broke against this line near Côte Dame Marie.[115] It quickly bogged down as the Americans were mowed down by woven belts of machine-gun fire at 'death valley', as they called the Vesle River. It took weeks of hard work before Pershing's forces were able to break the Kriemhild Line, outflank the Bois de Boulogne, and throw the Germans behind the Meuse.

In October the German Fifth Army supplied Ludendorff with an assessment of American forces. It praised the individual vigour and prowess of the American soldier, but found liaison between staffs and fighting forces to be 'inadequate'. While infantry and machine guns were helpless against American tanks, most of the latter were rendered *hors de combat* not by artillery but rather by mechanical breakdowns and the mud of shell craters. Interrogation of American prisoners revealed that most were 'naive in military and political matters' and merely followed the desires of their officers to crush 'German militarism'. Whereas they originally had seen the war as a 'happy picnic', this 'hurrah patriotism' had vanished in the Meuse-Argonne campaign. Most Americans were weary of the war and simply wanted to go home.[116]

This analysis notwithstanding, the Americans pressed on. To the great chagrin of the French, Pershing's First Army, now commanded by General Hunter Liggett, decided to liberate Sedan – site of the ignominious French defeat in 1870. There is no question that the Americans calculated the prestige factor in their decision. General Hugh A. Drum, Pershing's Chief of Staff, bluntly stated: 'General Pershing desires that the honor of entering Sedan should fall to the American First Army'.[117] But a jumble of orders and counterorders confused the commanders in the field, with the result that Pershing's favourite First Division 'advanced through' the American 42nd (Rainbow) Division by night – and momentarily took its commander, General Douglas MacArthur, prisoner![118]

The burlesque of Sedan could not obscure the fact that the outcome of the war was no longer in doubt. In mid-August Wilhelm II conceded that the game was up: 'We are at the end of our capabilities. The war must be ended'.[119] On 6 September Ludendorff accused his staff and front-line commanders of having lost the war; the next day he replaced his operations officer, Wetzell, with Major Joachim von Stülpnagel. The military situation deteriorated rapidly. The German Army lost 228 100 men in August; of these, 110 000 were listed as 'missing', that is, they had deserted. The number of divisions had shrunk from roughly 200 in March to 125 by the end of September; only 47 were deemed fit for combat. The Allies maintained 211 full divisions in the field, and their numbers grew steadily with the daily arrival of thousands of Americans.

Morale among German troops reached new lows. Fresh units moving up to the front were greeted even by the venerable Prussian Guards with shouts of 'strike breakers' and 'war prolongers'.[120] Major Ludwig Beck, a staff officer with Army Group German Crown Prince and destined to rebuild the Army under Adolf Hitler in the 1930s, compared German forces on the Western Front to a fragile 'spider's web of combatants'.[121] Although the Army's last Medical Report was compiled on 31 July, researchers of the German official history later estimated the number of shirkers or slackers at between 750 000 and 1 million for the last 2 months of the war. And while there are relatively few documented cases of soldiers openly disobeying orders, apparently hundreds of thousands simply refused to take risks.

General Heinrich Scheüch, head of the War Office and soon to take over the Prussian War Ministry, tried to comfort Ludendorff with the news that 637 000 men born in 1900 would soon join the ranks. Some officers on Ludendorff's staff suggested that Germany might resort to a *levée en masse* or even to guerrilla warfare to stem the Allied advance. They found few takers. Major von Leeb with Army Group Crown Prince Rupprecht expressed the view of many when he stated: 'The campaign has been lost, the military mistakes [made] have now come home to roost'. Leeb only hoped that 'diplomacy can save what there is to save'.[122] He, as well as fellow staff officers, knew that the Army was both morally and physically destroyed.

On 1 October Colonel von Thaer joined the General Staff just in time to receive a detailed operational review from Ludendorff. The latter was no longer concerned with prosecuting the war to a victorious conclusion, but rather with his role in history. Ludendorff began the meeting by expressing his fear that the Siegfried Line could be ruptured any day. 'The OHL and the German Army are finished; the war could no longer be won; rather, the final defeat was probably inescapably at hand.' Bulgaria had capitulated to the French General Franchet d'Esperey on 29 September; Austria–Hungary and Turkey were at the end of their endurance. Ludendorff reiterated that the Allies, with the help of nearly 3 million fresh American troops, could soon gain 'a *great* victory, a *breakthrough in grand style*'. 'One could *no longer* rely on the troops.' The bottom line was that the Army had to be spared a catastrophic defeat at all costs. There was only one solution: the Kaiser and the Chancellor had to 'request an armistice *without any hesitation*'. Lest staff officers not appreciate the full meaning of his words, the First Quartermaster-General repeated that 'prosecution of the war was senseless', and that only 'a *quick* end' to the war could save the Army from destruction. Closing the briefing, Ludendorff cynically suggested that the Kaiser be asked to bring to power '*those circles which we mainly have to thank* that things have come to this'. In other words, liberals and socialists were to be made ministers so that they would bear the burden for ending the war. '*They can now clean up the mess for which they are responsible.*'[123] Most staff officers broke down amidst sobbing and tears.

Few of those present at the meeting realized that Ludendorff had just laid the foundations of the infamous 'stab-in-the-back' (*Dolchstoss*) legend that was to dog German politics in the postwar period. Within 24 hours, Ludendorff dispatched Major Erich von dem Bussche-Ippenburg to Berlin to inform incoming Chancellor Prince Max von Baden and party leaders that the war had been lost. The Bulgarian front had collapsed. The Western Front threatened to cave in any day. There was no antidote to Allied tanks. And the manpower situation was so critical that the Army could not survive the winter. 'Every [delay] of 24 hours could worsen the situation.'[124] In short, Ludendorff demanded an immediate armistice on the basis of the Fourteen Points – which the General admitted he did not know, and which he now requested from the Foreign Office. Civilian leaders, who had been denied precise information on the military situation for 4 years by the *OHL* and the two dozen corps commanders at home, were now told to conclude peace at any price – and within a day.

Max von Baden became Chancellor on the evening of 3 October. Within 48 hours he dispatched a formal note to President Wilson requesting peace negotiations on the basis of the Fourteen Points. Wilson's reply of 8 October was diplomatic and polite, and merely requested clarification whether Imperial Germany in fact fully accepted the Fourteen Points as the basis for further discussions.[125] The Reich's ruling elite quickly embraced the President's measured words, much like a drowning person reaches for a lifeline. Ludendorff thought that Wilson's terms would allow him to keep Ukraine and the German-speaking parts of Alsace-Lorraine. The Foreign Office calculated that the Fourteen Points would permit Germany to regain its overseas colonies after the peace. Optimists in Berlin and Spa spied the chance to play Wilson off against hard-line Entente leaders such as Clemenceau and Lloyd George. A few even hoped to hoist the British on the President's petard concerning the 'self-determination' of peoples – read, the Irish question.

A second note of 14 October, in Wilson's own words, proved to be more 'frank and direct', and poured cold water on such rosy interpretations of the Fourteen Points. The President now demanded 'absolutely satisfactory safeguards and guarantees of the maintenance of the present military supremacy of the armies of the United States and of the Allies in the field', rebuked the Reich's 'illegal and inhumane' submarine warfare, and denounced the Germans' 'wanton destruction' of Flanders and France.[126]

In Berlin and Spa, panic set in with the arrival of the 'bombshell'. The Chancellor on 16 and 17 October quickly dispatched his closest advisor, Kurt Hahn, to The Hague to assure the American legation there that the new government intended to reform Prussia's antiquated constitutional system. Additionally, by way of this personal diplomacy, Max von Baden hoped to appeal directly to President Wilson to end the war on moderate and humane terms. At Spa, Ludendorff still favoured an immediate armistice to save the Army, but Hindenburg on 18 October assured military commanders that the front, both in France and at home, could be 'regarded as being secure'.[127]

More realistic synopses, however, prevailed. Few army leaders saw any hopes in renewing the war, and few diplomats expected more lenient treatment from Paris or London. On 20–1 October the German government formally appealed to Wilson for an armistice. It agreed to evacuate all occupied territories, but rejected the President's charges of 'illegal and inhumane actions' in occupied territories. It further pointed out that Germany was already revising its constitution along more democratic lines, thereby hoping to defuse American charges of 'Prussian militarism'. For the first time in its history, Germany accepted proposals by a foreign power as the basis for peace.

President Wilson's third note of 23 October removed any final illusions that the Germans may have had about a peace based on the Fourteen Points. Wilson demanded 'unrestricted power' to 'make a renewal of hostilities on the part of Germany impossible'. Moreover, he refused to negotiate with the 'King of Prussia' and his military minions, whose words could not be trusted, and instead stated that he would deal only with the 'veritable representatives of the German people who have been assured of a genuine constitutional standing as the real rulers of Germany'. The only terms to be offered to 'the monarchical autocrats of Germany' were 'surrender'.[128]

Neither statesmen nor soldiers in Germany ever understood what Wilson had meant in January 1917 by his formula 'peace without victory'. The President's fundamental policy, based on his conception of a just and lasting peace, remained consistent: the United States would enter the conflict one way or another to secure 'an equitable territorial settlement based on self-determination and a new world order based on collective security'.[129] The defeat of 'Prussian militarism' and 'autocracy' was part of that policy. The problem was that Wilson's personal style of diplomacy often was at odds with his idealistic pronouncements. His biographer, Arthur S. Link, admitted that the President 'exercised almost absolute personal control' over foreign affairs, that he often bypassed the State Department via private agents and advisers, that he at times conducted negotiations behind the backs of his Secretaries of State, and that overall he 'acted like a divine-right monarch in the conduct of foreign relations'. Secure in the knowledge that the American people had 'temporarily vested their sovereignty in foreign affairs in him',[130] Wilson saw himself as an instrument of divine purpose. He believed that his intellect was superior to that of both his associates and the German negotiators.

The President's third note stunned the Germans. Wilhelm II had already dismissed Wilson's second note as 'a piece of unmitigated frivolous insolence',[131] and Ludendorff on 23 October reacted to the third note by stating that he already found Prince Max's peace terms to have been 'beyond the bounds of what was militarily acceptable'. Ludendorff ranted to his staff about Wilson's and the Allies' 'boundless will of conquest and annihilation'.[132] Hindenburg concurred. At 10 p.m. on 24 October, he promulgated what amounted to a declaration of war on Prince Max's peace initiative. The Army's Order of the Day to all soldiers, read aloud to the General Staff to shouts of 'Long Live His Majesty, our King, Kaiser, and Warlord!', minced no words: 'Wilson's answer demands military capitulation. Thus for us soldiers it is unacceptable. . . . Wilson's answer can only amount to a challenge to continue to resist to the utmost of our capabilities'.[133] Obviously, Ludendorff and Hindenburg were quite willing to prolong the war in order to secure their vast annexations in the east and to maintain the Prusso-German ruling elite in power.

They found few takers and thus Prince Max was spared a confrontation with the *OHL*. On 26 October General Erich Ludendorff left his defeated Army in the field and fled in disguise to Sweden to pen his memoirs. Major von Leeb tartly commented: 'Therewith the mil[itary] dictatorship that until now has truly existed is at an end'.[134]

Chapter 10 Notes

1. Martin Middlebrook, *The Kaiser's Battle. 21 March 1918: The First Day of the German Spring Offensive* (London, Allen Lane, 1978), provides a vivid account of the opening day of the campaign.
2. See Heiger Ostertag, 'Die grosse Schlacht in Frankreich. Unternehmen Michael 21. März bis 4. April 1918', *Militärgeschichte* 3 (1993), p. 33; Oberkommando des Heeres, *Der Weltkrieg 1914 bis 1918*. 14: *Die Kriegführung an der Westfront im Jahre 1918* (Berlin, E. S. Mittler & Sohn, 1944), pp. 131 ff.
3. Otto Riebicke, *Was brauchte der Weltkrieg? Tatsachen und Zahlen aus dem deutschen Ringen 1914/18* (Berlin, Kyffhäuser-Verlag, 1936), p. 77.
4. Kurt Riezler, *Tagebücher, Aufsätze, Dokumente*, ed. Karl Dietrich Erdmann (Göttingen, Vandenhoeck & Ruprecht, 1972), pp. 459–60. Entry dated 15 April 1918.
5. Reichsarchiv, *Der Weltkrieg 1914 bis 1918*. 13: *Die Kriegführung im Sommer und Herbst 1917* (Berlin, E.S. Mittler & Sohn, 1942), pp. 324, 326.
6. Riezler, *Tagebücher, Aufsätze, Dokumente*, pp. 328–9.
7. BHStA, MA 3083. Report of 28 September 1917.
8. Reichsarchiv, *Der Weltkrieg 1914 bis 1918* 13, pp. 330–1.
9. *Der Weltkrieg 1914 bis 1918* 13, p. 397.
10. See Fritz von Lossberg, *Meine Tätigkeit im Weltkriege 1914–1918* (Berlin, E. S. Mittler & Sohn, 1939), pp. 315–16.
11. *Der Weltkrieg 1914 bis 1918* 14, pp. 77, 85.

12. Albrect von Thaer, *Generalstabsdienst an der Front und in der O.H.L. Aus Briefen und Tagebuchaufzeichnungen,* ed. Siegfried A. Kaehler (Göttingen, Vandenhoeck & Ruprecht, 1958), pp. 163, 169. Entries of 10 February and 19 March 1918.
13. BA-MA, W-10/50634 Generaloberst v. Einem, entry dated 16 February 1918.
14. *Der Weltkrieg 1914 bis 1918* 14, pp. 41–2.
15. BA-MA, PH 3/29 Übungskurs Sedan, September 1917.
16. BA-MA, PH 3/245 Ausbildungs-Lehrgänge Sedan 1917; see also PH 3/33 for a Seventh Army report on training dated 22 November 1917.
17. *Der Weltkrieg 1914 bis 1918* 14, p. 31.
18. BA-MA, PH 3/30 Übungskurs Sedan; 22–9 September 1917.
19. *Der Weltkrieg 1914 bis 1918* 14, pp. 29, 36, 720–1.
20. BA-MA, PH 5 I/46 Heeres OK: Kronprinz Rupprecht; 12 January 1918.
21. BA-MA, PH 5I/46 Heeres OK: Konprinz Rupprecht; Täuschungsplan of 24 February 1918.
22. BA-MA, PH 2/86 Kriegsministerium. Reichstagsmaterial; *Der Weltkrieg 1914 bis 1918* 14, p. 34.
23. Wolfram Wette, 'Reichstag und "Kriegsgewinnlerei" (1916–1918). Die Anfänge parlamentarischer Rüstungspolitik in Deutschland', *Militärgeschichtliche Mitteilungen* 36 (1984), p. 44. Daimler' stock rose from 317 at the end of 1913 to 630 by 1916, and 1350 late in 1917.
24. BA-MA, PH 20/19 Versorgungstruppen. Tanks.
25. BA-MA, PH 20/19 Versorgungstruppen. Ludendorff's order of 18 January 1918.
26. BA-MA, PH 20/19 Versorgungstruppen. Report of 3 May 1918. See also a report of April 1918 by the Second Army stressing the tanks' limited radius and restricted ammunition storage.
27. BA-MA, PH 6 I/28 VII AK (Gallwitz). Report of 28 April 1917.
28. BA-MA, PH 3/401. Generalstab. Memo of 8 March 1918.
29. BA-MA, PH 8 I/34 AOK IX. Tank Abwehr. A recent reinterpretation is T. H. E. Travers, 'Could the tanks of 1918 have been war winners?', *Journal of Contemporary History* 27 (1992), pp. 389–406.
30. Erich Ludendorff, *Urkunden der Obersten Heeresleitung über ihre Tätigkeit 1916/18* (Berlin, E. S. Mittler & Sohn, 1920), p. 641; and Bruce I. Gudmundsson, *Stormtroop Tactics: Innovation in the German Army, 1914–1918* (New York, Westport, and London, Praeger, 1989), pp. 149–52.
31. Cited in Holger H. Herwig, 'The Dynamics of Necessity: German Military Policy during the First World War', in Allan R. Millett and Williamson Murray, eds, *Military Effectiveness* (3 vols, Boston, Allen & Unwin, 1988) 1, pp. 101–2. See also Timothy T. Lupfer, *The Dynamics of Doctrine: The Changes in German Tactical Doctrine During the First World War* (Fort Leavenworth, Kans., U.S. Government Printing Office, 1981), pp. 41–9; and *Der Weltkrieg 1914 bis 1918* 14, pp. 45–6.
32. Cited in Crown Prince Rupprecht, *Mein Kriegstagebuch,* ed. Eugen von Frauenholz (3 vols, Berlin, Deutscher Nationalverlag, 1929) 2, p. 372.
33. *Der Weltkrieg 1914 bis 1918* 14, p. 88.
34. David F. Trask, *The AEF and Coalition Warmaking, 1917–1918* (Lawrence, University Press of Kansas, 1993), p. 53.
35. Wilhelm Deist, 'Der militärische Zusammenbruch des Kaiserreichs. Zur Realität der "Dolchstosslegende" ', in Ursula Büttner, ed, *Das Unrechtsregime. Internationale Forschung über den Nationalsozialismus* (2 vols, Hamburg, Christians Verlag, 1986) 1, pp. 105–6.
36. Ostertag, 'Die grosse Schlacht', p. 32.
37. *Der Weltkrieg 1914 bis 1918* 14, pp. 104–5.
38. BHStA-KA, HS 1964. 2. Bayer. Inft. Regt. Lt. Hermann Pürckhauer.
39. BHStA-KA, HS 1964, KTB Pürckhauer, 21 March 1918; *Der Weltkrieg 1914 bis 1918* 14, p. 131.

40. BHStA-KA, HS 1965. Lt. von LeSuire. Inf. Regt. #1. KTB 21. bis 23. März 1918.
41. Gudmundsson, *Stormtroop Tactics*, pp. 165–6.
42. BHStA-KA, HS 1964 KTB Pürckhauer.
43. BHStA-KA, HS 1965 KTB LeSuire.
44. BA-MA, W-10/50640 Tagebücher v. Hutier, entry for 31 March 1918.
45. Cited in *Der Weltkrieg 1914 bis 1918* 14, p. 162.
46. Walter Görlitz, ed., *The Kaiser and His Court: The Diaries, Note Books, and Letters of Admiral Georg Alexander von Mülller Chief of the Naval Cabinet, 1914–1918* (New York, Harcourt, Brace & World, 1961), p. 345. Entry dated 26 March 1918.
47. *Der Weltkrieg 1914 bis 1918* 14, p. 167.
48. Cited in Trask, *The AEF and Coalition Warmaking*, p. 64.
49. The deteriorating state of the German Army is documented in Germany, Nationalversammlung, *Das Werk des Untersuchungsausschusses der Verfassunggebenden Deutschen Nationalversammlung und des Deutschen Reichstages 1919–1930. Vierte Reihe. Die Ursachen des deutschen Zusammenbruchs im Jahre 1918. Zweite Abteilung. Der Innere Zusammenbruch* (19 vols, Berlin, Deutsche Verlagsgesellschaft für Politik und Geschichte, 1925–30), esp. vols 6 and 11.
50. *Der Weltkrieg 1914 bis 1918* 14, pp. 196–7.
51. Gerhard Ritter, *Staatskunst und Kriegshandwerk. Das Problem des 'Militarismus' in Deutschland* (4 vols, Munich, R. Oldenbourg, 1968) 4, p. 284.
52. Cited in *Der Weltkrieg 1914 bis 1918* 14, p. 244.
53. Erich Ludendorff, *Meine Kriegserinnerungen 1914–1918* (Berlin, E. S. Mittler & Sohn, 1919), p. 482.
54. Ostertag, 'Die grosse Schlacht', p. 35; *Der Weltkrieg 1914 bis 1918* 14, p. 254.
55. Riebicke, *Was brauchte der Weltkrieg?*, p. 83.
56. Generalfeldmarschall Wilhelm Ritter von Leeb, *Tagebuchaufzeichnungen und Lagebeurteilungen aus zwei Weltkriegen,* ed. Georg Meyer (Stuttgart, Deutsche Verlags-Anstalt, 1976), pp. 111, 112, 115. Entries dated 29 and 31 March as well as 6 April 1918.
57. BA-MA, Nachlass Groener, N 46, vol. 63. 'Ludendorff'.
58. Thaer, *Generalstabsdienst an der Front*, pp. 188, 196–7. Entry of 2 May 1918.
59. Lossberg, *Meine Tätigkeit im Weltkriege*, p. 321.
60. Rupprecht von Bayern, *Mein Kriegstagebuch* 3, p. 372.
61. BA-MA, W-10/50652 Kriegstagebuch v. Kuhl, entry for 31 March 1918.
62. *Der Weltkrieg 1914 bis 1918* 14, pp. 257–9.
63. *Der Weltkrieg 1914 bis 1918* 14, pp. 255–6, 283–4.
64. Cited in Deist, 'Der militärische Zusammenbruch', p. 115.
65. Rupprecht von Bayern, *Mein Kriegstagebuch* 3, p. 326; and 2, p. 387.
66. Thaer, *Generalstabsdienst an der Front*, p. 198.
67. Evelyn, Princess Blücher, *An English Wife in Berlin: A Private Memoir of Events, Politics, and Daily Life in Germany throughout the War and the Social Revolution of 1918* (New York, E. P. Dutton, 1920), p. 226.
68. Cited in *Der Weltkrieg 1914 bis 1918* 14, p. 506. Report of 15 April 1918.
69. BHStA-KA, HS 1959. Bayer. Inf. Regt. 15. Lt. Joseph Kübler.
70. BHStA-KA, HS 1972, Nr. 105. Lt. Willi Held.
71. Cited in Duff Cooper, *Haig* (2 vols, Toronto, Macmillan, 1935–6) 2, p. 273.
72. BHStA-KA, HS 2027. Oberlt. Simm. Schilderung über Tankbekämpfung der 4. Res. Feldart. Regt. 5.
73. BA-MA, PH 3/26 Angriffserfahrungen. 17 April 1918.
74. BA-MA, PH 2/24 Gasschiessen. Preuss. Heeresgasschule. August 1918.
75. Deist, 'Der militärische Zusammenbruch', p. 112. Figures from Germany, Reichskriegsministerium, *Sanitätsberichte über das deutsche Heer . . . im Weltkriege 1914–1918* (3 vols, Berlin, E. S. Mittler & Sohn, 1934–35) 3, pp. 781, 783.

76. BA-MA, W-10/50640 Tagebücher v. Hutier, entry for 20 May 1918.
77. Riebicke, *Was brauchte der Weltkrieg?*, p. 37.
78. BA-MA, W-10/50652 Kriegstagebuch v. Kuhl, entry for 5 June 1918.
79. *Der Weltkrieg 1914 bis 1918* 14, p. 398.
80. Cited in Trask, *The AEF and Coalition Warmaking*, p. 77.
81. BA-MA, PH 3/305. Sturmabteilung; report of June 1918.
82. Cited in *Dokumente aus geheimen Archiven*. 4: *Berichte des Berliner Polizeipräsidenten zur Stimmung und Lage der Bevölkerung in Berlin 1914–1918*, eds Ingo Materna and Hans-Joachim Schreckenbach (Weimar, Böhlau, 1987), p. 278.
83. Ritter, *Staatskunst und Kriegshandwerk* 4, pp. 382–3.
84. Army Group Archduke Albrecht on 8 August 1918 issued orders to keep Alsatians in line by threatening them with capital punishment even after the war, thus denying them a safe haven in Alsace; by seizing home and land; and by publishing their names. BA-MA, PH 5 I/75 AOK. Heeresgruppe Herzog Albrecht.
85. *Der Weltkrieg 1914 bis 1918* 14, pp. 430–1, 444, 514.
86. See Manfred Vasold, *Pest, Not und schwere Plagen. Seuchen und Epidemien vom Mittelalter bis heute* (Munich, C. H. Beck, 1991), *passim*.
87. Cited in *Der Weltkrieg 1914 bis 1918* 14, p. 445.
88. *Der Weltkrieg 1914 bis 1918* 14, pp. 479, 503.
89. Cited in *Der Weltkrieg 1914 bis 1918* 14, p. 490.
90. Cited in Marc Ferro, *The Great War, 1914–1918* (London, Routledge & Kegan Paul, 1973), p. 199.
91. Lossberg, *Meine Tätigkeit im Weltkriege*, pp. 344–7. Ludendorff apparently felt that his departure from the scene would lift enemy spirits and depress those of the German front and home. He threatened to resign if Lossberg pressed his demand for a strategic retreat. BA-MA, N 46, Nachlass Groener, vol. 156.
92. Crown Prince Rupprecht, *Mein Kriegstagebuch* 2, p. 402. Entry dated 25 June 1918.
93. *Der Weltkrieg 1914 bis 1918* 14, p. 523.
94. *Der Weltkrieg 1914 bis 1918* 14, p. 681.
95. BA-MA, W-10/50640 Tagebücher v. Hutier. Entries for 9 and 17 July, 10 August, 25 and 30 September 1918.
96. *Der Weltkrieg 1914 bis 1918* 14, Appendix 42.
97. BA-MA, Nachlass Groener, N 46, vol. 63. 'Ludendorff'. See also Lossberg, *Meine Tätigkeit im Weltkriege*, p. 346.
98. Wilhelm Groener, *Lebenserinnerungen. Jugend, Generalstab, Weltkrieg*, ed. Friedrich Hiller von Gaertringen (Göttingen, Vandenhoeck & Ruprecht, 1957), p. 347. Lossberg, *Meine Tätigkeit im Weltkriege*, p. 351, states: 'Not just 8 August 1918, but already 18. 7. 1918 was the critical turning point in the conduct of the war'.
99. Lossberg, *Meine Tätigkeit im Weltkriege*, pp. 350, 354. Ludendorff made his claim about 8 August in *Urkunden der Obersten Heeresleitung*, p. 547.
100. BHStA, MA 3085 Militär Bevollmächtigter Berlin. Schoen's report of 24 July 1918.
101. *Der Weltkrieg 1914 bis 1918* 14, p. 679.
102. See the splendid piece on this 'camouflaged military strike' by Wilhelm Deist in Wolfram Wette, ed., *Der Krieg des kleinen Mannes. Eine Militärgeschichte von unten* (Munich and Zurich, Piper, 1992), pp. 146–67.
103. Riebicke, *Was brauchte der Weltkrieg?*, pp. 51–2.
104. Thaer, *Generalstabsdienst an der Front*, p. 220.
105. BA-MA, PH 8 I/34. AOK 9. Tank Abwehr.
106. BA-MA, PH 20/19 Versorgungstruppen. Tanks.
107. *Der Weltkrieg 1914 bis 1918* 14, p. 525.
108. BA-MA, W-10/50640 Tagebücher v. Hutier, entry for 24 October 1918.
109. *Der Weltkrieg 1914 bis 1918* 14, pp. 517–20.

110. Trask, *The AEF and Coalition Warmaking*, p. 78.
111. BHStA, MA 3085 Militär Bevollmächtigter Berlin. Lerchenfeld's report of 28 September 1918.
112. Riebicke, *Was brauchte der Weltkrieg?*, p. 36. American forces according to *United States Army in the First World War 1917–1919*. 8: *Military Operations of the American Expeditionary Forces* (Washington, DC, U.S. Government Printing Office, 1948), pp. 131–5, 167, 235.
113. BA-MA, PH 5 I/52 AOK Gallwitz. Ludendorff's order, dated 11 September 1918. See also *Der Weltkrieg 1914 bis 1918* 14, pp. 599–602.
114. B. H. Liddell Hart, *The Real War 1914–1918* (Boston and Toronto, Little, Brown, 1930), p. 456.
115. See Trask, *The AEF and Coalition Warmaking*, pp. 122–3, 127–9; and Rod Paschall, *The Defeat of Imperial Germany 1917–1918* (Chapel Hill, Algonquin Books, 1989), pp. 163 ff.
116. BA-MA, PH 5I/52 Army Group Gallwitz. Report of 28 October 1918.
117. Drum to Pershing, 5 November 1918. *United States Army in the First World War*. 9: *Meuse-Argonne Operations of the American Expeditionary Forces* (Washington, DC, U.S. Government Printing Office, 1948), p. 385.
118. See the report of 7 November 1918 by General Charles P. Summerall, commander of the V Army Corps. *United States Army in the First World War* 9. Also Edward M. Coffman, *The War to End all Wars: The American Military Experience in World War I* (Madison, The University of Wisconsin Press, 1986), p. 351.
119. Cited in *Der Weltkrieg 1914 bis 1918* 14, p. 568. Dated 10 August 1918.
120. *Der Weltkrieg 1914 bis 1918* 14, p. 622; Lossberg, *Meine Tätigkeit im Weltkriege*, p. 356; A[ugust] von Cramon, *Unser Österreichisch-Ungarischer Bundesgenosse im Weltkriege. Erinnerungen aus meiner Tätigkeit als bevollmächtigter deutscher General beim k. u. k. Armeeoberkommando* (Berlin, E. S. Mittler & Sohn, 1922), p. 174.
121. Klaus-Jürgen Müller, *General Ludwig Beck. Studien und Dokumente zur politisch-militärischen Vorstellungswelt und Tätigkeit des Generalstabschefs des deutschen Heeres 1933–1938* (Boppard, H. Boldt, 1980), p. 326.
122. Leeb, *Tagebuchaufzeichnungen*, p. 138. Entry dated 30 September 1918.
123. Thaer, *Generalstabsdienst an der Front*, pp. 234–5. Leeb, *Tagebuchaufzeichnungen*, p. 140, quickly accepted that survival of the Army was the most important task at Supreme Command. 'The main thing now is not to allow a catastrophe to destroy the Army.' Entry for 3 October 1918.
124. Cited in Prinz Max von Baden, *Erinnerungen und Dokumente*, ed. Golo Mann (Stuttgart, Ernst Klett, 1968), pp. 322–3.
125. Arthur S. Link, ed., *The Papers of Woodrow Wilson* (69 vols, Princeton, Princeton University Press, 1965) 51, pp. 268–9.
126. Link, ed., *The Papers of Woodrow Wilson* 51, pp. 333–4.
127. BA-MA, PH 5 I/52 Army Group Gallwitz.
128. Link, ed., *The Papers of Woodrow Wilson* 40, pp. 402, 417–19.
129. Trask, *The AEF and Coalition Warmaking*, p. 167.
130. Arthur S. Link, *The Higher Realism of Woodrow Wilson and Other Essays* (Nashville, Tenn., Vanderbilt University Press, 1971), p. 83.
131. Cited in Ritter, *Staatskunst und Kriegshandwerk* 4, p. 441.
132. BA-MA, PH 5 I/52 Army Group Gallwitz. Ludendorff's opinions of 23 October 1918.
133. Cited in Ludendorff, *Urkunden der Obersten Heereseitung*, pp. 577–8.
134. Leeb, *Tagesbuchaufzeichnungen*, p. 148, dated 27 October 1918.

11

Defeat, 1918–19

We call the general strike of a defeated army the German revolution.

Walther Rathenau, 1918

Austria–Hungary and Germany had been defeated in the field by July 1918. Yet both continued the struggle into the autumn in the hope of a miracle. None came. In the Habsburg case, internal dissent destroyed the Army in August and September; in the Hohenzollern case, Allied hammer blows all along the Western Front battered the Army into submission by October. As early as 1 October, Kurt Riezler at the Wilhelmstrasse committed his darkest fears concerning the future to his diary: 'Slavery for 100 years. The dream of world power gone forever. The end of all hubris. The scattering of Germans throughout the world. Fate of the Jews.'[1]

The home front likewise had collapsed. Workers and veterans, women and children went about in rags, adult skeletons rummaging through garbage heaps to glean pieces of rotten meat, congealed blood, and decayed vegetables. The Allies estimated late in 1918 that an adult required at least 2500 calories per day to work; German labourers were down to 1000 calories, at best sufficient to nourish a 12-year-old child. More than 250 000 Germans had died of malnutrition in 1918 alone. In Austria–Hungary both the food supply and the transportation system had collapsed totally by October.

Finis austriae

On 17 August 1918 the peoples of the Dual Monarchy for the last time had a chance to observe Karl's birthday. The Kaiser spent the day at Reichenau, in the foothills of the Alps, and decorated a dozen generals with the coveted Knight's Cross of the Military Order of Maria Theresa. Archduke Friedrich in return presented Karl with a field marshal's baton that the *AOK* had taken along on Conrad von Hötzendorf's aborted Venetian campaign in the spring of 1918, with the intention of bestowing it on Karl in Vicenza or further south in Italy.[2] The hubris of the moment could hardly have escaped those present.

The truth is that the once venerable *k.u.k.* Army was no longer a fighting force. Of the Isonzo Army's 15 divisions, seven were at one-third, three at one-half, and only five even at two-thirds of full strength. Dysentery, malaria, and malnutrition had reduced the Army's rank and file to a pathetic shadow of its former self. The Sixth Army reported that its soldiers on average weighed 120 lbs. In mid-August Army Group Boroević warned headquarters at Baden that 600 to 800 men daily fell victim to malaria. Most soldiers had just one set of clothes, and these were but tattered rags. One regiment at the front noted that only every third man possessed a coat. Other units reported sentries manning their posts without underwear or trousers. Most soldiers went for days without meat or fat. 'In the morning and at night only black coffee without [sugar or cream]; at noon nutritionless dried vegetables and insufficient . . . ersatz bread, at best with a bit of cheese or pumpkin. Other fresh vegetables were only rarely to be had.' The Eleventh Army with understatement cabled the *AOK*: 'The troops are tired'. A soldier in Dalmatia informed his officer: 'We are not heroes, but beggars!'[3]

On 18 August General Arz von Straussenburg undertook what was to be the last formal assessment of the *k.u.k.* Army. His report was a strange mixture of naïvety and ignorance. The Chief of the General Staff finally appreciated that the Great War had taken on 'the characteristics of an economic struggle of survival', and accepted that it had become 'a question of the Monarchy's existence'. He now understood that modern industrial warfare demanded that the economic, political, and social components of the national polity be coordinated! Yet Arz staunchly defended the right of officers to preferential rations and accommodation, and declined to follow what he called the 'German example', whereby officers and men ate the same food at the front. Such an egalitarian turn was out of the question due to the 'differences in educational levels' between officers and men. How could one expect Austrian–German officers to consume food from kitchens staffed by different nationalities? The General found the prospect 'insufferable'. And what Austrian–German officer, Arz wished to know, would agree to serve in an army where officers and men ate from the same menu?

The Chief of the General Staff at least understood the dire straits in which his men found themselves. They received barely 100 g. of meat on

5 days of the week; vegetables at best twice a week; barely a pound of potatoes per week; and both men and horses were collapsing with alarming regularity due to the lack of food and fodder. No new sheets or tents, ice machines or water treatment plants had reached the front. Only 1.1 million of the required 8 million pairs of boots had been distributed to the soldiers in 1917–18. Arz promised that in future each Austrian division would have a bakery with 12 ovens (and 48 in the rear echelon) at all times.[4]

The General Staff had also received reports from the front concerning the Allied use of tanks, and in September it published instructions on how to deal with them. The tanks, Arz crowed, posed no danger to the troops. The best policy was simply to ignore them and to concentrate on the following infantry, 'the most dangerous opponent'. Friendly artillery would mop up the tanks – as it had done since 1914 with cavalry – once they had passed the front lines. Soldiers were instructed to dig fox holes in which to hide from the tanks' guns, and not to waste ammunition by firing on the mechanical monsters with machine guns.[5] It was fortunate for *Kamerad Schnürschuh* that he did not face British or French tanks along the Piave.

In fact, an eerie silence had descended over the southwestern front after the July battles. Both sides riveted their gaze to France, where they expected the war to be decided. When it became certain that the *Michael* offensive had failed and that the Allied and Associated Powers were about to storm the Siegfried Line and drive the Germans out of France, Italian General Diaz decided to go on the offensive. Diaz had at his command 51 Italian, 3 British, and 2 French divisions as well as a Czecho-Slovak and an American regiment; in all, 57 divisions with 704 battalions of infantry supported by 7700 guns and 6 million shells. The 22 divisions of this interallied force that were to spearhead the attack were moved up to the front between 26 September and 10 October.[6] Diaz planned to attack along the entire front, concentrating on the Piave in the direction of Vittorio Veneto. The assault, scheduled for 16 October, had to be postponed several times due to foul weather.

In the meantime, the Habsburg front was rapidly disintegrating. Army Group Pflanzer-Baltin began to withdraw from Albania on 1 October. The *AOK* ordered its troops to evacuate Venetia in mid-October. By the third week of October, General Kövess, commanding in Serbia, ordered a strategic retreat behind the Danube, Save, and Drina rivers. More than 100 000 men had been withdrawn from the Italian front, leaving a mere 400 000 – of whom but a third were combatants – to face the threatening Anglo-French-Italian assault. A wave of Spanish influenza hit railroad personnel in Vienna, making idle 8000 cars of rolling stock. Wild rumours of an impending armistice spread through the Army's ranks, and numerous ethnic units refused to obey orders to stand. National councils in the rapidly emerging new states of the Multinational Empire encouraged these developments: quasi-governments were established at Agram and Prague on 6 October. The Poles declared their independence from Vienna one day later.

Kaiser Karl undertook one final effort to end the war in order to save at least part of his inheritance. On 16 September and again on 4 October he appealed to President Wilson for peace on the basis of the Fourteen Points. The President's replies (to Berlin) were hardly encouraging, and they linked any Austro-Hungarian initiative to similar (and as yet not undertaken) efforts by Germany. Thus, on 16 October Karl launched a last-minute bid to reform the Empire and to save his throne. An Imperial Manifesto transformed the Austrian half of the Monarchy into a federal state wherein completely autonomous Romanian and Ruthene national councils would join their German counterpart. Neither Czechs nor Slovaks, Poles nor South Slavs paid any attention to the decree. And when Hungary threatened to curtail food shipments if Vienna attempted to extend the Manifesto to Transleithania, Karl quickly promised not to 'disturb the integrity of the lands of the Crown of St Stephen'.[7]

The Manifesto, rather than saving the Empire, proved to be its death warrant. Arz von Straussenburg suppressed its publication for several days, fearing that it would sow confusion among the officer corps. Karl lamely reassured that corps in an order-of-the-day that the special relationship that existed between it and the Crown would remain intact. By now, little that the Kaiser did mattered. On 19–20 October President Wilson rejected Karl's promise of 'autonomy' for the 'Czecho-Slovak' and the 'Jugo-Slavic' peoples and instead demanded their full independence.[8] Imperial-and-Royal orders and officials were soon ignored in Agram, Budapest, Laibach, Prague, Warsaw, and even Vienna. On 21 October the Parliament of Lower Austria voted to create a new German-Austrian state. In Budapest Károly's 'Independence and '48er Party' demanded termination of the 1867 Compromise. Karl refused all calls from his military to deploy force against the newly-emerging national states. On 23 October Croatian units rebelled in Fiume. Concurrently, other Croatian as well as Bosnian, Czech, Magyar, and Romanian formations left their posts in Venetia and headed home.[9] The *k.u.k.* Army was in a state of open revolt and informal dissolution.

General Diaz finally launched his long-awaited assault on 24 October 1918, the first anniversary of the start of the Battle of Caporetto. The Italian Fourth and Twelfth armies attacked in the direction of Monte Grappa north of Bassano, while the Eighth and Tenth armies crossed the middle Piave toward Vittorio Veneto. Surprisingly, Habsburg forces fought tenaciously for 2 days – and then melted away. Arz informed the Germans within 48 hours of the start of the Italian offensive that half his Army, 30 divisions, was in revolt. The Austrian official history of the war gives a long litany of divisions affected by dissolution between 26 and 27 October: the list included the 67th and 27th divisions at Asiago, the 34th and the 25th at Portule, the 16th in Sisemola, and the 5th in Borgo.[10] Recent studies suggest that the Czech 13th and 26th, the Bohemian 29th and 43rd, the Croatian 42nd and 57th divisions, and even units of the elite Austrian 3rd (Edelweiss) Division were also in rebellion.[11]

On 24 October Hungarian leaders appealed to *Honvéd* soldiers to lay down their arms and head home. Field Marshal von Krobatin called for an end to hostilities already the next day; Archduke Joseph followed with a similar plea on 26 October. At 9 a.m. on the morning of 28 October Field Marshal von Boroević demanded that the *AOK* conclude an armistice at any price to head off the 'anarchy' that would surely spell 'catastrophe for Monarchy and Army'.[12] Arz followed this advice within 4 hours. At 3:45 p.m. the *AOK* dispatched a military delegation to Triente to discuss terms with the Italians.

That same day, 28 October, Prague politicians proclaimed a Czecho-Slovak state; Slovak leaders concurred within 3 days. Austrian Galicia also announced on 28 October that it would join a new Polish state. One day later Croatia, Slovenia, and Dalmatia seceded from the Dual Monarchy. The German regions of Bohemia, Moravia, and Silesia declared the creation of an independent Austro-German Free State on 30 October. The following day War Minister Béla Linder of the new Hungarian National Council recalled Magyar troops, thereby formally abrogating the 1867 Compromise. On 31 October Karl issued a decree allowing all former Habsburg officers to accept employment with the emerging national states. Disgruntled soldiers in Budapest murdered former Prime Minister Tisza. The Swiss Ambassador in Vienna, Charles-Daniel Bourcart, caught the mood well in his last official report: 'Chaos reigns in the former Dual Monarchy'.[13]

In the meantime, the Austrian General Viktor Weber von Webenau worked feverishly to initiate armistice talks with Rome. It proved to be a risky undertaking. On 29 October the Italians fired on his emissary, Captain Kamillo Ruggerea, as the latter tried to approach their lines under a white flag. Two days later General Pietro Badoglio, Deputy Chief of the Italian General Staff, refused to receive a small delegation of German officers that included Captain Heinz Guderian, the future tank master of the Third Reich. Finally, just before midnight on 2 November, Karl accepted the Italian armistice terms worked out at the Villa Giusti, General Diaz' guest quarters near Padua; Weber von Webenau signed the document around 2 a.m. the next morning. The terms amounted to capitulation. The *k.u.k.* Army was to lay down its arms immediately and surrender half its artillery; to maintain only a skeletal force of no more than 20 divisions; to evacuate occupied lands; to release Entente prisoners of war; and to accord the Allies free access to the Austro-Hungarian transportation system (as a means of moving against Germany).[14]

But the Italians had cleverly stipulated that the Armistice took effect for them only at 3 p.m. on 4 November, and this allowed Diaz to mount a final attack designed to regain the 'honour' lost at Caporetto in 1917. The Italian 'victory' of Vittorio Veneto was won against an Empire that no longer existed, an Army that was incapable of fighting, and military units that consisted primarily of Slavs (Czechs, Slovaks, South Slavs, Poles, Ruthenes, Romanians) and Italians. Roughly 350 000 to 400 000 fleeing Austro-Hungarian soldiers from mainly rear-echelon forces as well as 24 generals fell into captivity in the space of 36 hours.[15] There is some evidence to suggest that the *AOK* at Baden had decided that captivity was preferable to starvation – and to having these ragged bands return home to loot the countryside.[16] Whatever the case, the Italians did not treat their prisoners well. The captured troops were kept in open-air camps and forced to do hard labour, with the result that about 30 000 died.

The Army's journey home quickly degenerated into chaos. Even Austrian units returning from the South Tyrol via the Inn Valley resorted to wide-scale looting and plundering of supply stores. At Innsbruck and Villach, the trains bringing back the veterans of the Italian campaigns were attacked by marauding bands of 'green cadres', bandits and thieves. Moreover, the trains were badly overcrowded, some 'looking in the distance like bees swarming', as one observer noted. 'Every train was fully occupied including the roofs, platforms, bumpers, running-boards, and locomotives. Hundreds of men paid the price [death] in tunnels, sharp turns, and low railway-bridges for their haste to return home.' Many of the revellers fired their rifles and set off hand-grenades.[17] An eye-witness recalled that the troops, 'once safe in Carinthia', simply threw away their rifles, insulted their officers, left their starving animals, and made for their homes in great haste. 'Soon thousands of helpless animals, thirsty and starving, stood about. . . . When fodder could no longer be procured, the gates were opened and the horses let loose to fend for themselves. . . . Droves of them roamed the streets of Klagenfurt, eating bark off the trees.'[18]

But the exodus did not end with the safe transport of veterans out of northern Italy. By 6 November, about 14 trains per day left Innsbruck, 18 Villach and Klagenfurt, and 32 Laibach to return 140 000 men to their homes in the new national states of the erstwhile Empire. By mid-

November, 400 000 soldiers had been trans-shipped out of the Inn Valley, 400 000 out of Carinthia, and 800 000 out of the Laibach basin. More than 460 000 Austrian troops from the Alps and the Tyrol marched home on foot.[19]

The price of Austria–Hungary's great folly had been horrendous: of the 8 million men mobilized, 1 015 200 had died, 1 943 000 had been wounded, and 3 748 000 had been hospitalized due to illness. Additionally, 480 000 of the 1 691 000 men taken prisoner had perished over the course of the 52 months of fighting.[20] A sympathetic historian of the *k.u.k.* Army in 1947 sought to write its epitaph:

> It was a good Army because it always understood how to do its duty. Wherever the belief in victory was lacking – and it was almost always lacking – it was replaced by good troop spirit and comradeship. It fought for the honour of the regimental flag, to please the colonel or captain, also for a decoration or a medal, and did not take a reverse too seriously for the special field rations remained in place and at home coffee houses and girls beckoned.[21]

Whether these cavalier thoughts were shared by the millions of casualties of the *k.u.k.* Army and their relatives remains questionable.

Josef Redlich – professor, minister, and liberal politician – visited Karl for the last time at Schönbrunn on the morning of 8 November. Pity overcame Redlich, though he was no monarchist. He found the 'poor young Kaiser' stripped of all authority and power, a solitary and pathetic figure amidst the baroque splendour of the Habsburg palace built by Karl VI and Maria Theresa, and once occupied by Napoleon I. The Army had been 'split into a million atoms'. Not a 'trace of the power' of the old Habsburg dynasty remained, 'neither in Vienna nor in Prague, neither in Budapest nor in Agram'. The dichotomy between Karl's current powerlessness and the grandeur of Schönbrunn 'symbolizes the deepest tragedy of earthly fame and human power'. Even the brilliant rococo portraits and the dazzling uniforms of the Kaiser's military entourage exuded but a 'breath of decay, the decay of a culture at once the finest but also recently grown tired'.[22]

On 10 September 1919 the victorious Allies in the Treaty of St Germain reduced Karl's inheritance to a small German-speaking rump centred at Vienna. The new Austrian Republic recognized the independence of Czechoslovakia, Yugoslavia, Poland, and Hungary. It ceded Austrian Galicia to Poland; the Trentino, the South Tyrol, Trieste, the Istrian Peninsula, and the Dalmatian islands to Italy; and Bosnia–Herzegovina to Yugoslavia. The army was limited to 30 000 men, the air force was abolished, and since Austria was cut off from the sea it no longer required a navy. In fact, Karl had turned over the Danube flotilla to Budapest and the Adriatic fleet to the Yugoslav Council. At Pola Captain Janko Vuković de Podkapelski became the new fleet chief. The Italians, angered at having been denied a major war prize and fearful that the Austrian naval threat in the Adriatic would be replaced by a Yugoslav, on 1 November sent a special operations team to Pola, where with two mines they blew up the flagship *Yugoslavia*, the former dreadnought *Viribus Unitis*. Austria was forbidden to seek closer relations with Germany, and in Article 177 of the Treaty accepted responsibility for starting the war and agreed in part to pay for its damages.

Hungary suffered a similar fate in the Treaty of Trianon, signed on 4 June 1920. It lost three-quarters of its former lands and two-thirds of its subjects. Budapest was forced to turn over Slovakia and Ruthenia to Czechoslovakia; Croatia–Slavonia and the Banat of Temesvár to Yugoslavia; and Transylvania as well as part of the Hungarian *pusta* to Romania. The Magyars were permitted an army of 35 000 men. Article 161 of the Treaty forced Hungary to accept responsibility for the war and to pay reparations.

Kaiser Karl renounced all political power on 11 November 1918, but refused formally to abdicate the throne. In March 1919, under British protection, Karl went into exile in Switzerland not far from the ruins of Castle Habichtsburg on the banks of the Aar River – the very spot from which his ancestors more than 6 centuries earlier had set out to rule Austria.

Finis prussiae

The German Army's demand of 3 October for an immediate armistice took Berlin's political leaders by surprise. Overnight, or so it seemed, the Reich had gone from victory to defeat. Its soldiers occupied Russia as far as the Caspian Sea. Belgium, Poland, the Baltic states, Ukraine, and Romania were German satellites. How could Ludendorff now demand an armistice? And at what price? At a press conference hastily assembled by the Supreme Command and the Foreign Office the following day, newspaper editors were briefed on the military situation. Having been fed mainly optimistic reports by the *OHL* for the past 4 years, they were utterly unprepared for the bleak prognosis and feared public reaction to the ill tidings.

Georg Bernhard, editor of the influential *Vossische Zeitung* and director of the powerful Ullstein publishing house, reminded the military that the populace was divided into two diametrically opposed camps: one painted the situation 'unduly black', the other 'so rosy that they insist on keeping Belgium'. Bernhard demanded that the *OHL* 'at the twelfth hour' finally tell the truth: 'How do we stand militarily?' Otherwise, a 'catastrophe', a collective psychological shock, would befall the German *Volk*. Representatives of other newspapers such as the *Deutsche Tageszeitung*, *Frankfurter Zeitung*, and *Kölnische Volkszeitung* likewise called for clarity. When the Foreign Office cautioned the press to avoid falling into either of the two antipodal camps, the conference became chaotic. Alexander Mozkowski of the Chemnitz *Allgemeine Zeitung* accused the government of lacking confidence in the media and of having manipulated the press for the course of the war. Thereupon Bernhard announced the conference closed and declared that he would no longer attend such briefings. The Supreme Command lamely suggested that the representatives of the press had 'lost their nerves'.[23]

Panic gripped Berlin. Slowly, the realization dawned that the war had been lost and that Germany's fate rested in the hands of the Allies. What kind of peace would they offer? What sort of future awaited 65 million Germans? Was there really no alternative to surrender? Would Berlin follow the example of Petrograd? Who would be the German Lenin?

On 7 October Walther Rathenau, head of German General Electric (AEG), published an article entitled 'A Dark Day' in Bernhard's *Vossische Zeitung*, wherein he sought to turn the tide at the last moment by calling for a '*levée en masse*, a rising of the people'. The Cabinet immediately dispatched General Scheüch, head of the War Office, to query Rathenau about the proposed '*défense nationale*' by 750 000 citizens. Rathenau now raised his call to 1.5 million *Bürger*, demanded that the Treaty of Brest-Litovsk be revised, that the U-boat campaign be called off, and that the Prussian War Ministry by reconstructed with 'citizens and soldiers'. Scheüch reported instead that Rathenau wished to see only 400 000 to 450 000 citizens called out for national defense.[24]

The Cabinet turned to the Supreme Command. On 9 October Ludendorff informed them that he saw no sense in a *levée en masse*; the Army already was short 70 000 replacements per month. Scheüch, who that same day was appointed Prussian War Minister, bravely put out a watchword, 'Every man should serve; every woman should work', but then conceded that he, too, saw no chance of success for Rathenau's mobilization of the nation.[25] Obviously, neither general wished to transform the old Imperial Army into a citizens' militia.

Instead, Scheüch optimistically held out the prospect that the 637 000 youths born in 1900 would soon join the ranks. But General Groener,[26] who succeeded Ludendorff as First Quartermaster-General of the Army on 29 October, quickly poured cold water on Scheüch's calculations.

Groener termed the 637 000 mark a 'highly imaginary figure', and instead suggested that the Army could at best gain 300 000 raw recruits; the rest were of questionable value. Groener also rejected the suggestion by some General Staff officers as well as Deputy Commanding Generals and Provincial Presidents that Germany embrace Rathenau's idea of a *levée en masse*, and reminded them that tens of thousands of wounded and invalided soldiers as well as 35 000 railway cars still awaited evacuation from the front.[27]

Last but not least, Groener lectured his staff that the Army was disintegrating: between 200 000 and 1.5 million soldiers were either 'missing' or had deserted; more than 40 000 'shirkers' were located at Maubeuge alone.[28] Austria–Hungary's collapse meant that its two infantry divisions would have to be pulled out of the Western Front on 29 October and sent home. Army Group Gallwitz reported on 31 October that thousands of soldiers refused to obey orders to fight.[29] Early in November the *OHL* conceded that it could muster barely a dozen fully-ready combat divisions between the Belgian Channel coast and the Upper Rhine. And a new, more deadly wave of Spanish influenza had hit almost one in every six Germans late in October 1918.

The final impetus for Germany's collapse came from the Navy. On 22 October Admiral von Hipper, the new fleet chief, concocted Operations Plan No. 19, which called for a suicidal sortie by the High Sea Fleet against the British Grand Fleet, augmented by five American super-dreadnoughts.[30] Germany's admirals hoped thereby to salvage the service's 'honour' and to assure the fleet's 'future existence'. Instead, on 29 October the stokers doused the fires in the boilers and raised the red banner of revolt on the dreadnoughts *König*, *Kronprinz Wilhelm*, and *Markgraf*. Officers reported further cases of insubordination on the dreadnoughts *Thüringen*, *Kaiserin*, and *Helgoland*. Few sailors sought to emulate Lenin's Russian revolution, and instead considered their actions more akin to a 'strike' against the military powers of Imperial Germany. Most demonstrated against the government's failure to end the war. Inexperienced in politics, Hipper dispatched the mutinous Third Squadron to Kiel, where its sailors immediately fomented revolution. Lübeck and Travemünde fell by 5 November, Hamburg the next day, followed by Bremen, Cuxhaven, and Wilhelmshaven on 6 November. From the ports, the sailors headed inland and kings, princes, and mayors throughout the Reich quietly surrendered their authority to them.

The naval rebellion, coming on the heels of President Wilson's third note and Hindenburg's Army Order of the Day, finally energized the politicians in Berlin. By 28 October, in a last-ditch attempt to save what could be saved by placating the Great Idealist in Washington, they had put the finishing touches on the first major revision of the Bismarckian constitution since 1871. Henceforth, the Chancellor would be responsible to the Reichstag. International treaties, the declaration of war as well as the conclusion of peace, and the appointment, promotion, and dismissal of officers would require the consent of both the Reichstag and the Federal Chamber. The Ministers of War likewise would have to answer to both federal houses. In short, the German parliament gained control over foreign and military affairs. The Kaiser's broad constitutional command powers (*Kommandogewalt*) and his monopoly over foreign and military matters were things of the past. But it was largely a classic case of too little and too late. Few Germans at the end of October cared for anything but an end to the war. The Commander of the XIV Deputy Army Command at Karlsruhe, General Isbert, on 30 October laconically commented that 'the broad masses only want peace, even if it is a peace at any price. . . . A sullen resignation has gripped them; they desire only peace and care little about what comes after that'.[31]

There remained the question of the Kaiser. The cult of personality surrounding Hindenburg (and even Ludendorff) had reduced Wilhelm II to an almost forgotten and meaningless figure, certainly by late 1916. The Supreme War Lord's command function had consisted largely in distributing bottles of pink 'victory' champagne to victorious generals. And Prince Max had conducted his diplomatic exchanges with President Wilson in October 1918 without the authority or even knowledge of the Kaiser. Wilson, in his third note of 23 October, had made it perfectly clear that he would not negotiate with the House of Hohenzollern. Still, the officer corps remained personally sworn to defend the Kaiser until death, and there seemed little escape from this oath. Wilhelm II still believed that he was German Emperor and King of Prussia by the Grace of God, and he steadfastly rejected all suggestions that he vacate the throne. 'A successor of Frederick the Great does not abdicate.'[32] The Kaiser by way of a handshake ordered his six sons to swear that they would not consider any form of succession.

On 29 October, on what proved to be his last day on German soil, Wilhelm II received from the Police President of Greater Berlin a lengthy report summarizing the mood in the capital since the start of Operation *Michael*. Apart from the obligatory assurances that Berliners would defend their Kaiser and King to their last breath, Oppen painted a dark picture. Deprived by military censors of precise news from the front, Berliners were shocked and depressed by newspaper reports stating that the offensive in France had failed. Police informers were unanimous that the populace yearned for peace at any price, that it was tired of the incessant squabbling in the Reichstag, and that it looked to President Wilson for 'salvation'.

Above all, Oppen apprised his sovereign of the deep 'social shifts' occasioned by the war. Large segments of the 'civil service and middle class' had been impoverished by inflation and rising prices, while industrial workers from the 'lower class' had done well financially. The former had been supplanted from their cabarets and wine bars by the latter 'and their female following'. But Oppen saved his greatest scorn for war profiteers – many of them allegedly Jewish. They flaunted their ill-gotten gains at the race tracks, dominated the theatres, and monopolized the new cinemas. 'No fur and no jewelry is too expensive for the war profiteer's wife or daughter.' Gambling and a brutalization of social intercourse characterized the new elite. The number of prostitutes in Berlin had risen from 3800 in August 1914 to 6100 in August 1918 – not counting the numerous 'casual hookers'. Murders and armed break-ins had reached 'shocking heights'; most were committed by deserters, soldiers on leave, unsupervised youths, and Russian-Polish labourers. Oppen reported that only the rich could play the black market, and that this 'embittered and angered' the less affluent. Moreover, it had resulted in an acrimonious split between city and countryside.

The war had radically changed the labour market. The Auxiliary Service Law of 1916 had forced unemployed males to accept work in factories and shops. Women had moved into jobs in offices, factories, and transportation – and had done 'surprisingly well', especially in the latter sector. Thirdly, about 20 000 Russian-Polish prisoners of war collected garbage in the capital and kept its gas and coal plants running. But especially the Jews among this group were addicted to gambling and engaged in 'profiteering and huckstering'; they would have to be 'ruthlessly repatriated' after the war.

In closing, Oppen lamented the decline in commerce and the trades as a result of the war. Shortages of raw materials, labour, and equipment hampered the traditional trades. Cobblers and carpenters, bakers and brewers were plagued by the lack of cotton, chemicals, paper, lumber, glue, malt, sugar, flour, and soap. One out of every two masters and three out of every four journeymen from among Berlin's 45 000 prewar artisans had been conscripted by the Army. Apprentices applied to enter the trades only at 20 per cent of prewar numbers as most headed off to high-paying jobs in war industries. What trades still existed did so only because countless wives had 'found the courage to keep their husbands' shops going'. Oppen bleakly concluded that not even massive postwar subsidies and loans would suffice to restore Berlin's commerce and trades to 1914 levels.[33]

There is no record of a response from the Kaiser. That same day he left Berlin for the last time in order to be near the officers of his General Staff at Spa, men sworn to uphold his throne.[34] Wilhelm II cheerily announced that he was prepared to march back to Berlin at the head of his troops in case of unrest in the capital. But he was to be bitterly disappointed by the reception that awaited him at Spa. Some officers wanted the Kaiser to seek an 'honourable' death at the head of a regiment at the front (if one could be found willing); others hoped that he would lead the High Sea Fleet in a 'death ride' against the Grand Fleet; and still others wanted him to place himself at the head of his troops and return to Berlin. Wilhelm II once more vowed that he would never 'desert the colours', and opined that when the chips were down, the armed forces and the people would rally to defend his German and Prussian thrones.[35]

To test this imperial hypothesis, General Groener on 9 November called an emergency session of 50 of his most senior army commanders at the Villa Fraineuse above Spa. Of the 50 commanding generals, 39 made it in time while 11 were delayed. Groener confronted them with two questions: 1. How did the soldiers feel about the Kaiser; would they possibly follow Wilhelm II and 'reconquer' the home front? And 2. How did the troops feel about Bolshevism; would they take up weapons against Bolsheviks at home?

The answers surpassed even the most pessimistic expectations. Of the 39 commanders, only one guaranteed that the soldiers stood squarely behind their Kaiser; 15 gave a qualified 'yes', while 23 bluntly stated that the men would not accompany their Supreme War Lord home. With regard to Bolshevism, 12 commanders demanded that peace and order among the ranks first be restored before they could speak for their troops; 19 doubted that the soldiers could be deployed against Bolsheviks; and eight stated that there was no hope of using regular Army units to quell political unrest at home. Over and over, Groener heard a single refrain: 'The troops are fully exhausted at the moment; only the ruins [of an army] are on hand'. The men needed rest, food, and clothes. 'The person of the Kaiser no longer played a role for the mass of soldiers.' Turning to his General Staff, Groener discovered that only one officer believed in the possibility of a fight for 'King and Fatherland'.[36]

With this, the issue was decided. It remained for Groener, a Württemberger, to inform the King of Prussia later that day: 'The Army will march home in peace and order under its leaders and commanding generals, but not under the command of Your Majesty for it no longer stands behind Your Majesty!' Wilhelm II pathetically demanded that Groener put this statement in writing. Colonel Heye, Groener's deputy, reassured the Kaiser that the Army would no longer 'fight at home or outside its borders'.[37] Hindenburg, in Groener's opinion, purposely opted to 'remain quietly in the shadows' while the Kaiser seemed oblivious to the 'seriousness of the situation'.[38] Within 24 hours, the imperial cream-and-gold train carried Wilhelm II quietly across the border into the Netherlands, thus ending 504 years of Hohenzollern rule in Brandenburg-Prussia-Germany. Hindenburg now announced that he was prepared to lead the armies home to save the fatherland from the 'Bolshevik danger of civil war' and to fight the Allies to the last man![39] He found no politician willing to sacrifice 65 million Germans for this whim.

In Berlin, Philipp Scheidemann of the SPD at noon on 9 November proclaimed the birth of a German republic from a balcony of the Reichstag. A delegation headed by the Centre Party leader Erzberger was dispatched to a forest near Compiègne, about 40 miles north of Paris, to receive the armistice terms of the Allied and Associated Powers, allegedly in accordance with the terms of President Wilson's fourth note of 5 November. The guns fell silent at 11 in the morning on the eleventh day of the eleventh month of 1918. The war was in its 1586th day.

About 9.3 million men died during the Great War – 3.6 million from the Central Powers and 5.7 million from the Allied and Associated Powers. For the latter, Russia led the list with 2.3 million men, followed by France with 1.9 million, Britain with 800 000, Italy with 450 000, and the United States with 126 000. Germany lost 2 036 897 men killed, 5 686 937 wounded, and 993 775 taken prisoner. One German soldier had died nearly every minute, 55 every hour, and 1331 every day of the war. One German soldier had been killed for every 35 inhabitants and one Austro-Hungarian for every 50.[40] In 1918 there were 507 000 war widows and 1 million fatherless children in the Reich. The conflict had cost the warring nations 759 million Marks per day – a total of 1 trillion, 37 billion, 942 million Marks.[41]

In contrast to Petrograd in 1917, there was no 'Red October' in Berlin in 1918. The Social Democrat Ebert, head of a provisional government, let it be known that he hated social revolution 'like sin'. On 10 November Ebert entered into an agreement with Groener, whereby the Army promised to bring its forces home in an orderly fashion while the government agreed to recognize the authority of the Prussian-German officer corps. Civil servants stayed at their posts. There was no purge of the officer corps, the diplomatic corps, the civil service, or the judiciary. Ernst Troeltsch, a noted theologian, captured the spirit of the German revolution: 'Not a person dead in defence of Kaiser and Reich! . . . On all faces one could read: Salaries will continue to be paid!'[42] Rathenau spoke of a 'revolution by accident', and percipiently linked the revolution to the Army's disintegration after March 1918. 'We call the general strike of a defeated army the German revolution.'[43]

On 28 April 1919 a special train carrying 160 German diplomats and civil servants left Berlin for Versailles.[44] The French intentionally slowed the train down for the greater part of its journey through the snow, sleet, and hoarfrost of Belgium and northern France so that its occupants could better take in the desolate landscape. Ruined villages and shell craters abounded. Emergency structures spanned rivers where once bridges had stood. Burned sheds, exploded munitions trains, rusted barbed wire, and charred ruins were omnipresent. Columns of German POWs deployed as forced labour waved at the train; French cleanup detachments stood in stony silence as the cars slowly rolled by. When the train arrived at Versailles the next day, the German peace delegation was received with icy formality and housed behind wooden board fences at the Hôtel des Réservoirs.

On 7 May French Premier Clemenceau opened the first and only meeting between Allied and German plenipotentiaries at Marie Antoinette's Trianon palace. His political agenda was straightforward: *Germaniam esse delendam*. In short, staccato sentences and with haughty disdain, the 'Tiger' warned the German delegation that 'the hour to settle accounts' was at hand, and then read the 80 000 words of the 440 articles of the proposed treaty. In May 1919 Chancellor Scheidemann's government debated the terms in Berlin – and eventually resigned rather than accept responsibility for the draconian settlement. When threatened with resumption of the war, the Germans dispatched Foreign Minister Hermann Müller and Transportation Minister Hans Bell to sign the Treaty of Versailles on 28 June 1919 in the Hall of Mirrors, where only half a century earlier Bismarck had created the German Empire. None of the 'men of 1914' – Kaiser Wilhelm II, Chancellor von Bethmann Hollweg, General von Moltke, or General von Falkenhayn – were present. Nor were the men of 1918 – Field Marshal von Hindenburg and General Ludendorff – at Versailles that day.

In fact, Hindenburg soon had more important matters on his mind. He appeared before a special Reichstag Committee of Enquiry late in 1919 to 'testify' on the narrow technical question of the timing of unrestricted submarine warfare in January 1917. Instead, ably assisted by Ludendorff, who had returned from his self-imposed Swedish exile, and the Conservative leader Helfferich, the Field Marshal turned his 'testimony' into a triumphant farce. Escorted by an honour guard, the 'wooden titan' took his place in a witness-box decorated with chrysanthemums tied with ribbons of the imperial colours of black-white-red. Hindenburg resolutely ignored the Committee's technical questions concerning the U-boat campaign and instead read a prepared statement. He swore under oath that none of the Kaiser, his government, or the General Staff had wanted war in 1914. Further, that as verified by no less an authority than an unnamed 'British general', the German Army in 1918 had been 'stabbed in the back' by the home front (Jews and Marxists, pacifists and socialists). Alluding to the ancient Germanic *Nibelungen* saga, which had last played a prominent role in the July crisis of 1914, Hindenburg concluded: 'Like Siegfried, stricken down by the treacherous spear of savage Hagen, our weary front collapsed'.[45] A stunned Committee of Enquiry was barely able to cross-examine the 'witness'. The *Dolchstosslegende* provided a powerful and convenient explanation for the loss of the war; it would be exploited by the Right in Germany throughout the 1920s to discredit the Weimar Republic.

The Treaty of Versailles proved to be a heavy mortgage for Germany's first democracy. France received Alsace and Lorraine. Belgium was restored to independence and given the former German frontier lands of Eupen, Malmédy, and Moresnet. Denmark eventually took northern Schleswig. Poland seized Posen, a large part of West Prussia, Upper Silesia, and a strip of land between Germany and East Prussia (the Polish Corridor), while Danzig became a 'free' city within the Polish customs union. And Lithuania in 1920 took the port of Memel. In all, Germany lost 13 per cent of its territory and 10 per cent of its inhabitants. Its colonies were handed to the Allies to govern as 'mandates' from the League of Nations. To show its 'good faith', the new German republic was to make an advance payment of 20 billion Marks in gold. But since Berlin lacked the requisite gold, the Allies took payment in kind from existing stocks and current production: 2.2 million tons of merchant shipping, 5000 loco-motives, 136 000 railway cars, 130 000 pieces of agricultural machinery, 135 000 head of cattle, 50 000 horses, 24 million tons of coal, and 15 million tons of dyestuffs.[46]

Germany's armed forces especially faced a bleak future under the terms of what was now popularly referred to as the 'Versailles *Diktat*'. Articles 159 to 213 stipulated that the Army was to be reduced to 100 000 men, conscription forbidden, the General Staff outlawed, and heavy artillery, military aircraft, and tanks proscribed. The Army had to destroy 59 897 artillery pieces, 31 470 trench mortars, 130 558 machine guns, and 6 million rifles as well as 15 714 aircraft and 27 757 engines. The Navy was allowed only six elderly battleships and barred from building new vessels over 10 000 tons. It was to hand over or destroy 26 capital ships and 315 U-boats. The Allies confiscated its merchant fleet.[47] Germany was not allowed an air force. An anonymous veteran of the Great War summed up the mental state of many soldiers in 1918–19: 'Peace, no longer a father-land, no Kaiser, no comradeship, divisiveness, no love of *Volk*, no pride, reviled, dishonoured, insulted, . . . despised'.[48]

The Treaty of Versailles also stipulated trials for about 100 so-called 'war criminals' on charges of 'acts against the laws and customs of war'.

The list ran from Wilhelm II (Article 227) down to most U-boat commanders (Articles 228–30).[49] But the Netherlands refused to turn the Kaiser over to the Allies for prosecution. Another 'war criminal', Hindenburg, in 1925 became the second (and last) President of the Weimar Republic. Most galling in the long run, Article 231 forced Germany to accept 'sole guilt' for starting the war, while Article 232 demanded that it pay all the costs of the war ('*la Boche payera*') incurred by all the victorious powers. One estimate is that Germany between 1919 and 1933 paid 148 139 300 000 Marks in reparations.[50]

Few Germans in 1919 harboured notions of eventual rebirth and restoration of military power. Colonel von Thaer, who had witnessed the final dénouement of the *OHL* at Spa in October 1918, spent several nights in January 1919 discussing the future with General Walther Reinhardt, a liberal officer about to assume command of the War Ministry. While Thaer was exceedingly pessimistic about the coming years, Reinhardt openly stated that 'the goal is and remains a free Germany, hopefully restored to its former borders, with [the] strongest, most modern army with [the] newest weapons. One must not let this goal recede from view for even one moment'. Thaer, taken aback, interjected that this surely was a vision of at best 3 decades down the road. 'No, far off the mark', Reinhardt countered. 'We must and will be in position to do so in 15 years.' The incoming War Minister assured Thaer that universal male conscription would be restored and rearmament undertaken, and that Germany would possess the most modern weapons 'on land, at sea, and in the air'. The Allies, Reinhardt cagily suggested, would be content to rest on their laurels 'and in 15 years all their weapons and equipment will be scrap iron'.[51]

Reinhardt had drawn cogent political consequences from the war and the revolution: nation and army needed to be brought into closer harmony before rebirth and resurrection could take place. Reichswehr planners throughout the 1920s argued that a future war was possible only if and when the nation stood shoulder to shoulder with its armed forces. Never again should generals soil their hands with collective bargaining, political infighting, food rationing, and patriotic instruction. Instead, they needed to concentrate their energies on what the historian Gerhard Ritter called *Kriegshandwerk* – the planning and conducting of war, their true vocation. In 1933 they found a political leader who shared that conception. Two years later, precisely as prophesied by Reinhardt, Germany announced universal male conscription and general rearmament.

Princess Blücher, that incisive diarist of events in Berlin during the war, as early as December 1918 at her remote retreat in the ancestral Blücher castle at Krieblowitz in Silesia, had detected among the Germans the need for a leader to take the place of the departed Kaiser. 'I believe myself that the German people in reality need something for their imagination – a figure-head that represents in some way the phantastic, the unusual, the ideal.'[52] The 'phantastic' and the 'unusual' came to power on 30 January 1933. Whether he was also the 'ideal' remains a matter of personal preference.

Chapter 11 Notes

1. Kurt Riezler, *Tagebücher, Aufsätze, Dokumente*, ed. Karl Dietrich Erdmann (Göttingen, Vandenhoeck & Ruprecht, 1972), p. 480.
2. A[ugust] von Cramon, *Unser Österreichisch-Ungarischer Bundesgenosse im Weltkriege. Erinnerungen aus meiner vierjährigen Tätigkeit als bevollmächtigter deutscher General beim k. u. k. Armeeoberkommando* (Berlin, E. S. Mittler & Sohn, 1922), p. 176.
3. Bundesministerium für Landesverteidigung, *Österreich-Ungarns Letzter Krieg 1914–1918*. 7: *Das Kriegsjahr 1918* (Vienna, Verlag der Militärwissenschaftlichen Mitteilungen, 1938), pp. 571–5; József Galántai, *Hungary in the First World War* (Budapest, Akadémiai Kiadó, 1989), p. 322.
4. ÖStA-KA, MKSM 25-1/9. 'Darstellung der materiellen Lage der Armee im Felde', 18 August 1918.
5. ÖStA-KA, MKSM 25-1/9. 'Verwendung und Bekämpfung von Tanks', 27 September 1918.
6. *Österreich-Ungarns Letzter Krieg 1914–1918* 7, p. 595.
7. Rudolf Kiszling, *Österreich-Ungarns Anteil am Ersten Weltkrieg* (Graz, Stiasny Verlag, 1958), p. 88; and Gunther E. Rothenberg, *The Army of Francis Joseph* (West Lafayette, Ind., Purdue University Press, 1976), p. 216.
8. Arthur S. Link, ed., *The Papers of Woodrow Wilson* (69 vols, Princeton, Princeton University Press, 1985) 51, p. 383.
9. See Kiszling, *Österreich-Ungarns Anteil*, pp. 89–90; Rothenberg, *Army of Francis Joseph*, p. 216.
10. *Österreich-Ungarns Letzter Krieg 1914–1918* 7, p. 611.
11. Richard Georg Plaschka and Karlheinz Mack, *Die Auflösung des Habsburgerreiches. Zusammenbruch und Neuorientierung im Donauraum* (Munich, R. Oldenbourg, 1970), p. 260.
12. Cited in *Österreich-Ungarns Letzter Krieg 1914–1918* 7, p. 632.
13. Cited in Manfried Rauchensteiner, *Der Tod des Doppeladlers. Österreich-Ungarn und der Erste Weltkrieg* (Graz, Vienna, and Cologne, Verlag Styria, 1994), p. 616. Linder's order is in ÖStA-KA, Nachlass Boroević, B/4.
14. Kiszling, *Österreich-Ungarns Anteil*, p. 93. See also Bruno Wagner, 'Der Waffenstillstand von Villa Giusti 3. November 1918', unpubl. diss., Vienna University 1970.
15. *Österreich-Ungarns Letzter Krieg 1914–1918* 7, p. 758. The official history pinpoints the numbers of POWs at 436 674 up to 11 November 1918.
16. Rothenberg, *Army of Francis Joseph*, p. 218.
17. *Österreich-Ungarns Letzter Krieg 1914–1918* 7, p. 760.
18. Cited in Arthur J. May, *The Passing of the Hapsburg Monarchy 1914–1918* (2 vols, Philadelphia, University of Pennsylvania Press, 1966) 2, p. 800.
19. *Österreich-Ungarns Letzter Krieg 1914–1918* 7, p. 764.
20. Kiszling, *Österreich-Ungarns Anteil*, p. 95. These figures are reprinted by Rothenberg, *Army of Francis Joseph*, p. 218. See also *Österreich-Ungarns Letzter Krieg 1914–1918* 7, p. 831.

21. Heinrich Benedikt, *Monarchie der Gegensätze. Österreichs Weg durch die Neuzeit* (Vienna, Ullstein Verlag, 1947), pp. 194–5.
22. Fritz Fellner, ed., *Schicksalsjahre Österreichs 1908–1919. Das politische Tagebuch Josef Redlichs* (2 vols, Graz and Cologne, Verlag Hermann Böhlaus Nachf., 1954) 2, p. 315.
23. See Wilhelm Deist, ed., *Militär und Innenpolitik im Weltkrieg 1914–1918* (2 vols, Düsseldorf, Droste Verlag, 1970) 2, pp. 1300–5.
24. Erich Matthias and Rudolf Morsey, eds, *Die Regierung des Prinzen Max von Baden* (Düsseldorf, Droste Verlag, 1962), pp. 92, 103.
25. Matthias and Morsey, eds, *Die Regierung des Prinzen Max von Baden*, pp. 118–19, 122–3.
26. General Oskar von Hutier, Eighteenth Army, had reduced the choice as follows: 'Groener? South German Democrat. [Max] Hoffmann? Jewish wife!' BA-MA, W-10/50640 Tagebücher v. Hutier, entry for 27 October 1918.
27. See Gerhard W. Rakenius, *Wilhelm Groener als erster Generalquartiermeister. Die Politik der Obersten Heeresleitung 1918/19* (Boppard, H. Boldt, 1977), pp. 26 ff.
28. Oberkommando des Heeres, *Der Weltkrieg 1914 bis 1918.* 14: *Die Kriegführung an der Westfront im Jahre 1918* (Berlin, E. S. Mittler & Sohn, 1944), pp. 666, 697, 760.
29. BA-MA, PH 5 I/52 Army Group Gallwitz.
30. BA-MA, Nachlass Hipper, N 162, vol. 9, p. 8. See Wilhelm Deist, 'Die Politik der Seekriegsleitung und die Rebellion der Flotte Ende Oktober 1918', *Vierteljahrshefte für Zeitgeschichte* 14 (1966), pp. 341–68.
31. Cited in Deist, *Militär und Innenpolitik* 2, p. 1329, n. 5.
32. Cited in Gerhard Ritter, *Staatskunst und Kriegshandwerk. Das Problem des 'Militarismus' in Deutschland* (4 vols, Munich, Verlag R. Oldenbourg, 1968) 4, p. 458.
33. Oppen to Wilhelm II, 29 October 1918. *Dokumente aus geheimen Archiven.* 4: *Berichte des Berliner Polizeipräsidenten zur Stimmung und Lage der Bevölkerung in Berlin 1914–1918,* eds Ingo Materna and Hans-Joachim Schreckenbach (Weimar, Hermann Böhlaus Nachfolger, 1987), pp. 297–303.
34. The most detailed account of the Kaiser's last days in office remains Alfred Niemann, *Revolution von Oben-Umsturz von Unten. Entwicklung und Verlauf der Staatsumwälzung in Deutschland 1914–1918* (Berlin, Verlag für Kulturpolitik, 1927), pp. 188 ff.
35. BHStA, MA 3085 Milit. Bevollmächtigter. Lerchenfeld's report dated 21 October 1918.
36. *Der Weltkrieg 1914 bis 1918* 14, p. 716.
37. *Der Weltkrieg 1914 bis 1918* 14, p. 717.
38. BA-MA, N 46 Nachlass Groener, vol. 63. 'Ludendorff'.
39. BA-MA, PH 5 I/52 Army Group Gallwitz. Hindenburg's note of 10 November 1918.
40. Otto Riebicke, *Was brauchte der Weltkrieg? Tatsachen und Zahlen aus dem deutschen Ringen 1914/18* (Berlin, Kyffhäuser-Verlag, 1936), pp. 97–102. The figures for Serbia were one out of every 11; France one out of every 28; Britain one out of every 66; Italy one out of every 79; Russia one out of every 107; and the United States one out of every 2000 inhabitants.
41. Riebicke, *Was brachte der Weltkrieg?*, p. 111.
42. Cited in Christian Graf von Krockow, *Die Deutschen in ihrem Jahrhundert 1890–1990* (Reinbeck bei Hamburg, Rowohlt, 1990), p. 123.
43. Walther Rathenau, *Kritik der dreifachen Revolution* (Berlin, S. Fischer, 1919), p. 9.
44. See Alma Luckau, *The German Delegation at the Paris Peace Conference* (New York, H. Fertig, 1971).
45. Paul von Hindenburg, *Aus meinem Leben* (Leipzig, S. Hirzel, 1920), p. 403. The British general referred to was probably Frederick Maurice or Neill Malcolm.
46. Gerd Hardach, *The First World War 1914–1918* (London, Allen Lane, 1977), p. 247.
47. Riebicke, *Was brauchte der Weltkrieg?*, pp. 107–8.
48. Cited in Wolfram Wette, ed., *Der Krieg des kleinen Mannes. Eine Militärgeschichte von unten* (Munich and Zurich, Piper, 1992), p. 120.

49. See Walter Schwengler, *Völkerrecht, Versailler Vertrag und Auslieferungsfrage. Die Strafverfolgung wegen Kriegsverbrechen als Problem des Friedensschlusses 1919/20* (Stuttgart, Deutsche Verlags-Anstalt, 1982).
50. Riebicke, *Was brauchte der Weltkrieg?*, p. 106.
51. Albrecht von Thaer, *Generalstabsdienst an der Front und in der O.H.L. Aus Briefen und Tagebuchaufzeichnungen 1915–1919,* ed. Siegfried A. Kaehler (Göttingen, Vandenhoeck & Ruprecht, 1958), pp. 284–5.
52. Evelyn, Princess Blücher, *An English Wife in Berlin: A Private Memoir of Events, Politics, and Daily Life in Germany throughout the War and the Social Revolution of 1918* (New York, E. P. Dutton, 1920), p. 302.

Bibliography

Archival sources

Vienna: Haus-, Hof- und Staatsarchiv. Politisches Archiv (HHStA, PA)

I. Allgemeines

536 Botschaftsberichte Berlin 1914–1918
592–93 Cabinet des Ministers. Protokoll 1913–1915
818 Liassa Krieg. Interne Massnahmen
837–44 Deutschland 1918. Liassa Krieg. Haltung Deutschlands
1064 Liassa Krieg
1499 Krieg geheim XLVII

III. Preussen (Berlin)

171–75 Preussen Berichte 1914–1918
173–75 Gesandschaft Berlin

VII. Gesandschaft Berlin

32–37 Korrespondenz mit Versch.
196–204 Separat Akten

VIII. England. Berichte 1913. Weisungen Varia 1914

Vienna: Österreichisches Staatsarchiv

A. Kriegsarchiv (ÖStA-KA)

Armeeoberkomando. Operationsbüro; AOK-Akten
475 Krieg gegen Rumänien
512 Korrespondenz Conrad-Falkenhayn
550 Italien
551 Russland
560 Vorbereitungen für den Krieg gegen Italien
561 Italien 1915

600 Berichte aus dem Deutschen Hauptquartier, 1914–1918
607 Berichte des deutschen Militärbevollmächtigten
679 Tagebücher der Operationsabteilung
Conrad-Archiv: A Nachlass Conrad
                B Flügeladjutant
Chef des Generalstabes 1913. Militärisches
Kriegsministerium 5A/61–191. 'Durchhalten über Winter 1917/18'
Militärkanzlei Seiner Majestät (MKSM):
      Faszikel 18, 44, 69, 70, 93; Sonderfaszikel 79
      'Standort des A.O.K. am 18. Juli 1917'
      Reports 1914, 1915, 1916, 1917, 1918
Neue Feldakten (NFA)
Operations-Büro Gen. Stab. Faszikel 26, 44, 59, 89a, 90, 91, 95
Nachlass Dankl (B/3)
Nachlass Boroević (B/4)
Nachlass Kundmann (B/15)
Nachlass Hartinger (B/428)
Nachlass Schneller (B/509)
Nachlass Kövess (B/1000)

B. Verwaltungsarchiv der Republik

Präsidium des K.K. Ministerium des Innern
      25–28/22 Kriegsschäden
      34–4/400 Vergütung von Kriegsschäden
      35–3/608 Forderungen
      25414–22/Galizien Plünderungen und Diebstähle

Bonn, Germany: Auswärtiges Amt, Politisches Archiv (AA-PA)

Deutschland 128 Nr. 1 secr. Bündnisvertrag zwischen Deutschland, Österreich-
      Ungarn und Italien (Dreibundvertrag)
Deutschland 143 secr. Militärische Besprechungen: Italien/Österreich,
      Rumänien
Deutschland 143 secr. Nr. 1. Zusammenarbeit der Oberkommandos der
      deutschen, italienischen und österreichischen Marine
Gesandschaft Wien. O. Dienst Instruction und Stellung des Militär-Attachés
Österreich 73. Militär-Angelegenheiten Österreichs
Österreich 73 secr. Militär- und Marine-Angelegenheiten Österreichs
Österreich 95. Beziehungen Österreichs zu Deutschland
Österreich 95 secr. Beziehungen Österreichs zu Deutschland
Nachlass Jagow

Koblenz, Germany: Bundesarchiv (BA)

Logbücher Bogislav v. Selchow
Nachlass Bülow

Nachlass Gothein
Nachlass Hertling
Nachlass Schwertfeger
R. 1 Reichinstitut für Geschichte des neuen Deutschland. Berichte v.
  Holtzendorff an Ballin. 16 vols.
R 43/II. Akten der neuen Reichskanzlei

Freiburg, Germany: Bundesarchiv-Militärarchiv (BA-MA)

MSg 1/1228, 2511–12 Nachlass v. Alten
MSg 1/1914, 2515–17 Tagebuch Kageneck
MSg 1/3251 Frhr. v. Lyncker. Kriegsbriefe
MSg 2/65 Tagebuch Feldwebel Schlubeck
MSg 2/626 Aufzeichnungen eines Stabsarztes Feld Laz. 201 Verdun
MSg 2/4537 Tagebuch Wilhelm Schulin
MSg 2/4705 Emmichs Tagebuch
MSg 109/7893 Graf v. Kageneck
PH 1 Militärkabinett. Mobilmachung 1914
PH 1/3 Mobilmachung 1914
PH 2 Kriegsministerium: Faszikel 14, 17, 69, 86, 88, 99, 114, 119, 180
PH 3 Generalstab: Faszikel 25, 26, 28, 29, 30, 33, 60, 245, 305
PH 3/328 Oberste Heeresleitung. Bericht Freiherr v. Freytag-Loringhoven
PH 5 I/46 Heeres-Oberkommando Kronprinz Rupprecht
PH 5 I/52 Armeegruppe Gallwitz
PH 5 I/75 Heeresgruppe Herzog Albrecht
PH 5 II/119 Generalstab. Erste Armee, Rückblick
PH 6 I/27, 255 VII. Armeekorps Münster
PH 6 I/28 VII. Armeekorps (Gallwitz)
PH 7/2 Stellvertr. Oberkommando VII
PH 8 I/34 Armeegruppe Kronprinz Wilhelm
PH 20/19 Versorgungstruppen
PH 21/24 Preussische Heeresgasschule
Nachlass Schlieffen (N 43)
Nachlass Einem gen. v. Rothmaler
Nachlass Groener (N 46)
Nachlass Haeften (N 35)
Nachlass Moltke (N 78)
Nachlass Müller (N 159)
Nachlass Hipper (N 162)
Nachlass Capelle (N 170)
Nachlass Levetzow (N 239)
Nachlass Seeckt (N 247)
Nachlass Tirpitz (N 253)
Nachlass Wandel (N 564)
Special Collection W-10 (in future RH 61): Kriegsgeschichtliche
  Forschungsanstalt des Heees, former Militärarchiv der DDR:

50220 Der Schlieffenplan (Wilhelm Dieckmann)
50368 Stimmung in der Heimat 1917/18
50397 Hindenburgprogramm und Hilfsdienstgesetz
50400 Zur Wirtschaftslage um die Wende 1917/18
50631 Tagebücher Beseler
50634 Generaloberst v. Einem (Kriegstagebücher- und Briefe)
50635 Falkenhayn-Tagebuch
50640 Tagebücher v. Hutier
50652 Kriegstagebuch v. Kuhl
50656 Tagebuch v. Plessen
50661 Kriegserinnerungen v. Tappen
51063 Plessen-Tagebuch

Munich, Germany: Bayerisches Hauptstaatsarchiv. Geheimes Staatsarchiv (BHStA)

Gesandschaft Berlin 1086–1095
Ministerium des Königlichen Hauses und des Äussern, MA 3076–3085, Militär
  Bevollmächtigter Berlin

Munich, Germany: Bayerisches Hauptstaatsarchiv, Kriegsarchiv (BHStA-KA)

Bayerischer Militärbevollmächtigter 265/III/114. Berichte an das Kriegs-Amt
HS 2543–2546. Tagebücher General von Wenninger
MKR 1765. Mobilmachung 1914. Politische Lage und Massnahmen. Nachrichten
MKR 1829–32 Berichte des bayerischen Militärbevollmächtigten
MKR 1835 Mitteilungen des Chefs des Generalstabes . . . der OHL
Handschriften Sammlung Nrs. 1958, 1959, 1964, 1965, 1972, 2027, 2112, 2156,
  2646, 2695 (Bayer. Infanterie-Leib-Regiment and Bayer. Inft. Regt. 1–15)

Stuttgart, Germany: Hauptstaatsarchiv

E 130. I. Staatsministerium. Niederschriften über Sitzungen von
  Reichstagsausschüssen 1915–1918. 5 vols.
J 47 Nachlass Conrad Haussmann 1857-1922

Potsdam (formerly East Germany): Zentrales Staatsarchiv

Reichskanzlei: Grosses Hauptquartier 21

Official documents

*L'Allemagne et les problèmes de la paix pendant la première guerre mondiale.
Documents extraits des archives de l'Office allemand des Affaires étrangères,*
  ed. André Scherer and Jacques Grunewald (4 vols., Paris, Presses
  Universitaires de France, 1962–1978).

Austria, Bundesministerium für Landesverteidigung, *Österreich-Ungarns Lettzter Krieg 1914–1918,* eds Edmund Glaise von Horstenau and Rudolf Kiszling (7 vols., Vienna, Verlag der Militärwissenschaftlichen Mitteilungen, 1931–8). *Dokumente aus geheimen Archiven.* 4: *Berichte des Berliner Polizeipräsidenten zur Stimmung und Lage der Bevölkerung in Berlin 1914–1918,* eds Ingo Materna and Hans-Joachim Schreckenbach (Weimar, Hermann Böhlaus Nachfolger, 1987).

Germany, Marinearchiv, *Der Krieg zur See 1914–1918* (18 vols, Berlin and Frankfurt, E. S. Mittler & Sohn, 1922–66).

——, *Der Krieg zur See 1914–1918. Der Handelskrieg mit U-Booten* (5 vols, Berlin, E. S. Mittler & Sohn, 1932–66).

Germany, Nationalversammlung, *Das Werk des Untersuchungsausschusses der Verfassunggebenden Deutschen Nationalversammlung und des Deutschen Reichstages 1919–1930. Vierte Reihe. Die Ursachen des Deutschen Zusammenbruchs im Jahre 1918. Zweite Abteilung. Der Innere Zusammenbruch* (19 vols, Berlin, Deutsche Verlagsgesellschaft für Politik und Geschichte, 1925–30).

Germany, Reichsarchiv, *Der Weltkrieg 1914–918. Die militärischen Operationen zu Lande* (14 vols, Berlin, E. S. Mittler & Sohn, 1925–44).

——, *Der Weltkrieg 1914 bis 1918. Kriegsrüstung und Kriegswirtschaft* (2 vols, Berlin, E. S. Mittler & Sohn, 1930).

——, *Schlachten des Weltkrieges in Einzeldarstellungen* (37 vols, Oldenburg and Berlin, Verlag Gerhard Stalling, 1921–30).

Germany, Reichskriegsministerium, *Sanitätsberichte über das deutsche Heer . . . im Weltkriege 1914/1918* (3 vols, Berlin, E. S. Mittler & Sohn, 1934–5).

Germany, *Verhandlungen des Reichstages. XII., XIII. Legislaturperiode.*

Great Britain, *History of the Great War: Military Operations,* ed. Sir James E. Edmonds (23 vols, London, Macmillan, 1922–48).

Great Britain, *History of the Great War: Naval Operations,* eds. Sir Julian S. Corbett and Henry Newbolt (5 vols, London, Longman, Green, 1920–31).

Österreich-Ungarns Aussenpolitik von der Bosnischen Krise 1908 bis zum Kriegsausbruch 1914. Diplomatische Aktenstücke des Österreichisch-Ungarischen Ministeriums des Äussern, eds. Ludwig Bittner and Hans Uebersberger (8 vols, Vienna and Leipzig, Österreichischer Bundesverlag für Unterricht, Wissenschaft und Kunst, 1930).

Protokolle des Gemeinsamen Ministerrates der Österreichisch-Ungarischen Monarchie (1914–1918), ed. Miklós Komjáthy (Budapest, Akadémiai Kiadó, 1966).

Scott, James B., ed., *The Reports of the Hague Conferences of 1899 and 1907* (Oxford, Clarendon Press, 1917).

United States Army in the World War 1917–1919 (17 vols, Washington, DC, U.S. Government Printing Office, 1948).

Ursachen und Folgen. Vom deutschen Zusammenbruch 1918 und 1945 bis zur staatlichen Neuordnung Deutschlands in der Gegenwart, ed. Herbert Michaelis and Ernst Schraepler (15 vols, Berlin, Dokumenten-Verlag Dr Herbert Wendler, 1958).

Memoirs, diaries, private papers

Arz von Straussenburg, Arthur, *Zur Geschichte des Grossen Krieges, 1914–1918. Aufzeichnungen* (Vienna, Rikola Verlag, 1924).

——, *Kampf und Sturz der Mittelmächte* (Vienna, J. Günther, 1935).

Auffenberg von Kamarów, Moritz, *Aus Österreichs Höhe und Niedergang. Eine Lebensschilderung* (Munich, Drei Masken Verlag, 1921).

Bach, August, ed., *Deutsche Gesandschaftsberichte zum Kriegsausbruch 1914. Berichte und Telegramme der badischen, sächsischen und württembergischen Gesandschaften in Berlin aus dem Juli und August 1914* (Berlin, Quaderverlag, 1937).

Baden, Prinz Max von, *Erinnerungen und Dokumente* (Stuttgart, Klett, 1968).

Bardolff, Carl von, *Soldat im alten Österreich. Erinnerungen aus meinem Leben* (Jena, E. Diederichs Verlag, 1938).

Bauer, Oberst [Max], *Der grosse Krieg in Feld und Heimat. Erinnerungen und Betrachtungen* (Tübingen, Osiander'sche Buchhandlung, 1922).

Bäumer, Gertrud, *Heimatchronik während des Weltkrieges* (Berlin, F. A. Herbig, 1930).

Beck, Ludwig, *Studien*, ed. Hans Speidel (Stuttgart, K. F. Koehler, 1955).

Bethmann Hollweg, Theobald von, *Betrachtungen zum Weltkriege* (2 vols, Berlin, Reimer Hobbing, 1919–21).

Blücher, Evelyn, Princess, *An English Wife in Berlin: A Private Memoir of Events, Politics, and Daily Life in Germany throughout the War and the Social Revolution of 1918* (New York, E. P. Dutton, 1920).

Briefwechsel Hertling-Lerchenfeld 1912–1917. Dienstliche Privatkorrespondenz zwischen dem bayerischen Ministerpräsidenten Georg Graf v. Hertling und dem bayerischen Gesandten in Berlin Hugo Graf von und zu Lerchenfeld, ed. Ernst Deuerlein (2 vols, Boppard, H. Boldt, 1973).

Broucek, Peter, ed., *Ein General im Zwielicht. Die Erinnerungen Edmund Glaises von Horstenau* (2 vols, Vienna, Cologne, and Graz, Böhlau, 1980).

Burián von Rajecz, Stephan, *Drei Jahre aus der Zeit meiner Amtsführung im Kriege* (Berlin, Ullstein, 1923).

Conrad von Hötzendorf, Franz, *Aus meiner Dienstzeit 1906–1918* (5 vols, Vienna, Leipzig, and Munich, Rikola Verlag, 1921–5).

——, *Private Aufzeichnungen. Erste Veröffentlichungen aus den Papieren des k. u. k. Generalstabs-Chefs*, ed. Kurt Peball (Vienna and Munich, Amalthea-Verlag, 1977).

Conrad von Hötzendorf, Gina, *Mein Leben mit Conrad von Hötzendorf. Sein geistiges Vermächtnis* (Leipzig, Grethlein & Co., 1935).

Cramon, A[ugust] von, *Unser Österreichisch-Ungarischer Bundesgenosse im Weltkriege. Erinnerungen aus meiner vierjährigen Tätigkeit als bevollmächtigter deutscher General beim k. u. k. Armeeoberkommando* (Berlin, E. S. Mittler & Sohn, 1922).

Cramon, A[ugust] v. and Paul Fleck, *Deutschlands Schicksalsbund mit Österrich-Ungarn. Von Conrad von Hötzendorf zu Kaiser Karl* (Berlin, Verlag für Kulturpolitik, 1932).

Czernin, Ottokar, *Im Weltkriege* (Berlin and Vienna, Ullstein, 1919).

Deist, Wilhelm, ed., *Militär und Innenpolitik im Weltkrieg 1914–1918* (2 vols, Düsseldorf, Droste Verlag, 1970).

Einem, Karl von, *Ein Armeeführer erlebt den Weltkrieg*, ed. J. Alter (Leipzig, von Hase & Koehler, 1938).

Falkenhayn, Erich von, *Die Oberste Heeresleitung 1914–1916 in ihren wichtigsten Entschliessungen* (Berlin, E. S. Mittler & Sohn, 1920).

English translation: *General Headquarters 1914–1916 and its Critical Decisions* (London, Hutchinson, 1919).

Fellner, Fritz, ed., *Schicksalsjahre Österreichs, 1908–1919. Das politische Tagebuch Josef Redlichs* (2 vols, Graz and Cologne, Verlag Hermann Böhlaus Nachf., 1953–4).

Freytag-Loringhoven, Hugo von, *Menschen und Dinge, wie ich sie in meinem Leben sah* (Berlin, E. S. Mittler & Sohn, 1923).

Gallwitz, Max von, *Meine Führertätigkeit im Weltkriege 1914/16* (Berlin, E. S. Mittler & Sohn, 1929).

——, *Erleben im Westen 1916–1918* (Berlin, E. S. Mittler & Sohn, 1932).

Geiss, Imanuel, ed., *Julikrise und Kriegsausbruch 1914: Eine Dokumentensammlung* (2 vols, Hanover, Verlag für Literatur und Zeitgeschehen, 1963–4).

Groener, Wilhelm, *Lebenserinnerungen. Jugend, Generalstab, Weltkrieg*, ed. Friedrich Hiller v. Gaertringen (Göttingen, Vandenhoeck & Ruprecht, 1957).

Hamilton, Ian, *Gallipoli Diary* (2 vols, London, Edward Arnold, 1920).

Helfferich, Karl, *Der Weltkrieg* (3 vols, Berlin, Ullstein, 1919).

Hill, Leonidas E., ed., *Die Weizsäcker-Papiere 1900–1932* (Berlin, Frankfurt, and Vienna, Propyläen Verlag, 1982).

Hindenburg, Paul von, *Aus meinem Leben* (Leipzig, S. Hirzel, 1920).

Hoffmann, Max von, *War Diaries and Other Papers* (2 vols, London, M. Secker, 1929).

Janssen, Karl-Heinz, ed., *Die graue Exzellenz zwischen Staatsräson und Vasallentreue. Aus den Papieren des kaiserlichen Gesandten Karl Georg von Treutler* (Frankfurt, Berlin, and Vienna, Propyläen, 1971).

Jünger, Ernst, *In Stahlgewittern. Ein Kriegsbuch* (Berlin, E. S. Mittler & Sohn, 1926).

Kaiser Karl, *Persönliche Aufzeichnungen, Zeugnisse und Dokumente*, ed. Erich Feigl (Vienna, Amalthea, 1984).

Krauss, Alfred, *Die Ursachen unserer Niederlage. Erinnerungen und Urteile aus dem Weltkrieg* (Munich, J. F. Lehmanns Verlag, 1921).

Leeb, Wilhelm Ritter von, *Tagebuchaufzeichnungen und Lagebeurteilungen aus zwei Weltkriegen*, ed. Georg Meyer (Stuttgart, Deutsche Verlags-Anstalt, 1976).

Lloyd George, David, *War Memoirs of David Lloyd George, 1914–1918* (6 vols, London, I. Nicholson & Watson, 1933–6).

Lossberg, Fritz von, *Meine Tätigkeit im Weltkriege 1914–1918* (Berlin, E. S. Mittler & Sohn, 1939).

Ludendorff, Erich, *Urkunden der Obersten Heeresleitung über ihre Tätigkeit 1916/18* (Berlin, E. S. Mittler & Sohn, 1920).

——, *Meine Kriegserinnerungen 1914–1918* (Berlin, E. S. Mittler & Sohn, 1919).

——, *Kriegführung und Politik* (Berlin, E. S. Mittler & Sohn, 1921).

Matthias, Erich and Rudolf Morsey, eds, *Die Regierung des Prinzen Max von Baden* (Düsseldorf, Droste Verlag, 1962).

Moltke, Graf [Helmuth], *Die deutschen Aufmarschpläne 1871–1890*, ed. Ferdinand von Schmerfeld (Berlin, E. S. Mittler & Sohn, 1929).

Moltke, Eliza von, *Generaloberst Helmuth von Moltke. Erinnerungen. Briefe. Dokumente 1877–1916. Ein Bild vom Kriegsausbruch, erster Kriegsführung und Persönlichkeit des ersten militärischen Führers des Krieges* (Stuttgart, Der Kommende Tag Verlag, 1922).

Neck, Rudolf, ed., *Arbeiterschaft und Staat im Ersten Weltkrieg 1914–1918* (2 vols, Vienna, Cologne, Stuttgart, and Zurich, Europa Verlag, 1964–8).

Pogge von Strandmann, Hartmut, ed., *Walther Rathenau: Industrialist, Banker, Intellectual, and Politician. Notes and Diaries 1907–1922* (Oxford, Clarendon Press, 1985).

Poincaré, Raymond, *Au service de la France—neuf années de souvenirs* (10 vols., Paris, Plon-Nourrit, 1926–33).

Rabenau, Friedrich von, ed., *Seeckt. Aus seinem Leben 1866–1917* (Leipzig, Hase & Köhler, 1938).

Reichold, Helmut and Gerhard Granier, eds., *Wild von Hohenborn. Briefe und Tagebuchaufzeichnungen des preussischen Generals als Kriegsminister und Truppenführer im Ersten Weltkrieg* (Boppard, H. Boldt, 1986).

Richert, Dominik, *Beste Gelegenheit zum Sterben. Meine Erlebnisse im Kriege 1914–1918*, eds Angelika Tramitz and Bernd Ulrich (Munich, Knesebeck & Schuler, 1989).

Riezler, Kurt, *Tagebücher, Aufsätze, Dokumente*, ed. Karl Dietrich Erdmann (Göttingen, Vandenhoeck & Ruprecht, 1972).

Rosner, Karl Peter, ed., *Erinnerungen des Kronprinzen Wilhelm. Aus den Aufzeichnungen, Dokumenten, Tagebüchern und Gesprächen* (Stuttgart and Berlin, J. G. Cotta, 1922).

Rupprecht von Bayern, Kronprinz, *Mein Kriegstagebuch*, ed. Eugen von Frauenholz (3 vols, Berlin, Deutscher Nationalverlag, 1929).

Schlieffen, Alfred von, *Gesammelte Schriften* (2 vols, Berlin, E. S. Mittler & Sohn, 1913).

Schwabe, Klaus and Rolf Reichardt, eds, *Gerhard Ritter. Ein politischer Historiker in seinen Briefen* (Boppard, H. Boldt, 1984).

Seeckt, Hans von, *Gedanken eines Soldaten* (Berlin, Verlag für Kulturpolitik, 1927).

Stürgkh, Josef, *Im Deutschen Grossen Hauptquartier* (Leipzig, Paul List Verlag, 1921).

Thaer, Albrecht von, *Generalstabsdienst an der Front und in der O.H.L. Aus Briefen und Tagebuchaufzeichnungen 1915–1919*, ed. Siegfried A. Kaehler (Göttingen, Vandenhoeck & Ruprecht, 1958).

The Kaiser and His Court: The Diaries, Note Books and Letters of Admiral Georg Alexander von Müller Chief of the Naval Cabinet, 1914–1918, ed. Walter Görlitz (New York, Harcourt, Brace & World, 1959).
The Papers of Woodrow Wilson, ed. Arthur S. Link (69 vols, Princeton, Princeton University Press, 1966–94).
Tirpitz, Alfred von, *Erinnerungen* (Leipzig, K. F. Koehler, 1919).
——, *Politische Dokumente. Deutsche Ohnmachtspolitik im Weltkriege* (Hamburg and Berlin, Hanseatische Verlags Anstalt, 1926).
Valentini, Rudolf von, *Kaiser und Kabinettschef. Nach eigenen Aufzeichnungen und dem Briefwechsel des Wirklichen Geheimen Rats Rudolf von Valentini*, ed. Bernhard Schwertfeger (Oldenburg, Stalling, 1931).
Wilhelm, Kronprinz, *Meine Erinnerungen aus Deutschlands Heldenkampf* (Berlin, E. S. Mittler & Sohn, 1923).
Wolff, Theodor, *Tagebücher 1914–1919*, ed. Bernd Sösemann (2 vols, Boppard, H. Boldt, 1984).

Books

Afflerbach, Holger, *Falkenhayn. Politisches Denken und Handeln im Kaiserreich* (Munich, R. Oldenbourg, 1994).
Albertini, Luigi, *The Origins of the War of 1914* (3 vols, New York and London, Oxford University Press, 1957).
Ashworth, Tony, *Trench Warfare 1914–1918: The Live and Let Live System* (London, Macmillan, 1980).
Asprey, Robert B., *The German High Command at War: Hindenburg and Ludendorff Conduct World War I* (New York, William Morrow and Co., 1991).
Augeneder, Sigrid, *Arbeiterinnen im Ersten Weltkrieg. Lebens- und Arbeitsbedingungen proletarischer Frauen in Österreich* (Vienna, Europaverlag, 1987).
Baumgart, Winfried, *Deutsche Ostpolitik 1918. Von Brest-Litowsk bis zum Ende des Weltkrieges* (Vienna and Munich, R. Oldenbourg, 1966).
Becker, Jean-Jacques, *The Great War and the French People* (Oxford, Berg, 1993).
Benedikt, Heinrich, *Monarchie der Gegensätze. Österreichs Weg durch die Neuzeit* (Vienna, Ullstein, 1947).
Berghahn, Volker, *Germany and the Approach of War in 1914* (New York, St. Martin's Press, 1973).
Bessel, Richard, *Germany After the First World War* (Oxford, Clarendon Press, 1993).
Brown, Malcolm and Shirley Seaton, *Christmas Truce* (New York, Hippocrene Books, 1984).
Bucholz, Arden, *Moltke, Schlieffen, and Prussian War Planning* (New York and Oxford, Berg Publishers, 1991).

Callwell, Charles E., *Field Marshal Sir Henry Wilson: His Life and Diaries* (2 vols., London, Cassell & Co., 1927).

Churchill, Winston S., *The World Crisis* (6 vols, London, Thorton Butterworth, 1923–31).

——, *The Unknown War: The Eastern Front* (New York, Charles Scribner's Sons, 1931).

Clausewitz, Carl von, *On War,* eds Michael Howard and Peter Paret (Princeton, Princeton University Press, 1984).

Coffman, Edward M., *The War to End All Wars: The American Military Experience in World War I* (Madison, The University of Wisconsin Press, 1986).

Cohen, Eliot A. and John Gooch, *Military Misfortunes: The Anatomy of Failure in War* (New York, Free Press, 1990).

Conze, Werner S., *Polnische Nation und deutsche Politik im ersten Weltkrieg* (Graz and Cologne, Böhlau, 1958).

Cooper, Duff, *Haig* (2 vols, Toronto, Macmillan, 1935–6).

Cornwall, Mark, ed., *The Last Years of Austria–Hungary: Essays in Political and Military History 1908–1918* (Exeter, University of Exeter Press, 1990).

Creveld, Martin van, *Supplying War: Logistics from Wallenstein to Patton* (Cambridge, Cambridge University Press, 1977).

Czermak, Wilhelm, *In deinem Lager war Österreich. Die österreichisch-ungarische Armee, wie man sie nicht kannte* (Breslau, W. G. Korn, 1938).

Daniel, Ute, *Arbeiterfrauen in der Kriegsgesellschaft. Beruf, Familie und Politik im Ersten Weltkrieg* (Göttingen, Vandenhoeck & Ruprecht, 1989).

Deák, István, *Beyond Nationalism: A Social & Political History of the Habsburg Officer Corps 1848–1918* (Oxford, Oxford University Press, 1990).

Dieckmann, Wilhelm, *Die Behördenorganisation in der deutschen Kriegswirtschaft 1914–1918* (Hamburg, Hanseatische Verlagsanstalt, 1937).

Eksteins, Modris, *Rites of Spring: The Great War and the Birth of the Modern Age* (Boston, Houghton Mifflin, 1989).

Epstein, Klaus, *Matthias Erzberger and the Dilemma of German Democracy* (Princeton, Princeton University Press, 1959).

Falls, Cyril, *The First World War* (London, Longmans, 1960).

——, *The Battle of Caporetto* (Philadelphia and New York, J. B. Lippincott Company, 1966).

Farrar, Lancelot L., *The Short-War Illusion: German Policy, Strategy & Domestic Affairs, August–December 1914* (Santa Barbara, Calif., ABC-Clio, Inc., 1973).

Feldman, Gerald F., *Army, Industry, and Labor in Germany 1914-1918* (Princeton, Princeton University Press, 1966).

Ferro, Marc, *The Great War, 1914–1918* (London, Routledge & Kegan Paul, 1973).

Fiala, Peter, *Die letzte Offensive Altösterreichs. Führungsprobleme und Führerverantwortlichkeit bei der öst.-ung. Offensive in Venetien, Juni 1918* (Boppard, H. Boldt, 1967).

Fischer, Fritz, *Griff nach der Weltmacht. Die Kriegszielpolitik des kaiserlichen Deutschland 1914/18* (Düsseldorf, Droste Verlag, 1961).
——, *Krieg der Illusionen. Die deutsche Politik von 1911 bis 1914* (Düsseldorf, Droste Verlag, 1969).
Foerster, Wolfgang, *Aus der Gedankenwerkstatt des deutschen Generalstabes* (Berlin, E. S. Mittler & Sohn, 1931).
François, Hermann von, *Gorlice 1915. Der Karpathendurchbruch und die Befreiung von Galizien* (Leipzig, K. F. Koehler, 1922).
French, David, *British Strategy & War Aims 1914–1916* (London, Allen & Unwin, 1986).
Führ, Christoph, *Das K.u.K. Armeeoberkommando und die Innenpolitik in Österreich 1914–1917* (Graz, Vienna, and Cologne, Böhlau, 1968).
Fussell, Paul, *The Great War and Modern Memory* (London, Oxford, and New York, Oxford University Press, 1975).
Gabriel, Richard A. and Karen S. Metz, *A History of Military Medicine* (2 vols, New York, Westport, and London, Greenwood Press, 1992).
Galántai, József, *Hungary in the First World War* (Budapest, Akadémiai Kiadó, 1989).
Garrison, Fielding, *Notes on the History of Military Medicine* (Hildesheim and New York, G. Olms, 1970).
Geiss, Imanuel, ed., *Juli 1914: Die europäische Krise und der Ausbruch des Ersten Weltkriegs* (Munich, Deutscher Taschenbuch Verlag, 1965).
Geyer, Michael, *Deutsche Rüstungspolitik 1860–1980* (Frankfurt, Suhrkamp, 1984).
Gibson, R. H. and Maurice Prendergast, *The German Submarine War, 1914–1918* (London, Constable, 1931).
Glaise von Horstenau, Edmund, *Die Katastrophe: Die Zertrümmerung Österreich-Ungarns und das Werden der Nachfolgerstaaten* (Vienna, Amalthea-Verlag, 1929).
——, *Franz Josephs Weggefährte. Das Leben des Generalstabschefs Grafen Beck. Nach seinen Aufzeichnungen und hinterlassenen Dokumenten* (Zurich, Leipzig, and Vienna, Amalthea-Verlag, 1930).
Golovin, Nicholas N., *The Russian Army in the World War* (New Haven, Conn., Yale University Press, 1931).
Gooch, John, *The Plans of War: The General Staff and British Military Strategy c. 1900–1916* (London, Routledge & Kegan Paul, 1974).
——, *Army, State and Society in Italy, 1870–1915* (New York, St Martin's Press, 1989).
Grant, Robert M., *U-Boats Destroyed: The Effect of Anti-Submarine Warfare, 1914–1918* (London, Putnam, 1964).
Gray, Colin S., *The Leverage of Sea Power: The Strategic Advantage of Navies in War* (New York, Free Press, 1992).
Groener-Geyer, Dorothea, *General Groener. Soldat und Staatsmann* (Frankfurt, Societäts-Verlag, 1955).
Gudmundsson, Bruce I., *Stormtroop Tactics: Innovation in the German Army, 1914–1918* (New York, Westport, and London, Praeger, 1989).

Guinn, Paul, *British Strategy and Politics 1914 to 1918* (Oxford, Clarendon Press, 1965).

Haber, L. F., *The Poisonous Cloud. Chemical Warfare in the First World War* (Oxford, Clarendon Press, 1986).

Halpern, Paul G., *A Naval History of World War I* (Annapolis, Naval Institute Press, 1994).

Handbuch der deutschen Militärgeschichte, ed. Militärgeschichtliches Forschungsamt (5 vols., Munich, Bernard & Graefe Verlag, 1979).

Hantsch, Hugo, *Leopold Graf Berchtold: Grandseigneur und Staatsmann* (2 vols., Graz, Vienna, and Cologne, Verlag Styria, 1963).

Hardach, Gerd, *The First World War 1914–1918* (London, Allen Lane, 1977).

Hazlehurst, Cameron, *Politicians at War, July 1914–May 1915. A Prologue to the Triumph of Lloyd George* (London, Cape, 1971).

Hecker, Gerhard, *Walther Rathenau und sein Verhältnis zu Militär und Krieg* (Boppard, H. Boldt, 1983).

Heller, Charles E., *Chemical Warfare in World War I: The American Experience, 1917–1918* (Fort Leavenworth, Kans., U.S. Government Printing Office, 1984).

Herwig, Holger H., *The German Naval Officer Corps: A Social and Political History, 1890–1918* (Oxford, Clarendon Press, 1973).

——, *'Luxury' Fleet: The Imperial German Navy 1888–1918* (London and Atlantic Highlands, NJ, Ashfield Press, 1987).

Herwig, Holger H. and Neil M. Heyman, eds., *Biographical Dictionary of World War I* (Westport, Conn., and London, Greenwood Press, 1982).

Herzfeld, Hans, *Die deutsche Rüstungspolitik vor dem Weltkriege* (Bonn and Leipzig, Kurt Schroeder, 1923).

——, *Der Erste Weltkrieg* (Munich, Deutscher Taschenbuch Verlag, 1968).

Herzog, Bodo, *60 Jahre Deutsche Uboote 1906–66* (Munich, J.F. Lehmanns, 1968).

Hirschfeld, Gerhard, Gerd Krumeich, and Irina Renz, eds, *Keiner fühlt sich mehr als Mensch . . . Erlebnis und Wirkung des Ersten Weltkriegs* (Essen, Klartext, 1993).

Hitler, Adolf, *Mein Kampf* (Munich, Frz. Eher Nachf., 1939).

Horne, Alistair, *The Price of Glory: Verdun 1916* (New York, Penguin, 1962).

Hoyer, Helmuth, *Kaiser Karl I. und Feldmarschall Conrad von Hötzendorf. Ein Beitrag zur Militärpolitik Kaiser Karls* (Vienna, Notring, 1972).

Hüppauf, Bernd, ed., *Ansichten vom Krieg. Vergleichende Studien zum Ersten Weltkrieg in Literatur und Gesellschaft* (Königstein/Ts., Forum Academicum, 1984).

Huston, James A., *The Sinews of War: Army Logistics, 1776–1953* (Washington, DC, U.S. Government Printing Office, 1966).

Janssen, Karl-Heinz, *Der Kanzler und der General. Die Führungskrise um Bethmann Hollweg und Falkenhayn (1914–1916)* (Göttingen, Musterschmidt, 1967).

Jeřábek, Rudolf, *Potiorek. General im Schatten von Sarajevo* (Graz, Styria, 1991).

Joll, James, *1914: The Unspoken Assumptions* (London, Weidenfeld and Nicolson, 1968).

Kabisch, Ernst, *Der Rumänienkrieg 1916* (Berlin, O. Schlegel, 1936).

Kann, Robert A., *Die Sixtusaffäre und die Geheimen Friedensverhandlungen Österreich-Ungarns im Ersten Weltkrieg* (Vienna, Verlag für Geschichte und Politik, 1966).

Keiger, John F. V., *France and the Origins of the First World War* (New York, St. Martin's Press, 1983).

Kennan, George F., *The Decline of Bismarck's European Order: Franco-Russian Relations, 1875–1890* (Princeton, Princeton University Press, 1979).

Kern, Stephen, *The Culture of Time and Space, 1880–1918* (Cambridge, Mass., Harvard University Press, 1983).

Kielmannsegg, Peter Graf, *Deutschland und der Erste Weltkrieg* (Stuttgart, Klett-Cotta, 1980).

Kilduff, Peter, *Germany's First Air Force 1914–1918* (London, Arms and Armour Press, 1991).

King, Jere Clemens, *Generals & Politicians: Conflict Between France's High Command, Parliament and Government, 1914–1918* (Berkeley and Los Angeles, University of California Press, 1951).

Király, Béla K. and Nándor F. Dreisziger, eds, *East Central European Society in World War I* (New York, Columbia University Press, 1985).

Kissinger, Henry, *Diplomacy* (New York, Simon & Schuster, 1994).

Kiszling, Rudolf, *Österreich-Ungarns Anteil am Ersten Weltkrieg* (Graz, Stiasny Verlag, 1958).

Kitchen, Martin, *The Silent Dictatorship: The Politics of the German High Command under Hindenburg and Ludendorff, 1916–1918* (New York, Croom Helm, 1976).

Kocka, Jürgen, *Facing Total War: German Society, 1914–1918* (Leamington Spa, Berg, 1984).

Kraft, Heinz, *Staatsräson und Kriegführung im kaiserlichen Deutschland 1914–1916. Der Gegensatz zwischen dem Generalstabschef von Falkenhayn und dem Oberbefehlshaber Ost im Rahmen des Bündniskrieges der Mittelmächte* (Göttingen, Musterschmidt, 1980).

Krieger, Rudolf, *Die Entwicklung des Conrad'schen Offensivdenkens* (Stuttgart, W. Kohlhammer, 1934).

Kuhl, Hermann von, *Der deutsche Generalstab in Vorbereitung und Durchführung des Weltkrieges* (Berlin, E. S. Mittler & Sohn, 1920).

Landwehr von Pragenau, Ottokar, *Hunger: Die Erschöpfungsjahre der Mittelmächte 1917–1918* (Zurich, Leipzig, and Vienna, Amalthea, 1931).

Lehnters Handbuch für Truppenführer. Kriegsausgabe (Berlin, E. S. Mittler & Sohn, 1917).

Lemke, Heinz, *Allianz und Rivalität. Die Mittelmächte und Polen im ersten Weltkrieg (Bis zur Februarrevolution)* (East Berlin, Akademie-Verlag, 1977)

Liddell Hart, B. H., *Reputations: Ten Years After* (Boston and Toronto, Little, Brown, 1928).

——, *The Real War 1914–1918* (Boston and Toronto, Little, Brown, 1930).

Lieven, D. C. B., *Russia and the Origins of the First World War* (New York, St Martin's Press, 1983).

Link, Arthur S., *The Higher Realism of Woodrow Wilson and Other Essays* (Nashville, Tenn., Vanderbilt University Press, 1971).

Linke, Horst Günther, *Das zaristische Russland und der Erste Weltkrieg. Diplomatie und Kriegsziele, 1914–1917* (Munich, Fink, 1982).

Linnenkohl, Hans, *Vom Einzelschuss zur Feuerwalze. Der Wettlauf zwischen Technik und Taktik im Ersten Weltkrieg* (Koblenz, Bernard und Graefe, 1990).

Lucas, James S., *Austro-Hungarian Infantry, 1914–1918* (London, Almark, 1973).

Luckau, Alma, *The German Delegation at the Paris Peace Conference* (New York, H. Fertig, 1971).

Lüders, Marie-Elisabeth, *Das unbekannte Heer. Frauen kämpfen für Deutschland 1914–1918* (Berlin, E. S. Mittler & Sohn, 1936).

Lupfer, Timothy T., *The Dynamics of Doctrine: The Changes in German Tactical Doctrine During the First World War* (Fort Leavenworth, Kans., U.S. Government Printing Office, 1981).

Mamatey, Victor S., *The United States and East Central Europe 1914–1918: A Study in Wilsonian Diplomacy and Propaganda* (Princeton, Princeton University Press, 1957).

Margutti, Albert von, *Kaiser Franz Joseph. Persönliche Erinnerungen* (Vienna, Manz'sche Verlags- und Universitätsbuchhandlung, 1924).

May, Arthur J., *The Passing of the Hapsburg Monarchy, 1914–1918* (2 vols, Philadelphia, University of Pennsylvania Press, 1966).

Meckling, Ingeborg, *Die Aussenpolitik des Grafen Czernin* (Vienna, R. Oldenbourg, 1969).

Menning, Bruce W., *Bayonets before Bullets: The Imperial Russian Army, 1861–1914* (Bloomington, Indiana University Press, 1992).

Michalka, Wolfgang, ed., *Der Erste Weltkrieg. Wirkung, Wahrnehmung, Analyse* (Munich and Zurich, Piper, 1994).

Middlebrook, Martin, *The First Day on the Somme: 1 July 1916* (London, Penguin, 1984).

——, *The Kaiser's Battle. 21 March 1918: The First Day of the German Spring Offensive* (London, Allen Lane, 1978).

Millett, Allan R. and Williamson Murray, eds., *Military Effectiveness* (3 vols, Boston, Allen & Unwin, 1988).

Mischke, Ferdinand Otto, *Vom Kriegsbild* (Stuttgart, Seewald, 1976).

Mommsen, Wolfgang J., *Max Weber und die deutsche Politik 1890–1920* (Tübingen, J. C. B. Mohr, 1959).

Monticone, Alberto, *Deutschland und die Neutralität Italiens 1914–1915* (Wiesbaden, Franz Steiner, 1982).

Morrow, John H., Jr., *German Air Power in World War I* (Lincoln, University of Nebraska Press, 1982).

Morton, Frederic, *Thunder at Twilight: Vienna 1913/14* (New York, Macmillan, 1989).

Mosse, George L., *Fallen Soldiers: Reshaping the Memory of the World Wars* (New York, Oxford University Press, 1990).

Moyer, Laurence V., *Victory Must Be Ours: Germany in the Great War 1914–1918* (New York, Hippocrene Books, 1995).

Müller, Klaus-Jürgen, *General Ludwig Beck. Studien und Dokumente zur politisch-militärischen Vorstellungswelt und Tätigkeit des Generalstabschefs des deutschen Heeres 1933–1938* (Boppard, H. Boldt, 1980).

Niemann, Alfred, *Revolution von Oben-Umsturz von Unten. Entwicklung und Verlauf der Staatsumwälzung in Deutschland 1914–1918* (Berlin, Verlag für Kulturpolitik, 1927).

Nowak, Karl Friedrich, *The Collapse of the Central Powers* (New York, E. P. Dutton, 1924).

Otto, Helmut, *Schlieffen und der Generalstab. Der preussisch-deutsche Generalstab unter der Leitung des Generals von Schlieffen 1891–1905* (East Berlin, Deutscher Militärverlag, 1966).

Pantenius, Hans Jürgen, *Der Angriffsgedanke gegen Italien bei Conrad von Hötzendorf. Ein Beitrag zur Koalitionskriegsführung im Ersten Weltkrieg* (2 vols, Cologne and Vienna, Böhlau, 1984).

Paschall, Rod, *The Defeat of Imperial Germany 1917–1918* (Chapel Hill, Algonquin Books, 1989).

Pedroncini, Guy, *Les Mutineries de 1917* (Paris, Presses universitaires de France, 1967).

Pitreich, Max von, *Der österreichisch-ungarische Bundesgenosse im Sperrfeuer* (Klagenfurt, Arthur Killitsch, 1930).

——, *1914: Die militärischen Probleme unseres Kriegsbeginnes. Ideen, Gründe und Zusammenhänge* (Vienna, Selbstverlag, 1934).

Plaschka, Richard Georg, *Cattaro-Prag. Revolte und Revolution. Kriegsmarine und Heer Österreich-Ungarns im Feuer der Aufstandsbewegungen vom 1. Februar und 28. Oktober 1918* (Vienna, Böhlau, 1963).

——, *Matrosen. Offiziere. Rebellen. Krisenkonfrontationen zur See 1900–1918* (2 vols, Vienna, Cologne, and Graz, Hermann Böhlaus Nachf., 1984).

Plaschka, Richard Georg, Horst Haselsteiner, and Arnold Suppan, *Innere Front. Militärassistenz, Widerstand und Umsturz in der Donaumonarchie 1918* (2 vols, Vienna, Verlag für Geschichte und Politik, 1974).

Poincaré, Raymond, *Comment fut déclarée la guerre de 1914* (Paris, Flammarion, 1939).

Porch, Douglas, *The March to the Marne: The French Army 1871–1914* (Cambridge, Cambridge University Press, 1981).

Quandt, Siegfried and Horst Schichtel, eds, *Der Erste Weltkrieg als Kommunikationsereignis* (Giessen, Köhler KG, 1993).

Rakenius, Gerhard W., *Wilhelm Groener als erster Generalquartiermeister. Die Politik der Obersten Heeresleitung 1918/19* (Boppard, H. Boldt, 1977).

Ramhardter, Günther, *Geschichtswissenschaft und Patriotismus. Österreichs Historiker im Weltkrieg, 1914–1918* (Vienna, R. Oldenbourg, 1973).

Rathenau, Walther, *Kritik der dreifachen Revolution* (Berlin, S. Fischer, 1919).

Rauchensteiner, Manfried, *Der Tod des Doppeladlers. Österreich-Ungarn und der Erste Weltkrieg* (Graz, Vienna, and Cologne, Styria, 1993).

Rechberg, Arnold, *Reichsniedergang. Ein Beitrag zu dessen Ursachen aus meinen persönlichen Erinnerungen* (Munich, Musarion Verlag, 1919).

Regele, Oskar, *Generalstabschefs aus vier Jahrhunderten. Das Amt des Chefs des Generalstabes in der Donaumonarchie. Seine Träger und Organe von 1529 bis 1918* (Vienna and Munich, Verlag Herold, 1918).

——, *Feldmarschall Conrad. Auftrag und Erfüllung 1906–1918* (Vienna and Munich, Verlag Herold, 1955).

——, *Gericht über Habsburgs Wehrmacht. Letzte Siege und Untergang unter dem Armee-Oberkommando Kaiser Karls I—Generaloberst Arz von Straussenburg* (Vienna, Verlag Herold, 1968).

Renouvin, Pierre, *La Crise européenne et la guerre mondiale* (Paris, Presses universitaires de France, 1962).

Riebicke, Otto, *Was brauchte der Weltkrieg? Tatsachen und Zahlen aus dem deutschen Ringen 1914/18* (Berlin, Kyffhäuser-Verlag, 1936).

Rieder, Heinz, *Kaiser Karl. Der Letzte Monarch Österreich-Ungarns, 1887–1922* (Munich, Callwey, 1981).

Riedl, Richard, *Die Industrie Österreichs während des Krieges* (Vienna, Hölder-Pichler-Tempsky, 1932).

Ring, Friedrich, *Zur Geschichte der Militärmedizin in Deutschland* (East Berlin, Deutscher Militärverlag, 1962).

Ritter, Gerhard, *Der Schlieffenplan. Kritik eines Mythos* (Munich, R. Oldenbourg, 1956).

English translation: *The Schlieffen Plan. Critique of a Myth* (New York, Frederick A. Praeger, 1958).

——, *Staatskunst und Kriegshandwerk. Das Problem des 'Militarismus' in Deutschland* (4 vols, Munich, R. Oldenbourg, 1964).

English translation: *The Sword and the Scepter: The Problem of Militarism in Germany* (4 vols, Coral Gables, Fla., University of Miami Press, 1969–71).

Rochs, Hugo, *Schlieffen: Ein Lebens- und Charakterbild für das deutsche Volk* (Berlin, Voss, 1921).

Rommel, Erwin, *Infantry Attacks* (Toronto, Stoddart, 1990).

Rothenberg, Gunther E., *The Army of Francis Joseph* (West Lafayette, Ind., Purdue University Press, 1976).

Schäfer, Theobald von, *Generalstab and Admiralstab. Das Zusammenwirken von Heer und Flotte im Weltkrieg* (Berlin, E. S. Mittler & Sohn, 1931).

Scheer, Reinhard, *Germany's High Sea Fleet in the World War* (London, Cassell, 1920).

Schwabe, Klaus, *Woodrow Wilson, Revolutionary Germany, and Peacemaking, 1918–1919. Missionary Diplomacy and the Realities of Power* (Chapel Hill and London, The University of North Carolina Press, 1985).

Schwarte, Max, *Der grosse Krieg 1914/1918* (Leipzig, Barth in Auslg., 1921).

Schwengler, Walter, *Völkerrecht, Versailler Vertrag und Auslieferungsfrage. Die*

Strafverfolgung wegen Kriegsverbrechen als Problem des Friedensschlusses 1919/20 (Stuttgart, Deutsche Verlags-Anstalt, 1982).

Seherr-Thoss, Hans C. von, *Die deutsche Automobilindustrie* (Stuttgart, Deutsche Verlags-Anstalt, 1974).

Seyfert, Gerhard, *Die militärischen Beziehungen und Vereinbarungen zwischen dem deutschen und dem österreichischen Generalstab vor und bei Beginn des Weltkrieges* (Leipzig, J. Moltzen, 1934).

Shanafelt, Gary W., *The Secret Enemy: Austria-Hungary and the German Alliance, 1914–1918* (New York, Columbia University Press, 1985).

Showalter, Dennis E., *Tannenberg: Clash of Empires* (Hamden, Conn., Archon Books, 1991).

Silberstein, Gerard E., *The Troubled Alliance: German–Austrian Relations, 1914 to 1917* (Lexington, The University Press of Kentucky, 1970).

Siney, Marion C., *The Allied Blockade of Germany 1914–1918* (Ann Arbor, The University of Michigan Press, 1957).

Smith, Leonard V., *Between Mutiny and Obedience: The Case of the French Fifth Infantry Division during World War I* (Princeton, Princeton University Press, 1994).

Sokol, Hans Hugo, ed., *Österreich-Ungarns Seekrieg 1914–18* (Zurich, Leipzig, and Vienna, Amalthea-Verlag, 1933).

Stegemann, Bernd, *Die Deutsche Marinepolitik 1916–1918* (Berlin, Duncker & Humblot, 1970).

Stegemann, Hermann, *Geschichte des Krieges* (4 vols, Stuttgart and Berlin, Deutsche Verlags-Anstalt, 1917–21).

Steglich, Wolfgang, *Bündnissicherung oder Verständigungsfrieden. Untersuchungen zu dem Friedensangebot der Mittelmächte vom 12. Dezember 1916* (Göttingen, Musterschmidt, 1958).

——, *Die Friedenspolitik der Mittelmächte 1917/18* (2 vols, Wiesbaden, Franz Steiner, 1964).

Steiner, Zara, *Britain and the Origins of the First World War* (New York, St Martin's Press, 1977).

Stevenson, David, *French War Aims Against Germany 1914–1919* (Oxford, Clarendon Press, 1982).

Stone, Norman, *The Eastern Front, 1914–1917* (New York, Charles Scribner's Sons, 1975).

Tobisch, Manfred, *Das Deutschlandbild der Diplomatie Österreich-Ungarns von 1908 bis 1914* (Frankfurt and Bern, Lang, 1994).

Toller, Ernst, *Gesammelte Werke* (5 vols., Munich, Hanser, 1978).

Trachtenberg, Marc, *History and Strategy* (Princeton, Princeton University Press, 1991).

Trask, David F., *Captains and Cabinets: Anglo-American Naval Relations, 1917–1918* (Columbia, University of Missouri Press, 1972).

——, *The AEF and Coalition Warmaking, 1917–1918* (Lawrence, University Press of Kansas, 1993).

Travers, Tim, *The Killing Ground: The British Army, the Western Front and the*

Emergence of Modern Warfare, 1900–1918 (London, Allen & Unwin, 1987).
——, *How the War was Won: Command and Technology in the British Army on the Western Front, 1917–1918* (London and New York, Routledge, 1992).
Trumpener, Ulrich, *Germany and the Ottoman Empire 1914–1918* (Princeton, Princeton University Press, 1968).
Tunstall, Graydon A., Jr., *Planning for War Against Russia and Serbia: Austro-Hungarian and German Military Strategies, 1871–1914* (New York, Columbia University Press, 1993).
Unruh, Karl, *Langemarck. Legende und Wirklichkeit* (Koblenz, Bernard & Graefe, 1986).
Urbánski von Ostrymiecz, August, *Conrad von Hötzendorf. Soldat und Mensch* (Graz, Leipzig, and Vienna, Ulrich Mosers Verlag, 1938).
Valiani, Leo, *The End of Austria-Hungary* (New York, Random House, 1973).
Vasold, Manfred, *Pest, Not und schwere Plagen. Seuchen und Epidemien vom Mittelalter bis heute* (Munich, C. H. Beck, 1991).
Vietsch, Eberhard von, *Bethmann Hollweg. Staatsmann zwischen Macht und Ethos* (Boppard, H. Boldt, 1969).
Vincent, C. Paul, *The Politics of Hunger: The Allied Blockade of Germany, 1915–1919* (Athens and London, Ohio University Press, 1985).
Wallach, Jehuda L., *The Dogma of the Battle of Annihilation: The Theories of Clausewitz and Schlieffen and Their Impact on the German Conduct of Two World Wars* (Westport, Conn., and London, Greenwood Press, 1986).
Weber, Frank G., *Eagles on the Crescent: Germany, Austria-Hungary, and the Turkish Alliance, 1914–1918* (Ithaca, NY, Cornell University Press, 1970).
Wegs, Robert J., *Die österreichische Kriegswirtschaft 1914–1918* (Vienna, A. Schendl, 1979).
Wendt, Hermann, *Verdun 1916. Die Angriffe Falkenhayns im Maasgebiet mit Richtung auf Verdun als strategisches Problem* (Berlin, E. S. Mittler & Sohn, 1931).
——, *Der italienische Kriegsschauplatz in europäischen Konflikten. Seine Bedeutung für die Kriegführung an Frankreichs Nordostgrenze* (Berlin, Junker und Dünnhaupt, 1936).
Werth, German, *Verdun. Die Schlacht und der Mythos* (Bergisch-Gladbach, Gustav Lübbe Verlag, 1979).
Whalen, Robert Weldon, *Bitter Wounds: German Victims of the Great War, 1914–1939* (Ithaca, NY, and London, Cornell University Press, 1984).
Wheeler-Bennett, John W., *Brest-Litovsk: The Forgotten Peace March 1918* (London, Macmillan, 1963).
Wildman, Allan K., *The End of the Russian Imperial Army: The Old Army and the Soldiers' Revolt (March–April 1917)* (Princeton, Princeton University Press, 1980).
Williamson, John G., *Karl Helfferich 1872–1924: Economist, Financier, Politician* (Princeton, Princeton University Press, 1971).
Williamson, Samuel R., Jr., *The Politics of Grand Strategy: Britain and France Prepare for War, 1904–1914* (Cambridge, Mass., Harvard University Press, 1969).

——, *Austria-Hungary and the Origins of the First World War* (New York, St. Martin's Press, 1991).

Williamson, S. R. and P. Pastor, eds., *Essays on World War I: Origins and Prisoners of War* (New York, Columbia University Press, 1983).

Wilson, Keith, ed., *Decisions for War: 1914* (London, UCL Press, 1995).

Wilson, Trevor, *The Myriad Faces of War: Britain and the Great War, 1914–1918* (Cambridge, Polity Press, 1986).

Wrisberg, Ernst von, *Heer und Heimat 1914–1918* (Leipzig, K. F. Koehler, 1921).

Wynne, G. C., *If Germany Attacks: The Battle in Depth in the West* (London, Faber & Faber, 1940).

Zabecki, David T., *Steel Wind: Colonel Georg Bruchmüller and the Birth of Modern Artillery* (Westport, Praeger, 1994).

Zechlin, Egmont, *Krieg und Kriegsrisiko. Zur deutschen Politik im Ersten Weltkrieg. Aufsätze* (Düsseldorf, Droste Verlag, 1979).

Zeman, Z. A. B., *The Break-up of the Habsburg Empire, 1914–1918: A Study in National and Social Revolution* (London, Oxford University Press, 1961).

Zwehl, Hans von, *Erich v. Falkenhayn, General der Infanterie. Eine biographische Studie* (Berlin, E. S. Mittler & Sohn, 1926).

Chapters in books

Allmayer-Beck, Johann Christoph, 'Die Träger der Staatlichen Macht', in Otto Schulmeister, *Spectrum Austriae* (Vienna, Herder, 1957).

Andrew, Christopher, 'France and the German Menace', in Ernest R. May, ed., *Knowing One's Enemies: Intelligence Assessment Before the Two World Wars* (Princeton, Princeton University Press, 1984).

Angermeier, Heinz, 'Der österreichische Imperialismus des Generalfeldmarschalls Conrad von Hötzendorf', in D. Albrecht et al., eds, *Festgabe für Max Spindler* (Munich, C. H. Beck, 1955).

Burchardt, Lothar, 'The Impact of the War Economy on the Civilian Population in Germany during the First and Second World Wars', in Wilhelm Deist, ed., *The German Military in the Age of Total War* (Leamington Spa, Berg, 1985).

Clay, Anthony, 'Robert Nivelle and the French Spring Offensive, 1917', in Brian Bond, ed., *Fallen Stars: Eleven Studies of Twentieth Century Military Disasters* (London, Washington, and New York, Brassey's, 1991).

Deist, Wilhelm, 'Der militärische Zusammenbruch des Kaiserreiches', in Ursula Büttner, ed., *Das Unrechtsregime: Internationale Forschung über den Nationalsozialismus. Festschrift für Werner Jochmann zum 65. Geburtstag* (2 vols, Hamburg, H. Christians Verlag, 1986).

——, 'Kiel und die Marine im Ersten Weltkrieg', in Jürgen Elvert, ed., *Kiel, die Deutschen und die See* (Stuttgart, Franz Steiner, 1992).

——, 'Verdeckter Militärstreik im Kriegsjahr 1918?', in Wolfram Wette, ed., *Der Krieg des kleinen Mannes. Eine Militärgeschichte von unten* (Munich and Zurich, Piper, 1992).

Fellner, Fritz, 'Die "Mission Hoyos" ', in Wilhelm Alff, ed., *Deutschlands Sonderung von Europa 1862–1945* (Frankfurt and New York, Lang, 1984).

French, David., 'Who Knew What and When? The French Army Mutinies and the British Decision to Launch the Third Battle of Ypres', in L. Freedman, P. Hayes, and R. O'Neill, eds, *War, Strategy and International Politics: Essays in Honour of Sir Michael Howard* (Oxford, Clarendon Press, 1992).

Geyer, Michael, 'German Strategy in the Age of Machine Warfare, 1914–1945', in Peter Paret, ed., *Makers of Modern Strategy from Machiavelli to the Nuclear Age* (Princeton, Princeton University Press, 1986).

Glaise von Horstenau, Edmund, 'Feldmarschall Conrad von Hötzendorf', in *Soldatische Wirklichkeit* (n.p., n.d.).

Hanák, Péter, 'Die Volksmeinung während des letzten Kriegsjahres in Österreich-Ungarn', in Richard Georg Plaschka and Karlheinz Mack, eds, *Die Auflösung des Habsburgerreiches. Zusammenbruch und Neuorientierung im Donauraum* (Munich, R. Oldenbourg, 1970).

Harrison, Richard W., 'Alexander Samsonov and the Battle of Tannenberg, 1914', in Brian Bond, ed., *Fallen Stars: Eleven Studies of Twentieth Century Military Disasters* (London, Washington, and New York, Brassey's, 1991).

Herwig, Holger H., 'Imperial Germany', in Ernest R. May, ed., *Knowing One's Enemies: Intelligence Assessment Before the Two World Wars* (Princeton, Princeton University Press, 1984).

——, 'Industry, Empire and the First World War', in Gordon Martel, ed., *Modern Germany Reconsidered, 1870–1945* (London and New York, Routledge, 1992).

——, 'Strategic uncertainties of a nation-state: Prussia-Germany, 1871–1918', in W. Murray, M. Knox, and A. Bernstein, eds, *The Making of Strategy: Rulers, Strategy, and War* (Cambridge, Cambridge University Press, 1994), pp. 242–77.

Lee, John, 'Sir Ian Hamilton and the Dardanelles, 1915', in Brian Bond, ed., *Fallen Stars: Eleven Studies of Twentieth Century Military Disasters* (London, Washington, and New York, Brassey's, 1991).

Leslie, John, 'Österreich-Ungarn vor dem Kriegsausbruch. Der Ballhausplatz in Wien im Juli 1914 aus der Sicht eines österreichischen Diplomaten', in Ralph Melville, ed., *Deutschland und Europa in der Neuzeit. Festschrift für Karl Otmar v. Aretin* (2 vols, Wiesbaden, Franz Steiner, 1988).

Pichkík, Karel, 'Der militärische Zusammenbruch der Mittelmächte im Jahre 1918', in Richard Georg Plaschka and Karlheinz Mack, eds, *Die Auflösung des Habsburgerreiches. Zusammenbruch und Neuorientierung im Donauraum* (Munich, R. Oldenbourg, 1970).

Plaschka, Richard Georg, 'The Army and Internal Conflict in the Austro-Hungarian Empire, 1918', in Béla K. Király and Nándor F. Dreisziger, eds, *East Central European Society in World War I* (New York, Columbia University Press, 1985).

Ritter, Gerhard, 'Die Zusammenarbeit der Generalstäbe Deutschlands und Österreich-Ungarns vor dem ersten Weltkrieg', in *Zur Geschichte und*

Problematik der Demokratie. Festgabe für Hans Herzfeld (Berlin, Duncker & Humblot, 1958).

Schäfer, Theobald von, 'Generaloberst von Moltke in den Tagen vor der Mobilmachung und seine Einwirkung auf Österreich-Ungarn', in *Die Kriegsschuldfrage* (Leipzig, Druck der Nord-Deutschen Buchdruckerei, 1925).

Schmidt-Brentano, Antonio, 'Die Österreichische beziehungsweise Österreich-Ungarische Armee von Erzherzog Carl bis Conrad von Hötzendorf', in Heinrich Lutz and Helmut Rumpler, eds., *Österreich und die deutsche Frage im 19. und 20. Jahrhundert. Probleme der politisch-staatlichen und sozialkulturellen Differenzierung im deutschen Mitteleuropa* (Munich, R. Oldenbourg, 1982).

Wegs, Robert J., 'Transportation: The Achilles Heel of the Habsburg War Effort', in Robert A. Kann, Béla K. Király, Paula S. Fichtner, eds, *The Habsburg Empire in World War I: Essays on the Intellectual, Military, Political and Economic Aspects of the Habsburg War Effort* (New York, Columbia University Press, 1977).

Wehler, Hans-Ulrich, 'Der Verfall der deutschen Kriegstheorie. Vom "Absoluten" zum "Totalen" Krieg oder von Clausewitz zu Ludendorff', in Hans-Ulrich Wehler, ed., *Krisenherde des Kaiserreichs 1871–1918* (Göttingen, Vandenhoeck & Ruprecht, 1970).

Williamson, Samuel R., 'Joffre Reshapes French Strategy', in Paul M. Kennedy, ed., *The War Plans of the Great Powers, 1880–1914* (London, George Allen & Unwin, 1979).

Articles

Angress, Werner T., 'Das deutsche Militär und die Juden im Ersten Weltkrieg', *Militärgeschichtliche Mitteilungen* 19 (1976), pp. 77–146.

Broucek, Peter, 'Der k.u.k. Delegierte im Deutschen Grossen Hauptquartier Generalmajor Alois Klepsch-Kloth von Roden und seine Berichterstattung 1915/16', *Militärgeschichtliche Mitteilungen* 15 (1974), pp. 109–26.

——, 'Chef des Generalstabes und Oberster Kriegsherr. Aus den Erinnerungen des Feldmarschalleutnants Alois Klepsch-Kloth von Roden, K.u.K. Delegierten im Deutschen Grossen Hauptquartier, 1915/18', *Mitteilungen des österreichischen Staatsarchivs* 27 (1974), pp. 385–401.

——, 'Die Deutschen Bemühungen um eine Militärkonvention mit Österreich-Ungarn (1915–1918)', *Mitteilungen des Instituts für Österreichische Geschichtsforschung* 87 (1979), pp. 440–70.

Buchfink, Ernst, 'Moltke und Schlieffen', *Historische Zeitschrift* 158 (1938), pp. 308–22.

Burchardt, Lothar, 'Die Auswirkungen der Kriegswirtschaft auf die deutsche Zivilbevölkerung im Ersten und im Zweiten Weltkrieg', *Militärgeschichtliche Mitteilungen* 15 (1974), pp. 65–97.

474   *The First World War*

Craig, Gordon A., 'The World War I Alliance of the Central Powers in Retrospect: The Military Cohesion of the Alliance', *Journal of Modern History* 37 (1965), pp. 336–44.

Deist, Wilhelm, 'Die Politik der Seekriegsleitung und die Rebellion der Flotte Ende Oktober 1918', *Vierteljahrshefte für Zeitgeschichte* 14 (1966), pp. 341–68.

Farrar, L. L., Jr., 'The Short-War Illusion: The Syndrome of German Strategy, August–December, 1914', *Militärgeschichtliche Mitteilungen* 12 (1972), pp. 39–52.

Glaise von Horstenau, Edmund, 'Feldmarschall Franz Graf Conrad von Hötzendorf zur 85. Wiederkehr seines Geburtstages', *Wehrwissenschaftliche Rundschau* 68 (1937), pp. 707–26.

Groote, Wolfgang von, 'Historische Vorbilder des Feldzugs 1914 im Westen', *Militärgeschichtliche Mitteilungen* 57 (1990), pp. 33–55.

Guth, Ekkehart P., 'Der Gegensatz zwischen dem Oberbefehlshaber Ost und dem Chef des Generalstabes des Feldheeres 1914/15. Die Rolle des Majors v. Haeften im Spannungsfeld zwischen Hindenburg, Ludendorff und Falkenhayn', *Militärgeschichtliche Mitteilungen* 35 (1984), pp. 113–39.

Herwig, Holger H., 'Admirals *versus* Generals: The War Aims of the Imperial German Navy 1914-1918', *Central European History* 5 (1972), pp. 208–33.

——, 'Tunes of Glory at the Twilight Stage: The Bad Homburg Crown Council and the Evolution of German Statecraft, 1917/18', *German Studies Review* 6 (1983), pp. 475–94.

——, 'From Tirpitz Plan to Schlieffen Plan: Some Observations on German Military Planning', *Journal of Strategic Studies* 9 (1986), pp. 53–63.

——, 'Disjointed Allies: Coalition Warfare in Berlin and Vienna, 1914', *The Journal of Military History* 54 (1990), pp. 265–80.

Herwig, Holger H., and David F. Trask, 'The Failure of Imperial Germany's Undersea Offensive Against World Shipping, February 1917–October 1918', *The Historian* 33 (1971), pp. 611–36.

Hillgruber, Andreas, 'Die Erwägungen der Generalstäbe für den Fall eines Kriegseintritts Italiens 1914/15', *Quellen und Forschungen aus italienischen Archiven und Bibliotheken* 48 (1968), pp. 346–64.

Höbelt, Lothar, 'Schlieffen, Beck, Potiorek und das Ende der gemeinsamen deutsch-österreichischen-ungarischen Aufmarschpläne im Osten', *Militärgeschichtliche Mitteilungen* 36 (1984), pp. 7–30.

Horne, John and Alan Kramer, 'German "Atrocities" and Franco-German Opinion, 1914: The Evidence of German Soldiers' Diaries', *Journal of Modern History* 66 (1994), pp. 1–33.

Jäschke, Gotthard, 'Zum Problem der Marne-Schlacht von 1914', *Historische Zeitschrift* 190 (1960), pp. 311–48.

Janssen, Karl Heinz, 'Der Wechsel in der Obersten Heeresleitung 1916', *Vierteljahrshefte für Zeitgeschichte* 7 (1959), pp. 337–71.

Kiszling, Rudolf, 'Die Entwicklung der österreichisch-ungarischen Wehrmacht seit der Annexionskrise 1908', *Berliner Monatshefte* 12 (1934), pp. 735–49.

——, 'Generalfeldmarschall Graf Schlieffen und die Kriegsvorbereitungen Österreich-Ungarns', *Wehrwissenschaftliche Mitteilungen* 64 (1933), pp. 153–9.

——, 'Bündniskrieg und Koalitionsführung am Beispiel der Mittelmächte im Ersten Weltkrieg', *Wehrwissenschaftliche Rundschau* 10 (1960), pp. 633–41.

——, 'Heer und Kriegsmarine in den letzten Jahrzehnten vor Ausbruch des Ersten Weltkrieges', *Österreich in Geschichte und Literatur* 6 (1963), pp. 251–60.

——, 'Feldmarschall Conrad v. Hötzendorf', *Österreich in Geschichte und Literatur* 8 (1964), pp. 157–67.

——, 'Die militärischen Vereinbarungen Österreich-Ungarns 1867–1914', *Österreich in Geschichte und Literatur* 10 (1966), pp. 427–35.

Krumeich, Gerd, 'Verstümmelungen und Kunstglieder. Formen körperlicher Verheerungen im 1. Weltkrieg', *Sozialwissenschaftliche Informationen* 19 (1990), pp. 97–102.

Lasswell, Harold D., 'The Garrison State', *The American Journal of Sociology* 46 (1941), pp. 455–68.

Mai, Gunther, 'Burgfrieden und Sozialpolitik in Deutschland in der Anfangsphase des Ersten Weltkrieges (1914/15)', *Militärgeschichtliche Mitteilungen* 22 (1976), pp. 21–50.

Martin, Gregory, 'German Strategy and Military Assessment of the American Expeditionary Force (AEF), 1917–18', *War in History* 1 (1994), pp. 160–96.

Meier-Welcker, Hans, 'Strategische Planungen und Vereinbarungen der Mittelmächte für den Mehrfrontenkrieg', *Österreichische Militärische Zeitschrift*, Sonderheft 2 (1964), pp. 15–22.

——, 'Die Beurteilung der Politischen Lage in Österreich-Ungarn durch Generalmajor von Seeckt im Sommer 1917', *Militärgeschichtliche Mitteilungen* 4 (1968), pp. 87–104.

Ostertag, Heiger, 'Die grosse Schlacht in Frankreich. Unternehmen Michael 21. März bis 4. April 1918', *Militärgeschichte* 3 (1993), pp. 31–7.

Otto, Helmut, 'Zum strategisch-operativen Zusammenwirken des deutschen und österreichisch-ungarischen Generalstabes bei der Vorbereitung des ersten Weltkrieges', *Zeitschrift für Militärgeschichte* 2 (1963), pp. 423–40.

Peball, Kurt, 'Der Feldzug gegen Serbien und Montenegro im Jahre 1914', *Österreichische Militärische Zeitschrift*, Special issue, 1 (1965), pp. 18–30.

——, 'Briefe an eine Freundin. Zu den Briefen des Feldmarschalls Conrad von Hötzendorff an Frau Walburga von Sonnleithner während der Jahre 1905–1918', *Mitteilungen des Österreichischen Staatsarchivs* 25 (1972), pp. 492–503.

Plaut, Paul, 'Psychographie des Krieges', *Beihefte zur Zeitschrift für angewandte Psychologie* 20 (Leipzig, Johann Ambrosius Barth, 1920), pp. 1–123.

Ritter, Gerhard, 'Der Anteil der Militärs an der Kriegskatastrophe von 1914', *Historische Zeitschrift* 193 (1961), pp. 72–91.

Röhl, J. C. G., 'Admiral von Müller and the Approach of War, 1911–1914', *The Historical Journal* 12 (1969), pp. 651–73.

Rüdt von Collenberg, Ludwig, 'Graf Schlieffen und die Kriegsformation der deutschen Armee', *Wissen und Wehr* 10 (1927), pp. 605–34.

Saul, Klaus, 'Jugend im Schatten des Krieges. Vormilitärische Ausbildung - Kriegswirtschaftlicher Einsatz - Schulalltag in Deutschland 1914–1918', *Militärgeschichtliche Mitteilungen* 34 (1983), pp. 91–184.

Schlieffen, Alfred von, 'Der Krieg der Gegenwart', *Deutsche Revue* 34 (1909), pp. 13–24.

Schulte, Bernd, 'Neue Dokumente zum Kriegsausbruch und Kriegsverlauf 1914', *Militärgeschichtliche Mitteilungen* 25 (1979), pp. 123–85.

Showalter, Dennis E., 'The Eastern Front and German Military Planning, 1871–1914 – Some Observations', *East European Quarterly* 15 (1981), pp. 163–80.

Stegmann, Dirk, 'Die deutsche Inlandspropaganda 1917/18. Zum innenpolitischen Machtkampf zwischen OHL und ziviler Reichsleitung in der Endphase des Kaiserreiches', *Militärgeschichtliche Mitteilungen* 12 (1972), pp. 75–116.

Stone, Norman, 'Army and Society in the Habsburg Monarchy, 1900–1914', *Past & Present* 33 (1966), pp. 95–111.

——, 'Moltke–Conrad: Relations Between the Austro-Hungarian and German General Staffs, 1909–1914', *Historical Journal* 9 (1966), pp. 201–28.

——, 'Die Mobilmachung der österreichisch-ungarischen Armee 1914', *Militärgeschichtliche Mitteilungen* 16 (1974), pp. 67–95.

Thoss, Bruno, 'Nationale Rechte, militärische Führung und Diktaturfrage in Deutschland 1913–1923', *Militärgeschichtliche Mitteilungen* 42 (1987), pp. 28–60.

Travers, T. H. E., 'Could the tanks of 1918 have been war winners?', *Journal of Contemporary History* 27 (1992), pp. 389–406.

Travers, Tim, 'The Somme July 1, 1916: The Reason Why', *MHQ: The Quarterly Journal of Military History* 7 (1995), pp. 62–73.

Trumpener, Ulrich, 'The Escape of the *Goeben* and *Breslau*: A Reassessment', *Canadian Journal of History* 6 (1971), pp. 171–86.

——, 'The Road to Ypres: The Beginnings of Gas Warfare in World War I', Journal of Modern History 47 (1975), pp. 460–80.

Turner, L. C. F., 'The Significance of the Schlieffen Plan', *The Australian Journal of Politics and History* 13 (1967), pp. 47–66.

——, 'The Role of the General Staffs in July 1914', *The Australian Journal of Politics and History* 11 (1965), pp. 305–23.

Ullrich, Volker, 'Entscheidung im Osten oder Sicherung der Dardanellen. Das Ringen um den Serbienfeldzug 1915', *Militärgeschichtliche Mitteilungen* 32 (1982), pp. 45–63.

——, 'Zwischen Verhandlungsfrieden und Erschöpfungskrieg. Die Friedensfrage in der deutschen Reichsleitung Ende 1915', *Geschichte in Wissenschaft und Unterricht* 37 (1986), pp. 397–419.

Van Evera, Stephen, 'The Cult of the Offensive and the Origins of the First World War', *International Security* 9 (1984), pp. 58–107.

Waldersee, Georg Graf, 'Über die Beziehungen des deutschen zum österreichisch-ungarischen Generalstabe vor dem Weltkriege', *Berliner Monatshefte* 8 (1930), pp. 103–42.

Wette, Wolfram, 'Reichstag und "Kriegsgewinnlerei" (1916–1918). Die Anfänge parlamentarischer Rüstungskontrolle in Deutschland', *Militärgeschichtliche Mitteilungen* 36 (1984), pp. 31–56.

Wittich, Alfred von, 'Zur Weltanschauung Conrads von Hötzendorf', *Militärwissenschaftliche Mitteilungen* 75 (1944), pp. 1–16.

Zechlin, Egmont, 'Ludendorff im Jahre 1915. Unveröffentlichte Briefe', *Historische Zeitschrift* 211 (1970), pp. 316–53.

Dissertations

Breiter, Marion, 'Hinter der Front. Zum Leben der Zivilbevölkerung im Wien des Ersten Weltkrieges', Vienna University 1991.

Degreif, Dieter, 'Operative Planungen des k.u.k. Generalstabes für einen Krieg in der Zeit vor 1914 (1880–1914)', Mainz University 1983.

Drofenik, Willi, 'General Alfred Krauss. Eine Biographie', Vienna University 1967.

Ernharth, Ronald L., 'The Tragic Alliance: Austro-German Military Cooperation, 1871–1918', Columbia University 1970.

Etue, George E., Jr., 'The German Fatherland Party, 1917–1918', University of California-Berkeley 1959.

Freiwirth, Paul K., 'Germany and Austria-Hungary as Allies, 1914–1916', University of Maryland 1961.

Fussek, Alexander, 'Minister Präsident Karl Graf Stürgkh', Vienna University 1959.

Hanks, Robert W., 'The End of an Institution: The Austro-Hungarian Army in Italy, 1918', Rice University 1977.

Heacock, Roger L., 'Diplomatic Relations Between the Austro-Hungarian Empire and the German Reich in World War I, 1916–1918: A Study Based on Documents from the Austrian State Archives', University of Denver 1967.

Hecht, Rudolf, 'Fragen zur Heeresergänzung der gesamten Bewaffneten Macht Österreich-Ungarns während des Ersten Weltkrieges', Vienna University 1969.

Hoettl, Volker, 'Die Beziehungen Conrads von Hötzendorf zu den deutschen Generalstabschefs 1914–17 auf politischem Gebiet', Vienna University 1968.

Hoffmann, Eduard P., 'Feldmarschall Boroevic von Bojna. Österreich-Ungarns Kriegsfront an den Flüssen Isonzo und Piave', Vienna University 1985.

Holden, Anne C., 'Bulgaria's Entry in the First World War: A Diplomatic Study, 1913–1915', University of Illinois 1976.

Hopwood, Robert F., 'Interalliance Diplomacy: Count Czernin and Germany, 1916–1918', Stanford University 1965.

Hoyer, Helmut, 'Kaiser Karl I. und Feldmarschall Conrad von Hötzendorf. Ein Beitrag zur Militärpolitik Kaiser Karls', Vienna University 1972.

Jeřábek, Rudolf, 'Die Brussilowoffensive 1916. Ein Wendepunkt der Koalitionsführung der Mittelmächte', 2 vols, Vienna University 1982.

Jones, David R., 'Imperial Russia's Armed Forces at War, 1914–1918: An Analysis of Military Effectiveness', Dalhousie University 1986.

Käs, Ferdinand, 'Versuch einer zusammengefassten Darstellung der Tätigkeit des österreichisch-ungarischen Generalstabes in der Zeit von 1906 bis 1914 unter besonderer Berücksichtigung der Aufmarschplanungen und Mobilmachungen', Vienna University 1962.

Leslie, John, 'Austria–Hungary's Eastern Policy in the First World War, August 1914 to August 1915', Cambridge University 1975.

Lewerenz, Lilli, 'Die deutsche Politik im Baltikum 1914–1918', Hamburg University 1958.

Mann, Josef, 'FML Blasius Schemua. Chef des Generalstabes am Vorabend des Weltkrieges 1911–1912', Vienna University 1978.

Mayer, Klaus, 'Die Organisation des KPQ beim k.u.k. AOK im Ersten Weltkrieg 1914–1918', Vienna University 1963.

Meelich, Helmut, 'Die Kriegswirtschaft Österreich-Ungarns 1914–1918. Wirtschaftsorganisation und Versorgungspolitik im Ersten Weltkrieg', Vienna University 1976.

Müller, Eugenie Maria, 'Der Konflikt Conrad Ährenthal', Vienna University 1978.

Schmölzer, Hildegund, 'Die Propaganda des Kriegspressequartiers im Ersten Weltkrieg', Vienna University 1965.

Ullreich, Josef, 'Moritz von Auffenberg-Komarów. Leben und Wirken 1911–1918', Vienna University 1961.

Vermes, Gabor, 'Count István Tisza: A Political Biography', Stanford University 1966.

Wagner, Bruno, 'Der Waffenstillstand von Villa Giusti 3. November 1918', Vienna University 1970.

Wassermair, Otto, 'Die Meutereien der Heimkehrer aus russischer Kriegsgefangenschaft bei den Ersatzkörpern der k. u. k. Armee im Jahre 1918', Vienna University 1968.

Waurisch, Gertrud, 'Kaiser Franz Joseph und Conrad von Hötzendorf in den Jahren 1906–1911', Graz University 1949.

Wegs, Robert, 'Austrian Economic Mobilization During World War I: With Particular Emphasis on Heavy Industry', University of Illinois 1970.

Index